Managerial
Economics

Managerial Economics

W. DUNCAN REEKIE
University of the Witwatersrand

JONATHAN N. CROOK
University of Edinburgh

Third Edition

Philip Allan

NEW YORK LONDON TORONTO SYDNEY TOKYO SINGAPORE

First published 1975 by

Philip Allan

66 Wood Lane End, Hemel Hempstead,
Hertfordshire, HP2 4RG
A division of
Simon & Schuster International Group

Printed and bound in Great Britain by
Dotesios Printers Ltd, Trowbridge, Wiltshire

British Library Cataloguing in Publication Data

Reekie, W. Duncan
 Managerial economics — 3rd ed.
 1. Managerial economics
 I. Title   II. Crook, Jonathan N.
 330'.024658   HD30.22
 ISBN 0–86003–174–8 Pbk
 ISBN 0–86003–070–9

---

3   4   5   93   92   90

For Ruth and Kate

Contents

Preface

Preface to Third Edition

If consumers can be relied on as assessors of a product's merits then we must thank our colleagues (teachers and students) who have prescribed and read this book for over a decade in at least four continents. In their judgement this book has been useful and successful and for that implied praise we are grateful. We must also express our thanks to our own students over the years, and to fellow teachers who have pointed out inadequacies, errors and omissions in earlier editions. We have tried to take on board many of their criticisms.

This edition has been thoroughly revised. In particular, the chapter on capital budgeting has been updated to take account of recent advances in the field; the Dorfman—Steiner Theorem has been reintroduced in a more practical, normative fashion; applications of theory are even more plentiful than hitherto; and the contribution of the corporate strategy and long-range planning literature has been acknowledged by an extensive discussion. The objectives of different stakeholders in the firm have been set in the context of the principal—agent problem; a more descriptively realistic analysis of costs has been included; and the econometrics of demand estimation has been simplified and made more intuitive, as has our explanation of linear programming. Our discussion of regional and monopoly policies which impinge on managerial decision making have been brought completely up to date.

Of course, there has been a cost in the light of these additions. We have eliminated many of the more trivial study questions, and some of the esoteric appendices of the previous edition. This has been necessary in order to contain the material within market-imposed physical and financial constraints. In the spirit of 'thinking marginally', we hope our readers will agree that the changes in this edition represent a move towards a new optimum.

W. DUNCAN REEKIE
University of the Witwatersrand
JONATHAN N. CROOK
University of Edinburgh
May 1987

PART I

Basic Concepts

1
Introduction to Maximisation and Optimisation

1.1 Maximising the Value of the Firm

Throughout this book we assume that the objective of the firm is to maximise profits. Other objectives have been attributed to managers and we shall discuss these in Chapter 3. Optimisation is the most desirable allocation of resources from the manager's point of view, given whatever goals he has. However, total optimisation, even by a profit-maximising firm, is so complex that we have to discuss partial optimisation of only one or a small number of the firm's activities and only in Chapter 16 will we return to total optimisation. In the remaining chapters we will concentrate on maximising the value of the firm by taking price decisions, investment decisions, manufacturing decisions, or whatever, on the assumption that conditions ruling elsewhere within the firm are held constant.

Profits can be viewed either as the excess of revenues over costs in the short run, or as the value of the firm having taken into account the time dimension. It is with this latter concept of profit that we will be primarily concerned.

Algebraically, the value of the firm can be expressed as follows:

value of the firm = present value of expected future profits or

$$PV_\pi = \frac{\pi_1}{1 + r} + \frac{\pi_2}{(1 + r)^2} + \frac{\pi_3}{(1 + r)^3} + \cdots + \frac{\pi_n}{(1 + r)^n}$$

$$= \sum_{t = 1}^{n} \frac{\pi_i}{(1 + r)^i} = \sum_{t = 1}^{n} \frac{(TR - TC)_t}{(1 + r)^t}$$

where $\pi_1, \pi_2, \ldots \pi_n$ are the expected profits for each year from 1 to n; r is the appropriate interest rate; and TR and TC are total revenues and total costs respectively. (The meaning of present value is discussed in the next subsection.)

3

Clearly, to maximise long-term profits in this way requires an understanding not only of what is meant by *TR, TC* and *r*, but also of the variables which can influence their magnitudes. The ability to control such variables, comprehend those which are beyond the firm's control, understand their interrelationships, and foresee or initiate changes in their values is the task of the manager and the subject matter of this book.

Present Value

Money has a time value. £1 received today is worth more than £1 to be received in the future. The sooner we receive money, the better off we are because the sooner we can invest it to earn interest. But how much more today's £1 is worth compared with £1 due in the future depends on the time interval and what can be done with the £1 in the interval. (It should be noted at this point that we are not discussing the impact of inflation on the real value of money. This is a separate issue which will be discussed in Chapter 16.)

Suppose we have currently available a sum of £1000 which we will term its present value or *PV*. We can invest this sum in the bank at let us say, an interest rate, *r,* of 10%. After one year we could withdraw from the bank both the original deposit and the accumulated interest; this would be our future receipt in year one, or R_1. That is:

$$R_1 = £1000 + (0.1)\,1000 = £1100$$

Generally

$$R_1 = PV + r(PV) = PV(1 + r)$$

Alternatively, if we did not withdraw the money but left it on deposit for a further year, then at the end of year two we could withdraw the following:

$$R_2 = £1100 + (0.1)\,1100 = £1210$$

Generally

$$R_2 = R_1 + (r)\,R_1 = R_1(1 + r) = PV(1 + r)^2$$

In like manner, *R* at the end of year three would be:

$$R_3 = PV(1 + r)^3$$

and at the end of year *n*:

$$R_n = PV(1 + r)^n$$

This process is called compounding. The above general formula is the compound interest formula, and it tells us the magnitude of a future receipt if we already know its present value and the interest rate.

The reverse procedure, where the future receipt and the interest rate are known, and the present value remains to be found, is known as discounting.

The discounting formula can be stated as:

$$PV = R_n/(1 + r)^n$$

This tells us the PV of a sum of money to be received n years hence, given a discount rate of r. When a stream of future receipts is expected, occurring at annual intervals, then the PV of the stream is the sum of the PVs of each receipt. That is:

$$\frac{R_1}{(1 + r)} + \frac{R_2}{(1 + r)^2} + \frac{R_3}{(1 + r)^3} + \cdots + \frac{R_n}{(1 + r)^n} = \sum_{i=1}^{n} \frac{R_i}{(1 + r)^i}$$

1.2 Two Rules of Marginal Equivalency

In attempts to indicate conditions which must be fulfilled for managers to allocate resources optimally within a firm, two general questions face managerial economists. Firstly, to what extent should a course of action be pursued and secondly, if insufficient funds prevent all actions from being carried out at the optimum level, to what degree should each be pursued?

Two theorems of marginal equivalency answer these questions:

1. A course of action should be pursued until its marginal benefits equal its marginal costs, that is where its marginal net benefits equal zero.
2. If no action can be pursued to the optimum extent, each different action should be pursued until they all yield the same marginal benefits per unit of cost.

Total, Average and Marginal Relationships

Theorem 1 is best explained by reference to Table 1.1.

Table 1.1

Units of Output	Total Profits £	Average Profits £	Marginal Profits £
1	5	5	5
2	16	8	11
3	31	10.33	15
4	49	12.25	18
5	63	12.6	14
6	72	12.0	9
7	74	10.57	2
8	67	8.37	− 7

Here we have the hypothetical total, average and marginal profit functions of a firm. Note that, if we know the total profit function, the average and marginal values can be readily derived. The average value is merely the total value divided by quantity. The marginal value at any output level is just the total value at that level less the total value at the immediately preceding output level. In other words, any total value is equal to the sum of all preceding marginal values.

Given this it is clear that if the marginal value is positive, then the total value will be rising. If the marginal value is negative, the total value will be falling. Therefore Theorem 1 is substantiated.

Diminishing Marginal Returns

Theorem 2 cannot be fully explained without reference to the law of diminishing marginal returns, which we will not examine in detail until Chapter 7. Briefly, the law states, that if the quantities of all inputs are held constant, but that of one input is increased, then the marginal output of that input will eventually decrease.

Suppose a businessman is pursuing two courses of action, A and B, and the marginal profit for the expenditure of £1 on A is £3.00 and on B is £3.50. It would be worth his while to transfer £1 of expenditure from A to B. So doing he would forfeit £3.00 of profits but gain £3.50 for no extra cost. It would pay him to continue reallocating his expenditure until both A and B provided the same marginal profit per pound. If he could not pursue each action to the extent that its marginal profit equalled zero, the final marginal profits would be positive.

Due to the law of diminishing returns, B's marginal yield relative to that of A would fall as more resources were allocated to it. Simultaneously as fewer resources were allocated to A, A's marginal yield would rise relative to that of B. Hence ultimately the optimal position of marginal equivalency would be reached.

1.3 Mathematical Methods

Relationships between economic variables can be expressed verbally, in a table, graphically or algebraically.

Marginal Analysis and Geometry

The relationships of Table 1.1 are expressed geometrically in Figure 1.1. The relationships between average profits and output (Q) and between marginal π and Q can be derived from the relationship between total π and Q.

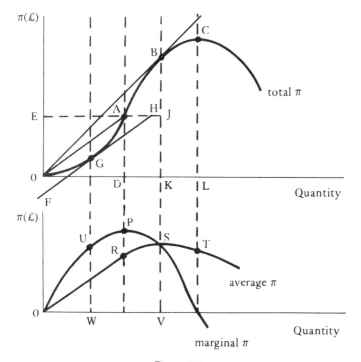

Figure 1.1

Marginal and Average Values

Average π are total π divided by Q. So in Figure 1.1 average π at output OD equals (distance AD/distance OD). Now the general formula for the slope of a straight line between two points, say A with co-ordinates (x_1, y_1) and B with co-ordinates (x_2, y_2) is $(y_2 - y_1)/(x_2 - x_1)$. Therefore since total π corresponds to the ys and Q to the xs, average π at OD equals the slope of OA. At any point on a total curve the corresponding average is the slope of the straight line from the origin to that point. Given this, we can see that the slopes (and hence average values) of straight lines from the origin to the total curve increase until output equals OK. Thereafter they decrease.

Marginal π is the increase in total π which results from a 1 unit increase in Q. Hence if AJ represented one unit, marginal π at output OD would equal BJ/AJ. If AJ was very much less than 1 unit, BJ would be smaller too and BJ/AJ would approximate the slope of a tangent to the total π curve at A. In general

$$\text{marginal } y = \frac{y_2 - y_1}{x_2 - x_1} = \frac{\Delta y}{\Delta x} \tag{1.1}$$

Now the slope of a curve at any point equals the slope of the tangent to the curve at that point. Thus at any point on the total curve the corresponding marginal figure is given by the slope of the line drawn tangent to the curve at that point. Marginal π at G is equal to the slope of FH, which equals WU in the lower half of the figure. Marginal π at B is equal to the slope of OB which equals VS, in the lower figure. Marginal π at C would equal zero, since there the total π curve is neither rising nor falling and so its slope would be zero. This is the point of maximum total π. After point C the slope of the total π curve is negative with corresponding implications for the marginal π curve.

Notice that at outputs up to OD, the gradient of the total π curve increases as Q increases, but thereafter the gradient decreases. Hence marginal π is maximised at OD.

It will already have been noted that average π and marginal π are equal at S, where the tangent to total π and the line from the origin to the output level on total π indicated by S are the same, namely OB. Before B, the slope of the total π curve at any point is greater than the slope of the line drawn from the origin to that point. After B, the reverse holds true. Consequently, up to point B, or S on the lower figure, the fact that marginal values are higher than average will result in continuously increasing average values. After S, since marginal values are lower than average the average curve will fall away.

Figure 1.2 shows the familiar marginal cost (MC) and average cost (AC) curves of elementary texts. In Figure 1.1 we showed how it was possible to obtain marginal and average values from a total curve. Here we will illustrate how total values can be derived from the average or marginal curves. (The arguments we will use would be equally applicable to Figure 1.1.) Since total cost equals average (unit) cost multiplied by the number of units produced, then at Q_1 total cost equals OA times OQ_1 which is the rectangle OQ_1CA. At

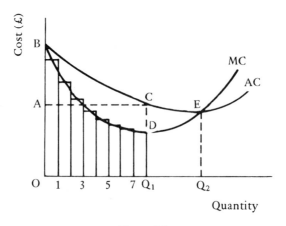

Figure 1.2

any point on an average curve the total value is equal to the rectangle inscribed under that curve which has the axes for one set of sides and the origin and the point on the curve as diagonally opposite points.

We have already defined a total value as the sum of all preceding marginal values. Thus the total cost of producing Q_1 (8 units) is the sum of the eight thin rectangles by which the MC curve is plotted, area $OBDQ_1$. At any point on a marginal curve the total value is equal to the area under the curve to the left of a vertical line dropped from the point on the curve to the x, or horizontal axis.

The above two propositions enable us to find a marginal curve when only an average curve is known. Consider Figure 1.3 where we have a linear demand, or average revenue, curve (AR). At Q_1 we know that total revenue is equal to the area contained by the rectangle $OACQ_1$. To draw in the (unknown) marginal revenue (MR) curve, we must do so in such a way that at Q_1 the total revenue represented by $OBDQ_1$ is equal to $OACQ_1$. This will only be so if the two triangles ABE and CDE are equal in area. Both triangles already have two angles of equal magnitude, irrespective of where BD cuts AC. (Each has a right angle, and the angles at E are the opposite angles of a vertex.) Consequently, for the two triangles to be of equal size and shape they now merely need to have an equal side. This is obtained by ensuring that BD cuts AC at its midpoint so that $AE = EC$. Given a linear average curve, the corresponding marginal curve is found by drawing in the straight line which begins where the average curve cuts the vertical, or y, axis and passes through the midpoint of any horizontal line from the average curve to the y axis.

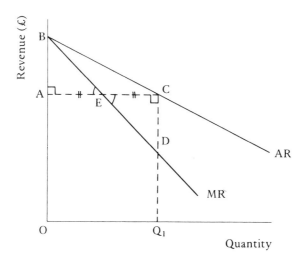

Figure 1.3

The problem of constructing a marginal curve from a non-linear average curve is more complex. For example, in Figure 1.4, we are given the average cost curve, *AC*. Rather than finding the marginal cost curve, *MC*, as such, we must approximate it by discovering a number of individual points on it. At output level Q_1, the corresponding marginal value for *X* is *Y*. This is found by drawing *AB*, the tangent to *X*. This can be regarded as a proxy linear average curve passing through *X* and relevant to Q_1. The corresponding linear marginal curve to *AB* is *AD*. At Q_1, *AD* has a value of *Y*. Similarly, at output level Q_2, the average value of *W* has a corresponding marginal value of *Z*. This value was found by constructing the lines *EF* and *EG* in the same way as *AB* and *AD*. This process can be repeated at different output levels until the position of *MC* is known with confidence.

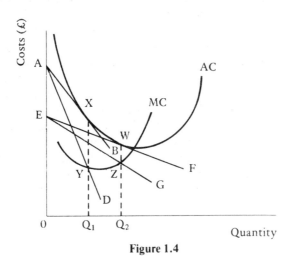

Figure 1.4

Marginal Analysis and Calculus

Often by representing a relationship by an equation we can find specific answers to certain problems. In these cases, calculus may be useful to locate maximum and minimum values. In this section we list some rules which are used in differential calculus.

Functions of one Variable

Earlier we argued that in our formula for marginal *y*, equation 1.1, as we reduced the size of the change in *x*, distance *AJ* in Figure 1.1 would become smaller and *BJ/AJ* would become a closer and closer approximation to the gradient of the total π curve at *A*. Now a derivative is a precise specification of the general marginal relationship $\Delta y/\Delta x$. It is the value of $\Delta y/\Delta x$ when

Δx is infinitesimally small. In this case we write:

$$\frac{dy}{dx} = \lim_{\Delta x \to 0} \left(\frac{\Delta y}{\Delta x} \right)$$

Hence if we know a total cost equation we can find the marginal cost at any output.

To find the derivative of a function we follow the rules which are given in Table 1.2. The proofs of these rules can be found in the Additional Reading at the end of this chapter.

To see how calculus allows us to find the maximum or minimum values of a function, consider Figure 1.5. At outputs less than OQ_1 the gradient of the total curve is negative, at OQ_1 its gradient is zero, at outputs Q_1 to Q_3 it is positive and at outputs greater than OQ_3 it is negative again. Therefore we can draw the curve representing the gradient, or first derivative or marginal values. At OQ_1 total π has a local minimum (*local* because there may be lower minima at outputs for which we have not drawn the curve): as Q increases from just below Q_1 to just beyond it π decreases but then rises. At C total π has a local maximum: as output increases from just below OQ_3 to just above OQ_3, total π rises at first but then decreases. Since at A and C the gradient is zero (because if we change Q by ΔQ, $\Delta \pi$ is zero, hence $\Delta \pi / \Delta Q$ is zero) if we set $d\pi/dQ = 0$ we have a necessary condition for a maximum or a minimum.

To distinguish between which of a maximum or a minimum we have, we use our observations about the gradients of the total curve at outputs just below and just above OQ_1 and OQ_3. Since in the former case as Q increased, the gradient changed from being negative to positive, the gradient must be *increasing*. But in the case of OQ_3 as Q increased, the gradient changed from being positive to being negative, so it must be *decreasing*. If the gradient is increasing as Q increases, the gradient of the gradient must be positive whereas if the gradient decreases as Q increases, the gradient of the gradient must be negative.

To find the gradient of the gradient of a function we find the first derivative of the first derivative, called the second order derivative and written $d^2\pi/dQ^2$ in this particular case. So we simply apply the rules of Table 1.2 to the first derivative.

For example:

$$\pi = aQ + bQ^2 - cQ^3$$

$$\frac{d\pi}{dQ} = a + 2bQ - 3cQ^2$$

$$\frac{d^2\pi}{dQ^2} = 2b - 6cQ$$

Our argument is summarised in Table 1.3.

Table 1.2   Some Simple Rules of Differentiation

RULE	EXAMPLES	DERIVATIVES
1. *Constant Rule* The derivative of a constant is zero.	$y = a$ $y = 9$	$dy/dx = 0$ $dy/dx = 0$
2. *Power Rule* The derivative of a power function is the power times any original constant times the independent variable to its original power less one.	$y = ax^n$ $y = 9x$ $y = 9x^2$ $y = 9x^3$	$dy/dx = nax^{n-1}$ $dy/dx = 9$ $dy/dx = 18x$ $dy/dx = 27x^2$
3. *Sums and Differences Rule* The derivative of a sum (difference between) of several terms is the sum (difference between) of the derivatives of these terms.	$y = g(x) + h(x)$ $y = 10 + 4x^2 - 3x^3$	$dy/dx = \dfrac{dg}{dx} + \dfrac{dh}{dx}$ $\dfrac{dy}{dx} = 8x - 9x^2$
4. *Product Rule* The derivative of the product of two terms is the first term multiplied by the derivative of the second, plus the second term multiplied by the derivative of the first.	$y = g(x)h(x)$ $y = 9x^2(2 - x)$	$\dfrac{dy}{dx} = g(x)\dfrac{dh}{dx} + h(x)\dfrac{dg}{dx}$ $\dfrac{dy}{dx} = 9x^2(-1) + (2-x)18x$ $= -9x^2 + 36x - 18x^2$ $= 36x - 27x^2$
5. *Quotient Rule* The derivative of a ratio function, equals the denominator multiplied by the derivative of the numerator, minus the numerator multiplied by the derivative of the denominator, all divided by the denominator squared.	$y = u/v$ where $u = g(x)$ $v = h(x)$ $y = (2 - x)/9x^2$	$\dfrac{dy}{dx} = \dfrac{1}{v^2}\left(v\dfrac{du}{dx} - u\dfrac{dv}{dx}\right)$ $\dfrac{dy}{dx} = \dfrac{9x^2(-1) - (2-x)18x}{81x^4}$ $= \dfrac{-9x^2 - 36x + 18x^2}{81x^4}$ $= \dfrac{9x^2 - 36x}{81x^4} = \dfrac{x-4}{9x^3}$
6. *Chain Rule* The derivative of a function of a function, such as $y = f(u)$ when $u = g(x)$, with respect to x, is equal to the derivative of y with respect to u, multiplied by the derivative of u with respect to x.	$y = f(u)$ where $u = g(x)$ $y = 2t^2$ where $t = x^3$	$\dfrac{dy}{dx} = \dfrac{dy}{du}\dfrac{du}{dx}$ $\dfrac{dy}{dx} = 4t.3x^2$ $= 4x^3.3x^2 = 12x^5$

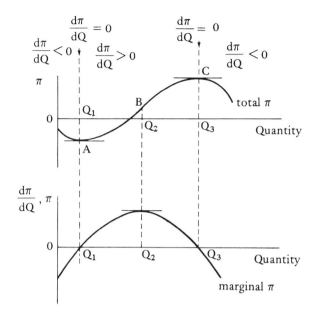

Figure 1.5

Table 1.3

If $y = f(x)$ then we have found:

A MAXIMUM if: $\dfrac{dy}{dx} = 0$ and $\dfrac{d^2y}{dx^2} < 0$

A MINIMUM if: $\dfrac{dy}{dx} = 0$ and $\dfrac{d^2y}{dx^2} > 0$

Functions of Several Variables

Unconstrained Optimisation In many cases a dependent variable depends on the values of *several* independent variables. For example a demand function:

$$Q = f(A,P)$$

where Q represents quantity demanded per period, A advertising per period and P, price.

To find the marginal effect of each independent variable on the dependent variable whilst holding the effects of the other variables constant we can use partial derivatives. A first order partial derivative of $Q = f(K,L)$ with respect to K is

$$\frac{\partial Q}{\partial K} = \lim_{\Delta K \to 0} \left(\frac{\Delta Q}{\Delta K}\right) \qquad \text{where } L \text{ is held constant.}$$

This is analogous to the first derivative of a function of one variable which we explained above.

To interpret a partial derivative geometrically consider Figure 1.6 where $Q = f(K,L)$ represents a surface. If we hold L constant at L_0, then Q can change only if K is changed. These changes are shown by the 'slice' BPL_0. The partial derivative $\partial Q/\partial K$ at a point equals the gradient of this slice at that point because from the above definition of $\partial Q/\partial K$ we can see it is the change in Q divided by the change in K when this tends to zero and L is held constant. Similarly $\partial Q/\partial L$ at a point represents the gradient of the slice K_0PC at that point if K is fixed at K_0.

To find a first order partial derivative we treat all of the independent variables as constants except for that with respect to which we are differentiating. We then simply apply the rules of Table 1.2. For example:

$$z = 25 + 3x^2 + 5xy - 2y$$

$$\frac{\partial z}{\partial x} = 6x + 5y$$

$$\frac{\partial z}{\partial y} = 5x - 2$$

To find the maximum of say, Q, as in Figure 1.6 we are geometrically trying to locate point P. We set $\partial Q/\partial L$ and $\partial Q/\partial K$ equal to zero. These conditions are necessary because if either was positive (negative) we could increase

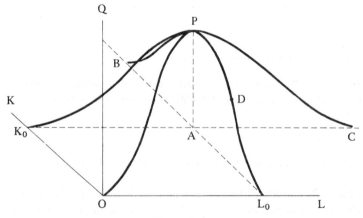

Figure 1.6

Q by increasing (decreasing) the relevant independent variable. In terms of Figure 1.6 we can see that the gradient of both of the slices K_0PC and BPL_0 equals zero at P, whereas at D, for example, $\partial Q/\partial K$ is positive so by increasing K we could increase Q. Hence D does not represent a maximum value of Q. However, note that we have explained only the necessary conditions for a maximum here. For the necessary *and* sufficient conditions the reader is referred to the Additional Reading list.

Constrained Optimisation   Managers often wish to maximise or minimise a function of certain variables given certain constraints on those variables. For example, minimise total cost (which depends on the quantities of inputs and their prices) subject to output being equal to a fixed level (which also depends on the quantities of inputs and their prices).

Two techniques can be used: the reduction method and the lagrangian multiplier method. Before describing each, however, let us gain a geometric interpretation of the problem. If we are given an equation $Q = f(K,L)$ which we wish to maximise given that $4K + 2L = 100$, the first equation may represent a dome and the constraint, a line, because it contains only two variables, K and L, and not three. This dome is represented in Figure 1.7 and the constraint by AC. Geometrically the problem is to locate a point on the dome which is furthest up from the base but vertically above AC. That is if we slice the dome by moving a knife vertically through it so that it cuts along AC, where will it touch the dome first?

The Reduction Method: To consider both methods consider the problem:

Maximise $z = 20x + 15y + 8xy - y^2 - x^2$ subject to $4x + 2y = 100$. Using the reduction method we would make, say, y the subject of the constraint equation, substitute it into the z function and treat the result as an unconstrained

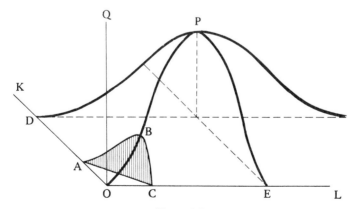

Figure 1.7

maximisation problem of one variable. Hence $y = 50 - 2x$

$$\therefore z = 20x + 15(50 - 2x) + 8x(50 - 2x) - (50 - 2x)^2 - x^2$$
$$= -1750 + 590x - 21x^2$$

$$\frac{\partial z}{\partial x} = 590 - 42x = 0 \qquad \therefore x = 14.05$$

$$\frac{\partial^2 z}{\partial x^2} = -42 < 0 \qquad \qquad \therefore \text{ a maximum.}$$

Substituting $x = 14.05$ into the constraint gives the optimum value of y to be 21.9. By substituting both of these values into the z function the maximum value of z is found to be 2394.05.

Notice that z could have been output, x and y quantities of capital and labour, and their coefficients 4 and 2 could have been their prices, with total cost equal to the 100. But often the constraints encountered are too numerous or too complex for the reduction technique to be practical, for example if in the last case we had four independent variables and constraints. A simpler method is the lagrangian multiplier method.

Lagrange Multiplier Method: In this technique the constrained optimisation problem is converted into an unconstrained problem. The technique is to re-arrange the constraint so that on one side we have the value zero, to multiply the resulting equation by an undetermined variable — the lagrangian multiplier — and to add this to the objective function. Hence for our last problem:

$$Z_\lambda = 20x + 15y + 8xy - y^2 - x^2 + \lambda(100 - 4x - 2y)$$

where Z_λ is the lagrangian function and λ the lagrangian multiplier. We then differentiate Z_λ with respect to x, y and λ and equate each derivative to zero to obtain three equations in three unknowns, x, y and λ. These equations are then solved simultaneously. To understand, recall that we wish to find values of x and y which give the largest possible value of z while still satisfying the constraint that $100 - 4x - 2y = 0$. If only values of x and y which fulfil the constraint are considered, the expression in brackets in the Z_λ function may be written as zero, and those values from this restricted set which maximise Z_λ will also maximise z (and do so subject to the constraint). Therefore, provided we could be sure that the constraint is fulfilled, we could treat the problem of finding x and y which give the constrained maximum of z as that of finding x and y which give the unconstrained maximum of Z_λ. Hence we would partially differentiate Z_λ with respect to each of x, y, and λ and equate the partial derivatives to zero. The multiplication of the rearranged constraint by λ guarantees that the constraint is fulfilled because, when Z_λ is differentiated with respect to λ and equated to zero, the constraint is obtained as one of the necessary conditions for the constrained maximum. Differentiation with respect to x and y completes the requirements for the unconstrained maximum as explained on page 13.[1] Hence we obtain:

$$\partial Z_\lambda / \partial x = 20 + 8y - 2x - 4\lambda = 0$$
$$\partial Z_\lambda / \partial y = 15 + 8x - 2y - 2\lambda = 0$$
$$\partial Z_\lambda / \partial \lambda = 100 - 4x - 2y = 0$$

Solving simultaneously gives $x = 14.05$, $y = 21.9$ and $z = 2394.05$, the same solutions as from the reduction method. If further constraints existed we would rearrange each, apply a different lagrange multiplier to each and proceed as before. (Note that λ represents the marginal change in z when the constraint — in the example, 100 — changes by one unit. Thus if z represents output and x and y are capital and labour with prices of £4 and £2 respectively, and the constraint represents the available budget to be spent on both inputs, then λ is the marginal product of money. It equals the increase in output if the budget were to be increased from £100 to £101. In the example, λ has a value of 41.8. If we increased the budget by £1 and allocated this optimally between additional X and Y, output would rise to 2436.01 units or approximately 42 units above its previous level. We would hire an additional 0.14 units of X and 0.30 units of Y.)

Additional Reading

Archibald, G.C. and Lipsey, R.G. (1967) *An Introduction to a Mathematical Treatment of Economics*, Weidenfeld and Nicholson.

Birchenhall, C. and Grout, P. (1984) *Mathematics for Modern Economics*, Philip Allan.

Casson, M. (1973) *Introduction to Mathematical Economics*, Thomas Nelson.

Chiang, A.C. (1984) *Fundamental Methods of Mathematical Economics*, McGraw Hill.

Dowling, E.T. (1980) *Mathematics for Economists*, McGraw Hill.

Glass, J. Colin (1980) *An Introduction to Mathematical Methods in Economics*, McGraw Hill.

Huang, D.S. (1964) *Introduction to the Use of Mathematics in Economic Analysis*, John Wiley.

Yamane, T. (1968) *Mathematics for Economists: An Elementary Survey*, Prentice Hall.

---

1   Notice that, given the fulfilment of the constraint, although we could write Z_λ $= 20x + 15y + 8xy - y^2 - x^2 + \lambda(0)$, we could not omit the $\lambda(0)$. This is because this expression already assumes the constraint *is* fulfilled, but we wish to *find* values of x and y which will fulfil it and expressions involving x and y are included in the constraint function.

APPENDIX 1
Partial Derivatives and Total Differentials

Given the equation:

$z = f(x,y)$

where x and y are independent, partial derivatives are defined as follows:

$$\partial z/\partial x = \lim_{\Delta x \to 0} \frac{\Delta z}{\Delta x} = \frac{f(x+\Delta x,\ y)-f(x,\ y)}{\Delta x}$$

$$\delta z/\partial y = \lim_{\Delta x \to 0} \frac{\Delta z}{\Delta y} = \frac{f(x,\ y+\Delta y)-f(x,\ y)}{\Delta y}$$

The former derivative represents the change in z per unit change in x where the latter is infinitesimally small. If x changes by such a small amount, dx, with y held constant, then the magnitude of the change in z is

$$dz = \frac{\partial z}{\partial x} \cdot dx$$

Similarly, if y changes by an infinitesimally small amount, dy, with x held constant, the magnitude of the change in z is:

$$dz = \frac{\partial z}{\partial y} \cdot dy$$

Hence, if both x and y change by dx and dy respectively, the total change in z equals:

$$dz = \frac{\partial z}{\partial x} \cdot dx + \frac{\partial z}{\partial y} \cdot dy$$

with is called the *total differential* of the z function. This expression may be denoted as:

$$dz = f_x.dx+f_y.dy$$

where $f_x = \partial z/\partial x$ and $f_y = \partial z/\partial y$.

2
Decision Analysis under Conditions
of Risk and Uncertainty

Most managerial decisions involve risk or uncertainty. In this chapter we firstly set out a framework for explaining decision theory, and secondly discuss the nature of certainty, risk and uncertainty. Thirdly the units in which the decision outcomes might be measured are explained. Measures of risk are described and fifthly we outline techniques for making decisions in situations of risk and uncertainty. Finally sequential decision making under risky conditions is discussed.

2.1 A Framework for Decision Making

Suppose a decision maker wishes to choose between a given number of alternative actions. The outcome of each will depend on both which action is chosen and which 'state of nature' occurs. A state of nature is a specific set of environmental factors which affect the value of an outcome. For example, the decision maker may wish to decide on which of two projects to pursue where the profits resulting from each depend on which of the following occurs: recession, mild slump, normal conditions, mild boom, and boom.

We can represent this decision maker's situation diagrammatically as in Table 2.1 where S_1 to S_5 represent the five states of the economy respectively, A_1, A_2 represent the pursuance of projects A and B respectively and O_{11} ... O_{25} represent outcomes.

This matrix can be generalised for any number of actions A_1 ... A_n and any number of states of nature S_1 ... S_q. We shall assume that the list S_1 ... S_q represents a complete list of mutually exclusive states of nature. (We also assume each state of nature is independent of the choice of action.) We may measure the outcomes in terms of money units or utility units as we discuss in Section 2.3.

19

Table 2.1

Actions	States of Nature				
	S_1	S_2	S_3	S_4	S_5
A_1	O_{11}	O_{12}	O_{13}	O_{14}	O_{15}
A_2	O_{21}	O_{22}	O_{23}	O_{24}	O_{25}

2.2 The Nature of Certainty, Risk and Uncertainty

Decision making situations may be classified in two ways: the degree of strategic interdependence between different decision makers and the degree of knowledge which a decision maker has about the occurrence of each state of nature. When a manager makes a decision this will always, to some extent, affect the outcomes of decisions made by other firms, hence interdependence between decision makers always exists. But *strategic* interdependence exists if the actions of other firms are explicitly taken into account by the first firm. Strategic interdependence is absent if the actions chosen by other firms are simply regarded, together with many other factors, as a state of the environment. For example, if there are so many firms that none can individually affect the product's price, then any one firm can decide on the quantity it wishes to sell without considering its effects on other firms' sales. But if only two firms existed in a market, strategic interdependence would exist because each would then try to predict its competitor's action. In this chapter we restrict ourselves to situations where strategic interdependence is absent.

There are three degrees of knowledge which a decision maker can have about the occurrence of each state of nature: certainty, risk and uncertainty, although the literature is not consistent in its treatment of the latter two. This chapter mainly follows the definitions of Luce and Raiffa (1957).

Certainty exists if the decision maker has complete knowledge of every relevant aspect of the decision situation and hence knows which outcome will result from each action. *Risk* exists if each action leads to one of several possible outcomes where the decision maker knows the probability of occurrence of each state of nature. Notice that the decision maker does not know which state of nature he *will* face but only the proportion of the total number of occasions on which each state of nature will exist if the situation frequently recurs.

The probability of occurrence of a state of nature may be calculated either *a priori*: before the states have occurred, or *a posteriori*: after the states have occurred on a certain number of occasions. In the former the probability may be deduced given certain knowledge. For example, the probability of the occurrence of a head when a coin is tossed may be deduced to be one half, given the knowledge that an unbiased coin has two sides. In the *a posteriori* case, a sample of occasions on which states of nature occurred is taken and the relative frequency of each state of nature calculated. This method assumes that the relative frequency of each state in the past is identical to that in the future. Alternatively a subjective probability of occurrence may be attributed to each state of nature on, for example, a subjective evaluation of one's experiences of similar past events. *Uncertainty* exists if the probability of each outcome occurring when any one action is chosen is either completely unknown or is not even meaningful.[1]

Thus the cases of certainty and uncertainty are two extremes of the degree of knowledge which a decision maker has as to the probability of occurrence of each state of nature. As the decision maker's confidence in his estimates of these probabilities decreases, the situation moves from certainty towards uncertainty. Most decisions are taken in situations between these two extremes.

2.3 Utility

The units in which the outcomes or payoffs may be measured are money or 'utility'. Given a situation of risk the decision maker may choose the action with the largest expected money value (*EMV*). This concept is detailed in Section 2.6. Briefly, an action's *EMV* is the probability of a state of nature occurring times its money outcome if that state occurred, aggregated for each state. But the ranking of actions by *EMV*s may not correspond to their ranking in terms of the manager's preferences. An extreme example of this is the St Petersburg Paradox. There one must decide how much to pay to take part in a gamble where a coin is tossed and one would receive £2^n if the first head occurred on the nth toss. The *EMV* of this gamble is infinity,[2] yet few would place their lifetime's earnings on such a bet. An alternative measure may more accurately represent a decision maker's preferences.

Von Neumann and Morgenstern (VNM) have proved that, given certain assumptions about a decision maker's behaviour, a specific technique exists to predict which of the two risky actions he will prefer. The technique involves the construction of an expected cardinal utility index for each action. Before

---

1   Luce and Raiffa include a fourth category: a combination of risk and uncertainty in which the probability of occurrence of each state of nature is determined *a posteriori* using objective data. We include this under *risk*.

2   EMV = (Probability of first head on first toss) × £2 +(probability of first head on second toss) × £2^2 +(probability of first head on third toss) × £2^3
       + . . .
     = (0.5) × 2+$(0.5)^2$ × 2^2+$(0.5)^3$ × 2^3 + . . .
     = 1 + 1 + 1 . . .
     = ∞

we explain the technique it is necessary to discuss VNM's concept of cardinal utility.

The Nature of VNM Cardinal Utility

Neoclassical cardinal utility (see Chapter 5) measures the intensity of satisfaction which an individual derives from an action. But VNM cardinal utility is very different (despite the identical use of words). It is a number associated with a payoff which enables one to rank payoffs in terms of those more and those less preferred by a decision maker. In what sense is the measure cardinal? To explain this we must distinguish between different types of measure.

Measures may either be associative, ranking or cardinal. The first is an identifying label. The second allows one to rank phenomena in terms of the index or measure. But it does not allow one to combine two or more rankings to produce an index which would be valid for the phenomena jointly. For example, suppose we have two ladders. Using a measure which ranks only height we would award a higher number to the taller ladder and a lower number to the shorter. Provided we always give a higher number to the taller ladder the actual numbers used do not matter. The measure will still rank the ladders correctly. But one cannot necessarily *combine* the actual numbers to compare this pair of ladders with another pairing of ladders. The third measure does allow one to combine the indices of a characteristic of two phenomena to predict whether or not the characteristics of the two together do or do not exceed the characteristics of another two. Such an index, for example metres, would enable us to predict whether the height of the two ladders, one extended from the other, would or would not exceed the height of a ceiling. The VNM index is a cardinal index in this sense. It permits the combination of utility indices of more than one payoff so that one can assess whether or not one set of joint payoffs is to be preferred to other combinations.

Construction of the Index

Here we construct the VNM utility index for a risky payoff, secondly for a certain payoff, and thirdly we compare indices of the former type. Suppose an entrepreneur is trying to decide between manufacturing denim jeans or cord trousers. Suppose the possible payoffs depend only on whether consumers' tastes are predominantly in favour of denim or of cords. Let the money payoffs (in £000) in each case be those shown in Table 2.2.

If, for jeans, the utility index of the £100,000 payoff is 1000 utils and 500 utils for the £40,000, and the respective probabilities are 0.7 and 0.3, then the expected utility of the introduction of this product is $0.7 \times 1000 + 0.3 \times 500 = 850$ utils. Similarly, in the case of the introduction of cords, if the utility index for each payoff is 690 utils for the £60,000 and 880 utils for the £80,000 then the expected utility for this product is $0.7 \times 690 +$

Table 2.2

	Tastes in favour of denim	Tastes in favour of cords
Probability	0.7	0.3
Denim jeans	100	40
Cords	60	80

$0.3 \times 880 = 747$ utils. In general, the expected utility of a risky action, A, $EUV(A)$, with two payoffs, π_1 and π_2, is:

$$EUV(A) = pU(\pi_1) + (1-p)U(\pi_2) \qquad (2.1)$$

where p and $(1-p)$ denote the probabilities of π_1 and π_2 occurring respectively, and $U(\pi_1)$ and $U(\pi_2)$ denote the utility indices for π_1 and π_2. But how does one evaluate $U(\pi_1)$ and $U(\pi_2)$?

To ascribe a utility number to a specific money payoff, say π_1, the decision maker is presented with a 'standard gamble' comparison. A risky action, say A_1, is considered as the yardstick for comparison. Its possible outcomes, X_1 and X_2, have probabilities of occurrence q and $(1-q)$ respectively. Arbitrarily chosen utility indices are then awarded to X_1 and X_2 so that the higher index is attributed to the outcome the decision maker prefers. Next, the decision maker is presented with a series of choices between the risky action, A_1, and the action A_2, which has the certain outcome of π_1 to which we wish to ascribe a measure of utility. That is, he is asked to compare $EUV(A_1) = qU(X_1)+(1-q)U(X_2)$ and $EUV(A_2) = 1.U(\pi_1)$. This choice situation is represented in Table 2.3.

The value of q is altered in the series of choice situations until the decision maker is indifferent between the two actions. If $U(X_1)$ is less than $U(X_2)$

Table 2.3

Actions \ State of Nature	S_1	S_2	Expected Utility
Probability	q	$(1-q)$	
A_1	$U(X_1)$	$U(X_2)$	$qU(X_1)+U(X_2)$
A_2	$U(\pi_1)$	$U(\pi_1)$	$1.U(\pi_1)$

then, as q increases from 0 to 1, the probability of gaining X_1 rather than X_2 is increased and $EUV(A_1)$ decreases from $U(X_2)$ to $U(X_1)$. At the value of q which renders the decision maker indifferent between the actions, both have the same utility index. So $EUV(A_1) = EUV(A_2)$ and therefore $U(\pi_1) = q . U(X_1) + (1-q)U(X_2)$. But, since $U(X_1)$ and $U(X_2)$ are known, albeit with arbitrarily chosen values, and q has been found by experiment, $U(\pi_1)$ can be calculated. The process can be repeated for $U(\pi_2)$. Both indices can then be substituted into equation (2.1) to find the utility index for action A.

Returning to the jeans and cords example, suppose we wish to find the utility which the entrepreneur associates with £100,000. We could formulate the standard gamble as a risky action with payoffs of £10 million and £10. Suppose the entrepreneur says he prefers £10m. to £10: we would arbitrarily assign utilities of, say, 19620 and 20 utils to each respectively. The entrepreneur is then given a series of choices between, on the one hand, the standard gamble and on the other hand a certain £100,000 where q, the probability of gaining the £10m. in the standard gamble, is progressively reduced until he is indifferent between the two. Suppose this value of q is 0.05. Then:

$$
\begin{aligned}
EUV(£100,000) &= EUV(\text{standard gamble}) \\
&= qU(£10 \text{ million}) + (1-q)U(£10) \\
&= (0.05 \times 19620) + (0.95 \times 20) \\
&= 1000 \text{ utils}
\end{aligned}
$$

The same procedure could be performed for the other possible outcome of the denim product and both 'utility' values substituted into an expression analogous to equation (2.1) to gain the EUV for denim jeans.

The third aim of this section is to compare the EUVs of two risky projects. The VNM theorem says that, provided the decision maker's preferences fulfil certain axioms, if these standard gamble procedures are followed, any risky project with a higher EUV than another is preferred. (For a proof of this theorem and the assumed axioms, see Baumol (1977), pp. 432−5.) In the case of the example, if the EUVs of the denim and cord jeans were 850 and 747 respectively, the entrepreneur would prefer the former.[3]

EUV compared with EMV

Decisions based on EUVs may differ from those based on EMV comparisons. Consider the relationship between money values and utility for a decision maker. Three cases are often distinguished: decreasing, constant and increasing marginal utility. If each extra £1 which the decision maker has increases his utility index by less than the previous £1, the marginal utility of money is decreasing. Therefore the gradient of the decision maker's utility function

---

3   Notice that the theorem does not say that the manager *should* prefer to manufacture denim jeans but that he *does*; the EUVs indicate his relative preferences.

is decreasing. If each £1 yields the same increase in utility as the previous £1, the *MU* of money is constant and hence so is the gradient of his utility function, and if the *MU* of money is increasing so also will the slope of the utility function. These cases are shown in Figure 2.1.

Holding everything else constant, each case implies a different attitude to risk by the decision maker. In the first case each extra £1 received adds less to utility than would be lost if he gave up £1. Therefore the decision maker would not bet on the success of a project where the possible money losses equal the possibly money gains and where each has a probability of 0.5 because the *EUV* of the bet would be negative. Such action is said to show risk aversion.

In the second case, each £1 gained yields the same utility as a £1 loss. Therefore the decision maker would be indifferent as to whether or not he took part in this gamble since its *EUV* is zero to him. Such behaviour is risk neutral. In the third case each extra £1 gained would add more to utility than would be detracted by the loss of £1. Hence the decision maker would be willing to engage in the gamble since its *EUV* would be positive. Such action is risk preferring or seeking.

If the decision maker's utility function is not a linear function of money, the *EMV* and *EUV* values may rank projects differently, whereas if this utility function is linear, the same ranking would result. To illustrate this inequality consult the following example. Suppose a manager has to choose between buying a satellite to put into orbit on the Space Shuttle or buying a government bond both costing £10,000. Suppose the only relevant states of nature are whether the satellite works perfectly or is slightly defective when in orbit, that the probability of the satellite working perfectly is 0.6, and that the bond is riskless. If the bond pays a 10% return, and the satellite investment is worth £15,000 if it works perfectly but only £6,000 if it is defective, the choice situation is represented in Table 2.4. The utilities associated with each money payoff have been derived from a figure like Figure 2.1. In terms of *EMV*s,

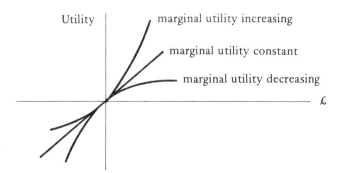

Figure 2.1

Table 2.4

Actions	States of Nature Probability	Satellite Works Perfectly 0.6	Defectively 0.4	E.V.
A_1 Satellite	*EMV*: (£000)	15.00	6.00	11.40
	EUV: Marginal utility decreasing	3.10	2.50	2.86
	Marginal utility constant	14.00	5.50	10.60
A_2 Bond	*EMV*: (£000)	11.00	11.00	11.00
	EUV: Marginal utility decreasing	3.00	3.00	3.00
	Marginal utility constant	10.20	10.20	10.20

the satellite project is preferred to the government bond since its *EMV* is greater than that of the latter. But if the *EUV*s are compared and if the manager is risk averse he would prefer the government bond, whereas if he is risk neutral he would prefer the satellite. In this particular example the ranking is also the same as that based on *EMV*s if the manager is risk seeking but in *other examples* a risk *seeking* utility function could lead to a reverse ranking compared with that of risk neutrality.

Throughout the remainder of this chapter each payoff will be presented in monetary units because these are more readily available to managers than utility indices.

2.4 Measurement of Risk

To explain the techniques which have been proposed to measure risk we introduce the concept of a probability distribution of outcomes resulting from a decision. This shows the relationship between the value of each possible outcome and the probability of its occurrence.

Consider the example in Section 2.1 where a manager has to choose between two projects where the profits from each depend on the forthcoming state of the economy. Suppose the manager wishes to maximise the *EMV* of profits and that he knows the probability of occurrence of each state of the economy. The situation is shown in Table 2.5.

Given that only five states of nature can occur, Figure 2.2 represents the probability distribution of the outcomes of each project. If there were a very large number of states of the economy then the number of columns in Table 2.5 would be much greater. With a very large number of points in the figure

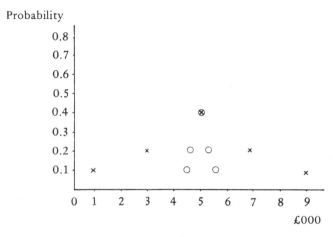

Figure 2.2

Table 2.5

States of Nature / Actions	Deep Recession	Stagnation	Normal	Mild Boom	Extreme Boom	EMV
PROBABILITY	0.10	0.20	0.40	0.20	0.10	
PROJECT A	1.00	3.00	5.00	7.00	9.00	5.00
PROJECT B	4.50	4.75	5.00	5.25	5.50	5.00

each representing a different payoff and each with a specific probability of occurrence, the probability of any particular value is much lower than in Figure 2.2. The resulting large number of points may then be approximated by a continuous line as in Figure 2 3.

Measures of the risk associated with an action relate to certain characteristics of the probability distribution of outcomes for that action. Crudely, the riskiness of any decision is measured in terms of the variability of its outcomes. The less dispersed the possible outcomes are from the expected value (i.e. the mean), the greater the probability that the actual outcome will be within a given range of that expected and hence the less risky the project.

Standard Deviation

The most common measures of risk are the standard deviation and coefficient of variation. The former may be calculated as:

$$\sigma = \sqrt{\sum_{i=1}^{n} P_i(X_i - \bar{X})^2}$$

where P_i = probability of outcome i
X_i = value of outcome i
n = number of outcomes
$\bar{X}$ = mean value of all outcomes
σ = standard deviation

The lower the standard deviation, the tighter the probability distribution of outcomes and the lower the risk, whereas the higher the standard deviation the greater the risk. From Table 2.5 we can see that in terms of standard deviations, project A is riskier than project B and in Figure 2.3 project X is riskier than project Y.

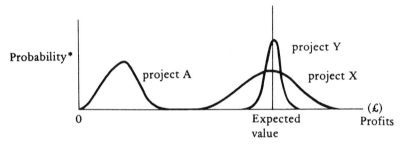

* More accurately 'probability density' (since the probability of any specific π value occurring is near zero, yet the area under the curve between two π values gives the probability of a π value in that range).

Figure 2.3

One criticism of this measure is that a manager may be more concerned with outcomes below the expected value than with outcomes above.[4] Therefore a measure of risk which more accurately corresponds to that experienced by a manager would be a measure which included only payoffs *below* the expected value. An example of such a measure is the 'semi-standard deviation' which is calculated as:

$$SSD = \sqrt{\sum_{i=1}^{k} P_i(X_i - \bar{X})^2}$$

4   A manager may be more concerned with avoiding outcomes well below the average than with obtaining outcomes well above it. Obviously, higher outcomes are more desirable than lower ones. But while very high outcomes only indicate more, rather than less, success, very low outcomes (e.g. large losses) could be *fatal* for the firm.

where P_i = probability of outcome i
    X_i = value of outcome i
    i = 1 ... k = the set of outcomes whose values are less than $\bar{X}$
    $\bar{X}$ = mean of all outcomes

However, it is usual for the standard deviation and semi-standard deviation to be correlated, so the latter may add little information which is omitted by the former.

A second criticism of the standard deviation (and also of the semi-standard deviation) is that two alternative actions may have probability distributions which intuitively seem to differ in riskiness but which have the same standard deviation. For example, suppose projects A and X in Figure 2.3 have the same standard deviation of £1,000 but A has an expected profit of £10,000, whereas X has an expected profit of £100,000. Using the standard deviation as a measure of risk, both A and X are equally risky, but this measure has not taken into account the greater expected return of X in comparison with A.

Coefficient of Variation

To standardise for different magnitudes of outcomes one can calculate the coefficient of variation for each project:

$$V = \frac{\sigma}{E(R)}$$

where $E(R)$ denotes expected profits. Using this crtierion project A is more risky than project X.

A limitation of these measures is that neither σ nor V give indications of other aspects of the probability distribution such as shape, yet shape may affect risk. For example, both distributions in Figure 2.4 share the same values for σ and V but the adoption of project A may result in profits between π_0 and π_2 whereas project B would not result in profits below π_1 but could result in profits as high as π_3. Therefore a more accurate assessment of the

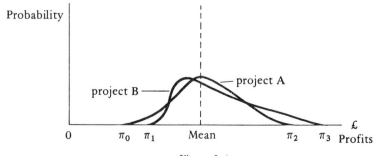

Figure 2.4

riskiness of a project may depend not only on σ and V, but also on the degree of skewness of the distribution, its range, modal outcome[5] and so on.

2.5 Decision Criteria Under Certainty

Here the decision maker knows which state of nature will occur. Therefore he can replace the payoffs which are possible for each action by the payoff which will occur. He can then choose the action with the largest payoff.

2.6 Decision Criteria Under Risk

In this case the decision maker is able to assign a probability distribution to the states of nature. The literature discusses several alternative criteria including the *VNM* Expected Utility Value (*EUV*) approach and the Expected Money Value (*EMV*) criterion. Here we concentrate on the latter.

Expected Money Value (EMV)

If the payoffs are retained in money units the decision maker would choose the action with the largest *EMV*. *EMV* is calculated as:

$$EMV(A_i) = P_1\pi_{i1} + P_2\pi_{i2} + \ldots + P_n\pi_{in}$$

$$= \sum_{j=1}^{n} P_j\pi_{ij}$$

where P_j is the probability of state of nature j

π_{ij} is the payoff which results from action i and state of nature j.

As we saw earlier, *EMV* corresponds to a specific case (that of risk neutrality) of the general utility index method of determining preferences. But this case may rarely exist in practice.

A criticism of the ranking of projects based on *EMV* is that it ignores the riskiness of each project. This was illustrated in Table 2.5 where two projects had the same *EMV*, but different distributions of possible payoffs. One alternative criterion to the use of *VNM* utilities is the use of expected return—risk analysis. The *EMV* and the risk of each action may be plotted on a diagram with these variables measured along each axis. Risk may be measured using any of the measures explained in Section 2.4. Figure 2.5 shows the result for the actions represented in Table 2.6.

---

5   The modal outcome is that with the greatest probability of occurrence.

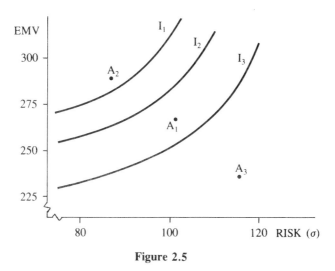

Figure 2.5

Table 2.6

Actions \ States of Nature	S_1	S_2	S_3	EMV
Probability	0.25	0.35	0.40	
A_1	100	300	350	270
A_2	300	400	200	295
A_3	400	100	250	235

The manager's preferences may be represented by indifference curves, for example lines I_1, I_2, I_3. Each indifference curve joins different combinations of *EMV* and risk between which the manager is indifferent. If the manager prefers a greater *EMV* with a given level of risk and also a lower level of risk given an *EMV*, then the indifference curves will have a positive slope. Combinations on curves closer to the top left-hand corner represent *EMV* — risk combinations which are preferred to those on curves closer to the lower right-hand corner because with any given level of risk the former curves indicate greater *EMV* than the latter. To accept greater risk and remain indifferent to their initial position a manager is assumed to require a greater *EMV*; that is, the manager is risk-averse. If the manager is risk-neutral, given a value of *EMV*, he would be indifferent between alternative levels of risk. Hence his indifference curves would be horizontal. If the manager is a risk seeker, he would prefer greater *EMV and* risk, therefore his indifference curves would have a negative slope. In Figure 2.5 we assume that for each additional unit of risk a manager experiences he requires a greater increase in EMV to remain indifferent compared with the original combination. Given the indifference curves in Figure 2.5 we predict that the manager would prefer action A_2.[6]

Finally, note that we have ignored the possibility that the earnings resulting from one action may be correlated with those of others. This possibility is considered in Chapter 12.

2.7   Decision Criteria Under Uncertainty

Several techniques can be used when the probability of each state of nature is unknown: for example, the maximin (or Wald) criterion, the minimax regret (Savage) criterion, the maximax criterion, the Hurwicz and the Laplace criteria. For each we shall use as an example the choice situation of Table 2.7.

Table 2.7

Actions \ States of Nature	S_1	S_2	S_3
A_1	1.0	2.0	9.0
A_2	-2.0	5.0	11.0
A_3	3.0	3.5	4.5

Maximin Criterion[7]

For each strategy the decision maker identifies the lowest payoff. The strategy with the largest of these 'lowest payoffs' is selected. In the example the lowest payoffs for strategies A_1, A_2 and A_3 are 1.0, -2.0 and 3.0 respectively. The decision maker would select A_3.

This criterion is 'conservative' or 'pessimistic' because it is a rule whereby the decision maker avoids the worst outcome. Some argue that since the criterion does not take account of the value of every payoff it can lead to unreasonable conclusions. For example, in Table 2.8 action A_3 would be chosen despite the very large possible payoffs of the alternatives.

6   Indifference curves are examined in detail in Chapter 5.
7   This criterion is identical to a minimax procedure on a payoff matrix of losses (or disutilities or costs).

Table 2.8

Actions \ States of Nature	S_1	S_2	S_3
A_1	2.9	10^4	10^7
A_2	2.9	10^4	10^{10}
A_3	3.0	3.1	3.1

Minimax Regret Criterion

Here the decision maker asks what would be the sacrifice if a particular state of nature occurred, but instead of having chosen the strategy with the greatest payoff given that state, he had chosen another. Hence, for each state of nature the difference between the maximum payoff and that for each action is calculated and placed in a new 'regret' matrix. For each action the largest regret is calculated and the action with the smallest of these is selected. Adoption of the criterion, therefore, avoids the greatest sacrifice of payoff if the chosen strategy turns out not to be the one with the highest payoff, given the state of nature which occurs. Thus this criterion can also be regarded as 'pessimistic'.

In the example, the regret matrix is shown in Table 2.9 and strategy A_1 would be chosen.

Table 2.9

Actions \ States of Nature	S_1	S_2	S_3	Row Maxima
A_1	2.0	3.0	2.0	3.0
A_2	5.0	0	0	5.0
A_3	0	1.5	6.5	6.5

Several criticisms have been made of this criterion. Firstly, it ignores information; specifically, it ignores all regrets except the largest for each strategy. But the action with the smallest of these may have regrets all of a similar size whereas the rejected actions may, apart from the largest regret, have much smaller ones than those of the chosen strategy. In this situation the criterion may be unreasonable.

Secondly, the criterion may select a strategy from a group of alternatives but would select a different strategy if the original group were depleted by one which was initially rejected. For example consider the case in Table 2.10. If all three strategies were available A_3 would be selected, as shown by the 'Regrets 1' matrix. But if only strategies A_2 and A_3 were available A_2 would be chosen not A_3 the original and still available choice.

Table 2.10

Actions	Payoffs S_1	S_2	S_3	Regrets 1 S_1	S_2	S_3	Row Maxima	Regrets 2 S_1	S_2	S_3	Row Maxima
A_1	21	11	1	0	11	18	18				
A_2	1	22	8	20	0	11	20	10	0	11	11
A_3	11	5	19	10	17	0	17	0	17	0	17

Maximax Criterion

Here the decision maker selects the largest payoff for each action and the action with the largest of these maxima. In Table 2.7 the largest payoffs are 9.0, 11.0 and 4.5 respectively. Hence the decision maker would select A_2. This criterion also ignores information: it would select a strategy even if the maximum payoff for that strategy only marginally exceeded that of others, even if the other possible outcomes from the selected action were very much or even dangerously lower.

Hurwicz α-Criterion

The maximin criterion selected only the worst outcome for each action whereas the maximax selected only the best. The Hurwicz α criterion is an attempt to use both. For each action an α-index, αI_i, is calculated where:

$$\alpha I_i = \alpha I_i + (1-\alpha)L_i$$
$$I_i, L_i = \text{the least and largest payoffs for action } i \text{ respectively}$$
$$\alpha = \text{a pessimism}-\text{optimism index}$$

The action with the largest α-index is selected. For example if $\alpha = \frac{1}{4}$ the α-indices for each action in the original example are, 7, $7\frac{3}{4}$ and $4\frac{1}{8}$ for A_1, A_2 and A_3 respectively, hence A_2 would be chosen.

The value of α may be derived by presenting the decision maker with hypothetical choices between A_1 and A_2 as in Table 2.11. The value of z is increased from 0 until the decision maker is indifferent between the two actions.

Table 2.11

States of Nature Actions	S_1	S_2	αI_1
A_1	0	1	$1 - \alpha$
A_2	z	z	z

When indifference is reached, the actions are assumed to have the same α index. Hence $(1 - \alpha) = z$ so, given z, α can be calculated. Notice that if $\alpha = 1$ the criterion is the maximin criterion whereas if $\alpha = 0$ it becomes the maximax criterion. Since the former is a pessimistic rule, whereas the latter is an optimistic rule, the derivation of the name 'pessimism–optimism' index is clear.

A criticism of this technique is that it also ignores information: only the largest and smallest payoffs are considered. Hence one action may be chosen in preference to the others despite the fact that all of its intermediate payoffs may be less than those of any other strategy.

Principle of Insufficient Reason (Laplace Criterion or Baye's Criterion)

This states that if one has no idea which state of nature is most likely to occur, then one should ascribe the same probability of occurrence to each. Hence if there are n states of nature, the probability of $1/n$ is ascribed to each, and the expected value for each strategy calculated. The strategy with the greatest expected value is chosen.

A criticism of this technique is that in practice there may be many different ways of listing states of nature where each way is complete and each state mutually exclusive. For example, the states of nature which affected the outcomes to the denim jeans/cords choice were given as 'tastes in favour of denim' and 'tastes in favour of cords'; hence, using the Laplace criterion, each state would have a probability of $\frac{1}{2}$, but possibly one should consider three relevant states: 'Tastes strongly in favour of denim', 'Tastes mildly in favour of denim', 'Tastes in favour of cords', each being ascribed a probability of $\frac{1}{3}$ and so on.

Mixed Strategies

Instead of choosing a pure strategy the decision maker could choose each strategy on a fixed proportion of occasions, the choice on each occasion being determined randomly. The payoffs for each state of nature in the mixed strategies would be those expected from the combination of actions. The pure strategies and the mixed strategies could all be compared on a maximin or minimax regret criterion for selection. For example, if the mixed strategy in Table 2.12 (taking a different example to that of Table 2.7) consists of A_1 and A_2 with probabilities $\frac{1}{3}$ and $\frac{2}{3}$ respectively, the payoffs for each state of nature are the sum of $\frac{1}{3}$ and $\frac{2}{3}$ times those of the pure strategies. When the maximin criterion is applied to this augmented matrix the chosen action is A_2.

Table 2.12

Actions \ States of Nature	S_1	S_2
A_1	30	15
A_2	60	30
$\frac{1}{3} A_1 + \frac{2}{3} A_2$	50	25

Cautionary Note

Note that in all of our payoff matrices the VNM utility index value could be substituted for each monetary value for use with any of our criteria. But of these criteria, the Principle of Insufficient Reason is the only one which is consistent with all of the VNM assumptions (see Baumol 1977).

2.8   Sequential Decisions: Decision Trees

A manager often has to decide between strategies where the outcomes depend on chance events and/or future choices whose outcomes themselves depend on chance and/or future choices and so on. Provided he has sufficient information concerning the probabilities of the outcomes of each chance event and of the values of every final outcome, decision trees are a method of calculating the *EMV* of each strategy.

Suppose a manager has to decide whether or not to develop a new product which has emerged from his research laboratory. He believes that the probability of successfully doing so in two years is 0.7 and hence the probability of either technological failure or inability to keep to his budgeted time span is 0.3. If successful, the pattern of net cash inflow will depend on whether he launches the product with high or low advertising, or whether he abandons the product. In the former two cases, demand may be high, medium or low with probabilities 0.5, 0.3 and 0.2 respectively if advertising is high, but 0.2, 0.3 and 0.5 respectively if advertising is low. High, medium and low levels of demand give net cash inflows of £8,000, £5,000 and £3,000 if advertising is high, but £8,500, £5,500 and £2,500 if it is low. Abandonment at this stage results in a loss of £1,000.

If, however, the development fails after two years, the manager must decide whether or not to engage in further efforts. If development is authorised this may also succeed or fail. Suppose the probabilities of these outcomes occurring, given earlier failure, are 0.3 and 0.7 respectively. If the development is successful on this occasion, again the manager must decide whether to launch and advertise heavily, advertise lightly or abandon. In the first two cases the probabilities of high, medium and low demand are 0.5, 0.3, 0.2 and 0.2, 0.3 and 0.5 respectively, with corresponding cash inflows of £7,000, £4,000, £2,000 and £4,500, £2,500 and £1,500. Abandonment at this stage results in a loss of £2,000. Abandonment in the very first place results in neither profit nor loss, whereas abandonment after an initial development failure results in a loss of £1,000.

The problem facing the manager is represented by the decision tree of Figure 2.6. Each square box represents a 'decision node', the branches from it indicating *decisions* made. The circles represent 'chance nodes', the branches represent *outcomes* which result from earlier decisions and which occur with certain probabilities. The numbers above the lines represent the probability of the next outcome occurring given that the previous chance node has been reached.

To make the decision on the basis of *EMV*s, the *EMV* for each action is calculated and the action with the greatest *EMV* is chosen. Each *EMV* is calculated on the basis that whenever a decision has to be made, the manager will choose that with the highest *EMV*. The method of analysing this type of problem is called 'rollback' or 'foldback' and consists of working from right to left, calculating the *EMV* of the outcomes for each decision and choosing the action with the highest *EMV* when the decision node is reached. This *EMV* is then applied to the probability of the outcome which led to the decision for which this *EMV* has been calculated, and so on until each of the original actions has an *EMV* attached to it.

Returning to the example and beginning in the top half of the figure, given that the development research was successful, the *EMV* of a heavily advertised launch is £6,100 (i.e. $0.5 \times 8000 + 0.3 \times 5000 + 0.2 \times 3000$). For similar reasons the *EMV* of a lightly advertised launch is £4,600. Since the *EMV* of abandonment at this stage is £ − 1,000, the largest *EMV* of a successful development stage is £6,100. In the central section, given an initial development failure, further research and eventual success, the *EMV*s of heavily and lightly advertised launches are £5,100 and £2,400 respectively, whereas abandonment results in a £2,000 loss. The largest of these *EMV*s i.e. at node

Figure 2.6

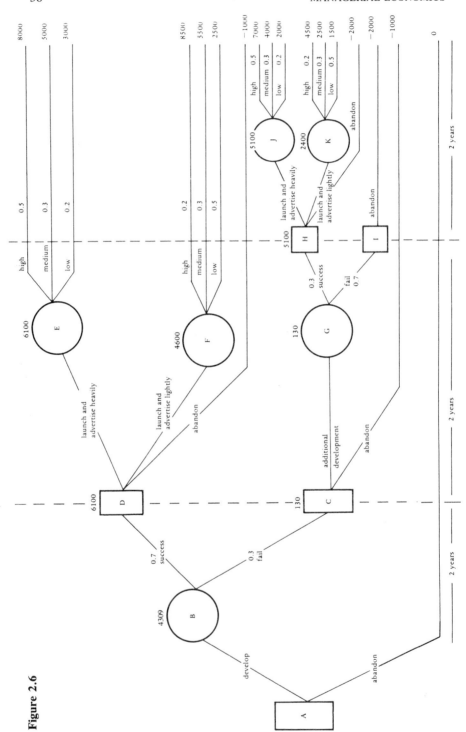

H, is £5,100. Since success in the second research attempt has an *EMV* of £5,100 and probability 0.3, whereas failure has an *EMV* of −£2,000 and probability 0.7, the *EMV* of additional development is £130, i.e. (0.3 × £5,100 + 0.7 × £−2,000). The largest of the *EMV*s of additional development (£130) versus abandonment (−£1,000) is the former. Hence this is the *EMV* at node *C*. By weighting the *EMV*s at nodes *C* and *D*, that of pursuing development initially is calculated. By comparing this (£4,309) with that of initial abandonment (£0) the manager can decide on his strategy.

Techniques for Adjusting the Present Value Formula for Risk

In Chapter 1 we defined the value of the firm as:

$$PV\pi = \sum_{t=1}^{n} \pi_t/(1+r)^t \qquad (A2.1)$$

However, π_t relates to expected, not certain, value: in the event, another value may occur. Hence, suppose a manager wished to choose between two projects. Let both projects have the same lifespan and the same expected profits in each year. But assume the risk associated with the annual earnings of one project is much greater than that of the other. The values of $PV\pi$ calculated using (A2.1) would be equal, but if the manager is risk-averse, he would prefer the lower-risk project. Hence, ranking the $PV\pi$ values would not indicate the manager's preferred project. In this appendix we explain three out of many methods which have been proposed to adjust equation (A2.1) to rank projects accurately when each project involves different levels of risk.[1]

I Certainty Equivalent Method

Using this method the manager attempts to derive a hypothetical value for $PV\pi$ where the π_ts are received with certainty such that he is indifferent between this $PV\pi$ and that of the risky stream. The expected profit for each year is estimated together with the degree of risk (as indicated by the coefficient of variation of the probability distribution of profits for that year). These expected values are converted to their hypothetical certainty equivalent values

---

1   We have ignored the possibility that the earnings of one project may be correlated with those of others. This possibility is considered in Chapter 12.

(that is, the value of π_t to be received with certainty and between which and the risky profit the manager would be indifferent). The *PV* of the stream of certainty equivalent values is then calculated.

The derivation of the certainty equivalent values can be explained by referring to an expected return–risk diagram. For example, in Figure A2.1 an expected return–risk indifference curve is presented. It shows combinations of expected return and risk between which the manager is indifferent and has the same properties as that shown in Figure 2.5. For reasons given earlier, if the manager is risk-averse, the curve will slope upwards; if he is indifferent to risk, the curve would be horizontal and if he enjoys risk, the curve would slope downwards. In the first case, curves further towards the top left-hand corner would represent combinations which the manager would prefer to those on the line we have drawn.

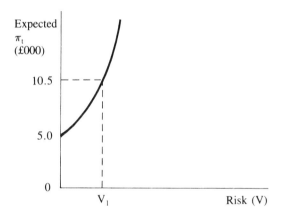

Figure A2.1

Returning to the certainty equivalent technique, if the risk level associated with a given level of expected profits is V_1 and the expected profits of a project in a particular year are £10,500, then if these points are both located on the curve, the manager is indifferent between the risky value and profits of £5,000 with no risk, i.e. certainty. Hence he would replace the £10,500 in his $PV\pi$ stream by £5,000.

In general, if π_t represents the risky return and π_t^* the certainty equivalent value of this, the PV formula would be modified to:

$$PV\pi = \pi_0^* + \frac{\pi_1^*}{(1+i)} + \frac{\pi_2^*}{(1+i)^2} + \ldots + \frac{\pi_n^*}{(1+i)^n} \qquad (A2.2)$$

where i equals the risk-free discount rate. The risk-free discount rate is used because the replacement of the risky return by its certainty equivalent fully compensates for any risk and so there is no need to make any further adjustment.

The certainty equivalent of £A with risk can be derived by repeatedly presenting the manager with choices between receiving this value with risk and successively smaller amounts to be received with certainty until indifference is reached.

Consider further the relationship between π_t and π_t^*. The certainty equivalent coefficient is defined as:

$$\alpha_t = \frac{\pi_t^*}{\pi_t} = \frac{\text{certain profits}}{\text{risky profits}} \Rightarrow \pi_t^* = \alpha_t \pi_t$$

Hence, if we knew the value of α_t and π_t, we could calculate π_t^*. Now, α is dependent on, amongst other things, the level of risk. In the above example with risk of V_1, $\alpha_t = 0.48$. If risk were higher than V_1, the risky profits, which have the same preference ranking as the certain £5,000, would be higher. Therefore the corresponding α would be lower (£5,000 divided by a number larger than £10,500). If the level of risk were less than V_1, the risky profits on the same indifference curve as the £5,000 would be less than £10,500; the value of α would be higher. Hence α lies between 1 (zero risk) and ∞ (very high level of risk). Plotting this relationship as in Figure A2.2 gives the 'α curve'.

If we knew that for a given level of risk the ratio of risky profit to its

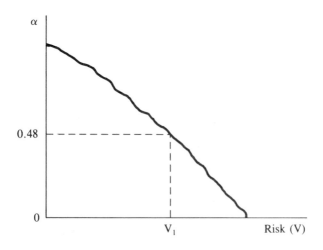

Figure A2.2

certainty equivalent, (α), was always the same regardless of the value of the certain profits or their time of receipt, i.e. the risk–return indifference curves were parallel in the vertical direction, then we could read off the α value for an anticipated level of risk. For example, with risk of V_1, the α value is 0.48. Hence the $PV\pi$ formula, equation (A2.2), would be written and calculated as:

$$PV\pi = \alpha_0\pi_0 + \frac{\alpha_1\pi_1}{(1+i)} + \frac{\alpha_2\pi_2}{(1+i)^2} + \ldots + \frac{\alpha_n\pi_n}{(1+i)^n}$$

However, it is possible that as a firm's circumstances change over time, the certainty equivalent of a specific risky return may change; that is, the α curve shifts and the α value changes. We would then need a new α curve for each time period.

II Risk-Adjusted Discount Rates

In this approach the discount rate is increased above the riskless rate, that is, the rate of return which could be gained for certain, by an amount depending on the degree of risk. Assuming that less rather than more risk is preferred, a risk premium is added to the riskless rate such that, given the level of risk, the manager is indifferent between the riskless rate and the adjusted rate with the premium added. We represent the relationship between the two in Figure A2.3. Here the manager is indifferent between a riskless rate, i, of 10% and the risk-adjusted rate, $i+k$, of 14% received with risk level V_1.

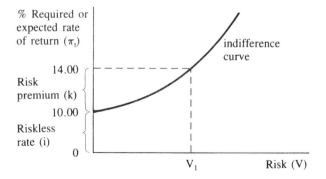

Figure A2.3

The *PV* formula is modified to be:

$$PV = \pi_0 + \frac{\pi_1}{(1+i_1+k_1)} + \frac{\pi_2}{(1+i_2+k_2)^2} + \ldots + \frac{\pi_n}{(1+i_n+k_n)^n}$$

where the values of i and k may differ between time periods.

This technique has a number of limitations when used in practice. Firstly, firms often group projects together according to their riskiness, potential investments in each group being ascribed the same value of k_t. However, it has been argued that the probability distributions of returns in each year are often not considered when the risk of each project is assessed. Secondly, the relevant risk−return indifference curve is not derived to calculate the appropriate value of k for each level of risk: the choice of k is often somewhat arbitrary. Thirdly, firms often apply the same values of i for every time period and likewise for k. This implies that the manager believes that the riskiness of expected future values of profits increases with time and at a constant rate. In fact, it might not. To understand this implication, remember that both the certainty equivalent and risk-adjusted discount rate give the same present value of a risky profit which is expected to be received in a given year. (They must do because they both adjust the *PV* of a risky receipt to equal that of a certain receipt which gives the same utility as the risky one.) Hence:

$$\frac{\alpha_t \pi_t}{(1+i)^t} = \frac{\pi_t}{(1+i+k)^t}$$

where α_t = certainty equivalent coefficient

$\quad i,k$ = risk-free discount rate and risk premium respectively: both assumed constant for all periods.

Cross-multiplication and cancelling π_t gives:

$$\alpha_t = \left(\frac{1+i+k}{1+i}\right)^t \tag{A2.3}$$

Hence

$$\alpha_1 = \frac{1+i+k}{1+i}$$

and by substituting this into (A2.3): $\alpha_t = (\alpha_1)^t$. Verbally, the further into the future we consider, the greater the adjustment to the risky profits that is implied to gain their certainty equivalent value. Further, since the adjustment for one further period is α_t multiplied by α_1,

$$\alpha_{t+1} = (\alpha_1)^{t+1} \qquad \text{(from equation A2.3)}$$
$$= (\alpha_1)^t \cdot \alpha_1 = \alpha_t \cdot \alpha_1$$

the adjustment is at a constant rate (α_1) for each additional period into the future we consider.

III Probability Distribution Approach

Using this technique, an expected *NPV*−standard deviation indifference map is drawn and points representing each project placed in it.[2] The possible values of cash flow in each year are each ascribed a probability of occurrence. These probabilities are conditional on the occurrence of a given cash flow in the preceding year. The overall probability of *NPV* for all the years is calculated and the expected *NPV* estimated using the formula:

$$E(NPV) = \sum_{i=1}^{n} NPV_i P(NPV_i)$$

where $P(NPV_i)$ = probability of NPV_i occurring and NPV_i = Net Present Value, estimate i. The standard deviation of the possible *NPV*s is calculated as:

$$\sigma(NPV) = \sqrt{[\sum_i (NPV_i - E(NPV))^2 \, P(NPV_i)]} \tag{A2.4}$$

To illustrate, consider a firm deciding whether it should market a large or a small car. For simplicity, assume the former operation will last only two years and that only three possible cash inflows can exist, given the value in the previous year. In year 0 the three cash inflows for the large car are £50, £75 and £100 with probabilities assessed by the management at 0.3, 0.4 and 0.3. In year 1, given that the previous year's figure was £50 and the possibilities of £75, £100, £125, the management estimates the probabilities of each as 0.2, 0.6 and 0.2.[3] This procedure is repeated for the other two possible values for year 0. The probability of each cash inflow in year 1 is the product of the probabilities that it and the previous year's value occurred. The situation is shown in the tree Figure A2.4.

The *NPV* of each pair of payoffs (in years 0 and 1) is calculated by discounting. Hence the first figure in column 3, 118.18, is the *NPV* of receipts of £50 in year 0 and £75 in year 1, i.e. 118.18 = 50+75/(1.1). Notice that the payoffs received in the current period (period 0) have not been discounted because there is no delay in their receipt, so no foregone interest has been lost. The remainder of the column is calculated similarly. The expected *NPV*

2    $NPV = -C_0 + \dfrac{\pi_1}{1+r} + \dfrac{\pi_2}{(1+r)^2} + \ldots + \dfrac{\pi_n}{(1+r)^n}$

   where C_0 = initial capital outlay of a project
   r = discount rate
   π_n = net cash inflow in year n, i.e. profits net of operating costs (see Chapter 12).
3   Notice that these probabilities are conditional on the cash inflow in the previous period. If the cash flows between periods are independent or perfectly correlated, equation (A2.4) can be simplified.

	Outcome	Probability of Outcome	NPV_i @ $r = 10\%$	$P(NPV_i).NPV_i$
0.3 / 50 : 0.2	75	$0.2 \times 0.3 = 0.06$	118.18	7.09
0.6	100	$0.6 \times 0.3 = 0.18$	140.91	25.36
0.2	125	$0.2 \times 0.3 = 0.06$	163.64	9.82
0.4 — 75 : 0.3	100	$0.3 \times 0.4 = 0.12$	165.91	19.91
0.4	150	$0.4 \times 0.4 = 0.16$	211.36	33.82
0.3	180	$0.3 \times 0.4 = 0.12$	238.64	28.64
0.3 \ 100 : 0.4	200	$0.4 \times 0.3 = 0.12$	281.82	33.82
0.4	210	$0.4 \times 0.3 = 0.12$	290.91	34.91
0.2	229	$0.2 \times 0.3 = 0.06$	300.00	18.00
year 0 : year 1				211.37

Figure A2.4

is found by summing the products of each *NPV* and its probability of occurrence, the first figure in column 4 equalling 0.06 × 118.18 and so on. The expected value is 211.37. The stages in calculating the standard deviation of the possible *NPV* values are shown in Figure A2.5. Hence the expected value and standard deviation for the large car may be plotted in a figure, each axis measuring each of these variables. Corresponding values may be calculated and plotted for the small car or any other investment. Indifference curves may be placed on the figure to establish a ranking of preferences between projects.

Column 1 P_i	Column 2 E(NPV)	Column 3 NPV_i	Column 4 $(NPV_i - E(NPV))^2$	Column 5 Column 4 × $P(NPV_i)$
0.06	211.37	118.18	8684.38	521.06
0.18	211.37	140.91	4964.61	893.63
0.06	211.37	163.64	2278.15	136.69
0.12	211.37	165.91	2066.61	413.32
0.16	211.37	211.36	0	0
0.12	211.37	238.64	743.65	89.24
0.12	211.37	281.82	4963.20	595.58
0.12	211.37	290.91	6326.61	759.19
0.06	211.37	300.00	7855.28	471.32
				3880.03

$\sigma(NPV) = \sqrt{3880.03} = 62.29$

Figure A2.5

IV A Note on Simulation

Hertz (1964) has proposed a technique for examining the probability distribution of possible *NPV*s for a project when the values of factors which affect each year's cash inflow are subject to risk. To illustrate, suppose a firm wishes to know the expected *NPV* and its coefficient of variation of a stream of earnings to be generated by a new plant to be set up to produce a new product. To calculate a value for the net cash inflow in each period the manager needs to know values of certain variables. Typically these are:

1. Market size
2. Selling price } MARKET ANALYSIS
3. Market growth rate
4. Market share

5. Investment required } INVESTMENT COST ANALYSIS
6. Residual value of investment

7. Operating costs } OPERATING AND FIXED COSTS
8. Fixed costs

9. Useful life of facilities

Values for factors 1−4 will enable revenue for each period to be calculated, values for factors 5−8 enable costs to be calculated, and the last variable indicates in how many periods net cash inflows will be received. Different firms may disaggregate these items to a greater or lesser extent.

Secondly, the probability distribution of the possible values of each factor is derived, using either past observations or by asking experts within the company for their subjective estimates. For example, although the marketing department may estimate the product's expected market share to be 15%, this is only one of many possible shares and the department is also able to give subjective probabilities that the share will lie in certain ranges, for example a probability of 0.10 that the share will be 15−18%, and so on. Thirdly, a computer is used to randomly select a value for each of the factors and to calculate the corresponding *NPV*. This is a hypothetical value based on the particular combination of market size, selling price, etc. chosen. The random selection is repeated hundreds or even thousands of times. When the resulting possible *NPV* values are plotted, they will form a frequency distribution of which the mean and standard deviation may be calculated. (The computer program would be written to take into account any dependence between the factors, for example the likelihood that if the selling price rose greatly the market share might decrease.) Hence, provided the assumed probability distributions of the factor values are accurate, the expected return and the risk associated with the new plant can be estimated.

Notice that simulation, as explained above, is simply a technique for deriving a project's probability distribution of possible *NPV* values from probability distributions of the factors which affect *NPV*. Simulation does not indicate which one of several such projects is preferred. To do this the manager has to compare the expected *NPV* and risk characteristics of different projects, preference between which may, in theory, be indicated by indifference curves.

This technique has a number of limitations. Firstly, the amount of computer programming required may lead to high labour costs compared to the value of the information obtained. If the technique is repeated for different projects, this cost per project will be reduced. Secondly, if the NPV distribution is highly sensitive to alterations in the factor distributions, little confidence can be placed in the overall results. However, the technique does enable a manager to examine the sensitivity of the *NPV* distribution to that of each factor in turn. He could alter the assumed distribution of, say, market share, the accuracy of which he is unsure about and then run the simulation exercise again. A comparison of the results with the original run would give some indication as to the sensitivity of the final *NPV* distribution to the factor distribution in question.

Additional Reading

Allen, D.E. (1983) *Finance: A Theoretical Introduction*, Martin Robinson.

Baker, A.J. (1981) *Business Decision Making*, Croom Helm.

Baumol, W.J. (1977) *Economic Theory and Operations Analysis*, Prentice-Hall.

Berry, R.H. and Dyson, R.G. (1980) 'On the negative risk premium for risk adjusted discount rates', *Journal of Business Finance and Investment*.

Bussey, L.E. (1978) *The Economic Analysis of Industrial Projects*, Prentice-Hall.

Clark, J.J., Hindelang, T.J. and Pritchard, R.E. (1979) *Capital Budgeting: Planning and Control of Capital Expenditures*, Prentice-Hall.

Friedman, M. and Savage, L.J. (1948) 'The utility analysis of choices involving risk', *Journal of Political Economy*, Vol. 56.

Grayson, C. Jackson (1960) *Decisions Under Uncertainty: Drilling Decisions by Oil and Gas Operators*, Division of research, Harvard Business School.

Hertz, D.B. (1964) 'Risk analysis in capital investment', *Harvard Business Review*.

Luce, R.D. and Raiffa, H. (1957) *Games and Decisions*, John Wiley.

Magee, J.F. (1964) 'Decision trees for decision making', *Harvard Business Review*, Vol. 42.

Magee, J.F. (1966) 'How to use decision trees in capital budgeting', *Harvard Business Review*, Vol. 44.

McGuigan, J. and Moyer, R.C. (1979) *Managerial Economics*, Castle House.

Moore, P.G. (1972) *Risk in Business Decision*, Longman.

Moore, P.G. (1976) *Anatomy of Decisions*, Penguin Books.

Peston, M. and Coddington, A. *Statistical Decision Theory*, CAS Occasional Paper No. 7.

Pratt, J.W., Raiffa, H. and Schlaifer, R. 'The foundations of decision making under uncertainty', an elementary exposition, *Journal of the American Statistical Association*, Vol. 59.

Robichek, A.A. and Myers, S.C. (1965) *Optimal Financing Decisions*, Prentice-Hall.

Ryan, T. (1978) *Theory of Portfolio Selection*, Macmillan.

Van Horne, J. (1977) *Financial Management and Policy*, Prentice-Hall.

3
Business Objectives

In this chapter we explain several models of the firm, each based on a different assumption concerning the managerial objective. We do this for two reasons. Firstly, these explanations help to clarify the reader's understanding of the necessary conditions which management must fulfil given sufficient information and varying objectives. Secondly, models help deduce comparative static predictions for a 'typical firm'. That is, a prediction of the qualitative changes in the equilibrium values of endogenous variables (those which the model explains) when exogenous variables (those outside the model) change. Examples of endogenous variables are price, output, profits, advertising and so on, and examples of exogenous variables are taxes, costs, and demand conditions. Such predictions, for example that when a lump sum tax rises the 'typical firm' will reduce output, would be useful to the government economist and to the trade association economist. If a firm believed that others in its markets fulfilled the assumptions of a particular model, then that model would allow it to make predictions as to their average response to such changes. Correspondingly, if a firm believes that it conforms to a particular model, then the predictions show in which direction managers should adjust their policy variables to continue to achieve their chosen goal.

A model is merely a description of reality in a simplified and highly abstract form. The number of factors which can affect firms' responses to an exogenous change is so large that it would be impossible to include them all. Therefore only the most essential factors can be included.

The factors which one includes are those which enable the model to fulfil the purpose for which it was designed. Therefore firstly, when the *prediction* of other firms' responses is the aim, the model adopted should be that which has achieved this aim more frequently than any other model. Secondly, when normative *prescriptions* are to be deduced, the model which assumes the goal most desired by management should be taken.

One may divide models into those with single-period and those with multi-period goals. In the former we consider models based on each of three maximising goals: profits, sales revenue and Oliver Williamson's utility model. The concept of satisficing is also discussed. In the second case we consider long-run maximisation of profit, sales and Marris's utility model. Finally, we discuss the extent to which managerial decisions deviate from those desired by owners.

3.1   The Single-Period Profit-Maximising Model

We assume here that the firm is a monopolist. The total revenue (TR) and total cost (TC) functions are as in Figure 3.1. To maximise profits, the firm must determine the output level at which the vertical distance between TR and TC is greatest. Geometrically this occurs where the gradients of the two curves are equal, as at Q_2. At outputs less than Q_2, a one unit increase in Q increases TR by more than TC, so such an increase would increase profits, π. At outputs above Q_2, an increase in Q would increase TR by less than TC: π would fall. Since the gradients of TR and TC are the values of marginal revenue and marginal cost, profit maximisation requires equality of these marginal values. The firm's total profit curve is obtained by subtracting TC from TR at each output level as shown in the lower part of Figure 3.1. Maximum profits occur where the profits curve peaks.

The level of the profit-maximising output can be derived using the calculus of Chapter 1. Suppose the TR and TC functions are:

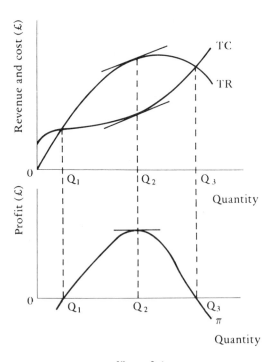

Figure 3.1

$$TR = 41Q - 2Q^2$$
$$TC = 4 + 5Q - 118Q^2 + 0.033Q^3$$

Now $\pi = TR - TC$

$$= 41Q - 2Q^2 - (4 + 5Q - 118Q^2 + 0.033Q^3)$$
$$= 36Q + 116Q^2 - 0.033Q^3 - 4$$

$$\frac{d\pi}{dQ} = 36 + 232Q - 0.1Q^2 = 0 \text{ for max.}$$

Solving for Q, one obtains -0.16 or 2320.16. Since output can never be negative, the profit-maximising rate of output is 2320.16 units.

$$d^2\pi/dQ^2 = 232 - 0.2Q$$

This is negative when $Q = 2320$. Therefore a maximum rather than a minimum value of profit has been found. Notice that since the first derivatives of TR and TC are MR and MC and that equality of MR and MC are necessary for profit maximisation, the equilibrium output can be found by equating these values.

The model may be used to predict what the response of management should be if an exogenous factor changes and if managers wish to continue maximising profits. If fixed costs, for example rent or rates, rise or if a lump sum tax is increased, TC rises by the same amount at every output level. Therefore the change in TC, when one additional unit of output is produced (i.e. MC) is unaltered at each output level. Since MR is unchanged, MC equals MR at the original output. So output should remain the same.

If variable costs such as the wage rate, or if a tax on every unit of output rise, the costs of producing one additional unit will be greater at every output level than it was originally. That is, the MC curve would rise. Since the MR curve remains the same, MC would equal MR at a lower output.

If a tax on profits increased, the post-tax profits curve would shift closer to the Q axis by an amount proportional to the original profits level. But since the tax increase is by the same percentage at every level of profits, the curve will still peak at the same output as before the tax rise. The profit-maximising output should remain the same. If the demand curve shifts, the profit-maximising output may fall, rise, or remain unchanged depending on the exact shift in the curve as is shown in Figure 3.2. In each case the demand curve shifts from D_0 to D_1, *ceteris paribus*.

3.2 Single-Period Managerial Models

Frequent criticisms were made of the profit-maximising model and managerial models were proposed as substitutes. One criticism was that profit maximising did not describe the goal to which managers aspired. Four main reasons

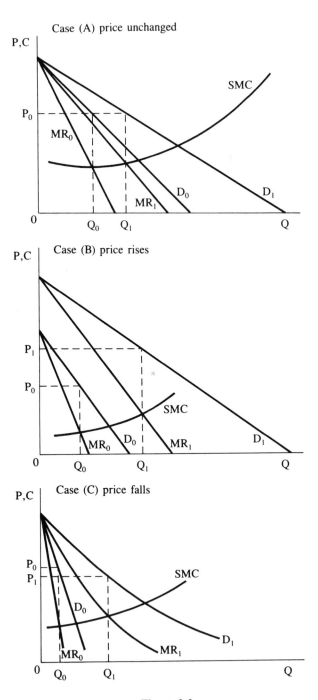

Figure 3.2

were put forward. First, firms may not be constrained by external forces to maximise profits. Studies have shown that in the large modern corporation there may be a divorce of ownership from control. Shareholders are diffuse and/or lacking in knowledge of the industries in which they invest. In addition an absence of competitive policies by existing firms can permit departures from profit-maximising behaviour by others. Secondly, it has been argued that firms do not and/or cannot actually maximise profits because managers do not know of the concepts of expected marginal revenue and marginal costs. They cannot predict the relevant future values, they are risk averse and intrafirm communication difficulties may prevent profit maximisation. Thirdly, it has been argued, both on the basis of evidence and *ad hoc* reasoning, that managers have goals other than single-period profits which they try to attain. A further criticism of the assumption has been that some of the comparative static predictions which may be deduced from it have been observed less frequently than those derived from alternative hypotheses. For example, the profit-maximising prediction that price and output would remain unchanged if fixed costs rose, appears to be less frequently observed than the prediction that such a rise would lead to a price rise, a prediction to be derived from Baumol's single-period model, to which we now turn.

Baumol's Single-Period Sales Maximising Model

Baumol has argued that businessmen, particularly in oligopolistic industries, aim to maximise their sales revenue. His assertion is based on public statements by businessmen and on a number of *a priori* arguments as to the disadvantages of declining sales: for example, fear of customers shunning a less popular product, less favourable treatment from banks, loss of distributors and a poorer ability to adopt a counter strategy against a competitor. In Figure 3.3, the

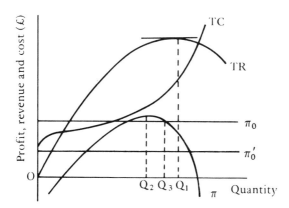

Figure 3.3

position is equal to an output level of Q_1 where the slope of the TR curve (marginal revenue) equals zero. In comparison, the profit-maximising output occurs when $MR = MC$, that is Q_2

However, as it stands this argument is incomplete. Baumol argued that there is some minimum level of profits, a profits constraint, which must be earned. This level is determined by a firm's desire to keep its dividends and share prices sufficiently high to keep existing shareholders quiescent and to enable it to raise new capital at a future date. Only after this profit constraint has been earned do profits become subordinate to sales in the firm's hierarchy of goals. This constraint is the line π_0 in Figure 3.3. If π_0 is above the level of profits which occur when $MR = 0$, as in the figure, the revenue maximiser is 'constrained'. The constrained maximiser in Figure 3.3 will produce at output level Q_3 where the constraint, π_0, is met. If π_0 was less than the profit where $MR = 0$, e.g. π_0' in Figure 3.3, then the revenue maximiser would be unconstrained and produce Q_1. Provided that π_0 is less than maximum profits, the sales maximiser will produce a greater output than the profit maximiser.

The first main difference between the profit maximiser and a constrained sales maximiser is that the latter will charge a lower price to sell the extra $(Q_3 - Q_2)$ output. If both have the same demand curve this must be true.

A second implication is that the sales maximiser will spend more on advertising than the profit-maximising firm. In Baumol's simplified explanation it is assumed that advertising does not affect a product's price. It does, however, lead to increased output sold (with diminishing returns) and it is assumed that advertising will always lead to a rise in TR; MR will never become negative. By assuming that advertising does not affect total non-advertising costs, and by measuring advertising expenditure also along the vertical axis, the TC line of Figure 3.4 is derived. Since advertising will always increase TR, the businessman will increase advertising until prevented by the profits constraint. In Figure 3.4, A_1 is the profit maximising level of advertising expenditure, which, if π_0 is less than maximum profits, will always be less than the constrained revenue maximiser's expenditure, A_2. This simplified Baumol model is inconsistent. If advertising leads to greater output sold, non-advertising costs would be expected to rise, yet Baumol, in his simplified version, assumed they would not. However, Baumol also refers to a three dimensional diagram which would enable the assumption of price constancy to be relaxed and to incorporate costs as varying with output. For simplicity we have omitted this treatment. (The reader is referred to the Additional Reading for many articles which have proposed solutions to this difficulty.)

The comparative static predictions[1] include that which is allegedly

---

1   All of the following comparative static predictions assume that the revenue maximiser does not adjust his advertising expenditure.

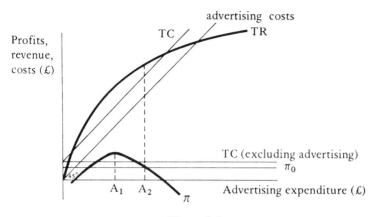

Figure 3.4

observed, of a rise in fixed costs leading to a rise in price. Assume an initial equilibrium in Figure 3.5 of output Q_1 for the constrained sales maximiser, and Q_3 for the profit maximiser, with the profits curve π_1. If fixed costs (or a lump sum tax) rise, the *TC* curve would rise by the same amount at each output, and the profits curve would fall parallel to its original position. Therefore the gradient of the profits curve is still zero at Q_3, the final profit-maximising output, but the profits constraint can be met only at a lower out-put, Q_2, the final constrained revenue maximiser's output. Since demand is unchanged, the constrained revenue maximiser would raise price to sell the reduced output, the profit maximiser would not.

If, *ceteris paribus*, variable costs or an output tax rose, both the profit maximiser and constrained revenue maximiser would reduce output. If variable costs rose, the cost of each additional unit of output would be greater than previously. Therefore the *TC* curve would pivot upwards about its intersec-tion with the vertical axis. Hence the profits curve would fall and by a greater

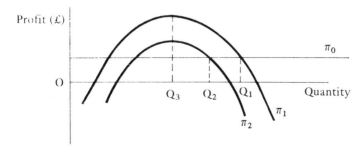

Figure 3.5

amount the larger the output, (because *TC* will have risen by a greater amount there). This shift is shown in Figure 3.6. The outputs of both the profit maximiser and the constrained revenue maximiser will both fall from Q_2 to Q_1 and Q_4 to Q_3 respectively.

Figure 3.7 shows that a similar situation arises when the rate of corporation tax increases. Compared with Figures 3.5 and 3.6, a corporation tax increase only shifts the profits curve downwards at each level of *profitable output*, and does it by the percentage tax increase (a varying absolute amount) not by a lump sum. Again, the constrained sales maximiser will raise his price and reduce his output, from Q_1 to Q_2, in order to meet the externally imposed profit constraint. The profit maximiser, however, must continue to produce at Q_3. Although his after-tax profits curve has now fallen from π_1 to π_2, Q_3 is still the output level at which the slope of π_2 equals zero.

Finally, the constrained revenue-maximising model predicts that a rise in demand will lead to a rise in output since the profits curve will shift upwards and cut the profits constraint at a greater output. The effect on price is unclear because the relative prices indicated by the 'before' and 'after' outputs depend on the position and shape of the initial and final demand curves. These positions and shapes we have not specified. The same predictions hold in the case of the profit maximiser.

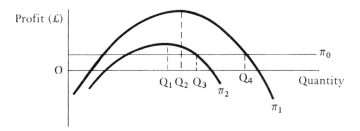

Figure 3.6

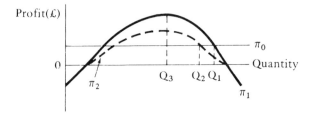

Figure 3.7

Oliver Williamson's Model of Managerial Discretion

Williamson's model depends on the same assumptions as Baumol's: a weakly competitive environment, a divorce of ownership from control, but a capital market imposed minimum profit constraint. Williamson argues that the most important motives of businessmen are desires for salary, security, dominance, and professional excellence. These can be gained by additional values of expenditure on staff, S, managerial emoluments, M, and discretionary investment, I_D. It is argued that these provide additional utility and it is utility, U, which managers aim to maximise. Hence the manager's goal is to maximise U where:

$$U = f(S,M,I_D)$$

The quality and number of staff (S) reporting to a manager enables him to gain promotion, salary and dominance and also security through greater confidence as to his department's survival, and greater professional excellence due to the better services which a larger staff can provide. Managerial emoluments (M), represent the type and amount of perquisites the manager receives (the lavish offices, personal secretary, expense account and so on) beyond the level necessary for efficient operation. The greater is M, it is argued, the greater the manager's status, prestige, and satisfaction. Discretionary investment expenditure (I_D) is that investment which exceeds that necessary to achieve the minimum post-tax profits demanded by shareholders (denoted π_0). Such spending allows managers to pursue their pet projects, personal investment preferences and to exercise their power — hence it provides utility.

Unlike the models presented earlier, Williamson's firm announces only 'reported' profits, whereas Baumol's and the profit-maximising firm report actual profits. Reported profits, the profits admitted by the firm, equal actual profits less M. M is deducted because it is an expenditure made and is also tax deductible. Notice that in Williamson's model, *actual* profits may not equal *maximum* profits if, as the model predicts, S exceeds the profit maximisation level.

Before explaining a simplification of the model, it is useful to outline these relationships using the above notation and where:

R = Revenue
C = Production cost
T = Tax
Actual profit: $\pi = R - C - S$
Reported profit: $\pi_R = \pi - M = R - C - S - M$
Minimum (post-tax) profit constraint: π_0
Discretionary investment: $I_D = \pi_R - \pi_0 - T$

Since the objective function of a Williamson firm consists of four variables, a completely satisfactory geometric treatment is not possible. Instead we present a simplified diagrammatic analysis of the equililbrium and comparative static predictions which will deviate slightly from the original whilst giving an indication as to the essential components. Williamson's model was initially presented mathematically. Such a treatment is beyond this text and the reader is referred to the references on page 81.

We begin our illustration of the equilibrium of the model by considering perks and ignoring expenditure on staff and π_0. Since $\pi_R = \pi - M$, if the maximum level of actual profit a firm could earn is given and π takes on this value, one could represent this relationship as in Figure 3.8. Because each £1 spent on perks reduces π_R by £1, this curve will have a gradient of -1 and is shown by the upper line. If a profits tax, rate t, is levied on π_R, the curve AB will pivot anticlockwise about point B. This is because, for every £1 diverted from perks to π_R, reported profit will increase by £1, but after tax, post-tax π_R will increase by only £$(1-t)$ because of the tax paid out by the firm. Therefore the slope of the new constraint is $-(1-t)$ which has a value which is closer to zero than AB. Finally, subtract a given profits constraint, π_0, from post-tax reported profit. Since at each level of perks post-tax reported profit decreases by the same amount, we arrive at a final constraint which is line DE, parallel to CB, but lower by the value of π_0. Along the vertical axis this line represents post-tax reported profit in excess of the minimum profits constraint which, by definition, is discretionary investment. Therefore line DE shows how management may exchange I_D for M and vice versa (given the maximum level of profits achieved) and still be sure of attaining the minimum profits constraint.

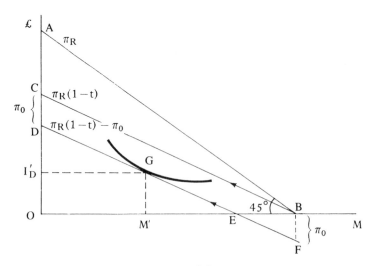

Figure 3.8

Now suppose that managerial utility depends only on perks and I_D and that the marginal utility of each is positive. If a manager is to retain the same level of utility when sacrificing I_D, he must take additional M. We can represent this trade-off by an 'indifference curve' as shown by the curved line in Figure 3.8. Such a curve shows combinations of M and I_D between which the manager is indifferent. If we assume that for each additional £1 taken as perks, management is prepared to give up only smaller and smaller amounts of I_D to remain equally satisfied, the indifference curves will be curved inwards as shown. Williamson assumed that management wishes to maximise its utility, and because both I_D and M yield utility, wishes to attain a combination of these which is on the highest indifference curve possible. However,[2] management can only gain combinations of I_D and M on the lowest line of Figure 3.8. Therefore the combination where this constraint line is tangential to the highest indifference curve possible denotes the utility maximising point: point G with I_D of I_D' and perks of M'.

We now turn to the staff expenditure and I_D trade-off and temporarily assume that there is no expenditure on perks. If sales staff expenditure, S, increases, output sold will increase. As S increases, reported profit will at first rise since each extra salesman increases output sold more than his predecessor. But eventually further sales effort will be less productive, leading to greater wage costs than revenue brought in. Therefore the relationship between reported profits and S is an inverted U-shape, as shown by P in Figure 3.9.

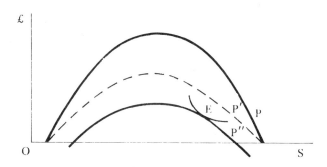

Figure 3.9

To derive the relationship between S and I_D instead of π_R, suppose that a profits tax is subtracted from the levels of profits shown by line P in Figure 3.9. The curve would become 'flatter' and at each level of S, the maximum

2   Given π, π_0 and t.

post-tax value of π_R would be less, as shown by the dotted curve, P', in Figure 3.9. But the level of S which corresponds to π_R of zero is unchanged, since the tax could not reduce a zero-reported profit. Hence curve P' in Figure 3.9 would have the same intercepts as originally. Finally, suppose that the minimum profits constraint is subtracted from P'. Then the level of adjusted profits corresponding to each value of S would be uniformly lower. Curve P' would shift downwards to give curve P''. Since the vertical axis of Figure 3.9 now represents post-tax reported profit in excess of the profits constraint, we have a curve showing the manager's trade-off between I_D and S given π, π_0 and t.[3] By applying an indifference curve to Figure 3.9, one can predict the utility-maximising combination of I_D and S: point E.

Now graphically put together the concepts of Figures 3.8 and 3.9 as shown in Figure 3.10. Since I_D is represented by the vertical axis in both cases, when the manager is maximising his utility, the value of I_D must be the same in both cases. The analysis of Figure 3.9 assumed no perks. This is shown by PH_1 in Figure 3.10b, the same as P'' in Figure 3.9. But if management decides to take perks, as it would if its utility-maximising position is shown as point X in Figure 3.10a, the level of I_D corresponding to each level of S in Figure 3.10b, would be reduced by that level of perks, in this case M'', from PH_1 to PH_2. Recall that I_D is calculated after perks have been subtracted. So, corresponding to each level of perks, there is a different level of the profit hill. Secondly, the original (Figure 3.8) analysis of Figure 3.10a assumed a given π (and so a fixed and known S). If S changes from the profit-maximising level of S_0 (as it would if G in Figure 3.10b were the new combination), π decreases. If S rises, say to S'', the I_DM curve would shift downwards parallel to itself, that is, to a line below $I_{D1}M_1$. This may affect the profit hill yet again, and so on. When the constraint lines in each figure are tangential to the highest indifference curve which can be reached, at the same level of I_D, then the indicated values of I_DM and S are the utility-maximising levels, given π_0 and t. Such combinations are shown by points C and D in Figure 3.10.

Notice that by definition a profit maximiser takes $M = 0$ (because M is defined as emoluments *in excess* of the profit-maximising value). If the management also has no preference for staff over and above the profit-maximising level, the values of I_D and S taken would be shown by point F in Figure 3.10b. If management has a preference for staff but not for emoluments, point E in Figures 3.9 and 3.10b would locate the optimum combination. If, as in the Williamson firm, management has a preference for I_D, S and M, then points C and D are chosen for reasons given earlier. If we assume that the indifference curves in both diagrams have the convex downwards shape

---

3   The I_DM and I_DS lines of Figures 3.8 and 3.9 have been derived under the assumption that both output and lump sum taxes are zero. This assumption is relaxed when we explain the comparative statics of the model.

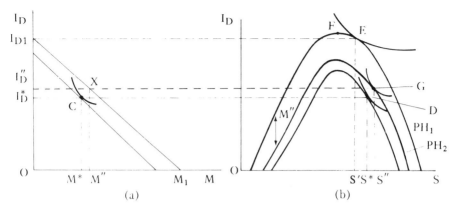

Figure 3.10

attributed to them, then in the Williamson firm the level of perks taken must be positive, and point D in Figure 3.10b must lie to the right and below point F. Therefore, the Williamson firm chooses a positive value of M, whereas the profit maximiser chooses a zero value, and the former also takes a higher value of S and lower value of I_D than the latter. Finally, a higher value of S corresponds to a higher value of output produced. Hence, since a Williamson firm would choose a higher S value than a profit-maximising firm, it would choose to produce a higher output.

Due to their complexity we explain the comparative static predictions of this model in an Appendix and summarise them in Table 3.1. This table compares the qualitative predictions which have been deduced from all the single-period models which have been explained.

3.3 Satisficing

Dissatisfaction with the profit-maximising model of economists prompted writers in other disciplines to develop models of the firm. One of the first of these was Simon in 1955. Simon argues that managers must always have imperfect knowledge on which to base decisions; that if full knowledge was available, the calculations involved in decision making would be too complex to be practicable; and that, given this and the other inevitable uncertainties surrounding decision making in reality, businessmen can never know whether they are maximising profits or not. Instead, he says, businessmen 'satisfice', they do not maximise, they aim merely at satisfactory profits.

What the satisfactory aspiration level of profits will be depends on past experience and will take account of future uncertainties. If it is easily attained, the aspiration level will be raised, if it proves difficult to attain, it will be

Table 3.1   Comparative Static Predictions Concerning Output

Increase in / Model	Lump Sum Tax (T↑)	Fixed Costs (FC↑)	Output Tax (Q₁↑)	Variable Costs (VC↑)	Corporation Tax (t↑)	Demand (D↑)
	Changes in Q:					
Profit Maximiser	0	0	↓	↓	0	↑
Baumol's Sales Revenue Maximiser	↓	↓	↓	↓	↓	↑
Williamson's Utility Maximiser	↓	↓	↓	↓	↑	↑

Note: ↑ = increase   ↓ = decrease   0 = no change

revised downwards. In either event managers will instigate 'search' behaviour to find out why actual performance differs from that aspired to so that remedial action can be taken. However, because of the cost of gleaning information, not all alternatives will be explored. A satisfactory alternative course of action will be selected — this probably will *not* be the profit-maximising alternative. (The cynic would argue that this is merely marginalist behaviour. One searches for the *best* course of action (*not* the satisfactory course), but only until the marginal cost of search equals the marginal benefits to be attained from the search.)

If neither search behaviour, nor the lowering of aspiration levels results promptly enough in the achievement of a 'satisfactory' situation then, Simon alleges, the manager's behaviour pattern will become one of apathy or of aggression. This model may seem a long way removed from managerial usefulness. This may be true, but it represents a major departure from traditional ways of thinking about how firms operate and may yet spawn results of utility. For example, it does knit in with the facts where businessmen price on a full cost basis, adding a satisfactory margin of profit, not knowing where the $MR = MC$ price and output combination is. It does help explain why some firms, faced with a falling market share, act more vigorously than competitors, in an attempt to halt the decline; while others, conversely, in the same situation, act as though they were commercially moribund.

3.4   The Multi-Period Profit-Maximising Model

Observation of management behaviour and business press has led several writers to argue that management goals are growth-centred. These writers have built a range of dynamic models which differ from the so called 'static' models of the firm which we have examined so far, and which help to deduce the optimum values of policy instruments for expansion minded firms. Thus, if we introduce the time factor into the profit-maximising model, the firm will be assumed to act in a manner which will maximise the present value of expected future profits, $[PV(\pi)]$.

Consider Figure 3.11 derived by Baumol. $PV(\pi)$ equals the difference between the present values of total revenue and total costs, $PV(TR)$ and $PV(TC)$ respectively. $PV(TR)$ and $PV(TC)$ are assumed to depend on the firm's growth rate of output, g. The firm chooses the value of g which maximises $PV(\pi)$. The $PV(TC)$ function is composed of two types of cost; output costs and expansion costs. Output costs are the ordinary, day-to-day operating and production costs. They are composed of fixed and variable costs; and if we assume constant returns to scale they will rise in a linear fashion as the firm's annual rate of growth rises. (If the firm has identified the optimum scale of plant, it can replicate that plant as often as required to meet any output growth needs.) On the other hand, expansion costs can be expected to rise more than proportionately as the rate of growth increases.

It is for this reason that the $PV(TC)$ function is displaying non-linear properties. One major reason for the disproportionate rise in expansion costs is the limited ability of management to administer efficiently a growing entity. Growth entails recruitment of new personnel at all levels of the firm. These must be trained and assimilated into the organisation. While new staff is being trained and gaining experience, inefficiencies arise. The greater the training task and the more new employees there are, then — given the fixed size of the original management team — the higher these inefficiencies become, and

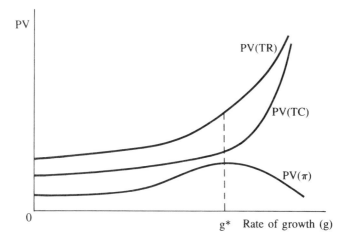

Figure 3.11

the firm's expansion costs rise accordingly. Expansion costs also rise dispropor-
tionately if the firm tries to shorten the time required to construct new fixed
plant capacity. 'Crash programmes' invariably raise unit costs. Also, ever
more rapid growth requires ever more capital to finance the expansion. Beyond
some level, the cost of capital will rise. For example, frequent issues of shares
to raise funds will force the price of equity down and so its cost of servicing up.

The $PV(TR)$ function also rises at an increasing rate as g increases. That
is, a firm which continuously grows at a relatively high rate will expect a
more than proportionately greater discounted sum of future revenue than a
firm which grows at a relatively low rate. This can be seen by formulating
the $PV(TR)$ equation:

Let R_t = revenue in period t
 t = 0: current period
 g = continuous growth rate of revenue and output

Then $PV(TR)^4 = R_0 + \dfrac{R_1}{1+r} + \dfrac{R_2}{1+r} + \ldots$

But $R_1 = R_0 + R_0 \cdot g = R_0(1+g)$
 $R_2 = R_1 + R_1 \cdot g = R_1(1+g) = R_0(1+g)^2$
and so on.

So $PV(TR) = R_0 + \dfrac{R_0(1+g)}{(1+r)} + \dfrac{R_0(1+g)^2}{(1+r)^2} + \ldots$

$$= R_0 \left\{ \frac{\frac{1}{}}{1 - \dfrac{(1+g)}{(1+r)}} \right\} = R_0 \left\{ \frac{(1+r)}{(r-g)} \right\} \tag{3.1}$$

$$= R_0(1+r)(r-g)^{-1}$$

(The sum of the geometric series $a + ak + ak^2 + \ldots + ak^n$ as $n \to \infty$ where 'a'
is a constant and k, a multiplicative factor, is $[a/(1-k)]$.)

If we partially differentiate this with respect to g, using rule 6 of Table
1.2 we derive:

$$\frac{\partial PV(TR)}{\partial g} = R_0(1+r)(r-g)^{-2}$$

which is positive because R_0 and $r > 0$ (assuming $r > g$). So the $PV(TR)$ curve
has a positive gradient. Now

---

4   In this formula we begin at $t = 0$, not $t = 1$ as in Chapter 1. This is because
     we assume here that revenue is currently being earned, whereas in Chapter 1
     we assumed that initial earnings were received at the end of period 1.

$$\frac{\partial^2 PV(TR)}{\partial g^2} = 2R_0(1+r)(r-g)^{-3}$$

is positive for the same reason. So the gradient of the $PV(TR)$ curve increases as g increases, that is the $PV(TR)$ curve bends upwards as shown in the figure.

The growth rate which achieves the management's goal is that where $PV(TR)$ exceeds $PV(TC)$ by the greatest amount: g^* in Figure 3.11. If g is increased beyond g^*, the increase in $PV(TR)$ is less than that of $PV(TC)$, so $PV(\pi)$ would fall. Marginal $PV(TR)$ is less than marginal $PV(TC)$. If g is below g^* but increased, $PV(TR)$ would increase by more than $PV(TC)$, so $PV(\pi)$ would rise. Marginal $PV(TR)$ exceeds marginal $PV(TC)$. So $PV(\pi)$ is maximised where these marginal present values are equal.

3.5 Multi-Period Managerial Models

John Williamson's Integrative Model

John Williamson developed a model which reconciled, at least for some cases, both the dynamic and single-period situations. Figure 3.12 illustrates the basis

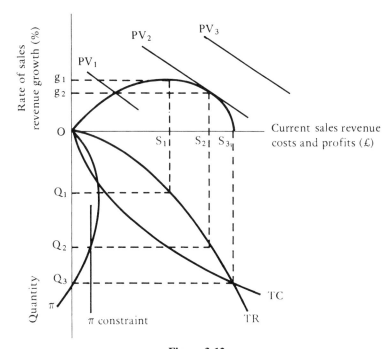

Figure 3.12

of some of his arguments, albeit in highly simplified form. The lower portion of the figure contains the single period π, TR and TC curves, but in an unusual position, the relevant axes having been rotated to the right by 90°. The upper portion of the figure plots the growth rate of current revenue, g (which may differ from that of output unlike the analysis of the last section) against current revenue. The curve OS_3 depicts the maximum obtainable g at different levels of current revenue.

Consider, firstly, the firm which wishes to maximise g. Growth requires funds to finance expansion. If we assume (not unrealistically) that the only funds available for expansion are internally generated profits, then g can only be maximised when current profits are at a maximum. Hence g_1, maximum growth, occurs at current sales level S_1, and output level Q_1. In like manner, g will be zero when profits are non-existent, at O and S_3. Thus a growth rate maximiser will produce at the same output level as a single-period profit maximiser.

Consider, secondly the revenue maximiser. In the single-period situation we observed that such a firm would produce more than the profit maximiser. In the multi-period setting, the maximiser of the present value of sales will also produce at a higher level in the single period than would the profit maximiser. To prove this we construct 'iso-present value' curves, PV_1, PV_2 and so on into the upper half of Figure 3.12. Any one of these lines joins points of equal present value of revenue, given the manager's discount rate. Whatever its shape each iso-present value line will slope down from the left to the right. This can be seen by considering equation (3.1). Given $PV(TR)$ and r, a rise in g will reduce the denominator of equation (3.1), hence necessitate a decrease in R_0. Similarly, given $PV(TR)$ and r, a rise in R_0 will increase the numerator and necessitate a fall in g. So for any iso-present value line, a rise in g necessitates a fall in R_0 and vice versa. For simplicity we present them as straight lines. Iso-present value lines further to the right than others represent greater present value. Again from equation (3.1), for any given values of g and r, a rise in R_0 implies a rise in $PV(TR)$.

The firm which wishes to maximise the present value of future sales will select that point on the curve flowing from O to S_3 which is compatible with the highest attainable iso-present value line. This means it will choose a point on the curve which is tangential to a PV line. Since the iso-PV lines slope from left to right, this point of tangency must be beyond the current sales level, S_1, where the OS_3 curve has a zero slope, for example S_2, on line PV_2.

Thus the maximiser of the present value of future sales will produce at an output level such as Q_2, which is in excess of the single-period profit maximising level of Q_1. The growth rate selected will be g_2, with a current sales level of S_2. It should be noted also, that the profit 'constraint' in Figure 3.12 is not externally imposed by the capital market as it was in the earlier models we examined. On this occasion the 'constraint' has been internally generated by the decisions of the managers themselves for sales to grow at rate g. Clearly, an external constraint must also be taken into account by management when they select their preferred growth rate. Failure to meet the external constraint could result in share prices being so low that they fail to reflect the profit potential of the firm's assets. In this situation the possibility of a takeover becomes real and, if activated, might well result in the incumbent management being removed from their posts.

Marris's Model

Marris has argued that managers aim to maximise their utility, which in this model depends only on the firm's growth rate, subject to a security constraint. Stockholders are assumed to be wealth maximisers. That is, they wish to maximise the present value of future expected dividends plus share price when they realise their value:

$$S_0 = \sum_{t=0}^{n} d_t/(1+r)^t + S_n/(1+r)^n$$

$$= \sum_{t=0}^{\infty} d_t/(1+r)^t \tag{3.2}$$

where S_0 = current share price
d_t = dividend per share received in year t
S_n = share price in year n
r = discount rate

Our discussion follows the original by Marris and its simplification by Radice and Hay and Morris. For simplicity Marris assumes that the firm's growth rate, g, once chosen, remains fixed indefinitely and that it relates to all characteristics of the firm: assets, profits, revenue, dividends and so on. Hence all ratios of these 'state' variables remain constant. (However the number of shares (N) is assumed constant.) Therefore we can rewrite equation (3.2) as:

$$S_0 = \sum_{t=0}^{\infty} \frac{d_0(1+g)^t}{(1+r)^t}$$

using similar reasoning as that preceding equation (3.1). Hence, since $d_0 = D_0/N$ where D_0 = total dividend payment, we can write:

$$S_0 = \sum_{t=0}^{\infty} \frac{D_0(1+g)^t}{N(1+r)^t} \tag{3.3}$$

Marris argues that there is a two-way relationship between g and profitability, P. In equation form:

$g = f(P)$ ... (supply-growth relationship) (3.4)
$P = \Phi(g)$ ... (demand-growth relationship) (3.5)

Consider the supply-growth relationship. Greater profitability allows faster growth because it allows more to be retained per period if the retention ratio is given, and hence more to be reinvested. Similarly Marris argued that the greater the profitability the greater the amounts of debt and equity which would be taken by the capital market per period. For simplicity the supply growth function is presented as a straight line as in Figure 3.13.

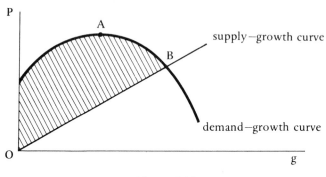

Figure 3.13

Consider now the demand growth equation. Marris argued that the main form of firm growth is diversification rather than increasing revenue from existing products. A new product may be a success, a failure, or in between. In the first case, revenue rises over time and eventually reaches a high level which increases only at the rate at which the market for the product increases. In the second case, revenue would rise only to a low level and then decrease. For simplicity we assume that all products are successful.

Marris argues that if a firm adopts the maximum diversification rate consistent with a given level of profitability, at relatively low rates of growth the relationship between P and g is direct. Several reasons are put forward for this. Firstly, growth and diversification at a slow rate rather than not at all will allow the relatively high profits of those products which are continually being introduced to be gained, rather than just the relatively low profits of old products. There would then always be some new products earning (temporarily high) monopoly profits. Secondly, up to a certain growth rate, managerial efficiency may increase with the firm's growth rate, because growth allows managers to face new interesting situations, and enables them to gain additional prestige and to exercise their ability, unlike the management of a firm with no growth.

However, eventually, greater rates of diversification result in successively lower profitability. Firstly, the methods of increasing the diversification rate reduce profitability by reducing total revenue or increasing total costs, relative to firm size. Such methods are: increasing advertising expenditure, greater R&D expenditure or lower prices. Secondly, as mentioned in Section 3.3, faster growth would require a faster growth rate of skilled management. This would mean that less time was spent by experienced staff in performing their original tasks and inefficiencies arise. These factors would outweigh those causing a direct relationship at lower growth rates. Hence as the growth rate increases, profitability would decrease.

For these reasons, equation (3.5) forms an inverted U-shape as shown in Figure 3.13. Since both equations (3.4) and (3.5) must be satisfied (there can only be one value for each of g and P) the chosen growth rate and profitability must be where both the demand-growth and supply-growth lines intersect, that is point B in Figure 3.13.

However, the exact position of the supply-growth curve merits more explanation. Its location depends on the subjective preferences of the management for security and tenure. At any level of profitability, the maximum growth rate depends on the level of retentions, increase in new debt and the rate of increase of new equity. Suppose the retention ratio is initially low and growth rate minimal. As the retention ratio rises, current dividends would fall if profitability remained unchanged, but their growth rate would increase. As the retention ratio (R) increases, the supply-growth curve will pivot clockwise since with no external finance: $g = R \cdot P$, that is $P = (1/R)g$. Now at first at successively higher retention ratios, the profitability increase, as predicted by Figure 3.13, would outweigh the reduction in dividends which would otherwise occur. Dividends and their growth rate rise and so, given the discount rate which shareholders apply to future receipts, the value of each share rises.

When the retention ratio has reached a level such that the supply-growth line passes through A, the firm will be maximising profitability. If retentions are further increased, current dividends will be lower due to lower profits and payout ratio, but their growth rate will outweigh this and the firm's market value will still increase. Eventually, still higher retention ratios would cause the decrease in dividends to outweigh the increase in growth rate in the share value formula (equation 3.3), and hence for the share value to fall. When the rate of increase of debt or new equity per period is increased, the analysis is more complex but the same results apply.

Marris explains the significance of a lower share price in terms of the 'valuation ratio'. A valuation ratio equals the total market value of the firm's shares (number of shares times their market price) divided by the book value of the firm's assets (valued at replacement cost).

Remembering that if by adopting a higher retention ratio etc, the higher growth rate eventually causes a lower share price, then given the number of shares and the book value of assets, the valuation ratio would be lower.

If the valuation ratio falls below the subjective valuation ratio put on the firm by a potential bidder, the latter will take over the firm. In short, a firm will be taken over if a buyer believes he can make more profitable use of the existing assets than the current managerial team and so increase its share price and valuation ratio. Since a takeover will jeopardise the jobs of those managers who opted for growth in the first place, managers will wish to keep their valuation ratio above a level where takeover is thought 'likely'.

Referring back to Figure 3.13, since management wishes to maximise the firm's growth rate subject to a minimum valuation ratio constraint, the relevant supply-growth line is that which is pivoted as far clockwise as managers believe leaves their firm safe from takeover. Policies which involve higher valuation ratios are also safe and therefore retentions policies leading to supply-growth curves anywhere within the shaded area of the figure are 'safe'.

Figure 3.14 presents the same arguments in a more explicit form. Point X indicates the point of maximum shareholder utility given that they wish to maximise their wealth and so make some trade-off between current dividends and capital gains. At point X equation (3.3) is maximised, share price is at its highest possible level and thus by definition so also is the firm's valuation ratio (as indicated by Figure 3.14). Managers too, however, are in a trade-off situation. They are not, like shareholders, comparing current dividends with future dividends, but rather job security against corporate growth. Their

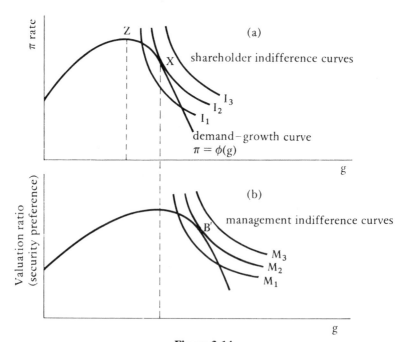

Figure 3.14

indifference curves are indicated by the lines labelled M_1, M_2 and M_3. Given the indifference curves of the figure, the managers of the firm will choose point B' and the appropriate growth rate/valuation rate combination. (B' in Figure 3.14 implies the same growth rate as B in Figure 3.13.)

However, managerial utility (M) is a function of security (the valuation ratio), and if the threat of takeover is high enough, the indifference curves labelled M will be close to horizontal and B' and X will coincide vertically (in Figure 3.14) and in Figure 3.13 the supply-growth line will pivot to the left maintaining the implication that B and B' still result in equal growth rates.

3.6 Recent Developments

Agency Costs

Recent literature has explored further some implications of the separation of a firm's ownership from its control. Many writers have argued that the relationship between 'owners' and 'managers' is a special example of an 'agency relationship'. That is, it is a contract where principals (owners) engage agents (managers) to perform services on their behalf and in so doing delegate considerable decision making authority to them. Assuming both principals and agents are utility maximisers, it is likely that an agent will act in such a way that, whilst maximising his own utility, he will not maximise that of the principal. For example, in Williamson's model, managers took more than the profit-maximising level of perks and in Marris's model, managers set a growth rate in excess of that which maximised the valuation ratio. The monetary value of the benefits foregone by the principal because the agent does not maximise his utility is called the 'residual loss' from the agency relationship.[5]

Jensen and Meckling (1976) represented the magnitude of the residual loss diagrammatically as follows. Assume that the manager gains utility from both money wages and the present value of perks. With a given technology and demand, any chosen combination of policy variables, e.g. price, output, etc., will result in particular cash inflows in future periods which in turn will determine the market value of the firm.[6] Given the manager's money wage, if he

---

5   Here the word 'residual' is used to indicate the total *agency costs* borne by the principal *less* those he incurs by 'bonding' (e.g. contract writing) and 'monitoring' (e.g. auditing) the agent.

6   Refer to equation (3.2). If both sides of the example are multiplied by the number of shares (N), we obtain the total market value of the firm on the LHS. By definition, the dividend per share is net cash inflow (NCF) multiplied by $(1 - \phi)$ where ϕ = retention ratio. Hence equation (3.2) implies:

$$MV = N \times \sum \frac{NCF_t(1 - \phi_t)}{(1 + r)^t}$$

which is clearly positively related to NCF.

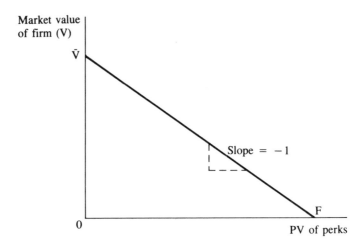

Figure 3.15

took only the value maximising level of perks and chose the value maximising level of price, etc., the firm's value would be maximised at, say, point $\bar{V}$ in Figure 3.15, where the downward-sloping line meets the vertical axis.[7] But a manager may take more perks than the level which maximises the firm's market value. If he does, and given the maximum market value of the firm, its *actual* market value will decrease because, by definition:

$$V = \bar{V} - P \qquad\qquad\qquad (3.6)$$

Where V = market value of firm
$\quad\;\; P$ = PV of perks
$\quad\;\; \bar{V}$ = maximum market value of firm.

Therefore, for each additional £1 by which the manager increases the PV of his perks, the market value of the firm decreases by £1. Similarly, from equation (3.6) we can deduce that if the manager takes all of the PV of profits as perks, the value of the firm would be reduced to zero: point F in Figure 3.15. (Of course, for each scale of firm there would be a different $\bar{V}F$ line parallel to the one shown. The $\bar{V}F$ line is analogous to the budget constraint of demand and cost theory discussed in Chapters 5 and 7.)

To illustrate the magnitude of the agency 'residual loss' we shall compare the value of a firm where the owner is also the manager (and hence, by definition, there is no agency relationship) with a case where there is such an agency relationship. Suppose, first, that the manager owns 100% of the equity of the firm. Then the maximum market value of his (100%) share in

7   For simplicity we assume that perks of zero maximise the MV of the firm.

the firm, given any level of perks, is shown by $\bar{V}F$ in Figure 3.15. This is because, if he increases the PV of his perks by £1 and the market value of the firm decreases by £1, the latter is *his* loss of wealth: he owns the entire firm. This line is reproduced in Figure 3.16. Suppose also that his indifference curves between utility and perks are as shown in Figure 3.16. To maximise his utility he will choose to take the PV of perks equal to F^* and correspondingly the value of the firm will be V^*: point X.

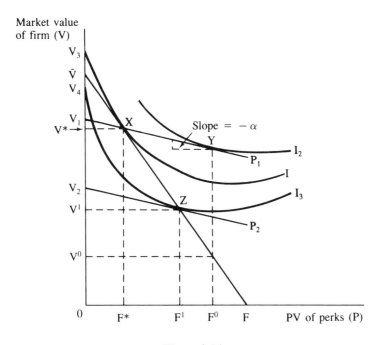

Figure 3.16

Secondly, suppose the owner (already at point X) sells some of his shares in the firm to an outsider but retains a proportion, α, of the firm's equity. In this case, if he — still being the manager — increases the PV of perks taken by £1, the market value of the firm decreases by £1. But, since he only owns α of the firm, the cost to *him* of taking extra perks is now lower than it was when he was the owner. The market value of *his* share decreases only by α £1, and α is less than 1.0. Hence the constraint which the manager (and now only part owner) faces in his choice of PV_{perks} and MV_{firm} has a slope of $-\alpha$, not -1 as had $\bar{V}F$. This constraint V_1P_1, however, must also pass through point X. This is because, if the individual wishes, he can still have that combination of perks and MV which he had before selling his shares. The share sale provides him with cash receipts $(1-\alpha)V^*$, the MV of his remaining shares αV^* and perks corresponding to F^*. The new constraint is shown as $V_1 P_1$ in Figure 3.16.[8] If the manager's indifference curves are unchanged, he will choose a greater PV of perks, F^0, (point Y) than when he owned the whole firm. Given equation 3.6, since the PV of perks has increased, the actual market value of the firm will decrease by this amount, i.e. from V^* to V^0.

However, share purchasers are not naive. If they believe that after purchase the manager will take perks in excess of F^*, and consequently that the value of the firm will then fall below V^*, they will only, at most, be prepared to pay $(1 - \alpha)$ times the new expected value of the firm. They will not be willing to pay as much as $(1 - \alpha)V^*$ for the shares.

Similarly, the owner/manager is aware that, with chosen perks of F^0, the firm would only have a value of V^0 and, while he is willing to sell for $(1 - \alpha)V^*$, he is not prepared to sell for $(1 - \alpha)V^0$. He will only be prepared to sell for $(1 - \alpha)$ times the new expected value of the firm, or above.

Given that the owner/manager wishes to sell $(1 - \alpha)$ of the firm, what price will be satisfactory to both parties to the trade? Jensen and Meckling show that it must be V^1, on a constraint line $V_2 P_2$ which passes through Z, a particular point on $\bar{V}F$ where the owner/manager has an indifference curve I_3, tangential to it.

To understand that this is mutually acceptable, consider Figure 3.17. If

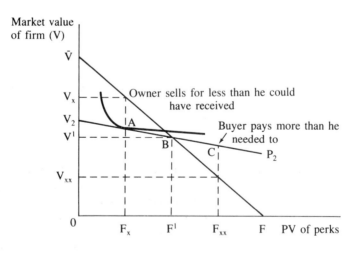

Figure 3.17

the point of tangency between V_2P_2 and an indifference curve were to the left of B, say A, the manager would take perks of F_x. If $(1-\alpha)$ of the shares were sold for $(1-\alpha)V^1$ but after their sale their value were V_x, the original owner would have sold the shares for less than he could have received for them. Alternatively, if the point of tangency were lower than B on V_2P_2, say C, the manager would take perks of F_{xx} causing the firm's value to be V_{xx}. If a new owner paid $(1-\alpha)V^1$ for his shares, he would have paid more than he need have. But if tangency occurred at B, the perks taken and firm value would be F^1 and V^1. In that case the buyer would pay a price and the original owner would receive a price reflecting what the shares were worth to each respectively.

In summary, we see that when a manager owns all the shares of a firm, the firm's value is V^* (in Figure 3.16). But when he owns only α of the shares, because he takes more perks than when the sole owner, the value of the firm and of his wealth is less than V^*: it is V^1. This reduction in the value of the firm is the 'residual loss' of the agency relationship which was created when the owner/manager sold some of his shares.[9] (Although, as Jensen and Meckling point out, this 'loss' is perfectly consistent with economic efficiency since the owner/manager would only incur it if he believed he could make himself better off by using the cash receipts $(1-\alpha)V^1$ elsewhere. Similarly, shareholders will only pay for the shares purchased if, in their judgement, this is the best alternative use of their cash resources.)

Managerial Discipline

Agency relationships, then, can result in agents — in this context managers — behaving in a way which does not maximise the welfare of principals — owners (at least as measured by V). The question arises as to whether there are any mechanisms which constrain the agent's behaviour to be closer to that of wealth maximisation of the principal than it would otherwise be. Two main constraints have been proposed. We have already discussed one: the takeover mechanism embodied in the Marris model. Manne (1965) called this the *market in corporate control*.

A second, put forward by Fama (1980), argues that managerial performance is encouraged by the existence of managerial labour markets within and between firms. Fama viewed the firm as a number of contracts between factors of production which specify what each input will do, how it relates to other inputs to produce outputs and how receipts from the outputs are divided between the inputs. A manager has a contract with the firm to supply his skills for an agreed rent — his wage. Wealth holders offer their money which

9 In terms of utility the agency cost to the owner/manager is V_3V_4 since this represents the reduction in market value which gives the same utility loss as the movement from point X to point Z in Figure 3.16.

is used to buy plant and machinery which is combined with other inputs. In return, wealth holders have a claim on a portion of the retained profits: the residual surplus. But the amount of their payment is unknown when they supply their cash: they bear risk. Hence Fama separates the manager from the risk bearer. The owner of each input of managerial skills, of manual skills, and of financial capital can change the firm to whom he rents. Workers look for new jobs and shareholders sell their shares in one company and buy them in another. In short, a firm is not owned by shareholders because the firm is a set of contracts made voluntarily by each input supplier. Therefore, argues Fama, 'control over a firm's decisions is not necessarily the province of security holders'. Shareholders will not necessarily force managers to follow their wishes. If shareholders disagree with managerial decisions, the former can sell their shares. Further, since one would expect shareholders to have a diversified portfolio, one would not expect a shareholder to be especially interested in interfering in managerial decisions in any one firm.

Nevertheless, high managerial performance is stimulated by *internal and external labour markets*. Management is not a monolith, but rather a group of self-interested persons seeking to displace others. Managers are in competition with fellow incumbents and outside challengers. As Fama (1980, pp. 291–4) points out, managers rent their wealth, or human capital, to the firm and the 'rental rates . . . signalled by the management labour market . . . depend on the success or failure of the firm'. Managers are 'sorted and compensated' (p. 292) according to performance. Since the firm is always in the market for new managers it must be able to explain to recruits how they will be rewarded. If the reward system is not responsive to performance, the firm will not be able either to recruit or retain the best managers. Conversely, but by the same argument, managers, especially top managers, have a stake in the firm's performance since the external market uses that as a means of determining their opportunity wage. In the internal management market, monitoring lower levels of management, gauging their performance and rewarding them is a normal management task. And this monitoring process operates upwards as well: 'Lower managers perceive that they can gain by stepping over shirking or less competent (seniors) . . . (while) in the nexus of contracts . . . each manager is concerned with the performance of managers above and below him since his marginal product is likely to be a positive function of theirs' (Fama, p. 293). However, although Fama has proposed these *a priori* hypotheses, which are persuasive, empirical evidence in their support is, in the nature of things, difficult to provide.

Conclusion

Although *a priori* arguments have been proposed as to why profit maximisation is or is not an accurate description of managerial goals, several replies have been made. Similarly, a certain amount of empirical evidence has been found both to support and to counter the predictions of most models. The reader is referred to the Additional Reading for references to this literature. Whether profit maximisation is the most accurate description of managerial goals is clearly debatable. However, it is an operational objective and will be the one assumed to hold in most of the following pages.

The Comparative Static Predictions of O. Williamson's Model of Managerial Discretion

Suppose that a lump sum tax is imposed. Because I_D is measured after tax, the $I_D S$ curve will shift downwards. The $I_D M$ line will also shift downwards because there is now less post-tax profit from which to pay perks or from which to spend on I_D. These movements are shown in Figure A3.1. The initial movement of the $I_D S$ line, if perks remain unchanged, is PH_1 to PH_2. But remember that, if additional (fewer) perks are taken, I_D, at each level of S, is decreased (increased). In Figure A3.1a management maximises utility by taking less in perks, therefore the $I_D S$ line would shift upwards to PH_3. In addition, any change in S would alter π and hence the position of $I_D M$ curve again. For simplicity this further move of the $I_D M$ line has been omitted from Figure A3.1 and from all further explanations of the comparative statics of this model. The qualitative predictions of the model depend on the shapes and positions of the indifference curves. Figure A3.1 has been drawn to yield the predictions which Williamson thought most likely. Values of $I_D M$ and S (and hence output) are reduced. A rise in fixed costs would have similar effects since I_D is defined net of all costs.

Suppose that an output tax is introduced. As output and correspondingly S is increased, the total value of tax paid will increase. Therefore, as S is increased, the greater the downward shift in the profits curve of Figure 3.9. Hence, assuming perks remain unchanged, the $I_D S$ line shifts downwards and to the left, as shown in Figure A3.2b, from PH_1 to PH_2. For each level of S there is a corresponding output and hence additional tax and hence reduction in I_D. Turning to the $I_D M$ line, there is similarly a specific reduction in post-tax profits from which to pay perks. Therefore, for each S level there is a different, now lower, $I_D M$ line due to the different tax payable. In Figure A3.2 we present the initial and final equilibria. As the figure is drawn, less expenditure is made on perks than originally. Therefore the final $I_D S$

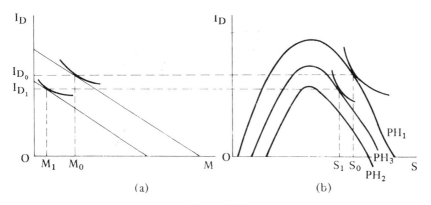

Figure A3.1

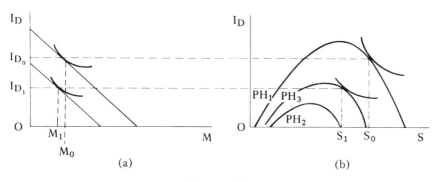

Figure A3.2

line will move upwards from PH_2 to PH_3.[1] Again, the predictions depend on the shape of the indifference curves. A rise in variable costs would lead to a similar analysis.

Consider a rise in profits tax. The profit hill will become 'flatter', as shown by Figure 3.9. Assuming M remains unchanged, this movement is from PH_1 to PH_2 in Figure A3.3b. Assuming S is unchanged, the I_DM line will pivot anticlockwise about point B in Figure A3.3a. To understand the reason for the pivot, look back to Figure 3.8. Originally, for every £1 diverted from perks to I_D, only £$(1-t)$ of additional I_D could be made because I_D depended on post-tax reported profits whereas perks were untaxed. But now t is higher. So, for every £1 by which M is reduced, I_D increases by even less than originally. However, to derive I_D, π_0 must be subtracted from $\pi_R(1-t)$ —

1   Notice also that, if S changes from its initial level, there is a further shift in the I_DM line due to a change in π. Again, for simplicity we have omitted this from our figure.

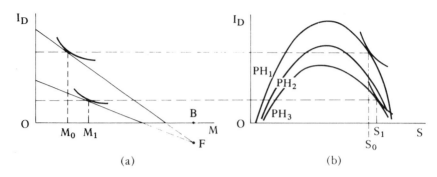

Figure A3.3

it was for this reason that the middle line of Figure 3.8 was shifted downwards. Hence, if π_0 is subtracted from a line flatter than that marked $\pi_R(1-t)$, we gain the same flatter line shifted downwards by π_0, that is, a line pivoted about point B. Point F in Figure 3.8 corresponds to point F in Figure A3.3a. Finally, since Figure A3.3a is drawn such that additional perks are taken, the profit hill, PH_2 in part (b) of the diagram, would shift downwards to PH_3. Again, the predictions depend on the shape of the indifference curves, our figure being drawn to yield the predictions derived by Williamson.

Lastly, suppose the demand curve shifted to the right. Each TR curve would pivot anticlockwise about its intersection with the vertical axis; hence the profit hill would shift upwards and become wider from PH_1 to PH_2 in Figure A3.4b. Secondly, since actual profits have increased, more could be spent on both I_D and perks. Hence the I_DM line moves to the right parallel to itself (the profits tax is unchanged). The initial and final equilibria, shown in Figure A3.4, are drawn to indicate those predictions deduced by Williamson. Since

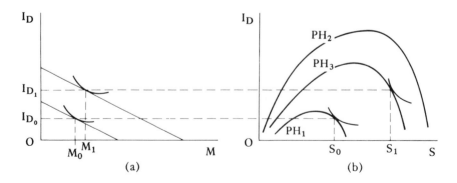

Figure A3.4

additional perks are shown to be taken, the final profit hill would be PH_3, not PH_2. Notice also that the additional S taken would lead to the I_DM curve to have shifted — a move we have ignored.

Additional Reading

Alchian, A.A. and Demsetz, H. (1972) 'Production, information costs, and economic organisation', *American Economic Review*, Vol. 62.

Baldwin, W.L. (1964) 'The motives of managers, environmental restraints, and the theory of managerial enterprise', *Quarterly Journal of Economics*, Vol. 78.

Baumol, W.J. (1967) *Business Behaviour, Value and Growth*, Harcourt, Brace & World Inc (revised edn).

Fama, E.F. (1980) 'Agency problems and the theory of the firm', *Journal of Political Economy*, Vol 88.

Hall, M. (1967) 'Sales maximisation, an empirical examination', *Journal of Industrial Economics*, Vol. 15.

Hall, R.C. and Hitch, R.J. (1939) 'Price theory and business behaviour', *Oxford Economic Papers*, No. 2.

Havemann, R. and De Bartolo, K. (1968) 'The revenue maximisation oligopoly model', *American Economic Reveiw*, Vol. 58.

Havemann, R. and De Bartolo, K. (1970) 'The revenue maximising oligopoly model: reply', *American Economic Review*, Vol. 60.

Hawkins, C.J. (1970a) 'On the sales revenue maximisation hypothesis', *Journal of Industrial Economics*, Vol. 18.

Hawkins, C.J. (1970b) 'The revenue maximisation oligopoly model; comment', *American Economic Review*, Vol. 60.

Hay, D. and Morris, D. (1979) *An Introduction to Industrial Economics*, Oxford University Press.

Heidensohn, K. and Robinson, N. (1974) *Business Behaviour*, Philip Allan.

Holl, P. (1975) 'Effect of control type on the performance of the firm in the UK', *Journal of Industrial Economics*, Vol. 23.

Holl. P. (1977) 'Control type and the market for corporate control in large US. corporations', *Journal of Industrial Economics*, Vol. 25.

Jensen, M.C. and Meckling, W.H. (1976) 'Theory of the firm: managerial behaviour, agency costs and ownership structure', *Journal of Financial Economics*, Vol. 3.

Kafoglis, M. and Bushnell, R. (1970) 'The revenue maximisation oligopoly model: comment', *American Economic Reveiw*, Vol. 60.

Koutsoyiannis, A. (1979) *Modern Microeconomics*, Macmillan.

Kuehn, D. (1976) *Takeovers and the Theory of the Firm*, Macmillan.

Lawriwsky, M.L. (1984) *Corporate Structure and Performance: The Role of Owners, Managers and Markets*, Croom Helm.

Machlup, F. (1967) 'Theories of the firm: marginalist, behavioural, managerial', *American Economic Review*, Vol. 57.

Manne, H.G. (1965) 'Mergers and the market for corporate control', *Journal of Political Economy*, Vol. 73.

Marris, R. (1971) 'An introduction to theories of corporate growth', in R. Marris and A. Wood (eds) *The Corporate Economy*, Macmillan.

Mueller, D.C. (ed) *Determinants and Effects of Mergers*, Oelgeschlager, Gunn and Hain, Cambridge, Mass.

Penrose, E. (1980) *The Theory of the Growth of the Firm*, Basil Blackwell (2nd edn).

Radice, H. (1971) 'Control type, profitability and growth in large firms', *Economic Journal*, Vol. 81.

Sawyer, M.C. (1979) *Theories of the Firm*, Weidenfeld and Nicolson.

Shipley, D.D. (1981) 'Pricing objectives of British manufacturing industry', *Journal of Industrial Economics*, Vol. 29.

Singh, A. (1971) *Takeovers*, Cambridge University Press.

Solow, R.M. (1971) 'Some implications of alternative criteria for the firm', in R. Marris and A. Wood (eds) *The Corporate Economy*, Macmillan.

Steer, P. and Cable, J. (1978) 'Internal organisation and profit: an empirical analysis of large UK companies', *Journal of Industrial Economics*, Vol. 27.

Waverman, L. (1968) 'Sales maximisation: a note', *Journal of Industrial Economics*, Vol. 17.

Wildsmith, J.R. (1973) *Managerial Theories of the Firm*, Martin Robertson.

Williamson, J. (1966) 'Profit, growth and sales maximisation', *Economics*, Vol. 33.

Williamson, O.E. (1967) *The Economics of Discretionary Behaviour*, Markham.

PART II

Knowing the Market

4
Forecasting

By definition the future is unknown. Yet managers must take decisions today which either depend on or affect conditions ruling tomorrow. Such decisions can be in the fields of investment, research and development, price, advertising, recruitment and so on, and involve the future values of variables like output demanded, wage rates, interest rates, consumers' income and the likely state of technology.

Business forecasting aims to reduce uncertainty about tomorrow, so that more effective decisions can be made today by providing predictions of future values of variables from past and present information. Usually future sales are predicted first, followed by other areas of corporate forecasting and planning.

In this chapter, several techniques for forecasting future values of many different variables are reviewed. Forecasting methods vary widely in their accuracy and sophistication (not necessarily synonymous terms) when applied to most variables. The manager's problem is, given his choice of variable to be predicted, to choose the most accurate technique subject to the nature of the forecast required, the availability of finance, data and expertise.

4.1 Surveys

Survey techniques can be used to provide short- to medium-term forecasts (up to 2 years hence) based on what people say they intend to do or what they expect will occur under specific circumstances. It is assumed that people's intentions and expectations can be accurately established and that attitudes can be collected in a way which enables predictions to be made. We present firstly the methodology of sales forecasting, and secondly a brief list of surveys of variables relating to UK macroeconomic activity.

Sales Forecasting

Despite the title of this section, it is to be emphasised that analogous procedures may be applied to forecasting future levels of wages, interest rates, fuel prices and so on. When forecasting sales, surveys (unlike the techniques described in Section 4.3 onward) have the advantage of being applicable to new, as well as established, products. A new product could be described to the respondent and his views towards it recorded.

1. *Surveys of Buyer Intentions*:   Customers are asked what they will purchase under various conditions, for example, price and income levels. However, this technique has many disadvantages. Firstly, response error may be significant. Buyers may be *unwilling* to give correct answers, either for reasons of privacy or commercial secrecy. They may be *unable* to give correct information because they have uncertain intentions or may change their minds after the survey. Because of the way in which the questions are phrased, or the way in which they are asked, or answers recorded, 'interviewer bias' may occur.

Secondly, these surveys are costly. Costs can be reduced by combining with other firms which are not competitors, sharing a questionnaire and hence asking fewer questions relating to one particular firm. But the amount of information obtained is then much less than using a firm-specific questionnaire. However, these 'omnibus' surveys can be useful to evaluate consumers' awareness of price, quality and other differences between products.

2. *Surveys of Sales Forces*:   Superficially, this technique has many advantages. Those who are closest to the market are questioned and their responses aggregated. It is cheap and easy to do, with the possible spin-off benefit of a self-selected target which may increase the motivation of the salesman.

However, disadvantages exist. Sales representatives suffer from either optimism or pessimism. One would expect this: the former because of a desire to appear dynamic, the latter because payments may depend on the amount by which actual sales exceed quotas based on forecasts. Hence estimates may be biased upwards or downwards. To correct these biases a record could be kept of each man's forecasts and achievements over a period. Possibly a consistent over- or under-prediction pattern will emerge. This 'normal' discrepancy for each could then be applied as a correction factor to each man's forecasts before aggregation, though care would have to be taken that the raw estimate did not contain any unusual factors specific to one man's territory, to which the correction should not apply. Other accuracy-improving techniques are often used. For example: informing each salesman of the accuracy of his past forecasts, providing each salesman with an independent forecast of GNP, basing part of the salesman's remuneration on the accuracy of his forecast and arranging for the salesman to discuss the reasons for his forecast with his immediate superior. In each case over-optimism or over-pessimism would be expected to be reduced.

3. *Surveys of Experts*:   Obtaining views from a group of specialists either outside the firm — for example, investment analysts, academics, consultants, or inside — for example, executives, has the possible advantages of speed and cheapness. (At its simplest, a succession of telephone calls may produce the required information.) And in intractable areas, such as forecasting future technological states where basic data are non-existent, it can provide, at worst, a range of different views to which the manager can adapt his thinking.

4. *Surveys Relating to Aggregated Items*:   A number of surveys of aggregated variables are published regularly in the UK. Whilst these may not relate to a manager's particular brand or inputs, they may relate to the product group of which his brand is a member, or to the type of inputs he uses. Examples of these surveys are:

Name of Survey	*Publisher/ Location*	*Regularity*	*Examples of Variables Included* *Expectations/Intentions Relating to:*
Industrial Trends	CBI	Monthly	Company's exports capital expenditure, new orders, numbers employed, output, stocks, average costs, average prices
Investment Intentions Survey	Dept of Industry	Twice yearly	Company's intended expenditure on land, buildings, vehicles, plant and machinery
Distributive Trades Survey	*Financial Times*	Monthly	Sales
Business Survey	CBI/EC	Monthly	Company's employment, stocks of raw materials, stocks of finished products, production, selling price, direction of change of new orders, direction of change of exports
Consumers' Confidence Survey	Gallup	Monthly	Consumer's expectations as to direction of change of income, the macroeconomy, prices, unemployment

Techniques

Individuals may be simply asked for estimates of future values of a variable under certain conditions or a range of values may be elicited from them and reduced to one value by the surveyor. Several techniques of the latter variety are used.

PERT Method (Programme Evaluation and Review Technique):   The respondent is asked for an optimistic, X_1, a most likely, X_2, and a pessimistic, X_3, estimate. A single estimate is derived by finding the weighted average of these three values. The weights 1, 4, 1 respectively for X_1, X_2 and X_3 are commonly used and based on past experience. Hence:

$$EV = (X_1 + 4X_2 + X_3)/6$$
$$\sigma = (X_3 - X_1)/6$$
$$\sigma = \text{standard deviation}$$
$$EV = \text{expected value of } X$$

This technique has the limitations that it is assumed that the respondent can produce three realistic estimates of the required types, which he may not be able to do. Secondly, it assumes that the optimistic, most probable and pessimistic values are normally distributed. If the respondent is biased this may not be so.

Decision Theory: In this case the respondent is asked both for several estimates of sales and the probability of each under different uncontrollable situations (states of nature). The expected value is calculated (see Section 2.6). Defects of this technique are that the assumptions that the executive can identify the relevant states of nature, and can estimate the probabilities of each, may not be valid. But the technique is based on value judgments with a more consistent basis than pure guesses.

Utility Theory: By presenting the respondent with a number of choice situations, the probability which he associates with each of several forecasts is formed. The most likely forecast is taken. For example the subject is told that his job depends on his accurate forecasting. He is presented with a choice between accepting two forecasts: (a) a 100% chance (certainty) of sales being £10,000 and (b) 1% probability of achieving sales of £50,000 (the estimate for which a probability is required) and 99% chance of nothing. If the subject chooses (b) the probability of the £50,000 forecast is raised until indifference between (a) and (b) is reached. This probability is assumed to be that associated with £50,000. A major problem with using this technique is the large amount of time required. It is useful when, say, executives are required to provide accurate forecasts from experience.

Delphi Technique: One way of increasing the accuracy of answers may be to provide feedback as in the Delphi technique. At its simplest, members of, for example, an executive panel are asked by letter to give their predictions of the likelihood of occurrence of specified events. Postal anonymity from other panel members minimises the impact of personal inhibitions on the making of speculations about the future. Panel members are then informed by letter of the outcome and in particular of the consensus. Dissenters are invited to explain their reasons for diverging and/or to modify their forecasts. This process may be repeated again, and the final range of outcomes regarded as a probabilistic forecast. At worst, however, the firm may have nothing better as a result of this exercise than a mere consensus of ignorance.

4.2 Experiments

Experiments can be used for deriving forecasts, especially when no information concerning consumers' past purchases of a product is available as, for example, when a new product is to be launched. Two main types are in use: test marketing and laboratory experiments.

Test Marketing

The firm finds a test area which is thought accurately to represent the market into which the product is to be introduced. The product is launched in the test market in a manner identical to that which the firm intends to use when and if the product is launched nationally. If more than one test area is used, alternative marketing tactics can be compared. For example, price, advertising, packaging and other controllable variables in the demand function can differ area by area. Sales can be compared at different levels of price, advertising and so on, or with different pack designs.

A major limitation of this technique is its high expense in both time and money. When examining a new product, a full-scale marketing exercise is required and a significant amount of output has to be manufactured. The test must last long enough to cover the repurchase cycle, otherwise false conclusions as to the demand beyond initial purchases may be drawn. For example, when a new product is launched sales might be higher than after the initial round of purchases (see Figure 4.1) because of the effect of unusually high initial advertising and novelty interest. When it is time to repurchase, both of these factors may be lower, but the consequent lower sales may not be predicted if the test exercise is prematurely terminated. The length of the cycle will of course vary with the nature of the product and may be so long, as in the case of consumer durables, as to preclude use of this technique.

Secondly, use of the technique increases the chances of prompt imitation on a national scale by a competitor. Thirdly, it is often difficult to find an

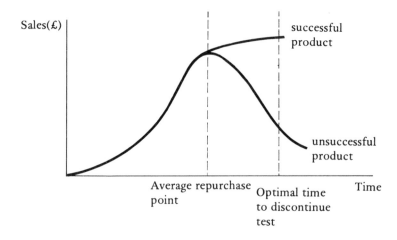

Figure 4.1

area which accurately represents the intended total market. Similarities should be present in socio-economic breakdown, age, occupational grouping, advertising media availability and so on. If no area which is sufficiently representative is found, adjustments, which enable further inaccuracies to creep in, must be made. In the United Kingdom, television regions are frequently chosen because the expenditure on advertising offered to the known population can be easily measured. Fourthly, if one considers only one market over time and unusual conditions occur during the test — for example, strikes by raw material suppliers, lay-offs by a major local employer — the results may not be representative of 'normal' conditions. Further, it is common for competitors to respond to a test marketing exercise with atypical behaviour. Competitors may lower prices or increase advertising so that again the test market results obtained are not representative of 'normality'. Finally if, for example, price is raised during the experiment, customers may be lost never to return when the product is nationally launched. However, the technique does enable one to draw conclusions from what customers do, as opposed to what they *say they will do*, as in the survey approach.

Experiments in Laboratories

One method of preventing unusual factors from making the results of a test marketing exercise unrepresentative of 'normal' demand conditions is to ask subjects to undergo shopping trips in a laboratory store and to record which and how much of each brand they would buy at different prices. Typically, a sample of subjects is selected as being representative of the intended target market. Secondly, each subject is asked to assess his or her relative preferences towards different existing brands of the product and is then exposed to advertising materials for both the new and established brands. Next, the subjects are given a fixed amount of money and asked to buy some of the product from a simulated store designed to be as close to a real shopping experience as possible. The quantity of the new brand purchased is recorded. Those respondents who choose the new brand are allowed to take it home and a later questionnaire records their repurchase intentions. The product's prices or other characteristics may be altered and the experiment repeated. Alternatively, a subject may be asked to undertake a number of hypothetical shopping trips whilst at a desk. Each is told they can imagine they have a given amount of money to spend. They are then asked how much of each item they would buy on each of a number of shopping trips from printed lists of available products.

One of the earliest proponents of these techniques was Pessemier who used it to obtain price–quantity combinations and so demand curves for various goods. However, the results may be biased by testing and selection effects. The former occurs when subjects alter their behaviour because they realise they are part of an experiment and their behaviour is being recorded. The latter occurs if the subjects who agree to take part are atypical of those in a potential market because they consist of those who are prepared to take part in tests.

4.3 Time Series Analysis

Each of this group of techniques uses only past values of a variable or the time period number to predict future values. There is no attempt to represent factors which causally affect the values of the variable. In the first two cases which we describe it is assumed that the historic relationship between past and future values will continue to hold.

1. Naive Methods

Many naive methods exist, their main advantage being their simplicity and cheapness. Examples are:

$$\hat{X}_{t+1} = X_t \qquad \text{the 'no change' model}$$
$$\hat{X}_{t+1} = X_t + \Delta X_t$$
$$\Delta \hat{X}_{t+1} = K\Delta X_t \qquad \text{the 'proportional change' model}$$
$$\hat{X}_{t+1} = a + b(t+1)$$

where $\hat{X}_{t+1}$ = the value of X which is forecast for period $t+1$; and $\Delta X_t = X_t - X_{t-1}$. K, a and b = constants to be estimated. Values of K, a and b may be estimated by plotting values of ΔX_{t+1} against ΔX_t (in the case of K) and X_{t+1} against $t+1$ (in the case of a and b) and fitting a line either by eye or by using regression techniques (see Chapter 6). K and b are the slopes of these lines, respectively, in the third and fourth equations and a is the intercept in the fourth equation.

Limitations of these methods are firstly that the assumed relationship may not accurately fit past values and so may not produce accurate forecasts. Secondly, because no causal factors are separately included, forecasts based on these techniques would not reflect unusual changes in such factors. For example, if competitors increased their advertising suddenly and greatly a firm's sales might then no longer be accurately forecast by this technique.

2. Time Series Decomposition

Use of this technique assumes that the value of a variable at a point in time can be decomposed into one or more of trend, T, seasonal, S, and cyclical, C, elements and a random element E. Variation due to each component may be represented graphically as in Figure 4.2 for the case of sales. Trend variation relates to long-term changes in, say, sales, due for example, to changes in population or technology etc. Cyclical variation occurs over a few years, whereas seasonal fluctuations occur within fixed intervals, such as a year. Random variations are those which may not be classified into other categories and may be due to unique events such as fires, war, strikes and so on. The forecaster assumes a relationship between the components, for example:

$$X_t = T_t + C_t + S_t \text{ or } X_t = T_t \cdot C_t \cdot S_t$$

Values of T, C and S are predicted for the next period and substituted into

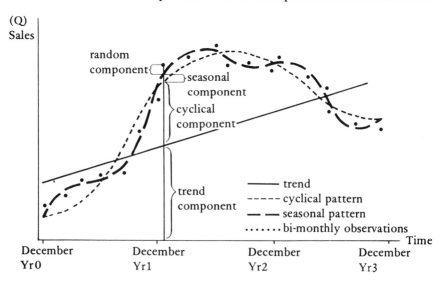

Figure 4.2

these equations to give a predicted value for X, $\hat{X}$. But how are these predictions derived? We shall explain this for the second (and most commonly used) equation. We shall use as an example the series in Table 4.1.

Stage 1: The T and C components are removed to estimate the values of S and E for each season. To do this a moving average (see the next section) is calculated where the number of terms equals the number of seasons in a year.

Because high values in a year have been averaged with low values, the variation in the data between seasons and due to random fluctuations is removed. So M_t, the moving average values, consist only of trend and cyclical components: $M_t = T_t \cdot C_t$. Dividing the actual values of X by the corresponding moving average gives S and E because:

$$X_t/M_t = (T_t \cdot C_t \cdot S_t \cdot E_t)/(T_t \cdot C_t) = S_t \cdot E_t.$$

So in Table 4.1 the corresponding moving averages and values of $S_t \cdot E_t$ are presented.

Stage 2: The randomness of the $E \cdot S$ series is now removed and the average index for each period is calculated. To do this the quarterly values of X_t/M_t are examined (for example, for spring, summer, autumn and winter of each of the last, say, seven years). The largest and lowest values for each quarter are deleted and the average for each quarter calculated (medial average). Both procedures remove randomness since this is more likely to be observed in the outliers than in more regular seasonal observations and the averaging procedure distributes randomness evenly over the elements in each average. These medial averages are scaled so that their sum equals 4 (i.e. their sum, on average, for each quarter). The M series represents the cyclical and trend pattern in the data (see Figure 4.2) whereas the M series multiplied by the seasonal indices gives the seasonal pattern, because each seasonal *index* equals the average (over several years) ratio of the corresponding seasonal value (i.e. $T_t \cdot C_t \cdot S_t$) to the cyclical and trend *value*. If the seasonal indices did not total 4, the average of the seasonal values within one year would not then equal the average cyclical and trend values over that year. That is, the *average* multiplicative factor applied to the M (cyclical and trend) values over one year would not equal 1. To ensure that they do, the quarterly medial averages are scaled as shown. In Table 4.1, to calculate the medial average for the first quarter, the values 0.972 and 1.149 were excluded and the remaining values averaged to a value of 1.004. Since the sum of all medial averages was 4.050, each is multiplied by 0.988 so that their sum totals 4, each individual value now being a seasonal index.

Stage 3: Remember that the moving average values consist of $T_t \cdot C_t$. We now wish to remove the cyclical factor for each quarter. To do this the trend value is calculated first. A common method of calculating a trend value is

Table 4.1

QU YR	Observed Values				4 Quarter MAs				(Actual/4 Quarter MAs) = S.E.				Total
	1	2	3	4	1	2	3	4	1	2	3	4	
1	310	500	490	610			477.5	607.5			1.026	1.004	
2	830	960	1040	1300	722.5	860	1032.5	1152.5	1.149	1.116	1.007	1.128	
3	1310	1400	1470	1630	1262.5	1370	1452.5	1525	1.038	1.022	1.012	1.069	
4	1600	1640	1650	1780	1585	1630	1667.5	1677.5	1.009	1.006	0.990	1.061	
5	1640	1660	1640	1700	1682.5	1680	1660	1647.5	0.975	0.988	0.988	1.032	
6	1590	1610	1560	1590	1635	1615	1587.5	1580	0.972	0.997	0.983	1.006	
7	1560	1580	1600	1720	1572.5	1582.5	1615		0.992	0.998	0.991		
Medial Average									1.004	1.006	0.998	1.042	4.050
Seasonal index									0.992	0.994	0.986	1.029	

1 Since these are quarterly MAs they should be centred at quarter $2\frac{1}{2}$ in every 4-quarter period. But because the observed values are divided by these MAs, the latter have been positioned at quarter 3.

to estimate a and b in:

$$T_t = a + bt$$

where t = time period, using regression or some other method. The value of M_t is then divided by T_t to give C_t:

$$\frac{M_t}{T_t} = \frac{T_t \cdot C_t}{T_t} = C_t$$

Suppose that in the example a and b are: 737 and 43 respectively. Then the C_ts can be calculated for each quarter.

Stage 4: To forecast we calculate

$$\hat{X}_{t+1} = \hat{T}_{t+1}\hat{C}_{t+1}\hat{S}_{t+1}$$

where $\hat{S}_{t+1}$ is the average index which was calculated earlier for the relevant, say, quarter. $\hat{T}_{t+1}$ is calculated using the above equation. $\hat{C}_{t+1}$ is calculated frequently from judgment based on a consideration of past cyclical components.

Hence, in the example, since we wish to predict a figure for the first quarter of year 8, $\hat{S}_{t+1}$ is the index for $Q1$, i.e. 0.992, $\hat{T}_{t+1}$ is 1984 from the above equation, and if we believe $\hat{C}_{t+1}$ will be 0.840 the prediction is: 1653.

These techniques require only past values of the variables which are usually readily available. They can be performed quickly by using a computer, the forecaster needing only moderate analytical skills, and their performance for 12-month forecasts has in the past been good. But a limitation of these techniques is that any causal factor which in the past has changed regularly (or remained constant) may change irregularly in the future (or vary), but the effects of these changes would not be allowed for by these models. Secondly, since past information must be available, the demand for new products cannot be calculated. Furthermore, the prediction of the cyclical component requires an additional technique such as an indicator (see Section 4.4) or a survey of expert opinion.

3. Smoothing Techniques

Moving Averages

Use of these techniques also assumes that each observed value consists of a regular element and a random element. By averaging several successive values the random element is assumed to be removed. Various methods may be followed, but at their simplest the most recent smoothed value is used as the forecast. If a four-period moving average is used, each value is calculated according to the formula:

$$M_t = \tfrac{1}{4} q_t + \tfrac{1}{4} q_{t-1} + \tfrac{1}{4} t_{t-2} + \tfrac{1}{4} q_{t-3} \qquad (4.1)$$

For example, consider the data in Table 4.2. The last moving average can be used as the forecast for January 1988. This is a short-term forecasting method. If the most recent moving average is taken as the forecast for the succeeding March or June, the errors would be likely to be larger than for forecasts for earlier months since no observations nearer the forecast date than December would enter the calculation.

Table 4.2

	Month		Forecast 6-Month Moving Average
1987	January	20	
	February	15	
	March	40	
	April	20	
	May	40	
	June	60	
	July	40	32.5
	August	45	35.8
	September	70	40.8
	October	50	45.8
	November	90	50.8
	December	70	59.2
1988	January		60.8

One limitation of the simple moving average is that, if the observed values begin to follow a steeper trend between periods t and $t+1$, the moving average which includes the tth observation will be below this observed value for period $t+1$. This is because the forecast for period $t+1$ is the moving average of the six previous (and, on average, lower) values. If the trend continues to remain upwards, the moving averages used as a forecast will always be below the line joining the observations. This is because, when used as a forecast one month into the future, the moving average for six values will be placed one month after the most recent value. But, given the upward trend, the observed value in period $t+1$ will be above the average of the previous six observations. This is shown in Figure 4.3 (which uses different observations compared with Table 4.2). Forecast A is the average of observations 1 to 6 and so is below observation 7. For this reason simple moving averages are most suited to short-term (up to three months hence) forecasts when the trend is less likely to be significant than over longer periods. Corrections for a rising or falling trend may be used, and the reader is referred to the additional reading for these.

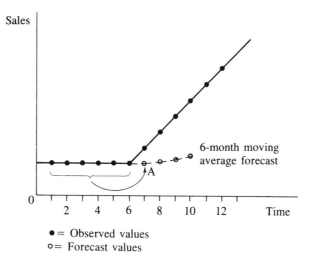

Figure 4.3

Exponential Smoothing

In the example shown in Table 4.2 the forecast for January equalled the average of the observed sales for July to December where *each had the same weight*. This is generally the case with simple moving averages (see equation 4.1). But any change in trend will be observed in the most recent figures before later ones. Therefore a more accurate forecast would be obtained if the most recent observations were given greater weights than more distant observations. A formula which achieves this would be:

$$M_t = a_1 q_t + a_2 q_{t-1} \ldots + a_{12} q_{t-11} \qquad (4.2)$$
$$\text{where } a_1 > a_2 > a_3 > \ldots > a_{12}$$

and in order that M_t may be a true average,

$$a_1 + a_2 + a_3 + \ldots + a_{12} = 1.0$$

To forecast sales, the same procedure as in the simple moving average case is followed except that the weights in the moving average formula are exponentially declining. To do this, the value given to each a is typically chosen to form a geometric progression — each is chosen to be a constant fraction of the one preceding it. Thus, if the fraction were four-fifths, then:

$$a_1 = 0.2, \ a_2 = 0.16, \ a_3 = 0.128, \text{ and so on.}$$

The equation for the moving average would then be written:

$$M_t = 0.2 \, [q_t + 0.8 q_{t-1} + (0.8)^2 \, q_{t-2} + \ldots + (0.8)^n \, q_{t-n}]$$

and M_t would be taken as the forecast for period $t+1$.

Adaptive Filtering

The last two types of moving averages both use equation (4.2) to smooth past observations. In both cases the weights are subjectively chosen by the forecaster and then remain fixed for every moving average which is calculated for a given set of data. Alternatively, when adaptive filtering is used, the magnitude of the forecast error when one moving average is calculated is used to adjust the weights to calculate the next moving average. To explain further, consider a forecast for period $t+1$ which equals the moving average calculated for the preceding three periods:

$$F_{t+1} = a_1 q_t + a_2 q_{t-1} + a_3 q_{t-3}$$

Using any set of weights, the first moving average is calculated using observations for periods 1, 2 and 3, giving a forecast for period 4. This forecast is compared with the observed value in period 4. The magnitude of the error is inserted into a formula which will select values for a_1, a_2 and a_3 which will minimise this error. The new weights are used to calculate the forecast for period 5 using observations for periods 2, 3 and 4 and the process is repeated.

Whilst this method is likely to be more accurate than the other moving average techniques described, it is also less tractible. As with all moving average techniques, it does not allow the manager to predict the seasonal or cyclical component of his sales levels.

4.4 Barometric Techniques

Mechanical extrapolation implies that the future is some sort of extension of the past. Barometric techniques, however, are based on the idea that the future can be predicted from certain events occurring in the present. Formally, they involve statistical indicators, usually time series, which, when combined in certain ways, provide indications of the direction in which the economy, or certain industries in it, is going.

Leading Indicators

These tend to reflect future changes. For example, in Figure 4.4, births lead blazer sales and a lagged correlation coefficient could be calculated. In a situation of this sort, blazer sales can be forecast by examining the birth rate pattern five years earlier.

Leading indicators are often used to forecast cyclical changes in macroeconomic variables. Common leaders of overall business cycle

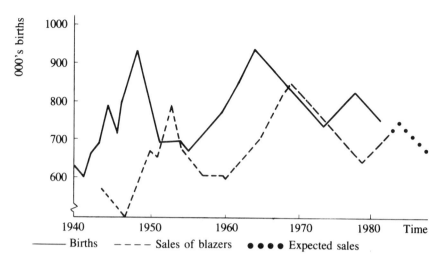

Figure 4.4

movements include stock market prices, the average working week in manufacturing and new orders for machine tools. Many indices are published in *Economic Trends*, the *National Institute of Economic and Social Research Review, The Economist* and the *Financial Times*.

A major problem in using this technique is to find the relevant indicator for the purpose. Since past values are required if one wishes to forecast using this technique, it cannot be used for new product forecasts. Moreover, an unusual change in a factor which is causally related to the forecasted variable, but not to the indicator, may render predictions by the latter very inaccurate (for example if five-year olds start wearing wind cheaters rather than blazers due to a change in tastes or competitive strategies by competitors, the birth rate will not accurately predict blazer sales). Alternatively, for the same reason, the lag between indicator and event may change. Thirdly, an indicator may move, a manager may react but find too late that the movement was merely a quirk of no real significance. Fourthly, in practice indicators have not always accurately shown the magnitude of changes in forecast variables, even when and if they have indicated turning points.

Coincident Indicators and Lagging Indicators

These coincide with or fall behind general economic activity or market trends. Their value is not in forecasting but rather in confirming, or refuting a few months afterwards the validity of the leading indicator used as an indicator of business cycles. Common examples of coinciding indicators are GNP itself, employees in manufacturing, industrial production and retail sales. Common examples of laggards are manufacturers' stock levels and consumer credit outstanding.

Diffusion Indices

Diffusion indices were developed to try to overcome the problem that a movement in one indicator is of unknown significance at first. To calculate a diffusion index, the percentage of a group of chosen leading indicators which have risen (or fallen) over the last period is plotted against time. When the index exceeds (or falls below) 50%, most of the indicators have risen (fallen or remained unchanged) and hence predict a rise (fall or no change) in the forecast variable. So by combining several indicators, a small movement of no consequence in one would be outweighed by others. If the indicators used are sub-units of one larger one, for example housebuilding starts in each county, where all counties are equally significant, the diffusion index resembles the rate of change of the aggregated variable. Hence the percentage of, say, regional or county house-start indicators showing growth would decrease when the rate of increase of national house-starts decreases, (albeit total house-starts may still be increasing). Since the *rate of increase* would decrease before *total house-starts fall*, the diffusion index which shows this rate would decrease before the aggregate house-starts indicator falls.

A limitation of these indices, when used in the United States to forecast business cycles, has been that the lead time between changes in those indicators which have usually been chosen, and turning points in the business cycle, has been very short: many peak early in the cycle, remain stable and then fall dramatically during the downturn. The inclusion of more indicators to increase the lead time has rendered their interpretation difficult. Secondly, a decrease in the index may be erroneously taken as an indication of a downturn in the forecast variable, if for example, it decreases but still remains above 50%. But a manager would not, at the time of the decrease, be aware of the value to which it eventually is to descend. For these reasons diffusion indices should complement not replace other forecasting techniques.

Composite Indicators

These consist of a weighted average of several indicators. The inclusion of several indicators reduces the likelihood that a movement in it is insignificant or random.

The use of composite indices to forecast business cycles in the UK has been studied by O'Dea and the Central Statistical Office, the latter producing indicator series quarterly. O'Dea removed the trend and then smoothed each indicator series using a moving average method. Secondly he subjectively ascribed weights to each of five desirable indicator characteristics and attributed scores to each indicator according to the degree to which it fulfilled each characteristic. These characteristics were economic significance, cyclical conformity, timing stability, smoothness and currency. By multiplying an indicator's score on a characteristic by the appropriate weight and summing, the overall weight for the indicator in the composite was obtained.

The CSO removed the trend from a large number of possible indicators and selected a small number which were leading, coincident with and lagged the reference cycle according to nine characteristics. Each was inverted where appropriate and adjusted to form an index with a common amplitude about 100. Each composite indicator was then formed using equal weights for each constituent series. *Economic Trends* currently publishes monthly values of longer and shorter leading indicators as well as coincident and lagging indicators.

4.5 Econometric Models

When using these techniques one is trying to predict a future value of a variable by examining future values of other variables which are causally related to it. For example, to predict the future demand for a model of a car ($\hat{Q}^D_{t+1}$) one would substitute the future values of factors which are causally related to it, say, its price ($\hat{P}_{t+1}$), advertising by the manufacturer ($\hat{A}_{t+1}$, competitors' advertising (AC_{t+1}), and aggregate personal disposable income ($\hat{Y}_{t+1}$), into a formula which relates demand to these variables.

The first stage in the method is to hypothesise which variables causally affect the forecast variable and the form of the mathematical relationship between them. Such hypotheses may be deduced from economic theory or proposed on the basis of past empirical evidence. For example one might hypothesise a linear form for the above demand problem:

$$Q^D_t = \alpha + \beta_1 P_t + \beta_2 A_t + \beta_3 AC_t + \beta_4 Y_t + \epsilon_t$$

Secondly the values of α, β_1, and so on are estimated. (See Chapter 6 for an explanation of regression techniques.) The equation which best represents behaviour in the past is assumed to represent it in the future. Future values of P_t and so on are then predicted and substituted into the equation.

Notice that the equation does not include *every* possible independent variable which might determine the value of Q^D_t; it is an abstraction. So even if the linear form accurately represents the relationship (which it may not), substitution of values of P_t, A_t, AC_t and Y_t into the model may not give values for Q^D_t which equal those realised. The differences are represented by the ϵ_t (error) variable. This is a general property of regression models.

Econometric models may consist of only one equation (a single equation model) if such a form represents the causal relationship sufficiently adequately for the purpose in hand. But often theory may predict that an independent variable in one equation will causally affect the dependent variable *and vice versa*. In these cases a complete system of equations representing the causal relationships between these variables must be specified: a simultaneous model.

Sumultaneous models consist of two types of variables: endogenous and exogenous and two types of equations: behavioural equations and identities. Endogenous variables are those which are explained or predicted by the model and exogenous variables are those which are determined by factors which are not predicted by the system. Behavioural equations represent how people or physical processes are expected to behave — allowing for the possibility that they might not do so in the hypothesised way — whereas identities are relationships which are necessarily always correct.

To illustrate such a model consider the following simplified model of the economy where GNP is defined as the sum of consumption, investment and government expenditure:

$$Y_t = C_t + I_t + G_t \tag{4.3}$$

Consumption is hypothesised to be positively related to GNP:

$$C_t = \alpha + \beta Y_t + \epsilon_t \tag{4.4}$$

Investment is hypothesised to be negatively related to the interest rate but positively related to past periods profits:

$$I_t = \gamma - \delta r_t + \theta \pi_{t-1} + \epsilon_t \tag{4.5}$$

where Y_t = GNP in period t
      C_t = Actual consumption in period t
      I_t = Actual net capital investment in period t
      G_t = Actual government expenditure in period t
      π_{t-1} = Actual profits in period $t-1$
      ϵ_t = Disturbance term in period t
      $\alpha, \beta, \gamma, \delta, \theta$ = constants, which in practice will be estimated.

Equation (4.3) represents the definition of GNP, hence it is an identity. Equations (4.4) and (4.5) represent causal relationships which are simplifications and abstractions: for example values of Y_t substituted into equation (4.4) will not very often give completely accurate predictions for C_t because of random disturbances ($\epsilon_t s$). Hence these equations are behavioural. Notice that in equation (4.4) values of Y_t determine values of C_t but from equation (4.3) an increase in the value of C_t will increase Y_t, *ceteris paribus*.

The advantages of these models are firstly, that they attempt to explain why a variable attains different values and hence can include unusual changes in independent variables unlike the other techniques discussed so far. Secondly, unlike the time series approach, the econometric approach may enable managers to forecast the effects of changes in policy variables if they are included as independent variables. Thirdly, unlike barometric models, estimates of the *values* of variables are predicted. Fourthly, the accuracy of the model can be improved as predicted values are compared with realised values.

Finally, it is important to note that the use of econometric models and that of surveys and experiments are not necessarily alternatives. Surveys and experiments *may* be used to derive the data which can be used to estimate the coefficients of an econometric model. In addition, if the model requires values of exogenous variables for the period of the forecast, some method of deriving these values must be used, for example, surveys, indicators, time series and so on.

4.6 Input—Output Analysis

By examining the industrial source of inputs into the production process of every industry in an economy, and by making certain assumptions about the production function in each, the use of IO analysis enables managers to gain an indication of the likely effects on the demand for the output of their industry (and of others) of a change in final demand by consumers, the government and foreign countries. To understand how this is achieved, the nature of certain IO matrices and their use in forecasting is explained.

Suppose, for simplicity, that an economy consists of two industries: manufacturing and services, and also governmental, exports, and household sectors. (For simplicity, we have assumed that imports are zero.) Suppose that the revenue and expense accounts of each of the two industrial sectors are as shown in Table 4.3. This table shows, in the case of manufacturing, for example, the values of inputs purchased from all other industries including itself, the expenditure it made on wages and taxes, and the resulting profits. Also shown are sales to each industry and to households, the government and foreign countries.

But rearranging the information in Table 4.3, an IO *transactions matrix* may be constructed (Table 4.4). This shows the values of transactions which have occurred between any two sectors over a given period. The value of transactions may be shown in terms of quantities or money. Each sector listed vertically represents the origin of an input and each column its destination. The table can be divided into four quadrants. The top left-hand corner represents transactions between industries. The equivalent quadrant for the United Kingdom has 99 industries included and so a 99 row by 99 column quadrant is required. The top right-hand corner shows the values of outputs of each industry which were finally demanded. The lower left-hand corner shows the payments which were made for primary inputs to the two industries (i.e. value added), that is, inputs not produced by industries shown in the top left-hand corner. GNP may be calculated by either summing the final demand — export expenditure plus government expenditure plus household expenditure — or by summing the total value added (equals total factor payments). The lower right-hand corner would show values of primary inputs taken by the final demand sectors. (We have assumed that these figures equal zero for simplicity.)

Table 4.3

_____ MANUFACTURING _____			
Purchases from Manufacturing	30	Sales to Manufacturing	30
Purchases from Services	15	Sales to Services	10
Government (Taxes)	60	Exports	30
Wages	145	Sales to Government	90
Profits and Depreciation	40	Sales to Households	130
TOTAL	290	TOTAL	290

_____ SERVICES _____			
Purchases from Manufacturing	10	Sales to Manufacturing	15
Purchases from Services	5	Sales to Services	5
Government (Taxes)	30	Exports	10
Wages	91	Sales to Government	40
Profits and Depreciation	20	Sales of Households	86
TOTAL	156	TOTAL	156

_____ GNP ACCOUNTS _____			
INCOME		_EXPENDITURE_	
From Government (Taxes)	90	Exports	40
From Wages	236	By Government	130
From Profits and Depreciation	60	By Households	216
TOTAL	386	TOTAL	386

Note: Expressed in £ million.

To understand how IO aids the forecaster, it is useful to explain the *direct inputs technology matrix*. This is a matrix in which each value shows the amount of an input required to produce £1's worth of the corresponding output. To construct this matrix and to use it to forecast, it is assumed that prices and technology remain constant over the forecast period, that factor inputs are used in constant proportions, and that constant returns to scale prevail. Table 4.5 shows the *direct inputs technology matrix* for Table 4.4. Each value

Table 4.5 Direct Inputs Technology Matrix

	Inputs to Manufacturing	_Inputs to Services_
Manufacturing	0.103	0.064
Services	0.052	0.032

Table 4.4 IO Transactions Matrix (£ million)

	PRODUCERS		FINAL DEMAND			Gross Output
	Inputs to Manufacturing	Inputs to Services	Exports	Government	Households	
Manufacturing	30	10	30	90	130	290
Services	15	5	10	40	86	156
Government Wages	60	30				90
	145	91				236 } GNP = 386
Profits and Depreciation	40	20				60
Gross Input	290	156				

GNP = 386

has been derived by dividing the corresponding value in the transactions matrix by the gross input (= gross output) of the relevant industry, i.e. by the row or column total. For example, to produce £1 of manufacturing output, £(15/290) = £0.052 of service output is needed. Since prices are always constant by assumption, this ratio always represents the same quantity, and since a constant state of technology and constant returns are assumed, this quantity will not vary due to technological change or with the magnitude of total manufacturing output.

Suppose now that the demand for manufacturing goods by the *final demand* sectors is forecast to increase by £1 million and that for services is expected to remain the same. By multiplying this value by each coefficient in the technology matrix, the initial increase in the input from each industry, which is necessary to produce this additional manufacturing output, is calculated. Hence £(1m. × 0.103) = £103,000 of additional manufacturing output (as well as the £1 million) will have to be produced; as will £(1m. × 0.052) = £52,000 of additional service industry output. However, this is just the first round of increases. Each of these increases will require additional inputs from the other sector. The additional £103,000 of manufacturing output will require £(103,000 × 0.013) = £10,609 of manufacturing inputs and further service inputs. The additional £52,000 of service inputs would need further service and manufacturing inputs. Each of these further inputs would need ever more inputs from each sector, though the requirements diminish as we consider successive rounds. An analogous argument would apply if, instead of the final demand for one industry changing, those of several industries changed.

When the first and all successive increments in each industry's outputs is included we obtain the direct and indirect inputs technology matrix per £1 of final demand.[1] This is analogous to the direct inputs technology matrix except that the values show the total (i.e. first round plus all future round effects) inputs per unit of final demand produced. The direct plus indirect matrix for Table 4.4 is shown in Table 4.6. By multiplying the value of final demand for any industry's output by each value separately down the corresponding column, and summing these products, the gross output from that industry which is necessary to supply the final demand is estimated. Hence, to supply a final demand of £1m. for manufacturing and zero for services

Table 4.6   Direct and Indirect Inputs Technology Matrix

	Inputs to Manufacturing	*Inputs to Services*
Manufacturing	1.119	0.074
Services	0.060	1.037

requires £1.119m. and £0.60m. of manufacturing and service industry outputs respectively.

The costs of data collection for the construction of an IO transactions matrix are too great in relation to the benefits for collection by individual firms. Consequently, firms use the tables published by government statistical agencies, which only produce information at the industry, not the firm, level. Hence the technique will not give predictions of the quantity demanded from an individual firm. However, the technique will produce predictions of the demand for industry outputs which in turn may help a firm predict its own demand. A firm can also compare the identities of its customers with those of its industry as a whole and similarly those of its suppliers. Such comparisons may suggest where potential customers may be gained or generate ideas for combining inputs in different and more efficient proportions.

IO has other limitations as a forecasting tool. Firstly, the assumption of constant returns to scale may not hold in all industries, so the expansion of one industry's output may not have the predicted effect on that of another.

1   The values of the necessary increase in gross output of each industry to fulfil any increase in final demand may be derived by solving certain simultaneous equations. The input of industry i, per unit of output by industry j, a_{ij} (the values in the direct inputs technology matrix), when multiplied by the output of the purchasing industry, X_j equals the *total* input into j by i, that is, $a_{ij}X_j$. Hence by adding such values for every industry which purchases from one specific industry, and also the final demand for that industry, F_i, the gross output from i is obtained. Hence the transactions matrix of Table 4.4 can be represented as:

$$a_{11}X_1 + a_{12}X_2 + F_1 = X_1 \qquad \text{(i)}$$
$$a_{21}X_1 + a_{22}X_2 + F_2 = X_2 \qquad \text{(ii)}$$

and in general $\sum\limits_{j=1}^{n} a_{ij}. \ X_j + F_i = X_i$

where a_{12} = value of input 1 necessary to produce £1 of output 2, and so on; X_1 = gross output of industry 1, and so on; F_1 = total final demand for industry 1, and so on. In general, the transactions matrix can be written as:

$$A\underline{X} + \underline{F} = \underline{X}$$

where A is an $n \times n$ matrix of direct input technical coefficients
       $\underline{X}$ is an $1 \times n$ vector of industry outputs
and $\underline{F}$ is an $1 \times n$ vector of final demands

Rearranging gives:

$$\underline{F} = (I-A)\underline{X} \Rightarrow (I-A)^{-1}\underline{F} = \underline{X}$$

where I is the unitary matrix.

The 'direct and indirect inputs technology matrix per £1 of final demand' is $(I-A)^{-1}$. So, given a vector of forecasted future final demands and the a_{ij}s of the direct input technology matrix, the vector of industry outputs can be calculated.

Secondly, relative prices of different industry outputs may change between the date on which the transaction matrix was assembled and the date of the forecast. In response, the actual physical flows of outputs in the transactions matrix and so the direct and indirect inputs technology matrix may have changed. In addition, since technology matrices are calculated in money values, such a change in relative prices would mean that the forecast of future money values of each industry's output was based on the wrong ratio in the transactions matrix. Thirdly, if technology changed over time, the inputs from one industry per unit output of another might change; again, the forecast would be based on an inappropriate transactions matrix. Whilst techniques have been developed to reduce at least the last two sources of error, they cannot remove it entirely.

4.7 Markov Chains

When highly simplified, the Markov chain method of prediction is to multiply current values by the proportion by which they are expected to change, in order to derive their expected values for the next period. To explain the procedure we consider the example of the sellers of each of three brands (the only brands of the product which are sold) where each wishes to predict his market share at the end of the next — say — month, which is March.

Transition Probabilities

Suppose that the seller of each brand notices that between January 31 and February 28, sales of his brand have changed. Suppose also that each seller has been able to discover the original and final brand which each switching customer previously bought and now buys. A table (similar in construction to an input—output transactions matrix) may be used to represent the known flow of customers: Table 4.7. The number of customers on January 31 and February 28 for each brand are shown in the left-hand and right-hand columns and the difference between these two consists of the difference between customers gained (shown in the second column) and those lost (shown in the third column). Hence the value '100' of 'A' row, 'B' column in the losses section shows that 100 customers switched from brand A to brand B. Some customers will be retained. They will number the difference between the original number and those lost, as shown in Table 4.8.

Since each figure in the losses section of Table 4.7 shows the number of customers which switched from each particular brand to another, the probability that any one customer will switch from one particular brand to another may be calculated by dividing the relevant figure in the loss section of Table 4.7 by the row total for January. Hence the probability that any one customer would switch from brand A to brand B between January and February was

Table 4.7 Flow of Customers

Brand	Number of Customers on Jan 31	Gains from			Losses to			Number of Customers on Feb 28
		A	B	C	A	B	C	
A	800	0	150	200	0	100	150	900
B	1000	100	0	100	150	0	300	750
C	1400	150	300	0	200	100	0	1550

Table 4.8 Derivation of Retentions

Brand	Number of Customers on Jan 31	Gains	Losses	Number of Customers on Feb 28	Retentions
A	800	350	250	900	550
B	1000	200	450	750	550
C	1400	450	300	1550	1100

0.125 ($= 100/800$) and that for a switch from brand A to brand C was 0.188 ($= 150/800$).

The probability that any customer will be retained by a brand equals the number retained by that brand divided by the number who originally bought the brand. Hence the probability of retention between January and February for brands A, B and C was, respectively 550/800, 550/1000, and 1100/1400.

If we place each of the probabilities which we have derived in the last two paragraphs in the same position as the numerator in their calculation was placed in the *losses to* section of Table 4.7, we obtain the *transition probability matrix:* Table 4.9.

Table 4.9 Transition Probability Matrix

Brand	A	B	C
A	$0.688 \left(= \dfrac{550}{800}\right)$	$0.125 \left(= \dfrac{100}{800}\right)$	$0.188 \left(= \dfrac{150}{800}\right)$
B	$0.150 \left(= \dfrac{150}{1000}\right)$	$0.550 \left(= \dfrac{550}{1000}\right)$	$0.300 \left(= \dfrac{300}{1000}\right)$
C	$0.143 \left(= \dfrac{200}{1400}\right)$	$0.071 \left(= \dfrac{100}{1400}\right)$	$0.786 \left(= \dfrac{1100}{1400}\right)$

Prediction

One Period: To predict market shares it may be assumed that their future values depend only on customers' switching behaviour over the last period (a first-order Markov chain), on behaviour over the last two periods (a second-order Markov chain) *or* on behaviour over even more past periods. In this chapter we discuss only a first-order process; the reader is referred to the Additional Reading for higher-order chains. Hence it is assumed that the probability that a customer switched from one specific brand to another brand in the last period *equals* the probability that he will make that switch in the next period.

Therefore to predict the market share of, say, brand A on March 31 we calculate:

$$\left\{\begin{array}{l}A\text{'s expected market}\\ \text{share constituted by}\\ \text{customers retained}\\ \text{by } A\end{array}\right\} \ + \ \left\{\begin{array}{l}A\text{'s expected market}\\ \text{share constituted by}\\ \text{customers expected}\\ \text{to switch from } B \text{ to } A\end{array}\right\} \ + \ \left\{\begin{array}{l}A\text{'s expected market}\\ \text{share constituted by}\\ \text{customers expected}\\ \text{to switch from } C \text{ to } A\end{array}\right\}$$

Now

A's expected market share constituted by customers retained by A	$= (A$'s propensity to retain customers) $\times (A$'s current market share)	$= 0.688 \times 0.281$ $= 0.193$
A's expected market share constituted by customers expected to switch from B to A	$= (A$'s propensity to attract customers from $B)$ $\times (B$'s current market share)	$= 0.150 \times 0.234$ $= 0.035$
A's expected market share constituted by customers expected to switch from C to A	$= (A$'s propensity to attract customers from $C)$ $\times (C$'s current market share)	$= 0.143 \times 0.484$ $= 0.069$
		Total $= 0.297$

Notice that A's propensities to retain customers, to attact them from B and to attract them from C are the probabilities given in the first column of the transition probability matrix.

To predict the market share of brand B on March 31 we would similarly calculate:

$$\left\{\begin{array}{l}B\text{'s expected market}\\ \text{share constituted by}\\ \text{customers retained}\\ \text{by } B\end{array}\right\} \ + \ \left\{\begin{array}{l}B\text{'s expected market}\\ \text{share constituted by}\\ \text{customers expected}\\ \text{to switch from } A \text{ to } B\end{array}\right\} \ + \ \left\{\begin{array}{l}B\text{'s expected market}\\ \text{share constituted by}\\ \text{customers expected}\\ \text{to switch from } C \text{ to } B\end{array}\right\}$$

and for C:

$$\left\{\begin{array}{l}C\text{'s expected market}\\ \text{share constituted by}\\ \text{customers retained}\\ \text{by } C\end{array}\right\} + \left\{\begin{array}{l}C\text{'s expected market}\\ \text{share constituted by}\\ \text{customers expected}\\ \text{to switch from } A \text{ to } C\end{array}\right\} + \left\{\begin{array}{l}C\text{'s expected market}\\ \text{share constituted by}\\ \text{customers expected}\\ \text{to switch from } B \text{ to } C\end{array}\right\}$$

Each of these terms would be calculated in the analogous way to that explained for A.

Instead of setting out the problem in this spacious way one could use matrix algebra. The predicted market shares could be calculated as the product of the row vector of current shares (for example of A, B and C) times the transition probabilities matrix. (A row vector is simply a collection of numbers which are arranged side by side in a row.) In the case of the example:

$$(0.281\ 0.234\ 0.484)\begin{pmatrix}0.688 & 0.125 & 0.188\\ 0.150 & 0.550 & 0.300\\ 0.143 & 0.071 & 0.786\end{pmatrix} = (0.297\ 0.198\ 0.503) \tag{4.6}$$

By performing this multiplication we would derive[2]:

$$\left\{\begin{array}{ccc}0.281 \times 0.688 & 0.281 \times 0.125 & 0.281 \times 0.188\\ +0.234 \times 0.150 & +0.234 \times 0.550 & +0.234 \times 0.300\\ +0.484 \times 0.143 & +0.484 \times 0.071 & +0.484 \times 0.786\\ = \quad (0.297 & 0.198 & 0.503)\end{array}\right.$$

The left column of this matrix is identical to the arithmetic above for the prediction of A's share. This is because this matrix representation is simply a graphically different, though logically the same, way of presenting the calculation. The second and third columns are identical to the arithmetic which we would, if space was allowed, have written to predict the future shares of B and C.

Further Periods: The above method is general for the prediction of, say, market shares, one period into the future. For convenience let us represent the row vector for the current period t by Z_t and the matrix of transition probabilities which relate to the changes between t and $t+1$ by $P_{t,t+1}$. Then generalising equation (4.6) we have

$$Z_t \cdot P_{t,t+1} = Z_{t+1} \tag{4.7}$$

Therefore, if a prediction two periods into the future, say to April in the above

2   The formula for the product of a 1×3 matrix times a 3×3 matrix is:

$$(a_{11}\ a_{12}\ a_{13})\begin{pmatrix}b_{11} & b_{12} & b_{13}\\ b_{21} & b_{22} & b_{23}\\ b_{31} & b_{32} & b_{33}\end{pmatrix}$$

$$= (a_{11}b_{11} + a_{12}b_{21} + a_{13}b_{31}\ \ a_{11}b_{12} + a_{12}b_{22} + a_{13}b_{32}\ \ a_{11}b_{13} + a_{12}b_{23} + a_{13}b_{33})$$

example, is required, one would apply the method for a one-period prediction to the forecasted value for March. If the transition probabilities are assumed
to remain the same between April and March as between February and March,
then the shares for April could be predicted as:

$$(0.297\ 0.198\ 0.503) \begin{pmatrix} 0.688 & 0.125 & 0.188 \\ 0.150 & 0.550 & 0.300 \\ 0.143 & 0.071 & 0.786 \end{pmatrix} = (0.304\ 0.182\ 0.511)$$

$$(4.8)$$

The left hand row vector shows the predicted shares for March. Therefore
it is the product of the row vector of shares for February (the current period)
times the transition probability matrix. Hence to derive equation (4.8) the
current period shares have been multiplied by the transition probability matrix
twice. That is:

$$\underline{Z}_{\text{April}} = \underline{Z}_{\text{Feb.}} P_{\text{Feb.,Mar.}} P_{\text{Mar.,Apr.}} = \underline{Z}_{\text{Feb.}} P^2_{\text{Feb., Mar.}} \text{ if } P_{\text{Feb.,Mar.}} = P_{\text{Mar.,Apr.}}$$

In general

$$\underline{Z}_{t+n} = \underline{Z}_t \cdot P^n_{t,t+1}$$

$$(4.9)$$

$$\text{if } P_{t,t+1} = P_{t+1,t+2} = P_{t+2,t+3} \cdots P_{t+n-1,t+n}$$

Equilibrium Conditions

Suppose the transitional probability values are assumed to remain constant
and that values of say, market shares, are predicted further and further into
the future. After a large number of predictions, forecast shares may not change
between one period's values and those predicted for the next period. An
equilibrium would exist. For example, if the market shares of our three brands
are predicted for later months using the same transitional probabilities matrix
the forecasts are as shown in Table 4.10. From this table it can be seen that
the absolute difference between the predicted share for each month and its
predecessor decreases the further into the future the forecast month is.

To find the possible equilibrium values consider equation (4.9) (which
it is recalled is a generalisation of all the previous prediction manipulations).
If we consider how to predict the values of our market shares, just one period
hence say, $t+1$, but now call that future period the period when values reach
their equilibrium values, we have:

$$\underline{Z}_{t=\text{equil period}} = \underline{Z}_{t-1=(\text{equil period})-1} \cdot \underline{P}_{t-1,t}$$

Expanding this and substituting the market shares transition probability matrix
for P we have:

$$(A_t,\ B_t,\ C_t) = (A_{t-1}\ B_{t-1}\ C_{t-1}) \begin{pmatrix} 0.688 & 0.125 & 0.188 \\ 0.150 & 0.550 & 0.300 \\ 0.143 & 0.071 & 0.786 \end{pmatrix}$$

Table 4.10

	Share	A Share in one Month Minus Share in Previous Month	Share	B Share in one Month Minus Share in Previous Month	Share	C Share in one Month Minus Share in Previous Month
February	0.281		0.234		0.484	
March	0.297	+0.016	0.198	−0.036	0.503	+0.019
April	0.304	+0.007	0.182	−0.016	0.511	+0.008
May	0.310	+0.006	0.174	−0.012	0.513	+0.002

where A_t, B_t, C_t are the market shares of A, B and C respectively, in period t. Hence by matrix multiplication:

$$A_t = A_{t-1}0.688 + B_{t-1}0.150 + C_{t-1}0.143$$
$$B_t = A_{t-1}0.125 + B_{t-1}0.550 + C_{t-1}0.071$$
$$C_t = A_{t-1}0.188 + B_{t-1}0.300 + C_{t-1}0.786$$

But in equilibrium, predictions of successive values are the same, that is $A_t = A_{t-1}$, $B_t = B_{t-1}$ and $C_t = C_{t-1}$. Hence:

$$A = 0.688A + 0.150B + 0.143C \Rightarrow -0.312A + 0.150B + 0.143C = 0$$
$$(4.10)$$
$$B = 0.125A + 0.550B + 0.071C \Rightarrow 0.125A - 0.450B + 0.071C = 0$$
$$(4.11)$$
$$C = 0.188A + 0.300B + 0.786C \Rightarrow 0.188A + 0.300B - 0.214C = 0$$
$$(4.12)$$

and since the sum of all market shares equals 1.000:

$$A+B+C = 1 \Rightarrow A+B+C-1 = 0 \tag{4.13}$$

Hence there are three unknons A, B and C and four equations. Dropping one equation and solving the remaining three simultaneously gives the equilibrium market shares of brands A, B and C as 0.316, 0.169 and 0.515 respectively. (A note of caution is in order. Equilibrium values may not exist and/or may not be unique. The reader is referred to the Additional Reading for a discussion of the conditions under which this occurs.)

Evaluation

One limitation of the use of Markov chains as a predictive device is that the variable to be forecast must relate to one of a finite number of known states where the sum of all values for each state totals 1. For example, the market share of 1 of 3 brands may be forecast, the sum of shares equalling 1. Thus the prediction of future sales in £s *per se* is not suitable for the technique. In addition it follows that it must be conceptually possible for the system to move from one state to another. Thus customers could move as above from brand *A* to brands *B* and/or *C*. But how the future level of own or rival prices could be predicted using the technique is not possible to ascertain as the technique is described here.

Thirdly, the technique is expensive. Information concerning the initial values of variables as well as the transition probabilities must be acquired. In the case of market share information this may necessitate a costly market research study.

4.8 Usage

A number of studies have examined the popularity of different forecasting techniques and the contexts in which they are used. These studies differ in

Table 4.11   Wheelwright−Clarke and Sparkes−McHugh Surveys

Authors Country Publication Date	*WHEELWRIGHT & CLARKE* *USA* *1976*		*SPARKES & McHUGH* *GB* *1984*	
	% who use it	*% of those familiar with it who use it*	*% who use it*	*% of those with an awareness & working knowlege who use it*
Salesforce estimates	67	74	n/a	n/a
Juries of Executive Opinion	77	82	72	76
Customer Surveys	48	57	57	n/a
Naive, Trend Extrapolation,			58	63
Moving Averages,	65	75	57	58
Exponential Smoothing,			11	13
Adaptive Filtering, Time				
Series Decomposition				
Box−Jenkins[1]	24	40		
Econometric Methods				
Single Equation	70	76	10	12
Simultaneous Models	57	65		

1. The Box−Jenkins technique is a highly complex method whereby a forecast value of, say, sales is based on sales in various past periods and past values of a variable whose value on any one occasion was randomly determined. An example of the model used is:
$S_t = \phi_1 S_{t-1} + K + e_t + \theta_1 e_{t-1}$ where S_t is sales in period t, e_t is a random variable, K, ϕ_1, and θ_1 being constants to be estimated.

the techniques considered, size of firms in the sample, the function of the respondents within their company, the variables to be forecast, and the results presented. However, Table 4.11 presents the results of two recent studies. In both surveys the jury of executive opinion, and various mechanistic extrapolation techniques, were popular. But the British firms used econometric models and sophisticated time series models (Box–Jenkins techniques) far less than their American counterparts. The British survey concludes that, whilst American firms had 'by the mid 1970s . . . made substantial progress in the application of forecasting methods . . . the same cannot be said for British firms', and it found 'a lack of knowledge of specific techniques' in the British sample.

Table 4.12 reports the techniques which Sparkes and McHugh (1984) found were being used by a sample of British managers for each of four types of variables. Of the techniques shown in the table the most frequently used to forecast market size and share were 'surveys' and 'executive assessment' respectively. The most popular technique used for forecasts for production/stock control and for financial planning was also 'executive assessment'. Unfortunately, the sample relates to large firms (most had sales above £5m. per annum), was sent only to accountants within firms, and was small (around 65 respondents).[3]

Table 4.12 Techniques: Number of Responses

	Executive Assessment	Trend Analysis	Moving Averages	Surveys	Exponential Smoothing	Regression & Correlation
Market Size	2	1	0	15	2	2
Market Share	32	17	12	6	0	0
Production/ Stock Control	10	3	8	0	2	0
Financial Planning	20	3	3	0	1	0

3   This survey is the most up-to-date British survey with which the authors are familiar. For a more specific study relating to sales forecasting techniques, see Mentzer, J.T. and Cox, J.E. (1984), *Familiarity, Application and Performance of Sales Forecasting Techniques*, Journal of Forecasting, Vol. 3(1).

Table 4.13

	Surveys	Test Markets	Naive	Simple Moving Averages	Exponential Moving Averages	Time Series Decomp.	Adaptive Filters	Box–Jenkins	Single Equation Econometrics	Simultaneous Equation Econometrics	Leading Indicators	Input–Output
TIME HORIZON												
1 month	✓	n/a	✓	✓	✓	✓	✓	✓	✓	✓		
1–3 months	✓		✓	✓	✓	✓	✓	✓	✓	✓		
less than 2 years			✓			✓	✓	✓	✓	✓	✓	
more than 2 years			✓									✓
ACCURACY												
Predicting pattern	5	n/a	1	2	3.5	5	7	10	8	10		6
Predicting turning points	8		3	0	0	3	6	8	4	6	5	0
(0 = lowest, 10 = highest)												
COSTS												
Development	n/a	n/a	0	1	0.5	4	4	8	6	8	0	10
Running	n/a		n/a	1	0	4	7	10	6	8	n/a	10
(0 = lowest, 10 = highest)												

Source: Adapted, with changes from Wheelwright and Makridakis (1980), Table 15.1.

4.9 Summary

A number of forecasting techniques have been reviewed, mainly in the context of sales forecasting. It has been emphasised that different techniques are applicable in different situations. However, a comparison of the techniques, in general, according to different criteria is given in Table 4.13.[4]

4   For a comparison of characteristics of forecasting techniques for sales forecasting, see Chambers, J., Mullick, S.K. and Smith, D.D., (1971) *How to Choose the Right Forecasting Techniques*, Harvard Business Review, pp. 45–74. We have not reproduced this here because it is now a little dated.

APPENDIX 4
New Product Forecasts

Test marketing and consumer surveys are examples of techniques already discussed which can be used to help in forecasting sales of new products before national launch. Another technique is life cycle segmentation analysis.

Life Cycle Segmentation Analysis

Market segmentation is always useful but is especially so for difficult problems such as new product sales forecasts. Business tactics differ at each stage of the product life cycle, so we want to know when the product will be at any one stage of this cycle. But the cycle will be proceeding at different rates in different market segments, so timing of tactics will differ also according to the segment concerned.

All products were once new to the market-place. As time passes their sales rise from zero to a maximum after which they go into a decline situation, when they will ultimately be withdrawn from the market.

New product sales tend to follow an S-shaped curve. Such cuves fit the sigmoidal formula $R = k/(1 + e^{-(a+b)t})$, where k, a, b and e are constants determined from the data, R is sales revenue, and t is time. But this formula is almost useless in predicting the course of such a curve until it at least begins to turn over at the top, or unless maximum sales, the compulsory turning point and its timing can be forecast with confidence.

In short, mathematics is apparently of little help in forecasting what a product's sales will be, since almost all of the product life-cycle curve must be known before a formula can be applied to it. This may be of historic interest but is clearly of little value to the manager who wants to know how to react to or to influence the future course of events.

Figure A4.1 shows a typical life-cycle curve divided into five stages. The length of each stage will vary product by product. Some products, such as Rubik cubes, which are heavily dominated by fashion, may pass through all five in a matter of months. Others, like the motor car, may last for several years, with decline arrested (or even reversed) by the regular introduction of new models or the tapping of new market segments.

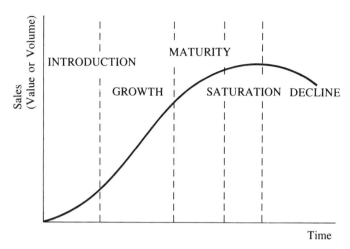

Figure A4.1

The phenomenon of market segmentation gives a clue as to how the product life-cycle concept can be practically harnessed for marketing decisions. First, we shall examine what elements of the mix are important at different stages of the cycle, and second, how segmentation can help identify which stage of the cycle we are at and hence which tactic or tactics to concentrate on.

Mickwitz has suggested that the relevant elements in the marketing mix are as follows:

1. Introduction — quality has the greatest marketing impact, then advertising; price and service have the least.
2. Growth — early adopters have now already purchased, buyer resistance is now being met, advertising is the most effective weapon, then quality.
3. Maturity — most price-insensitive buyers have now bought, rivals have entered the market, so price elasticity has become very much higher, then advertising, quality and service.
4. Saturation — price is no longer important, because it is already low; product differentiation, in quality, packaging, or intangibly through advertising becomes important, as does service.
5. Decline — the problem now is to find new product uses and advertise them; quality and service will have some impact; price very little.

Figure A4.2 presents Mickwitz's arguments in diagrammatic form. The intuitive logic behind the model is credible, and it may well be applicable in many (if not all) cases. However, the problem of identifying the time at which the various stages of the life cycle begin and end remains. This is where market segmentation again comes into its own.

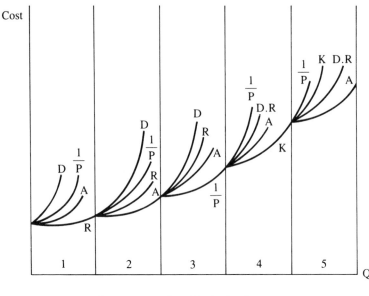

1 = Introduction   C = Marketing Input cost
2 = Growth   Q = Sales
3 = Maturity   R = Quality
4 = Saturation   A = Advertising
5 = Decline   1/P = Price Inverted
                          D = Service
                          K = Packaging

Source: P. Kotler, Market Decision Making, Holt, Rhinehart and Winston, New York, 1971, p. 83

Figure A4.2

Market segmentation is always useful, but is especially so for difficult problems such as product life-cycle analysis. Business tactics differ at each stage of the product life cycle, so we want to know when the product will be at any one stage of this cycle. But the cycle will be proceeding at different rates in different market segments, so timing of tactics will differ also according to the segment concerned. The problem of projecting the curve into the future, and so helping to answer the question of what tactics to adopt, can be simplified if we ask an associated question. Who should these tactics be directed at during the course of the cycle? By segmenting the market it may be possible to find well-developed curves in one or two segments, providing some indication of how less-developed curves in other sectors may be expected to progress.

If one knows the total market potential and the total potential in each segment, and if one knows how quickly the first segment is maturing, one can make estimates of similar or modified diffusion rates for the remaining segments and so, in aggregate, for the total market.

A major problem is to pinpoint the early adopters and then define the segment through which the new product will next diffuse. Will it be a trickle effect down the social classes? Or through, up or down, the age groups? Or will it be diffused broadly through middle and skilled working classes, as with TV, rather than through the poor or very rich classes? The example in Figure A4.3 of the life cycle for a new consumer durable shows saturation occurring earliest in the upper socio-economic (AB, followed by C_1) groupings. The social grade definitions are based on those used by the British Institute of Practitioners in Advertising. These are (for men only):

AB   Higher managerial, administrative or professional.
B   Intermediate managerial, administrative or professional.
C_1 Supervisory or clerical, junior managerial, administrative or professional.
C_2 Skilled manual workers.
DE   D Semi- and unskilled manual workers.
     E State pensioners or widows (no other earner), casual or lowest grade
       workers.

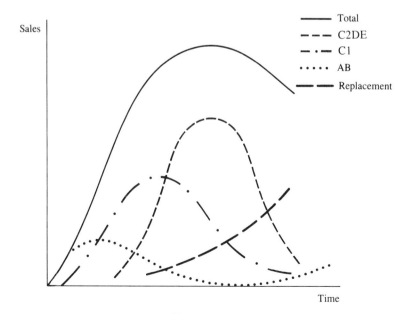

Figure A4.3

Additional Reading

Aaker, D.A. and Day, G.S. (1983) *Marketing Research*, 2nd edn., Wiley.

Barker, T. (1985) 'Forecasting the economic recession in the United Kingdom, 1979–1982: a comparison of model-based ex ante forecasts', *Journal of Forecasting*, Vol. V, No. 2.

Butler, W.F. and Kavesh, R.A. (eds) (1966) *How Business Economists Forecast*, Prentice-Hall.

Chisholm, R.K. and Whitaker, G.R. (1971) *Forecasting Methods*, Richard D. Irwin.

Georgoff, D.M. and Murdick, R.G. (1986) 'A manager's guide to forecasting', *Harvard Business Review*, January–February.

Gordon, R.A. (1962) 'Alternative approaches to forecasting: the recent work of the National Bureau', *Review of Economics and Statistics*, 44(3).

Gross, C.W. and Peterson, R.T. (1976) *Business Forecasting*, Houghton Mifflin.

Hadley, G. and Kemp, M.C. (1972) *Finite Mathematics in Business and Economics*, North Holland.

Haitovsky, Y., Treyz, G. and Su, V. (1974) *Forecasts with Quarterly Macroeconometric Models*, National Bureau of Economic Research.

Levin, R.I. and Kirkpatrick, C.A. (1980) *Quantitative Approaches to Management*, McGraw-Hill.

Lewis, J.P. (1962) 'Short-term general business conditions forecasting: some comments on method', *Journal of Business*, 35(4).

Makridakis, S., Wheelright, S.C. and McGee (1983) *Forecasting: Methods and Applications*, John Wiley.

Miernyk, W.H. (1965) *The Elements of Input–Outut Analysis*, Random House.

Nevin, J.R. (1974) 'Laboratory experiments for estimating consumer demand: a validation study', *Journal of Marketing Research*, Vol. 11.

O'Dea, D.J. (1975) *Cyclical Indicators for the Postwar British Economy*, Cambridge University Press.

Pessemier, E. (1960) 'An experimental method of estimating demand', *Journal of Business*.

Sawyer, A.G., Worthing, P.M. and Sendak, P.E., (1979) 'The role of laboratory experiments to test marketing strategies', *Journal of Marketing*, Vol. 43.

Sparkes, J.R. and McHugh, A.K. (1984) 'Awareness and use of forecasting techniques in British industry', *Journal of Forecasting*, 3(1).

Suits, D.B. (1962) 'Forecasting and analysis with an econometric model', *American Economic Review*, No. 52.

Surrey, M.J.C. (1971) *Analysis and Forecasting of the British Economy*, Cambridge University Press.

Tull, D.S. and Hawkins, D.I. (1987) *Marketing Research: Measurement and Method*, 4th edn, Macmillan.

Wallis, K.F., Andrews, M.J., Bell, D.N.F., Fisher, P.G., and Whitley, J.D. (1984) *Models of the UK Economy*, Oxford University Press.

Wheelwright, S.C. and Makridakis, S. (1980) *Forecasting Methods for Management*, 3rd edn., Wiley.

Economic Trends (1975) No. 257, March, HMSO.

5
Demand Theory

The nature of demand for the firm's goods in the market place is the foundation on which all a manager's decisions must ultimately rest. Failure to meet market demand is the ultimate management failure. In this chapter we examine the theory of demand. We begin in the traditional manner by analysing the individual's (or the individual household's) demand and then move on to an examination of total market demand. In practice, of course, it is not individual demand which managers are interested in, but either market or firm demand. Market behaviour, however, is merely the behaviour of aggregates of individuals.

5.1 Traditional Consumer Theory

The satisfaction a consumer gets from a good or service is called utility. A consumer will allocate his expenditure among the range of purchase options facing him in such a way that his total utility is maximised. The two inter-related theories of demand which we will present to support this statement, however, differ in their approach to utility. The cardinal theory assumes that the satisfaction a consumer gets from a range of products can be measured by cardinal numbers in units sometimes designated as 'utils'. Thus a consumer might get 6 utils of satisfaction from one unit of product A and only 4 utils from one unit of product B. The ordinal theory, more realistically, argues that satisfaction is a subjective concept incapable of precise measurement. The problem can be circumvented, however, by distinguishing between greater and lesser levels of utility. It is assumed only that the consumer can rank, not measure, the degree of satisfaction associated with a range of commodities.

The Cardinal Approach

Although it may not be realistic to measure utility, we can make plausible assumptions about how utility changes as consumption alters. In any given time period an increase in consumption of a product will provide an increase in total utility.

After a certain consumption rate (the satiation rate) total satisfaction will decrease as ever more of the product is consumed. There will also be a point where, as consumption increases, total utility increases, but at a decreasing rate. Diminishing marginal utility will exist. An increase in consumption of one unit of the product results in an increase in total utility less than that provided by the previous unit. A consumer may derive considerable satisfaction from purchasing a television set. The same, or even greater, (marginal) satisfaction may be obtained from a second set, as family squabbles over which channel should be viewed can now be avoided. A third set, however, while it might provide the added convenience of bedroom viewing, would have a lower marginal utility than the first two sets. The basic satisfaction of owning a TV, the opportunity to view where no opportunity had previously existed, would not be provided. A fourth set would have a still lower marginal utility. A fifth set might take the total utility function beyond its satiation rate. The consumer would be in the situation of having more sets than there are rooms in the house.

Figure 5.1 displays the type of utility surface we have been discussing for two products, A and B. The points of inflection indicate where

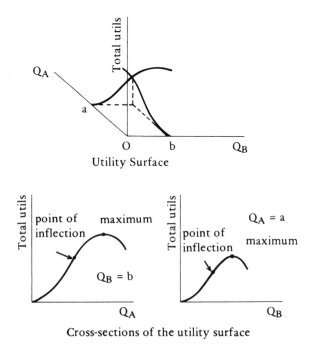

Figure 5.1

diminishing marginal utility for both A and B sets in (other things equal). The maximum values similarly indicate the saturation rates of consumption.

How much of each of the products facing a consumer will he choose to purchase? Since the consumer will have a given budget to spend, it is unlikely that he will be satiated. Assume the consumer is faced with a choice of n products. The total utility he would receive in a given period depends on the quantities he consumes of those goods. The consumer's utility function is:

$$TU = f(Q_1, Q_2, \ldots, Q_n)$$

where TU is total utility, and Q is the quantity consumed per period of any commodity from 1 to n.

The consumer's budget, however, will impose the following constraint on his utility function:

$$M = P_1Q_1 + P_2Q_2 \ldots + P_nQ_n$$

where M is the total amount of money available to the consumer and P the price of any commodity from 1 to n. To maximise utility is a standard optimisation problem. The decision variables are Q_1 to Q_n and M is a constraint on the Q_n choices. Set up the following Lagrangian equation

$$TU_\lambda = f(Q_1, Q_2 \ldots, Q_n) + \lambda(P_1Q_1 + P_2Q_2 + \ldots + P_nQ_n - M)$$

To find the values of Q_1 to Q_n, and of λ, which maximise TU, take the first derivatives of TU with respect to each and set the results equal to zero. Thus:

$$\frac{\partial TU_\lambda}{\partial Q_1} = \frac{\partial f}{\partial Q_1} + \lambda P_1 = 0 \tag{5.1}$$

$$\frac{\partial TU_\lambda}{\partial Q_2} = \frac{\partial f}{\partial Q_2} + \lambda P_2 = 0 \tag{5.2}$$

$$\ldots \ldots \ldots \ldots$$

$$\frac{\partial TU_\lambda}{\partial Q_n} = \frac{\partial f}{\partial Q_n} + \lambda P_n = 0$$

$$\frac{\partial TU_\lambda}{\partial \lambda} = P_1Q_1 + P_2Q_2 \ldots + P_nQ_n - M = 0$$

In principle, a solution can be found (provided second order conditions are also satisfied) and values for Q_1 to Q_n obtained accordingly. In practice, inability to measure utility generally makes this an impossible empirical exercise. However, we obtain useful insights from manipulation of equations (5.1) and (5.2). Transfer the second term to the right-hand side in each, divide the first equation by the second, and we obtain:

$$\frac{\partial f/\partial Q_1}{\partial f/\partial Q_2} = \frac{P_1}{P_2}$$

But $\partial f/\partial Q_1$ is the marginal utility (MU_1) of commodity 1 (by definition), and $\partial f/\partial Q_2$ is the marginal utility (MU_2) of commodity 2. So:

$$\frac{MU_1}{MU_2} = \frac{P_1}{P_2} \text{ and } \frac{MU_1}{P_1} = \frac{MU_2}{P_2}$$

From these results we can say that the consumer will allocate his budget between two (or more) products, so that the *MU*s of the products are proportional to their prices. Or, alternatively, the *MU*s should have the same ratio to each other as do the prices of the products.

Finally, to illustrate, award the following numbers to this last equation:

$$10/£2 = 15/£4$$

In this situation, where equality does not hold, the consumer should reallocate his spending away from *A* towards *B*. £2 more spent on *B* provides additional marginal utility of 10. £4 less on *A* results only in a utility sacrifice of 15. This process of reallocation of spending should continue until marginal equivalency per pound spent is again attained. Diminishing marginal utility will ultimately reduce the *MU* attainable from *B* and conversely, raise that attainable from *A*.

The Ordinal Approach

The use of consumer indifference curves enables us to adopt the ordinal approach to demand theory. Here the consumer is called on only to rank his preferences, not to measure them.

Consider Figure 5.2 which is an indifference map for the only two avail-

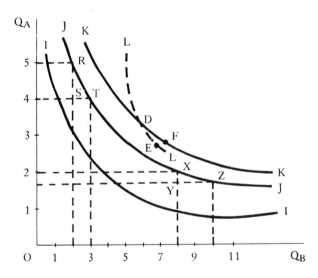

Figure 5.2

able goods, *A* and *B*. An indifference curve such as *JJ* is defined as the locus of points, each of which represents a combination of commodities such that the consumer is indifferent between any of these combinations. Thus the consumer will receive the same level of satisfaction or utility at either point *R* (5 units of *A* and 2 of *B*) or point *X* (2 units of *A* and 8 of *B*). In Figure 5.2 we assume, first, that the consumer has not passed the satiation rate of consumption. He will always prefer to have more of *A* and/or *B*. Thus any indifference curve which lies above and to the right of another represents some higher level of satisfaction. Also, as a result of this, each indifference curve must have a negative slope (for example, if *R* and *T* present identical utilities, but *R* involves a higher level of consumption of good *A*, then *T* must involve a higher consumption of good *B* to compensate for the lower total utility provided by *A*).

Second, we assume that our consumer's choice is rational. In other words, if *T*, *X* and *Z* are any three product combinations, and if the consumer is indifferent between *T* and *X*, and between *X* and *Z*, then the consumer is also indifferent between *T* and *Z*. There is consistency in, and transitivity between the consumer's preferences. As a result, indifference curves cannot intersect. (Consider the indifference curves *LL* and *KK* intersecting at *D*. Point *F* is preferred to point *E*, since it lies above and to the right of *E*. But the consumer is indifferent between *F* and *D*, since they both lie on *KK*, and in turn is indifferent between *D* and *E*, since *they* both lie on *LL*. Thus, by our rationality assumption, the consumer must be indifferent between *E* and *F*. Since he cannot both prefer *F* to *E* and be indifferent between them, indifference curve intersection is an impossible contradiction.)

Third, a diminishing marginal rate of substitution (*MRS*) is assumed. The *MRS* of product *B* for product *A* is the number of units of *A* whose satisfaction can be made up for by a unit gain in *B*. For a particular combination of *A* and *B* this equals the absolute value of the slope of the indifference curve at that point. Alternatively, consider the arc *RT*, the *MRS* (*B* for *A*) is *RS/ST*. Now consider two points such as *R* and *X*. At *R*, the consumer has a relatively large supply of *A* and a small supply of *B*. At *X* the converse holds. Therefore, at *R* the marginal utility (*MU*) of *B* will be high, relative to that of *A*, the commodity in plentiful supply. At *X* the *MU* of *A* will be higher relative to that of *B*. So at *R* the consumer is willing to give up one unit of *A* to obtain one unit of *B*. But at *X*, where *A* is scarcer and *B* more plentiful than at *R*, he is only willing to forfeit *XY*/2 units of *A* to obtain one unit of *B*. As a consequence of this diminishing *MRS* (*RS/ST* > *XY/YZ*) of *B* for *A*, indifference curves are convex to the origin.

Finally, we will show that the *MRS* of *B* for *A* is equal to the ratio of their marginal utilities.

If arc *RT* is sufficiently small, the utility loss in moving from *R* to *T* is $MU_A \times RS$ (the number of units of *A* given up). Similarly, the utility gain in moving from *R* to *T* is $MU_B \times ST$. Since the consumer is indifferent between

R and *T*, the gain and loss offset each other:

$$MU_A \times RS = MU_B \times ST \text{ thus } RS/ST = MU_B/MU_A$$

and so $MRS \equiv$ the slope of $JJ \equiv \Delta A/\Delta B \equiv MU_B/MU_A$. (Remember that since the movement *R* to *S* involves a reduction in Q_A, *RS* is negative. But we defined the *MRS* to equal the absolute value of the slope of the indifference curve, so we have written $MRS \equiv$ the slope of JJ. Similarly ΔA is negative but marginal utilities positive. So we have written $\Delta A/\Delta B \equiv MU_B/MU_A$.)

The ordinal approach to demand theory requires two more pieces of information, the income of the consumer and the prices of the commodities. This information is provided by the budget line (or price line) $M/P_A \, M/P_B$ in Figure 5.3. The budget line is the locus of combinations of *A* and *B* which can be purchased when the consumer spends his entire money income and the prices of *A* and *B* are given. Any point within the area $O \, M/P_A \, M/P_B$ is a possible choice of combinations for the consumer, but there he will not have spent all of his available budget. The point M/P_A indicates the number of units of *A* the consumer can buy if he spends his entire budget, *M*, on commodity *A* at the price P_A. Similarly M/P_B indicates the maximum units of *B* he could purchase.

The (negative) slope of the budget line is numerically equal to the inverse of the ratio of the prices of *A* and *B*. Thus:

$$\text{slope} = \frac{\Delta A}{\Delta B} = \left(\frac{M}{P_A} \Big/ \frac{M}{P_B} \right) = \frac{P_B}{P_A}$$

Given an income for an individual, plus his utility function, can we say what

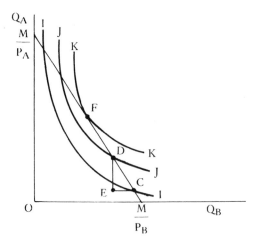

Figure 5.3

purchase combination will be most satisfying for him? The optimal position is that which yields highest utility. Within the range of choice available, the highest attainable indifference curve will be the one tangential to the price line. At point C the MRS is such that he can give up EC units of B in the market and obtain DE units of A in exchange. But he is better off at D than at C. He is on a higher indifference curve. Consequently he will move to point D. Moreover, he will not stop at D. He will only reach equilibrium, the position which cannot be improved on, when he reaches F.

At F the slope of the indifference curve KK and the budget line are equal. But the slope of KK at F is equal to the MRS of B for A at that point and:

$$MRS = MU_B/MU_A = \Delta A/\Delta B$$

And the slope of the price line at F equals P_B/P_A. Therefore, in equilibrium:

$$\frac{MU_B}{MU_A} = \frac{P_B}{P_A} \quad \text{or} \quad \frac{MU_B}{P_B} = \frac{MU_A}{P_A} \tag{5.3}$$

which is the position of marginal equivalency arrived at using the cardinal utility approach.

Income and Price Changes

Figure 5.4 summarises the impact on the budget line of an income change and of a price change. After an income increase, the original budget line MT moves out along each axis to $M'T'$, and does so parallel to the original line. OM' can now be bought of A, or OT' of B, rather than OM or OT. On the other hand, if the price of commodity B were to decrease then the effect would be the same as an increase in income.

The budget line would move to the right, to T', but would do so pivoting

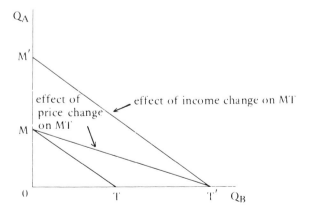

Figure 5.4

around the original point *M*. More of *B* could now be bought, *OT'* rather than *OT*, but the maximum amount of *A* which could be purchased would remain *OM*.

Now examine Figure 5.5. Here we have the family of budget lines *MT*, *M' T'* and *M" T"* tangential to a family of indifference curves. Through the points of tangency we have drawn the income–consumption curve. This shows the way in which consumption varies when income increases and prices remain constant. Such lines generally slope up and to the right. Sometimes, in the case of inferior goods, they will eventually bend back towards the left as the good is replaced by higher quality goods when income increases. (If the inferior good is plotted on the *y*-axis, of course, this line will bend down to the right.) Examples of these could be the replacement of mince by steaks in a family's diet, or the use of air travel rather than long-distance bus journeys.

From the income–consumption curve we can derive an Engel curve: named after the nineteenth century statistician who investigated the effects of income changes on consumer expenditure patterns. Engel curves for each of commodities *A* and *B* can be obtained from Figure 5.5. The points of tangency through which the income–consumption curve passes each provide three pieces of information: income, consumption of *A*, and consumption of *B*. Plotting consumption against income for any one commodity, other things held constant, provides an Engel curve.

If we now assume money income to be fixed, Figure 5.5 shows the effects of a price change. Here, product *B* is reduced in price on two occasions.

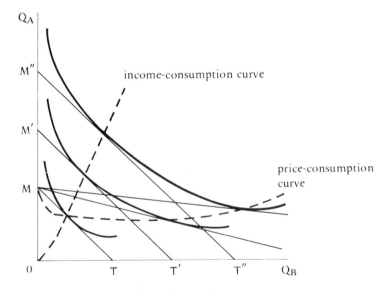

Figure 5.5

Again, the points of tangency between the indifference curves and the three price lines (on this occasion pivoted around M) are joined to trace the price–consumption curve.

As we move from lower to higher indifference curves, the price–consumption curve lies to the right of the income–consumption curve. This highlights the fact that not only does the fall in price of a commodity have a similar effect to an income increase but it also changes relative prices. In other words, the optimal MRS of B for A must also alter if $MU_B/MU_A = P_B/P_A$ is still to hold. There is, therefore, a tendency to substitute the commodity whose price has fallen for others whose price has not fallen as much or at all. The former effect is the *income effect* of a price change; the latter is the *substitution effect*.

In Figure 5.6 we show how these two effects can be separated from each other. The consumer's budget is M, and the price of A is P_{A1} and of B, P_{B1}. Equilibrium is originally at point D on curve II, where Q_{B1} units of B are bought. When P_{B1} falls to P_{B2} the budget line pivots to the right and the new equilibrium point is E, on curve JJ, where Q_{B2} is purchased. This movement, Q_{B1} to Q_{B2} is the *total effect* of the price change.

One way to isolate the substitution effect is to identify what substitution would take place if the final price ratio were to reign with no change in the consumer's real income (or utility). To do this we draw in price line $M'M'$, parallel to $M/P_{A1} M/P_{B2}$. This is tangential to II at F, the same indifference curve as that on which point D lies. The distance from Q_{B1} to Q_{B3} can be regarded as the substitution effect. It is the change in quantity demanded of

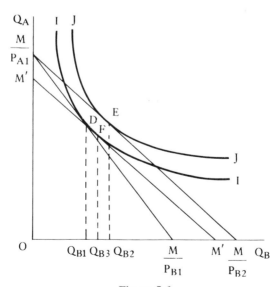

Figure 5.6

B resulting from a change in *B*'s price, holding constant the consumer's real income (or satisfaction).

The distance Q_{B3} to Q_{B2} is the income effect. Formally, it is the change in quantity demanded, exclusively associated with a change in real income, commodity prices and money income being held constant (that is the *MRS* and the price ratio are the same at both *F* and *E*).

Deriving the Demand Curve

Figure 5.7 depicts the manner in which the demand curve is derived from this analytic system. In the upper half of the figure a price–consumption curve is traced in, by connecting the three points where the family of price lines are tangential to the family of indifference curves. The three price lines *MT*, *MT'* and *MT''*, are drawn given a fixed price for commodity *A* and prices P_1, P_2 and P_3 respectively for commodity *B*.

In the lower half of the figure the quantity scale for commodity *B* is reproduced. The vertical axis, however, is now used to plot the relevant prices of *B*. If we connect the points P_1Q_1, P_2Q_2, and P_3Q_3 we obtain the demand curve for *B*.

This demand curve illustrates the first law of demand, namely that the quantity demanded will vary inversely with price, other things being equal

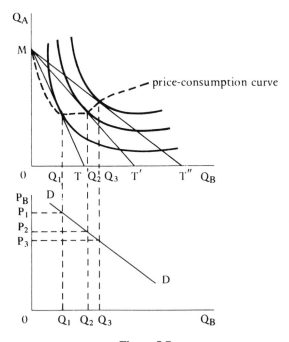

Figure 5.7

(and ignoring the exception of those inferior goods where the negative income effect is so strong it outweighs any negative substitution effects. Such goods, a peculiar type of inferior good known as Giffen goods are rarely, if ever encountered.)

The Additive Properties of Individual Demand Schedules

The usual assumption is that individual demand curves can be horizontally summed to produce a market demand curve for the good concerned. This approach assumes that each consumer's satisfaction associated with the consumption of the good is completely independent of the number of other consumers purchasing the same good. Liebenstein terms this approach a functional view of demand, which interprets demand as being based upon qualities inherent in the commodity itself. But what if there are external or non-functional effects? He suggests the following have an impact on utility: (a) the bandwagon effect, (b) the snob effect, and (c) the Veblen effect.

Liebenstein's Reservations

1.   The Bandwagon Effect

The bandwagon effect refers to the extent to which the demand for a commodity is increased because other people are purchasing the same good. It represents the desire to be fashionable. Given this assumption, each individual consumer's demand schedule is likely to be influenced by the level of overall demand in the market. We could analyse this by drawing up such individual demand curves under the assumption that each person thinks that the market demand will be at a given level. The summing of all these demand schedules in the usual fashion gives us a market demand such as curve D_a in Figure 5.8. D_a is drawn on the consumer's assumption that market demand will be OA. On the other hand, if consumers assume market demand to be OB, then D_b is the outcome. And, likewise, D_n is the sum of the individual curves when consumers assume a market demand of ON.

   If consumers are right in their expectation that OA will be the level of market demand, then the price in the market would be P_1 at point E_a. Curve D_a then traces out demand at various market prices, given that assumption. But if market demand turns out to be, say, OB, then as soon as consumers realize this they will start operating on demand curve D_b since this is consistent with the view that overall demand is OB. Again, if they are correct in this, there is only one price which is consistent with demand curve D_b and a level of market demand OB and that is price P_2. Given knowledge of market demand, one point only on each of these 'demand curves' is operative, and a line joining these unique points, marked D_M, traces out the true market demand curve taking into account the bandwagon effect.

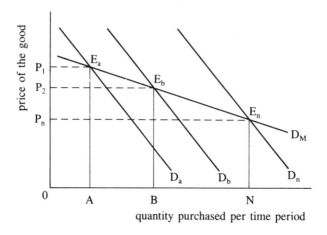

Figure 5.8 The Bandwagon Effect

The effect in this case leads to a market demand curve which is much more responsive to changes in price (i.e. is more elastic) than the simple adding of individuals' demand schedules would suggest.

2.   The Snob Effect

The snob effect can be seen as the reverse of the bandwagon effect. Once again we assume that the demand schedule of an individual consumer is influenced both by the price of the good and by his estimate of the size of the overall market demand. But in this case the relationship between the size of the market and the quantity demanded is reversed. The snob prefers exclusivity and hence the larger the estimated size of the market the less inclined he is to buy. The analysis proceeds exactly as before. It is assumed that it is possible to draw up an individual's demand schedule on the basis that market demand is expected to be at a particular level, and that all such individual curves can be summed to produce a market demand curve. Thus D_a in Figure 5.9 represents the market demand for the good given the consumer's expectation that the overall market size is OA, and so on, as previously. Once again only one price is consistent with curves D_a, D_b and D_n respectively. This is so since consumers switch to the relevant alternative demand curve once they realize that market size is different from either OA, OB or ON. The only difference from the bandwagon effect is that, as the level of market size increases, the true market demand schedule falls more rapidly, at all prices, as some snobs drop out of the market which they regard as becoming less exclusive.

Once again, Liebenstein concludes that simply adding individual demand schedules, ignoring what he calls external effects, leads to an inaccurate estima-

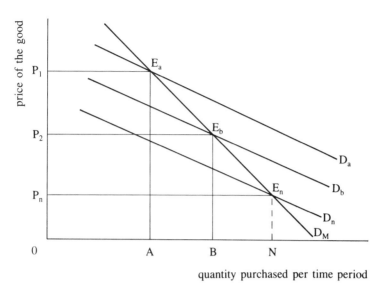

Figure 5.9 The Snob Effect

tion of demand and, in this case, demand is less responsive (i.e. less elastic; see later in this chapter) to a price change than otherwise would be predicted.

3. The Veblen Effect

Finally, Liebenstein describes the Veblen effect, which is based upon Veblen's theory of conspicuous consumption. Here we distinguish between the good's functional utility and the utility attached to its price; the latter may be considered the conspicuous consumption element. It is this conspicuous component of price which allegedly matters; it is assumed that the higher the conspicuous price the more other people are impressed, and so the greater the satisfaction of the purchaser.

Each consumer has a demand schedule. On the basis of expected conspicuousness of price, prices could be termed P_1, P_2 and P_n, and these curves can be aggregated to produce market demand curves D_1, D_2 and D_n, depending on the conspicuous price. Again, only one point on these aggregated demand curves is relevant, as shown in Figure 5.10. If consumers expect the conspicuous price to be P_1, the demand curve will be D_1, but if it turns out to be P_2, they will move up to operate on demand curve D_2, and so on. If conspicuous consumption is an important determinant of demand for the good, the higher the conspicuous price the higher the demand at all price levels. A line can then be drawn through the expected conspicuous price level of each of these demand curves and this produces the 'true' demand curve D_y. The remarkable feature of this demand curve is that it is upward-sloping.

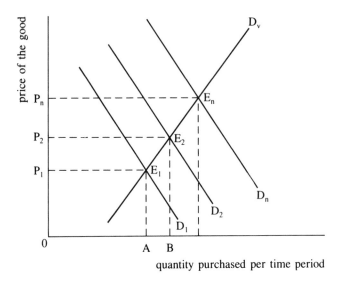

Figure 5.10 The Veblen Effect

This suggests that an upward-sloping demand curve is conceivable, at least for certain ranges of prices on certain luxury goods. If the price of the good is reduced sufficiently we might expect more normal consumers to enter the market; they will not be concerned with conspicuous effects, the Veblen effect will be reduced to zero, and the customary downward-sloping demand curve will emerge.

We have seen that, in certain circumstances, demand curves might indeed slope upwards, that adding individual demand schedules does not necessarily lead to a clear picture of market demand if there are external effects. It is also conceivable that all these external effects might be simultaneously operating and, to a certain extent, counterbalancing. However, these effects explicitly occur only when other things are not equal, so the first law of demand still holds.

It is true also that short-term speculative effects might lead to a temporary increase in quantity demanded, as people lay in stocks in anticipation of a price rise. Even here, however, the first law is not violated, since people are buying more today at a lower price than tomorrow's price is expected to be.

5.2 Becker's Development of Demand Theory

Up to this juncture we have developed the theory of market demand upon the assumption that the individual consumers who go to make up the market in aggregate are rational in their behaviour (that is they display consistency in and transitivity between their preferences). This assumption is not proven but is generally accepted on the grounds that whatever irrationality any one individual may display, the behaviour of large numbers of such individuals in the market closely approximates what it would be if each of them were rational.

Gary Becker has provided a theoretical basis for the law of demand for the market (that is that quantity demanded is inversely related to price) which does not require the assumption of individual rationality. Rather it rests on probabilistic expectations of aggregate behaviour; his theory can thus be applied using the consumer panel data which is a common tool of market researchers.

Another attraction of the Becker model is that it enables demand curves to be derived which examine the impact on quantity demanded of a price change alone. Only the substitution effect is of interest. Unlike Figure 5.7 where money income was held constant, in Becker's analysis real income is held constant. Since it is the real income constant version of the demand curve which is estimated in most econometric studies of demand relationships, it seems appropriate to place emphasis on theory which is immediately relevant rather than on the combined income substitution effect demand curve of Figure 5.7.

Moreover, Becker, when maintaining real income constant in order to isolate the substitution effect, uses a different device from that employed in Figure 5.6. There real income was equated with constant utility. An 'income-compensated' price line $M'M'$ was drawn in, parallel to $M/P_{A1} M/P_{B2}$, thus reflecting the new relative prices, but tangential to the original indifference curve II, so maintaining real income, or at least utility. An alternative approach (developed originally by Slutsky, as opposed to the constant utility approach just described which was developed by Hicks) is to draw in an income-compensated price line which would enable the consumer to buy the same 'basket of goods'. Real income represents purchasing power, and if the consumer's purchasing power is retained unchanged, after a shift in relative prices, then real income is constant. Again, since it is the ability to buy a measurable 'basket of goods' and not reach a hypothetical indifference curve which is the aim of income compensation, the Becker approach is yet another step nearer to managerial applicability than the conventional ordinal and cardinal approaches already discussed.

Consider Figure 5.11. The original budget line pivots to the left as the result of a price rise from P_{B1} to P_{B2} for product B. The original basket of goods purchased is represented by point X. Now assume that there is no change in the consumer's real income as a result of the price change. To do this we draw in the budget line $M'M''$ passing through X and parallel to $M/P_{A1} M/P_{B2}$. In other words, $OM'M''$ encloses the purchase opportunity combinations open to the consumer after an income-compensated increase

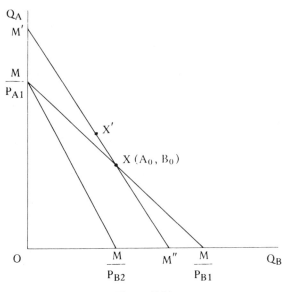

Figure 5.11

in the price of commodity B. Since $M'M''$ has a higher relative price for B and a lower one for A than does $M/P_{A1} \, M/P_{B1}$, the set it encloses offers more opportunity to consume A and less opportunity to consume B than does the set enclosed within $O \, M/P_{A1} \, M/P_{B1}$. Now, no matter what the consumer's decision rule, $OM'M''$ offers a smaller *opportunity* to consume more than B_0 of B, and a greater *opportunity* to consume more than A_0 of A.

Any rational decision rule which relates choice to 'availability' would necessarily lead the consumer to choose less of B than B_0 and more of A than A_0 out of $OM'M''$. The market demand curve would have a negative slope.

What of the 'irrational' decision rules which are said to be so prevalent amongst consumers? What of the impulse purchaser, the inert consumer, the otherwise inefficient consumer?

Becker regards the impulse purchaser as not being subject to a preference system. Such a consumer 'consults' only a probability mechanism. The individual's decisions cannot be determined in advance, but the average consumption of a large number of independent consumers would tend to be at the middle of the price line (say X) which is the statistically expected purchase combination pattern of a single consumer. However, after an income-compensated price rise in B, the budget line becomes $M'M''$, the mid-point of which is X', the average location of individual consumers distributed along it. X' is to the left of X and must always be so. Thus the downward sloping to the right of the demand curve is also implied by impulsive behaviour, at least in markets with large numbers of consumers (or for an individual consumer over a sufficiently long series of purchases).

This may perhaps be better understood using numbers. Assume 1000 consumers with identical incomes of £100 can each purchase goods A or B, both priced at £1. In total 100,000 As or 100,000 Bs could be bought. But given random distribution of preferences 50,000 of each good will be purchased (some consumers buying more of one than the other but the law of large numbers will ensure this averages out over the total). If the price of B is now increased to £2, only 50,000 Bs can be bought or 100,000 As. However, given the original market basket of 50,000 of each good, a new budget of £150 would have to be awarded to each consumer to enable them to maintain their real incomes. Such a budget would enable the consumers as a whole to purchase 150,000 As or 75,000 Bs at either extreme of the budget line. If incomes are again spent randomly the result would be a market basket of 75,000 As and 37,500 Bs.

What of the inert consumer? The brand loyal purchaser who apparently will purchase nothing but a particular product and always avoid all others? After a price change, consumers originally in the region $M/P_{A1}\, X$ may wish to remain there. But those along $X\, M/P_{B1}$ are now denied this possibility since it lies outside $OM'M''$. Those consumers, who have above average consumption of B would have to reduce their purchases, since OM'' is the maximum permitted by $M'M''$. Those relatively less inert consumers driven out of the area $X\, M''\, M/P_{B1}$ will be forced into $M'X\, M/P_{A1}$. So even inert behaviour leads to negatively inclined market demand curves.

5.3 The Demand Function

We are now in a position to move from the demand curve for an individual to that for a market, and from the market demand curve to the demand function. The first of these is conceptually simple. The market demand curve is obtained by horizontally aggregating all of the individual demand curves. Clearly, if any of the individual curves shift or change shape, the market demand curve will respond accordingly. Moreover, the market curve could also shift as a result of a change in the number of consumers in the market.

The demand function specifies the relationship between quantity demanded and all the variables which determine demand. The demand curve is merely that part of the function which relates price and quantity demanded.

The Determinants of Demand

The following nine variables are likely to be influential in determining the demand for most commodities:

P the market price of the good
T consumer tastes and preferences
Y the level of consumer incomes

P_s the prices of substitutes
P_c the prices of complements
E consumer expectations regarding prices, income and product availability
N number of potential consumers
O all other factors which may influence demand related to the product's specific characteristics

The effect of these on demand can be expressed in the form of the following non-specified equation:

$$Q = f(P, T, Y, P_s, P_c, E, N, O)$$

where Q is quantity demanded. Demand functions can be specified either for an individual firm or for the entire market in which the firm operates. The list of independent variables would differ in each case. One important difference would be the inclusion of variables representing competitors' activities in the firm's demand function (for example, competitors' advertising levels would probably be negatively related to the firm's demand). Even where a variable is common to the two functions, the parameter would probably differ. For example, suppose we had the following linear specified demand function:

$$Q = \hat{\alpha} + \hat{\beta}_1 P + \hat{\beta}_2 Y + \hat{\beta}_3 P_c + \hat{\beta}_4 N + e$$

The terms $\hat{\alpha}, \hat{\beta}_1, \hat{\beta}_2, \hat{\beta}_3, \hat{\beta}_4$ and e are constants, or parameters, calculated from past data. The value of $\hat{\beta}_4$ will be different if the function is for the market or for the firm — in the case of the firm $\hat{\beta}_4$ will be smaller. Only if the firm was a monopoly controlling the entire market would N, number of consumers, have an identical impact on the quantity demanded.

We will now expand on a number of these variables, and also on some additional determinants of demand.

Price, Income and Price Indices

Price is the amount of money given in exchange for a good or service. Money, however, is not a reliable yardstick with which to measure what must be given up to activate a trade. In consequence economists usually think of prices and incomes as measured in terms of some standard real good or 'numeraire'. In a two good world, with goods A and B given pound prices of £6 and £2 respectively, then if one A is bought £6 is given up, which could have been used to buy 3 Bs. Thus the B price of A is 3 Bs, or $P_A/P_B = 3$. Where there are n goods there are $n - 1$ other non-money goods than the one under study. In reality then it is customary to express the real (or relative) price of a good as the ratio of its absolute money price to some average price of all other goods. The average used is usually one of the various available price indices.

In cross-section studies of a demand function (that is studies at a point in time) the numeraire can frequently be ignored. In time series studies (i.e. over time) the numeraire is critical, since not only may general price inflation be present, but there is no reason why relative prices should move in step with the average. For example, if between 1970 and 1980 the money level of a person's salary doubled, but the retail price index rose from 100 to 150, is that individual better or worse off? Clearly he is better off. His real wage, the real price at which he is selling his labour has risen, not by 100% certainly, but by 33.33%. Where he earned £100, he now earns £200, but that £200 in 1980 will not buy £200 of 1970 goods, it will only buy £200 of 1980 goods. The price index increase tells us that in 1980 he must give up £150 to buy the equivalent of real goods which £100 could have bought in 1970. But even after maintaining his real purchases in 1980 by spending £150, our hypothetical individual still has £50 left, he is 33.33% better off than in 1970.

Similarly two products whose money prices had risen from £50 to £65 and from £100 to £155 between 1970 and 1980 can be compared. Both experienced a monetary, absolute price rise. To ascertain whether or not their real prices rose it is necessary to divide by the relevant numeraire. Thus the first product rose in price from £50/1.0 to £65/1.5 = £43.33 in 1970 pounds. The second rose from £100/1.0 to £155/1.5 = £103.33 in 1970 pounds. In 1980 fewer real goods and services would have to be given up to acquire the first good than were given up in 1970 (the amount fewer being represented by what £6.66 could buy in 1970). Conversely the second product had risen in price in real terms by over 3% in 1970 goods and services.

Two main price indices used by econometricians are the Retail Price Index (RPI) and the Gross Domestic Product (GDP) deflator. The first is essentially a Laspeyres or base-weighted index, the second is a variant of the Paasche or current year index. The RPI is constructed from sample family expenditures in a given base year. At its most simplistic the base year value (of 100) is then compared with some succeeding year's value, the only variables which are assumed to change being the prices of the original sample market basket. Thus:

$$RPI_0 = \frac{\sum_i^n P_{io}Q_{io}}{\sum_i^n P_{io}Q_{io}} \times 100 = 100 \quad \text{and} \quad RPI_1 = \frac{\sum_i^n P_{it}Q_{io}}{\sum_i^n P_{io}Q_{io}} \times 100$$

where P_i is the money price of good i, Q_i is the quantity bought, the subscript o is the base year and t is some future period. Clearly changes in the composition of the market basket due to innovation, obsolescence and product improvement are ignored. More subtly, the very fact that some prices rise or fall relative to others means people buy less or more of the good in question. This first law of demand is ignored by base year indices. It assumes that relatively higher priced items will continue to be bought in the same quantities as before. Substitution is ignored and thus the impact of average price inflation is exaggerated by the RPI. The defects of the current year index are the inverse of those of the base year index. Average price inflation is understated. The commodities bought in the current period are different in kind and quality from those bought in an earlier period. It is calculated thus:

$$\text{Paasche Year Index}_t = \frac{\sum\limits_{i}^{n} P_{it} Q_{it}}{\sum\limits_{i}^{n} P_{io} Q_{it}} \times 100$$

which, for the base year, 0, is:

$$PYI_o = \frac{\sum\limits_{i}^{n} P_{io} Q_{io}}{\sum\limits_{i}^{n} P_{io} Q_{io}} \times 100 = 100$$

where t is the current year.

Tastes and Preferences

Factors that shape consumers' preferences (that is influence the nature of the indifference map) embrace many determinants of consumption. For example, they include socio-economic factors such as age, sex, education, marital status, position in the domestic life cycle (for example, newly married, growing family, or middle-aged with no child dependants), and financial factors such as the disposition of wealth between liquid and illiquid assets. Tastes can change as a result of innovation and of advertising, and more fundamentally, as a consequence of changing values and priorities and rising living standards. Conversely, the existence of stable behaviour patterns, namely habits, means that changes in prices or incomes, or other variables may not have an immediate effect on demand but will be subject to a time lag.

Expectations

A consumer's expectations may influence his purchase behaviour. Thus if he anticipates that prices will rise in the near future, he may purchase now to avoid paying the higher price. Similarly, he may make a large value purchase now with a view to paying for it later out of expected increases in income.

Derived Demand

The demand for some goods is derived from the demand for others. The demand for newsprint is derived from the demand for newspapers. The demand for typewriters is derived from the demand for secretaries. In other words, when examining the demand for intermediate goods or capital goods (newsprint and typewriters, say) it will prove worthwhile also to study demand in the markets for the final goods (newspapers and secretaries) to which they are related.

Elasticities: Their Meaning and Value

A typical demand function for a commodity may be written thus:

$$Q = f(P, Y, P_s, P_c) \tag{5.4}$$

What the manager wants to know is how sensitive demand is to changes in the independent variables in the firm's demand function. The measure of responsiveness we use in demand analysis is elasticity. The general definition is that elasticity equals the percentage change in quantity demanded attributable to a given percentage change in an independent variable. So for any variable X, elasticity is given by:

$$\frac{\Delta Q/Q \ 100}{\Delta X/X \ 100} = \frac{\Delta Q}{\Delta X}\frac{X}{Q}$$

This equation measures arc elasticity, namely the elasticity over some finite range of the function. There is consequently more than one value for both X and Q. Generally, the average value of both X and Q over the range in question will be used, thus:

$$\text{arc elasticity} = \frac{\Delta Q}{\Delta X}\frac{(X_2 + X_1)/2}{(Q_2 + Q_1)/2} = \frac{\Delta Q}{\Delta X}\frac{X_2 + X_1}{Q_2 + Q_1}$$

At the limit, where ΔX is very small, $\Delta Q/\Delta X = \partial Q/\partial X$. This enables us to calculate elasticity at a point, such as X_1, Q_1:

$$\text{point elasticity} = \frac{\partial Q}{\partial X}\frac{X_1}{Q_1}$$

The partial derivative sign is used since we are interested in finding out the impact on quantity demanded of a change in X, holding all other factors constant.

Price Elasticity

Point price elasticity of demand, η is:

$$\eta = \frac{\partial Q_1 P_1}{\partial P_1 Q_1}$$

Before examining the importance of this concept it is worth discussing how a value for η, or any other elasticity, can be obtained in practice.

Our non-specified demand equation (5.4) becomes a model when it is expressed in mathematical form. The two most common specified demand equations are those which assume a linear relationship between Q and the independent variables, and those which assume a multiplicative association. For these two, equation (5.4) would be expressed respectively as:

$$Q = \alpha + \beta_1 P + \beta_2 Y + \beta_3 P_s + \beta_4 P_c + \epsilon \tag{5.5}$$

and

$$Q = \alpha . P^{\beta_1} Y^{\beta_2} P_s^{\beta_3} P_c^{\beta_4} \epsilon \tag{5.6}$$

which transforms to the linear logarithmic equation:

$$\log Q = \log \alpha + \beta_1 \log P + \beta_2 \log Y + \beta_3 \log P_s + \beta_4 \log P_c + \omega \tag{5.7}$$

where $\log \alpha$, β_1, β_2, β_3 and β_4 are constants to be calculated from past data. Multiple regression equations of this sort are to the managerial economist what the laboratory is to the chemist. They permit the equivalent of controlled experimentation. They have the attribute that other variables can be held constant when the relationship between a pair of variables is being studied.

We can calculate the point price elasticity from equation (5.5) by taking its partial derivative with respect to price, thus:

$$\frac{\partial Q}{\partial P} = \hat{\beta}_1 \quad \text{therefore} \quad \eta = \frac{\partial Q}{\partial P} \frac{P}{Q} = \hat{\beta}_1 . \frac{P}{Q} \tag{5.8}$$

where $\hat{\beta}_1$ is the estimated value of β_1.

Thus point elasticity can always be obtained from a linear demand function for variable X by multiplying the regression coefficient or parameter of variable X by the value of X/Q at that point. Given that the value of P/Q on a linear demand curve will vary, being higher at higher prices and lower at lower prices, η in turn will also vary in a similar fashion.

Since equation (5.6) can be transformed into the linear logarithmic equation (5.7), it can still be estimated using linear least squares regression techniques. Another useful factor of multiplicative demand functions is that they have constant elasticities over their full range. These elasticities are given by the coefficients estimated in the regression analysis. For example, writing the estimated form of equation (5.6) as:

$$Q = \hat{\alpha} . P^{\hat{\beta}_1} . Y^{\hat{\beta}_2} . P_s^{\hat{\beta}_3} . P_c^{\hat{\beta}_4} . e \tag{5.9}$$

and differentiating this with respect to price, we obtain:

$$\frac{\partial Q}{\partial P} = \hat{\beta}_1 . P^{\hat{\beta}_1 - 1} . \alpha . Y^{\hat{\beta}_2} P_s^{\hat{\beta}_3} P_c^{\hat{\beta}_4} e$$

and so, multiplying both sides by P/Q, we obtain:

$$\frac{P}{Q}\frac{\partial Q}{\partial P} = \eta = \hat{\beta}_1.P^{\hat{\beta}_1-1}.\alpha.Y^{\hat{\beta}_2}P_s^{\hat{\beta}_3}.P_c^{\hat{\beta}_4}.e\,\frac{P}{Q} \qquad (5.10)$$

If we now substitute equation (5.9) for Q in equation (5.10) we have:

$$\eta = \hat{\beta}_1.P^{\hat{\beta}_1-1}.Y^{\hat{\beta}_2}.P_s^{\hat{\beta}_3}.P_c^{\hat{\beta}_4}.e\,\frac{P}{P^{\hat{\beta}_1}.Y^{\hat{\beta}_2}.P_s^{\hat{\beta}_3}.P_c^{\hat{\beta}_4}.e}$$

which on cancellation is simply $\eta = \beta_1$. So $\eta = \beta_1$, the exponent of price in equation (5.6). Since this is not a function of the P/Q ratio, it is constant. This constancy applies for all the variables in a multiplicative demand relationship. Clearly, a demand function cannot be forced into a curvilinear relationship, but when it does occur, it removes the problem of variable elasticities from the manager's decision situation.

As shown above, when a multiplicative demand function is estimated, the question of the price at which we wish to calculate elasticity does not arise, η has the same value at all prices. But as equation (5.8) shows, this is not the case with a linear demand curve.

Often price elasticity is calculated at the mean values of P and Q which occur in the sample of observations when the coefficients were estimated. Hence the mean value of Q, $\bar{Q}$ — and of P, $\bar{P}$, — would be substituted in equation (5.8) to give:

$$\eta = \hat{\beta}_1\,\frac{\bar{P}}{\bar{Q}}$$

Price elasticity is of prime importance in indicating the effect on revenue of a price change. Revenue can rise, fall, or remain the same after a price change. There are three ranges of price elasticity, and two limiting cases. These are:[1]

1. $\eta = \infty$ This is the case of the perfectly elastic demand curve. Elasticity is infinite. The demand curve is a horizontal line, parallel to the quantity axis.

2. $\eta > 1$ The case of elastic demand. A reduction in price will result in a more than proportionate increase in quantity demanded. Total revenue will rise.

3. $\eta = 1$ The case of unitary elasticity. The demand curve is a rectangular hyperbola. The product of P and Q (total revenue) is constant, irrespective of the level of P.

4. $\eta < 1$ The case of inelastic demand. A reduction in price will result in a less than proportionate increase in quantity demanded. Total revenue will fall.

1   Since $\Delta Q/\Delta P$ is negative, η always has a negative value. Conventionally, however, the algebraic sign is ignored.

5. $\eta = 0$ The case of the completely inelastic demand curve. Elasticity
    is infinitely inelastic. The demand curve is a vertical line,
    parallel to the price axis.

The key factor, then, is the effect of a price change on revenue. Figure
5.12 depicts a linear demand curve of varying elasticity from $\eta = \infty$ to $\eta = 0$.
Marginal revenue (MR) is positive so long as total revenue (TR) is rising, and
becomes negative when TR falls. If one knows price and price elasticity of
demand at a point, then the value of MR can also be computed. Thus:

$$TR = PQ$$

$$MR = \frac{dTR}{dQ} = P\frac{dQ}{dQ} + Q\frac{dP}{dQ} = P + Q\frac{dP}{dQ}$$

Multiply throughout by P/P

$$MR = P\left(1 + \frac{Q}{P}\frac{dP}{dQ}\right) \qquad = P\left(1 + \frac{1}{\eta}\right) \qquad (5.11)$$

which is our desired result.

No profit-maximising businessman would lower his prices in the inelastic
range of his demand curve. Elasticity measures are vital information in the
taking of price decisions. Some products, such as necessities, will have

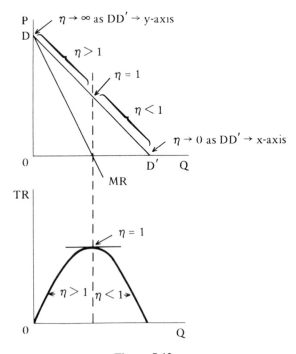

Figure 5.12

relatively inelastic demand. Within limits they must be bought whatever the price. Others, such as luxury items, will have much more elastic demands, and the market place will be more price sensitive.

Absolutely inexpensive products will have less elastic demand curves than more expensive ones. It will not be worth the consumer's while to waste a large amount of time and energy worrying about price. Derived demand will be less elastic than primary demand. A rise in the price of machine tools will result in only a relatively small fall in the quantity demanded. Buyers of machine tools will find it difficult, at least in the short run, to find substitutes for machine tools with which to manufacture their final products.

Elasticities of demand are also used in public policy decisions. For example, over the years the tobacco and liquor industries have argued that demand for their products was relatively elastic. So any increase in excise duty by the government would merely result in a decreased quantity demanded and so a lower revenue for both the industries and the government. The government, on the other hand, has argued that demand is relatively inelastic, and that a gross price increase would raise the revenue of the Exchequer.

Income Elasticity

The income elasticity of demand, η_y, can be calculated from equation (5.5) by taking its partial derivative with respect to income, thus:

$$\frac{\partial Q}{\partial Y} = b \qquad \text{so } \eta_y = \frac{\partial Q}{\partial Y} \frac{Y}{Q} = b \frac{Y}{Q}$$

Income and quantity purchased typically move in the same direction. So η_y is generally positive. The exceptions to this generalisation are inferior goods. When 'income' is included in a demand equation it can be measured on an aggregate, *per capita* or a per household basis.

'Income' can be national income, or GNP, personal income, disposable (after tax) income, or discretionary income (the surplus remaining after regular commitments on food, housing and other essential recurring expenses). GNP may be the most suitable measure of income in a demand model for machine tools; disposable income may be apposite for a clothing demand model; and discretionary income may well be the most suitable in a model of the demand for beer.

Knowledge of income elasticity is a vital piece of management information. Low income elasticity ($\eta_y < 1$) implies that the company will to some degree be insulated from the vicissitudes of business activity in the economy as a whole. This is the case, for example, with most necessities such as food-stuffs. High income elasticity, however, implies that a rise in income will be accompanied by a more than proportionate rise in the quantity demanded of the product concerned ($\eta_y > 1$). This will be the case with the demand for luxury commodities such as holidays abroad, audio equipment, expensive restaurants, and so on. Firms whose demand functions have high income elasticity of demand will pay particular attention to forecasting and tabulating expected levels of future economic activity.

Figure 5.13 shows a set of three Engel curves for a hypothetical household. For non-durable luxuries no expenditure is recorded at the lowest income levels. When expenditure commences it rises faster than income ($\eta_y > 1$). The income elasticity of necessities, however, is less than unity. In the case of durable luxuries, such as colour TVs, η_y is again greater than unity, but the Engel curve is stepped, indicating threshold levels of demand. Up to a certain level of income there is virtually no demand for the product, but beyond it will almost certainly be acquired. Similarly, demand for a second set barely exists until another threshold income level is attained.

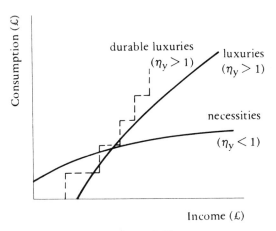

Figure 5.13

Cross-elasticity

The demand for most goods is influenced by the prices of other commodities. Thus the demand for butter is influenced by the price of margarine (a substitute). The demand for cassettes is influenced by the price of tape decks (a complementary good). As the price of cassette decks falls, their quantity demanded will rise and, in turn, the demand for tapes will increase.

Again using equation (5.5) we can calculate the cross-elasticity of demand with respect to a substitute good (η_{xs}) and with respect to a complementary good (η_{xc}) as follows:

$$\eta_{xs} = \frac{\partial Q}{\partial P_s}\frac{P_s}{Q} \quad \text{and} \quad \eta_{xc} = \frac{\partial Q}{\partial P_c}\frac{P_c}{Q}$$

The cross-elasticity of demand for substitutes is always positive. Q and P_s

will always move in the same direction. Conversely, the cross-elasticity of demand for complements is negative. Q and P_c will be inversely related. When two commodities are unrelated, cross-elasticity of demand will be zero or near-zero.

5.4 Conclusions

In this chapter the theory of demand has been outlined. The first law of demand: that quantity demanded is inversely related to price (other things equal) was stated and explained. (Alleged exceptions such as 'snob' goods or 'prestige' goods assume that the characteristics of the good as perceived by the consumer change as prices change: other things are not equal. Similarly, Giffen goods — if they exist — confuse income and substitution effects. The law of demand relates only to substitution effects. A further 'exception' was mentioned when consumer expectations were discussed. If people buy more today because they expect prices to be higher tomorrow, even if today's price is unchanged, then the first law is actually affirmed not denied. Recall that 'price' is relative price. Relative to expected prices, today's prices are lower and consistent with the first law of demand — people will buy more.)

The second law of demand, that consumers will be more responsive to a price change in the long than in the short run was also mentioned but not detailed. Long-run price elasticity is greater than short-run price elasticity. First, it takes time for people to adjust their buying patterns. Second, time must pass before people notice a price change. Thus a rise in home heating costs will result first in people cutting consumption of the relevant fuel. In the longer term, however, they will switch their fuel source and change the type of heating equipment they have in their houses: so cutting the consumption of the relatively expensive fuel still further.

In Chapter 6 it will be shown how the principles learned here can be put into effect.

Additional Reading

Baird, C.W. (1975) *Prices and Markets: Microeconomics*, West.

Baumol, W.J. (1977) *Economic Theory and Operations Analysis*, 4th edn., Prentice-Hall.

Becker, G.S. (1962) 'Irrational behaviour and economic theory', *Journal of Political Economy*, Vol. 70.

Liebenstein, H. (1950) 'Bandwagon, snob and Veblen effects in the theory of consumer's demand', *Quarterly Journal of Economics*, Vol. 64, No. 2, pp. 183–207.

Palda, K.S. (1969) *Economic Analysis for Marketing Decisions*, Prentice-Hall.

Veblen, T. (1899) *The Theory of the Leisure Class*, Allen and Unwin (1971).

6

Techniques for Demand Estimation

In Chapter 1 it was shown that to maximise profits a manager must produce that output at which $MR = MC$. In the last chapter it was shown that one method of deriving the MR function was to estimate the coefficients in the demand function, make price the subject of the equation, multiply it by Q and differentiate with respect to Q. If the value of MR was required at a particular value of Q, that Q value could be substituted into the MR function, or alternatively, the value of P and the price elasticity of demand, as in equation (5.11). However, knowledge of demand price elasticity requires knowledge of the coefficient of P. The coefficients of the other independent variables must also be known to predict their profit-maximising levels (if they are policy variables) or to predict the likely effects on TR and profits of changes in these variables (if they are exogenous).

The question arises as to how these coefficients may be estimated. This is the subject of this chapter. Chapter 7 will include a section on the measurement of cost functions, so the reader then has an idea as to how he might determine the profit-maximising values of certain policy variables for his firm.

6.1 Survey and Experimental Methods

These techniques may be used to derive values of the quantity demanded at different values of the independent variables. In the case of surveys, these quantities relate to intended purchases, whereas in the case of experiments they relate to actual purchases under known or partially known conditions. (Often a firm may have to estimate the values of competing firms' policy variables rather than receiving this information from competitors.) In either case sufficient information may be collected from which to estimate arc elasticities of demand by deriving values of quantity demanded at say, different prices, whilst holding constant all other variables which could affect demand. Where the experiment is in the field and not in the laboratory, however, the manager is unlikely to be able to derive even one elasticity of demand from the information gained, since other relevant variables in addition to, say, own price, are likely to have varied when price was changed.

These techniques give arc rather than point elasticities. They do not provide us with coefficients in the demand function. Hence they do not prescribe a method for predicting the quantity demanded for combinations of values of explanatory variables other than those on which the manager already has information. The most commonly used methods of deriving the coefficients of a firm's demand function *given* the information which has been collected by, for example, surveys of consumers, experts, suppliers or by experiments, come under the heading of Regression Techniques.

6.2 Regression Techniques

In this section we firstly explain the technique when the quantity demanded in a period, t, is hypothesised to be a function of only one independent variable, say price, in the same period. Secondly, the method is generalised to the case of several independent variables. Thirdly, some complications are explained. Fourthly, the identification problem is considered; and fifthly, two examples are explained.

Overview

Suppose it is believed that the demand function for a product is of the form:

$$Q^D = \alpha + \beta P \tag{6.1}$$

Observations on the price and corresponding quantity demanded in each of, say, 30 weeks have been collected. We may plot these observations as in Figure 6.1. To obtain a value for each of α and β we wish to find a straight

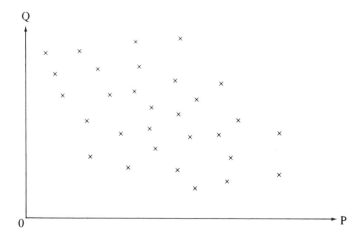

Figure 6.1

line which according to some criterion 'best fits' these points. One method of deriving such a line would be to fit one by eye. A major problem with this is that different people would fit different lines to the same points: no uniform criterion is being used. One of the most commonly used criteria is the method of Ordinary Least Squares (OLS). The use of OLS is based on a statistical model.

In this statistical model it is assumed that, for any given value of price, P_t, the corresponding quantity demanded, Q_t, is given by the equation:

$$Q_t = \alpha + \beta P_t + \epsilon_t \qquad (6.2)$$

where ϵ_t is a stochastic term. That is, on any one occasion (i.e. value of t) the value of ϵ is determined by chance, but the distribution of its possible values is assumed to have certain characteristics (to be explained later). In fact, ϵ could take on any one of an infinite number of *possible* values. Therefore, for a given price, Q_t could also take on one of an infinite number of *possible* values.

But why *in practice* might we think that a stochastic term should be added to equation (6.1)? Well, for every observation to fit equation (6.1) we would require that Q_t is affected only by P_t, that all persons in the groups to which the equation relates always behave exactly according to the equation (in the sense of always having the same values of α and β), that the true function is linear, and that all observed values of Q_t and P_t are measured completely accurately.

In reality, these conditions are unlikely to hold. Firstly, it is likely that equation (6.1) omits variables which affect Q_t, such as advertising and so on. For completely accurate representation of behaviour the model would have to include every variable which could possibly affect Q_t. So the equation would have to include a very large number of variables. Either in theory or in practice it may not be possible to include them all and to estimate their coefficients, for several reasons. For example, some of these variables may not be known. Secondly, there may be no technique to measure them — for example, tastes, expectations, and so on. Thirdly, the influence of each may be so small that conventional computational techniques would round their coefficient down to zero. Another major reason why the observations may not exactly fit the hypothetical model is that the true relationship may be nonlinear. Finally, the observed values may have been inaccurately measured. So even if equation (6.1) were the true relationship, the erroneous observations would misfit it.

Returning to the statistical model, equation (6.2) may be represented graphically, as in Figure 6.2. In the figure, equation (6.2) is represented by the continuous line which, let us assume, could theoretically be fitted to *every possible* sample of pairs of values of P_t and Q_t generated by consumers' behaviour. Figure 6.2 also shows a pair of P, Q values from this infinite number of possible pairs. For any such pair, for a given value of P_t, the value of

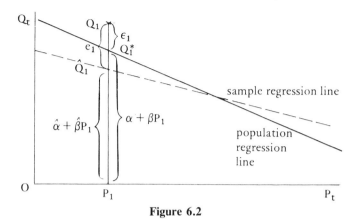

Figure 6.2

Q differs from that on the continuous line by ϵ_t. For example, for P_1 the statistical model shows a value for Q_1 of Q_1^* ($=\alpha+\beta P_1$) whereas the value in the sample which corresponds to P_1 is Q_1. Notice that Q_1 differs from Q_1^* by ϵ_1.

We have said that the continuous line in Figure 6.2 represented the linear equation which fits *every possible* sample of pairs of values of P_t and Q_t. Such a collection of values is called the *population*. The *population* of P_t and Q_t values is hypothetical in the sense that in practice no one could possibly observe every pair: there is an infinite number of them. What is observed is a sample of P_t, Q_t values such as, for example, over the last 30 weeks. However, when using OLS, we assume that equation (6.2) represents the process generating each sample. Furthermore, statisticians have proved that, given certain characteristics of the ϵ term in equation (6.2), we can make inferences about the α and β using merely a *sample of P_t, Q_t values. The manager's aim therefore is to estimate values of α and β which relate to the population of P_t and Q_t values using only a given sample of observations.*

Suppose we 'fit' a straight line to the sample data. It is highly unlikely that each P_t, Q_t pair will lie on the line: there will be an error called a residual, e_t. For example, in Figure 6.2, if P_1, Q_1 is an observed pair of values, Q_1 differs from the value predicted by the sample regression line for P_1 by the amount e_1. The residual values reflect both the factors which were assumed to affect ϵ_1 and the difference between the line fitted to the sample data and that assumed to apply to the population. These two lines differ because the former is calculated from a *sample* of observations, whereas the latter relates to the population of *all possible values*.

For clarity, a model which generates the *population* is denoted:

$$Q_t = \alpha+\beta P_t+\epsilon_t \tag{6.3}$$

The equation which has been 'fitted' to a *sample* is denoted:

$$Q_t = \hat{\alpha} + \hat{\beta}P_t + e_t \qquad\qquad (6.4)$$

Since $\hat{\alpha}$ and $\hat{\beta}$ may not equal α and β respectively, for a given value of P_t, e_t may not be equal ϵ_t.

Procedural Stages

When using regression analysis the procedural stages are as follows:

1.   Choice of Variables

In this stage the manager decides on the variables which he believes are included in the population model. A manager may derive a list of the variables to be included in a number of ways. For example, economic theory of the consumer, as explained in Chapter 5, predicts that an individual's demand for a good is related to its price, the prices of other goods, his/her income and tastes. Tastes can rarely be measured, but since advertising of own and rival products may affect tastes, advertising expenditure may be included instead. Alternatively, *a priori* reasoning or evidence either from casual observation or from studies of the demand for other goods or services may suggest further variables. Typically an assumed model would include the above variables. Additional variables, which may differ according to the product of interest, may be added. For example, the demand for volume drinks and ice cream is likely to be related to the weather, whereas that for washing-up liquid is not. The demand for a consumer durable is likely to be related to the interest rate on consumer credit and anticipated future income. The demand for investment goods is likely to be related to company profitability. For consumer products population may be a relevant variable. Finally, it should be noted that, for reasons to be explained, the identity of variables to be included in the model may be restricted by statistical considerations.

2.   Form of the Model

At this stage the manager decides on the functional form of the assumed model. Many alternative forms are available. Two examples, the linear and multiplicative forms, were discussed in Chapter 5 (see equations 5.5 and 5.6 respectively). If the manager is to use the OLS technique, his choice of form is constrained to one which, in the version to be estimated, is linear. Hence OLS can be applied to the multiplicative demand function (equation 5.6) because it can be converted to a linear form by taking logarithms of both sides. However, some functional forms cannot be linearised.

3.   Obtaining the Data

For some variables, e.g. personal disposable income, data can be obtained from government agencies (e.g. the Central Statistical Office) or private data-collecting companies (e.g. advertising data from MEAL).[1] But for some variables the data may not be available at all, or at a sufficiently disaggregated level for the model. In these cases it may have to be collected by survey or experiment.

4. Estimating the Parameters of the Model

Suppose that the manager strongly believes that the statistical population model relating every possible quantity demanded to given values of his product's price can be represented by:

$$Q_t = \alpha + \beta P_t + \epsilon_t$$

(We have deliberately chosen only one right-hand side variable for simplicity.) Estimates of α and β, $\hat{\alpha}$ and $\hat{\beta}$ respectively can be calculated by certain formulae, the *OLS estimators* of α and β. These estimates are based on finding those values of $\hat{\alpha}$ and $\hat{\beta}$ which minimise the sum of *squared* residual values. (Remember that for a given value of P, the residual is the difference between an observed value of Q and that predicted by the sample as shown in Figure 6.2.) Hence:

$$e_t = Q_t - \hat{\alpha} - \hat{\beta} P_t \quad \text{(from equation 6.4)}$$

$$\Rightarrow \sum_{t=1}^{n} e_t^2 = \sum (Q_t - \hat{\alpha} - \hat{\beta} P_t)^2$$

Differentiating with respect to $\hat{\alpha}$ and $\hat{\beta}$ using the chain rule (rule 6 in Table 1.2) for a turning point:

$$\frac{\partial \Sigma e_t^2}{\partial \hat{\alpha}} = \sum_{t=1}^{n} 2(Q_t - \hat{\alpha} - \hat{\beta} P_t)(-1) = 0 \text{ for a min} \qquad (6.5)$$

and

$$\frac{\partial \Sigma e_t^2}{\partial \hat{\beta}} = \sum_{t=1}^{n} 2(Q_t - \hat{\alpha} - \hat{\beta} P_t)(-P_t) = 0 \text{ for a min} \qquad (6.6)$$

Rearraning equations (6.5) and (6.6) and solving for $\hat{\beta}$ and $\hat{\alpha}$ gives[2]

$$\hat{\beta} = \frac{n(\sum_{t=1}^{n} P_t \cdot Q_t) - (\sum_{t=1}^{n} P_t)(\sum_{t=1}^{n} Q_t)}{n(\sum_{t=1}^{n} P_t^2) - (\sum_{t=1}^{n} P_t)^2} \qquad (6.7)$$

1   Media Expenditure Analysis Ltd.
2   See any standard econometrics text for the intervening steps.

and

$$\hat{\alpha} = \frac{\Sigma Q_i}{n} - \hat{\beta} \frac{\Sigma P_i}{n} \qquad\qquad (6.8)$$

into which equation (6.7) or the estimated value of $\hat{\beta}$ is substituted. An example
of the calculation of $\hat{\alpha}$ and $\hat{\beta}$ using these estimators is given in Table 6.1.

In practice, a manager would not perform these calculations by hand but
would use one of a large number of statistical packages which are available
for use on computers of all sizes from personal computers to mainframes.
Such packages not only produce values of $\hat{\alpha}$ and $\hat{\beta}$, but also a large number
of interpretative statistics which may be used to assess the applicability of
the population model to the situation in hand.

The fifth stage is to interpret the estimated sample regression line. This
is sufficiently important to occupy an entire section of our chapter, but is
rather difficult. The reader may skip this section with only a small loss of
continuity.

Interpretative Statistics

We begin this section by considering in depth the assumptions which form
the classical linear regression model, the statistical model behind OLS.

Table 6.1

Q	P	PQ	P^2
10	2	20	4
7	3	21	9
8	6	48	36
6	7	42	49
7	10	70	100
4	11	44	121
42	39	245	319

$$\bar{Q} = 7 \quad \bar{P} = 6.5$$

Using formulae (6.7) and (6.8),

$$\hat{\beta} = \frac{6(245) - (39)(42)}{6(319) - (39)^2} = \frac{1470 - 1638}{1914 - 1521} = -0.427$$

$$\hat{\alpha} = 7 + (0.427)(6.5) = 9.776$$

$$Q = 9.776 - 0.427P$$

This example is used to illustrate the calculation of $\hat{\alpha}$ and $\hat{\beta}$ from sample data. When
used in practice, many more observations would be needed.

1. Assumptions of the Classical Linear Regression Model

When using a model like: $Q_t = \alpha + \beta P_t + \epsilon_t$, we make the following assumption about the way the P_ts are generated:

A(i)   For any given set of values of t, the values of P_t are prescribed. That is, the P_t values are not regarded as 'randomly' generated but as fixed (or predetermined) values.

Given this assumption, the corresponding values of Q_t consist of the sum of two parts:

(a) a prescribed quantity, $\alpha + \beta P_t$ and
(b) an unpredictable deviation from (a), ϵ_t, which, *a priori*, can take on any one of an infinite number of possible values. The probability of each value of ϵ_t occurring is given by a particular probability distribution.[3]

We also make assumptions about ϵ_t. If these assumptions together with A(i) are valid, then firstly, the OLS estimators have certain desirable properties which other estimators do not have and secondly, one can make inferences about the *population values* of α and β from *mere sample observations*. These assumptions are:

A(ii) For any given value of t, the possible values of ϵ_t are normally distributed.

If one could take one value of P_t and repeatedly record every possible value of Q_t associated with it, since the factors which determine the ϵ_t values may differ on each occasion, the values of

---

3   Strictly speaking, we should refer to a 'probability density function'. Without using the name we loosely explained the nature of a p.d.f. on pp. 27–28. In fact Figure 2.3 is a p.d.f. To recap, suppose a random variable X could take on a finite number, say 5, of specific values and that the probability of each was known. Then one could draw a histogram of the probability of each value occurring against that value. If the number of possible values of X is increased, the probability of each occurring will decrease. If the number of possible values of X tends to infinity as, for example, if X could take on any positive real number, the probability of each will tend to zero. However, the probability that X will take on a value between two values would not be zero since there would be a large number of possible values of X within any range. A p.d.f. encloses an area equal to 1. The area under the curve and between two values equals the probability that X will take on a value in that range.

The variable measured along the vertical axis, $f(x_0)$, multiplied by a *fixed* and very small value, dx, approximately equals the probability that x will take on values within $dx/2$ of any x_0 along the horizontal axis. That is, the probability of x taking values in any *given* small range around any value x_0 is proportional to $f(x_0)$.

ϵ_t and hence Q_t would differ. The ϵ_t values for the given P_t would be normally distributed.

A(iii) For any given value of t, the expected value of ϵ_t is zero.

   That is, the average of the possible population values of ϵ_t which correspond to the given value of P_t, is zero.

A(iv) The variances of the distributions of ϵ_ts for difference values of t are all the same.

   Suppose for a given value of t the variance of the probability density function of the associated ϵ_t is calculated. If this exercise is repeated for every possible value of t, the resulting variances will be the same. The possible values of Q_t will be equally dispersed at low as at medium and high prices.

The implications of the above assumptions may be represented graphically as in Figure 6.3 where the three specific values of P_t have been chosen. The straight line is simply a demand curve and the curved line at each price shows the distribution of the errors made, when predicting quantity. If all the possible hypothetical population values of ϵ_t associated with each P_t could be recorded and their distribution constructed, it would be normal in each case and have the same variance and mean of zero.

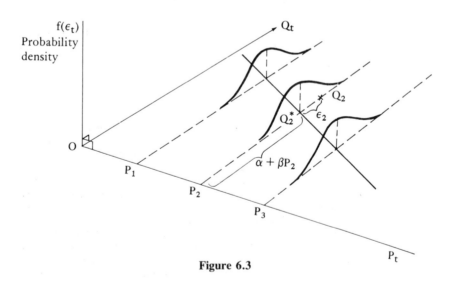

Figure 6.3

A(v) The ϵ_ts associated with one value of P_t are independent of those associated with any other value of P_t.

   This implies that the values of the ϵ_ts at different ts are uncorrelated. If the population demand curve underpredicts demand in one period, for example because of a sudden fall in a competitor's price, this does not make it any more likely that it will under or over estimate it in the next period. (This is a restricted explanation of assumption A(v). A fuller analysis is given on pages 167–169.)

Notice that the hypothesised validity of these assumptions — specifically assumption A(iii) — allows the population model to be rewritten by taking expectations of both sides of equation (6.2). Hence:

$$E(Q_t) = E(\alpha + \beta P_t + \epsilon_t) = E(\alpha) + E(\beta P_t) + E(\epsilon_t)$$

But α and β are constants and P_t takes on fixed values. Hence[4] $E(\alpha) = 1\alpha$ and $E(\beta P_t) = 1\beta P_t$. Also $E(\epsilon_t) = 0$ by assumption A(iii). Thus:

$$E(Q_t) = \alpha + \beta P_t + 0 = \alpha + \beta P_t \qquad (6.9)$$

But $E(Q_t)$ is the mean of all possible Q_t values given P_t (bearing in mind that at a given P_t, Q_t could take on different values depending on the value of ϵ_t). Therefore *the straight line in Figure 6.3 which can be labelled as equation (6.9), cuts each dotted line corresponding to a specific P_t at the average value of Q_t associated with it.* So Q_2^* is the mean of all of the possible Q_2 values which are associated with P_2.

2. Significance of Estimated Coefficients

If different samples are taken from the population and substituted into the formula for $\hat{\beta}$, the calculated values are almost certain to differ from each other and from that which would fit the population. Similarly, this is likely for $\hat{\alpha}$.

It can be shown that, if assumptions A(i) and A(iii) hold, the *expected values* of the $\hat{\alpha}$ and $\hat{\beta}$ values are, respectively, the population values of α and β. This implies that, if every possible sample of size n is taken and the values of $\hat{\alpha}$ and $\hat{\beta}$ calculated for each, the average of the $\hat{\beta}$ values would equal the value of the desired population coefficient, and similarly for $\hat{\alpha}$. It can also be shown that, if assumption A(ii) holds, the calculated values of $\hat{\alpha}$ and $\hat{\beta}$ from repeated samples are normally distributed if n is large (conventionally 'large' is over 30). Therefore the distribution of, say, $\hat{\beta}$ values may be shown by Figure 6.4. Furthermore, the standard deviation of this distribution and of the distribution of $\hat{\alpha}$ values from sample data may be estimated. We will denote these estimates $S_{\hat{\alpha}}$ and $S_{\hat{\beta}}$ for $\hat{\alpha}$ and $\hat{\beta}$ respectively.

In practice, estimates of α and β are gained from a single sample. Therefore, since each sample may give a different estimate, it is useful to know whether, in the light of a single sample, we can accept the hypothesis that α and/or β are really specific values which we may choose. This is done using a 't' test.

---

4   It will be recalled from Chapter 2 that the expected value of a variable X is $E(X)$ $= p_1 X_1 + p_2 X_2 + \ldots$ where p_1 is the probability that X takes on the value X_1 etc.

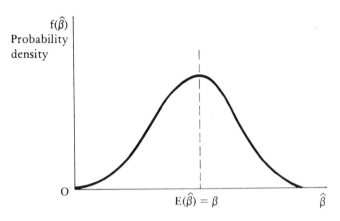

Figure 6.4

If $\hat{\alpha}$ and $\hat{\beta}$ are calculated from a sample, one can transform these estimates to form t-statistics:

$$t_{\hat{\alpha}} = \frac{\hat{\alpha} - \alpha^*}{S_{\hat{\alpha}}} \sim t_{\phi = n - K} \quad \text{for } \hat{\alpha} \tag{6.10}$$

$$t_{\hat{\beta}} = \frac{\hat{\beta} - \beta^*}{S_{\hat{\beta}}} \sim t_{\phi = n - K} \quad \text{for } \hat{\beta} \tag{6.11}$$

each having $n - K$ degrees of freedom where n is the sample size and K is the number of estimated parameters. In the case of our single independent variable model $K = 2$ ($\hat{\alpha}$ and $\hat{\beta}$).

The t-distribution is a probability distribution.[5] That is, the area between any two values of t is the probability that a value of t derived from a random sample will lie between these values, the total area under the curve equalling one. This point is represented diagrammatically in Figure 6.5 which shows a t-distribution (with $\phi = 20$ degrees of freedom). The probability that a value of t exceeds 2.086, $P(t > 2.086)$, is 0.025. Similarly $P(-t < -2.086) = 0.025$ because the t-distribution is symmetric. These and other values of t can be obtained from Student's t-tables in any statistics text.

To test the hypothesis that the population value, β, is a specific value, β^*, despite the value estimated from the sample being $\hat{\beta}$, one tests the null hypothesis:

$$H_0 \quad \beta = \beta^*$$

5   Strictly speaking, a probability density function.

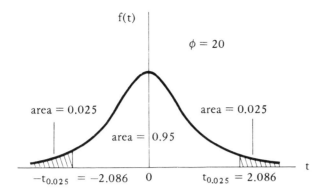

Figure 6.5

against the alternative hypothesis:

$$H_1 \quad \beta \neq \beta^*$$
$$\text{or} \quad H_1 \quad \beta > \beta^*$$
$$\text{or} \quad H_1 \quad \beta < \beta^*$$

depending on which alternative relationship is of interest. In practice H_1 is the hypothesis whose validity we wish to establish whereas H_0 is everything else.

Next, we calculate the t-statistic of equation (6.11) and compare it with a critical t-value from the theoretical t-distribution (given in the Tables in any statistics text). The comparison made depends on which alternative hypothesis we put forward. Suppose, for example, H_1 is $\beta \neq \beta^*$. That is, the 'true' value of β is *larger or smaller* than β^*. If the calculated t-statistic exceeds the critical t where $P(t > t_{\text{critical}} \text{ or } -t < -t_{\text{critical}}) = 0.05$, e.g. if $|t| > 2.086$ in Figure 6.5, then the probability that the calculated t-value would be observed if $\beta = \beta^*$ is less than 0.05. So if we have such a t-value, and we reject the hypothesis that $\beta = \beta^*$, there is probability of less than 0.05 that we have done the wrong thing. If we accept that a probability of rejecting a hypothesis when it is true (a 'type I error') of 0.05 is sufficiently low to accept this risk, we reject H_0: $\beta = \beta^*$ 'at the 0.05 level' (or at $\alpha_1 = 0.05$) and accept H_1. Notice that we have compared our calculated t with both positive and negative values of t-critical. This was done because our alternative hypothesis was the β is *larger or smaller* than β ($\beta \neq \beta^*$) and so it did not matter if β fell in either tail of the theoretical t-distribution.

Suppose, on the other hand, that we adopted the second alternative hypothesis: H_1: $\beta > \beta^*$. Then we would only be interested in whether or not the population value of β is greater than β^*, not whether it is greater *or smaller*. In this case the t-statistic is compared with a t-$_{\text{critical}}$ which cuts an area of

0.05 from only the right-hand tail of the theoretical t-distribution. If the sample $\hat{\beta}$ were less than β^* and so the calculated t were negative, the test would not be performed: one could not accept H_1 that β is greater than β^* regardless of the value of t. Finally, if H_1 were $\beta < \beta^*$ and if the calculated t were negative (because $\hat{\beta} - \beta^*$ was negative) this would be compared with minus t-$_{\text{critical}}$ which cuts 0.05 from the *left-hand* tail of the t-distribution. The same procedure is used to test corresponding hypotheses about α.

Often a manager may wish to test whether or not β is equal to or differs from zero. That is, he may wish to test: H_0: $\beta = 0$ against H_1: $\beta \neq 0$. This would be done by following the above procedure and substituting $\beta^* = 0$ into the t-calculation. The economic relevance of this test is that if one could reject H_0, then the independent variable would be accepted as affecting the dependent variable. If H_0 could not be rejected, then one would accept that the independent variable does not affect quantity demanded. So even if the estimated $\hat{\beta}$ gave a large elasticity of demand (see Section 5.3) we could not reject[6] the idea that, because the scatter of observations was so wide and hence $S_{\hat{\beta}}$ so large, the elasticity was in fact zero. The importance of this test will become especially apparent when multiple regression is explained and some independent variables, which are less likely than price to be related to Q_t, are also included. Examples of the testing of the significance of β are shown in Table 6.2.

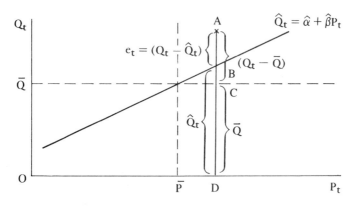

Figure 6.6

6   Although one may not be able to reject the hypothesis that $\beta = 0$, acceptance of this hypothesis may still be wrong. If one accepts a hypothesis which is in fact false, one has committed a 'type II error'. Unfortunately, in most statistical testing the probability of committing a type II error depends on the correct value of the parameter under test, which is unknown. Notice that, in general, it is *not* the case that: $1 - (\text{Probability of a type I error}) = \text{Probability of a type II error}$.

Table 6.2

A demand function for widgets has been estimated using OLS as:

$$Q_t = 1000 - 0.500 \ P_t \quad n = 28$$
$$(0.200)$$

Q_t = Quantity of widgets sold in week t
P_t = Price of widgets sold in week t
n = Number of observations

The term in brackets is the estimated standard deviation of $\hat{\beta}$

Test of Significance of $\hat{\beta}$

$H_0 : \beta = 0$
$H_1 : \beta \neq 0$

Set $\alpha_1 = 0.025$
$P(|t| > 2.056) = 0.025$
from t-statistics tables where $\phi = 28 - 2$
(one for each of $\hat{\alpha}$ and $\hat{\beta}$)

$\therefore |t\text{-critical}| = 2.056$

$$\frac{\hat{\beta} - 0}{S_{\hat{\beta}}} = \frac{-0.500}{0.200} = t_{\phi = 26}$$

$$|t_{\phi = 26}| = 2.500$$

$$|t_{\phi = 26}| = 2.500 > 2.056 = $$
$$|t\text{-critical}, \ \phi = 26|$$

Reject H_0 at $\alpha_1 = 0.05$

---

3. Goodness of Fit

The coefficient of determination, R^2, allows one to examine how closely the estimated equation fits the sample data. Suppose we plot sample observations of Q_t and P_t, one combination of which is shown in Figure 6.6. For each observation the difference between the observed Q_t and the mean of the sample values, $\bar{Q}$, may be calculated.[7] These differences are due to differences in P_t and to differences in e_ts as is shown in the figure. This may be understood by noting that:

---

7 One could have used the value $Q_1 = 0$ instead of $Q_1 = \bar{Q}$ since all one needs is a value of Q_t.

$$AC \quad = \quad BC \qquad + \ AB$$

$$(Q_t - \bar{Q}) \quad = \ (\hat{Q}_t - \bar{Q}) \qquad + \ e_t$$

Difference	Difference	Residual
between	between	
actual and	predicted, i.e.	
mean	that explained	
	by regression	
	line and mean	

In general terms we wish to measure how much of the total variation in *AC* values is made up of variation in *BC* values (i.e. changes predicted by the sample line) and how much is made up of variation in *AB* values (i.e. unexplained residuals). It may seem that an indication of the goodness of fit could be obtained by examining the proportion of the total deviation (sum of the deviation for each observation) which is explained by the regression line:

$$\frac{\text{Sum of explained deviation}}{\text{Sum of total deviation}} = \frac{\text{Sum of } BC \text{ values}}{\text{Sum of } AC \text{ values}} = \frac{\sum_{t=1}^{n} (\hat{Q}_t - \bar{Q})}{\sum_{t=1}^{n} (Q_t - \bar{Q})}$$

But the sum of *AC* values is $\Sigma (Q_t - \bar{Q}) = 0$. However, if the deviations are squared, all negative values become positive and it can be shown that:

$$\sum_{t=1}^{n} (Q_t - \bar{Q})^2 = \sum_{t=1}^{n} (\hat{Q}_t - \bar{Q})^2 + \sum_{t=1}^{n} e_t^2 \qquad (6.12)$$

Total Sum	Regression	Residual Sum
of Squares	Sum of	of Squares
(*SST*)	Squares	(*SSE*)
	(*SSR*)	

The coefficient of determination is defined as the proportion of total variation, *SST*, which is explained by the estimated regression line and hence by variations in P_t:

$$R^2 = \frac{SSR}{SST} = \frac{\sum_{t=1}^{n} (\hat{Q}_t - \bar{Q})^2}{\sum_{t=1}^{n} (Q_t - \bar{Q})^2} \qquad (6.13)$$

Hence an R^2 of 0.8 means that 0.8 of the total variation in the sample data about its mean was accounted for by variation in P_t about its mean. If our observations all lie on the regression line, $Q_t = \hat{Q}_t$, so by equation (6.13) $R^2 = 1$. The regression line explains 100% of the variation in Q_t. Since all of the points lie on the regression line, this is the value of R^2 one would expect.

At the other extreme, R^2 could equal zero. A necessary condition for this is that changes in the value of P_t would not lead to a change in the predicted value of Q_t, $\hat{Q}_t$. That is, the sample regression line would have a slope of zero: $\hat{\beta} = 0$. Then, the BC values of Figure 6.6 would be zero, so from equation (6.13) R^2 would be zero.[8] Examples of cases where the sample regression line would have a zero slope are shown in Figure 6.7. Notice that in Figure 6.7b, despite $R^2 = 0$, there is a systematic relationship between P_t and Q_t, but it is not a linear one.

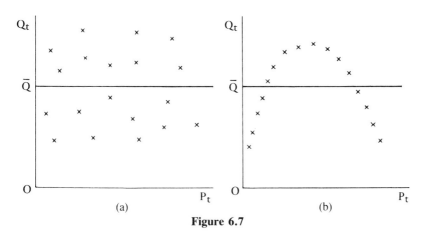

(a)   (b)

Figure 6.7

4. F-test

On pages 160–163 we explained how, with reference to equation (6.2), the null hypothesis H_0: $\beta = 0$ could be tested using a t-test. A different test statistic, the F-statistic, could also be used to test exactly the same hypothesis against the two-tail alternative.[9] Briefly, it can be shown that:

$$\frac{\Sigma \ (SSR)^2/(K-1)}{\Sigma \ (SSE)^2/(N-K)} \sim F_{\phi1 \ = \ K-1, \ \phi2 \ = \ N-K}$$

where K = number of estimated constants
N = number of observations

The F-statistic has a different probability distribution for every combination of degrees of freedom. Given the degrees of freedom, a calculated value of

8   The case where all of the observations lie along the horizontal line $\bar{Q}$ is an exception to this statement. In this case $Q_t = \bar{Q}$ and $\hat{Q}_t = \bar{Q}$, therefore the value of R^2 is indeterminate.
9   We familiarise the reader with this test here so that (s)he will more readily understand the test when its more common usage is explained in a more complicated context.

F is compared with a critical value which cuts off an area under one tail of the F distribution equal to the chosen probability of a type I error. Since both SSR and SSE must be positive, the F-statistic is positive. Therefore, although the alternative hypothesis is $\beta \neq \beta^*$, the critcal value of F is chosen so that the probability of gaining a larger value is the probability of a type I error. (The theoretical F distribution is contained in most statistics texts.) This means that, if α_1 is set at 5% then, given the null hypothesis, the chance of obtaining an F value in excess of F critical is 5% or less. This is too low a probability to accept so we reject the null hypothesis with the probability of having done the wrong thing of 5% or less. Consider, for example, the demand calculations in Table 6.1. The null hypothesis is $H_0: \beta = 0$ against $H_1: \beta \neq 0$. The α_1 is set at 0.05. The $F_{calculated}$ is 5.949 with $(K-1) = 1$ and $(N-K) = (6-2) = 4$ degrees of freedom. The value of $F_{critical, 1, 4} = 7.71$ (see any statistics test). Since $F_{calculated} < F_{critical}$ the null hypothesis is rejected.

This F test allows an inference to be made concerning R^2. For each sample of P, Q values an R^2 may be calculated. These will almost certainly differ between different samples: there will be a population of an infinite number of possible values of R^2. If on the basis of a sample the null hypothesis $\beta = 0$ cannot be rejected, it is accepted. But just as we argued that if $\beta = 0$, then $R^2 = 0$, so we say that if $\beta = 0$, R^2 in the population is zero. None of the variation in Q is explained by variation in P. If the null hypothesis can be rejected, R^2 in the population is not equal to zero and variation in P 'explains' a statistically significant proportion of the variation in Q.

Multiple Regression

So far we have discussed demand functions with only one independent variable. But the theory from Chapter 5 and *ad hoc* theorising suggest that the quantity demanded is likely to be determined by several independent variables in addition to price, such as advertising expenditure, consumers' incomes etc. The use of OLS estimators in such cases is just an extension of the one independent variable case. A population model assumed by the manager might be:

$$Q_t = \alpha + \beta_1 P_t + \beta_2 A_t + \beta_3 Y_t + \epsilon_t$$

where P_t = price of own good in period t; A_t = advertising expenditure in period t; Y_t = consumers' income; ϵ_t = error term; and values of α, β_1, β_2 and β_3 are estimated from a sample of observations. The estimated relationship is:

$$Q_t = \hat{\alpha} + \hat{\beta}_1 P_t + \hat{\beta}_2 A_t + \hat{\beta}_3 Y_t + e_t \qquad (6.14)$$

The OLS estimators of the coefficients are derived in the same way in these cases as in the case of one independent variable. e_t is made the subject of equation (6.14), both sides of the equation are squared, summed and differentiated with respect to $\hat{\alpha}$, $\hat{\beta}_1$, $\hat{\beta}_2$, $\hat{\beta}_3$ etc. The derivatives are each set equal to zero, so that the sum of squared errors is a minimum, and then solved for $\hat{\alpha}$, $\hat{\beta}_1$, $\hat{\beta}_2$, $\hat{\beta}_3$ etc. to derive the normal equations. For simplicity we present only the formulae for the case of two independent variables:

$$\hat{\alpha} = \bar{Q}_t - \hat{\beta}_1\bar{P}_t - \hat{\beta}_2\bar{A}_t$$

$$\hat{\beta}_1 = \frac{(\Sigma p_t q_t)(\Sigma a_t^2) - (\Sigma a_t q_t)(\Sigma p_t a_t)}{(\Sigma p_t^2)(\Sigma a_t^2) - (\Sigma p_t a_t)^2}$$

$$\hat{\beta}_2 = \frac{(\Sigma a_t q_t)(\Sigma p_t^2) - (\Sigma p_t q_t)(\Sigma p_t a_t)}{(\Sigma p_t^2)(\Sigma a_t^2) - (\Sigma p_t a_t)^2}$$

where $p_t = (P_t - \bar{P})$; $q_t = (Q_t - \bar{Q})$; and $a_t = (A_t - \bar{A})$. The assumptions of the statistical model are analogous to those for the single variable case, with two additions. These are, firstly, that there is no exact linear relationship between any two independent variables and, secondly, that the number of observations on each variable exceeds the number of coefficients to be estimated.

In addition, as in the single variable case, each sample is likely to give a different value for the same coefficient. To test whether the population value differs significantly from a given value, the same procedures are used, although the formulae for the denominator of each t-statistic, $S_{\hat{\alpha}}$, $S_{\hat{\beta}1}$, $S_{\hat{\beta}2}$ etc., incorporate terms which relate to the additional independent variables. The F-statistic may also be used to test the null hypothesis H_0: $\beta_1 = \beta_2 = \beta_3 = \ldots = 0$ against the alternative hypothesis that this is not true. If this null hypothesis is accepted, the manager would conclude that any variation in any or all of the independent variables would have no effect on Q. If the null hypothesis is rejected, then he would conclude that the variation in any or all of the independent variables *would* have an effect on Q.

Violations of Assumptions

In practice, the behaviour patterns of consumers may not correspond to the assumptions of the statistical population model. In these situations the statistical tests we have outlined are not valid. In particular these are the problems of autocorrelation, heteroscedasticity and multicollinearity. This section may also be omitted without great loss of continuity.

Autocorrelation   Autocorrelation is said to occur when the population values do not fulfil assumption A(v) that the ϵ_ts associated with any one value of P_t are independent of those associated with any other value of P_t. (If P_t takes on just one value per t, then autocorrelation would occur if ϵ_t was correlated with ϵ_{t-1}.) If we take the residuals, the e_ts, as proxies for the ϵ_ts of the population we can illustrate the phenomenon as follows.[10] If the model's over- or underprediction varied cyclically about zero, e.g. due to the competing price changing in a cyclical manner, the inaccuracy this month would be correlated with that for next month, the month after that, etc. Autocorrelation is then said to exist.

If the error in this period is correlated only with that of last period, then *first order* autocorrelation is said to occur. If the error of this period is correlated with that in the last period *and* in the previous period too, *second order* is said to exist.

Further understanding of the nature of autocorrelation can be gained by considering how it can be detected. One can distinguish between positive and negative autocorrelation. Positive autocorrelation occurs when, as claimed above, an error in one period is relatively high and so is that in the next period, or when an error in one period is relatively low, and so is that in the next period. Hence if we plotted e_ts against time (and taking e_ts as proxies for ϵ_ts) we would expect a 'herd like' pattern. Such a case is shown in Figure 6.8a. Negative autocorrelation occurs when, if an error in one period is relatively high, that in the next period is relatively low and *vice versa*. So if we plotted e_ts against time we would expect a 'saw tooth' pattern, for example as shown in Figure 6.8b.

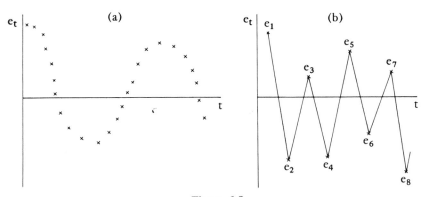

Figure 6.8

Since autocorrelation can vary in degree, examining a figure may not give a very clear indication of its existence. Fortunately, a more accurate test for first order autocorrelation is available: the Durbin–Watson test. The DW statistic is:

10 Autocorrelation would *not* exist if the quantity demanded this month were higher than that predicted by our estimated model because of a sudden reduction in a competitor's price (such a P not being included in our model) when such errors are not contemporaneously correlated.

$$d = \frac{\sum\limits_{t=2}^{n} (e_t - e_{t-1})^2}{\sum\limits_{t=1}^{n} e_t^2}$$

It can be shown that if the e_ts are free of first order autocorrelation then d = 2. However, the test is slightly different from comparing the calculated d with 2. The following rules have been established where $d*$ = the calculated value of d:

if $d* < d_L$: accept that first order positive autocorrelation exists
if $d* > d_u$: accept that no first order autocorrelation exists
if $d_L < d* < d_u$: the test is inconclusive

where d_u and d_L are given in the DW statistic table in any econometric text for the relevant number of observations, n, and number of independent variables, K'. (We have considered only the commonest type of autocorrelation: positive. Tests for negative autocorrelation are similar — see the Additional Reading. Tests in addition to the DW test are also available.)

If autocorrelation exists, then the variance of the $\hat{\beta}$ values which could be derived from every different sample of P_t and Q_t would be likely to be underestimated. Since this is the denominator in the t-statistic relating to the significance of the difference between the estimated β in our sample and that of the population, this t-statistic is likely to be overestimated. So the t-statistic might suggest we should reject the idea that, say, $\beta = 0$, when in fact we should not.

Several methods of reducing autocorrelation have been proposed depending on its cause. In the competitor's price example above the cause was the omission of an important autocorrelated variable. In this case one should add the missing term. If the cause is that one has estimated a linear equation when a multiplicative equation would be more appropriate then the latter should be estimated. If, however, we believe the autocorrelation would not be solved in these ways, various methods of estimating first difference equations can be used.

Heteroscedasticity Heteroscedasticity occurs when the population values do not fulfil assumption A(iv): that the ϵ_ts associated with each P_t have the same variance. For example, if in the context of the model, $Q_t = \alpha + \beta P_t + \epsilon_t$, the population variance of the quantity demanded was larger at higher values of price than at lower values, heteroscedasticity would exist. The possible Q_t values would be more dispersed around the regression line at higher levels of P_t than at lower levels of P_t, as shown in Figure 6.9.

If heteroscedasticity exists, it can be shown that the formulae for the variances of the OLS estimators $\hat{\alpha}$ and $\hat{\beta}$ are incorrect. Hence one could not use these variances to perform t-tests of the significance of these coefficients.

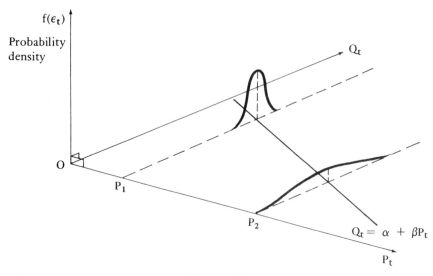

Figure 6.9

For proposed tests for the existence of heteroscedasticity and possible solutions to the problem the reader is referred to the Additional Reading. However, notice from its definition that if heteroscedasticity exists then one would also expect the observed residuals to be, say, more widely dispersed at a specific high value of P_t than at a low value.

Multicollinearity   Multicollinearity can occur only in models with more than one independent variable. Multicollinearity exists if any independent variable is correlated with another or is linearly related to several others. For example, suppose our hypothesised demand model contained both advertising expenditure by our firm and that by our competitors as two separate variables. Since in reality the advertising expenditures of most firms in the same market usually rise and fall together, these two variables are likely to be correlated. If multicollinearity exists, the variance of the estimates of β_1, β_2 and so on is greater than if there is no multicollinearity. So if we estimate β_1, β_2 etc., these estimates, and hence the corresponding elasticities of demand, could be *very* different from those in the population.

Notice that since most independent variables which one might wish to include in a demand function are correlated to some extent, the problem is not whether it exists but how serious it is. Multicollinearity is very difficult to remove. One might remove one or more of the correlated variables, relying on those retained to represent the changes in those omitted. Alternatively one might combine variables together. Either way, estimates of separate regression coefficients for each variable and hence the elasticity of each could not then be calculated.

The Identification Problem

One can never be quite sure in the statistical measurement of demand that
what one is measuring is 'demand'. For example, we are not justified in considering the line *AB* in Figure 6.10 to be a demand curve. The four price:
quantity points which *AB* connects were recorded historically and may, but
need not, represent points on the same demand curve. The data available are
insufficient to make such an assertion.

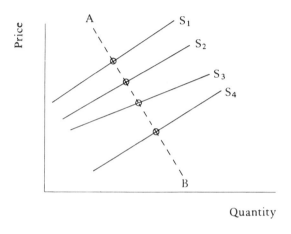

Figure 6.10

AB may represent a stable demand curve intersecting a shifting supply
curve at four different points (Figure 6.10), or it may merely be a regression
line produced by the movement of both demand and supply (Figure 6.11).
This regression line has no meaningful equivalent in static theory. A demand
curve shows the relationship between price and quantity demanded, all other
things being equal. A supply curve shows the relationship between price and
quantity supplied, all other things being equal. In Figure 6.11 non-price
variables in both the supply and demand functions have changed between the
points in time when the data were observed.

If we erroneously interpret *AB* as the demand curve, nonsense forecasts
can result. A price rise, if *AB* was the demand curve, might appear an attractive proposition. In Figure 6.12, raising price from P_4 to P_3 would apparently result in a fall in sales of only Q_4 to Q_3. Given the price increase, a
quantity reduction of this magnitude may well be justified. In reality, of course,
such a price rise, given the demand conditions of D_4, would be unacceptable
to the market place.

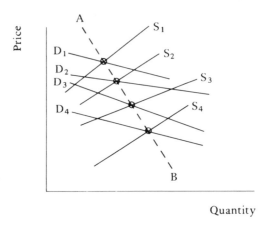

Figure 6.11

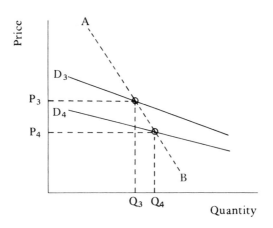

Figure 6.12

Given this simultaneous relationship how can the demand function be unscrambled (or identified) and separated from the other relationships present? Identification is possible only in certain circumstances.

First, identification is not possible if, over a period of time, neither of the two curves change their shape or position. In such a situation all the intersection points would coincide, or at least cluster so close together that no discernible pattern would result.

Second, identification of demand is not possible if the supply curve remains unchanged over time but the demand curve alters its position. A series of intersection points would be produced, but they will describe only the shape of the supply curve (which is thus identified) but not the demand curve.

Third, identification of demand is possible if the demand curve remains unchanged but the supply curve changes its position over time. This would be the situation in Figure 6.10 if *AB* was the demand curve, drawn from the relevant intersection points. But in Figure 6.10 the supply curve would then be unidentifiable.

Fourth, identification of demand is possible if information exists to explain why and by how much each curve has shifted between data observations. For example, the position of the demand curve may be affected by *per capita* disposable income. The position of the supply curve may be affected by the price level of a basic raw material. (If cost conditions in an industry rise or fall markedly in a period of stable demand, then a situation similar to Figure 6.10 may arise.)

A simultaneous equation estimation procedure can then be employed to establish what relationship exists between the four variables: quantity, price, *per capita* disposable income and raw material cost. The system is identified if it is possible to obtain by so doing an equation representing either of the demand Q_t^D or supply Q_t^s functions:

$$Q_t^D = f(p_t, Y_t) \quad Q_t^s = f(p_t, C_t)$$

where Y_t = personal disposable income in period t and C_t = raw material cost in period t.

If, however, the calculations provide an equation containing all four variables then the system is not identified. A mongrel function has been obtained. *A priori* our verbal model of the preceding paragraphs tells us that neither the demand nor supply functions contain both of the independent variables, raw material cost and *per capita* disposable income.

The corollary of this argument is that one of a pair of simultaneous relationships will be identified if it lacks a variable which is present in the other relationship.

The foregoing can also be illustrated graphically and intuitively. Consider the following historical data:

Year	1	2	3	4	5	6	7	8	9	10
Quantity demanded ('000)	3.0	12.0	4.0	8.0	8.8	10.0	6.6	2.5	1.0	4.5
Price (£)		2.3	4.0	1.5	4.5	3.3	6.0	7.1	6.5	8.0	8.0
Personal Disposable Income *per capita* (PDI)(£)	3000	6200	3500	5200	5000	6200	5900	4000	4000	5200
Raw Material Cost (per unit)(£)	2.0	1.0	1.5	1.5	1.0	1.5	2.2	2.7	3.1	2.7

The price and quantity information is plotted in Figure 6.13. We know that the points observed are the result of the interaction of supply and demand

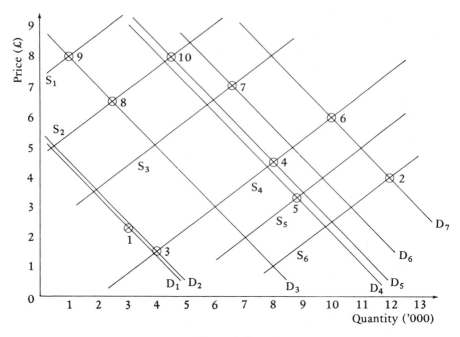

Figure 6.13

but as yet the relationship is unidentified. Quantity demanded however, is a function not only of price but also of income. Moreover, it seems reasonable to assume that income is not present in the supply function. Quantity supplied, on the other hand, is a function of price and raw material cost. The latter is unlikely to affect demand. (We are ignoring any correlation between personal disposable income per head and raw material cost.)

If this is so and we are convinced that income is the only variable which makes for substantial shifts in the demand curve, then it follows that points 2 and 6 are on one demand curve; points 4 and 10 are on a second and 8 and 9 are on a third. In each case PDI is the same. The remaining points are all on separate demand curves. Similarly, if we are convinced that raw material cost is the only variable which can lead to shifts in the supply curve then points 3, 4 and 6 are on one supply curve, and 8 and 10 are on another, while the other points are each on different supply curves.

Now consider points 2 and 6. Since they are on the same demand curve they have been located by shifts in the supply curve. But the supply curve shifted whilst the demand curve remained stationary because the level of raw material cost changed and raw material costs affect quantity supplied *not* quantity demanded. A similar explanation applies to points 4 and 10 and 8 and

9. (In fact, in the cases of the remaining points, 1, 2, 5 and 7, we believe they lie on separate demand curves because of differences in income.) Now notice that it is because a variable which shifts the supply curve is excluded from the demand function that we are able to 'identify' the latter. (A similar explanation applies to the supply function. Because the supply function *excluded* income, a variable which the demand function *includes*, the former is also thus identified.)

Examples

In this section we present two examples of the use of regression techniques in the estimation of demand functions.

Reekie and Blight: the demand for beer

Reekie and Blight proposed the model:

$$Q_t = \alpha + \beta_1 \frac{P_{Bt}}{P_{At}} + \beta_2 \frac{A_{Bt}}{A_{At}} + \beta_3 \frac{A_{Ct}}{A_{At}} + \beta_4 W_t + \beta_5 \frac{Y_t}{Y_{At}}$$

$$+ \beta_6 T_t + \beta_7 S_t + \beta_8 \frac{P_{Ct}}{P_{At}} + \epsilon_t$$

where

P_{Bt} = retail price index of beer in period t
P_{At} = retail price index for all goods other than beer, period t
P_{Ct} = retail price index for all other alcoholic drinks, period t
A_{Bt} = advertising expenditure on beer, period t
A_{Ct} = advertising expenditure on all other alcoholic drinks, period t
A_{At} = advertising price index for TV and press, period t
W_t = daily mean temperature, period t
Y_t = personal disposable income per head, period t
Y_{At} = retail price index for all goods, period t
T_t = trend dummy variable
  = 0: January−March and July−September
  1: April−June
  2: October−December

Notice that this model includes variables which would be predicted by consumer theory: product price, price of substitutes and income. Tastes are difficult to measure in practice but one would use advertising messages to affect them. Similarly the trend dummy variables were included to represent any long-term changes in tastes towards or away from beer.

Reekie and Blight's model includes variables which we would expect to be excluded from the supply function, for example, advertising and income. Similarly, it excludes variables which we would expect to be included in a supply function, for example: prices of inputs, wage rates, interest rates and so on. Therefore we would expect the parameters of the model to relate to the *demand* function rather than to the supply function, i.e. it is identified.

Using OLS, the following estimated equation was obtained:

$$Q_t = 3.18 - 1.355 \left(\frac{P_B}{P_A}\right)_t + 0.004 \left(\frac{A_B}{A_A}\right)_t + 0.019 \left(\frac{A_C}{A_A}\right)_t$$

$$\quad\quad\quad\quad (0.64) \quad\quad\quad\quad\quad (0.32) \quad\quad\quad\quad\quad (2.66)^*$$

$$0.057 W_t + 0.085 \left(\frac{Y}{YA}\right)_t + 0.085 T_t$$
$$(5.84)^* \quad (0.10) \quad\quad\quad\quad (1.22)$$

$$+ 0.019 S_t + 0.371 \left(\frac{P_C}{P_A}\right)_t \quad R^2 = 0.57$$
$$\quad\quad\quad\quad\quad\quad\quad\quad\quad\quad\quad DW = 2.05$$
$$(0.287) \quad (0.173) \quad\quad\quad\quad N = 60$$

The estimated coefficients all have the signs which one would expect, except for the real advertising of competing products variable. However, by comparing the critical t-statistic (2.00 for a two-tail alternative hypothesis) with those calculated, it can be seen that the null hypothesis that the population coefficient equals zero can be rejected only for two variables: temperature and competitors' advertising. Comparison of the calculated Durbin Watson statistic with the corresponding theoretical values in DW tables indicates that the errors are not auto-correlated. *A priori* one might expect that the advertising variables may be correlated and so might the price variables. It is possible therefore that the insignificance of some of these variables is due to multicollinearity. Further analysis of the data would be needed to confirm this view.

Cowling et al: Instant Coffee

Cowling *et al* proposed various models[11] one of which was:

$$Q_{Ct} = \alpha \left(\frac{P_{Ct}}{P_{Tt}}\right)^{\beta_1} A_{Ct}^{\beta_2} Y_t^{\beta_3} X_{Ct}^{\beta_4} \epsilon_t \quad\quad\quad\quad (6.15)$$

where

---

11 Cowling *et al* propose other, more complete, models than the one we describe here. However, these more complete versions are too complex for this chapter.

Q_{Ct} = consumption of instant coffee per head in period t
P_{Ct} = price of instant coffee of constant quality, period t
P_{Tt} = price of instant tea of constant quality, period t
A_{Ct} = advertising goodwill[12] towards instant coffee sellers, period t
Y_t = real personal disposable income per head, period t
X_{Ct} = quality of coffee
ϵ_t = stochastic error in period t

Notice that this model includes variables which we would expect to be excluded from the supply function, and excludes variables which we would expect to be included in a supply function. Therefore the *demand* function is identified.

The logarithms of both sides of equation (6.15) were taken to convert the model into a linear form (see Chapter 5). This was necessary since *OLS* can only be applied to linear equations. Using *OLS* they obtained:[13]

$$\log Q_{ct} = \begin{array}{cc} 9.78 & -1.78 \log P_{ct} & -2.93 \log X_{ct} \\ (8.72) & (-8.47) \quad PTt \quad (-6.19) \end{array}$$

$$+ \begin{array}{cc} 1.05 \log Y_t + & 0.017 \log A_{ct} \\ (2.27) & (0.547) \end{array} \quad \begin{array}{c} R^2 = 0.94 \quad F = 88.07 \\ DW = 1.97 \quad N = 36 \end{array}$$

(The number in brackets beneath an estimated coefficient is the t-statistic.)

All of the variables, with the exception of quality (X_c), have the sign which we would predict *a priori*. All are statistically different from zero, except for advertising.

As shown in Chapter 5, the elasticities of demand can be obtained from a demand function in double-log form by considering the estimated coefficient on the relevant variable. Hence the estimated elasticities are given in Table 6.3.

Table 6.3

	Relative Price	Quality	Income	Coffee Advertising
Elasticity	-1.78	-2.93	$+1.05$	NS

12 Advertising goodwill, i.e. the sum of past advertising expenditures, each deflated to allow for, e.g. forgetfulness and discounted (see Chapter 13) was included rather than current advertising expenditure because it was believed that past *as well as* current advertising expenditure is likely to affect current demand.
13 A number of seasonal dummy variables were included in the estimated equation, but their estimated coefficients were not reported by Cowling *et al.*

Additional Reading

Allard, R.J. (1974) *An Approach to Econometrics*, Philip Allan.

Bird, J.W.N. (1982) 'The demand for league football', *Applied Economics*, Vol. 14.

Cowling, K., Cable, J., Kelly, M., and McGuinness, T., (1975) *Advertising and Economic Behaviour*, Macmillan.

Eastman, B.D. (1984) *Interpreting Mathematical Economics and Econometrics*, Macmillan.

Gujarati, D. (1978) *Basic Econometrics*, McGraw-Hill.

Haines, B. (1978) *Introduction to Quantitative Economics*, Allen & Unwin.

Koutsoyiannis, A. (1977) *Theory of Econometrics*, (2nd edn) Macmillan.

Lewis-Beck, M. (1980) *Applied Regression Analysis: An Introduction*, Sage Series: Quantitative Applications in the Social Sciences, Vol. 22, Sage.

Naylor, T.H. (1981) 'Experience with corporate econometric models: a survey', *Business Economics*, January.

Reekie, W.D. and Blight, C. (1982) 'An analysis of the demand for beer in the United Kingdom', *Journal of Industrial Affairs*, Vol. 9, No. 2.

Stewart, M.S. and Wallis, K.F. (1982) *Introductory Econometrics*, 2nd edn, Basil Blackwell.

Wonnacott, T.H. and Wonnacott, R.J. (1977) *Introductory Statistics for Business and Economics*, (2nd edn) John Wiley.

Working, T. (1927) 'What do statistical demand curves show?', *Quarterly Journal of Economics*, (41).

PART III

Short/Medium-Term Decisions

7
Cost Theory and Measurement

The traditional theory of costs is derived from, amongst other things, the theory of production. Hence we discuss production theory prior to cost theory. Production theory concerns the relationship between factor inputs and output and allows us to derive the conditions to be fulfilled for an output to be produced at minimum costs. Cost theory concerns the relationship between various measures of costs — marginal, average and total — and their determinants, such as output, and so on. To apply these concepts to a particular firm, its cost function must be estimated. Thus the final section of this chapter is devoted to techniques of cost function measurement.

7.1 Production Theory

In economic terms production is an activity which creates or adds value or utility. Therefore production theory can be applied to storage, distribution and service activities as well as to manufacturing. Various non-manufacturing production activities add utility by, for example, changing place, ownership or saving time whereas manufacturing adds utility by changing the form of inputs.

A production function is a mathematical relationship which specifies the maximum quantity of output which can be obtained with a given quantity of each input. When presenting a production function two assumptions are made. Firstly, technology is invariant. (Technological change would alter the relationship between inputs and outputs which is represented by a production function which excludes a 'state of technology' term. If technology changes are also to be related to outputs, a variable representing this factor would have to be included in the function.) Secondly, it is assumed that inputs are used at maximum levels of efficiency.

Notice that since the production function relates inputs to *maximum* outputs, production processes, which for certain combinations of inputs do not produce as much output as another process, would not be represented by the function.

In general a production function may be represented as:

$$Q = f(K, L, Z_1 \ldots Z_n, \lambda)$$

where Q = maximum quantity of output per period; K = quantity of capital used per period; L = quantity of labour used per period; $Z_1 \ldots Z_n$ = quantities of other inputs used per period; and λ = a returns to scale parameter (to be explained below). For simplicity consider only a one output, two input case.

Figure 7.1 shows a production function in graphical form. It forms a surface OK_0XL_0. For example, suppose inputs of L_1 and K_0 of labour and capital respectively produce a maximum output of Q_1. The point representing this L, K, Q combination may be located by drawing a line up vertically by an amount representing Q_1 from the point where perpendiculars to each axis from K_0 and L_1 intersect. Repeating this process for every different L and K combination gives the surface.

Before explaining why the surface has the shape ascribed to it, notice that it can be represented in two rather than three dimensions by the use of isoquants. An isoquant is a locus of points, each representing a combination of quantities of two inputs and all such combinations producing the same output. (They are analogous to indifference curves in Chapter 5.) Since all points on any one isoquant represent the same output, they must all be on the surface at the same distance in the vertical direction from the base.

Such points can be located by passing a series of planes through the production surface parallel to the OKL plane. Each such plane would represent a different level of output. For example, planes have been passed through the surface at output heights Q_1 and Q_2. Any point along the curve Q_1Q_1, or along the curve Q_2Q_2, represents an equal output quantity of Q_1 and Q_2 respectively. When these output curves are transposed vertically downwards

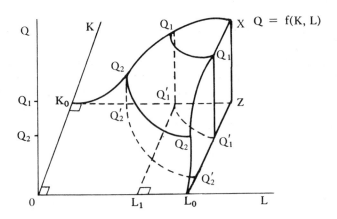

Figure 7.1

on to the *OKL* plane and indicated by the dashed curves $Q'_1Q'_1$ and $Q'_2Q'_2$, we have begun to construct an isoquant map. In geographic terminology, each such isoquant is a contour line on the hill of production.

The gradient of an isoquant (a negative value since it generally slopes from left to right) at a particular point equals the marginal rate of technical substitution of labour for capital at that point. The *MRTS* of *L* for *K* is the amount of *K* that must be given up for every one additional unit of *L* taken on such that output remains unchanged, i.e. *MRTS* (*L* for *K*) $= -\Delta K/\Delta L$. The minus sign is added because ΔK is negative but the amount of *K* *given up* in the *MRTS* is a positive amount. As ΔL becomes very small this ratio becomes (minus) the gradient of an isoquant, $-dK/dL$.

The *MRTS* of *L* for *K* equals the ratio of the marginal product of labour to the marginal product of capital. To understand this, suppose the input of *K* is reduced. The input of *L* must be increased if output is to remain unchanged and both the initial and final combinations of *K* and *L* are to remain on the same isoquant. The decrease in output due to the reduction in *K* (if *L* is not increased) is: $dQ = MP_K dK$, where MP_K is the marginal product of *K*, and *dQ* and *dK* are very small changes in *Q* and *K* respectively. If *L* is increased (but *K* remains fixed), the increase in output is $dQ = MP_L dL$ where MP_L is the marginal product of labour. *dK* and *dL* (both greatly magnified) are shown in Figure 7.2. For both initial and final combinations to be on the same isoquant:

$$MP_L dL + MP_K dK = 0 \Rightarrow \frac{MP_L}{MP_K} = -\frac{dK}{dL} = MRTS_{L \text{ for } K}$$

The minus sign is initially introduced here since the output reduction due to the reduction in *K* definitionally equals the output *increase* from the compensating *L* taken on.

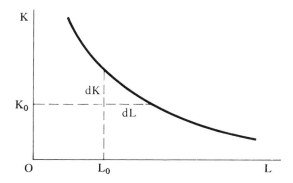

Figure 7.2

Since (minus) the gradient of an isoquant equals MP_L/MP_K, when MP_L is zero, so is the gradient of the isoquant, i.e. it is horizontal. If MP_K is zero, the isoquant has an infinite gradient, i.e. it is vertical. If we joint points on successive isoquants where each marginal product is zero, the enclosed area is called the economic region of production. This is shown in Figure 7.3 where the lines Q_1, Q_2, Q_3 denote isoquants.

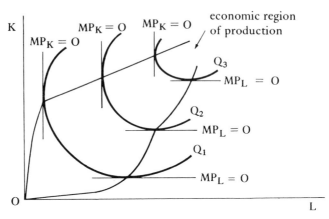

Figure 7.3

Within the economic region of production, isoquants have certain properties:

(i) The *MRTS* of L for K along any isoquant decreases as the quantity of L taken increases.

As K is decreased by, say dK in Figure 7.2, but L is held constant, MP_K increases according to the 'law' of diminishing returns. But, for the same reason if L is increased by, say, dL in Figure 7.2 MP_L decreases. Hence if K is decreased and L is increased by these amounts simultaneously MP_L/MP_K must then decrease and so *MRTS* decreases.
(ii) Isoquants further from the origin indicate greater output. Within the economic region, the marginal products of both factors are positive by assumption. Therefore increasing one factor, holding the other fixed, will increase output. But plotting the new combination on an isoquant map places it further from the origin than the original combination.
(iii) Isoquants have a negative slope.
Since the marginal products of both factors are positive, so is their ratio. But as shown above, the ratio of marginal products equals the negative of the gradient of an isoquant, so minus the ratio of marginal products equals the gradient.

Finally, notice that regardless of whether they are in the economic region of production or not, isoquants cannot intersect, for analogous reasons to those which explain why indifference curves cannot intersect.

Short-run Analysis: The Law of Diminishing Returns

The 'law' of diminishing returns states that as additional units of one factor are employed, all other input quantities held constant, a point will eventually be reached where each additional unit of that input will yield diminishing increases in total product, i.e. the marginal product of that factor will decrease.

This 'law' is a generalisation from observed events. On *a priori* grounds it is highly plausible. If a field or factory is held constant in size, the continued addition of labour cannot be expected to produce constant increments in output. At its most trite, the men will get in each other's way.

The 'law' can be represented graphically. Since a marginal value of a function is the gradient of that function, the gradient of the graph of output against inputs of, say, labour will eventually decrease as labour is increased. This is shown in Figure 7.4a. In Figure 7.4a it is assumed that increasing returns to labour occur at low levels of labour input. In terms of Figure 7.1, if capital input is held constant at K_0, and only the input of labour varied, a curve of the shape of that in Figure 7.4a would be traced as is shown (in Figure 7.1), by the 'slice' K_0XZ. As L is increased, the curve shows initially the assumed increasing returns to labour and eventually diminishing returns. The increase in output when one factor is fixed and the other increased can be shown in an isoquant diagram. In Figure 7.4b, the input of capital is fixed at $\bar{K}$, and the output produced when different levels of L are employed is shown by line $\bar{K}B$. Finally note that the 'law' relates to any factor, not just labour. Hence the same assumed relationships are shown by the 'slices', $L_0XZ, L_1Q_1Q'_1$, etc.

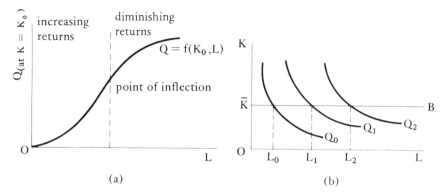

(a)   (b)

Figure 7.4

Long-run Analysis: Returns to Scale

In the long run, the quantities of all factors can be varied. Returns to scale
relate to changes in output when all inputs change by the same proportion.
Three alternative possibilities exist:

(i) Increasing returns to scale (*IRS*) — the proportionate change in output is greater than the proportionate change in inputs.
(ii) Constant returns to scale (*CRS*) — the proportionate change in output equals the proportionate change in inputs.
(iii) Decreasing returns to scale (*DRS*) — the proportionate change in
output is less than the proportionate change in inputs.

Each case may be represented graphically. In Figure 7.5 a ray, *OZ*, from
the origin with constant gradient joins a combination of *K* and *L* where *K/L*
is constant. Therefore if both factors changed by the same proportion the ray
would indicate both the final and original combinations simultaneously. Suppose the firm initially uses K_0 and L_0 of capital and labour to produce Q_0 output. Now suppose quantities of both inputs are doubled, $2K_0$ and $2L_0$ being
represented by *OB*. If *IRS* exist, output would now exceed $2Q_0$. Therefore
the $2Q_0$ isoquant would lie closer to the origin along *OZ* than *OB* since less
than $2K_0$ and $2L_0$ would be needed to produce it. If *CRS* exist, output would
equal $2Q_0$ so the $2Q_0$ isoquant would go through point *B*. If *DRS* exist, output would be less than $2Q_0$. Therefore the $2Q_0$ isoquant would intersect *OZ*
further from the origin than *OB* since more than $2K_0$ and $2L_0$ would be
needed to produce it.

A production function can exhibit *IRS*, *CRS* and *DRS* over different ranges
of input levels. It can also show *IRS* if inputs were changed by a given common multiple; and *DRS* if the inputs were changed by the same multiple. This

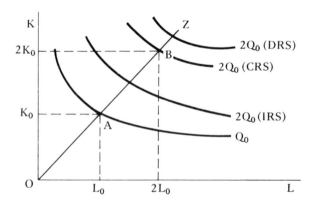

Figure 7.5

apparent paradox is due to the fact that the former property relates to one ray whereas the latter can only be observed on two different rays.

Homogeneous Production Functions

Some production functions have the property of *homogeneity*. That is, if all inputs are multiplied by a constant, λ, the new output is λ to the power V times its original value. Hence suppose: $Q = f(L,K)$. If $Q^* = f(\lambda L, \lambda K)$ implies $Q^* = \lambda^V.f(L,K) = \lambda^V.Q$, then the production function is defined as homogeneous of degree V.

It can be seen that, if $V = 1$, the function exhibits *CRS* because multiplying all inputs by λ results in λ times as much output. If V is less than 1, then *DRS* exist since multiplying all inputs by λ results in less than λ times as much output, whilst V greater than 1 indicates *IRS*.

Example One specific form of homogeneous function frequently discussed is the Cobb−Douglas production function:

$$Q = a.L^b.K^c \tag{7.1}$$

where a,b and c are constants, and where b plus c sums to unity. To see that this is homogeneous, multiply both inputs by a constant, λ. Hence the new output, Q^1, equals

$$
\begin{aligned}
Q^1 &= a(\lambda L)^b(\lambda K)^c &=& a\lambda^b L^b \lambda^c K^c &=& \lambda^{(b+c)} a L^b K^c \\
&= \lambda^{(b+c)}Q &=& \lambda Q \text{ (when } (b+c) \text{ equals unity)}
\end{aligned}
$$

When $(b+c)$ equals unity, this function is homogeneous of degree one, so it exhibits *CRS*.[1]

If equation 7.1 is differentiated with respect to L and K (separately), we obtain the marginal products of L and K respectively. Thus:

---

1 Note a homogeneous function always has a given value of v (returns to scale). A non-homogeneous function may exhibit varying returns to scale. For example, if L and K are multiplied by λ, we cannot factorise λ^v out from: $Q = 80L + 50K + 40LK - L^3 - K^3$. Notice that by substituting various values of K and L into this equation, at relatively low inputs a doubling of each input more than doubles output (*IRS*) whereas at higher levels of inputs doubling both results in less than double output (DRS) as follows:

L	K	% Δ in both inputs	Q	% Δ in Q
1	1		154	
2	2	100	404	262
.	.		.	
.	.		.	
7	7		2184	
14	14	100	4172	191

$$\partial Q/\partial L = baL^{b-1} K^c \quad \text{and} \quad \partial Q/\partial K = caL^bK^{c-1}$$

It can be seen that the marginal products are functions of L and K: a result which has often been observed in reality. Note also that the Cobb—Douglas function has the desirable property that when logarithms are taken of both sides of the equation a linear equation results to which the regression techniques of Chapter 6 may be applied to estimate a, b and c.

The Cost Minimising Combination of Inputs

Managers may wish to determine the combination of inputs to gain the maximum output that can be produced, given total cost, or the combination of inputs which minimises the total cost (TC) of producing a given output. To do this, given the production function, he needs the prices of factors. Given these prices, different combinations of two inputs which all have the same TC, can be represented by an isocost line. Since the total cost of each input equals its (given) price times the quantity of it used, we may (in the case of 2 inputs, K and L) write:

$$TC = P_KK + P_LL \tag{7.2}$$

If TC is fixed at TC_0 regardless of the quantities of inputs used, as along any isocost (or budget) line, equation (7.2) is a straight line. If $K = 0$, then $L = TC_0/P_L$. If $L = 0$ then $K = TC_0/P_K$. The slope of the line is $-P_L/P_K$ which is constant for all quantities of each input because their prices are constant. Such a line is shown in Figure 7.6. If TC is increased to TC_1, the intercepts of the line move further from the origin because $(TC_1/P_L) > (TC_0/P_L)$ etc. Hence isocost lines further from the origin denote greater total costs, given factor prices.

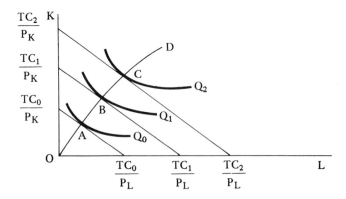

Figure 7.6

Given the production function and factor prices, the input combination which would result in a given output being produced at least total cost occurs where the relevant isoquant is just tangential to the lowest isocost curve possible. If an isocost line lies anywhere above the relevant isoquant, there exists a still lower isocost line which relates to less of both inputs to produce the chosen output. Hence it relates to lower total costs. Such a combination is shown by point A in Figure 7.6 for output Q_0; B for Q_1 and so on. Conversely to produce the maximum output given TC, the input combination corresponding to the isoquant furthest from the origin, which is also tangential to the relevant isocost line, is chosen. If an isoquant lies anywhere below the chosen isocost line, there exists another which just touches the isocost and which is further from the origin and so represents greater output. Such input combinations are also shown by points A to C in Figure 7.6.

Since each of these conditions is fulfilled when an isocost is tangential to an isoquant, and since the gradient of an isocost is $-P_L/P_K$ and that of an isoquant $-MP_L/MP_K$, these conditions are fulfilled when

$$-\frac{P_L}{P_K} = -\frac{MP_L}{MP_K} \Rightarrow \frac{MP_K}{P_K} = \frac{MP_L}{P_L} \tag{7.3}$$

This result can be derived mathematically in the case of any finite number of factors (not just two). We may write the production function as:

$$Q = f(I_1, I_2 \ldots I_n)$$

where Q is total output and I_i is the quantity used of commodity or factor i ($i = 1 \ldots n$). The total cost equation (equation 7.2) may be generalised to:

$$TC = P_1 I_1 + P_2 I_2 + \ldots P_n I_n$$

Suppose the firm wishes to minimise the total cost of production subject to the constraint that $Q = Q^*$. Therefore we may use the lagrangian multiplier technique of Chapter 1:

$$TC_\lambda = P_1 I_1 + P_2 I_2 + \ldots P_n I_n + \lambda [Q^* - f(I_1, I_2 \ldots I_n)]$$

$$\frac{\partial TC_\lambda}{\partial I_1} = P_1 - \lambda \frac{\partial f}{\partial I_1} = 0 \tag{7.4}$$

$$\frac{\partial TC_\lambda}{\partial I_2} = P_2 - \lambda \frac{\partial f}{\partial I_2} = 0 \tag{7.5}$$

$$\cdot \qquad \cdot \qquad \cdot \qquad \cdot$$
$$\cdot \qquad \cdot \qquad \cdot \qquad \cdot$$

$$\frac{\partial TC_\lambda}{\partial I_n} = P_n - \lambda \frac{\partial f}{\partial I_n} = 0 \tag{7.6}$$

$$\frac{\partial TC}{\partial \lambda} = Q^* - f(I_1, I_2 \ldots I_n) = 0 \tag{7.7}$$

This system of $n+1$ simultaneous equations can be solved and values of I_1 to I_n obtained (provided second-order conditions are satisfied). To solve the system, the price term is made the subject of equations (7.4) and (7.5) for example, and the latter equation is divided by the first:

$$\frac{P_1}{P_2} = \frac{\partial f/\partial I_1}{\partial f/\partial I_2}$$

Since $\partial f/\partial I_1$ is the marginal product of input 1, MP_1, and similarly $\partial f/\partial I_2$ equals MP_2 we have:

$$\frac{P_1}{P_2} = \frac{MP_1}{MP_2} \Rightarrow \frac{MP_1}{P_1} = \frac{MP_2}{P_2}$$

Note that in the case of the Cobb−Douglas function for K and L (see equation 7.3) it can be shown that[2]

$$\frac{K}{L} = \frac{\text{Exponent on } K \cdot P_L}{\text{Exponent on } L \cdot P_K}$$

This allows us a short cut for finding the inputs to maximise output given TC, or to minimise TC given output. Thus, for the function $Q = 1.2\, L^{0.6} K^{0.4}$, the ratio of K/L which does this is:

$$\frac{K}{L} = \frac{0.4\, P_L}{0.6\, P_K} \tag{7.8}$$

If the TC equation is:

$$1000 = 2L + K \tag{7.9}$$

that is, $P_L = 2$ and $P_K = 1$, we have from (7.8) that:

$$K/L = 0.4 \times 2/0.6 \times 1 \Rightarrow K = 4/3L \tag{7.10}$$

Substituting (7.10) into (7.9) we have:

$$2\,\frac{MP_L}{P_L} = \frac{MP_K}{P_K} \Rightarrow \frac{MP_L}{MP_K} = \frac{P_L}{P_K} \Rightarrow \frac{baL^{b-1} K^c}{caL^b K^{c-1}} = \frac{P_L}{P_K}$$

$$\Rightarrow \frac{b\,K}{c\,L} = \frac{P_L}{P_K} \Rightarrow \frac{K}{L} = \frac{c\,P_L}{b\,P_K}$$

$1000 = 2L + 4/3 \ L \Rightarrow L = 300$; $K = 400$ (by substitution in (7.9))
and $Q = 403.9$.

The maximum output which can be produced with a given budget of £1,000
is approximately 404 units per period.

If the prices of some, but not all, inputs change, factor substitution is likely.
Consider initially the *maximisation of output, given total cost*. Suppose, in
a two-input production function such as Figure 7.7, that the price of input
L decreased. Then the slope of the isocost line (with quantities of K and L
on the vertical and horizontal axes respectively) equals $-P_L/P_K$ and, following a decrease in P_L, will pivot from AB to AC. The initial combination of
inputs which maximises output for a given total cost changes from L_0K_0 to
L_1K_1 (X to Z).

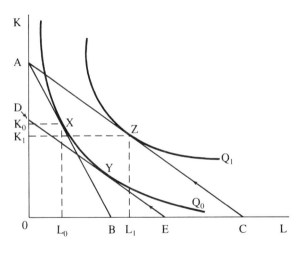

Figure 7.7

This change can be decomposed into substitution and output effects
analogous to the substitution and income effects of indifference curve theory.
The former is the change in the quantities of inputs due purely to a change
in their relative prices. The latter is the change in the quantities of inputs
required to produce the new output which the total cost can now pay for.
To isolate each effect diagrammatically, construct a hypothetical isocost line
(DE) with the same slope as AC, but tangent to the Q_0 isoquant, e.g. at Y.
Since DE is parallel to AC, its slope represents the new input price ratio,
and since it is tangent to the original isoquant, its point of tangency with Q_0
indicates inputs needed to produce the original output. The change in inputs
from point X to point Y is the substitution effect. The difference between lines
DE and AC is purely due to the change in output, since their slope (the input

price ratio) is the same. The remaining change in inputs (from Y to Z) represents the output effect.

Alternatively, *minimising total cost given output* would involve only the substitution effect. Here the new isocost line would be tangent to the original isoquant. Hence in Figure 7.7 the movement from X to Y with the new budget line DE represents lower total costs than AB (because it is lower than AC, which in turn represents the same budget as AB, given the new lower price of L).

However, neither of these explanations is complete. A change in a factor price may shift the marginal cost curve which in turn would alter the profit-maximising output. This further output change must be taken into account.

Finally, a change in demand, factor prices given, may also cause the profit-maximising output to change. Depending on the production function and hence the pattern of isoquants, this may cause a change in the ratio of factor inputs. The locus of points where different isocost lines with the same factor prices are tangential to successive isoquants is called the 'long-run expansion path' of the firm. In Figure 7.6 the line ABC is an expansion path.

Optimum Input Combinations Whilst the fulfilment of equation (7.3) guarantees that any *chosen* output is produced at minimum total cost, this is not sufficient for profit maximisation. This is because the fulfilment of equation 7.3 is not sufficient to imply that the profit-maximising output is being produced. Equation (7.3) is necessary but not sufficient for profit maximisation. To deduce the *profit-maximising* levels of each input, notice that the inverse of the terms in equation (7.3) also equal marginal cost of output (MC_Q):

$$\frac{P_K}{MP_K} = \frac{P_L}{MP_L} = \ldots = MC_Q \qquad (7.11)$$

To prove this, suppose an additional ΔL units of L are hired and its output is, say, ΔQ (the input of K is kept constant). The cost of the additional ΔL units is $P_L \Delta L$ (where P_L is fixed, assuming that each input is bought in a perfectly competitive market). Therefore, the change in total cost per unit change in output, i.e. MC_Q, equals:

$$\frac{P_L \Delta L}{\Delta Q} = \frac{P_L.1}{\Delta Q/\Delta L} = \frac{P_L}{MP_L}$$

Q.E.D.

The profit-maximising output requires that $MR_Q = MC_Q$. Hence, from equation (7.11):

$$\frac{P_K}{MP_K} = \frac{P_L}{MP_L} = \ldots = MC_Q = MR_Q \qquad (7.12)$$

$$\Rightarrow P_K = MP_K.MR_Q = MRP_K \qquad (7.13)$$
$$P_L = MP_L.MR_Q = MRP_L \qquad (7.14)$$

where MRP_K and MRP_L denote the marginal revenue products of capital and labour respectively. Since equation (7.12) implies that the firm is producing the profit-maximising level of output and is using the combination of inputs which does this at minimum cost, fulfilment of equation (7.12) is necessary and sufficient for profit maximisation. Note that equation (7.14) is simply the condition that the marginal cost of labour (P_L) equals the marginal revenue of an additional unit of labour, the latter being the change in total output when a unit of labour is hired times the change in total revenue received when that number of additional output units is sold. Equation (7.13) has the same interpretation for capital.

7.2 Cost Curves

When considering costs it must be remembered that the economist's concept of cost cannot be obtained from normal accounting data. The economist views cost as opportunity cost whereas the accountant measures cost historically (see Chapter 16).

Traditional Theory

In the traditional theory of costs, the same distinction is made between short- and long-run costs as was mentioned briefly in our discussion of production theory. Recapping, the short run is a period of time which is so short that quantities of only certain factors of production can be changed. The long run is a time period which is sufficiently long for the quantities of all factors to be varied. Examples of inputs which are fixed in the short run are: plant, certain administrative and managerial personnel and land. Examples of inputs which can be varied in the short run are raw materials, operating personnel and fuel. The long run may vary in length between industries because the length of time required to gain certain inputs may vary with their nature. For example, 'premises' to an aluminium smelting works may take years to acquire because they may have to be built, whereas 'premises' to a market research agency may either be built more quickly, or because of the relatively more readily available supply of office space, they could also be rented more easily than an aluminium smelter.

Derivation of Cost Curves

Total costs, TC, depend on the quantities of inputs used by a production process, and their prices. They also assume that inputs are combined in the most productive way to obtain the outputs; as implied by the production function.

Therefore total costs can be said to depend on the level of output, input prices and technology (which the production function assumes is fixed and so omits). This is the case when all inputs can be varied in quantity. But if some inputs are immediately variable, whilst others have fixed and specific values, output may be *less than it could be* from the quantities of inputs used. The former situation relates to the long run and the latter to the short run because of the variability of some inputs and fixity of others. Cost curves represent the relationship between output and cost, other variables such as technology and input prices, being assumed constant.

Short-run Cost Curves

Short-run total costs (*STC*) at each output equal the sum of short-run total fixed costs, (*TFC*) and short-run total variable costs (*STVC*).

(i) Total fixed costs (*TFC*) consist of the *TC* of factors which cannot be varied in the short run. This being so, *TFC* do not differ with output, but are constant. Fixed costs do not exist in the long run, when all inputs can be varied.

(ii) Short-run total variable costs, (*STV*) consist of the *TC* of factors which can be varied in the short run and hence differ at different levels of output. The shape of the *STVC* curve can be derived graphically from the expansion path of the firm *provided* both factors on the axes of the isoquant diagram are the only variable inputs in the short run. Assuming this to be the case, as in Figure 7.8 where all inputs other than fuel and wage labour are assumed constant, the *STVC* can be derived by plotting the *STVC* values, TVC_0, TVC_1, TVC_2, etc, against the corresponding output levels. The results are shown in Figure 7.9a.

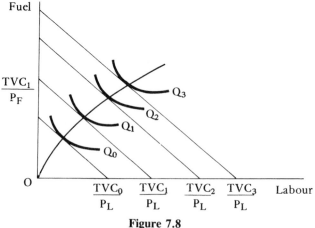

Figure 7.8

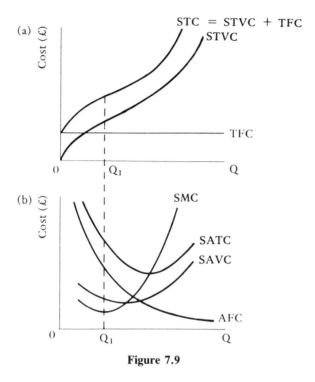

Figure 7.9

The deduction of the shape of the *TVC* curve from a production function is *most simply* illustrated if we assume that only one factor (say wage
labour), is variable and all others fixed. Assuming increasing returns to
this factor at low levels of utilisation, and that eventually the law of
diminishing returns applies, the relation between total output and labour
input was shown in Figure 7.4(a). If the horizontal axis is multiplied by
the (constant) wage rate P_L, it now measures *STVC*. To obtain the *STVC*
curve in its conventional position simply rotate Figure 7.4(a) anticlockwise
by 90° about the origin and then turn it over about the $STVC(= P_L \times L)$
axis (now vertical) as if it were the left-hand page of a book and we wished
to examine the previous page. A curve of similar shape to that in Figure
7.9a is obtained.

The shape of the *STVC* curve is determined by the productivity of
the variable factor(s). Up to Q_1 in Figure 7.9a, *STVC* increases at a
decreasing rate, because, with constant input prices, the marginal productivity of the variable input(s) is increasing. Beyond Q_1, the *STVC*
increases at an increasing rate as the marginal productivity of the variable
input(s) decreases. Below Q_1 the fixed input(s) are being under-utilised
by the variable input, beyond Q_1 the fixed input(s) are being
over-utilised.

(iii) Average fixed costs (AFC), are defined as: $AFC = TFC/Q$.

(iv) Short-run average variable costs $(SAVC)$, are defined as: $SAVC = SATC/Q$.

(v) Short-run average total costs $(SATC)$, are defined as: $SATC = STC/Q$.

(vi) Short-run marginal costs (SMC), are defined as the change in TC resulting from a one unit change in Q: $SMC = d(STC)/dQ$.

Since TFC does not vary with output, SMC equals the derivative of $STVC$: $SMC = d(STVC)/dQ$.

Graphically the AFC, $SAVC$, $SATC$, and SMC curves can be derived from the corresponding TC and TVC curves in the way shown in Chapter 1. The AFC curve takes the shape shown because the fixed TFC level is being spread over an increasing level of output.

The Long Run

In the long run all costs are variable, there is no fixed cost curve. The long-run total cost curve (TC), can also be derived graphically from an isoquant diagram if there are only two inputs. For example, suppose the only two inputs are capital and labour as shown in Figure 7.6. Assuming that factor prices are constant, the LTC curve may be derived by plotting each output against the corresponding level of TC: TC_0, TC_1, TC_2 etc. The LTC curve shows the minimum level of total cost for which each output can be produced when any combination of inputs may be chosen.

The LTC curve can be related to the STC curve in the case of two inputs by using isoquants. In Figure 7.10 with capital fixed at $\bar{K}$, AB shows quantities of L, which together with $\bar{K}$, are necessary to produce each output. For example, L_1^s of L is necessary to produce Q_1. In the long run with K variable, OC shows the quantities of each input necessary for each output. Hence L_1^l of labour with K_1^l of capital is necessary to produce Q_1. But the total cost of K_1^l and L_1^l is TC_1 whereas that of $\bar{K}$ and L_1^s is TC_2. Because the isoquant marked Q_1 has a decreasing gradient as L increases, TC_1 is less than TC_2. Moreover since isoquants generally have decreasing gradients at higher levels of L (as drawn), the short-run expansion path involves a higher total cost for a given output than the long-run expansion path, except at one combination of K and L. In the case of plant scale $\bar{K}$, this exception occurs at output Q_0 where long-run and short-run expansion paths intersect. Now since with plant $\bar{K}$, STC exceed LTC at outputs above and (it can be similarly shown) below Q_0, we can state that with K fixed at $\bar{K}$ the STC curve will lie above the LTC curve at all outputs except Q_0. By repeating this argument, it can be shown that for each level of K there is an STC curve which is tangential to the LTC curve at one output level but is otherwise above the LTC. Since there are many different values of K along an expansion path,

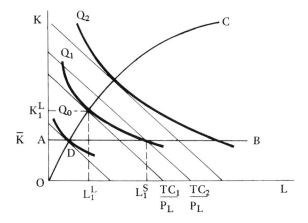

Figure 7.10

each usually corresponding to a different value of Q, the tangencies occur at different outputs.

The *LAC* curve can be derived from the *LTC* curve using the methodology of Chapter 1. It can also be derived by forming the envelope of different *STC* curves, each relating to different quantities of fixed factors. Consider Figure 7.11. A firm is faced with the choice of renting one of four factories for a period of a year. The *ATC* curves for the four factories over a period of a year are ATC_1, ATC_2, ATC_3 and ATC_4 in respective order of increasing size of plant. Suppose the firm expects to produce output level Q_3. Then it will pay to rent the plant with cost curve ATC_3. Both plants ATC_2 and ATC_4 are capable of producing Q_3, but could only do so at a much higher unit cost.

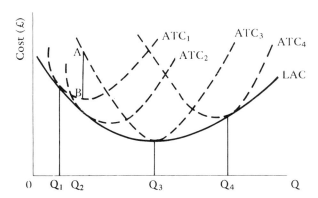

Figure 7.11

Given that it has rented ATC_3 then, this becomes the firm's short-run AC curve for the period of the year. Suppose, however, that it ends up producing output level Q_2, then its unit cost will be represented by the distance Q_2A. If output Q_2 persists, then in the long run (i.e. after the expiry of the one year rental) it will pay the firm to rent plant size ATC_2 and produce at unit cost level Q_2B.

Thus, in the long run, the firm's long-run average cost curve is represented by the tangential segments of all the short-run curves. When the choice of plant size is infinite, as might be the case when the firm can design and build from scratch a new plant, then the tangential points of these short-run curves become one smooth (envelope) curve of the type indicated by LAC.

The optimum size of plant is ATC_3. The minimum point on ATC_3 is tangential with the minimum of LAC. This is the case for no other plant size. Thus, for example, while no plant would be as efficient at ATC_1 in producing output Q_1 (the point of tangency between LAC and ATC_1) other plants *would* be more efficient than ATC_1 in producing output level Q_3 where ATC_3 is at a minimum. Only at the optimum plant size (of ATC_3) will it ever pay a firm to produce at minimum unit cost!

So far we have not explained why the traditional theory of costs predicts that the LAC is U-shaped. This is our next task.

Economies of Scale

The traditional theory of costs predicts that the LAC will decline as outut is initially increased because of the occurrence of economies of scale. These may be real or pecuniary. Real economies of scale occur when, due to the technology of available processes, with given input prices the average input per unit of output measured in terms of average cost declines. It is this phenomenon that the traditional theory of costs derives from production theory. The theory of costs derives the LAC under the assumption of constant factor prices. However, in practice, pecuniary economies — lower input prices for bulk purchases — have been observed. The incorporation of such phenomena into the theory of production would complicate matters, but would contribute to an even more steeply sloped LAC than that predicted by the traditional theory. Several causes of real economies of scale have been proposed:

Specialisation The larger the output the greater will be the opportunities for, and advantages of, specialisation of labour and machinery. The division of labour into specialised tasks permits the hiring of people with greater skills/knowledge of their one function rather than the hiring of persons with a range of skills and consequently a possibly lower level of expertise for each function. Specialists could not be hired at lower outputs because they would then be under-utilised. Secondly, specialisation reduces the time spent moving between types of work. Thirdly, specialised workers are more likely to have ideas for more efficient techniques or machines to increase their efficiency than less specialised workers.

Indivisibilities   A plant is indivisible if, when its output is reduced below a certain level, the required inputs remain constant. At high outputs a large plant may be more efficient than a small plant, but at outputs below its threshold a large plant's productivity will decrease eventually to below that of a smaller plant. To understand this, suppose that to produce a product two alternative processes can be used, one large, one small, with the following production function:

	Input of	*Input of*	*Output of*	*TC*	*AC*
	K	L	Q	$P_K=1, P_L=1$	$(=TC/Q)$
Process A	1	1	1	2	2
Process B	10	10	20	20	1

Both processes are assumed to have constant returns to scale. Each process can be used to produce any output rate. Given *CRS*, doubling inputs will always double the output for each process. Therefore, given input prices, the average cost of process A will be £2 for all levels of output above zero. Process B has a constant average cost of £1 per unit for outputs above 20. For outputs less than 20, however, the same amount of L and K is required as at 20, i.e. 10 of labour and 10 capital; therefore its total cost remains constant. With lower output[3] AC therefore rises. It can be seen that, when output is as low as 10, the AC of process B equals that of A, whereas at lower outputs still, the AC of B would be even higher than that of A. The LAC curve predicted by these arguments is shown in Figure 7.12.

Geometric relationships   For many types of equipment, running and construction costs are approximately proportional to equipment surface area, whilst output is approximately proportional to capacity. Examples are tanks, pressure vessels, ships, pipes and other containers. Because of the form of the mathematical relationship between surface area and volume, multiplying the surface area by k will lead to volume increasing by a multiple greater than k. Hence the ratio (surface area/volume) will decrease and correspondingly so will average cost. For example, if the length of each side of a rectangular tank is doubled, the surface area will increase four times, but its volume will increase eight times. In the case of a sphere, the surface area varies with volume to the power 2/3 so costs may be expected to be proportional to output to the power two thirds. Much empirical evidence supports this two-thirds relationship which is used by engineers when designing process equipment.

---

3   To reduce process B's output below 20, either some of the inputs will have to stand idle for some period or output is destroyed.

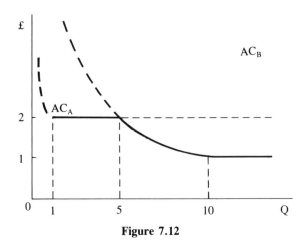

Figure 7.12

Stochastic economies   Stochastic economies occur when a firm wishes to hedge against an uncertain event. For example, if a firm wishes to maintain a spare machine to be used if a breakdown among a large number of machines occurs then it can be shown that the proportionate increase in the number of spare machines is less than that of the number of machines actually in service. Likewise, a firm using several identical machines will have to stock proportionately fewer spare parts than firms with only one, and similar economies can exist for stocks of raw materials, finished goods, labour and monetary resources.

Diseconomies of Scale

The traditional cost theory predicts that the *LAC* curve will, after a certain output, slope upwards due to diseconomies of scale. *Technical factors* are unlikely to produce diseconomies of scale. If inefficiencies arise as a result of over-large plant size, they can be avoided by replicating units of plant of a smaller size. (One example of this is turbine blades. If an over-large turbine is constructed, the ends of the blades will travel at a speed near that of sound. The strains imposed on the blades at this speed increase more than proportionately with turbine capacity.) Technical factors are more likely to limit the sources of scale economies than act as a source of diseconomies. However sources of diseconomies are arguably associated with managerial problems and labour relations.

Management problems   It is often argued that coordination costs increase more than proportionately with output. Firstly, as the number of hierarchical levels of decision taking from supervisor upwards increases, information may be distorted as it passes up to or down from the relevant decision maker even if all individuals have cost minimisation as their aim. Secondly, the number of decisions which require Board or a co-ordinator's approval will increase with scale while the capacity of the Board or decision maker to make decisions remains fixed, i.e. the peak co-ordinator suffers from 'bounded rationality' (see Williamson 1970) — limits on the rate at which he can absorb and process information. Less time per decision is allocated, with poorer decisions likely. These two reasons have been called 'control loss' by Williamson (1967). Thirdly, if those lower in the hierarchy have goals other than profit maximisation, they may follow them to a greater extent in large firms when they are less closely monitored (as they may be if there are many hierarchical levels between them and their managerial monitor).

Counter-arguments have been made to some of the points. Scherer argues that the accuracy of information passing from operative to decision maker has improved greatly over the last few decades due to technological innovation, better techniques of accounting and budgetary control, computer-supported management information systems. But it is unclear, *a priori*, whether the improvement has led to equal degrees of managerial efficiency at all output rates.

Changes in organisation structure may also affect efficiency. We need not restrict the analysis to single-division or one-product firms. Williamson (1975) has distinguished between several types of structure. The U (Unitary) form structure consists of each function being organised into a separate division, each answering to the Chief Executive as shown in Figure 7.13a.

Alternatively, the M (Multidivisional) form structure consists of separate divisions reporting to the Head Office, each division having within it subsections which perform each function, as shown in Figure 7.13b. An important characteristic is that operating and strategic decision making processes are separated and the appropriate mechanisms for control are used.

Williamson argues that the U-form is the appropriate structure for small to medium-sized firms. But at medium to large firm sizes, the M form becomes more efficient. If further hierarchical levels are introduced into a U-form firm's structure, then at large sizes 'control loss' increases. Bounded rationality limits the ability of the Head Office to make efficient decisions. Further, the heads of each functional division may liaise with Head Office in order to increase its capacity — this is likely to change the decisions which would otherwise have been made in favour of the more politically persuasive divisions and not necessarily the optimal profit-maximising ones. In addition, due to control loss, individual division heads may have greater scope for following their own non-profit objectives such as sales, staff expenditure, discretionary investment, and perks (see Chapter 3). Product and capital market competition may restrict this discretion but will do so to a lesser degree in markets where monopoly power exists or where shareholders lack the information necessary to assess their managers' performance accurately.

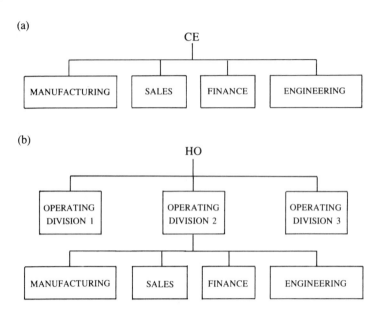

Figure 7.13

If the *U*-form is replaced by the *M*-form structure, efficiency is (*ceteris paribus*) likely to be greater. Firstly, operating decisions are made by each separate division, not by the Head Office. The Head Office therefore has more time to devote to the (fewer) strategic decisions, and information (up or down the organisation) needs to pass through fewer hierarchical levels.

Secondly, the Head Office advises on and monitors the performance of each division, so increasing the control over divisional behaviour. Thirdly, the divisions compete between themselves for resources, so encouraging greater efficiency in current resource usage and also better allocation of resources for future use. This will be so if proposals for investment in new projects or expansion are evaluated by the Head Office on the basis of the rate of return on past and current projects. Since managers often want to expand (see Chapter 3) they will operate as efficiently as possible today in order to attain resources to grow tomorrow. Fourthly, since the divisional heads do not enter into Head Office decision making, less partisan decisions are made.

Labour Relations

Some have argued that, as scale increases and operatives become separated by a greater number of hierarchical levels from decision makers, they become more alienated and morale decreases. In this case strikes may be expected to be more frequent than in small firms and the control loss due to firm size may make it more difficult for decision makers to deal with such dissension.

Secondly, if a large firm requires more labour than a smaller firm, it may bid up local wages compared with a smaller firm and/or it may have higher transport costs because of the need to transport workers over a greater distance to the plant.

Andrews' Theory of Costs

Some writers have argued that the actual cost curves which firms face have different shapes from those of the Traditional Theory. In particular, Andrews (1949) has argued that for all practical purposes SACs are downward-sloping with firms planning excess capacity and that the *LAC* never turns up.

Short Run

The Short Run is the maximum period of time which is too short for the machine with the largest capacity to be replaced. Costs are divided into indirect costs which do not vary continuously with output, and direct costs relating to inputs which do so vary.

Average Indirect Costs   Indirect costs include: the salaries of administrative staff and of all managers, wear and tear of machinery and plant, and the cost of premises and of the land on which they are located. It is argued that each machine will have a maximum possible output per period. If several processes are involved in manufacture, several small machines at one stage of the process may be required to produce the required output for a larger-capacity machine either earlier or later in the production process.

Andrews argues that the largest machine is installed with capacity in excess of that of the smaller processes which supply it. There are two reasons for this. Firstly, reserve capacity will be required to maintain output when breakdowns occur. Secondly, very large plant is time-consuming and disruptive to install. Capital in excess of planned output is installed so as to meet any demand expansion with less disruption and delay than replacement would involve.

Small machines will have less reserve capacity in proportion to planned output than the largest machine because the former can be replaced much more quickly than the latter. Secondly, stochastic economies will necessitate a smaller proportion of such small machines to be held in reserve for breakdowns than for the largest machine.

If, in the short run, capacity is kept constant, the total cost of such inputs is constant. Hence if output increases, average indirect costs (*AIC*) decrease. When the capacity of smaller machines is reached, say at Q_1 in Figure 7.14, then either multiple labour shifts will be worked, which will increase average direct (not *indirect*) costs, or additional lower capacity machines will have to be installed. If the former decision is taken, the *AIC* will continue to decrease until output Q_0, the capacity of the largest machine, is achieved, say, at point *B*. If the latter decision is taken, the total indirect costs will increase at Q_1 so their average value will increase — as shown by curve *CD*. The

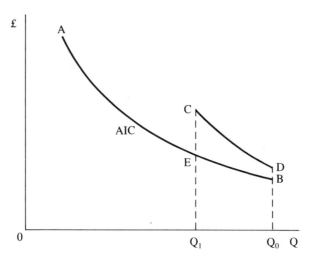

Figure 7.14

AIC curve would then be *AECD* and not *AB*. When the total capacity of the smaller machines reaches that of the largest, further output expansion is precluded in the short run.

Average Direct Costs   Direct costs are those of inputs whose quantities vary with output: employees engaged in manufacturing processes, and raw materials. Andrews argued that the *ADC* curve has a 'flat-bottomed' *U*-shape as shown in Figure 7.15. Considering labour costs first, at low and intermediate levels of output (below Q'), if additional direct labour is hired by hiring a greater

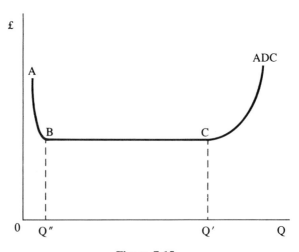

Figure 7.15

number of individuals, their productivity will remain constant. This is because the capacity of small machines with which they work can be increased and because there is excess capacity in the largest process. Therefore the diminishing returns to labour which were predicted by the traditional theory do not occur. Hence, if the wage rate is constant, the *ADC* of labour is constant. If very high rates of output were considered, e.g. above Q' in Figure 7.15, this may necessitate hiring the same individuals *for longer periods per day*, i.e. overtime. This may be necessary because the capital of the largest machine when using a single shift has been reached, or because of a lack of available labour. In this case we would expect their average productivity to be lower than without overtime and the average wage rate to be higher. Hence average direct labour costs would be higher. Secondly, average direct raw material costs are predicted to be constant at intermediate outputs given their price, but to be greater at very low[4] output rates, e.g. below Q'', due to greater wastage. Hence, at outputs below Q'', the *ADC* is decreasing, so the *MC* must be below *ADC*; and from a consideration of the total cost curve it can be shown that the *MC* is rising.[5] Between Q'' and Q' *ADC* is constant and so equals *MC*. Above Q' *ADC* increases so *MC* is above *ADC* and it can be shown that *MC* is increasing as well.

---

4   Also at very high output rates due to higher machinery breakdowns, etc.
5   This can be understood more clearly by noting that, from the shape of the *ADC* curve in Figure 7.15, the shape of the *TDC* curve is:

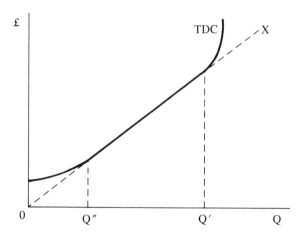

At outputs below Q'', *ADC* exceeds that above Q'' hence the *TDC* curve lies above line *OX* for these outputs. But, since *ADC* is constant over the outputs Q'' to Q', $TDC/Q = k$ where k is a constant, so $TDC = k . Q$ thus $ADC = MC(=k)$. Hence in this region *TDC* has a constant slope. Above Q' *ADC* exceeds the level between Q'' and Q' so *TDC* is greater than that given by line *OX*. By examining the slope of the *TDC* line itself and of rays from the origin to the *TDC* line, the shape of the *MC* curve in Figure 7.15 can be deduced.

Average Total Costs   *ATC* are derived by adding the *ADC* and *AIC* values at each output. The *ATC* will decrease with increases in output until just after Q' where the effects of reserve capacity are exhausted, and increase thereafter (see Figure 7.16). (As in the Traditional Theory, normal profits are included in the *AIC* values.) The minimum level of *ATC* will occur at a slightly larger output than Q' because, if output is increased slightly beyond Q', the decrease in *AIC* will at first exceed the increase in *ADC*. For larger increases in output beyond Q' the reverse is true, hence the *ATC* will rise.

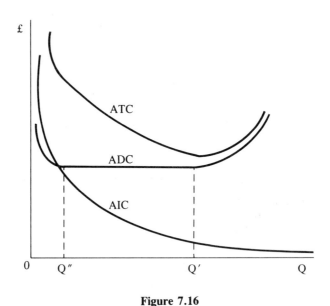

Figure 7.16

Long-Run Costs

In the long run the firm can vary the quantity of all inputs including the largest capacity machine. Andrews distinguishes between technical and managerial costs of production.

Technical Costs   These are the costs of all inputs other than management. Average technical costs decrease — firstly, due to specialisation and indivisibilities. Secondly, average repair costs may decrease due to stochastic economies (referred to above) and specialisation of labour. Thirdly, at high output rates the firm may make its own raw materials or inputs. Hence it may benefit from any economies of scale in this earlier activity if before expansion the benefits of such scale economies were retained by the supplier due to any monopoly power.

Managerial Costs   These are defined as all costs except technical costs. Andrews argued that a firm contained several managerial levels. For each level there is an appropriate management technique and each technique is applicable to a range of output rates. Within the output range to which a technique is appropriate, average managerial costs will decrease as output increases since the costs of the same-sized managerial group are divided by greater levels of output. If a larger output range for which a new technique is most appropriate is considered, initially average managerial costs will exceed those relating to the size of the management group using the previous technique. This is because the number of managers has increased greatly, but output by only a relatively small amount. But, again, average managerial costs decrease as output within this range rises. If the scale of output increases greatly, average managerial costs are argued to decrease and eventually to increase but at a decreasing rate as more levels of management are inserted. If the technical and managerial costs are summed, Andrews predicts that, as scale increases, then at first average costs decrease: both types of costs decrease; but eventually average costs become constant as falling technical costs are offset by rising managerial costs. This L-shaped *LAC* curve is shown in Figure 7.17.

Empirical work by Bain[6] and others has suggested that firms actually do produce below 100% capacity. (Depending on authors, the estimates range from an average of 66% up to 80%.) At any output, the *LAC* level (see Koutsoyiannis 1979) is that corresponding to a plant used at such a proportion of its capacity. Hence the actual level of costs, when this proportion of excess capacity exists (by design) and when the firm can choose any combination

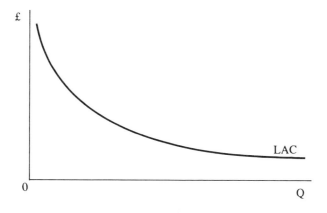

Figure 7.17

6   Bain, J.S. (1956) *Barriers to New Competition*, Harvard University Press.

of inputs (i.e. the long run), will be as shown in Figure 7.18. The *LAC* cuts the *SAC* curves at 66% of the capacity of the latter: points *A*, *B*, and *C* on the three *SAC*s shown. It would be possible to produce a level of output above that indicated by the fitted *LAC*. But firms typically do not do this because it would reduce their excess capacity which is required for the reasons explained on page 203 above.

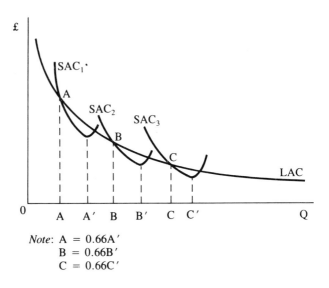

Note: A = 0.66A'
       B = 0.66B'
       C = 0.66C'

Figure 7.18

The Learning Curve

In the above theories of costs it has been assumed that the level of labour force skill applicable at each output rate is given. However, empirical evidence suggests that even if the output *per period of time* is constant, as a greater cumulated output is produced, the productivity of labour increases. Hence the level of *LAC* decreases with cumulated output *over time*.

This phenomenon was originally observed by Alchian[7] for the US aircraft manufacturing industry. He found that the general empirical relationship which best fitted his data was of the form:

$$\log L = a + b \log N \tag{7.13}$$

where *L* denotes labour input per unit of output and *N* denotes the cumulated

7   Alchian, A. (1963) 'Reliability of progress curves in airframe production', *Econometrica*, 31(4).

number of airframes produced. Diagrammatically, this is shown in Figure 7.19. (Other studies have found slightly different equations to be more appropriate.)

Baloff[8] argues that the learning curve relates to the initial start-up phases of a product's manufacture, and is horizontal by the time the 'steady-state' phase of operation is reached. In the long run the manager would wish to know the equilibrium level of productivity level k in Figure 7.19, and therefore would wish to estimate the value of a in equation (7.13).

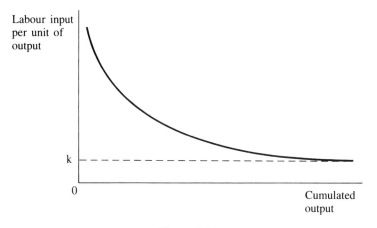

Figure 7.19

There are several reasons why productivity initially increases: for example, the development of greater skill and short cuts by a large range of personnel including machine operators, supervisors, salesmen, quality control and maintenance personnel. Engineers may redesign process machinery: for example, Abell and Hammond (1979) report that the semiconductor industry's average cost falls by 70–80% when cumulated output doubles. Product specifications may be changed slightly, perhaps to conserve raw materials or reduce machine time per item.

Apart from the relatively labour-intensive US airframe construction industry, Baloff quotes many US industries where equation (7.13), albeit with different values of b, is consistent with productivity growth — for example in the highly mechanised manufacturing industries such as steel, glass, containers, and electrical conductors. The Boston Consulting Group has estimated learning curve equations for a range of products to which we shall return in Chapter 13.

8 Baloff, N. (1966) 'The learning curve — some controversial issues', *Journal of Industrial Economics*, 14.

7.3 Measurement of Cost Curves

Short Run

Before discussing possible techniques for estimating SR cost curves we briefly recap on their nature. An SR cost curve shows the relationship between cost per period and the output per period which gave rise to it. The product is homogeneous, and input prices, the state of technology and the size of plant are fixed. A change in any of these last three variables would cause an SR cost curve to shift.

Two methods have been used to estimate SR cost curves: statistical cost analysis and the engineering approach, most studies having used the former. For ease of explanation we present the engineering approach under long-run analysis.

Statistical Cost Analysis

In this method, accounting data on *STC* or *STVC* are regressed on the corresponding output, both having been adjusted so as to fulfil the assumptions of the theoretical curve as closely as possible. The observations may be cross-sectional or in time series. The former consist of one observation relating to one period for each of a large number of firms, all having the same plant capacity but operating at different outputs. Time series data consist of a series of observations each relating to the same firm with the same plant operated at different outputs over different periods.

Use of this technique presents a number of problems which must be overcome, and the technique itself has been criticised as not isolating the theoretical function.

Firstly, theoretical cost curves relate to opportunity costs whereas accounting data do not. What the firm forgoes when choosing the output of a product is important to know when comparing outputs of alternative products. Secondly, when using cross section data, the accounting conventions must be the same across firms, otherwise a given output could be recorded as having incurred different costs even though all of the assumptions of the theory were fulfilled. In practice different accountants do not always classify the same items in costs.

Thirdly, theory requires the output in each period to be related to the costs it gave rise to. This involves estimating the portion of accounting costs in a period which were not due to current output and to establish the period to which they belonged. Usually this is not possible by examining what the cost entry in the accounts was attributable to, and estimates must be based on the views of engineers as to when events, which gave rise to certain costs, are likely to have occurred. For example, machinery may need repairing because of decay due to use and decay due simply to time. There may be much leeway as to when repairs may be made, hence they may be made long after the relevant output. Here there is a problem of finding which output the repairs are to be associated with (output may have varied greatly between the last and most recent repairs) and in finding how much of the accounting costs are due to usage (which is the relevant figure) and how much to obsolescence. Similarly, theoretical costs include depreciation of fixed capital due to usage but not due to obsolescence and time. But in practice accountants usually adopt a method or methods of depreciation, which are intended to recapture the historical expenditure on the machine. The value which was estimated for usage cannot be extracted by examining the calculation of such figures because such a value was never separately estimated.

Fourthly, theoretical costs relate to a homogeneous output but most firms produce several products. In many cases separate cost and output figures for each product have not been collected and/or the products jointly use some of the same processes, so the collection of such data would be difficult. Two commonly used methods of solution are to add independent variables into the cost function which represent the differing characteristics of each product which might affect costs and secondly to create an index of multiproduct output. The latter usually consists of a weighted average of the outputs of each product in which the weights consist of an index of each product's average direct costs. Staehle has criticised this multiproduct index by arguing that a spurious correlation of output with costs is created, because costs are entering both the independent and dependent variables. A virtual identity is being 'tested'.

Fifthly, when time series data are being used, the analyst must decide on the unit of time to which each observation relates. The shorter the period, the more difficult it is accurately to match output with cost. The longer the period the greater the chance of omitting fluctuations in output during such a period because a total would be taken instead of a separate figure for each subperiod. Staehle[9] has argued that use of an average output rate during an accounting period rather than a smaller unit of time (so short that the ratio of output to inputs is constant in each) biases the cost curve towards linearity. Johnston has shown that the occurrence of this is likely to be rare.

Sixthly, the *STVC* curve is constructed under the assumption that technology is fixed. Therefore to identify this curve, each firm in a cross-section study must be using plant with the same technology and so must the firm at every period in the sample when time series are used. In neither case is this condition likely to hold. In a time series regression the assumption of constant technology may be false, despite the fact that the firm has the same capacity because more productive parts and improvements may have been introduced. If such changes are not allowed for in the function, one would obtain a curve

9 H. Staehle (1953) 'The measurement of statistical cost functions: an appraisal of some recent contributions' in *Readings in Price Theory*, Allen & Unwin.

which really crossed successive SR curves as they shifted downwards due to change. Also in practice this problem may render the selection of the total observation period very difficult. The greater the period's length the greater the probability that plant size will change.

Johnston[10] argues that in cross-section studies, the residual term of the regression equation[11] would incorporate differences between firms in the degree of efficiency with which each uses its stock of knowledge. Those which use it well would be averaged with those which do not. Therefore when using regression analysis a weaker requirement is adequate: that each firm has the same stock of knowledge.

Seventhly, the *SRTC* curve is constructed on the assumption that factor prices and quality and managerial efficiency, are given. In practice, when using time series data these assumptions are also unlikely to hold. Changes in factor prices are likely over months, or even within a day in some cases such as fuel. Greater labour skill and changing raw material quality are likely, as is a change in the degree to which management pursues efficient use of a plant to produce a given output and changes in factor prices, both over the business cycle. A rise in factor prices would, everything else being equal, cause the same output to be produced at different levels of cost over the observation periods. The usual procedure in this case is to deflate expenditure on each factor in each period so that all SR expenditure is calculated at the prices of a specific period, i.e. in pounds of constant purchasing power. Alternatively, the input quantities are calculated and multiplied by their prices in a given period. Johnston[12] has shown that these procedures may cause bias by raising costs above their true value.

Johnston also argues that the net effect of other changes which persist over time can be taken into account by including, *t*, a time trend as an independent variable. For example, as time passes the educational standard of the labour force may increase. This is usually not done for factor price changes because their effects are important and may more accurately be included by the above procedures.

In cross section data factor prices may differ between firms in different locations (as may the quality of inputs obtainable for the same price). Such differences would distort the results because, again, everything else equal, output at different locations would be produced at different costs. In these cases Koutsoyiannis argues that accuracy may be partially restored by including an independent variable relating to location.

Having decided what to do about the above difficulties, the analyst proceeds to specify the cost function which he wishes to estimate. The theoretical

10   J. Johnston, *Statistical Cost Analysis*, p. 27.
11   See Chapter 6 for an explanation of the residual term.
12   J. Johnson, *op. cit.* pp. 170–6.

cost function is cubic in form with output as the independent variable:

$$STVC_t = \beta_1 Q_t + \beta_2 Q_t^2 + \beta_3 Q_t^3 + \epsilon_t$$

Inclusion of a constant, α, and changing the dependent variable to STC would enable an estimate for costs which do not vary with output, i.e. TFC, to be made.

If the econometrician believes that other functions are more appropriate to his firm then he should estimate these. Most studies have estimated cubic, quadratic and linear functions with respect to output.

Long-run Cost Curves

A long-run cost function represents the relationship between cost and output when all inputs are variable in quantity. It is constructed under the assumption that only current technology is used and factor prices and quality are both fixed. Output units are assumed to be homogeneous, produced at the lowest possible cost and using any quantities of inputs which are necessary. Three measurement techniques have been used: statistical cost analysis, the engineering approach and the survivor technique.

Statistical Cost Analysis

As in the estimation of short-run curves TC may be regressed against the relevant output, both adjusted to fulfil the above assumptions as closely as possible. Again time series or cross-sectional observations may be used. Each observation of the former type would relate to the costs and outputs of a single firm, but the total observations would be taken over a sufficiently long period that output levels and all inputs have varied considerably. Each cross-sectional observation would relate to a different firm during a short period and the sample would be chosen so that the range of capacity outputs would be considerable. Hence firms with different quantities of inputs which are fixed in the short run would be included.

Many problems which are likely to occur in the estimation of short-run curves also occur when long-run curves are estimated. The first five problems cited in the case of SR cost curve estimation also apply to long-run cost curves. Similarly factor prices must be constant for all firms in a cross section sample and for each time series observation. In addition, as in the short-run case, the theoretical long-run cost curve requires only the current technology to be used. Since time series observations in long-run estimation need to be very long, this assumption is especially unlikely to hold. In cross-sectional data the assumption is also unlikely to be valid because many firms will be using technologies of different ages. Plants are almost certainly not continually updated. However, greater division of labour which large size may allow, may enable large firms to use current technology more efficiently.

It may allow them to use larger and more productive machines. This effect should not be removed since it does not represent a difference between firms in the modernity of the technology available to them.

Further, the theoretical curve is constructed on the assumption that each output is produced using the plant which produces it at lowest cost. In cross section data, even if every firm used current technology, many firms at a point in time will not have adjusted their plant size(s) to fulfil this assumption: output may fluctuate much faster than plant size and/or some or all managers may be inattentive to possible cost reductions. Therefore in some cases the output may be produced on an *SAC* curve at a point away from the *LAC*, i.e. Q_0 with SAC_1 in Figure 7.20. Since costs which are below the *LAC* (or *LTC*) for a given output are by definition unattainable, the observation can only lie on or above the long-run cost curve. Hence the estimated curve is likely to lie above the true one. This is shown in Figure 7.20 where points *A*, *B*, *C*, and *D* are observed, cost-output combinations to which the incorrect *LAC* curve, *LAC**, has been fitted.

When cross-section data is used an interpretation problem may arise. If the *LAC* is estimated to have an *L* shape, as most studies have found, it is not clear which of two hypotheses is correct. That is whether (a) economies of scale exist or (b) economies of scale do not exist and those firms which have operated on the *LAC* have grown to their currently large size leaving those who operated above the *LAC* to remain so at their original size. Johnston[13] has argued that in general, for past studies, the former hypothesis is more likely than the latter for three reasons. Firstly, many past studies have related to public utilities which because of their legal monopoly have not grown by competing with other firms. Secondly, it is not necessarily the

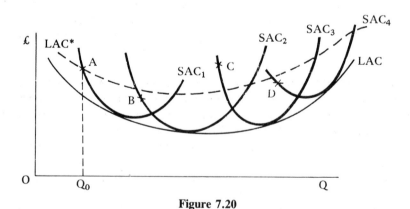

Figure 7.20

13   J. Johnstone, *op. cit.* p. 188.

case that a small low cost firm remains low cost when it expands. Low cost after expansion often necessitates complete reconstruction of a plant. Thirdly, a conclusion must be based on all of the relevant evidence. Both the empirical results *and* theory indicate economies of scale.

Finally Friedman[14] has argued that relating cost to output rather than to say, capacity, renders the 'regression fallacy' likely. It is argued that on average small firms are likely to produce at relatively low percentages of capacity, whilst large firms are likely to produce at relatively high percentages of capacity. Even if the *SAC* curves of all firms lie along a horizontal *LAC* curve, the lower capacity utilisation of small firms would be likely to cause them to have higher average costs than large firms. The resulting *LAC* indicates economies of scale despite a horizontal *LAC* curve.

Engineering Cost Curves

In its purest form the technique involves the derivation of a relationship between output and inputs for each stage of production on the basis of physical, chemical and engineering 'laws'. This 'production function' may, if there are only two inputs, be presented as a series of isoquants. Stage two is to find the minimum level of total costs which, given factor prices, is necessary to produce each output. If there are only two inputs, an isocost line may be applied to the 'isoquants' as in Section 7.2. The minimum total cost necessary to produce each output may be plotted against that output to derive the total cost curve.

To derive short-run cost curves the plant etc, is assumed given and the production function for the variable inputs is calculated. The minimum costs of producing each output are correspondingly deduced. In practice, it is usually impossible to derive production functions from scientific laws. Instead engineers, managers and cost accountants are asked to calculate the lowest costs of producing selected hypothetical levels of output on the basis of their experience of working with the techniques of their industry. They are told to assume that any currently available production technique may be incorporated. Some items within the estimate may be based on scientific laws, others not.

This method has several weaknesses. The first two relate to the measurement of *LAC*s, the third to *LAC*s and *SAC*s. Firstly, engineers have less knowledge of the costs at scales which differ greatly from those in which they work, even if these techniques are known by others. Therefore inaccuracies are likely to occur when estimated *LAC* curves are extrapolated to

---

14   M. Friedman (1955) 'Comment' in Universities National Bureau Committee for
     Economic Research: *Business Concentration and Price Policy*, Princeton University Press.

scales at which no respondents operate. Secondly, common procedure is to extrapolate from the verified technical relationship which holds for a small pilot plant to one for a large scale plant. Such extrapolation may involve error and many past studies which have adopted this approach have subsequently been shown to have underestimated the levels of *LAC* at extrapolated outputs.

Thirdly, since the technique essentially involves consideration of technical relationships associated with production processes, it does not yield estimates for managerial, administrative or research costs. Similarly, it is unlikely to give accurate estimates for service industries which are relatively labour intensive rather than relying on, for example, relationships between surface areas and volumes of receptacles.

However, the engineering approach has the advantages of deriving cost curves on the basis of a given state of technology and given factor prices.

The Survivor Technique

Use of this technique (as proposed by Stigler) assumes that the firm (or plant) operates in a highly competitive market. It also assumes that only those firms which produce at the minimum average cost possible will, in the long run, survive. Others will make less than normal profits and leave the size class either by exit from the industry or growth or contraction. Hence firms in those firm size classes which are losing their share of industry capacity have higher average costs than firms in those size classes which are increasing their share. Therefore, by determining the firm sizes in the latter category, one determines the range of sizes over which costs are lower than those at any other sizes. Firm size is measured by *share* of industry capacity or of output, rather than by absolute capacity or output because this will nullify the effects of changes in factors which affect all size classes.

An advantage of this technique is that it can relate only to a *plant* rather than to a firm. Therefore the difficulties of dividing joint costs of different products produced by a firm and of constructing a multiproduct output index, do not exist (provided the plant produces a single product).

Shepherd points out several limitations of the technique. Firstly, survival depends on profits and not just costs. Profits may be influenced by non-minimal costs due to market imperfections, for example restrictive agreements or barriers to entry preventing potential competition from potential entrants. Firms of non-optimal size could exist and may even grow. Similarly, if a range of sizes is found to have an increasing market share, one cannot assume the *LAC* is flat in this region. Cost may vary with size, but, due to some impediment to competition, so may revenue.

In addition, multiplant and single-plant firms are not distinguished. Plant level survival may be due to parent companies financing losses of plants which are too small or too large to have minimum average costs.

Thirdly, the technique does not indicate the level or shape of the *LAC* but only the range of firm (or plant) sizes at which average costs are lowest.

Fourthly, the technique yields implausible results if the firm (or plant) size distribution remains unchanged: all sizes of firm would be predicted to have minimum average costs.

Fifthly, factor prices and technology are likely to change over the observation period. Depending on the nature of the technical changes, the output at which firms (or plants) achieve lowest average costs may be changing. The same applies to factor prices. In addition, on a practical note, if a firm uses the Census of Production in the United Kingdom, the most relevant size measure available is employment. Technical change may alter the employment–output ratio. Therefore, even if the predicted optimum firm size in terms of *employment* remained constant, the lowest cost *output* may have been changing.

Sixthly, the technique assumes that all firms (or plants) experience the same environmental conditions. Lower input prices in one region may enable suboptimally sized firms to exist there. However an advocate of the technique would reply that in the long run such inefficiency would be competed away.

The technique also assumes that all firms have the same objectives. If they do not, inefficient firms may exist. But notice that if one firm is a profit maximiser and inefficiency is well known, only other firms whose behaviour is close to profit maximisation will survive.

Finally, because survival depends on factors which are excluded from the traditional theory of *LAC*, the concept of efficiency to which the technique relates differs from that of the *LAC* curve. Examples of such factors which are implicitly considered by the technique but which are explicitly excluded from the traditional analysis are *size related* flexibility to uncertainty, economies in R&D and labour relations.

Additional Reading

Abell, D.F. and Hammond, J.J. (1979) *Strategic Market Planning*, Prentice-Hall.

Andrews, P.W.S. (1949) *Manufacturing Business*, Macmillan.

Boston Consulting Group (1972) *Perspectives on Experience*, BCG.

Dean, J. (1976) *Statistical Cost Estimation*, Indiana University Press.

Ferguson, C.E. and Gould, J.P. (1975) *Microeconomic Theory*, Richard D. Irwin.

Friedman, M. (1955) 'Comment' in Universities National Bureau Committee for Economic Research, *Business Concentration and Price Policy*, Princeton University Press.

Gravelle, H. and Rees, R. (1981) *Microeconomics*, Longman.

Haldi, J. and Whitcomb, P. (1967) 'Economics of scale in industrial plants', *Journal of Political Economy*, 75(4).

Johnston, J. (1960) *Statistical Cost Analysis*, McGraw-Hill.

Koutsoyiannis, A. (1979) *Modern Microeconomics*, Macmillan.

Lancaster, K. (1974) *Microeconomic Theory*, Rand McNally.

Pratten, C.F. (1971) *Economies of Scale in Manufacturing Industry*, Cambridge University Press.

Rees, R. (1973) 'Optimum plant size in United Kingdom industries: some survivor estimates', *Economica*, (40).

Saving, T. (1961) 'Estimation of optimum size of plant by the survivor technique', *Quarterly Journal of Economics*, (75).

Scherer, F.M., Beckenstein, A., Kaufer, E. and Murphy, R.D. (1975) *The Economics of Multiplant Operations*, Harvard.

Shepherd, W.G. (1967) 'What does the survivor technique show about economies of scale?', *Southern Economic Journal*, (34).

Silberston, Z.A. (1972) 'Economies of scale in theory and practice', *Economic Journal*, Supplement, Vol. 82.

Smith, C.A. (1955) 'Survey of the empirical evidence on economies of scale', in Universities National Bureau Committee for Economic Research, *Business Concentration and Price Policy*, Princeton University Press.

Stigler, G.J. (1958) 'The economies of scale', *Journal of Law and Economics*, (1).

Williamson, O. (1967) 'Hierarchical control and optimum firm size', *Journal of Political Economy*, 75(2).

Williamson, O. (1970) *Corporate Control and Business Behaviour*, Prentice-Hall.

Williamson, O. (1975) *Markets and Hierarchies*, Collier Macmillan.

Williamson, O. (1986) *Economic Organisation*, Wheatsheaf.

8
Linear Programming

Linear programming is a technique used to solve maximisation or minimisation problems in the presence of constraints. This is precisely the intention of the lagrangian multiplier techniques described in Chapter 1. Why then did we not discuss linear programming in the introductory chapter, and what distinguishes it from the calculus techniques described there? Firstly, lagrangian techniques can only handle *exactly equal* constraints. Thus, a lagrangian problem might be formulated so as to minimise cost, subject to the constraint that exactly 100 units of total output were produced. A corresponding linear programming (*LP*) problem would be formulated so as to minimise cost provided that *no less* than 100 units of total output were produced. Secondly, the lagrangian technique can be applied when both the objective function and the constraints are nonlinear, whereas the *LP* method requires that both sets of equations be linear.

Thirdly, the *LP* technique has much in common with production theory, and comprehension will be increased if it is examined now, after we have studied the economic theory of production, rather than before. Initially, however, we will examine the dissimilarities.

8.1 Least-Cost Input Combinations

What differences are there between *LP* analysis and the classical production function? Firstly, the classical production function assumes that there is an infinite number of processes available to choose from. In turn, this implies that the firm can smoothly and continuously substitute one input factor for another. More realistically, *LP* analysis restricts the number of alternative processes to whatever finite number is relevant, and the possibility of continuous substitution is thus disregarded. Secondly, *LP* analysis restricts itself to one particular variant of the production function, namely the linear homogeneous production function. The expansion path of such a production function is always a straight line through the origin. That is, at given input prices, the optimal proportions of the firm's input factors will not change with the size of the input budget. Economies and diseconomies of scale are not present in such a situation since costs rise linearly with output.

219

Assume the firm is producing a single product using two input factors Y and Z. Also assume there are three alternative production processes A, B and C, available to the firm each of which uses a different but fixed combination of Y and Z. In Figure 8.1 the three 'process rays' OA, OB and OC join up points representing units of output. Thus A_2, B_2 and C_2 all represent two units of output, but are produced by processes A, B and C respectively, using the quantities of inputs which are indicated by their respective positions on the YZ plane. Because there are constant returns to scale $OA_1 = A_1A_2 = A_2A_3$, and so on. Similarly, $OB_1 = B_1B_2 = B_2B_3$ and $OC_1 = C_1C_2 = C_2C_3$. (There is, however, no reason why OA_1 should equal either OB_1 or OC_1 in geometric distance.)

If we now join the points of equal output, A_1 with B_1 with C_1 and so on, then we have constructed a family of production isoquants, identical to the isoquants of our discussion in the last chapter. This statement requires both qualification and expansion. Each point on B_6C_6 (for example) corresponds to a *combination* of processes B and C which produces the same output as OB_6 units by process B or OC_6 units by process C.

This is proved by taking any point P on line B_6C_6 and drawing a line through P parallel to OB (the result would be the same if the line were drawn parallel to OC). This intersects OC at C_4 indicating that four units should be produced using process C and the remaining two using process B, since $C_4P = B_4B_6$ as opposite sides of a parallelogram, and $B_4B_6 = OB_2$. (This implies the important economic assumption that simultaneous use of two processes will neither enhance nor detract from input–output relationships of the two individual processes.) A similar exercise could be performed on any of the

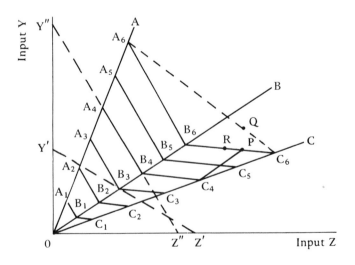

Figure 8.1

isoquant segments connecting points such as A_6 and C_6 on rays OA and OC which would represent combinations of processes A, B and/or C which produced the same output as OA_6 or OC_6. This, however, is wasteful and will never occur in an optimal situation. For consider any point Q on A_6C_6. Corresponding to any such point there will be points such as R on $A_6B_6C_6$ which lie below and to the left of Q. Thus R uses less of *both* Y and Z than does Q, but both R and Q yield the same outputs. Therefore Q can be ignored as far as the $A_6B_6C_6$ isoquant is concerned.

This conclusion points to another similarity between *LP* analysis and production theory. Although the *LP* production isoquants have kinks or corners (which calculus techniques cannot handle) their slopes are generally negative and they are convex to the origin. In other words, while *LP* analysis rules out diminishing returns to scale, the type of diminishing returns associated with the diminishing marginal rate of substitution of one input for another is embraced by it.

To Figure 8.1 we can add isocost lines. $Y'Z'$ and $Y''Z''$ represent two possible such lines. For the relative price levels indicated by $Y'Z'$, process B is optimal at output level B_3. $Y''Z''$ is drawn parallel to the isoquant segment A_4B_4. Here either process A or B, or any combination is optimal, with a total output of 4 units.

So far we have assumed that there are no constraints imposed on the ability of the firm to obtain inputs at constant prices. Clearly this is unrealistic. Firms have access only to limited amounts of machinery, floor space, labour or whatever at any one time, irrespective of their cash resources. The effects of such limitations are illustrated graphically in Figure 8.2. The maximum obtainable amounts of Y and Z are indicated by the Y and Z constraints respectively. The production possibilities open to the firm are represented by the shaded area bounded by the constraints and the process rays OA and OC.

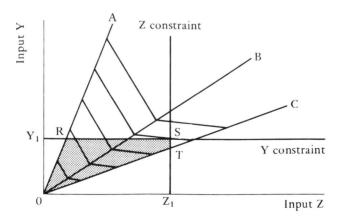

Figure 8.2

(*Y* and *Z* cannot be combined in proportions other than those on the rays, or between the rays, when processes are combined.) The area *ORST* is known as the *feasible space*. If the firm is trying to maximise output subject to the *Y* and *Z* constraints, it should operate where the feasible space touches the highest possible isoquant. This will be at point *S*. By constructing the relevant parallelogram the appropriate combination of processes *B* and *C* can be found which will enable this isoquant to be reached.

8.2 Optimising the Output Mix

Here we will broaden our discussion and move away from the single product situation to the more common multiproduct firm. We will consider a firm with three inputs *X*, *Y* and *Z*, and two outputs, products *A* and *B*. The firm wishes to maximise profits and, subject to input availability constraints, needs to determine the optimal quantities of *A* and *B* which will achieve this goal.

We will first examine the position geometrically, then algebraically and finally using the Simplex method. Clearly, the list of variables could be extended well beyond five, were it not for geometric complexity.

(i) The Geometric Approach

The typical *LP* problem is set out under the following headings:

> *The objective function*
> *The constraints*
> *The non-negativity requirements*

Let us set these out for our hypothetical example.

The Objective Function   The objective is to maximise profits. In *LP* problems 'profits' refer to 'contribution profits' (i.e. total revenue less variable costs). Fixed costs are ignored. However, since fixed costs are constant irrespective of output, the output level which maximises contribution profits also maximises profits net of fixed costs. (See Chapter 16 for a fuller discussion on contribution analysis.) Unit contribution equals price less average variable cost; if this is £2 for *A* and £3 for *B* then the objective function can be written thus:

$$\text{maximise } \pi_c = £2Q_A + £3Q_B \tag{8.1}$$

where π_c is total contribution profit and Q_A and Q_B are the quantities produced of *A* and *B* respectively.

The Constraints   To obtain the constraint equations we need to know how many units of the inputs *X*, *Y* and *Z* are available in each period. Say these are 20, 25 and 30 respectively. Coupled with this we need to know how many units of each of X, Y and Z are required to produce, respectively, one unit of the outputs A and B. Say these are 2, 3 and 0 for A and 5, $2\frac{1}{2}$ and 12 for B. The constraint equations can now be written thus:

$$2Q_A + 5Q_B \leqslant 20 \text{ (available units of } X) \tag{8.2}$$
$$3Q_A + 2\tfrac{1}{2}Q_B \leqslant 25 \text{ (available units of } Y) \tag{8.3}$$
$$12Q_B \leqslant 30 \text{ (available units of } Z) \tag{8.4}$$

The Non-Negativity Requirements Clearly no one making a graphic analysis would ever recommend negative outputs. However, in a complex algebraic problem solved by means of a computer, it may appear 'logical' to recommend certain negative outputs to maximise the objective function. Mathematically this might be possible; in practice it is nonsense. (Graphically it implies merely going to the left of the vertical and below the horizontal axis.) To ensure that this nonsense result does not occur, the following equations are included in the system:

$$Q_A \geqslant 0 \tag{8.5}$$
$$Q_B \geqslant 0 \tag{8.6}$$

Geometrically, the first step is to determine the feasible space. Figure 8.3 illustrates how this is done by drawing the corresponding lines of equations (8.2), (8.3) and (8.4) on the AB plane. The shaded area $OPRST$ represents the feasible space. Only points within this area meet all the constraints and also the non-negativity requirements.

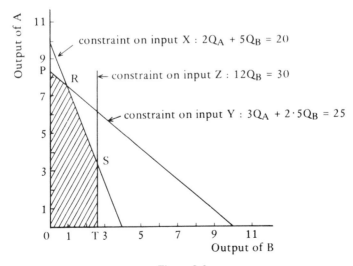

Figure 8.3

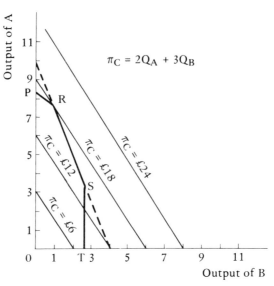

Figure 8.4

Next we must graph in the objective function, equation (8.1). This is illustrated in Figure 8.4 by the family of isocontribution lines. Each such line satisfies equation (8.1) and plots all possible contributions of A and B which produce a constant total contribution profit.

The solution to our problem becomes obvious when the feasible space *OPRST* is superimposed on Figure 8.4. Maximum contribution profits are £18 which are achieved by the output mix of products A and B indicated by point R.

If $\pi_c = $ £18 had the shape indicated by the dashed line parallel to segment *RS*, the optimal solution would then have been any point between and including R and S. For the algebra involved in *LP* analysis this last conclusion is important. Given the linearities involved in the analysis, optimal solutions occur at 'corners' of the feasible space, or along the whole of one boundary face (R to S in Figure 8.4, A_4 to B_4 in Figure 8.1). Since the firm will be indifferent as to where on the highest attainable isocontribution line it lies, it can restrict its algebraic computations to only the corner points of the feasible region and, accordingly, ignore the near infinite number of solutions within that region.

(ii) The Arithmetic Approach

To the *LP* format with which the previous subsection was introduced, one other concept must be added: *slack variables*. These account for that amount of any input which is unused. In our example the firm had three inputs X, Y

and Z. Consequently we introduce three slack variables S_X, S_Y and S_Z, one for each input. This enables us to rewrite each constraint relationship as an equation, not an inequality. Clearly, any slack variable which has a zero value at the optimal solution point is a possible bottleneck or limitation on production and profitability increases. Conversely, a positive value for a slack variable at the optimal point is indicative of possible excess capacity. Slack variables can never have negative values so this must be built into the non-negativity requirements.

Our illustrative problem can now be specified as follows:

$$\text{maximise } \pi_c = \pounds 2Q_A + \pounds 3Q_B \tag{8.1}$$

subject to the constraints

$$2Q_A + 5Q_B + S_X = 20 \tag{8.7}$$
$$3Q_A + 2\tfrac{1}{2}Q_B + S_Y = 25 \tag{8.8}$$

and

$$12Q_B + S_Z = 30 \tag{8.9}$$

where

$$Q_A \geqslant 0 \tag{8.5}$$
$$Q_B \geqslant 0 \tag{8.6}$$
$$S_X \geqslant 0 \tag{8.10}$$
$$S_Y \geqslant 0 \tag{8.11}$$
$$S_Z \geqslant 0 \tag{8.12}$$

The problem at this point is underdetermined. There are more unknowns $(Q_A, Q_B, S_X, S_Y, S_Z)$ than there are equations to be solved (8.7, 8.8, 8.9).

This dilemma is overcome by two basic propositions underlying linear programming. First, in almost all *LP* problems, an optimal solution can be found by considering only the corner locations of the feasible space. This point has already been explained. Second, at each corner the number of variables with a non-zero value exactly equals the number of constraint equations. Consider again Figure 8.3. At O, Q_A and Q_B are zero but S_X, S_Y and S_Z must have positive values. At P, Q_B and S_Y are zero but Q_A, S_X and S_Z must have positive values. Similarly at R, only S_Y and S_X are zero. At S, only S_Z and S_X are zero and at T, only S_Z and Q_A have zero values. Such solutions are called 'basic'. Given the first proposition it can be seen that we require the optimal 'basic feasible solution' (*BFS*).

We can say that, in almost all cases, the optimal *BFS* will have as many non-zero valued variables as the number of constraints. But how to find it? One method might be to calculate the profit at every corner and choose the largest. Hence consider corner O, the origin. Substituting Q_A and Q_B equal to zero in equations (8.7), (8.8), and (8.9) we obtain:

$$S_X = 20$$
$$S_Y = 25$$
$$S_Z = 30$$
π_C in equation (8.1) equals zero

At P, Q_B and S_Y equal zero, so we have:

$$2Q_A + S_X = 20$$
$$3Q_A \qquad = 25$$
$$\qquad S_Z = 30$$

Thus

$$Q_A = 8\tfrac{1}{3}$$

and by substitution

$$S_X = 20 - 16\tfrac{2}{3} = 3\tfrac{1}{3}$$
π_C in equation (8.1) equals £16$\tfrac{2}{3}$

At R, S_Y and S_X equal zero, so we have:

$$2Q_A + 5Q_B = 20$$
$$3Q_A + 2\tfrac{1}{2}Q_B = 25$$
$$12Q_B + S_Z = 30$$

Thus

$$Q_A = 10 - 2\tfrac{1}{2}Q_B$$

and by substitution

$$3Q_A + 10 - Q_A = 25$$

Thus

$$Q_A = 7\tfrac{1}{2}, \; Q_B = 1, \; S_Z = 18$$
π_C in equation (8.1) equals £18

At S, S_Z and S_X equal zero, so we have:

$$2Q_A + 5Q_B = 20$$
$$3Q_A + 2\tfrac{1}{2}Q_B + S_Y = 25$$
$$12Q_B = 30$$

Therefore

$$Q_B = 2\tfrac{1}{2}$$

and by substitution

$$2Q_A = 20 - 12\tfrac{1}{2}$$

Therefore

$$Q_A = 3\tfrac{3}{4}$$

and by substitution

$$11\tfrac{1}{4}+6\tfrac{1}{4}+S_Y = 25$$

Therefore $S_Y = 7\tfrac{1}{2}$

π_C in equation (8.1) equals £15

At T, S_Z and Q_A have zero values, so we have:

$$5Q_B+S_X = 20$$
$$2\tfrac{1}{2}Q_B+S_Y = 25$$
$$12Q_B = 30$$

Therefore

$$Q_B = 2\tfrac{1}{2}$$

and by substitution

$$S_X = 20-12\tfrac{1}{2} = 7\tfrac{1}{2}$$
$$S_Y = 25-6\tfrac{1}{4} = 18\tfrac{3}{4}$$
$$\pi_C \text{ in equation (8.1) equals £7}\tfrac{1}{2}$$

This confirms our geometric result that the optimum level of π_C is £18 at point R. S_Y and S_X equal zero there and so indicate potential bottlenecks in the use of resource inputs Y and X. S_Z, on the other hand, has a value of 18, signifying possible idle resources which could be more fruitfully employed. The optimal output mix is 1 unit of B and $7\tfrac{1}{2}$ units of A.

(iii) Simplex Method

A limitation of the arithmetic method in practice is that the number of corners may be *very* large indeed. Fortunately, a method of selecting corners which yield progressively higher profits is available: the Simplex method. We firstly explain the algebraic version of the technique and, secondly, a quicker matrix version.

Algebraic Version

Stage 1 To choose an initial *BFS* from which to progress to other corners one might choose that of producing neither A nor B. The slack variables then equal the total available quantities of each input: $S_X = 20$, $S_Y = 25$, $S_Z = 30$. This *BFS* may be represented as:

$$Q_A = 0$$
$$Q_B = 0$$
$$S_X = 20 - 2Q_A - 5Q_B = 20 \tag{8.13}$$

$$S_Y = 25 - 3Q_A - 2\tfrac{1}{2}Q_B = 25 \qquad (8.14)$$
$$S_Z = 30 - 0Q_A - 12Q_B = 30 \qquad (8.15)$$
$$\pi_c = 2Q_A + 3Q_B = 0 \qquad (8.16)$$

and this represents the origin in Figure 8.4.

Stage 2 But profits can be increased. From equation (8.16) it can be seen that every additional unit of B produced would give an additional £3 of profit, and every additional unit of A, £2 of profit. From equations (8.13) to (8.15) one can see that sufficient inputs are available to produce several units of B and/or of A. To select which of A or B to produce we compare their marginal profits: £2 and £3 respectively. B's marginal contribution exceeds A's. Therefore we increase Q_B. But by how much?

If we increase Q_B from zero we add Q_B to our basis (the non-zero variables). To keep the solution 'basic', i.e. a corner, we must reduce the value of an existing non-zero solution variable to zero. But which? The question of which existing basis variable to reduce and by how much Q_B is to be increased, are solved together.

In equation (8.13), if we keep Q_A equal to zero, each additional unit of B will reduce S_X by 5 units. Only 20 S_X units are available. Therefore if we use all of S_X to produce only B, we could produce only $20/5 = 4$ B units. From equation (8.14) each additional unit of B will reduce S_Y by $2\tfrac{1}{2}$ units. Since only 25 S_Y units are available, if we use all of them to produce only B, we could produce only $25/2\tfrac{1}{2} = 10$ units. Similarly if we used all of S_Z to produce B the maximum we could produce is only $30/12 = 2\tfrac{1}{2}$ units. Because output of B requires inputs X, Y and Z, each of which has a limited supply, the maximum B which can be produced is the smallest of 4, 10 and $2\tfrac{1}{2}$, i.e. $2\tfrac{1}{2}$. Greater output than this would violate constraint (8.12). Therefore Q_B is increased by $2\tfrac{1}{2}$ units and S_Z reduced to zero.

To examine the effects of changes in the values of variables which now equal zero on those variables which are currently included in the basis, we wish to have equations (8.13) to (8.15) with only Q_A and S_Z on the right-hand side. To do this, the variable which has just been introduced into the basis is made the subject of the equation whose dependent variable has been reduced to zero. This is substituted into the other constraint equations. Hence since Q_B is being introduced and S_Z reduced to zero equation (8.15) becomes:

$$Q_B = \frac{30}{12} - S_Z/12 = 2\tfrac{1}{2} - S_Z/12 \qquad (8.17)$$

which is substituted into equations (8.13) and (8.14). So we have, for inputs X, Y and Z respectively:

$$S_X = 20 - 2Q_A - 5(2\tfrac{1}{2} - S_Z/12) = 7\tfrac{1}{2} - 2Q_A + \tfrac{5}{12}S_Z \qquad (8.18)$$
$$S_Y = 25 - 3Q_A - 2\tfrac{1}{2}(2\tfrac{1}{2} - S_Z/12) = 18\tfrac{3}{4} - 3Q_A + \tfrac{5}{24}S_Z \qquad (8.19)$$
$$Q_B = 2\tfrac{1}{2} - S_Z/12 + 0Q_A \qquad (8.17)$$

The expression for Q_B is also substituted into the profits function:

$$\pi_c = 2Q_A + 3\left(2\tfrac{1}{2} - S_Z/12\right) = 7\tfrac{1}{2} + 2Q_A - \tfrac{1}{4}S_Z \tag{8.20}$$

Since Q_A and S_Z are zero, by substitution into equations (8.17) to (8.19) the values of S_X and S_Y can be derived (we already know $Q_B = 2\tfrac{1}{2}$). Hence our second *BFS* is:

$$Q_A = 0, \; Q_B = 2\tfrac{1}{2}, \; S_X = 7\tfrac{1}{2}, \; S_Y = 18\tfrac{3}{4}, \; S_Z = 0$$

Notice that this solution relates to point T in Figure 8.4.

Stage 3   Profits can again be increased. From equation (8.20) it can be seen that every additional unit of Q_A will contribute £2 to profits. To decide the value of Q_A and the variable in the *BFS* to be replaced, we proceed as before. From equations (8.18) and (8.19) the maximum amounts of A which can be produced by reducing S_X or S_Y to zero are $\dfrac{7\tfrac{1}{2}}{2} = \dfrac{15}{4}$ and $\dfrac{18\tfrac{3}{4}}{3} = 6\tfrac{1}{4}$ units respec-

tively. Equation (8.17) is unusual. Additional A does not affect Q_B, so an 'infinite' amount of Q_A could be produced and still fulfil the constraint. The maximum Q_A value which can be produced within all constraints is $3\tfrac{3}{4}$ units. Producing $3\tfrac{3}{4}$ units of A uses all of the slack in input X, i.e. $S_X = 0$.

To examine the effects of changes in basis variables on non-basis variables, we wish to have equations with S_X and S_Z on the right-hand side. Since Q_A is being introduced and S_X removed from the basis, equation (8.18) is rearranged to become:

$$Q_A = \tfrac{15}{4} - \tfrac{1}{2}S_X + \tfrac{5}{24}S_Z = 3\tfrac{3}{4} - \tfrac{1}{2}S_X + \tfrac{5}{24}S_Z \tag{8.21}$$

This is substituted into equations (8.19) and (8.17). These, together with equation (8.21) become, for inputs X, Y and Z respectively:

$$Q_A = 3\tfrac{3}{4} - \tfrac{1}{2}S_X + \tfrac{5}{24}S_Z \tag{8.21}$$

$$S_Y = 18\tfrac{3}{4} - 3(3\tfrac{3}{4} - \tfrac{1}{2}S_X + \tfrac{5}{24}S_Z) + \tfrac{5}{24}S_Z = 7\tfrac{1}{2} + 1\tfrac{1}{2}S_X - \tfrac{10}{24}S_Z \tag{8.22}$$

$$Q_B = 2\tfrac{1}{2} - \frac{S_Z}{12} \tag{8.23}$$

The expression for Q_A is also substituted into equation (8.20):

$$\pi_c = 7\tfrac{1}{2} + 2(3\tfrac{3}{4} - \tfrac{1}{2}S_X + \tfrac{5}{24}S_Z) - \tfrac{1}{4}S_Z = 15 - S_X + \tfrac{5}{24}S_Z \tag{8.24}$$

Since S_X and S_Z are zero, by substitution we find $S_Y = 7\tfrac{1}{2}$ and $Q_B = 2\tfrac{1}{2}$. Q_A is known to be $3\tfrac{3}{4}$. So our third *BFS* is:

$$Q_A = 3\tfrac{3}{4}, \; Q_B = 2\tfrac{1}{2}, \; S_X = 0, \; S_Y = 7\tfrac{1}{2}, \; S_Z = 0$$

Notice that this represents point S in Figure 8.4.

Stage 4   Again profits can be increased. The coefficient on S_Z indicates that by using one unit less of input Z, i.e. increasing S_Z by one unit, π will increase by $\frac{4}{24}$ units. By how much should S_Z be increased? From equation (8.23) we can see that the maximum by which S_Z could be increased is $2\frac{1}{2}/\frac{1}{12} = 30$ since then B is no longer produced. From equation (8.22) the maximum value which S_Z could take is $7\frac{1}{2}/\{\frac{10}{24}\} = 18$, then all slack in Y would be used and S_Y would become zero. From equation (8.21) additional S_Z allows additional B to be produced, not less. Therefore equation (8.21) does not indicate a constraint on the increase in S_Z. The lowest of 18 and 30 is 18. Therefore S_Y is reduced to zero.

To investigate the effects of changes in the two zero-valued variables S_X and S_Y on the positive variables, S_Z is made the subject of equation (8.22):

$$S_Z = 18 + \tfrac{18}{5}S_X - \tfrac{12}{5}S_Y \qquad (8.25)$$

This is substituted into the other two constraints and the profits function. Equations (8.21) to (8.24) become respectively:

$$Q_A = 3\tfrac{3}{4} - \tfrac{1}{2}S_X + \tfrac{5}{24}(18 + \tfrac{18}{5}S_X - \tfrac{12}{5}S_Y) = 7\tfrac{1}{2} + \tfrac{1}{4}S_X - \tfrac{1}{2}S_Y \qquad (8.26)$$

$$S_Z = 18 + \tfrac{18}{5}S_X - \tfrac{12}{5}S_Y \qquad (8.25)$$

$$Q_B = 2\tfrac{1}{2} - \tfrac{1}{12}(18 + \tfrac{18}{5}S_X - \tfrac{12}{5}S_Y) = 1 - \tfrac{3}{10}S_X + \tfrac{1}{5}S_Y \qquad (8.27)$$

$$\pi_c = 15 - S_X + \tfrac{1}{6}(18 + \tfrac{18}{5}S_X - \tfrac{12}{5}S_Y) = 18 - \tfrac{2}{5}S_X - \tfrac{2}{5}S_Y \qquad (8.28)$$

Substituting $S_X = S_Y = 0$ into these equations the fourth *BFS* is derived:

$$Q_A = 7\tfrac{1}{2}, \ Q_B = 1, \ S_X = 0, \ S_Y = 0, \ S_Z = 18$$

Notice that this represents point R in Figure 8.4.

In equation (8.28) the coefficients of both variables are negative. If S_X or S_Y is increased π_c would fall. Therefore the *BFS* is the optimal one.

The Matrix Version

The algebraic method of substituting one equation into others may be very time-consuming when the number of constraints, and hence equations, is large. When using the matrix version all of the above steps are performed, but by setting out the constraints and objective function in a matrix-like tableau and by using certain rules, time is saved.

Stage 1   A Simplex tableau is constructed representing the constraints and objective function. Table 8.1 shows the first tableau in our production problem. Essentially it represents equations (8.13) to (8.16) of our first *BFS* above. The row beginning 'Basis' names the variables to which each column relates. The column marked 'Basis' contains the names of variables with non-zero values in the solution, i.e. the current 'basis'. Q relates to the constants of each constraint equation. Hence the constant in the equation of

Table 8.1 First Tableau

C_j			2	3	0	0	0
	Basis	Q	Q_A	Q_B	S_X	S_Y	S_Z
0	S_X	20	2	5	1	0	0
0	S_Y	25	3	$2\frac{1}{2}$	0	1	0
0	S_Z	30	0	$\boxed{12}$	0	0	1
	Z_j	0	0	0	0	0	0
	$C_j - Z_j$		2	3	0	0	0

which S_X is the subject is 20. The columns marked Q_A, Q_B, S_X, S_Y and S_Z (excluding the Z_j and $C_j - Z_j$ rows) all contain the corresponding (negative of the) coefficients of the constraint equations (8.13) to (8.15). Hence the number '2' in column Q_A, row S_X indicates that in the equation whose subject is S_X, (8.13), the coefficient of Q_A is -2 etc. This implies that if Q_A increases by one unit, S_X *decreases* by 2 units. If the tableau figure had been -2 corresponding to a value in the equation form of $+2$, a one unit increase in Q_A would have necessitated an *increase* in S_X by 2 units. Whenever the sign in these tableau rows is positive (negative), then a one unit increase in the column variable indicates a decrease (increase) in the row variable.

The row and column marked C_j contains the coefficients of each variable in the objective function. Each of these coefficients shows the increase in profit due to a unit increase in the corresponding variable, provided that no profit is sacrificed when the variable is increased. Such a sacrifice may occur when, to fulfil a constraint, an increase in one variable is only possible when the value of another is reduced. The row marked Z_j shows these sacrifices. The value of Z for a column is calculated by multiplying each element in the column by the corresponding C_j value of the basis variable in its row, and summing the results. Hence Z for the Q_A column equals $(2 \times 0) + (3 \times 0) + (0 \times 0) = 0$. The reason for this is as follows. If Q_A increases by one unit, S_X is reduced by 2 units, as explained above. But variations in S_X do not affect profits: it has a coefficient of zero in the original profit function. Therefore a one unit rise in Q_A, though reducing S_X by two units, would not alter profits because of its effects on S_X. Similarly, a one unit rise in Q_A would reduce S_Y by 3 units. But again S_Y does not affect profits, so this reduction would not affect profits. Finally, a one unit rise in Q_A does not affect S_Z. Summing these reductions in profits totals zero. This is repeated for every column including the Q column. The Z value in the Q column equals total profits for the current *BFS*. It is the sum of the products of the value (the Q) of each variable in the basis and their coefficients in the profits equation.

Since a change in net (contribution) profits equals the increase in gross (contribution) profits (C_j), minus the sacrifice necessary to achieve it (Z_j), $C_j - Z_j$ represents the change in net profits due to a unit increase in the column variable. Thus in the Q_A column, a unit increase in Q_A does not necessitate a reduction in a profit-adding variable (as explained above, $Z = 0$) but does directly increase gross profit, as shown by its $+2$ coefficient in the profit function (the C_j row). Therefore a unit increase in Q_A results in a net profit increase of £$(2 \times 1) - (2 \times 0)$ which is $C_j - Z_j$. Similarly, a unit increase in Q_B results in a net profit increase of £$(3 \times 1) - [(5 \times 0) + (2\frac{1}{2} \times 0) + (12 \times 0)] = £3$.

Stage 2   The $C_j - Z_j$ row indicates that because the signs of the figures for Q_A and Q_B are positive, an increase in either will increase net profits. Since the figure for Q_B exceeds that of Q_A, the marginal contribution of the former exceeds that of the latter and therefore should be increased. To decide which slack to reduce to zero we compare the maximum amounts of B which can be produced if all of each slack is used, as was done in the algebraic method. Each element in the Q column (the constant in the constraint equations) is divided by the corresponding element in the column of the replacing variable. Hence the maximum amounts of B which can be produced by reducing S_X, S_Y or S_Z to zero are 4, 10 and $2\frac{1}{2}$ respectively. (Notice that we wish to rank only the non-negative values of these maxima because a negative value of any choice variable or slack is contrary to the non-negativity constraints.) Therefore to avoid violating constraint (8.9) S_Z is to be reduced to zero.

In the algebraic version, the next step was to make Q_B the subject of the S_Z equation and to substitute this into the other constraint and profit equations. Exactly the same process is completed in the matrix version by 'pivoting'. Firstly, one finds the element which is in the column of the variable to be introduced (Q_B) and the row of the variable to be replaced (S_Z), i.e. 12. This is the 'pivot'. In each tableau the pivot has been marked by a box.

The second tableau (Table 8.2) (which represents the equations in Stage 2 of the algebraic method) is derived thus:

(i)   *to find the new elements in the new pivotal row*: divide each element in the old pivotal row by the pivot.

Table 8.2   Second Tableau

C_j			2	3	0	0	0
	Basis	Q	Q_A	Q_B	S_X	S_Y	S_Z
0	S_X	$7\frac{1}{2}$	[2]	0	1	0	$-5/12$
0	S_Y	$18\frac{3}{4}$	3	0	0	1	$-5/24$
3	Q_B	$2\frac{1}{2}$	0	1	0	0	$1/12$
	Z_j	$7\frac{1}{2}$	0	3	0	0	$1/4$
	$C_j - Z_j$		2	0	0	0	$-1/4$

(ii) *to find the new elements in every other row including the the $(C_j - Z_j)$ row*

$$\begin{Bmatrix} \text{new element} \\ \text{in row } i, \\ \text{column } j \end{Bmatrix} = \begin{Bmatrix} \text{old element} \\ \text{in row } i, \\ \text{column } j \end{Bmatrix} - \frac{\begin{Bmatrix} \text{old element} \\ \text{in row } i, \\ \text{pivotal column} \end{Bmatrix} \times \begin{Bmatrix} \text{old element in} \\ \text{pivotal row,} \\ \text{column } j \end{Bmatrix}}{\text{pivot}}$$

Hence the row corresponding to input X in the first tableau becomes, in the second tableau:

	Q	Q_A	Q_B	S_X	S_Y	S_Z
$S_X =$	$7\frac{1}{2}$	2	0	1	0	$-\frac{5}{12}$

$= \quad 20 - 5(\frac{30}{12}) = 2 - 5(\frac{0}{12}) = 5 - 5(\frac{12}{12}) = 1 - 5(\frac{0}{12}) = 0 - 5(\frac{0}{12}) = 0 - 5(\frac{1}{12})$

(iii) to find the new elements in the Z_j row: multiply each element in one column by the corresponding new value in the C_j column and sum. Repeat for each column.

The Z_j row would be calculated as in Tableau 1. In each column each new element would be multiplied by the coefficient in the original profits equation of the variable in the same row, but in the column marked 'Basis'. These products would then be summed. Hence the Z value for the Q_A column would become $(2 \times 0) + (3 \times 0) + (0 \times 3) = 0$. Again each element except in the Z_j and $C_j - Z_j$ rows, if it has a positive sign would correspond to a negative in the constraint equation. Thus the $+2$ in the Q_A column S_X row, indicates that a one unit increase in Q_A *decreases* S_X by (2×1) units. But from the profits equation we can see that S_X does not affect profits. So the 3 unit decrease in S_X has a £$(2 \times 0) \times 3$ effect on profits.

The $(C_j - Z_j)$ row could also be calculated as for Tableau 1. However, including $(C_j - Z_j)$ in the pivoting procedure saves time. Notice that in Tableau 2 the net marginal profit of Q_B of £0 differs from the marginal gross profit in the profit function of £3. The reason for this is that the former equals $C_j - Z_j$, the latter C_j. A unit increase in Q_B does not necessitate a reduction in S_X or S_Y: the elements in the Q_B column, S_X and S_Y rows, are zeros. But the rise in Q_B would violate the third constraint unless one unit of Q_B was simultaneously removed: the element in the Q_B column, Q_B row is 1. This reduction would cause a £3 loss in gross profits since the coefficient of Q_B in the profits function is £3. However, the one unit rise in Q_B would raise profits by £3 for the same reason. The result is a net rise of £0 in profits. It is this net rise which is indicated by the $C_j - Z_j$ row.

Since only those variables in the 'basis' are non-zero, the column shows the values of the non-zero solution variables. Thus our second *BFS* is:

$$Q_A = 0, \ Q_B = 2\frac{1}{2}, \ S_X = 7\frac{1}{2}, \ S_Y = 18\frac{3}{4}, \ S_Z = 0$$

Notice that the second tableau is analogous to equations (8.17) to (8.20) of the algebraic method.

Stage 3   The $C_j - Z_j$ marginal net profit row shows that profits can again be increased by increasing Q_A. To decide which of the basis variables to reduce to zero, we again divide the Q column elements by the elements in the Q_A row. The smallest of these quotients is $3\frac{3}{4}$ corresponding to S_X. Therefore S_X is reduced to zero and Q_A increased to $3\frac{3}{4}$.

Again to examine the effects on the new basis variables of further changes in the new non-basis variables, we pivot and form the third tableau, Table 8.3. Since Q_A is being increased and S_X reduced, the pivot is the element in the Q_A column, S_X row: 2. Hence the elements in the pivotal (top) row are all divided by 2. Those in other rows follow procedures (ii) and (iii) above. Thus the new elements in the second row become:

$$\text{Vars} \qquad \begin{array}{c} Q \\ 7\frac{1}{2} \end{array} \qquad \begin{array}{c} Q_A \\ 0 \end{array} \qquad \begin{array}{c} Q_B \\ 0 \end{array} \qquad \begin{array}{c} S_X \\ -1\frac{1}{2} \end{array}$$

$$18\frac{3}{4} - \frac{3 \times 7\frac{1}{2}}{2} \quad 3 - \frac{3 \times 2}{2} \quad 0 - \frac{3 \times 0}{2} \quad 0 - \frac{3 \times 1}{2}$$

$$\begin{array}{cc} S_Y & S_Z \\ 1 & 10/24 \end{array}$$

$$1 - \frac{3 \times 0}{2} \quad -5/24 - 3\frac{\left(-\frac{5}{12}\right)}{2}$$

The $C_j - Z_j$ row is similarly found.

Again since all non-basis variables are zero, the coefficients in the third tableau give the third *BFS*: $Q_A = 3\frac{3}{4}$, $Q_B = 2\frac{1}{2}$, $S_X = 0$, $S_Y = 7\frac{1}{2}$, $S_Z = 0$. Notice that the third tableau is analogous to equations (8.21) to (8.24) of the algebraic method.

Stage 4   The marginal net profits row indicates that profits can still be increased if S_Z is increased. Dividing each element in the Q column by the

Table 8.3   Third Tableau

C_j			2	3	0	0	0
	Basis	Q	Q_A	Q_B	S_X	S_Y	S_Z
2	Q_A	$3\frac{3}{4}$	1	0	$\frac{1}{2}$	0	$-5/24$
0	S_Y	$7\frac{1}{2}$	0	0	$-1\frac{1}{2}$	1	$\boxed{10/24}$
3	Q_B	$2\frac{1}{2}$	0	1	0	0	$1/12$
	Z_j	15	2	3	1	0	$-4/24$
	$C_j - Z_j$		0	0	-1	0	$4/24$

corresponding element in the S_Z column suggests that S_Y is to be reduced to zero and S_Z increased to 18.

Again to examine the effects on the new basis variables of further changes in the new non-basis variables, we pivot. Since S_Y is being reduced and S_Z increased, the pivot is the element in the S_Z column, S_Y row: $\frac{10}{24}$. Table 8.4 shows the fourth tableau. Thus the fourth *BFS* is:

$$Q_A = 7\tfrac{1}{2}, Q_B = 1, S_X = 0, S_Y = 0, S_Z = 18$$

Table 8.4 Fourth Tableau

C_j			2	3	0	0	0
	Basis	Q	Q_A	Q_B	S_X	S_Y	S_Z
2	Q_A	$7\frac{1}{2}$	1	0	$-1/4$	$1/12$	0
0	S_Z	18	0	0	$-18/5$	$24/10$	1
3	Q_B	1	0	1	$3/10$	$-1/5$	0
	Z_j	18	2	3	$4/10$	$2/5$	0
	$C_j - Z_j$		0	0	$-4/10$	$-2/5$	0

In the fourth tableau there are no variables with positive coefficients in the net marginal profits $(C_j - Z_j)$ row. Therefore profits cannot be increased by increasing any variable. The negative elements relating to S_X and S_Y indicate that a reduction in their values would increase profits. But S_X and S_Y cannot be reduced: they are already zero and negative values would violate the non-negativity constraints on them. Therefore the fourth *BFS* is the optimal solution. Notice that the fourth *BFS* as calculated by the matrix version is identical to that of the algebraic version and the graphical and arithmetic methods.

Finally notice that to decide whether the replacement of one variable in the basis by another would increase π_c we looked for variables whose marginal net profit, i.e. whose coefficient in the $(C_j - Z_j)$ row was positive. Since the elements in this row can be derived by pivoting without separate calculation of the Z_j row, there is no need repeatedly to recalculate the latter. (Calculation of the Z_j row was included to facilitate our interpretation of the $(C_j - Z_j)$ row.)

8.3 The Dual

For every *LP* problem (the primal) there is a corresponding dual problem. The dual consists of the primal problem which has been changed in five respects.

(i) If the objective function in the primal is to be maximised (minimised), that of the dual is to be minimised (maximised).

(ii) The primal variables are replaced by new variables.

(iii) The maximum (or minimum) value of each input in the constraint equations in the primal become the coefficients of the new variables in the objective function in the dual.

(iv) Whereas the coefficients in each column in the primal constraint equations are related to the same (old) variable, each is placed along a row and relates to a different new variable.

(v) The $\leqslant$ ($\geqslant$) signs are reversed (but of course, the non-negativity conditions remain). Hence the primal and dual of our production problem are:

<table>
<tr><td>Primal</td><td>Dual</td></tr>
</table>

Maximise: $\pi_c = 2Q_A + 3Q_B$ Minimise: $C = 20P_X + 25P_Y + 30P_Z$
subject to: $2Q_A + 5Q_B \leqslant 20$ subject to: $2P_X + 3P_Y \geqslant 2$
         (availability of   (available π_c from A)
           input X)
        $3Q_A + 2\frac{1}{2}Q_B \leqslant 25$ $5P_X + 2\frac{1}{2}P_Y + 12P_Z \geqslant 3$
         (availability of   (available π_c from B)
           input Y)
        $12Q_B \leqslant 30$ $P_X \geqslant 0$
         (availability of $P_Y \geqslant 0$
           input Z) $P_Z \geqslant 0$
         $Q_A \geqslant 0$
         $Q_B \geqslant 0$

In matrix form the primal can be read horizontally and the dual vertically from the following matrix:

<table>
<tr><td></td><td colspan="5" align="center">PRIMAL</td></tr>
<tr><td></td><td>VARIABLES</td><td>A</td><td>B</td><td>RELATION</td><td>CONSTANTS</td></tr>
<tr><td></td><td>X</td><td>2</td><td>5</td><td>$\leqslant$</td><td>20</td></tr>
<tr><td>DUAL</td><td>Y</td><td>3</td><td>$2\frac{1}{2}$</td><td>$\leqslant$</td><td>25</td></tr>
<tr><td></td><td>Z</td><td>0</td><td>12</td><td>$\leqslant$</td><td>30</td></tr>
<tr><td></td><td>RELATION</td><td>$\geqslant$</td><td>$\geqslant$</td><td></td><td>Minimise C</td></tr>
<tr><td></td><td>CONSTANTS</td><td>2</td><td>3</td><td>Maximise π_c</td><td></td></tr>
</table>

To interpret the dual problem economically, we begin with the constraints of the production example. In the primal the coefficient of the Q_B term in each constraint equals the number of units of the corresponding input which are needed to produce a unit of B. Hence 5 units of X are needed to produce one unit of B (from constraint 1) as are $2\frac{1}{2}$ units of Y and 12 units of Z. Let P_X represent the shadow price for input X. (The 'shadow price' is the imputed profit each unit of X yields. Corresponding interpretations relate to shadow prices P_Y and P_Z.) Then the total value of inputs which are needed to produce a unit of B is $5P_X$ for X plus $2\frac{1}{2}P_Y$ for Y plus $12P_Z$ for Z.

Turning to the right-hand side of each inequality in the dual, notice that this was originally the coefficient of the corresponding variable in the objective function in the primal. Hence from the π function of the primal, £3 of profit were made for every unit of B produced overall. Therefore, the second inequality in the dual states that the total value of inputs needed to produce a unit of B must be greater than or equal to the profit which the B unit yields. A similar interpretation applies to the first constraint in terms of the output of A.

Finally, the coefficients in the objective function of the dual were originally the maximum available quantities of each input in the primal. Therefore when multiplied by the corresponding shadow prices and summed one obtains the total value of all inputs which are available to the firm. This is the objective function of the dual. Hence the dual problem is to choose values of the shadow prices for each input which minimise the total cost of inputs, subject to the requirement that the value of inputs to produce a unit of each product is no less than the profits which that unit yields.

To solve a minimisation problem, such as the dual of a maximisation primal, one can again use the Simplex method. When the constraint inequalities show the right-hand side to be 'greater than' the constant, we must add surplus variables to change the inequality to an equation. These are negative slack variables analogous to the positive slack variables of the primal. We will call these surplus variables $L_1 \ldots L_n$.

Secondly, in the (maximising) primal a readily available first basis existed: the slack variables (i.e. the graphical origin). When the problem is one of minimisation, if we try to take $Q_A = Q_B = 0$ as our first BFS we would obtain only the surplus variables as having non-zero values. But these would be negative and so unfeasible. Thus to obtain our first basis we add artificial variables $A_1 \ldots A_n$ to each constraint. To these is attributed a coefficient of unity. The same variables $A_1 \ldots A_n$, are introduced into the objective function with a very large coefficient (M) relative to those of the other variables. Because these *artificial* variables are positive, they can be used as (part if not all of) our first basis.

The dual of our production problem is now:

Minimise: $\quad C = 20P_X + 25P_Y + 30P_Z + 0L_1 + 0L_2 + MA_1 + MA_2$

Subject to: $2P_X + 3P_Y - L_1 - 0L_2 + A_1 + 0A_2 = 2$
$\qquad\qquad 5P_X + 2\frac{1}{2}P_Y + 12P_Z - 0L_1 - L_2 + 0A_1 + A_2 = 3$

The top section of Table 8.5 shows this problem in tableau form with the two artificial variables taken as our first basis.

Table 8.5 Tableaux for Minimisation Problem

	C_j		20	25	30	0	0	M	M
C_j	Basis	Q	P_X	P_Y	P_Z	L_1	L_2	A_1	A_2
1									
M	A_1	2	2	3	0	-1	0	1	0
M	A_2	3	5	$2\frac{1}{2}$	[12]	0	-1	0	1
	Z_j		$7M$	$5\frac{1}{2}M$	$12M$	$-M$	$-M$	M	M
	$C_j - Z_j$		$20-7M$	$25-5\frac{1}{2}M$	$30-12M$	$+M$	$+M$	0	0
2									
M	A_1	2	2	[3]	0	-1	0	1	0
30	P_Z	$\frac{1}{4}$	$\frac{5}{12}$	$\frac{5}{24}$	1	0	$-\frac{1}{12}$	0	$\frac{1}{12}$
	Z_j		$2M+12\frac{1}{2}$	$3M+6\frac{1}{4}$	30	$-M$	$-2\frac{1}{2}$	M	15
	$C_j - Z_j$		$7\frac{1}{2}-2M$	$18\frac{3}{4}-3M$	0	M	$2\frac{1}{2}$	0	$M-15$
3									
25	P_Y	$\frac{2}{3}$	$\frac{2}{3}$	1	0	$-\frac{1}{3}$	0	$\frac{1}{3}$	0
30	P_Z	$\frac{1}{9}$	[$\frac{5}{18}$]	0	1	$\frac{5}{72}$	$-\frac{1}{12}$	$-\frac{5}{72}$	$\frac{1}{12}$
	Z_j		25	25	30	$-\frac{75}{12}$	$-\frac{30}{12}$	$6\frac{1}{4}$	15
	$C_j - Z_j$		-5	0	0	$\frac{75}{12}$	$\frac{30}{12}$	$M-6\frac{1}{4}$	$M-15$
4									
25	P_Y	$\frac{2}{5}$	0	1	$-\frac{12}{5}$	$-\frac{1}{2}$	$\frac{1}{5}$	$\frac{1}{2}$	$-\frac{1}{5}$
20	P_X	$\frac{2}{5}$	1	0	$3\frac{3}{5}$	$\frac{1}{4}$	$-\frac{3}{10}$	$-\frac{1}{4}$	$\frac{3}{10}$
	Z_j	18	20	25	12	$-7\frac{1}{2}$	-1	$7\frac{1}{2}$	11
	$C_j - Z_j$		0	0	18	$7\frac{1}{2}$	1	$M-7\frac{1}{2}$	$M-11$

The Simplex procedure is followed in exactly the same way as in the maximisation case with one exception. Since we wish to minimise a function, we introduce into the basis the variable corresponding to the most negative $C_j - Z_j$ value. Such a variable would reduce cost more per unit than would any other variable. The artificial variables would not appear in the final solution because their C_j values of M would make their $C_j - Z_j$ values less negative than those of other variables.

Selection of the basis variable to be replaced is again based on a comparison of the constant (i.e. the value in the Q column) divided by the corresponding element in the pivotal column. These ratios equal the maximum amount of profit which can be ascribed to each unit of the input in the column, provided that no variables become negative. Thus since P_Z is the new variable to be introduced into the basis (on the $C_j - Z_j$ criterion) the ratios of elements in the Q column to their corresponding elements in the P_Z column are 2/0 and 3/12. Thus the maximum amount of profit ascribable to Z is £∞ and £3/12 in the case of the outputs of A and B respectively. Since we wish both constraint equations to hold with non-negative variable values, the maximum value we can give to P_Z is £3/12 indicating that A_2 is to be reduced to zero. Increasing P_Z by more than this would, as shown by the equation representing the first constraint, reduce A_Z to a negative value, so violating the non-negativity constraint.

Table 8.5 also shows the second, third and fourth tableaux. The final *BFS* is $P_X = 2/5$, $P_Y = 2/5$, $P_Z = 0$, $L_1 = 0$, $L_2 = 0$, which gives a value of $C = £18$. Notice that the solution value of the objective function in the primal is identical with that of the dual. This is always the case. The shadow price of Z is zero. Input Z is not fully employed, and so has a positive slack variable in the primal. Other things equal, what are additional units of Z worth to the firm? In terms of impact on profit, they would have a zero value because they could not increase total output. But X and Y, which are fully employed (zero slack in the primal), do have a positive value, since if the firm could obtain more of them, they could be combined with Z to increase output of A and B and so π_c. What are the values of X and Y at the margin? The imputed values, or shadow prices, are equal to £$\frac{2}{5}$. That is, if an additional unit of either X or Y could be obtained, the firm could increase its π_c by £$\frac{2}{5}$ and so could afford to pay up to that price for a marginal unit input of either X or Y.

We can rewrite the surplus variable of the first constraint as:

$$L_1 = 3P_X + 2P_Y - 2$$

Since $3P_X + 2P_Y$ denotes imputed price and the 2 is the resulting profit, the surplus represents the net 'loss' of using X and Y in A production. The L value for the most profitable product is zero. Therefore all other L values represent opportunity costs of using X and Y in the production of the corresponding output. In the example, since $L_1 = L_2 = 0$, the cost of production

9
Price Policy

The topic of price has always stood at the centre of economic discussion. This chapter begins in the traditional way by examining how profit-maximising businessmen set prices under conditions of varying market structures. The meaning of price discrimination is explained and ways in which firms can take advantage of discriminatory opportunities under, for example, conditions of innovation and product differentiation are detailed. The problems of oligopolistic interdependence and price leadership are looked at. Finally the question is raised as to what role, if any, costs do and should play in price decisions.

9.1 Market Structure and Price Behaviour

Perfect Competition

The characteristics of perfect competition are well known: large numbers of buyers and sellers, none of whom is powerful enough to make a transaction (or withhold from one) which affects the going market price. Products are homogeneous, information about terms of sale is freely available on both sides of the market, and firms have perfect freedom to enter or leave the industry. Under these circumstances firms will accept the going market price, they will be price takers, not price makers, and as such their only decision is to settle on the quantity of output which will maximise their individual profit levels.

This is illustrated in Figure 9.1. Market price will be determined by the interaction of the industry supply and demand curves, SS and DD. The individual firm, which faces the horizontal demand curve of perfect competition, will accept price level P_1, and set its output level at Q_1 where price (which in this case is the same as marginal revenue) equals marginal cost.

Had the minimum point of the firm's AC curve lain below its demand curve, abnormal profits would have been earned, entrants would have been tempted into the industry, and the supply curve, SS, would have fallen downwards to the right until a new and lower equilibrium market price had been arrived at, such that abnormal profits could no longer be earned. The reverse procedure would occur if the market price had been below the

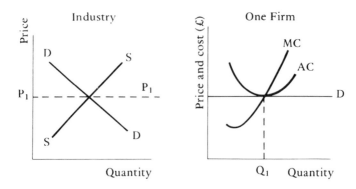

Figure 9.1

minimum level of the firm's *AC* curve. Marginal firms would leave the industry and the market price would rise.

Perfect competition, however, rarely occurs in reality. It is sometimes argued to be present in certain agricultural and other markets, but its prime value to the businessman is the insight it gives into the impact of demand conditions, competition, entry and changing supply conditions on the limits of pricing discretion.

Monopoly

Pure monopoly, like perfect competition, is rare. It implies the sale of a product with no close substitutes by a single firm. The firm here, unlike a perfect competitor, is a price maker, not a price taker. Given the assumption of profit maximisation, a monopolist will price at the point on the demand curve beneath which his marginal revenue and cost curves intersect. In Figure 9.2a this is at price level P_1, given an output level of Q_1. Figures 9.2b and 9.2c show respectively a monopolist's profit-maximising price and output positions when minimum average costs are achieved and when monopoly profits are zero.

In practice it is rare for a firm to be in a situation where it can have such freedom of action as the words 'price maker' suggest.

Few products have no close substitutes. For example, coal and oil, and copper and aluminium are pairs of products between which there is a high cross-elasticity of demand, and so where, if firms set a monopolistically high price, considerable switching of consumer choice might occur. Similarly, even in the absence of close substitutes, firms may hesitate to charge the monopolistic, profit-maximising price from fear of attracting entrants into the industry and so inducing price-cutting competition.

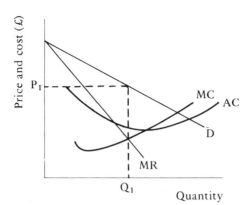

Figure 9.2a

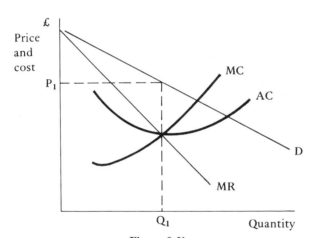

Figure 9.2b

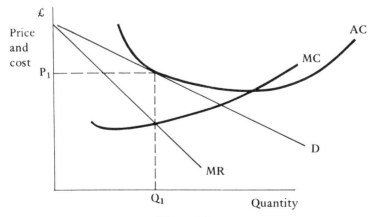

Figure 9.2c

Monopolistic Competition

The writings of Chamberlin on monopolistic competition were one of the major theoretical advances of the 1930s. Most firms do have competitors, but even so, most firms do produce products which are to some degree different from those of their competitors. This fact of economic life produced a degree of dissatisfaction with the polar models of perfect competition and pure monopoly, and it was hoped that the theory of monopolistic competition would improve the realism and utility of economic theory.

The main assumptions of monopolistic competition are first, the presence of large numbers of firms each of which produces a slightly different product from its rivals, thus consumer preferences and so downward-sloping demand curves emerge; second, there is keen rivalry between the firms.

Figure 9.3 illustrates the typical outcome for one such monopolistic competitor. The firm faces two types of demand curve, d_1d_1 and DD. At price P_1 and output Q_1 the firm can assume, given that it initiates a price change, one of two things. Either its rivals will match such a price change, or they will ignore the change. d_1d_1, the more elastic demand curve, rests on the latter assumption, DD on the former.

Given appropriate marginal revenue and marginal cost curves the firm may, to reach the point of marginal equivalency, cut its price from P_1 to P_2 and hope in so doing to increase output to Q_2. It will feel safe in doing this since, given a large number of firms, it assumes that it can act independently of its rivals. As a small firm in the presence of many, it will hope to pass its price cut on unnoticed by competitors. It will hope to move down d_1d_1.

However, because of keen rivalry between firms, the price cut will inevitably be matched. The relevant demand curve is, in fact, DD; d_1d_1 is obsolete and it will 'slide' down DD to position d_2d_2, at output level Q_3.

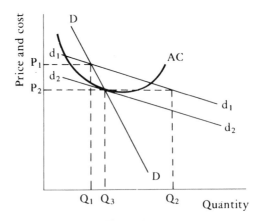

Figure 9.3

Supernormal profits attract entry. *DD* will move left. If losses result, exit and rightwards movement of *DD* will take place. This process will continue until *dd* is tangential to the firm's *AC* curve, no abnormal profits are being made, and there is no incentive, either to cut prices or for new firms to enter the industry. (Note that this outcome is not unlike, indeed it is highly similar to that of Figure 9.2c.)

9.2 Discriminatory Pricing

The Theory: Third Degree

Any monopolist selling one product to two or more different markets or market segments with different price elasticities of demand can always earn at least as much profit as a similar monopolist selling to one market of similar aggregate size, and probably can earn more. He can earn as much profit by setting $MR = MC$ and subdividing the total output between the two markets at the same (profit-maximising) price. However, he also has the possibility of charging different prices in the different markets, and if this is more profitable he will do so. Figure 9.4 shows how this can be done. AR_1, MR_1, AR_2 and MR_2 are, respectively, the demand and marginal revenue curves for markets 1 and 2. ΣMR is the aggregate marginal revenue curve obtained by summing MR_1 and MR_2 horizontally. MC is the firm's marginal cost curve, drawn on the assumption that the firm is producing only one product in one plant location.

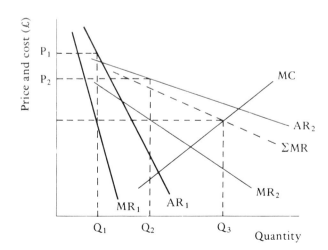

Figure 9.4

The profit-maximising rules for the firm are as follows:

1. Set $\Sigma MR = MC$ to obtain the point of most profitable output i.e. Q_3.
2. Subdivide Q_3 between the two segments, not by equating the prices with the price which could be obtained by travelling vertically up from Q_3 to the aggregate demand curve, but by equating the marginal revenues in each segment with the marginal revenue indicated by the intersection of MC with ΣMR. (If this is not done then it would pay the firm to transfer output from the segment where MR is lower to that segment where it is higher, until equality was obtained, at a given fixed total output.)
3. This results in different, discriminatory prices, P_1 and P_2, being charged in the two segments provided the price elasticity of demand differs between the two markets at a common price. (We can predict which segment will pay the higher price algebraically. Given that $MR = P(1 + 1/\eta)$ then if MR_1 is to equal MR_2 the higher the value of η the lower will be the price.) Thus leakage must be minimal or customers in market 2 will buy at price P_2 and resell to customers in market 1 at a price between P_1 and P_2. Hence the seller must have some degree of monopoly power for price discrimination to be profitable. In a perfectly competitive market arbitrage would equalise price differentials.
4. The product must be homogeneous to obtain a single MC curve.
Or
5. Any cost involved in sealing off the segment to prevent leakage must be less than the extra revenue which can be obtained by practising discrimination.

Notice that the demand in each market is represented by a separate demand curve. This is not the case with two other types of price discrimination which are distinguished in theory.

First Degree

In this case the firm is assumed to know the demand curve which each customer has for its product and charges each the highest price which the consumer is willing to pay for each unit. Hence consumer A would be willing to pay more for the first unit of a good than for the second, and so on. In terms of the aggregate demand curve for the product, since each additional unit sold increases TR by the price of that unit (the price for earlier units remaining higher), the demand curve is also the MR curve. As with third-degree discrimination, a necessary condition for profitable first-degree discrimination is that arbitrage is prevented. In addition, each customer must have a different reservation price for each unit otherwise (s)he would not be willing to pay a different price for each unit. The same amount of TR and aggregate output would result if the producer offered a certain quantity to a consumer for one and only one price equal to the area under the consumer's demand curve up to that output: a 'take it or leave it price'.

Second Degree

In second degree price discrimination there is no price distinction between consumers, but there is between 'blocks' of output. An additional block of units will be produced only if the *TR* from its sale exceeds the *TC* from its production.

The Practice

Stigler has defined price discrimination as 'the sale of technically similar products at prices which are not proportional to their marginal costs'. This definition enables us to get away from the strictly homogeneous product examined in the figure and to understand how price discrimination can be practised more actively by actually incurring costs to seal off market segments. There are at least six different situations in which different prices can be charged for basically the same product, viz. when differences occur in: quantity, product type, location, time, product use, and stage of market development. The management task is to spot such opportunities as exist if and when there are different segments with different degrees of demand elasticity and with minimal leakage. The following list of examples is by no means exhaustive.

Quantity   Discounts are often awarded by firms to customers who buy in bulk. The granting of discounts may be made to large customers as a *quid pro quo* for the cost saving per unit the firm can make as a result of the bulk sale.

   Alternatively, a discount may be awarded in return for a function which the customer implicitly carries out on behalf of the firm. Thus, a wholesaler typically receives a larger discount from a manufacturer than does a retailer since the wholesaler performs several marketing functions, such as salesmanship, storage and distribution to retail outlets, on behalf of the manufacturer. It should be noted, however, that the charging of different prices as a result of the granting of discounts is only price discrimination as strictly defined, if, and only if, the net prices are disproportional to the marginal costs of the trades made.

Product type   Market segments have different demand elasticities because buyers differ, for example, in preferences, in incomes, in tastes, in the information about products which they receive, and in the way that they process that information. These differences can be capitalised on by varying slightly the basic product, either tangibly, or intangibly through advertising, but doing so at an incremental cost less than the incremental revenue which can be gained by so doing. Thus, any price insensitivities which may be present in a market segment may be reinforced, while simultaneously the product differences make it less likely that leakage will occur.

Examples can be seen in any car manufacturer's product list where the same basic car is sold for a range of prices which are ostensibly justified to the segments concerned by the difference in engine size, numbers of carburettors, vinyl roof covering and other 'extras', which albeit adding to the manufacturing cost, generally do so by a smaller amount than can be added to the price.

Location   At least three types of price discrimination by location may be distinguished.

Uniform delivered pricing.   The same delivered price is charged at all destinations regardless of the buyer's location. Since the marginal costs of supplying a customer closer to a plant will be less than the marginal costs for a distant customer, price discrimination occurs. An example of this is the Asda chain of superstores which charges identical prices in each outlet in the entire UK for identical products.

Zone pricing.   In this case the seller divides a country into geographic zones and charges the same delivered price in each zone, but between zones the price differs. Two groups of buyers are discriminated against. Firstly, the marginal transport costs to those buyers nearest the seller within any one zone would be less than those to a seller on the far boundary of the zone. Secondly, two buyers, one on either side of a boundary, would have almost identical marginal transport costs but would be charged different prices.

Freight equalisation pricing.   The seller charges the buyer a transport cost which the buyer would pay if he bought from the nearest supplier. One way

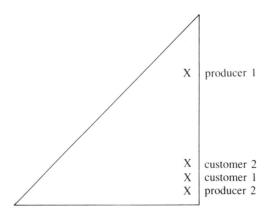

in which this may operate is where the seller quotes a delivered price which covers the transport cost from his competitor's plant and pays the transport cost from his own plant. Hence in the diagram above (which crudely represents a map of Britain) producer 1 charges customer 1 a lower price than he charges customer 2 because customer 1 is closer to producer 2 than is customer 2 and so would incur lower transport costs from producer 2's plant. Hence $p_1 < p_2$. But the marginal costs resulting from transporting an additional unit from producer 1's plant is greater for customer 1 than for customer 2 because of the greater distance from producer 1 to customer 1 compared with that to customer 2. Hence $MC_1 > MC_2$. Therefore $p_1/MC_1 < p_2/MC_2$ and so price discrimination occurs.

Time For price discrimination to be practised by time, the product must be non-storable, otherwise leakage will occur. For example most people prefer to take their holidays in July or August, not in April or October. Thus a higher price can be charged at the peak periods when demand is less elastic. The lower prices in the off-peak periods simultaneously encourage a smoothing of demand, help utilise overheads, such as aircraft and hotels, in slack times, and take the strain off overloaded facilities.

The pricing practices of the electricity industry with its on-peak and off-peak tariffs is a similar case, although in this instance we again see the danger of equating price differences with price discrimination. At off-peak periods only the highly efficient, low marginal cost nuclear powered stations are working and are providing the base load. As demand rises through the day first the oil-fired stations, and finally the coal-fired stations are brought on stream. In other words, the on-peak user is not only paying a higher price, but is consuming coal-generated electricity which has the highest marginal cost of all.

The extent of price discrimination, if any, can only be identified by knowledge of the precise and relevant cost and price schedules.

Product Use The same product can be used by different people, with different price sensitivities, in different ways. Thus the same seat on a public transport vehicle is 'used' differently by a child than by an adult. If the full fare was charged for the child, however, the parent might not take the child on the journey. The demand elasticity of the two users differs. Similarly, telephones used for business purposes by business firms are 'used' differently from those of domestic households. The business firm presumably regards the telephone as a 'must', the household may regard it as more of a luxury and so a higher tariff can be charged to the business user.

New Product Pricing Price discrimination can also be practised by stage of market development. This introduces the problem of new product pricing and how to price the product as it progresses through the various stages of the product life cycle (see Figure A4.1).

Joel Dean has argued that the choice lies somewhere between the two conceptual extremes of a skimming policy and a penetration policy.

Skimming Policy   This is a policy of relatively high prices, plus heavy promotional expenditures in the early stages, and progressively lower prices at later stages in the life cycle. Dean suggests that it will be of primary value when the following conditions hold good:

(a) The product is a major departure from alternatives previously available, since then demand will be relatively price-inelastic due partly to a desire to be 'one up on the Jones's' and partly to product unfamiliarity, and so a resulting inability to link price with cost so that a judgment can be made as to what sort of price is 'fair'.

(b) When little is known about the elasticity of demand of the various market segments, price can be gradually lowered from a high level until the optimum level is attained; the opposite procedure, starting with a low price and discovering after the event that the market would willingly have paid a higher price is difficult to reverse without considerable loss of consumer goodwill.

(c) Starting with a high price is a good way of breaking the market up into segments with different demand elasticities; the profitable 'cream' can be 'skimmed' from the least price-sensitive segment before making successive price reductions and skimming, in turn, the progressively more price-sensitive segments.

(d) High initial prices may not necessarily be the most profitable long-run policy, but they may be necessary to generate the highest possible cash flow early in the product life cycle, in order to contribute to tooling-up, research and development, and promotional costs.

Penetration Pricing   This is a policy of relatively low prices on market launch. Given that the product life cycle is S-shaped it should be adopted with a view to long-run not short-run profits. The bottom part of the S with low unit sales has still to be passed through, irrespective of price level. This policy, Dean suggests, is of primary value when:

(a) there is a high price elasticity of demand, enabling the mass market to be penetrated quickly and so, correspondingly, abbreviating the length of time before the life cycle curve begins to accelerate upwards,

(b) there are substantial unit cost savings as a result of a large throughput,

(c) the firm wishes to discourage new and rival entrants.

When the life cycle reaches the stage of market maturity and saturation, however, some entrants will most probably have appeared, design and production technology will be stabilising, competing products will not be dissimilar and the situation may well be approaching the condition known as oligopoly.

A Numerical Example

The calculus can be used to accomplish price discrimination provided that the firm knows its TC functions and the demand functions for the markets it is selling to. Thus, with two markets X and Y, TR_x and $TR_y = P_xQ_x$ and P_yQ_y respectively. Differentiation provides MR_x, MR_y and MC. For optimal price discrimination the three must be set equal to each other. Each of these equations are sterling values expressed in terms of Q. Thus Q_x and Q_y are found and P_x and P_y from the demand functions. As an illustration, let:

$$P_x = 2 - Q_x, \; P_y = 3 - 2Q_y$$

and $\quad MC = Q + 0.1$

where $\quad Q = Q_x + Q_y$

then $\quad MR_x = 2 - 2Q_x$ $\hfill (9.1)$

and $\quad MR_y = 3 - 4Q_y$ $\hfill (9.2)$

and $\quad MC = Q_y + Q_x + 0.1$ $\hfill (9.3)$

(Note: MR can be obtained from TR by differentiating.)

Solving (9.1), (9.2) and (9.3) simultaneously, we obtain:

$$Q_x = 0.47 \text{ and } Q_y = 0.49$$

and from the demand equations:

$$P_x = 1.53 \text{ and } P_y = 2.02$$

From this we can obtain the firm's TR, namely:

$$1.53 \times 0.47 + 2.02 \times 0.49 = £1.71$$

and if the TC equation had been $0.1 + 0.5Q^2 + 0.1Q$
then TC would be $0.1 + 0.5(0.47 + 0.49)^2 + 0.1(0.47 + 0.49) = £0.66$
Hence total profit is £1.05.

What if the firm had refused to price-discriminate? This means it would have let $P_y = P_x$ at $MR = MC$. Our analysis tells us that profits would have been lower. Let us prove this. Maximise:

$$\pi = TR - TC$$

subject to $P_y = P_x$ or $P_y - P_x = 0$

If we use the Lagrange multiplier we have:

$$\begin{aligned}
\pi_\lambda &= 2Q_x - Q_x^2 + 3Q_y - 2Q_y^2 - 0.1 - 0.5Q_x^2 - 0.5Q_y^2 - Q_xQ_y - 0.1Q_x \\
&\quad - 0.1Q_y + \lambda(2 - Q_x - 3 + 2Q_y) \\
&= 1.9Q_x - 1.5Q_x^2 + 2.9Q_y - 2.5Q_y^2 - 0.1 - Q_xQ_y + \lambda(-1 - Q_x + 2Q_y)
\end{aligned}$$

let $\quad \dfrac{\partial \pi_\lambda}{\partial Q_x} = 0 = 1.9 - 3Q_x - Q_y - \lambda$ $\hfill (9.4)$

$$\frac{\partial \pi_\lambda}{\partial Q_y} = 0 = 2.9 - 5Q_y - Q_x + 2\lambda \qquad (9.5)$$

and $\frac{\partial \pi_\lambda}{\partial \lambda} = 0 = -1 - Q_x + 2Q_y$ \qquad (9.6)

Solving simultaneously gives $Q_y = 0.65$, $Q_x = 0.3$, $\lambda = -0.3$ and hence $P_x = 1.7$, $P_y = 1.7$ and $\pi = £0.965$.

9.3 Oligopolistic Interdependence

Oligopoly exists when a few large firms compete against each other. How does this affect behaviour? In a word, interdependence — an interdependence of policies and decisions which is recognised by each oligopolist. Any decision one firm makes, be it on price, on product or on promotion, will affect the trade of competitors and so result in countermoves. As a result, one's competitors' behaviour will depend on one's own behaviour, and this must be taken account of when decisions are made.

This interdependence makes prediction difficult and so advice as to optimal decision taking is in turn very hard to give. Kinked demand curve theory is often used to explain the behaviour patterns of oligopolists. Price leadership and non-price competition are methods used to remove or to lessen the uncertainties of interdependence which surround their decisions. Insights can also be provided by the theory of games.

The Kinked Demand Curve

The assumption behind the theory of kinked demand is that each oligopolist will act and react in a way that keeps conditions tolerable for all members of the industry. This is most likely to occur where products are very similar. As a consequence, prices must be similar, otherwise if one firm is selling at a lower price than competitors, these competitors will be forced to lower their prices to match his. Alternatively, the lower priced firm will raise his price to match the levels of the remaining oligopolists. The firm will probably realise that it is better for him to accommodate his rivals rather than start a price war. Sticky prices tend to result with firms unwilling to raise prices; and unwilling to cut prices from fear of initiating a price war.

Figure 9.5 uses the pair of demand curves dd' and DD', which are the relevant curves for one oligopolist drawn on the assumptions, with which we are now familiar, of rivals price matching in the case of DD', and ignoring price changes in the case of dd'. Given a price of P_1, the oligopolist, on the arguments laid out above, will assume that the relevant demand curve for his situation is the combination of the two segments dX and XD', namely dXD' with a kink indicating price stability at X.

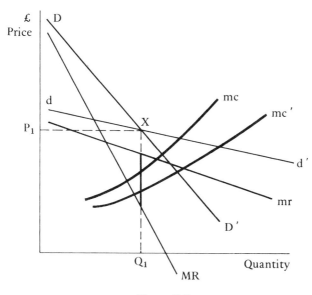

Figure 9.5

In an inflationary situation or in a time of high demand, this analysis can possibly help explain why oligopolistic prices tend not to be stable, but to be frequently altered and that in an upward direction. In such circumstances the individual oligopolist may believe that the kink is reversed. The relevant demand curve becomes DXd'. Oligopolists will follow one another's price increase. The public relations of this during inflation is, of course, easy. The firms merely need to express regret at the unavoidable passing on of increases, real or imagined, in the prices they pay for inputs.

Conversely, if one oligopolist has surplus capacity in conditions of high demand, he can cut his price to generate extra output in the relative confidence that his fellow oligopolists will continue to work at full capacity at the original price.

In Figure 9.5 moreover, it is clear that cost conditions can change (e.g. from MC to MC') with no alteration of marginal equivalency. This is due to the vertical 'gap' in the relevant marginal revenue curve. Marginal revenue is denoted by mr to the left of the vertical XQ_1 (and is derived from dd') and is denoted by MR to the right of this position (being derived from DD'). Similarly, demand conditions can change (as indicated by a rightward or leftwards movement in the demand curve dXD') with no change in the pricing implications given by the equivalency of marginal revenues and costs (as in Figure 9.6).

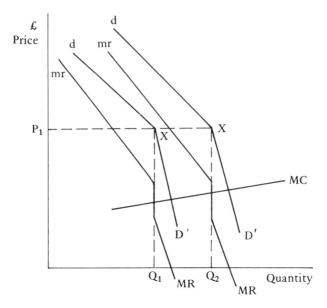

Figure 9.6

Reducing Interdependence

Oligopoly tends to reduce the freedom of action a firm has in taking price decisions. One way to regain some measure of initiative is to reduce the cross-elasticity of demand between one's own products and one's rivals by means of product differentiation. The differences can be real or illusory, and will generally be backed by advertising in order to reinforce any consumer preferences, and so relative price independence, which might emerge.

Non-price competition of this sort has considerable attractions to the oligopolists. It makes it less likely that he will lose sales if his rival cuts prices, or if he raises them. Moreover, if a firm takes the initiative in non-price competition, the time lag which must elapse before competitors can produce an effective countermove is relatively long.

A price cut can be matched instantaneously and so the competitive advantage it brings is eliminated. A new product variation or a changed advertising campaign, however, cannot be countered so rapidly.

Reducing Uncertainty through Price Leadership

Another alternative open to the firm is to opt out of the uncertainty surrounding pricing decisions in oligopoly by deliberately choosing a pattern of price parallelism. This is a situation where one firm takes the initiating role in all price changes in the relative confidence that others will follow, matching his lead. Three types of price leadership are commonly distinguished in the literature: dominant firm price leadership, collusive price leadership and barometric price leadership. The first of these has no apparent initial connection with oligopolistic market structure, but is still of relevance here. Firstly, it is the model for which a theory has been most elegantly developed, but secondly, and more importantly, it is a situation which has a strong tendency to devolve into an oligopoly.

Dominant Firm Price Leadership

This model rests on the assumption that the industry is composed of one large firm and a competitive fringe of small firms. The dominant firm sets the price, the others follow and sell all they can at that price. The dominant firm, the price leader, supplies the remainder of the market which is not satisfied by the fringe companies. Thus, although he is a price leader, he is a quantity follower. (Implicitly his price is just marginally higher than that of the fringe.)

Figure 9.7 illustrates how the leader determines his profit-maximising price given these assumptions. D_m is the market demand curve. ΣS_{cf} is the supply curve of the competitive fringe.

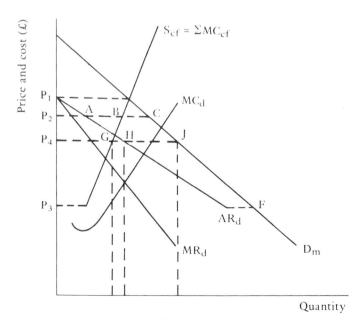

Figure 9.7

It is the amount estimated by the leader which will be supplied by fringe firms at various prices. It is equal to the sum of the individual MC curves of the fringe firms, in as much as they lie above their respective average variable cost curves. Thus, at price P_1 the dominant firm would sell nothing; the fringe would be willing and able to supply all the market's needs at that price.

At price P_2 total demand is equal to P_2C, the fringe would produce P_2B, leaving BC to be supplied by the dominant firm. If on the line P_2C the point A is placed such that $P_2A = BC$, then point A is on the dominant firm's demand curve where the price is P_2. This can be repeated for a series of prices and series of points like A to produce the dominant firm's demand curve, AR_d. Any price below P_3 is below the foot of the supply curve of the competitive fringe. Below this price they would not cover their average variable costs and so would refuse to supply. Consequently, the dominant firm's demand curve becomes the market demand curve below P_3, namely the line $P_1AR_dFD_m$.

The dominant firm will set its price at P_4, where $MR_d = MC_d$. The fringe will accept this price, and produce the quantity $P_4G = HJ$, leaving P_4H to be produced by the dominant firm.

This situation, however, could be one of unstable equilibrium. It may move either towards monopoly or oligopoly. If the price set allows positive profits to the fringe companies, entry will be encouraged at the expense of the dominant firm's market share; also fringe firms will be motivated to expand, either by merger or internally, to obtain the benefits of scale economies, again at the expense of the dominant firm's position.

Alternatively, the dominant firm may deviate from this pattern of leadership in price and followership in quantity, and change his objectives from short-run profit maximisation to one of aggressive long-run profit maximisation. In other words, aggressive price cutting may enable him to put many of the fringe firms out of business, enabling him to capture a monopoly or near monopoly share of the market.[1] There are other alternatives to these strategies which are discussed below under the topic of 'entry barriers'.

To apply calculus to the dominant firm model is not difficult. Consider a case where there is a fringe, c, of 20 firms. Suppose each such firm has:

$$MC = 10 + 8q \tag{9.7}$$

where q = output for each fringe member.

---

1   It is this fear of entry which may make the dominant firm reduce price to P_3 where entry is no longer profitable. The firm would expand until its MC had shifted rightwards and coincided with the foot of the LAC, whether it be L- or U-shaped. The dominant firm's relevant demand curve would then be P_3FD_M. It was from an argument of this nature and his theory of costs (see pp. 203–208) that Andrews argued that demand is effectively a horizontal line over the relevant range and price a constant mark-up over an L-shaped LAC.

$$\Rightarrow \Sigma\, MC = 10+0.4Q_c$$

(horizontal aggregation implies an unchanged intercept and a slope 20 times as gentle as that of an individual firm.)[2] For each fringe member,

$$P = MC$$

Hence

$$P = 10+0.4Q_c$$
$$\Rightarrow Q_c = S_{cf} = 2.5P-25 \tag{9.8}$$

Let the market demand be:

$$P = 50-Q \tag{9.9}$$
$$\Rightarrow Q = 50-P \tag{9.10}$$

AR_d is equation $(9.10)-(9.8)$ or

$$Q_d = 75-3.5P \tag{9.11}$$
$$\Rightarrow P = 21.43-0.29Q_d \tag{9.12}$$

and (with slope doubled)

$$MR_d = 21.43-0.58Q_d \tag{9.13}$$

Let $MC_d = 12$
Then for profit maximisation by the dominant firm: $MR_d = 12$ and we obtain $Q_d = 16.26$ units.
By substitution in (9.12) P for the dominant firm is £16.78.
By substitution in (9.8) Q_c for the fringe is 16.71 units.
Hence total Q is 33.04 units. By substituting this value in the market demand function (9.9) we obtain a market price of £16.75 (except for rounding errors) so verifying our results.

Collusive Price Leadership

When oligopoly is established, collusive price leadership may emerge. The co-ordination of prices which is apparent to the outside observer may well, of course, not require explicit but merely tacit collusion. An implicit recognition by all firms that one of them is taking the initiative with group interests in mind is all that is required. The leader may well be the largest firm in the group, and historically may also have been a 'dominant firm'. Where one seller has a larger share than others, the others may feel it sensible to match any increase he makes. If they do not he may rescind his increase, the smaller

---

2   When horizontally aggregating we set $MC_1 = MC_2 = \ldots = MC_n$ and add the corresponding qs. Hence from equation (9.7) $q = (MC-10)/8 \Rightarrow Q_c = q_1 + q_2 + \ldots + q_{20} = 20q = [20/8][MC-10] \Rightarrow MC = 10+0.4Q_c$.

firms will have gained little or nothing by way of increased sales, and will have forgone the increased revenue available had they raised their prices in line with the original increase. Similarly, smaller sellers are also likely to follow the leader's price reductions.

It is also probable that the leader is or has been the lowest cost seller. Low costs enable a firm to take the initiative in lowering price, and other sellers have little alternative but to follow. On the other hand, however, such cost advantages have to be tempered by statesmanship. Otherwise, setting a price which is too low for some higher cost rivals might trigger off a price war which could leave all firms, including the leader, worse off then they need have been. The beneficiary would be the firm with the greatest financial reserves, not necessarily the price leader.

Barometric Price Leadership

The leader with a large market share and low cost levels is not only plagued with the difficulties of exercising 'statesmanship' within the group, but he may also be regarded as highly suspect by the outside 'watchdogs' of industry such as the Director General of Fair Trading and the Monopolies and Mergers Commission. This may make him reluctant to accept the role of leader and the mantle may fall to another, smaller firm, the 'barometric' leader.

The barometric price leader is a firm which is followed even if it does not have a substantial market share. While it need not be the lowest cost firm in the industry, it certainly must be an efficient firm. The barometric firm, to maintain a leadership position, must be acknowledged by the rest of the group as a company which has a 'nose' for detecting changes in demand or cost conditions. His price alterations in reaction to such changes must be in accord with the common interests of the other sellers in the group. The barometric leader has little or no power to impose his decisions on the group and as a result his leadership may not be prolonged. The leadership may move from firm to firm, or price leadership and parallelism may even break down.

Game Theory

The theory of games, when first published by Von Neumann and Morgenstern raised new hope, as yet unrealised, that a definitive solution to the oligopoly problem might be available. Game theory moves away from predictions of rivals' countermoves based on experience or on probabilistic estimates towards a deductive approach based on the determination of the most profitable countermoves which will be made towards one's own 'best' strategy and to derive the relevant defensive measures. Generally game theory is restricted to duopoly. In itself this is a major limitation to its practicality.

Two-Person, Zero-Sum Game

In the zero (or constant) sum game, what one player or firm loses the other wins; the size of the cake is fixed. Consider two profit-maximising oligopolists, A and B, with profits directly related to market share. The problem is to arrive at a price aimed at yielding the largest market share for A while bearing in mind that B has an identical aim. Assume, simplistically, that all of A's possible prices are known, and that their outcomes can be evaluated making due allowances for each of the (known) price options of B. This information is summarised in a payoff matrix for A and analysed in terms of maximin for him and minimax for B. Table 9.1 illustrates this. A's alternative prices (or other strategies) are denoted by S_{A1}, S_{A2} and S_{A3}; B's by S_{B1} to S_{B4}. The payoffs are the market shares A will obtain for each combination of such pure strategies. A similar payoff matrix could be constructed for B, the basis for constructing it, given a zero-sum game, being merely that B's market share, for any given pair of prices will equal 100% less A's market share.

Table 9.1 A's Market Share (%)

		B's Strategies			
		S_{B1}	S_{B2}	S_{B3}	S_{B4}
A's Strategies	S_{A1}	50	55	65	70
	S_{A2}	40	45	60	65
	S_{A3}	30	40	55	60

A maximin approach for A will be chosen since he assumes that B will be doing his best to ensure that, for A, the worst possible competitive situation will occur. Conversely, Table 9.1 can be analysed for B on minimax principles. B will look for the best outcome for A (and so the worst for himself) in each column. The worst of these (minimax), and so the best of the worst from B's viewpoint, will be chosen. A will consequently select strategy S_{A1} and B strategy S_{B1}.

When S_{A1} and S_{B1} respectively are chosen, both A and B have their worst fears realised, but neither will wish to change his decision. Such an equilibrium is known as a saddle point. (Clearly, of course, a maximin strategy, although safe, is not the most profitable alternative when one's rival is not himself well-informed on the available strategies and/or is not himself a prudent decision taker!)

Pure strategy saddle points (which occur where a value is a row minimum and a column maximum) need not exist. Consider Table 9.2. Here A has a maximin strategy of S_{A1} and B a minimax strategy of S_{B2}. This is not a saddle

Table 9.2 A's Market Share (%)

		B's Strategies		
		S_{B1}	S_{B2}	S_{B3}
A's Strategies	S_{A1}	50	55	65
	S_{A2}	60	45	40

point since the maximin strategy combination of S_{A1}, S_{B1} does not coincide with the minimax strategy combination of S_{B2}, S_{A1}. This is not an equilibrium situation since, given the opportunity to choose anew, if B thought A would stick to S_{A1}, B would select instead S_{B1}. Acting on this, A will select S_{A2} rather than S_{A1}. But B could, in turn, anticipate this reasoning process by A and so would actually choose S_{B3}. Once again A would carry his reasoning a step further, and so on. In this situation unlike a saddle point, the maximin and minimax strategy combinations of the duopolists do not coincide.

One can, however, devise a *mixed strategy* for such situations. Mixed strategies are combinations of pure strategies whereby each pure strategy is selected with a given probability. The objective is to compute the relevant expected maximin (and minimax) strategy combination payoff. This expected payoff is the weighted average of the payoffs which would have been obtained had the respective pure strategies been chosen. The weights are the probabilities with which the pure strategies have been chosen.

To prevent B predicting with certainty which strategy A will adopt, A will select his pure strategies randomly with a probability of p_i. The problem is to select p_i so as to maximise the minimum expected gain. If B should select S_{B1}, A's *expected* gain would be 50% multiplied by the relevant value of p_1, plus 60% times the relevant value of p_2, or $\sum_{i=1}^{2} p_i . M_{iB1}$, where M_{iB1} is A's market share under i conditions of S_{B1}. Given that *some* mixed strategy exists that will assure an expected gain of at least X, then A will want to set p_i so that $\sum_{i=1}^{2} p_i . M_{iB1} \geqslant X$. X is unknown but it must be greater than 50% since, given Table 9.2, 50% is the worst possible result for A under S_{B1}. In a similar manner, the choice of p_i must be made so that if B selects S_{B2} or S_{B3} then $\sum_{i=1}^{2} p_i . M_{iB2} \geqslant X$ and $\sum_{i=1}^{2} p_i . M_{iB3} \geqslant X$. As probabilities it must also be true that $p_i \geqslant 0$ and $\sum_{i=1}^{2} p_i = 1.0$.

What we have now are the elements of the following linear programming problem:

maximise X subject to the constraints

$$0.5 \ p_1 + 0.6 \ p_2 - X \geqslant 0$$
$$0.55p_1 + 0.45p_2 - X \geqslant 0$$
$$0.65p_1 + 0.4 \ p_2 - X \geqslant 0$$
$$p_1 + p_2 = 1.0$$

and the general non-negativity requirements[1]

$$p_1, p_2 \geqslant 0$$

The solution of this problem is $p_1 = 0.57$ and $p_2 = 0.43$ which gives a value for X of 55%, A's expected maximin market share. Simultaneously, of course, B will be equally anxious to minimise A's expected payoff. His problem can be stated thus:

minimise X' subject to the constraints

$$0.5p_1' + 0.55p_2' + 0.65p_3' - X' \geqslant 0$$
$$0.6p_1' + 0.45p_2' + 0.4 \ p_3' - X' \geqslant 0$$
$$p_1' + p_2' + p_3' = 1.0$$

and the non-negativity requirements

$$p_1', p_2', p_3' \geqslant 0$$

The solution to this problem is $p_1' = 0.75$, $p_2' = 0$, $p_3' = 0.25$ which gives a value for X' of 55%. It is obvious that for both A and B to reach their objectives X must equal X'. This, in fact, has been shown to hold. A and B will each choose their pure strategies at random, subject only to the values of the respective probabilities. Strategy S_{B2} will never be employed. Over a sufficiently long time period or number of observations, A will achieve an average market share of 55% and B one of 45%. The random element is essential since if A, for example, merely followed S_{A1} non-randomly for 57% of the time and S_{A2} non-randomly for 43% of the time, then a regular pattern of choice might emerge. B might detect this regularity and take advantage of it.

---

1   In this example p_1 and p_2 must both be > 0 to avoid either strategy being selected alone. It has already been noted that such a choice is unstable. Hence when introducing slack variables into the three expressions to render them equations, we have four equations and six unknowns. The basic LP assumption for algebraic solution is that any two of the unknowns equal zero at a corner. Hence only 4 unknowns and 4 equations will exist (p. 225). Solutions are then obtained for X, letting any two such variables equal zero and selecting the solution which provides the greatest value for X. Since p_1 and p_2 must be greater than zero, only equation systems with two of the slack variables equal to zero need be considered. These values can be checked by the interested reader. Manual calculation requires subtraction of the three slack variables, S_1, S_2 and S_3 from the constraints to provide four constraint equations.

This result means that there will always exist a pair of mixed strategies which constitute an equilibrium pair in the sense that neither party can do any better for himself while the other also pursues such an optimal mixed strategy.

Two-Person Non-Constant-Sum Games

Games of this sort, in which some outcomes are more favourable to the participants jointly than others, are called non-constant-sum games or the 'prisoners' dilemma' case. Consider the combined game theory payoff matrix of Table 9.3. Firm A's strategies and their payoffs are in the bottom left hand corner of the relevant square, and firm B's in the top right. Both are profit maximisers. The incentives to engage in some form of collusion are high. If both firms raise prices each will make a profit of £10.

Table 9.3

		B	
		price up	*price down*
A	*price up*	10 10	20 −15
	price down	−15 20	6 6

Conversely, the incentive to cheat on the collusive agreement is also present. If either A or B reduces prices alone, profits will rise from £10 to £20. The firm which does not reduce price, however, will soon follow or it would be forced into a £15 loss.

Thus non-constant-sum games provide many insights into the theories of kinked demand, pricing and price leadership. They are not, however, as fertile in providing normative solutions as we might wish.

Collusive Pricing and Cartels

To avoid the uncertainties of pricing decisions and the downward pressure on prices which competition exerts, firms frequently come to express or implied agreements to maintain prices at a similar level. Although express agreements are frequently declared illegal under the provisions of the Fair Trading Act, the same end result is often aimed at by means of tacit collusion.

Individual firms, however, frequently find it worthwhile to break out of any such agreement, whether tacit or overt. There are three reasons for this: the 'free rider' problem, varying cost conditions, and shifting demand patterns.

Figure 9.8 illustrates the first of these problems. In panel (b) D_I represents the industry demand curve. S is the market supply curve, obtained by aggregating horizontally the MC curves of the numerous independent sellers in the industry. Without collusion the market price would be P_1 and the quantity produced and sold would be Q_1 where $P = MC$. Any single seller would produce and sell Q_4 units, where $Q_4 = Q_1/n$ where $n =$ the number of (equal sized) firms in the market. If any single seller were to sell an additional unit, his marginal revenue would be insignificantly different from P_1. For the group as a whole, however, MR would be significantly below market price. (Geometrically this is obscured in the figure since the quantity axis in panel (a) is a 'stretched out' version of the same axis in the second.)

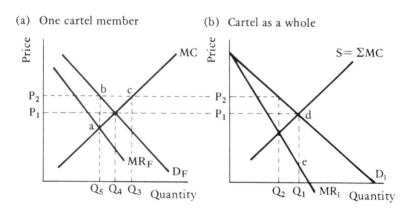

(a) One cartel member   (b) Cartel as a whole

(Quantity axes drawn on different scales.)

Figure 9.8

If the sellers collude as a single monopoly, the profit-maximising price–output combination is P_2Q_2 where $\Sigma MC = MR_I$. As long as all firms have identical MC curves, P_2 is also the optimum price for the individual cartel member. Since we are assuming that all sellers act in concert, when one reduces quantity there will be a perceptible effect on price. If a single seller acted alone, his demand curve would be almost horizontal at P_1, but since what any one does they all do, D_F, the 'share-of-the-market' curve is the relevant demand curve.

Had the two panels in the figure been drawn on the same (quantity) scale, the distance $(Q_1 - Q_2)$ would be n times as great as $(Q_4 - Q_5)$. Given concerted action the profit-maximising output for the single firm is Q_5 at the cartel price P_2 where $MC = MR_F$. Now joint profit maximisation has been made possible, 'free riding' can occur.

Each colluder is expected only to supply Q_5. This is a quota which somehow the cartel must enforce. But each firm realises that if he alone supplies more than Q_5, the effect on price will be negligible. P_2 is the price each firm must take. If a firm acts alone, P_2 is his marginal revenue curve. The quantity that then maximises profit (under these changed assumptions and given that others continue to price at P_2) is Q_3. The individual seller makes a profit gain of abc. Since this opportunity is open to all, the probability is very high that one or a few firms will seize it. A cartel may be a 'gentleman's agreement' but, as Stigler pithily pointed out, 'the participants seldom are, or long do'. Each firm will be tempted to gain a 'free ride' on the anti-competitive behaviour of his fellows. Since profits attract entrepreneurs like honey attracts bees then, unless a sufficiently powerful overseeing body can enforce the output quotas and/or inhibit new entry, the cartel will inevitably crumble. Generally only a state or government agency has such far-reaching inquisitorial powers of inspection and enforcement.

In Figure 9.8 we assumed that each firm's MC curve was in the same position so that equal quotas resulted in equal marginal costs. Suppose, however, that marginal costs vary. Assume as in Figure 9.9 that there are only two sellers and that the collusive agreement is that each will supply half the quantity demanded at each price. D_F is consequently the 'share-of-the-market' demand curve for each firm and the MR curve for the group as a whole. MR_F is each firm's perceived marginal revenue curve and MC_A and MC_B are the MC curves for firms A and B.

The optimum prices for A and B are thus different, namely P_A and P_B.

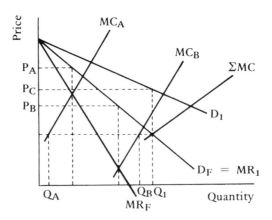

Figure 9.9

They will disagree over which price should be set for the group. Moreover, the cartel's optimum price, P_C, is not the optimum for either of the two firms. Cartel profits are maximised, not when the quantity to be produced is necessarily divided equally, but rather $MR_1 = \Sigma MC$, given when optimum output Q_1 is divided so that $MC_A = MC_B$ in order that each firm might have the same marginal cost. (If $MC_A \neq MC_B$ at any output level, then output reallocation should take place between the two firms until the marginal equivalency condition again holds. Without such reallocation the cartel would not be minimising costs and so would not, even if operating at the profit-maximising output level, be maximising the difference betwen revenue and costs.) Thus, if an output of Q_1 and a price P_C could be agreed upon, the cartel would face formidable difficulties in allocating output in the profit-maximising manner. Firm A would wish to produce more than Q_A and B less than Q_B. Again only an agency with strong powers of coercion could ensure that the cartel would not disintegrate. Again this is likely only if some governmental body exercises industrial oversight.

The problem of maintaining cartel prices is further enhanced if to the temptations of cheating and the problems of varying costs is added the hazard of shifting demand. Figure 9.10, a variant of which was first suggested by Scherer, illustrates this and shows how the problem is at its most intense in the case of firms with high fixed or overhead costs. Figure 9.10 shows two firms with identical demand curves D_1 (representing boom conditions) and D_2 (representing slump). For simplicity D_2 and MR_1 are deemed to be graphically identical. In panel (a) a firm with low fixed costs is represented and in (b) a firm with high fixed costs.

In both cases profit-maximising behaviour in boom conditions requires identical prices of P_1 and outputs of Q_1.

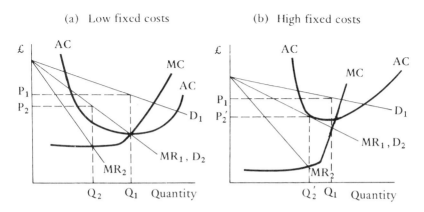

Figure 9.10

Although *MC* is constant for both firms up to the same level of output (or designed capacity of the firms' plants) because of their different cost structures it is much higher in the low fixed cost case than in the other case. As a consequence, when demand falls to D_2, the low fixed cost firm will contract output substantially and price at P_2. The high fixed cost firm will reduce price to P_2', and output, at Q_2', will be larger than at Q_2. However, although both firms are still pursuing profit-maximising behaviour the high fixed cost firm is now barely breaking even, but the low fixed cost firm is still making a significant absolute profit (albeit lower than before). If the high fixed cost firm is a member of a cartel the temptation to free ride at P_2' will be greater than for the low fixed cost firm. The more demand falls, the greater this temptation becomes for either firm.

9.4 Barriers to Entry

It might appear that successfully colluding oligopolists can charge a price considerably in excess of their average costs. In other words, price may equal, or approach, the level which would hold if the industry was a monopoly. In conditions of perfect and monopolistic competition, price cannot for long exceed average cost since the appearance of new entrants to the industry will exert downward pressure on prices. Writers such as Bain and Sylos-Labini, have extended this and argue that this relationship, between price and cost, exists throughout the entire economy; that it exists in the short run as well as the long; and that it requires merely the threat of entry, not actual entry, to enable it to hold.

If so, then relatively sticky but follow-my-leader pricing policies, ending up at a fairly high and near monopolistic level, need not necessarily occur in oligopoly, provided only that the threat of entry is strong or, what is the same thing, barriers to entry are low.

The theory of entry barriers rests on one principal assumption known as the Sylos postulate. This alleges that potential entrants expect established firms to maintain their output levels (i.e. reduce their price to accommodate the entrant) in the face of entry, and that this expectation is, in the event of entry, actually fulfilled. Figure 9.11 illustrates how a potential entrant can calculate where his demand will lie if he is considering entering a given industry. *DD* is the demand curve for the industry. Existing firms are producing Q_1 units of output at price P_1. Given the Sylos postulate an entrant must increase the industry's total output and therefore the industry's price must fall by a sufficient amount to clear both Q_1, and the additional output of the entrant. Effectively, therefore, the entrant's demand curve is that segment of the total industry demand curve to the right of the ruling price. This will be P_1D_1 if the ruling price is P_1, or P_2D_2 had the ruling price–output combination been P_2Q_2. To ascertain whether or not to enter an industry a

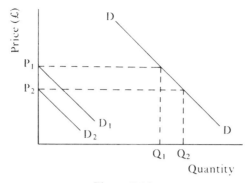

Figure 9.11

potential entrant will compare this demand curve with his particular cost function.

Entry barriers are of three main types. Product differentiation or consumer preference barriers, absolute cost advantages, and scale economies. Analytically, the former two can be grouped together. Preference barriers and absolute cost barriers are present if established firms have lower average unit costs than potential entrants at any given output level. Thus, to overcome preference barriers, entrants might have to spend more highly on advertising or research and development than existing firms.

To overcome absolute cost barriers they may have to pay higher input prices than established firms, as, for example, when an established firm controls a scarce input such as a patent right or a raw material source from which royalties or discriminatory prices can be extracted. Scale economy barriers exist when there is a declining $LRAC$ for the product in question which makes it difficult for a smaller firm to enter the market, given its substantially higher costs; or alternatively precludes entry by a large firm if the market is of a given size, and any unsatisfied demand can only be met by a small firm. Where such entry barriers exist, 'under the Sylos postulate, there is a well defined maximum premium that oligopolists can command over the competitive price' (Modigliani). The lower are the entry barriers, the closer is the price to the (perfectly) competitive level.

This is illustrated in Figures 9.12 and 9.13. In Figure 9.12 absolute cost barriers exist. The entrant's average total cost curve, ATC_E, is higher than that of established firms, ATC_F. Established firms can produce at a price–output combination of P_1Q_1 and the demand curve confronting the entrant is consequently P_1D_1. At no point on that curve can an entrant possibly make a positive profit. Had established firms been selling at price P_2, output Q_2, then the entrant's demand curve would have been P_2D_2 and entry would have occurred, pushing price down once more to the entry-deterring level. The height of the entry barrier is measured by the difference between the entry-

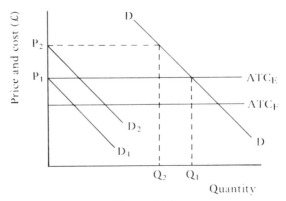

Figure 9.12

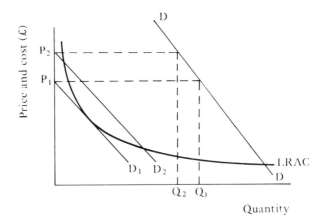

Figure 9.13

deterring price and the ATC_F curve. This difference is in turn dependent on the difference between the two ATC curves.

In Figure 9.13 the $LRAC$ curve available to all firms in the industry is displaying scale economies. The entry-deterring price–output combination is P_1Q_1.

The demand curve P_1D_1 facing a potential entrant at no time allows him to make a positive profit. Again, had established firms been producing at price P_2, output Q_2, then the entrant's demand curve would have been P_2D_2 and a substantial range of output over which profits could be made would have induced entry, pushing price down again to the entry-deterring or limit price. The height of the entry barrier is measured by the vertical difference between P_1 and the $LRAC$ curve at output Q_1.

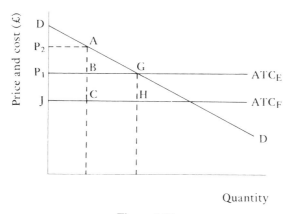

Figure 9.14

The practical effectiveness of this barrier is clearly dependent upon a combination of factors including the price elasticity of demand, the scale at which the *LRAC* levels off or begins to rise, and the size of the market itself. (In other words in quantitative terms, and given the axes scales, the effectiveness of the barriers will vary with the slope of the firm's demand curve, the slope and position of the *ATC* curve, and the position of the industry demand curve.)

What of the impact of time on the price decisions? In reality a time lag will occur while a new entrant establishes his production capacity prior to actually moving into the market place. Prices can then be set above the limit level while still maintaining the Sylos assumption. Figure 9.14 illustrates the nature of the calculation which will be made. Assume the existence of absolute cost barriers to entry and assume also a zero discount rate. It will pay the existing firms to charge the short-run profit-maximising ($MR = MC$) price of P_2, rather than the entry deterring price of P_1 if in so doing the profits for the period before entry, plus the profits for the period after entry, are greater than the profits which could be earned at P_1 for the total period to which the industry demand curve applies. Thus P_2 will be charged initially (and P_1, of necessity, after entry) if, in algebraic terms:

P_2ACJ (for the period before entry) + P_1BCJ (for the period after entry) is greater than P_1GHJ (for the total period)

Moreover, as Worcester has pointed out, the Sylos postulate can again hold but profit-maximising pricing and not limit pricing may be optimal even if entry barriers are low or non-existent. Thus in Figure 9.15 a monopolist (A) sets an initial profit-maximising price P_A. But because entry is easy, firms B, C and D subsequently enter the industry in successive periods. Firm A, by charging P_A initially, maximises profits over time, maintains output at Q_A

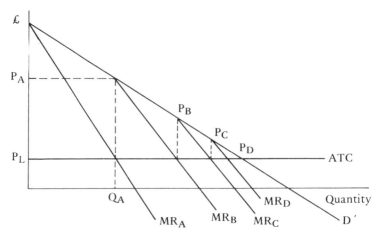

Figure 9.15

and so the dominant share. To have charged the entry deterring price of P_L would not have maximised discounted profits and would simply have perpetuated a worthless (to the firm) monopoly. Over time the original firm's price falls to P_B (when *B* enters) to P_C (when firm *C* enters) and so on.

Whether or not the Sylos postulate is valid is, of course of major relevance to entry and pricing decisions. Established firms might, for example, contract rather than maintain output levels in the face of entry. This means, of course, that entry will be much more attractive and so more likely to occur than under the Sylos postulate assumptions. The price received by an entrant would be the same as that ruling at entry, or at worst, if lower, not as low as it would be under the Sylos assumption. On the other hand, it could be argued that to contract output in the face of entry is a relatively unrealistic assumption. It implies that established firms will generously allow an entrant to take whatever share of the market he pleases while they themselves lose sales, and possibly incur higher unit costs as a result of their reduced throughput. The Sylos postulate and the discussion above seems more realistic.

The third assumption which could be made is, from the point of view of entrants, the most pessimistic of all. Established firms might be expected to and also be able to take aggressive defensive reaction in the face of entry. Heavy, but temporary price cutting, heavy advertising or other predatory tactics by established firms could well drive a relatively weak entrant out of the market. This assumption, of course, removes the possibility of obtaining definitive solutions as was sometimes done under the Sylos postulate. What the ruling price will be, whether entry will occur or not, what the post-entry price might settle at, will all depend on the relative competitive strengths of the entrant and established firms. These matters can be determined only instance by instance by observation, not *a priori*.

Alternatively, instead of attacking the limit price as 'too low' in wealth-maximising terms (as in Figures 9.14 and 9.15) one could argue as does McGee, that it is 'too high', in which case the Sylos postulate is again removed from centre stage. For example consider Figure 9.16. This is a typical 'limit price', 'scale economy barrier' model.

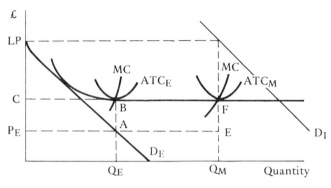

Figure 9.16

LP is the limit price. The industry is currently in the hands of a mono-polist with a plant size indicated by ATC_M. To achieve a plant size of minimum efficient scale an entrant would require plant ATC_E. If he constructed such a plant and the Sylos postulate held, he would make a loss of P_ECBA in perpetuity. But, if so, and he is really determined to enter, the existing firm would make the even larger loss of P_EEFC which is an irrational long-term situation.

Again no definitive price policy for either entrant or existing firm is apparent. But serious doubts are cast on the logic of the limit price models.

If firms do price as monopolists, and if entry does occur and it cannot be predicted in which direction the existing firm's prices and outputs will move, is a counsel of despair the only answer? Given profit maximisation the dominant firm model can be adapted to aid decision taking and prediction. Consider, in Figure 9.17, a monopoly producing Q_M. After entry by one or more smaller firms the original firm's 'residual' demand can be calculated as in Figure 9.7. Its new price and output levels will depend on where its (unchanged *MC*) curve intersects its revised *MR* curve. Only if *MC* is in the position MC_2 will output remain unchanged. With MC_1 and MC_3 output would fall or rise respectively (from Q_1 to Q_1' and from Q_3 to Q_3'). Whether prices would rise or fall would depend on the positions of the demand curves. With MC_2 and MC_3 price would undoubtedly fall. MC_1 provides an ambiguous outcome.

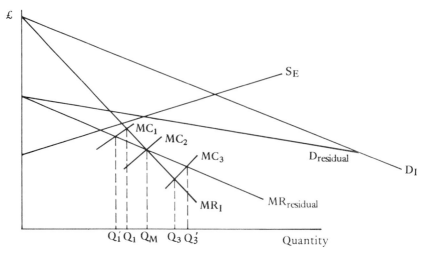

Figure 9.17

Osborne's Approach to Optimal Pricing

The above analysis suggested that the firm would face a choice between (a) setting a monopoly price until entry 'washed away' the monopoly profits; and (b) setting a limit price in perpetuity.

Osborne, however, pointed out that the optimal price will *always* be below the monopoly price albeit it can be above the limit price. This must be so if potential entrants' reactions are also accounted for.

The Sylos postulate is retained in Osborne's argument. But existing firms also take account of entrants' possible reactions and select an 'optimal' price in the light of these reactions. P_o (the optimal price) will always be below P_m (the monopoly price) but may equal or exceed the limit price, P_L. This is illustrated in Figure 9.18. D is the market demand curve, ATC_F existing firms' costs and ATC_E the potential entrants' costs. P_m and P_L are the monopoly and limit prices respectively, with Q_m and Q_L being the corresponding quantities. Osborne alleges the choice is not between P_m and P_L, but between P_L and some price P_o where $P_m > P_o \geq P_L$. An entrant's anticipated profits would be zero if P_L were selected. At higher prices entrants could make profits. Further, the higher the pre-entry price, the larger entrants' outputs would be. The output levels of the entrant corresponding to different pre-entry prices can be inferred from the diagram. At P_m the output level would be $Q_m Q_L$. At P_L the entrant's output level would be zero, and so on. The range of the output levels at the different pre-entry prices can then be subtracted from the market demand curve to yield the demand curve of Figure 9.18 (hence the distance $YP_m = Q_m Q_L$). *This dashed demand curve*

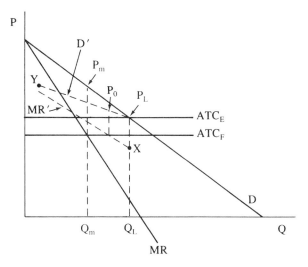

Figure 9.18

is D', the existing firms' demand curve having taken into account the reactions of entrant firms if existing firms charge prices ranging from P_m to P_L. When the relevant *MR'* curve is drawn in, P_o is duly established. P_o exceeds P_L. Had ATC_F been lower and (for example) passed through point X, then P_o and P_L would have been equal.

Spence's Excess Capacity Model

Recent developments concerning entry and limit pricing have concerned entry *deterrence* rather than entry *barriers*. In the former case a firm adopts a pre-entry policy which would commit it to follow a specific post-entry strategy. This post-entry strategy would prevent the entrant from making normal profits. One such model was proposed by Spence (1977).

Spence argues that a firm may construct excess capacity in advance of use during periods of growth, and suffer excess capacity during demand.contraction. If, instead of the Sylos postulate, potential entrants believe the established firm would increase output to use up excess capacity, this would lead price to be bid down to *SAC*. The entrant would expect to make only normal profits and so would not enter. Since pre-entry output is less than the threatened post-entry output, the pre-entry price is higher than the post-entry price. Hence the established firm may be able to set a pre-entry price which yields supernormal profits whilst entry is deterred, and without the existence of a barrier to entry in terms of economies of scale or absolute cost differences.

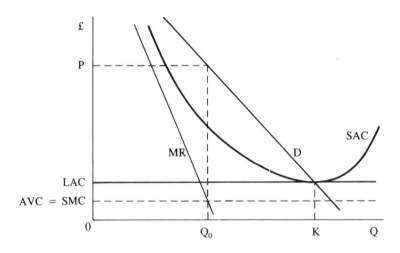

Figure 9.19

Spence's argument is explained with reference to Figure 9.19. For simplicity we assume constant $AVC = SMC$ and constant LAC at all outputs. Suppose the firm constructs capacity K. It could set $MR = SMC$, so producing Q_o, and at the same time threaten to increase output to level K if entry occurs. Notice that, because there is no entry barrier, the limit price under the Sylos postulate would be LAC with no supernormal profits. So, if entrants hold the Spence assumption, the established firm can make greater long-run profits than if entrants hold the Sylos assumption.

9.5 Schelling's Approach to Entry, Strategy and Conflict

Thomas Schelling, although writing as long ago as 1960, has provided very useful insights into oligopolistic interdependence, game theory models and entry behaviour. In the latter case he enables the analyst to move from the somewhat constricting Sylos postulate. For example, it seems not unreasonable (as Osborne has already suggested) that firms will not hold to P_L but rather will move to some higher accommodating price.

If a large potential entrant does not believe the limit price will be maintained it will enter irrespective, confident, rightly or wrongly, that its (large) addition to industry output will not depress price significantly. Threats of price cutting and output stability (Sylos) which are not believed will not deter entry. Scherer (p. 246) paraphrases Schelling's argument from the nuclear deterrent analogue thus:

If the Soviet Union invaded ... Europe, would the United States retaliate

... knowing that the Soviets would respond in kind ... If not, the ... deterrent is not credible, and it must be replaced by other barriers to entry such as ... conventional forces. There is more ... assume that a nuclear response to conventional aggression would be irrational ... If, however, US leaders have committed their reputations ... or if emotional behaviour ... displaced sober analysis, escalation might progress to ... nuclear weapons. Fear ... of such an *irrational* response contributes to deterrence ..., the US has something to gain by cultivating the impression that it will act irrationally or that events will get out of control ... By making irrational actions seem more likely ... one may move nearer the rational goal of averting the contingency. This is the so-called *rationality of irrationality* (emphasis added).

This argument can be extended to markets. Cartel discipline can crumble because of entry. Established firms will want to avoid this. To avoid a price war due to entry they may actively try to suggest they do *not* fear a price war. Thus, they may even on occasion actively indulge in such a war against new entrants in order to discourage still more entrants in a future period. To return to Scherer: 'Fear of irrational action, then, ... may be what deters the potential new entrant.'

The 'equilibrium' (of nuclear 'peace') in terms of lack of entry (or in terms of tacit collusion or cartelisation actually succeeding despite our remarks suggesting cartels are unstable on p. 263) is further explained by Schelling with three reasons. These are ready communications, the presence of lags, and the nature of rivalry dynamics. Again Schelling uses the nuclear warfare analogy.

In nuclear war hostile actions are known of near instantaneously as, indeed, are moves towards hostilities. Similarly in price warfare, price cuts are difficult to conceal. As a result, nations and firms find it possible to 'wait and watch' and this can continue indefinitely. Second, a nuclear attack (or a price cut) can often be responded to with near simultaneity. There is no lag period of any consequence. Hence potential aggressors realise they have 'little to give and much to lose' and so do not initiate aggressive action. Third, rivalry can be continuous or one-off. When it is continuous, joint profit maximisation behaviour is claimed by Scherer (p. 163) to be more likely. This is because repetition and stability permit easy learning and promote low cost cooperation and trust. Further, if the rivalry is continuous, an aggressive move today can be countered with retaliation tomorrow. In one-off rivalry such retaliation is not so feasible and so there is less motivation to refrain from aggression.

9.6 The Role of Cost

Many surveys have suggested that businessmen practice cost-plus pricing.

That is, some mark-up is added to average cost to obtain unit selling price. This seems a straight contradiction of the $MR = MC$ rule. It appears totally to ignore demand and makes no concession to competition, actual or threatened. Moreover it involves circular reasoning. If volume sold depends on price (as it does in demand analysis) but price depends on cost (as in cost-plus pricing) then how can price be determined, since cost depends on volume sold (as it does in cost analysis)? However, closer inspection of mark-up pricing reveals that businessmen choose a mark-up which they deem 'necessary' or 'appropriate' and so the paradox is resolved. There need be no conflict between the accountants' rules of pricing and the economic point of view.

Recall that in profit maximisation $MR = MC$. Then

$$MR = \frac{dTR}{dQ} = \frac{dPQ}{dQ} = \frac{QdP}{dQ} + P \quad \text{and } MC = \frac{dACQ}{dQ} = \frac{QdAC}{dQ} + AC$$

$$\therefore Q\frac{dP}{dQ} + P = Q\frac{dAC}{dQ} + AC$$

$$\therefore P = Q\frac{dAC}{dQ} + AC - Q\frac{dP}{dQ}$$

$$= AC + Q\left(\frac{dAC}{dQ} - \frac{dP}{dQ}\right)$$

Now assume constant costs such that $MC = LRAC$. Then

$$P = AC - Q\frac{dP}{dQ}$$

$$\therefore \frac{P-AC}{P} = -\frac{Q}{P}\left(\frac{dP}{dQ}\right) \qquad = \frac{1}{\eta}$$

Thus the left-hand side of this expression (the mark-up under cost-plus pricing) is higher the less elastic is demand and *vice versa*. The more price elastic a product is, the lower is its mark-up. Thus cost-plus pricing can simply be a synonym for $MR = MC$.

9.7 Incremental Pricing

Just as cost-plus pricing can be regarded as a rule of thumb which may result in *de facto* marginalist behaviour, so can incremental pricing. The difference is that incremental analysis is adopted in the explicit belief that marginal equivalency principles are optimal and that opportunity costs must be taken into account. Marginalism is acted upon, it is not achieved by default. Again, however, as with cost-plus pricing, the method of adopting these concepts is a crude one rather than one depending on any (relatively) sophisticated calculus.

It is assumed that demand and cost functions are not known, or would be too costly to find. Given this, incremental analysis is used as a low-cost marginal equivalency surrogate. In general, incrementalism requires that estimates be made of any

1. changes in total revenue
2. changes in total costs

and/or

3. changes in both total revenue and costs

which are consequential to any decision to change prices or advertising, to add or drop products, or to undertake any particular investment. This sounds easy. But implementation requires great care. In particular,

(a) opportunity costs must be considered
(b) fixed costs must be considered

Thus, if the decision under consideration were to reduce sales of other items in the firm's product line, then that foregone alternative would have to be included in the cost. Overhead costs, however, will generally be incurred regardless. These must, therefore, be disregarded in costing out a decision's consequences relative to its benefits. Only variable or out-of-pocket expenses should be included. In addition, any long-run effect on the firm's prospects must be taken note of. And, furthermore, general management must be aware of and coordinate incremental decisions. If someone did not take such coordinating authority, incrementally attractive decisions would be made which in aggregate would prove to be mutually exclusive. Or, alternatively, many such decisions could be taken, all of which could make a contribution to fixed costs but, in total, overhead commitments might never be met.

9.8 Sealed-Bid Pricing

When firms tender for contracts under a sealed-bid system the main problem is estimating the probable bids of competitors. 'Guesstimates' of these can be obtained from a variety of sources. What sort of level of bids have they submitted in the past? What are their current cost levels? Does trade gossip suggest they are working above or below full capacity? Is their plant and equipment modern and low-cost or obsolete and costly to operate? Alternatively, even if their plant is modern and their variable costs low, was the capital cost so great that they must keep the plant in continuous operation to recoup their fixed costs? In short, how keen are they to obtain business? With this sort of information a pay-off matrix of the kind shown in table 9.4 can be constructed. Here we have hypothetical data with four price choices and an assumed unit cost of £8.

Profits, over time, will be maximised with the £11 bid. Over a run of

Table 9.4 Sealed-Bid Pricing

Bid	Profit	Probability of our bid winning the contract	Expected pay-off
(1)	(2)	(3)	(2) × (3)
£	£		£
10	2	0.9	1.8
11	3	0.7	2.1
12	4	0.5	2.0
13	5	0.3	1.5

contracts we assume that we will win 70 per cent of them with bids of £11 and lose 30 per cent. This provides an average or expected profit for every contract we bid for (whether we win it or not) of £2.10 per unit. Obviously this type of analysis is only useful if market conditions are fairly repetitive; this need not be the case. In addition, if our firm requires certain or near-certain profits in the short run then a bid of £10 or less should be made. This will not maximise long-run profits but it will generate near-certain business.

Additional Reading

Archibald, G.C. (1959) '"Large" and "small" numbers in the theory of the firm', *Manchester School of Social and Economic Studies*.

Ferguson, C.E. and Gould, J.P. (1975) *Microeconomic Theory*, Irwin.

Harowitz, I. (1970) *Decision Making and the Theory of the Firm*, Holt Rinehart and Winston.

Koutsoyiannis, A. (1979) *Modern Microeconomics*, (2nd edn), Macmillan.

McGee, J.S. (1980) 'Predatory pricing revisited', *Journal of Law and Economics*, Vol. XXIII.

Needham, D. (1978) *The Economics of Industrial Structure, Conduct and Performance*, Holt Rinehart and Winston.

Osborne, D.K. (1973) 'On the rationality of limit pricing', *Journal of Industrial Economics*.

Scherer, F.M. (1980) *Industrial Market Structure and Economic Performance*, (2ns edn), Rand McNally.

Schelling, T.C. (1960) *The Strategy of Conflict*, Harvard University Press.

Spence, A.M. (1977) 'Entry, capacity, investment and oligopoly pricing', *Bell Journal of Economics*, Vol. 8.

Stigler, G.J. (1966) *The Theory of Price*, (3rd edn), Macmillan.

10
Public Utility Pricing

The nationalised industries occupy a large part of the British economy. Many of them are statutory monopolies. Pricing where $MR = MC$ does not then at first sight appear to maximise economic welfare. As a result, the problem of laying down criteria for the management of these enterprises looms large in the list of priorities of any government.

10.1 The Theory

Welfare economists argue that the general guideline laid down for nationalised industry pricing should be that of price equal to long-run marginal cost.

The rationale for this is illustrated in Figure 10.1. A private monopolist would operate at output level Q_1 and price P_1. Consumer surplus is equal to the area ABP_1 and producer surplus or monopoly profit to the area GP_1BF. If the monopolist is now compelled to operate where $P = MC$, output rises to Q_2, price falls to P_2 and consumer surplus becomes the triangle ACP_2. Producer surplus is now the area GP_2C. At P_2 the sum of producer's and consumer's surplus, ACG, is maximised. The result of the change in price policy is a net welfare gain equal to BCF.[1] In other words, the objective of public utility pricing is assumed to be the maximisation of total social benefits over total social costs, where social benefits are measured by the willingness of the market to pay as indicated by the demand curve.

If the rule of marginal cost pricing is followed, the question is raised as to the extent to which long-run and short-run marginal costs will conflict. The answer is that they will not if the industry adopts an appropriate investment policy. The explanation of this assertion has several stages and will lead us into some areas of difficulty over the sheer practicability of $P = MC$ as a management guideline.

1   The allocative virtues of pricing at marginal cost in a regulated industry depend on the assumption that prices in every other industry are already equal to MC. This is unrealistic and 'second best' adjustments must be made. Interested readers can pursue this digression in the Additional Reading listed at the end of this chapter.

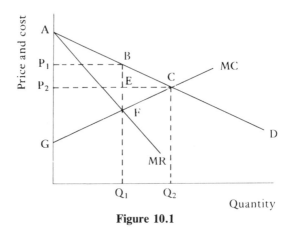

Figure 10.1

First, it is a truism that when short-run average cost (*SAC*) equals long-run average cost (*LAC*) then at that output level both short-run (*SMC*) and long-run (*LMC*) marginal costs are equal. Figure 10.2 shows the *SMC* and *LMC* at Q_1, Q_2 and Q_3, positions of declining, constant and rising *LAC*s respectively. The legitimacy of Figure 10.2 is easy to justify. At Q_1, Q_2 and Q_3, *SAC = LAC* and so, therefore, short-run total cost (*STC*) is equal to long-run total cost (*LTC*). But at outputs below and above each of Q_1, Q_2 and Q_3 the relevant *SAC* exceeds *LAC*, therefore *STC* exceeds *LTC*. Since, in addition, both the *LTC* and *STC* have positive gradients (production of additional output always increases *TC*) they must be tangential at Q_1, Q_2 and

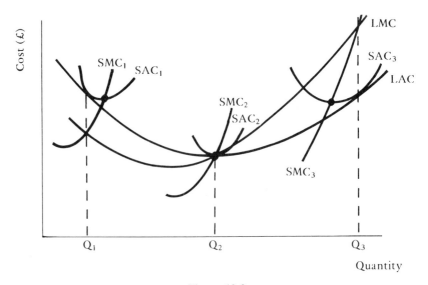

Figure 10.2

Q_3. Since their gradients equal their marginal values, tangencies at Q_1, Q_2 and Q_3 imply that $SMC = LMC$ at these outputs. Analogous arguments apply to all other outputs at which $LAC = SAC$.

The appropriate investment policy avoids a conflict between SMC and LMC and so the optimum plant size occurs where the two are equal, given $P = MC$. The rule which brings this about states that either:

(a) if at the output level for existing capacity for which $P = SMC$, $SMC > LMC$, then new capacity should be constructed or, conversely
(b) if at the output level for existing capacity for which $P = SMC$, $SMC < LMC$, then disinvestment should take place.

This is so because, if the rule is obeyed, economic welfare is maximised: the marginal benefits of expansion (or contraction) are equated with the marginal costs of that expansion (or contraction). The benefits of marginal output (in terms of willingness to pay) are equal to $(P_1 + P_2)(Q_2 - Q_1)/2$, where P_1, P_2, Q_1 and Q_2 are the original and revised prices and quantities respectively. In Figure 10.3 we demonstrate how this is arrived at.

Total consumer utility at $P_1 = OABQ_1$; total utility at $P_2 = OACQ_2$. Thus in terms of price the benefits of the marginal output $(Q_2 - Q_1)$ equal BCQ_2Q_1. But

$$
\begin{aligned}
BCQ_2Q_1 &= BDQ_2Q_1 - BDC \\
&= P_1(Q_2 - Q_1) - \tfrac{1}{2}(EBDC) \\
&= P_1(Q_2 - Q_1) - \tfrac{1}{2}(P_1 - P_2)(Q_2 - Q_1) \\
&= (Q_2 - Q_1)(P_1 - \tfrac{1}{2}P_1 + \tfrac{1}{2}P_2) \\
&= (P_1 + P_2)(Q_2 - Q_1)/2 \\
&= (SMC_1 + SMC_2)(Q_2 - Q_1)/2 \text{ (if } P = SMC)
\end{aligned}
$$

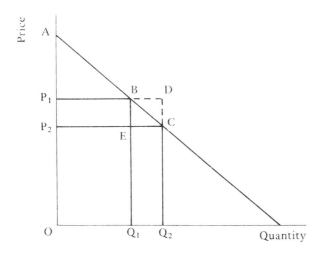

Figure 10.3

The marginal benefits of expansion would then equal the short-run marginal costs of expansion. But the cost of marginal output is $K + r(Q_2 - Q_1)$ where K is the incremental capital cost and r the unit running cost. The cost of expansion, $K + r(Q_2 - Q_1)$, is consequently equal to long-run marginal cost inclusive of the capital costs of fixed asset acquisition. Expansion is worthwhile if the marginal benefits (SMC) exceed the costs (LMC). Contraction and disinvestment is to be preferred in economic welfare terms if the costs (LMC) exceed the benefits (SMC). And so our investment rule is justified and the seeming conflict between SMC and LMC resolved.

Serious practical problems must now be examined. In decreasing cost industries, a firm following the investment and pricing rules laid down would be unable to cover its average costs. In short, a private monopolist forced to abide by such rules would go out of business.

In Figure 10.4 with plant SAC_1, pricing at SMC results in a profit earning P_1Q_1 price–output combination. But $SMC > LMC$ at P_1Q_1 and welfare will only be maximised when investment takes place and a plant size with a cost structure equal to SAC_2 is attained. Then $P = SMC = LMC$ at P_2Q_2.

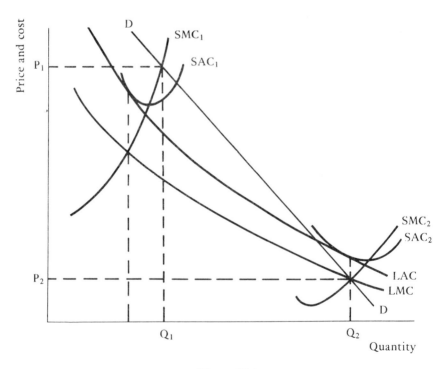

Figure 10.4

However, the firm is now making a loss and given our guidelines there is no way in which it can avoid this.

One solution is to price at marginal cost and subsidise the firm. Consumers can then choose an economically optimal amount of the service or product, based on $P = MC$, and the industry will be kept solvent. This is only practicable, however, if the money to pay the subsidy can be obtained without distorting resource allocation elsewhere. This is easier to say than to accomplish. Moreover, a subsidy redistributes income away from those who are taxed in order to raise the subsidy towards the users of the subsidised industry. This can only be equitable if those so taxed are also those who are subsidised. If a redistribution does occur, the quantity demanded may well be in excess of the quantity which would have been consumed had no subsidy been provided.

The ideal solution is for each person to pay the same price ($P = MC$) for the units he consumes at the margin, the deficit to be made up by each consumer accepting a share of it according to the valuation he places on the goods or services consumed. This could be done either by each individual consumer paying the appropriate lump sum relevant to his consumer surplus, or by his paying different intra-marginal prices pitched to contribute an identical net amount. These alternatives would not affect the individual consumer's marginal decision about consuming another unit. However, the information on each consumer's demand function is simply not available to enable such a system to operate at low cost.

A more practical way to leave consumers free to decide how much of a good they want to buy at MC and still pay sufficient to cover the deficit, is to operate some form of two-part tariff.

One part will be a unit price equated with marginal cost, the other a flat rate unaffected by use. This places on consumers the burden of meeting all the costs of the service they use but does not distort marginal choice, as pricing at average cost would do. However, such a system may prevent potential consumers from using the service if, at the margin, they are willing to pay MC per unit but not the flat fee for using the service at all.

Thus marginal cost pricing by nationalised industries (or government regulated but privately owned monopolies) is not the panacea to monopoly distortions it might at first appear to be. Superficially it would appear to provide government with the answers to such an industry's price–output decisions and to its levels of net investment. In practice, the situation is complicated by 'second best' considerations in that the rationale for marginal cost pricing, 'first best' conditions, demands that it is practised everywhere else in the economy. In decreasing cost industries the presence of a deficit if $P = MC$ raises questions of both efficiency and equity. Finally, the whole discussion rests on the assumption that managerial and technical efficiency will be continuously maximised. The effect on managerial efficiency of the provision of subsidies to eliminate deficits is ignored.

Peak Load Pricing

Marginal cost pricing theory has possibly made its greatest contribution to pricing practices in those public utilities where demand varies over time. The utility to which this statement has most relevance is electricity generation. Demand periodicity is of much less relevance in industries with a storable product. Electricity is the classic non-storable product with widely fluctuating demand.

Conceptually, there are two cases which can be distinguished in the peak load pricing problem. These are the firm peak case and the shifting peak case. In the firm peak case there is one peak period and differential prices (on- and off-peak) do not eliminate it. In the shifting peak case differential prices, if incorrectly applied, can result in the off-peak period becoming the peak.

The Firm Peak Case

Consider two independent demand curves for equal duration subperiods (say night and day) for electricity. Assume an inherited plant with a fixed maximum output of Q_d and constant unit running costs of r. What pricing policy will result in optimum use of the available capacity? Figure 10.5 shows that the prices should be P_N and P_D.

This pricing policy maximises the net total social benefits as measured by willingness to pay in a way no other pricing arrangement would. Geometrically these are equal to the area $(AEr + BCDr)$. At night, price is equal to $SMC = r$. During the day, price acts as a rationing device to allocate the service to those consumers who place most value on it in terms of willingness to pay. Here price is equal to the vertical portion of the SMC curve.[2]

The next question is what is the optimum capacity in the firm peak case? For simplicity, assume given and constant plant lives so that capital costs can be represented in an annual equivalent form. Running costs are equal to $r = SMC$. Capital costs are equal to k, and so $LMC = r + k$ (subject to $SMC = r$, a condition which will only hold up to a given plant's output limit).

In Figure 10.6 two possible plant sizes with maximum outputs of Q_D and Q_D' are shown. If capacity size Q_D was constructed, prices would be $r(P_N)$ and P_D for night and day respectively. However, this does not comply with the

2   This portion of the SMC curve is not equal to the cost of producing one extra unit, which is r. However, at Q_D it is not possible to produce a further unit owing to the rigidity of the plant. The relevant cost concept after Q_D is that of the opportunity cost of the marginal user, not that of the next best productive use of the resources. At Q_D the marginally excluded consumer puts the value of the resources in their current use at P_D.

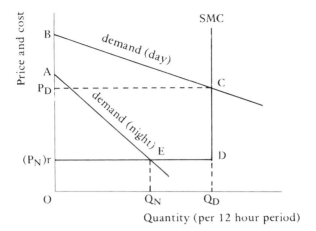

Figure 10.5

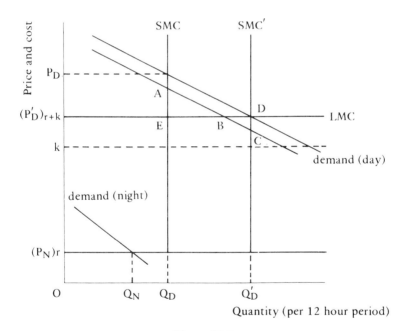

Figure 10.6

investment rule that *SMC* and *LMC* should be equated. In this instance, where $P = SMC$, $SMC > LMC$ and so new capacity should be constructed. The optimal size will be at Q'_D where again the night price will be P_N but the daytime price will be $P'_D = r + k = LMC = SMC'$. In the firm peak case, all capacity charges (k) are borne by the on-peak consumer. The off-peak consumer merely pays for his appropriate share of the running costs.

Up to this juncture we have made the implicit assumption that there are no indivisibilities in plant size. Thus if plant size Q_D is too small, in terms of the investment rule, then it is possible to build precisely the size of plant necessary to enable the conditions $P = SMC = LMC$ to be adhered to, as with plant size Q_D'. Let us drop this assumption and consider the situation which arises if Q_D and Q_D' are the only two plant sizes which it is commercially or technologically possible to construct over the relevant output range. All the conditions in Figure 10.6 remain unchanged, except daytime demand, which we will now assume to be represented by the line passing through the points A, B and C.

Neither plant size, under these circumstances, will permit the equating of $P = SMC = LMC$. Which plant is to be preferred? If Q_D is chosen, a daytime price of A would be selected, compared with the 'ideal' (given no indivisibilities) price of B. Net social benefits equal to the area ABE will have been forfeited. Conversely, if a plant to produce Q_D' is selected, a daytime price of C would be charged compared with the 'ideal' price of B, and a corresponding ideal plant size. Net social benefits equal to the area BDC will have to be forfeited. Given these circumstances, a plant will be chosen which minimises these notional losses of social benefits. Thus if $ABE > BDC$ then the plant size with capacity Q_D' will be constructed.

The Shifting Peak Case

In the shifting peak case, the nature of demand in the subperiods is such that both are responsible for capacity changes. Consequently, merely charging off-peak users for running costs can result in the quantity they demand being higher than that of the on-peak segment. In Figure 10.7, if night time users are charged r, the required capacity is Q_N. If daytime users are charged $r + k$, the required capacity is only Q_D.

The correct procedure is to use the entire 24-hour demand cycle. Vertical summation of the demand curves is required. Similarly, the cost curves must be aggregated vertically. The running costs, r, are consequently doubled. Capacity costs, of course, are unaffected. If an additional unit of capacity is provided for one cycle it is also available for the other. Thus the LMC for the 24-hour cycle is equal to $2r + k$.

Optimal capacity is consequently Q_A where the aggregate demand curve intersects the 24-hour cycle LMC schedule and simultaneously the SMC curve appropriate to a plant capacity of Q_A. Optimal pricing policy can then be found by referring to the component parts of the aggregate demand curve, namely P_D and P_N for day and night respectively. In the shifting peak case, the off-peak consumers do contribute to capacity costs, and do so in propor-

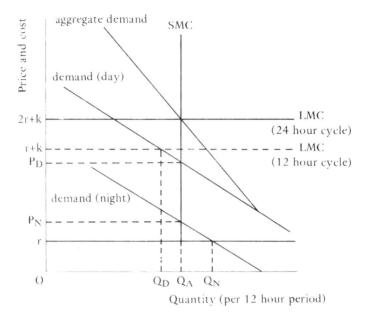

Figure 10.7

tion to the strength of their demand relative to the on-peak users. Again our investment rule has been complied with: $P_N + P_D = 2r + k = LMC$ (24 hours) $= SMC$.

In Figure 10.8 we relax the assumption of completely rigid plants and build in the more realistic consideration that output in a given plant can be increased, albeit at a rising marginal cost.

If plant 1, SMC_1, was inherited, the optimal prices would be P_N^1 and P_D^1 for night and day respectively. To ascertain whether investment or disinvestment is warranted, the sum of these prices must be compared with LMC where SMC_1 intersects LMC. In this case $P_N^1 + P_D^1$ is greater than LMC at Q_1 (where $LMC = SMC_1$), consequently expansion is warranted. When plant size 2 with SMC_2 is reached, optimal capacity has also been attained. Where prices equal SMC_2, P_N^2 and P_D^2, their sum equals LMC which in turn equals SMC_2. Neither with plant 1 or plant 2 has capacity been fully utilised in any of the four 12-hour periods examined. (Full utilisation would be Q_1 and Q_2, respectively.) Unlike Figure 10.7, an aggregate demand curve has not been used. With continuous cost functions the equality of $P = SMC$ occurs at different output levels, and consequently vertical aggregation of price at the same output level is inapposite.

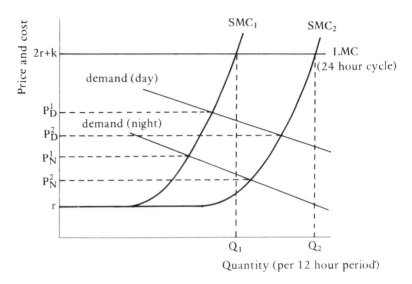

Figure 10.8

10.2 Controlling the Return on Capital

An alternative approach to the natural monopoly problem is to release the
public utility from the requirement to price at *MC*, and instead require it to
maximise profitability subject to a constraint on its rate of return. One model,
provided by Stein and Borts, assumes that the regulatory objective is to bring
profits down to the competitive level as indicated by a zero margin above
long-run average costs.

How would a public utility react if such a constraint were imposed by
government? Four possible alternatives suggest themselves. First, as a parallel
to the natural monopoly situation with a subsidy at $P = MC$, the firm might
simply raise costs above the minimum efficient level (X – inefficiency and/or
some other form of managerial or organisational slack would arise).
Second, if the firm operated in markets other than that in which it holds a
monopoly, it might reduce its rate of return to near zero in the latter and,
if it possessed some market power in the former, price its products in such
a way that cross-subsidisation would enable monopoly rents to be reaped in
the firm as a whole, albeit not (apparently) from the public utility. Third,
the firm might keep its return on capital down to the desired level, not by
reducing prices and profits, but rather by raising its capital base by ineffi-
ciently and unnecessarily using excess or obsolete (and hence high-cost) capital
equipment. Finally, and as a variant on this third point, the firm might even
operate on its production possibility frontier (that is, at full technological

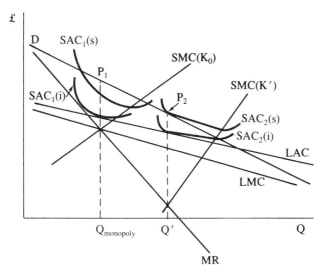

Figure 10.9

efficiency on the product transformation curve) but be too capital-intensive to permit allocative (i.e. $P = MC$) efficiency.

This is illustrated in Figure 10.9. Consider a firm operating with a capital stock of K_0 at $Q_{monopoly}$ where $MR = SMC(K_0) = LMX$ and a cost of capital embodied in the short-run average cost curve $SAC_1(i)$ equalling i *together with* the relevant gap between D **and** SAC_1. There is no incentive for the firm to expand output at price P_1 and profits are duly maximised. The social optimum of $P = MC$ has not been obtained, however. Expansion should take place for this to occur. Now impose a return on capital constraint of $s\%$ where s, although greater than i, must not be exceeded. This has the diagrammatic effect of raising SAC_1 to $SAC_1(s)$.

P_1 must be reduced since it permits abnormal profits. Abnormal profits only disappear when plant size is raised from SAC_1 to SAC_2, a capital stock of K' against the original smaller stock of K_0. With plant size SAC_2, profit-maximising behaviour results in $SMC(K')$ being equated with MR. Price is P_2, output is Q', and the profitability constraint of $s\%$ is satisfied. Economically, the *perceived* cost of capital to the firm has been reduced. Originally it was i plus the relevant abnormal profit. After regulation the best available alternative yielded only s. The price of capital is apparently lower, consequently more capital is employed. But at Q', $SMC < LMC$ suggesting that the firm is over-invested in capital equipment. The labour:capital ratio is socially non-optimal. This is so since, if at $Q' LMC > SMC$, then what is foregone by producing with one extra unit of capital (LMC) is greater than what is foregone by producing with one extra unit of labour (in the short run capital is a fixed input). Alternatively:

the actual cost of capital   the price or cost of
divided by its   > labour divided by its
marginal product   marginal product

or, symbolically,

$$i/MP_k > W/MP_L$$

where W is the wage rate. Rearranging,

$$MP_k/i < MP_L/W$$

which implies that output could be raised by shifting one pound of resources from capital to labour. Control of the rate of return has resulted in a production technique which is too capital-intensive.

10.3 The Current Practice and Privatisation

The theoretical approach of section 10.1 was the officially approved method of tackling nationalised industry prices in the UK from 1967 to 1978 (when one government White Paper replaced another). The 1967 White Paper has been described as impracticable. The 1978 White Paper is vague. Financial targets are now set for each industry, and these will vary by industry. Day-to-day management decisions, however, are left to the industries themselves.

The level of financial target will take into account, but need not be the same as the Required Rate of Return (RRR) to be used for investment appraisal. The RRR is intended to reflect the opportunity cost of capital in the economy, but the financial target may be varied with the government's political views of the industry's objectives.

The financial target set by government will (except in the case of industries such as steel where the market is not monopolised) determine the general level of prices charged by the industry. An adequate level of nationalised industry profit is regarded as essential to enable the industries to contribute to their own investment programmes and thus minimise borrowing from other sectors of the economy. The RRR does not exclude basing prices, where appropriate, on SMC, but it puts considerably less emphasis on this than heretofore.

Since the early 1980s the government has adopted an additional and alternative strategy to that of regulation of the public utilities. This is the policy known popularly as 'privatisation'. Privatisation includes denationalisation (sale of state assets to the public), deregulation (permitting competition with state monopolies) and contracting out (franchising to public or private companies the production of goods and services financed by the state). To the extent that firms are 'privatised' in these ways *and are not state regulated* by either marginal cost pricing rules (as is often the case in the USA) or by rate of return regulation (as with British Telecom), the profit-maximising guidelines of other chapters will again hold (subject to our discussion on managerial objectives in Chapter 3 and any competition policy guidelines as detailed in Chapter 15).

Additional Reading

Brittan, S., Kay, J.A. and Thompson, D.J. (1986) 'Privatisation', *Economic Journal*, Vol. 96, pp. 18–38.

Kay, J., Mayer, C., and Thompson, D. (1986) *Privatisation and Regulation — the UK Experience*, Oxford University Press.

Stein, J.L. and Borts, G.H. (1972) 'Behaviour of the Firm under Regulatory Constraint', *American Economic Review*, No. 62.

Webb, M.G. (1973) *The Economics of Nationalised Industries*, Nelson.

Williamson, O.E. (1966) 'Peak load pricing and optimal capacity under indivisibility constraints', *American Economic Review*, No. 56.

Cmnd. 3437 (1967) *Nationalised Industries, A Review of Economic and Financial Objectives*, HMSO.

Cmnd. 7131 (1978) *The Nationalised Industries*, HMSO.

11
Advertising Decisions

Here we shall examine one of the most controversial and publicly visible business practices: advertising. First we shall very briefly look at the contentious relationship between advertising and price. Next, and in more detail, we shall discuss the theory and practice of setting advertising budgets in order to maximise profits. Finally, how that advertising budget, once determined, can be allocated between different media is discussed. Here strong emphasis is placed on how the marginal equivalency principles of managerial economics are actually applied in practice. Because of the wealth and sophistication of market and advertising research data in the real-life market place, the practical usefulness of managerial economics is seldom exceeded in any other decision-making area.

11.1 Advertising and Price

Casual observation suggests that advertising can be a means to entry. It can reduce prices through increased competition and by encouraging large-scale, low-cost production. By increasing consumer information it can facilitate price comparison, increase demand elasticity and so result in competitively induced lower prices.

The alternative argument is that advertising can and does encourage brand loyalty and so lowers consumer price sensitivity. Branding provides consumers with a guarantee of product quality and consistency — poor brands can be avoided. Such 'quality information' may not be so cheaply accessible by any other route.[1]

---

1   If a cheaper route were readily and universally available, entrepreneurs would provide product information *and* the product at a lower price than is paid by consumers when they buy the product and the advertisement as a joint and inseparable package. This, of course, does happen, although not frequently. For example, for years Marks and Spencer never advertised the St. Michael brand. Restaurant and hotel information is provided by organisations separate from the firms themselves: for example the motoring organisations' handbooks. Similarly, the Consumers' Association publishes *Which?* However, these are exceptions.

The next few paragraphs show how advertising can raise prices. But it must be remembered that the discussion assumes, with no justification, that demand for the product could exist without advertising (and if demand did not exist there would be no price to raise!). Figure 11.1 (based on an argument by Williamson) provides a summary of the considerations leading businessmen to advertise in order to permit the level of the entry-deterring price to be raised. L is the entry-deterring or limit price in the absence of advertising, where entry barriers are limited to scale economies or absolute cost advantages. In the absence of advertising, entry will occur if price is raised above L. If only a small amount of advertising is engaged, the limit price will be little affected since the advertising will not be particularly effective, or if it is, entrants will find it easy to equal. This is illustrated in Figure 11.1(a) by the relatively flat shape to the curve LB (plotting entry-deterring price) when only a small movement has been made along the x, or advertising, axis. As existing firms increase their advertising, however, new entrants would also have to incur substantial advertising investment in order to break down existing firms' goodwill, while simultaneously creating their own.

This makes it possible for existing firms to charge a higher price than L without attracting entry, and the entry-deterring price curve LB rises quite sharply. After a point, diminishing returns to advertising may set in, and the

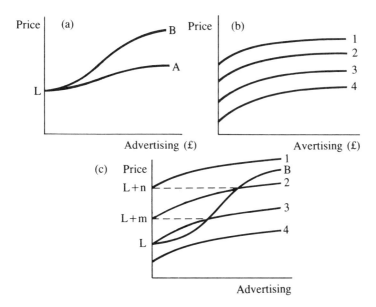

Figure 11.1 (a) How the limit price may vary with advertising. (b) Sales isoquants at different price-advertising combinations. (c) Maintenance of output and raising of price through advertising.

curve begins to level off. Curve LA has a similar, but gentler shape. This curve would apply in industries where advertising is not so effective as an entry barrier (e.g. compare cigarettes, where brand loyalty induced by advertising is high, with flour sales to the bakery trade, where customer choice is made largely on the basis of price or service).

Figure 11.1(b) shows a group of equal output curves. Each is a locus of price-selling expense combinations which are capable of inducing sales of the same output level. They slope upwards from left to right initially, because more advertising is required to sell the same output at higher prices. After a point, increasing advertising is less effective as a compensating mechanism for price increases, and the slope becomes less steep. Higher curves represent lower outputs since, given advertising, as price rises, output falls. Figure 11.1(c) superimposes the previous two diagrams, one on the other. This shows how a firm originally producing quantity 3 at price L can raise its price to level $L+m$ without inducing entry, while maintaining constant output. (Price could be raised still further to $L+n$, but in this instance sales would have to be forfeited by moving from isoquant 3 to isoquant 2.)

11.2 Theoretical Approaches to Budget Determination

Figure 11.2 shows how sales and profits may vary with advertising expenditure. Even with zero advertising, some sales will be achieved by a firm. Little impact on sales is made when advertising is indulged in at fairly low levels, since the expenditure is so low as to pass unnoticed by the majority of potential customers. After a point, however, successive increments in advertising expenditure will produce more than proportionate increments in sales. The sales revenue or response curve begins to rise steeply. The firm has crossed the threshold level below which its advertising level will pass unnoticed, and is reaching the stage where it can take advantage of economies of scale in advertising. Specialists in copywriting and design can be employed. Advertising research can be engaged in. More efficient media can be used. For example, a firm with £1000 to spend may be able to purchase for that sum one page in a paper with 10,000 readers, giving it a cost per contact of 10p. Such a firm would be precluded from taking a page in a five million readership paper at a cost per page of £50,000, but an average cost per contact of only 1p. Eventually, the sales response curve will move out of this exponential phase, diminishing returns to advertising expenditure will set in, and while the curve will continue to rise, it will do so less than proportionately and, as a whole, will take on an S-shaped appearance. The diminishing returns will be due to fixity in size of the target market. Sales saturation will be approached; those customers most amenable to persuasion will already have bought, and only the less willing prospects will remain.

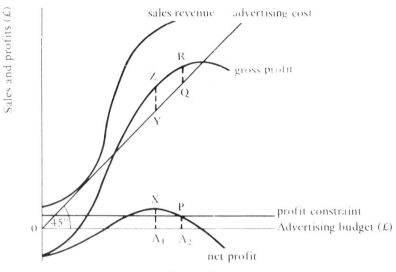

Figure 11.2

Given that the two axes of Figure 11.2 are drawn on the same scale, a 45° line can be drawn through the origin, and the vertical distance from any point on it to the x-axis can then usefully be represented as advertising cost. This equals the distance on the x-axis from where the intersection occurs to the origin. With knowledge of costs other than advertising costs for each sales level, the profit curve gross of advertising expenditure can be drawn. The net profit curve can also be inserted. The boat-shaped area between the gross profit curve and the 45° line equals net profits.

The profit-maximising firm will consequently produce at that sales level where net profits are maximised, XA_1, which is where advertising costs will equal YA_1 which equals a budget of OA_1. The model can readily be adapted to aid budget determination in firms with motives other than profit maximisation. For example, consider a Baumol-type profit constraint. A single-period sales maximiser would then set a budget equal to OA_2, a level which would achieve a higher sales response than OA_1, but a lower resulting profit.

This model, however, has several practical and theoretical disadvantages.

1. It assumes that advertising can be varied smoothly and continuously. In fact, this is not so. An advertising campaign may be increased or decreased in extent, but this can only be done in discrete 'lumps'. One insertion more or less in a magazine campaign, for example can represent an increase or decrease of several hundred pounds in expenditure. Similarly, quality may vary.

2. It takes no account of the fact that sales vary with elements in the

marketing mix other than advertising: price and quality, choice of distribution channel and product variety can all produce a different pattern of outcome under varying circumstances.

3. No account is taken of other costs, such as manufacturing or distribution expenditures.

4. It assumes that revenue and cost functions can be constructed, that the relationship between advertising and sales is known. This is rarely the case.

5. No account is taken of the possible reactions of rivals.

6. The fact that advertising today can result in sales tomorrow, and that today's sales will to some extent depend on past activity is ignored. It is a single-period model.

7. Advertising varies in quality, effectiveness and appeal, often in a manner unrelated to the level of advertising expenditure.

We will examine some of these critiques in more detail.

The payoff to advertising depends not only upon how the market responds to the firm's advertising, but also upon how competitors react. One way to embrace this difficulty is to use a matrix as in Table 11.1. Here we have three alternative budget levels, a single competitor, and three alternative advertising responses by that competitor. The payoffs in the table can be resulting profits (as here), sales, market share, attitude change by consumers, or whatever criterion the firm decides to set as the objective of its advertising effort. The advertising budget can now be selected by whatever decision rule is most appropriate given the managerial circumstances. (For example the maximax, maximin, the minimax regret, the maximum likelihood, and the expected value rules.)

This analysis can also be developed further to take account of the problem of outguessing the intelligent competitor. In other words, a game theory approach could be adopted. For example, assume a two-person constant-sum game, with a total available profit of £6.2 million. This implies, somewhat unrealistically, that the total profits available in the market are unrelated to advertising expenditures, but that each firm's share of these total profits is directly proportional to its relative advertising budget.

Table 11.2 indicates the competitor's payoff matrix. Under these cir-

Table 11.1 The Firm's Resultant Profit (π, £'000)

		Competitor's Advertising Budget (£'000)		
		100	200	300
Alternative Advertising	100	5000	3000	1500
Budget Levels	200	4600	3300	2900
(£'000)	300	3800	3500	3100

Table 11.2 The Competitor's Resultant Profit (π, £'000)

		Advertising Budget Levels (Original Firm) (£'000)		
		100	200	300
The Competitor's	100	1200	1600	2400
Alternative Budget	200	3200	2900	2700
Levels (£'000)	300	4700	3300	3100

cumstances, and given that both firms adopt the maximin criterion, one firm would set its budget equal to £300,000. The competitive firm would do so also. This would be the equilibrium position. Neither firm could improve its payoff by altering its budget.

Then there is the defect that the model does not take into account the time factor. Advertising can be likened to capital expenditure in that it not only generates sales and profits today, but will continue to do so into the future as a result of the creation of the asset of goodwill. Like all capital assets, the carry-over effects of advertising will wear out. Consumers will forget the original advert, future competitive advertising will obtrude, and so on. Consequently, advertising budgeting can be likened in a way to the capital investment decision.

A simple example of this approach has been suggested by Simon who suggests that the assets advertising creates will depreciate at a constant rate into the indefinite future. In addition, there will be sales in the current period even if present advertising is zero, due to the carry-over effects of past advertising. His model runs as follows:

let k = the constant rate of depreciation
r = the firm's cost of capital
A_0 = the advertising budget in the current period
ΔS_0 = the increment in sales (net of all costs except advertising) generated in the current period by A_0
PV_s = the present value of all present and future net sales generated by A_0

Then

$$PV_s = \Delta S_0 + \frac{\Delta S_0(1 - k)}{1 + r} + \frac{\Delta S_0(1 - k)^2}{(1 + r)^2} + \ldots$$

$$+ \frac{\Delta S_0(1 - k)^\infty}{(1 + r)^\infty} = \sum_{t=0}^{\infty} \frac{\Delta S_0(1 - k)^t}{(1 + r)^t} = \frac{\Delta S_0(1 + r)}{r + k}$$

which is a variant of Simon's basic formula.[2]

The principle of marginal equivalency then tells us to continue advertising in the current period until the increase in PV_s due to ΔA_0 is just equal to ΔA_0. The present value of profits earned by current-period advertising is:

$$PV_\pi = PV_s - A_0$$

This model is attractive and conceptually simple. However, to the normal difficulties of specifying the sales response from a given volume of advertising is added the need to award a depreciation rate, k, and a cost of capital, r. Not all advertising will have the same decay or depreciation pattern. Some, such as institutional advertising or corporate image advertising (e.g. sponsorship of Grand Prix racing cars by cigarette companies) will have little immediate impact on sales and so a low ΔS_0, but such promotion will presumably also have a low value for k.

11.3 Practical Models

The approaches to advertising budget determination examined so far are imperfect. Many firms turn to less rigorous but more practical methods for

2   This is proved as follows:

$$PV_s = \Delta S_0 + \frac{\Delta S_0(1 - k)}{1 + r} + \frac{\Delta S_0(1 - k)^2}{(1 + r)^2} + \ldots + \frac{\Delta S_0(1 - k)^\infty}{(1 + r)^\infty} \qquad \text{(i)}$$

Now multiply throughout by $(1 - k)/(1 + r)$:

$$\frac{PV_s(1 - k)}{1 + r} = \frac{\Delta S_0(1 - k)}{(1 + r)} + \frac{\Delta S_0(1 - k)^2}{(1 + r)^2} + \frac{\Delta S_0(1 - k)^3}{(1 + r)^3} + \ldots +$$

$$+ \ldots + \frac{\Delta S_0(1 - k)^\infty}{(1 + r)^\infty} \qquad \text{(ii)}$$

Now if equation (ii) is subtracted from equation (i) we obtain:

$$PV_s - \frac{PV_s(1 - k)}{1 + r} = \Delta S_0$$

Therefore

$$PV_s = \Delta S_0 \left[\frac{1}{1 - (1 - k)/(1 + r)} \right]$$

$$= \Delta S_0 \left[\frac{1 + r}{(1 + r) - (1 - k)} \right]$$

$$= \frac{\Delta S_0(1 + r)}{r + k}$$

which is the desired result.

setting their advertising budget. Four of the more common ones have been described by Joel Dean. These are:

(a) The percentage-of-sales approach
(b) All-you-can-afford approach
(c) Competitive-parity approach
(d) Objective-and-task approach

Percentage-of-Sales

Ease of decision taking is a major advantage in this approach. The advertising budget is set at a level equal to some predetermined percentage of past or anticipated sales. The added attraction of apparent safety is present in that sales receipts and advertising outlays tend to coincide. However, no guide is given as to what percentage should be chosen and it seems probable that the 'dead hand of the past' will be a powerful influencer of choice. Firms will tend to choose that percentage which they traditionally use. Ideally, of course, the budget should be set in such a way that the outlay maximises the return from resulting sales. There is no reason why some arbitrary and consistent percentage of sales will achieve this aim.

The approach rests on some other illogicalities, particularly with regard to the sales base from which the budget is calculated. The use of future sales as the base from which to calculate the percentage has at least some rationale (although achieved sales will depend on many other factors as well as advertising expenditure). The same cannot be said for the use of past sales. Advertising is meant to cause sales in the future, not be the result of sales in the past. Yet this is the implication when budgets are set at some percentage of past sales.

All-you-can-Afford

Here the firm spends on advertising up to the limits of its cash resources. The reasoning behind this approach bears a strong resemblance to newer models of the firm.

Oliver Williamson, for example, suggests that firms must meet some 'minimum profit' level in order to maintain expected shareholder earnings and equity prices in the stockmarket, and to carry out essential investment expenditure. Above this minimum level, however, management will spend corporate resources on factors which increase its own utility. In so much as each manager obtains utility from the number of staff personnel reporting to him, then managers will attempt to increase the size of the firm in order to increase, in turn, the size of their staff establishment. Clearly, one means of increasing firm size is to use these profits above the profit-maximising level of advertising.

In practical terms this could mean that the advertising budget is set as the result of some sort of dialogue between the firm's financial and marketing directors. Certainly, one apparent advantage is that the approach sets a definite ceiling on what will be spent. The ceiling, of course, may be well above the profit-maximising level. Conversely, it is not inconceivable that the ceiling may be below the optimal level. Profitable market openings might be present in forthcoming periods for which past profit levels are insufficiently high to support an optimal advertising budget. In such cases the firm might be better advised to borrow resources for advertising, rather than be limited to 'what-it-could-afford'.

Competitive-Parity

This method again has the attraction of apparent security. The firm spends on advertising at the same percentage of sales, assets, market share or some other variable, as its competitors in the same industry. On the assumption that the relevant data can be obtained, the method has the advantage of simplicity. However, with the differing degrees and directions of corporate diversification, it seems unlikely that any one firm can identify itself completely with a group of firms all of whom are allegedly competing in precisely the same market.

For example, a paint manufacturer mainly selling to the painting trade will require different levels and styles of advertising from another firm selling primarily to the do-it-yourself market. Further, the first firm could be diversified in a small way into wallpaper production, the second might be operating in a wholly unrelated industry. Even if appropriate comparisons can be made, there is no reason why the budget selected should be optimal.

The method can also breed complacency, which could be rudely shattered if one aggressive firm decided to break ranks, and gained a substantial competitive advantage before sleepier rivals reacted. Similarly, a smaller firm which unthinkingly followed the industry pattern might find itself below a threshold level of advertising where its voice just could not be heard. Such a threshold is an absolute not a relative barrier.

Objective-and-Task

The previous three methods implied that allocation of the total budget by product, region and advertising medium followed the determination of the total budget. This approach tackles budget determination in the reverse order. The firm first defines the objectives it wants the advertising to attain. For example, the objective may be to achieve sales of product A in territory Z of some specified amount. Secondly, the advertising tasks which must be done to reach the objective are defined. The programme could, for example, take the form of a media campaign, say, six inserts in the local paper serving territory Z in a specified period. Finally, the tasks are costed, the costs aggregated and so the budget obtained.

Up to a point, of course, this is only a slight advance over the percentage-of-sales approach. Once again, the tasks to attain a given objective will usually be defined in terms of what it apparently took to attain some similar objective in the past. Thus, in the example given, six inserts in the paper serving territory Z will probably be chosen to attain the specified sales of product A only because six inserts had achieved that result in the preceding period. The question of whether five or seven inserts would be more profitable than six will probably not be asked, and if it were, the choice to change from six might well be made more in hope than in certainty. But, given the current state of knowledge (or lack of it), this is rather an unfair criticism. Ideally, the tasks to be determined should be related to the objective to be attained, and not to any recorded relationship between the two in past periods. However, past relationships are very often the only starting point from which to work, given the difficulties involved in predicting future sales response to future advertising.

One slight modification to this approach would, apart from the practical constraints already mentioned, bring it closer to the theoretical ideal of marginal equivalency of revenues and costs. The relevant question is whether an objective is worth pursuing in terms of the cost. With this considered in the approach, then only the more profitable objectives would be chosen, and the firm would be moving towards attainment of a profit-maximising advertising budget. The company would, of course, still be none the wiser as to whether marginal increases or decreases in expenditure on prescribed tasks would result in any particular objective becoming more or less profitable.

Experimental Method

This method is very similar to using a test market. A different level of advertising expenditure is set in different representative markets. The price, product quality, and so on are held fixed. The difference in sales between the markets is assumed to be the effect of the difference in advertising spend. Alternatively the advertising expenditure can be varied over time in one market, the differences in sales, again, being ascribed to this cause. The optimum budget is then chosen. The limitations of this technique are similar to those of test marketing: high cost, extraneous factors may nullify the results and a long time period may be required, so rendering the results possibly out of date.

Usage

Surveys suggest that the popularity of these methods has changed over the last 10–15 years in both the US and the UK. Table 11.3 shows some of the results from the most recent UK study. This shows, firstly, that many firms

Table 11.3 Percentage of Firms Which Use Method Regularly

	Sample	Consumer Goods	Industrial Goods	Services
What we can afford	48.8	50.5	54.1	41.8
Objective and task	39.6	43.0	39.8	35.8
Percentage of expected sales	38.3	56.6	33.0	28.7
Experimentation	13.7	16.6	7.3	17.0
Desired share of voice	11.5	17.5	5.4	11.3
Match competition	8.5	12.8	4.3	8.2
Accept agency proposal	4.3	4.0	4.6	4.1
Number of replies: 1,690				

Source: Derived from Hooley and Lynch (1985).

actually use a combination of methods. Secondly, the most popular methods overall are the 'all-we-can-afford', 'objective-and-task' and 'percentage-of-expected-sales' methods. Thirdly, service firms use the 'what-we-can-afford' approach less than consumer or industrial goods firms, whilst a greater proportion of consumer goods firms uses 'percentage-of-expected-sales' than the percentage of firms in the other two industries. 'Experimentation' and 'desired share of voice' are more popular among consumer goods and service firms than among industrial firms. The 'objective-and-task' method is equally popular for all groups.

11.4 The Theory and Practice of the Optimum Promotional Mix

Sales Response Isoquants and Marginal Equivalency

For any given advertising budget, the well-known principle of marginal equivalency states that it will be optimally allocated between the media when

$$MSR_1/P_1 = MSR_2/P_2 \ldots = MSR_n/P_n$$

where *MSR* represents the marginal sales response resulting from the last unit of advertising, in one particular medium, denoted by the appropriate subscript from the series $1, 2, 3, \ldots n$, where n represents the total number of available media. P represents the price of purchasing one unit of the medium in question.

This is so, since if the ratios are not equal as in

$$MSR_1/P_1 > MSR_2/P_2$$

then it would pay to remove some advertising effort from medium 2 and transfer it to medium 1. This may be more clearly understood if numbers are assigned. Consider that medium 1 is TV and 2 is newspapers. Consider that, in each, an extra showing or insert costs £100. Assume that spending an extra £100 on TV will bring in an extra £2000 sales, but in newspapers an extra £100 will only produce an extra £1000 sales. Thus

£2000/£100 > £1000/£100

With a fixed budget it would pay to switch £100 from newspaper to TV advertising. £1000 of sales would be forfeited through less advertising in the press, but £2000 would be gained through the higher level of TV advertising. A net gain of £1000 would result. Ultimately, of course, continuing to switch advertising in this way from the press to TV will produce diminishing returns to TV advertising. The ratio MSR_1/P_1 will fall. Conversely, spending less on the press will tend to raise the ratio MSR_2/P_2. When the two ratios are equal the budget is optimally allocated.

The same conclusion can be illustrated graphically. Here we use isoquants to join up points of equal sales response to advertising.

Figure 11.3 shows an example of an isoquant map constructed for this purpose. The budget line MM joins up those combinations of full-page press adverts and 15-second TV slots which can be purchased with the given budget. On the assumption that the costs of the media to the firm do not vary with the amount spent, MM will be a straight line.

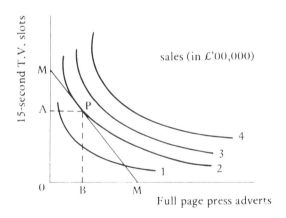

Figure 11.3

The profit-maximising advertiser will allocate his budget in such a way that he purchases A units of TV time, and B pages of press space. At this point, P, the budget line is tangential to the highest attainable (£200,000) sales response isoquant.

At P, the slope of the isoquant and the slope of the budget line are equal.

That is, the marginal rate of substitution of press for TV equals:

$$\frac{MSR_{Press}}{MSR_{TV}} = \frac{\Delta TV}{\Delta Press} = \frac{P_{Press}}{P_{TV}} \text{ or } \frac{MSR_{Press}}{P_{Press}} = \frac{MSR_{TV}}{P_{TV}}$$

which is again the position of marginal equivalency (ignoring the negative signs implied by the slopes).

Up to this juncture we have merely adapted the production function for advertising purposes. Now we must move beyond the normal stopping point of these expositions. The production function assumes a given technology, but any technology embraces a variety of possible and known techniques. In real-life manufacturing there are always a variety of techniques open to the manager, not merely a variety of capital–labour input combinations. For example, the sources of supply for capital equipment are themselves diffuse. Thus items of machinery which are fundamentally similar often vary slightly one from the other in manner of use, quite apart from the range of labour inputs the manager can select to work each machine. Similarly, in real-life advertising there is always a variety of known message designs available for use, not merely a variety of, say, press–TV combinations using only one design type.

The typical graphical production function isoquant is oversimplified. In order to take account of differing techniques of manufacturing or, in this case, differing message designs, some modifications are essential. In the area of general production theory, Feller has suggested the use of an arrangement of isoquants similar to that of Figure 11.4. We will adapt this figure specifically for advertising purposes. The isoquants represent the same level of sales response obtainable not only with differing media combinations, but also with differing message designs. D_1, D_2 and D_3 represent three different design types. The thick 'envelope' isoquant, D_1D_3, is the only isoquant relevant for the manager, since any part of an isoquant lying above the envelope curve would require at least more of one medium, and not less of the other medium, to produce a given sales level, than would be required by some other known, existing message design. (The isoquants in Figure 11.3 are all implicitly envelope isoquants for the relevant sales responses, as in Figure 7.3 they are 'envelopes' for a range of techniques.)

With a budget line, AA, the profit-maximising advertiser would select message design D_1, and would combine his media in the proportions indicated at the point of tangency A_1. If the costs of TV and press advertising altered, say press became cheaper and TV more expensive, then the same budget could possibly buy the input combinations indicated by BB. Not only will media substitution take place as the advertiser moves to B_1 from A_1, but message design will also alter from D_1 to D_2.

This analysis is not in the least inconsistent with reality. It is rather an attempt to bring theory closer to real life.

Theory neglects advertising creativity. Yet the sales effect of advertising

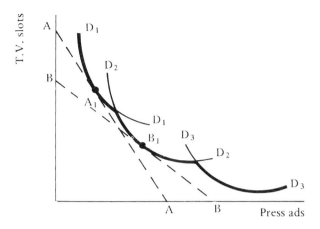

Figure 11.4

depends heavily on this. The term 'creativity' refers to what the advertiser says (message content) and to how he decides to say it (message form).

Some flesh may now be put on the bones of Figure 11.4 by means of the following highly simplified illustration. Consider an advertiser with problems of media selection and message design (content and form). The content decision could involve a choice, say, between a highly descriptive advertisement with a lengthy exposition at one extreme, and a cryptic, abbreviated presentation of product-associated attributes at the other. The form decision could imply a choice, say, between a 'hard sell' approach and a witty, playing down of the advertised product.

Thus, isoquant D_1D_1 could represent varying combinations of press and TV advertisements which result in an equal sales response, given a message design D_1, which is a combination of minimum information and maximum wry wit. D_2 could represent a message design which is a combination of lengthy exposition and the 'hard sell'. D_3 could be maximum humour plus maximum information, and so on.

So with media cost line AA, message design D_1 would be chosen — minimum information, maximum wit — at media combination point A_1. This is not an implausible position. When TV is cheap relative to the press, as it is with cost line AA, then other things equal, TV will tend to be used relatively more by the advertiser than will the press. If this is so, then the message design which will be the most effective will be that which is relatively most suited to TV, and least to the press. Conversely, when the press is cheap relative to TV, as with cost line BB, then media substitution will take place as indicated in the shift from A_1 to B_1. When such a movement is made towards buying relatively more press advertisements and fewer TV ones, then it should not be unexpected that a change in message design will occur from one suitable to TV to one more suited to the press.

D_2 is a more suitable message design than D_1 if the press is the more attractive medium economically, and *vice versa*. Closely reasoned arguments require relatively large amounts of supporting information, and time for that information to be digested by the potential consumer. Newspapers provide the advertiser with the ability to put over large amounts of information and give the reader as long as he himself needs to assimilate it. TV adverts, on the other hand, are of necessity brief, and cannot be perused in depth at the discretion of the individual viewer.

D_1, however, is probably a more suitable message design when TV is the more economically attractive. Here TV will tend to be used relatively more than the press, and the strengths of TV can be exploited by the appropriate message design. Voluminous information is precluded, but a lesser quantity of information may be all that is required, given the added impact of visual motion and aural stimulation. Moreover, if, as some have suggested, people tend to be less willing to accept the credibility of advertising messages on TV than they do in the press, then it could be that the 'hard sell' will generate ill-will towards the advertiser, while a humorous approach might knit in better with the credulity attitudes people bring to their advertisement viewing habits.

Media Planning in Practice

The difficulties involved in predicting the sales response from any advert or run of adverts often forces managers to turn to highly pragmatic, imprecise tools of media planning.

Media characteristics (such as colour, motion, sound and print) and suitability for promoting the product in question will be assessed. Costs will be obtained, and a decision taken on the basis of whether or not the appropriate potential consumers are being reached at an acceptable level of expenditure. Within a fixed budget this (reach) must in turn be balanced against frequency of advert appearance, and both against continuity, or length of campaign. Media scheduling, in other words, is often solely a matter of managerial intuition, albeit based on close and intimate knowledge of the product, the market and the available media. In short, there are four variables in media planning and (given a budget) an expenditure change in one implies a corresponding expenditure reduction or increase in one or more of the others, namely:

1. reach
2. frequency
3. continuity
4. impact

Sinclair defines 'impact' as the physical media characteristics required for the product given either its nature or the nature of the target market.

Given the application of production function theory to the problem of the media mix, it is not surprising that one of the most commonly used tools is linear programming. Figure 11.5 illustrates the application of linear programming to the media mix decision. The process rays D_1, D_2, D_3 and D_4, can now more properly be regarded as representing the differing message design types of Figure 11.4. The press and TV constraints indicate the physical limits of insertions in each of these media. If the press was a weekly paper, for example, the constraint would be 52. The TV constraint might be 312 slots given a six-evening week (for some products manufacturers consider it worthwhile advertising on TV only on the nights before a possible shopping day, namely Sunday to Friday evenings inclusive). BB is the budget line and, within the constraints, the highest attainable sales response isoquant is bb, on process ray D_2, at the media mix indicated by point P.

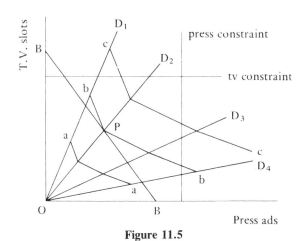

Figure 11.5

More generally this can be written as follows:

$$\text{maximise sales} = \sum_{i=1}^{n} R_i Q_i \tag{11.1}$$

subject to the constraints

$$\sum_{i=1}^{n} C_i Q_i \leqslant B$$

$$Q_i \leqslant L_i$$
$$Q_i \geqslant 0 \text{ for } i = 1, 2, 3, \ldots n$$

where Q_i = the number of unit adverts or insertions in medium i; R_i = the sales response of a single insertion in medium i; C_i = the cost per insertion in medium i; B = given total advertising budget; L_i = a predetermined (or physical) limit of insertions in medium i.

Unfortunately, the situation is not quite so straightforward as the above discussion implies. Some of the obstacles to the immediate application of production function theory in this way are intrinsic in the linear programming technique, others are implicit in the uncertain nature of the relationship between advertising and sales. For example, the following (false) assumptions have been made:

the sales response to a medium insertion is constant
the time factor is non-relevant
sales response per insertion is known
costs of media insertions are constant
there is no media interaction
the number of insertions is a continuous variable.

We will now examine each of these assumptions in more detail.

The S-shaped Sales Response Function

We have already seen, in Figure 11.2, that there comes a point when there are diminishing returns to scale of advertising. The linear programming model ignores this possibility. The unrealism of this assumption can be readily and intuitively shown. Consider equation (11.1). The model can be solved by finding the value R_i/C_i, the sales response per pound, for each medium.

The optimal solution is then to select the medium with the highest value of R_i/C_i and spend on it up to the limit of either B or L. If B is not exhausted, then the remainder should be spent on the medium with the second highest R_i/C_i ratio.

However, it is highly unlikely that spending the budget on only one, or a few, media represents the 'true' optimum. One way out of this difficulty is to adopt the procedure of 'piecewise' linear programming. The non-linear response function is split up into a piecewise linear equivalent. Figure 11.6 illustrates this discussion and equation (11.2) shows how the linear programming model of equation (11.1) would be adapted accordingly, thus:

$$\text{maximise sales} = \sum_{i=1}^{n} [R_{i1}Q_{i1} + R_{i2}(Q_{i2} - Q_{i1}) + R_{i3}(Q_{i3} - Q_{i2})] \quad (11.2)$$

subject to the constraints

$$\sum_{i=1}^{n} C_i Q_i \leqslant B$$

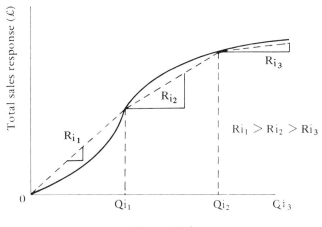

Figure 11.6

$$Q_i \leqslant L_i$$
$$Q_{i3} > Q_{i2} > Q_{i1} \geqslant 0$$

The Time Factor

The problem of media scheduling (whether to advertise more heavily, for example, on a Monday or a Friday, in January or October) can be overcome by adding a time subscript to each Q_i, so specifying the total exposure, $R_{it}Q_{it}$, over each medium and over time. This does not, however, cope with the second aspect of time, namely the positive impact of replication and the negative one of forgetfulness. We will offer one possible counter to this criticism in the next few paragraphs.

Exposure and Awareness as a Proxy for Sales Response

The exact relationship between advertising and sales is rarely if ever known. Econometric demand equations and test marketing exercises are two common means of attempting to ascertain what the sales response to any given level of advertising might be. Both, however, are essentially *post hoc* in nature. For *ante hoc* decision making, exposure to an advert, or awareness of its appearance, are commonly used proxy measures of advertising effectiveness, the plausible rationale behind this being that exposure of a potential customer to an advert is more likely to result in a sale than non-exposure.

Unfortunately, readership survey data (or viewership for TV) is of limited assistance to most advertisers wishing to measure the extent of exposure to their campaign. Most campaigns have more than one insertion in the media. As a result, while readership may give some idea of the reach of a one-shot campaign, it will prove to be inadequate for measurement of reach and of frequency of exposure in a campaign with two or more shots.

The term 'opportunity to see' (OTS) with regard to an advert means just that. For example, consider a campaign with four inserts in a women's weekly magazine, which has an average readership of 7.5 million. The total target population is all women, say 20 million. Assume the same 7.5 million read the magazine week by week, and the other 12.5 million never see it. Then the situation in Table 11.4, case 1 exists. This is a very unlikely distribution. In reality, some women will subscribe to the publication faithfully week by week, others will see it frequently but not consistently, while still others will be only spasmodic readers. Furthermore, some journals will have a more loyal readership than others. The results that this might have on the frequency distribution of OTSs throughout the target population are illustrated in cases 2 and 3 of the table.

Table 11.4

Total population of women 20 million = 100%	Members of total population with:				
	zero OTS	one OTS	two OTSs	three OTSs	four OTSs
Journals with identical average readership of 7.5m.					
Case 1: Totally loyal readership	12.5m (62.5%)	—	—	—	7.5m (37.5%)
Case 2: High readership loyalty	50%	5%	10%	15%	20%
Case 3: Low readership loyalty	40%	20%	20%	10%	10%

In all three cases illustrated, the total readership potential is $4 \times 7.5m = 30$ million readers. But, in fact, in case 1, only 7.5 million read the magazine, albeit on four consecutive occasions. In case 2, 10 million people saw the magazine at least once, but only 4 million saw it four times, while in case 3, 12 million saw it at least once, but only 2 million four times. Clearly, the advertiser with a run of adverts in a medium is interested in these sorts of data, the total and distribution of OTSs throughout the population, and not merely readership.

The data in Table 11.4 can be obtained from the National Readership Survey (NRS). Thus in column 1 of the table we have the *reach* figures. (Similar data are available for TV viewers and radio listeners from the Broadcasters' Audience Research Board (BARB). Further, the real-life data collected are broken down regionally and by socio-demographic groups. In other words, table 11.4 is unrealistically simple. Collection techniques range from questionnaires to electronic meters attached to TV sets.

To return to our example, given that the target market is all 20 million women, reach is $7.5/20 = 37.5\%$ in each of cases 1, 2 and 3. However, reach alone is not enough, and the NRS questionnaire results provide the type of data required to construct the remaining columns of Table 11.4. Namely the OTS (or in the case of radio and TV, OTH (hear) or OTV (view)) figures. thus we obtain the *frequency* data.

At this juncture many media planners would stop and set themselves tasks (as in the objective and task budget determination technique) embodying also the impact and continuity variables. Typical objectives could be schedules such as (a) to reach a minimum of 37.5% of the target market over the campaign period or (more complex) (b) to reach a minimum of 20% of the target market with a frequency of 4 occasions per month between August and December and a monthly frequency of 3 times between January and July. These tasks would then be costed against the rate cards of the selected media and the budget chosen. To evaluate schedules against each other comparing permutations of reach times and frequency a *Gross Rating Point* (GRP) can be used. GRP is simply reach times frequency. Thus, in cases 2 and 3 of Table 11.4 respectively, the GRPs are:

$$5\% + 2 \times 10\% + 3 \times 15\% + 4 \times 20\% = 150$$
$$20\% + 2 \times 20\% + 3 \times 10\% + 4 \times 10\% = 130$$

So the case (2) journal has a higher GRP value than case (3), despite having identical average readership figures. (Note: the neat whole number OTS figures of Table 11.4 will not occur in practice — rather, on average, fractional figures will be obtained.)

We can now go one stage further, however. The information in Table 11.4 can be converted into a projected advertising effectiveness (not sales) response function. From the Gallup Organisation (UK) (in the USA Daniel Search Inc.), the regularly published survey data can provide the average noting (or awareness) score in the particular publication in some past period by ads similar in style, size, colour, position, and so on, to the one the firm is considering inserting. This average is then taken as the probability that such an ad's OTS potential will or will not be transformed into 'opportunities taken'.

Consider an ad with a predicted noting score of, say, 50%. A prediction of the response function for a four-insertion campaign in the women's magazine described in case 2 is required. The first step is demonstrated in Table 11.4 which indicates how the OTS distribution is converted into the more relevant distribution of opportunities taken, or exposures actually received by readers. By the normal theory of probability, half of those having one OTS will see the ad, and half will not. Similarly, of those having two OTSs, one half will see it once, one quarter twice and one quarter not at all, and so on for the higher values of OTSs.[3]

The next stage is to 'specify the response function' from the 'ad exposures received' figures.

This is done by assigning values to the different numbers of exposures. Manifestly, the 15.63% of the total population in Table 11.5 who receive two exposures will be more affected by the advertising than the 18.13% who receive only one exposure. To transform each exposure datum to an appropriate effectiveness equivalent or response value requires modifying it by an appropriate weight. The weights should reflect the S-shaped sales response function, thus taking into account increasing, then ultimately decreasing, returns in advertising effectiveness. Table 11.6 shows how a response function can be specified using arbitrary weights[4] to transform the advert exposure data of Table 11.5.

Column 4 of Table 11.6, marginal response values, refers only to that incremental proportion of the population effectively reached by one more or one less exposure. The cumulative response values are then easily calculated from the marginal data. The cumulative data can be compared with the

Table 11.5

Estimate of opportunities taken (ad exposures received)	All housewives	Members of population with:				
		zero OTS	one OTS	two OTSs	three OTSs	four OTSs
	100%	50%	5%	10%	15%	20%
0	58.12%	50%	2.5%	2.5%	1.87%	1.25%
1	18.13	—	2.5	5	5.63	5
2	15.63	—	—	2.5	5.63	7.5
3	6.87	—	—	—	1.87	5
4	1.25	—	—	—	—	1.25

3   These proportions relate to the products of (a) the corresponding binomial probabilities of a certain number of successes from a given number of opportunities (where the probability of success in each case is 0.5) and (b) the percentage of the population with 0, 1, 2, 3 ... OTS values. Hence they can be determined from the binomial probabilities table in a statistics text.

4   For illustrative purposes it has been assumed that for a four-insert campaign, increasing returns to advertising inserts have been succeeded by diminishing effectiveness. Clearly, the use of the entire length of the S-shaped function to base weights on in this way may not be valid until many more inserts have been made. This can only be judged on the merits of the case. It is possible, for example, that a pattern such as 0.1, 0.6, 0.8, 1.0 would have been more appropriate here (increasing followed by constant returns).

Table 11.6

(1)	(2)	(3)	(4)	(5)
Ad exposures	Relative effectiveness of exposures (arbitrary weights)	% Target group reached	Marginal response value 2 × 3	Cumulative response values
0	0	58.12	0	0
1	0.1	18.13	1.813	1.813
2	0.4	15.63	6.252	8.065
3	0.8	6.87	5.496	13.561
4	1.0	1.25	1.25	14.781

S-shaped sales response function of Figure 11.2. Intermedia comparisons and decisions can then be effectively made on lines very similar to those suggested by the marginal-equivalency formula. The disadvantages of using arbitrary weights will be partially neutralised for comparison exercises of this sort if an identical system of weighting is used for calculating each medium's response function. Furthermore, it is highly probable that assigning weights in this manner provides more realistic information for decision takers than not doing so at all. Failure to do so implies constant returns to advertising exposure, a most unlikely situation.

Column 4 provides values for R_{i1}, R_{i2}, and so on, for equation (11.2) which can be used as proxies for (the otherwise unknown) sales response data, and which also embrace the impact of replication of advertisement exposure. It does not, however, take into account the fact that exposure effectiveness *per capita* diminishes over time due to forgetfulness.

Media Discounts

The linearity assumptions of linear programming models ignore the not uncommon practice of media owners to award volume cumulative discounts to customers after a given size of purchase in a medium. This gives rise to sharp discontinuities in the total cost function. This inability is a significant problem at all times but particularly when a multi-product firm is deriving its media plan. (In the theory of production the budget line is no longer straight but becomes convex to the origin.)

Media Interaction

Linear programming also makes the unrealistic assumption that there is no media interaction. Media interaction can be of two varieties. First, there is straightforward audience duplication. Thus a potential customer can be exposed to an ad for the same product in both the Daily Express and on television. Conceptually, this is relatively easy to embody in the media planning model. For example, if the probability of a Daily Express reader noting a given ad is 0.8, and the probability of that same reader noting the relevant TV ad is 0.6, then the probability of that individual (or group of individuals) noting them both is the product of the two probabilities, namely 0.48.

More problematically, there is the problem of media synergy, or its obverse. For example, if £1000 of press advertising in isolation results in 10 units of effectiveness and, similarly, £1000 of TV advertising in isolation results in 10 units of effectiveness, but £2000 of advertising evenly split between the two media and carried out simultaneously results in more or less than 20 units of effectiveness then synergy or its obverse has occurred.

For example, a person who normally ignores press advertising may be encouraged to study a press advert in some detail if he has seen the same product advertised on TV the previous evening. He might, perhaps, want to digest at leisure product information in the press which is something the transience of a TV advert precludes. When this occurs in production theory, the convexity of the output isoquants to the origin becomes more pronounced. Thus a given budget line would be tangential to a higher isoquant. The converse would occur if the advertising response functions reacted in a negative manner.

The Integer Nature of Insertions

Linear programming is unable to cope with non-continuous input variables. The only (imperfect) practical way to overcome this is the somewhat unsatisfactory method of 'rounding off' to the nearest whole input unit. This weakness also highlights the inappropriateness of our linear programming analogy of Figure 11.5, where we compared the process rays with the message design envelope isoquants of production theory in Figure 11.4. Message designs, however, cannot be uniquely identified; they merge imperceptibly. Moreover, in practice, the message design which, by all rational reasoning, is most appropriate for a given media mix, might prove to be highly successful if used in a wholly unconventional media pattern. Such is the unpredictability of the creative factor.

Nevertheless, despite the many difficulties this chapter has enumerated, because of the vast availability of survey and other market research data, advertising is an area where the reasoning of managerial economics can readily, and fruitfully, be applied.

The Dorfman−Steiner Theorem

So far, in the discussions on price and advertising, we have generally held price constant while varying advertising, and vice versa. The Dorfman−Steiner theorem permits variation in both. (Indeed, other variables, such as research and development expenditures, which also affect output, can be embodied in the general model — see Needham 1975).

Algebraically, the theorem states that profit maximisation occurs when

$$\eta = \mu$$

where η = price elasticity of demand

$\quad\mu$ = marginal sales effect of advertising (i.e. the marginal change in sales revenue due to a marginal change in advertising expenditure)

Let p = price
$\quad q$ = quantity demanded
$\quad a$ = advertising expenditure
$\quad c$ = average production costs (assumed constant)
$\quad\pi$ = profits

During the proof process several interesting implications emerge. The firm desires to maximise profits

$$\pi = pq - cq - a \qquad (A1)$$

where $q = f(p,a)$
and $\quad \partial q/\partial p < 0$ (the demand curve slopes down)
and $\quad \partial q/\partial a > 0$ (advertising shifts the demand curve outwards)

Price and advertising are independent variables, so $\partial p/\partial a = 0$, while total cost ($cq$) is a function of output, so:

$$cq = C = g(q) = g[f(p,a)].$$

But production cost is also independent of advertising, so $\partial(C)/\partial a = 0$. With these assumptions we can rewrite equation (A1) as:

$$\pi = p[q(p,a)] - C(q) - a \qquad (A2)$$

To choose the values of p and a that will maximise profits, equation (A2) must be differentiated with respect to each and the resultant equations set equal to zero:

$$\frac{\partial \pi}{\partial a} = \left(p \frac{\partial q}{\partial a} + q \frac{\partial p}{\partial a} \right) - \left(\frac{\partial C}{\partial q} \cdot \frac{\partial q}{\partial a} \right) - 1 = 0$$

using rules (5) and (6) from Chapter 1. Hence:

$$\frac{\partial \pi}{\partial a} = p \frac{\partial q}{\partial a} - \frac{\partial C}{\partial q} \cdot \frac{\partial q}{\partial a} - 1 = 0 \tag{A3}$$

(Recall p and a are independent variables.) And

$$\frac{\partial \pi}{\partial p} = \left(p \frac{\partial q}{\partial p} + q \frac{\partial p}{\partial p} \right) - \left(\frac{\partial C}{\partial q} \cdot \frac{\partial q}{\partial p} \right) = 0 \tag{A4}$$

Equation (A3) can be rearranged by factorising $\partial q / \partial a$ out of the expression and recalling that $\partial c / \partial q$ equals MC. Since AC is assumed constant, i.e. not varying with output, $MC = AC$. Hence:

$$\frac{\partial q}{\partial a} (p - c) = 1$$

Now multiply through by a/pq to obtain:

$$\left(\frac{a}{q} \cdot \frac{\partial q}{\partial a} \right) \frac{(p - c)}{p} = \frac{a}{pq} \tag{A5}$$

The first term in brackets is the advertising elasticity of demand, η_a. The second term is the mark-up obtained over average costs, and the right-hand side is the firm's advertising: sales (or A/S) ratio. If c is regarded as marginal costs, then the second term is known as the Lerner index of monopoly power, which records the firm's 'power' to raise its price above marginal cost.

Thus we can see from equation (A5) that profit-maximising advertising expenditure depends on:

1. The advertising elasticity of demand. The greater this is, the greater advertising should be (to maintain the equation's equality).
2. The firm's sales revenue (pq). The greater this is, the greater advertising will be.
3. The firm's monopoly power as measured by the Lerner index. The greater this is, the greater advertising will be.

If we now return to equation (A4) and multiply through by p/q we obtain:

$$\left[p \times \left(\frac{p\partial q}{q\partial p} \right) + \frac{pq}{q} \right] - \left[\frac{\partial C}{\partial q} \left(\frac{\partial q}{\partial p} \frac{p}{q} \right) \right] = 0 \qquad (A6)$$

Given that the expressions in curved brackets are by definition equal to price elasticity of demand $(-\eta)$ we can rewrite equation (A6) as:

$$p(-\eta) + p - c(-\eta) = 0$$

or

$$(p-c)\,(-\eta) = -p$$

which, if divided throughout by $(-p)$ and by η, results in:

$$\frac{p-c}{p} = \frac{1}{\eta} \qquad (A7)$$

So, by substituting (A7) into (A5), we have:

$$\frac{\eta_a}{\eta} = \frac{a}{pq} = \frac{a}{S} \qquad (A8)$$

The firm's a/S ratio will be higher, the lower is price elasticity of demand. To obtain the formal Dorfman−Steiner result of:

$$\eta = \frac{p\partial q}{q\partial p} = \mu = p\,\frac{\partial q}{\partial a}$$

we simply expand and manipulate equation (A8). Thus:

$$\frac{a}{q}\,\frac{\partial q}{\partial a} \cdot \frac{1}{\eta} = \frac{a}{p \cdot q}$$

$$= \frac{p\partial q}{\partial a} = \mu = \eta$$

Q.E.D.

Additional Reading

Broadbent, S. (1980) *Spending Advertising Money*, (3rd edn), Business Books.
Dean, J. (1951) *Managerial Economics*, Prentice-Hall.
Dorfman, R. and Steiner, P. (1954) 'Optimal advertising and optimal quality', *American Economic Review*, December.
Economist Intelligence Unit (1986) *Is your Advertising Budget Wasted?*

Feller, I. (1972) 'Production isoquants and the analysis of technological and technical change', *Quarterly Journal of Economics*, Vol. XXCVII.

Hooley, G.J. and Lynch, J.E. (1985) 'How UK advertisers set budgets', *International Journal of Advertising*, Vol. 4.

Montgomery, D. and Urban, G.L. (1969) *Management Science in Marketing*, Prentice-Hall.

Needham, D. (1975) 'Market structure and firms' R&D behaviour', *Journal of Industrial Economics*, Vol. 23, No. 4.

Needham, D. (1976) 'Entry barriers and non-price aspects of firms' behaviour', *Journal of Industrial Economics*, Vol. 25, No. 1.

Reekie, W.D. (1981) *The Economics of Advertising*, Macmillan.

Simon, J. (1969) *The Management of Advertising*, Prentice-Hall.

Sinclair, Roger (1985) *Make the Other Half Work Too*, Macmillan.

Williamson, O.E. (1963) 'Selling expense as a barrier to entry', *Quarterly Journal of Economics*, Vol. 77, No. 1, February.

PART IV

Medium/Long-Term Decisions

12
Capital Budgeting

There are three main problems involved in financial economics: investment selection, method of funding investments once selected, and dividend policy towards corporate shareholders when investments begin to bear fruit.

12.1 Investment Appraisal

Investment appraisal handles three main types of capital outlay problem. First, is expansion advisable? Would it be profitable to add to our existing stock of plant or equipment? Second, is replacement of obsolete, but mechanically adequate, capital stock worthwhile? Finally, if the answers are positive, should we rent or buy the new machinery or factory space? There are two traditional methods of solving these problems, the return on capital method and the pay-back period. The more recent alternative, however, is to use one of the discounted cash flow techniques.

A project's *return on capital* (*ROC*) is its expected profit, less depreciation, but before tax, expressed as a percentage of capital outlay. Thus, the return on capital for a machine which is to cost £1000, produce £200 of profit per year, and is depreciated by the straight line method over ten years, would have its *ROC* calculated as follows:

Forecasted Profit	£200
Less Depreciation (10% × £1000)	£100
Net Pre-Tax Return	£100

Thus $ROC = 100/1000$ as percentage $= 10\%$.

Provided the company considered 10% to be adequate, the project would be approved. With alternative projects from which only a limited number could be chosen (because of shortage of funds, or because projects were mutually exclusive) then the *ROC* for each would be ranked and those with highest values selected.

As detailed here, this technqiue has a number of drawbacks. First, it takes no account of profit variability from year to year. The forecasted figure could, of course, be calculated by averaging the varying forecasts for a range of years. Second, no guidance is given as to what system of depreciation the firm should employ. Our example used the straight line method. There is no reason why the reducing balance system would not have been equally appropriate; nor why 9% or 11% as a depreciation rate would be less or more appropriate than the 10% used. Third, no indication is given as to how capital outlay itself should be defined. For example, should the receipt of government investment grants or tax allowances be deducted? Fourth, no account is taken of the effect of differing asset lives. Thus, two projects with identical capital outlays might have *ROC*s of 9% and of 16%. The latter, however, might provide returns for only two years before replacement became essential or before the profit opportunity vanished. On the other hand, if the 9% project continued to provide its return for 25 years, it could well be a more attractive and sensible alternative. The technique as defined, however, would select the 16% project irrespectively. Finally the possibility of reinvesting returns in subsequent projects in later periods is ignored.

A project's *pay-back period* is the number of years required for accumulated profits, gross of depreciation, to equal the capital cost of the asset. Thus the pay-back period in our earlier illustration (outlay £1000, annual profit £200) would be five years. If a choice had to be made between projects, then they would be ranked in diminishing order of attractiveness and the projects with the briefest pay-back periods selected.

There are two major difficulties. No account is taken of earnings received after the pay-back period expires. Thus, other things being equal, a project which ceases on the expiry of its pay-back period of five years, is regarded as more attractive than a project with a six-year pay-back which also continues to earn well into its ninth year of life. Second, all future payments are given equal weight. Thus no distinction would be made in the relative attractiveness of two projects, each with a three year pay-back and each with a £1000 outlay where earnings were received in three annual increments of £900, £50 and £50, or £50, £50, and £900.

Discounted cash flow (DCF) techniques overcome the various difficulties associated with the two traditional methods. Each of the deficiencies is taken into account and reduced consistently to one figure which is truly comparable, project by project.

Both *DCF* methods make use of the present value formula of Chapter 1, viz:

$$PV = \frac{\pi_1}{1+r} + \frac{\pi_2}{(1+r)^2} + \frac{\pi_3}{(1+r)^3} + \ldots + \frac{\pi_n}{(1+r)^n} = \sum_{i=1}^{n} \frac{\pi_i}{(1+r)^i}$$

To work through the full formula is tedious and a common short-cut is to use a table of discount factors (see Appendix at the end of this chapter). This enables us to give a value to each term provided that π and r are known.

There are three basic steps. First, profits are calculated for each year of the project's estimated life. These are obtained from sales and cost forecasts, calculated after tax. Thus, variability of profit year by year is explicitly taken into account. Second, the depreciation is not deducted. All capital expenditure will be included in the final cash flow calculation, so no provision to build up a fund to cover the original outlay will be required. Thus the problems of how to handle depreciation in the traditional methods are taken account of. Third, investment grants and allowances are included in the appropriate year's cash flow. The relevant future receipt or cash flow for each year can then be calculated as in the example in Table 12.1.

Table 12.1

Year	Profits (Sales-cost, less Tax)	Investment Allowances	Proceeds from Sale of Plant as Scrap	Cash Flow
1	10	20	—	30
2	30	10	—	40
3	30	—	—	30
4	25	—	—	25
5	10	—	—	10
6	10	—	10	20

Table 12.2 shows what the present value of the project would be at three given and different interest rates (r). The discount factors are taken from the Appendix — they are, quite simply, the relevant reciprocals of $1/(1+r)^i$.

The two alternative *DCF* techniques, net present value (*NPV*) and internal rate of return (*IRR*), both generally provide the same outcome or result.

Table 12.2

Year	(1) Cash Flow	(2) Discount Factor for 5%	Relevant PV (1×2)	(3) Discount Factor for 6%	Relevant PV (1×3)	(4) Discount Factor for 7%	Relevant PV (1×4)
1	30	0.952	28.56	0.943	28.29	0.935	28.05
2	40	0.907	36.28	0.890	35.6	0.873	34.92
3	30	0.864	25.92	0.840	25.2	0.816	24.48
4	25	0.823	20.57	0.792	19.8	0.763	19.1
5	10	0.784	7.84	0.747	7.47	0.713	7.13
6	20	0.746	14.92	0.705	14.1	0.666	13.32
	£155		£134.09		£130.46		£127.0

The rules for the use of the two are as follows:

(1) A project is worthwhile if the *NPV* is greater than zero (where *NPV* is defined as the project's present value less its capital outlay),[1] or

(2) A project is worthwhile if its *IRR* is greater than the cost of capital to the company (where *IRR* is defined as that discount rate which will render the project's *NPV* equal to zero).

Reconsider Table 12.2, given that the capital outlay required is exactly £130.46. The *NPV* is positive (£134.09 − £130.46) at a 5% interest rate. The project is worthwhile. At 7%, *NPV* is negative (£127.00 − £130.46) and so the project is not attractive. Alternatively, the project's *IRR* is exactly 6%. Thus the project is worthwhile at any cost of capital to the company below 6%. At a cost of capital over 6%, the company would be paying more for the capital than it would receive as a return from the project.

Figure 12.1 shows the *NPV* function for the project of Table 12.2 varying with the discount interest rate, *r*. Both methods indicate that the project is worthwhile at any cost of capital less than 6%. The *NPV* is positive at all points to the left of the 6% discount rate. The *IRR* is 6% exactly, the point where the *NPV* function cuts the discount rate axis.

In Figure 12.2 the firm is faced with three alternative projects, *A, B* and *C*. In this situation of project choice, either technique provides the same answer. At a discount interest rate of *x*, each project has a positive *NPV*, yet the *NPV* of *C(c)* is more attractive than *b* or *a*, the *NPV*s of *B* and *A* respectively. Similarly, *C*'s *IRR*, *c'*, is greater than either *a'* or *b'*.

One disadvantage of the *IRR* technique is that it requires trial and error calculation until a zero *NPV* is reached and so the *IRR* discovered. This is laborious, but it does mean that it can be calculated before a decision is taken on what the cost of capital is, against which the *IRR* is to be compared. The *NPV* calculation is a one-off job, but only if the cost of capital, the discount rate *r*, is known.

Table 12.3 summarises much of this discussion.

---

1   The underlying reason for the *NPV* rule is that *NPV* is the value today of the surplus which the project earns over the amount the firm could earn by putting its money into the next-best project (which would give a rate of return equal to *r*). To understand this, consider a project costing £10 with a single cash inflow of £22 in year one. Let the return on the best alternative project be 10%. The cash inflow of the £22 is worth only £20 (= 22/1.10) today, that is, after we have removed the amount we could have earned with the best alternative project during our one year's wait. But our project cost £10. So the value today, of the project net of its outlay *and also after the opportunity cost has been removed*, is £20 − £10 = £10. But notice how this was obtained:

$$-10+[22/(1+r)]$$

in other words: *NPV*.

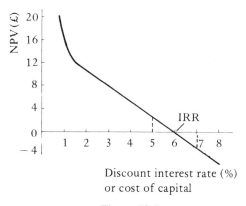

Figure 12.1

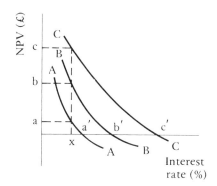

Figure 12.2

12.2 Conflict Between the DCF Techniques

Capital Rationing

Although the *NPV* and *IRR* techniques appear to be simply the opposite sides of the same coin they can and do give conflicting results. Consider Figure 12.3. A group of projects is arranged in descending order of attractiveness by their respective *IRR*s. *MCC* is the marginal cost of capital. The heavy line on the histogram shows the *IRR* of the marginal project. Clearly the firm should invest £7000 up to and including project *E*.

However, in any given period the firm is unlikely to have an unconstrained budget available for capital investment, in which case it may prove better to accept several smaller projects which fully utilise the budget, rather than accept one large project which leaves part of the budget unused. Thus in Figure

Table 12.3 Discounted Cash Flow Formulae and their Uses

(a) *Expansion Decisions*

Go ahead if $NPV > 0$

i.e. if $NPV = \displaystyle\sum_{i=1}^{n} \frac{FR_i}{(1+r)^i}$ − capital outlay > 0

or Go ahead if *IRR* > cost of capital

(b) *Rent or Buy Decisions*

Rent if the *PV* in this case is greater than the *NPV* in case (a) and is also > 0.

i.e. if $PV = \displaystyle\sum_{i=1}^{n} \frac{(FR\text{-rental charge})_i}{(1+r)^i} > 0$

Clearly, no capital outlay is deducted from the *PV* in this case.
or Rent if *IRR* is greater than the *IRR* in case (a).

(c) *Decisions on Replacement or Continuity with Existing Plant*

Here the book value of existing plant should be ignored. It is irreversible and cannot be altered by today's decisions. Marginal equivalency principles will be adhered to and sunk costs ignored if actions are taken only when the benefits exceed the costs. Thus it pays to replace existing plant if the following condition holds (and *vice versa*):

$\displaystyle\sum_{i=1}^{n} \frac{(\text{Cost savings due to new equipment})_i}{(1+r)^i}$

$+$ scrap value of old plant today

$+ \dfrac{\text{scrap value of new equipment in year } n}{(1+r)^n}$

$>$ capital outlay on new equipment

$+ \dfrac{\text{scrap value of old plant in year } n}{(1+r)^n}$

Note: All of the above formulae can be adjusted for risk and uncertainty using the techniques
  described in Appendix 2A. Alternatively, if the Capital Asset Pricing Model is used to
  calculate 'r', then risk is explicitly embodied in the formulae (see pp. 339–362).

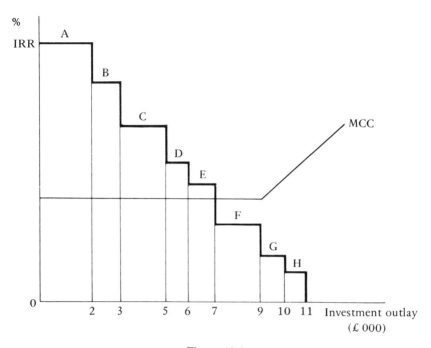

Figure 12.3

12.3 the firm might have only £4000 to invest. Should it undertake *A*, *B* and *D*, *A* and *C*, or *A* and *B* with an unused £1000? Each of these three courses of action is acceptable by the *IRR* method. The appropriate choice is the one which provides the highest *NPV* to the firm. Suppose the *NPV*s and other relevant information are as summarised in Table 12.4. The profitability index (i.e. the ratio of the gross present value of future cash flows to the original

Table 12.4

Project	Initial Outlay (£)	NPV	Profitability Index	Ranking Profitability Index	NPV	IRR
A	2000	1000	1.5	1	1	1
B	1000	400	1.4	2	3	2
C	2000	700	1.35	3	2	3
D	1000	250	1.25	4	4	4
E	1000	200	1.2	5	5	5
idle balance*	1000	0	1.0	6	6	6

* invested at cost of capital, i.e. *MCC* in Figure 12.3

outlay) is clearly a useful shorthand device when appraising projects using
the *NPV* method: it merely needs to exceed unity for us to know that the *NPV*
will be positive, thus the higher the index, the more attractive in relative (but
not absolute) terms is the project. The index emphasises not only the *NPV*
of a project, but also the efficiency with which the project generates that *NPV*
from each pound invested. In this example, the optimal choice is *A* and *C*,
providing an *NPV* of £1700, rather than *A, B* and *D* providing an *NPV* of
only £1650.

Mutually Exclusive Projects

On other occasions also, the *IRR* and the *NPV* methods can give contradic-
tory results. This is not of importance if there is no capital rationing, and
if we are merely trying to find out whether a project is worthwhile. If both
methods say the project is attractive, then it can be gone ahead with. But it
does matter if two or more mutually exclusive projects are being compared
and a rank order is desired to permit choice of one and rejection of the others.
Graphically, this situation is illustrated in Figure 12.4. With a cost of capital
of *V*, project *A* has a higher and more attractive *NPV*. Yet project *B*, with
an *IRR* of *Z* is more attractive than project *A* with an *IRR* of only *Y*.

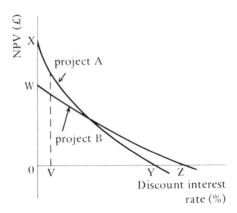

Figure 12.4

The conflict arises because of differences in the time patterns of the cash
flows of each project. In *NPV* terms project *A* is preferred at lower interest
rates because its receipts are achieved relatively later. (Tomorrow's cash is
worth less than today's because of discounting, and the higher the discount
rate and/or the further away 'tomorrow' is, the more true this becomes.) Project
B, with cash flows received relatively earlier, consequently becomes more

attractive at higher discount rates. In *IRR* terms, project B is consistently more attractive at $Z\% > Y\%$.

Consider the two projects C and D outlined in Table 12.5, given a cost of capital of 3%.

Table 12.5

	Year	Outlay (year 0)	1	2	3	NPV	IRR
i	Project C	100	120	0	0	16.4	20%
ii	Project D	110	0	0	140	18.1	8.5%
iii	D – C	10	– 120	0	140	1.7	4%

If correct assumptions are made about the implicit compounding of interest, the *NPV* and *IRR* techniques can be reconciled. Several methods of comparing like with like are available. First, and most simply the *NPV* method compares today's pounds with today's pounds, thus favouring project D. Secondly, the two projects can be compounded forward to a *common terminal date*. (Project C's income of £120 in year 1 is available for reinvestment at that point at the cost of capital.) In year 3 project D yields £140 less £120.2 (the initial £110 outlay compounded forward to year 3) which equals £19.8. Project C's £120 compounded forward is worth £123.6 by year 2 and £127.3 by year 3 from which we subtract £109.3 (the initial £100 outlay's value in year 3) to obtain £18. Again project D is preferred. Third, project D's *IRR* is 8.5%. Project C, however, returns 20%, but only for one year. Subsequently it returns 3%, the cost of capital or the return on the best available alternative investment opportunity. In addition, D has a greater initial outlay than C. The return from this additional £10 must be included with those of the £100 to facilitate comparison. We assume this £10 is invested at (the best available rates) the cost of capital to give an inflow of £10.9 in year 3 only. By adding this to the £127.3 to give £138.2 and finding the rate which discounts this to equal the £110 initial outlay, the *corrected IRR* of C is found to be 7.9%. This is less favourable than D's 8.5%. Finally, the *NPV* and *IRR* techniques can be reconciled using the method known as the *incremental hypothetical project*.

If project C is chosen at the opportunity cost of D, then the implication is that the £10 'saved' by not investing in D is invested at 3%, the best alternative use. If D is chosen, however, that 'incremental' £10 has an *IRR* greater than 3%, namely 4% (calculated as in row *iii* of Table 12.5). In other words, D provides all that C can provide in terms of *NPV* ($18.1 = 16.4 + 1.7$) but provides 1% more ($4\% - 3\%$) on the additional £10 which is required to finance it. Again project D is the optimal choice.

Dual Rates of Return

Simultaneous calculation of two *IRR*s for one project is not common but it can happen and ambiguity arises. Figure 12.5 illustrates the phenomenon.

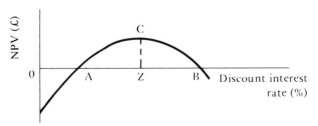

Figure 12.5

With a cost of capital of Z, the project has a positive *NPV* of C. Yet two *IRR*s are present, A and B. Since $OZ > OA$, this project should be rejected. Yet, if *OB* is taken as the *IRR*, the project should be gone ahead with. The reason for the duality of answers is the two reversals of sign in the net cash flow during the project's life. When this occurs, the *IRR* method will often (not always) produce ambiguous results. The reason this happens lies in the mathematical construction of the discounting formula itself. Consider a three-period project with outlay K and income π. The *IRR* is that value for r which renders

$$K - \frac{\pi_1}{1+r} - \frac{\pi_2}{(1+r)^2} = 0$$

or $K(1+r)^2 - \pi_1(1+r) - \pi_2 = 0$

Let $(1+r) = x$, and K, π_1, and π_2 be a, b and c respectively, then

$ax^2 - bx - c = 0$

In short, this is merely a quadratic equation where two possible values for x, i.e. $1+r$, may occur. In short, the *IRR* formula has the same number of roots as the power value of the discounting denominator. Most of these multiple roots will be either negative or hypothetical (e.g. $\sqrt{-2}$). The Change of Sign Rule described by the mathematician Descartes can be adapted to the *IRR* formula to state that there will be as many positive roots for $(1+r)$ as there are changes in the sign of the cash flow. Thus, if after the initial outlay there are only positive cash flows, there will be only one positive root for $(1+r)$ and hence only one value for r itself. On occasions, however, negative cash flows can be expected in a project's life.

For example, some North Sea oil rig construction yards on the West Coast of Scotland were built in deep water sea lochs. Permission to build these yards during the height of the rig construction boom in the 1970s was given on the understanding that the firms would return the countryside to its original condition when the yards were closed. Open cast coal mining has similar environmental reclamation constraints. Consider a project with the following cash flow and a cost of capital of 10% as in row 1:

	Outlay	Year 1	Year 2	Year 3	Year 4
Row 1	− 1000	+1000	+2000	+1500	−1100
Row 2	− 1000	+1000	+2000	+ 500	0

The problem of multiple roots can be avoided by limiting the number of sign changes to one as in row 2. In *NPV* terms rows 1 and 2 are identical. £1100 spent in year 4 is the same as £1000 spent in year 3. The former is simply discounted to year 3 values using the 10% discount rate.

12.3 Capital Structure

So far we have not considered how the cost of capital is selected for use in the discounting approach. Here we will discover that the value for r is intimately connected with the decision as to how to raise the capital with which the firm is funded.

The Cost of Capital

The cost of capital is the discount rate which should be used in the formula for calculating a project's *NPV*. It is the yardstick with which the *IRR* of a project is compared. It enables the manager to apply marginal equivalency principles to the investment decision. Projects can be ranked in diminishing order of attractiveness by *IRR* and each undertaken until the *IRR* of the marginal project equals its cost of capital.

Thus, it is a marginal cost. It is the cost of capital of the marginal project. This project will only be gone ahead with if the benefits it will produce are equal to the benefits forgone by failing to invest in (and so forfeiting the return from) the best available alternative investment opportunity. It is, therefore, an opportunity cost. It is the return available on the best alternative project. This is a figure which is easier to describe than to determine, however. It is not, for example, the ruling market interest rate. That would only be the cost of capital if there was a perfect capital market. Then a firm could borrow or lend without limit and without risk. Given unlimited capital, any project yielding a rate higher than the market rate would already have been undertaken. Only then would the highest obtainable rate anywhere, the opportunity cost, be the market rate.

Even if the capital market was perfect, a further difficulty would arise. Lending rates and borrowing rates tend to differ. Borrowers usually have to pay more than they would receive as lenders. At its simplest, this is accounted for by the presence of a middleman. Which rates should be chosen? If the only alternatives are borrowing and lending, then the lending rate is the cost of capital, if the money to be invested would otherwise have been lent out to the market given an absence of outstanding debt. The borrowing rate is the best available alternative return (or avoidable cost) if the money to be used in the project would otherwise have been allocated to repay a debt.

In addition, the cost of obtaining money is not always static as the quantity borrowed rises. Sometimes the cost rises as more is borrowed. In such circumstances it is the marginal cost of borrowing which is the cost of capital.

Finally, the cost of capital cannot equal the market rate for the simple reason that the market rate is not unique, but can have a range of values depending on the source from which funds are raised. Each source (for example, debentures, ordinary shares, loans, retained earnings, and so on) has a different interest requirement. There is no reason why any of them should be equal to the rate offered by the best available alternative investment opportunity. Moreover, which source of new capital a firm will use will depend upon its attitude to capital gearing, to fixed interest charges and to any tax advantages which may accrue by using one method rather than another. (Current tax law permits the charging of loan interest against profits before the levying of Corporation Tax. Dividends, however, are deducted from profits after the calculation of Corporation Tax. Other things being equal, for this reason alone loan stock is a more attractive form of financing than equity. It reduces the base figure on which Corporation Tax must be paid and so reduces the firm's tax bill and, correspondingly, increases the after-tax income available for distribution or for reinvestment.)

The Debt:Equity Ratio and Gearing

The practical advantages and disadvantages of one method of financing *vis à vis* another are, of course, taken into account in the theoretical concept of the cost of capital. Since this theoretical cost is difficult to determine for reasons discussed above, practical alternatives have been devised which are useful approximations to the firm's true cost of capital.

The so-called 'traditional' approximation is to take the weighted average of the firm's earnings yield calculated before tax[2] and the rate of interest payable on any fixed interest capital.

2   The earnings yield is the net profit earned per share expressed as a percentage of the market price of a share. Generally, it is calculated after Corporation Tax, hence the use of the word net. For cost of capital purposes, it is usually grossed up to include Corporation Tax liability. This is done to ensure that the cost difference between the two sources of funds due to differences in tax treatment is not overlooked.

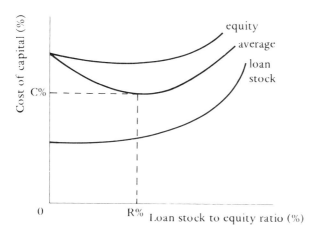

Figure 12.6

This is illustrated in Figure 12.6 for a continuous range of gearing (loan:equity) ratio alternatives. The cost of capital of a company financed solely by equity would be the earnings yield itself. The 'average' and the 'equity' cost curves intersect at this point. In the impossible event of a company being solely financed by debentures, the 'average' and 'loan stock' cost curves would intersect at a loan:equity ratio of 100%. Why do the curves have the positions and shapes indicated? The fixed interest on loan stock cost curve starts off at a relatively low level. Since loan stock holders legally have first call on the profits of a company in the pecking order of distribution, they are traditionally assumed to have chosen a less risky form of investment alternative than equities and consequently they expect and are entitled to a lower rate of return than the equity holder. As the gearing ratio increases, however, the degree of risk assumed by loan stock holders also increases. By definition, the surplus of total profits accruing to equity holders will have become absolutely smaller. Since this is the bond holder's 'cushion' in the event of a downturn in the fortunes of the firm, they will demand a slightly higher return to compensate for this. After a point this increase in reward will not compensate for increasing risk and the gentle rise in the early stages of the loan stock curve will become dramatic and sharp. Table 12.6 expresses this argument in figures.

Two firms are shown each with £1000 of capital assets, each experiencing a profits fall from £200 to £100 in a given two-year period. Each distributes its total surplus to its shareholders. The only difference between the two is in their gearing ratios. Hi-Gear Ltd, the firm with the higher debt:equity ratio, is less favourably placed to maintain payments of loan interest in the face of a profit downturn. (The initial cushion is £110, compared to Lo-Gear's £100; for a similar profit downturn, this falls to only £10, a proportionately larger fall than Lo-Gear's which drops only to £90.)

Table 12.6

Hi-Gear Ltd			Low-Gear Ltd		
Capital Structure			Capital Structure		
100 £1 Ordinary shares		100	900 £1 Ordinary shares		900
900 10% Debentures		900	100 10% Debentures		100
		£1000			£1000
	Year 1	Year 2		Year 1	Year 2
Profits	200	100	Profits	200	100
Less loan interest	90	90	Less loan interest	10	10
Dividend	110	10	Dividend	190	90
Dividend yield	110%	10%	Dividend yield	21%	10%

The equity cost curve in Figure 12.6 will be higher to begin with because of the intrinsic difference in risk. As the debt:equity ratio rises, the return demanded by shareholders will also rise. Higher gearing increases the risk to the equity holder as well as to the debenture holder. In this case, the increased risk is due to the increased variability of the residual left to pay shareholders with. (Hi-Gear Ltd, for example, experiences a 100% fall in dividend yield between years 1 and 2. Lo-Gear suffers a drop, under identical circumstances, of only 11%.)

The traditionalist view, therefore, is that moderate levels of gearing reduce the cost of capital, higher levels increase it. Just as management tries to minimise production and marketing costs at any given output level, so too it should try to minimise financing costs. This means, first, selection of the appropriate gearing structure. Cost of capital is minimised at $C\%$, a gearing ratio of $R\%$. Second, the average cost of capital curve is dependent on the positions of both the loan stock and the equity cost curves. If either of these can be shifted downwards, then the average itself will fall.

The Modigliani—Miller View

The main challenge to the above arguments has come from Modigliani and Miller (MM). They argue that the cost of capital is independent of capital structure. The main MM proposition is that the average cost of capital is constant (not U-shaped) and is equal to the cost of equity in a company with a zero loan:equity ratio.

They argue that this must be so since, if otherwise equally risky companies differ in market value and gearing ratio, then investors will sell investments (shares or debentures) in the higher valued firms and buy investments in the lower valued. This arbitrage process is profitable so long as differences in market value (and so total yield from any one firm) persist.

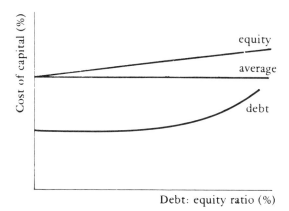

Figure 12.7

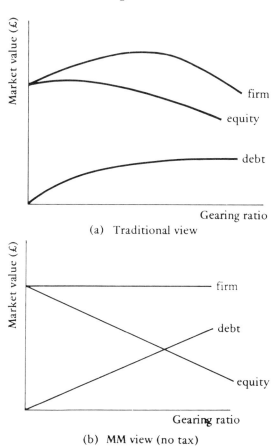

(a) Traditional view

(b) MM view (no tax)

Figure 12.8

Given that ungeared firms are in the list of options open to investors, then the uniform level at which the cost of capital will settle will be the cost of equity in such firms. Figure 12.7 illustrates the MM view of the cost of capital. Figure 12.8 compares the MM and traditional views of how the value of the firm varies.

The MM model rests on a number of highly restrictive assumptions. Corporate taxation is disregarded. Earnings retention and so corporate growth is zero. Total assets are given, only their method of funding may change. For any firm, each investor has the same expectations as to earnings before interest (π_{BI}). π_{BI}, in turn has a zero growth rate. Company operating risk is deemed constant over time and independent of gearing. The firm's life span is infinite. Investors operate rationally in a perfect capital market, and each individual is able to borrow or lend at the same rates as would quoted companies. To show the model in operation let:

S = total market value of equity
B = total market value of debt
V = $B+S$
I = interest payments
g = growth rate
N = number of shares outstanding
P_0 = current share price
D_0 = current dividend
I/B = K_d = cost of debt (see pp. 333 and 338)

$$\frac{D_0}{P_0} = K_e = \text{cost of equity given that } g = \text{zero (see pp. 332-3 and 338-9)}$$

$$= \frac{D_0(N)}{P_0(N)} = \frac{\pi_{BI}-I}{S} = \frac{\pi}{S}$$

where π = earnings after interest, and all of the above expressions are in their perpetuity form. The weighted average cost of capital, K_w, under either the traditionalist or MM views is:

$$K_w = (W_d \times K_d) + (W_e \times K_e)$$

where $W_d + W_e = 1.0$

$$\therefore K_w = (B/V \times K_d) + (S/V \times K_e)$$
$$= (B/V \times I/B) + (S/V \times \pi/S)$$
$$= I/V + \pi/V = \pi_{BI}/V$$

Now suppose that 2 firms exist identical in every respect except market values and gearing. The share price of the more highly valued company will be bid down by shareholders selling their shares, and the share price of the lower valued company will be bid up by shareholders buying its shares. This will continue until the market values of both companies are equal. This is because, without increasing his risk, each shareholder can increase his income by such arbitrage. When the market values become equal, shareholders can no longer increase their income in this way and equilibrium is reached. K_w is now the same for each firm irrespective of gearing.

To see this, recall that

$$K_{w1} = \frac{\pi_{Bl1}}{V_1} \text{ and } K_{w2} = \frac{\pi_{Bl2}}{V_2}$$

for firms 1 and 2. If they are identical for V_1, V_2 and their gearing ratios, then because V_1 comes to equal V_2 through arbitrage, and since $\pi_{Bl1} = \pi_{Bl2}$ because the firms are identical, then the weighted average costs of capital, K_{w1} and K_{w2} must also be equal.

Numerically, consider firms A and B prior to an MM arbitrage process. Each has a par and market value as shown. This assumes an identical equity capitalisation rate of 10% despite gearing differences. Thus:

	A		B	
	Par Value	Market Value	Par Value	Market Value
Equity	5000	7500	10,000	10,000
Debt (5%)	5000	5000	—	—
	£10,000	£12,500	£10,000	£10,000

B has a dividend of £0.1 per share, a pay out of £1000 for an earnings yield of 10%. A has a dividend of £0.15 per share, a pay out of £750 for an earnings yield of 10%. In addition A must pay out £250 in interest. As a consequence of A's higher gearing, its total market value is higher at £12,500, reflected in this example exclusively in equity prices. As the traditional approach would predict A's weighted average, cost of capital at 8% is lower than B's at 10%.

(For A, $K_w = \frac{\pi_{Bl}}{V} = \frac{1000}{12,500} = 8\%$. For B, $K_w = 10\%$.)

But any individual investor who held, say, 50 A shares in his personal portfolio, could improve his position by selling them and acquiring B shares in their place. Thus as in columns i and iii:

| | Before Sale | | After Sale | |
| | i | ii | iii | iv |
		(equilibrium)		(equilibrium)
A shares (50)	£75	£50	nil	nil
B shares	nil	nil	125	100
dividend received	£7.5	£7.5	£12.5	£10
debt (personal)	nil	nil	50	50
gearing ratio of portfolio	75:50	50:50	75:50	50:50
interest due (personally)	nil	nil	£2.5	£2.5
income (net)	£7.5	£7.5	£10	£7.5

The investor in this case has maintained the gearing ratio of his portfolio at 75:50 by borrowing £50 to enable him to purchase a total of 125 B shares. As a consequence his net income rises from £7.5 to £10. He will continue to do this until no further gain can be made. Thus, at its simplest, if B's market price and par values remained the same, but A's share price fell to par because of continuous selling, then when A's total market value reached £10,000, no further arbitrage would take place, and both firms would have a weighted average cost of capital of 10%. Columns ii and iv show how arbitrage would no longer be worthwhile in such circumstances. Note that in both comparisons the gearing ratios are held constant in order to hold portfolio risk constant.

The Cost of Debt

The cost of debt, $I/B = K_d$, in the weighted average cost of capital equation is obtained by adjusting it for tax. Thus the after tax cost of debt is $K_d = I/B(1-t)$ where t is the rate of corporation tax. Thus, for tax reasons, debt is cheaper than equity and MM and traditionalists agree that the overall cost of capital is U-shaped when gearing takes place. MM, however, attribute this solely to the tax effect, and not at all to the pure leverage effect. More precisely, I should equal the present value of all interest payments and any principal repayment and K_d should be the *IRR* which equates the value of I with the proceeds to the firm of the issue of debentures.

The Cost of Equity

The cost of ordinary shares in the cost of capital calculations is 'the minimum rate of return' the firm 'must earn on the equity-financed portion of its investments in order to leave unchanged the market price of its stock' (Van

Horne). This is the firm's expected earnings yield or rate of return shareholders expect to earn over the years from holding shares of the firm.

Thus it can be found by calculating the value of r in the following equation:

$$P_0 = \frac{D_0}{1+r} + \frac{D_0(1+g)}{(1+r)^2} + \frac{D_0(1+g)^2}{(1+r)^3} + \ldots + \frac{D_0(1+g)^n}{(1+r)^{n+1}}$$

which simplifies to $P_0 = D_0/(r-g)$, or

$$r = \frac{D_0}{P_0} + g = K_e \tag{12.1}$$

where D_0 is the current level of dividend, P_0 the current market price and g the expected constant growth rate of dividends per share.

This model (often known as the Gordon dividend growth model) assumes, of course, that dividends will grow at a rate of g compounded to infinity. It also assumes an efficient capital market: that is that P_0 reflects all available information about the economy, the financial markets and the particular company concerned. In turn this implies that P_0 adjusts quickly and smoothly to new information. P_0 thus only moves randomly (the random walk) around its 'intrinsic value', the intrinsic value itself adjusting solely to informational changes. Neither of these assumptions is necessarily correct, and although modifications to g can be embodied in the original equation before solving for r, these too must involve inexact estimation.

12.4 The Cost of Equity and Portfolio Theory

An alternative approach to measuring the cost of equity, r, is the capital asset pricing model (CAPM) approach. Given certain assumptions, the required rate of return is the same as the discount rate calculated using the Gordon dividend growth model. Moreover, it also embraces any risk involved in the potential shareholding (or investment project). Hence no further adjustment for risk to the *NPV* formula is required.

When an investor decides to adopt a certain mix of securities (or range of investment projects), he does so under conditions of less than full information. If we ignore uncertainty and assume that conditions of actuarial risk apply, then it is conceptually possible that a decision taker could use the expected utility maximisation model of Chapter 2. To do so would require knowledge of each individual project's or security's risk and return profile. The entire probability distribution of the possible returns of each security or project would have to be known and so would the utility function of the decision maker.

Furthermore, since the returns of different securities may or may not be correlated over time, any particular portfolio's returns will vary according to its mix of securities. Thus the expected utility maximisation model would have to be extended to the choice of the optimal portfolio or set of securities. Each set in turn would have an expected (mean) return and risk (standard deviation). The firm or decision maker would then choose the portfolio which maximises his expected utility.

In principle this requires that every possible portfolio mix be examined, and that the expected utilities be calculated from the total probability distribution of possible returns given the utility of wealth of the investors. The investor can then choose the portfolio providing the highest expected utility. To obviate this enormous data requirement, Markowitz suggested that the possible values of a security's risky *NPV* will have a *normal* probability distribution. Such a distribution is, of course, identifiable by only two elements: the mean and the variance. (The variance, σ^2, is the square of the standard deviation, σ.) This, as we shall see, reduces the data requirement problems to a more manageable level.

Since the mean and variance provide in summary all the information about a normal frequency distribution for one asset or project, we can move on to consider a two-or-more security portfolio.

Expected Returns

Let proportion x of the investor's resources be invested in firm A and $(1-x)$ in firm B. The portfolio's expected return $\bar{r}_p$ can then be expressed as:

$$\bar{r}_p = x\bar{r}_A + (1-x)\bar{r}_B \qquad (12.2)$$

The *portfolio's* mean return is simply the weighted average of returns on *individual shares* (or investments) where the weights are the percentages of resources attributed to each. Thus, if the returns for A and B are as shown in Table 12.7, then $\bar{r}_A = 9.5\%$ and $\bar{r}_B = 12\%$ respectively.

Variances

The variances for A and B are calculated from the general formula:

$$\sigma^2 = \sum_i (r_i - \bar{r})_p^2 \qquad (12.3)$$

Table 12.7

Probability (p)	A(%)	B(%)
0.25	12	22
0.25	20	10
0.25	10	4
0.25	−4	12

Hence $\quad \sigma_A^2 = 0.25(0.025)^2 + 0.25(0.105)^2 + 0.25(0.005)^2$
$$+ 0.25(-0.135)^2 = 0.007475 \ (\sigma_A = 8.6\%)$$

Likewise $\quad \sigma_B^2 = 0.0042$

The relevant risk measure of the portfolio (in terms of its standard deviation around $\bar{r}_p$) will clearly depend not only on $\bar{r}_A$, $\bar{r}_B$, on σ_A and σ_B, but *also on whether all possible returns for A and B are or are not expected to be positively or negatively correlated with each other*, and on the strength of that correlation. Thus, unlike the calculation of $\bar{r}_p$, portfolio risk is *more than* just the weighted average of the relevant securities' standard deviations or variances. Rather, we are interested in how the distributions of returns do or do not move in unison.

This is the basis of what is now called portfolio theory. It distinguishes between two types of risk: systematic and unsystematic. The former (systematic risk) cannot be avoided by security investors, since it affects financial markets in totality (e.g. general economic conditions, government policy changes at a macro level, and so on). Unsystematic risk, however, is peculiar to the security or firm concerned. This type of risk will include strikes, innovations, management quality, the state of industry rivalry and the like. Unsystematic risk can be 'diversified away' in any individual's portfolio since shares with a high level of such risk can be offset against low-risk shares. Figures 12.9, 12.10 and 12.11 illustrate the effect of such diversification.

In Figure 12.9 the returns for firms A and B fluctuate over time (for example A and B could be producers of ice cream and umbrellas). Their returns are perfectly inversely correlated. Notice that the investor does not know whether returns on A or B will be high or low next period, but only that *if* they are high for A, they will probably be low for B and vice versa. By appropriately diversifying ownership between A and B an investor can guarantee for himself (assuming a perfectly negative correlation) an unvarying (i.e. riskless) return of $Y\%$. This is known as risk removal or *risk reduction*.

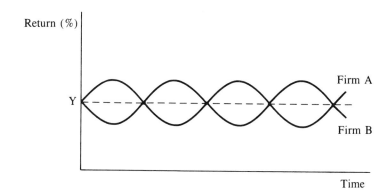

Figure 12.9

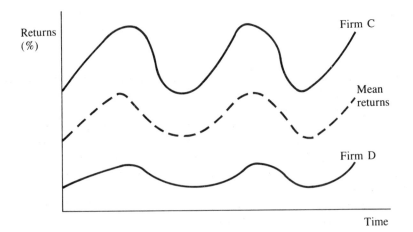

Figure 12.10

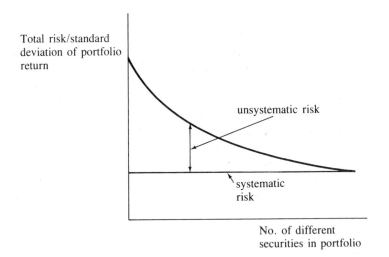

Figure 12.11

It should be noted that this is not the same as *risk averaging*. For example, in Figure 12.10, firms *C* and *D* have perfectly *positively* correlated returns over time (albeit *C* has both bigger returns on average and a higher level of risk as indicated by their variability). By appropriately diversifying his portfolio between *C* and *D* an investor can risk average. The fluctuation amplitude of the dashed line is less than that of the returns pattern for *C* but greater than that for *D*.

The risk which can be reduced (or averaged) is, of course, limited to unsystematic risk. Thus even an investor with a portfolio such as that in Figure

12.9 will not actually find that his returns are static and consistent over time as the figure indicates. Rather, the dashed line at Y will continue to rise and fall in line with the stock market as a whole. That is, the systematic risk component cannot be eliminated.

Figure 12.11 shows how appropriate portfolio diversification can reduce unsystematic risk close to zero, but never risk as a whole. That is, if the capital market is efficient (i.e. investors are rational and well informed, transaction costs and obstacles to investment or disinvestment are zero, no participant is large enough to affect a security's price, and all investors have similar expectations) then it follows that at the margin investors will have constructed portfolios whose overall risk is effectively limited to the systematic component (Figure 12.11).

This explains why, in Table 12.7, the σ for a diversified portfolio of A and B is less than σ for a specialised holding of either A or B. This is what we would expect successful diversification to accomplish. But we would also expect riskier assets to have higher returns as in Figure 12.10. However, A with a σ of 8.6% has a lower return at 9.5% than B with σ of 6.5% and return of 12.0%. This paradox is resolved when we discover that σ is not an appropriate measure of risk when individual securities can be combined (as in most cases in real life they can) with others into portfolios. As Brealey and Meyers put it: 'Since investors can diversify away unique risk, they will not demand a higher return from stocks that have above-average unique (i.e. unsystematic) risk. But they *will* demand higher return from stocks with above-average *market* (i.e. systematic) risk.'

In statistical terms the reason is that covariance, rather than variance or standard deviation, is the appropriate measure to gauge the riskiness of an individual security relative to a diversified portfolio. This can be proved or illustrated numerically, intuitively, or with more sophisticated statistical theory. Here we will use numerical and intuitive illustrations.

The covariance is simply a measure of the way the two random variables, for example r_A and r_B, move in relation to each other. When the covariance σ_{AB} is positive the variables move in the same direction, and when negative in opposite directions. The covariance is important since it measures the contribution of a single security's returns to total portfolio risk.

There are two factors which, statistically, affect the value of σ_P, given the returns on each stock. These are (a) the proportion of resources devoted to each stock and (b) the correlation between these returns. We shall consider these in turn.

(a) Proportion of Resources in Each Stock (x)

As the number of securities in a portfolio rises and the share of each (x) decreases, the portfolio variance decreases and approaches the average feasible covariance. The 'average feasible' covariance is, of course, at the limit, the covariance of the stock market as a whole.

Consider first a numerical example based on the securities A and B of Table 12.7. A 50:50 mix of products A and B provides a return midway between the returns to be expected from specialisation, but in addition a lower level of risk (as measured by σ_P) than specialisation in *either* A or B (measured by σ_A and σ_B) would provide. A and B have standard deviations of 8.6% and 6.5% respectively, whereas σ_P is only 5.3% (see Table 12.8). Risk reduction, not risk averaging, has taken place.

Naturally, the manager need not choose to have a product mix composed only of A or B on a 50:50 basis. Any mix is possible. Some possibilities are listed in Table 12.8, and Figure 12.12 plots the resulting mean and standard deviation. It can be shown that

$$\sigma^2{}_P = x^2\sigma^2{}_A + (1-x)^2\sigma^2{}_B + 2x(1-x)\rho_{AB}\sigma_A\sigma_B \tag{12.4}$$

σ_A and σ_B are known from Table 12.7, and that ρ_{AB}, the correlation coefficient, is calculated from the returns data relating to r_A and r_B in Table 12.7, and it equals -0.04, while $\sigma_A\sigma_B = 8.6\% \times 6.5\% = 0.0056$.

Column 3 $(\bar{r}_p)$ of Table 12.8 is simply the weighted average of $\bar{r}_A$ and $\bar{r}_B$ taken from the results of Table 12.7 $(\bar{r}_A = 9.5\%$ and $\bar{r}_B = 12\%)$. Column 4 (σ_p), however, is not the simple weighted average of the individual σ_A and σ_B values derived from Table 12.7 $(\sigma_A = 8.6\%$ and $\sigma_B = 6.5\%)$. That would only be so if the returns were perfectly correlated (pure risk *averaging* would have taken place). But we have already seen (Figures 12.9 and 12.10) that risk *reduction* is achieved by diversification, not simply risk averaging.

Why does this result in the use of equation (12.4) for σ_p^2 in Table 12.8 rather than the intuitively apparent use of a weighted average? To understand

Table 12.8

Percentage in A	Percentage in B	$\bar{r}_p(\%)$	$\sigma_p(\%)$
100	0	9.5	8.6
75	25	10.0	6.4
50	50	10.75	5.3
25	75	11.5	5.6
0	100	12.0	6.5

Note: The product portfolio risk and return figures were calculated thus (for the 50:50 case):

$$\bar{r}_p = (0.5 \times 0.095) + (0.5 \times 0.12)$$
$$= 10.75\%$$
$$\sigma_p^2 = (0.25 \times 0.007475) + (0.25 \times 0.0042)$$
$$+ 2.0 \cdot 5.0 \cdot 5(-0.04)\,0.0056$$
$$= 0.001869 + 0.001 - 0.000112$$
$$= 0.00276$$
$$\Rightarrow \quad \sigma_p = 5.3\%$$

equation 12.4 consider a two stock portfolio. The variance, σ_P^2 is calculated from the following four cell matrix which shows the covariation between any two stocks.

	A	B
A	$\sigma_{A,A}$	$\sigma_{A,B}$
B	$\sigma_{B,A}$	$\sigma_{B,B}$

This can be re-expressed as:

	A	B
A	σ_A^2	$\rho_{AB}\sigma_A\sigma_B$
B	$\rho_{AB}\sigma_B\sigma_A$	σ_B^2

since it is a statistical definition that the correlation coefficient, $\rho_{AB} = \sigma_{AB}/\sigma_A\sigma_B$. Each of these cells is respectively the covariance between A's returns and A's returns, between A's and B's returns, between B's and A's returns and between B's and B's returns. The portfolio variance is obtained by summing the four cells having first weighted each cell by the relevant pro- portions of total funds invested in A (x) and B ($1-x$). Thus in the top left cell the weight is x^2 and in the bottom right it is $(1-x)^2$. (Since we are dealing with σ_P^2 not σ_P). In the top right and bottom left cells the appropriate weighting factor is $x(1-x)$ in each cell. Hence equation 12.4 is derived. Notice from Table 12.8 that given ρ_{AB}, increasing the proportion of the portfolio which is devoted to B (from 0%) increases the value of $\bar{r}_p$ but leads at first to a reduction in σ_p before an increase (see Figure 12.12).

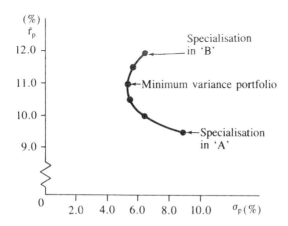

Figure 12.12   Trade-off between mean and standard deviation

In the multi-security case, the number of possible covariances, of course, increases. This can be illustrated in a matrix thus:

$$
\begin{array}{llll}
\sigma_{A,A} & \sigma_{A,B} & \sigma_{A,C} & \cdots\cdots \sigma_{A,M} \\
\sigma_{B,A} & \sigma_{B,B} & \sigma_{B,C} & \cdots\cdots \sigma_{B,M} \\
\sigma_{C,A} & \sigma_{C,B} & \sigma_{C,C} & \cdots\cdots \sigma_{C,M} \\
\quad\cdot & \quad\cdot & \quad\cdot & \qquad\cdot \\
\quad\cdot & \quad\cdot & \quad\cdot & \qquad\cdot \\
\quad\cdot & \quad\cdot & \quad\cdot & \qquad\cdot \\
\quad\cdot & \quad\cdot & \quad\cdot & \qquad\cdot \\
\quad\cdot & \quad\cdot & \quad\cdot & \qquad\cdot \\
\sigma_{N,A} & \sigma_{N,B} & \sigma_{N,C} & \qquad\sigma_{N,M}
\end{array}
$$

In a two-product portfolio, we have two variances (σ_B^2 and σ_A^2) and two covariances ($\sigma_{A,B}$ twice). In a three-product portfolio, the top left-hand corner, there are nine possible covariances, three are variances (σ_A^2, σ_B^2 and σ_C^2) and six are 'pure' covariances ($\sigma_{A,B}$, and $\sigma_{A,C}$ and $\sigma_{B,C}$, all twice). Similarly, a four-asset portfolio has four variance terms and twelve covariance terms. As the number of variance terms equals the number of securities (n) while the number of covariance terms equals ($n^2 - n$) then, as we form ever larger portfolios, the covariance terms become relatively more and more important.

So, as n increases, the value σ_p^2 approaches the average covariance: first, because equation (12.4) becomes ever more dependent on the covariance rather than on individual variances; second, the individual variances not only become less numerous relative to the number of covariances but also less important, given that they are weighted by the squares of the fraction of the portfolio they comprise and this fraction is an ever diminishing one. So, if the average covariance were zero, then all risk, not only unsystematic risk, could be eliminated by sufficiently broad diversification. Since security returns do not move wholly independently, however, market or systematic risk will never fall to zero.

Thus not only numerically, but also intuitively, it is clear that a covariance measure, rather than standard deviation alone, is the appropriate risk measure for a security relative to a diversified portfolio.

(b)   The Correlation Between Returns

Now that a method has been developed for calculating the risk and return for a portfolio, we must ask: (1) what happens if A and B are independent of each other, i.e. if σ_{AB} is zero? (2) what if they are perfectly correlated? (3) how do we find the product mix which minimises risk? and (4) are we limited to the series of points traced out by the curve in Figure 12.12?

The statistical definition of the correlation coefficient, ρ, helps answer some of these questions. The correlation coefficient ρ_{AB} between two independent variables is

$$\rho_{AB} = \frac{\sigma_{AB}}{\sigma_A \sigma_B} \qquad (12.5)$$

Clearly, if the returns from the two products or securities are independent, namely if σ_{AB} is zero, then so too will be ρ_{AB}. Conversely, if the returns are perfectly correlated, ρ_{AB} will equal unity.

In the example of Tables 12.7 and 12.8 the covariance was negative. This indicated that r_A and r_B tended to move in opposite directions. (Had σ_{AB} been positive it would have indicated the returns moved simultaneously in broadly the same direction.) Hence if both securities are purchased, there is less risk than if only one is. The gains appearing at any one time on A tend to offset the losses (or relative downward profit movements) occurring at the same time for B, and vice versa. A and B had returns which were negatively correlated.

What would have been the situation had they been *perfectly* correlated (positively or negatively)? Consider the data given in Table 12.9 for securities Y and X respectively. If we were now to plot a mean–variance return trade-off graph as in Figure 12.13, given differing levels of investment in the products in question, we would obtain the dashed line joining points X and Y. If $\rho_{xy} = +1$ this can be shown to be a straight line. The expected return on the portfolio mix as x changes from 100% to 0% moves from 2.25% to 0.625%. The standard deviation also changes from that of X to that of Y. The slope of this line can be found thus:

$$\text{slope of } XY = (r_y - r_x)/(\sigma_y - \sigma_x)$$

$$= \frac{2.25 - 0.625}{1.92 - 0.96} = 1.69$$

Conversely, if the returns between X and Y are perfectly *inversely* correlated ($\rho_{xy} = -1$), the trade-off between mean and standard deviation would be the dashed line XZY. At the appropriate security mix one security's fluctuation

Table 12.9

Probability	$r_Y(\%)$	$r_X(\%)$
0.25	−0.5	0.0
0.25	0.0	1.0
0.25	1.0	3.0
0.25	2.0	5.0

$\sigma_x = 1.92 \qquad \sigma_Y = 0.96 \qquad \rho_{xy} = 1.0$

$\sigma_{xy} = \rho_{xy}\, \sigma_x\, \sigma_y$

$\bar{r}_x = 2.25 \qquad \bar{r}_y = 0.625$

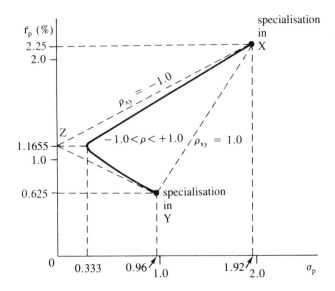

Figure 12.13 Risk—return trade-off: two products

of returns would be exactly offset by the others. This can also be proven mathematically. Usually, however, since securities never vary wholly independently of each other because of systematic risk, neither extreme holds and correlation is less than perfect. The general slope of the mean—variance opportunity set will be the solid curve *XY*.

The Opportunity Set

This *opportunity set*, or *minimum variance boundary*, is the locus of risk and return combinations offered by a portfolio of risky products which yield the minimum variance for a given rate of return. The line is normally convex, i.e. bounded by triangle *ZXY*. Indeed, any set of portfolio combinations formed by two risky products, less than perfectly correlated, must lie inside this triangle, and hence must be convex.

Figure 12.14 (originally devised by Eleanor Morgan) provides a simple way of understanding how the two-security opportunity set is derived (with given values of $\bar{r}_x$, $\bar{r}_y$ and ρ_{xy}). In quadrant I the horizontal axis shows how portfolio returns (given securities x and y) can range from $\bar{r}_x$ when the investor has 100% of his funds invested in x, to $\bar{r}_y$ when he specialises in y. Alternative portfolio mixes provide a portfolio return, $\bar{r}_p$, which is a weighted average of $\bar{r}_x$ and $\bar{r}_y$.

Quadrant II contains a 45° reference line with both axes displaying the proportion of x and/or y the investor holds. Quadrant III plots the portfolio

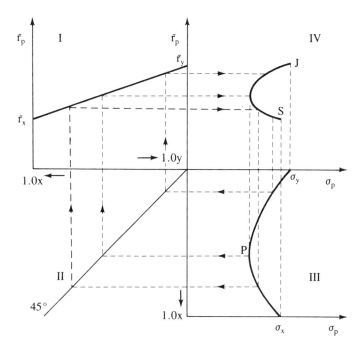

Note: This figure was based on an idea originally devised by Eleanor Morgan of the University of Bath.

Figure 12.14

risk σ_p, which can range from σ_x to σ_y. But here the relationship is not linear as in quadrant I. Since by assumption the returns on x and y are at least partly negatively correlated, *portfolio risk is not averaged* between σ_x and σ_y, *it is reduced*. (Had the correlation been negative unity, point P, the point of minimum risk would have lain on the vertical axis). The risk—return opportunity set can now be constructed graphically in quadrant IV by selecting any points in quadrant III, tracing them to their corresponding values in quadrant I and linking the relevant horizontal lines in quadrant I with the appropriate verticals from quadrant III. If this is done for sufficient points the minimum variance boundary, *JS*, is obtained.

The Capital Market Line and Efficient Portfolios

Figure 12.15 illustrates the opportunity set of an investor showing all possible portfolios of securities as perceived by him, not simply two. The efficiency boundary, *XZ*, is convex to the upper left of the figure (note that the phrases efficiency boundary, opportunity set, and minimum variance boundary tend to be used interchangeably). Any portfolio below and to the right

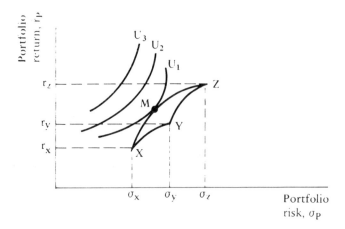

Figure 12.15

of this line is a possibility to the investor, given his available funds. They are not, however, 'efficient' in that other portfolios on *XZ* are possible with lower levels of risk (given an expected return) or higher returns (given a level of risk).

The opportunity set is made up of a series of convex curves, each representing different portfolio blends of a given list of securities. Thus the addition to or deletion of a particular security from a portfolio might result in a curve such as *XY* as opposed to *YZ* or *XZ*.

The line *XY* could represent all combinations of securities *X* and *Y*, *YZ* all combinations of securities *Y* and *Z*, *XZ* all combinations of securities *X* and *Z*. The *area* enclosed by *XYZ* represents all possible combinations of all three securities. Portfolios composed of only one security are indicated by the points *X*, *Y* and *Z* respectively, and have the return and risk values indicated in the figure. (In this simplified example a two-security portfolio of some mix of *X* and *Z* is everywhere superior to any three-security portfolio composed of *X*, *Y* and *Z*. This, of course, need not be the case. It will depend on each security's risk and return characteristics and their covariances with each other. It is more probable that *XZ* would be a multi-security portfolio.) The optimum portfolio, given any investor's utility function and degree of risk aversion or preference, is obtained by superimposing the risk–return indifference curves (discussed in Appendix 2, Figure A2.3) on Figure 12.15. In this instance the highest attainable utility is given by point *M* on U_1, where U_1, U_2, U_3, are the investor's indifference curves.

We saw that, as the number of products in a portfolio increases, the risk which any one contributes to the portfolio reduces exclusively to the covariance risk. That is, the portion of a security's risk not correlated with the portfolio as a whole can be avoided at no cost. No rational investor will pay a premium for a security with diversifiable risk. But since *covariance* risk cannot be diversified away, the investor will pay such a premium: or what is the same thing, expect a higher return.

CAPM and the Cost of Equity

The *capital asset pricing model* (CAPM) uses this principle to price risky securities. If it is assumed that all hold an effectively diversified or 'market' portfolio, then part of a security's risk — the 'unsystematic' component — will have been diversified away. Only the undiversifiable 'systematic' risk will remain, as measured by the covariance between the returns on the security and those on the market portfolio, which by definition cannot be diversified away. Thus securities will be priced in equilibrium, according to their non-diversifiable systematic risk (normally termed their beta (β) coefficient). A risk-free security earns a return equal to the risk-free rate, and a risky product earns an additional premium in proportion to its beta coefficient. For any individual security, j, then, the total expected rate of return is the completely risk-free rate i plus some premium, r^*. Thus:

$$i + r^* = \bar{r}_j \qquad (12.6)$$

What is the value r^* (the price of systematic risk), and how can it be calculated? It is to this question we now turn.

Unfortunately, most investors are unlikely to be aware of the efficiency boundary, far less the optimum point on it. The concepts can be given greater practical usefulness, however, if we add to our analysis the possibility of risk-free securities such as government bonds, where the cash return is certain. When this alternative is available, in order to determine the optimal portfolio we draw a straight line from the risk-free rate, i, tangential to the efficiency boundary as in Figure 12.16. The line itself shows the proportions of the risk-free security and portfolio N which can be held. Now only one portfolio mix of risky securities, N, not an infinite number as before, is considered. If the investor is also able to borrow or lend at the risk-free rate, then this line has a higher utility than the efficiency boundary. To the left of N the investor would invest part of his funds in the portfolio mix designated by N and the remainder in the risk-free security. To the right of N, he would hold only portfolio N and borrow additional funds at rate i to invest still further in it.

Thus, for example, investor A cannot improve his utility by either borrowing or lending. He will invest all his resources in portfolio N. Investor C, however, has a different utility function. U_{C1} indicates the highest level of utility he can achieve while remaining on the efficiency frontier. But if C moves from the portfolio mix indicated by that tangency point and instead invests all his resources in portfolio N *and* borrows funds at the risk-free rate i, and invests this sum in N, he can increase his return (and probably his risk)

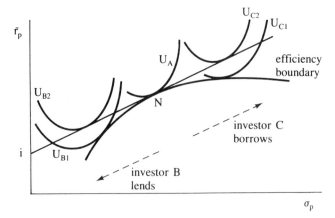

Figure 12.16

and his utility to the tangency point of U_{C2} and the straight line. (A numerical example for C might be an individual with wealth of £100, initial interest of £20 = 20%, who borrows £50 at i = 5% and invests the £150 in N at 18%, giving a return of £27 less the servicing charge on his borrowing of £2.50, so providing £24.50 as a return on his personal wealth of £100, i.e. 24.5%.)

Conversely, B, who is probably more risk-averse, would initially choose a portfolio indicated by the tangency point of U_{B1}. He could be earning, say, 8% or £8 on an investment of £100. He could increase his utility by moving to U_{B2} as follows. He takes, for example, £50 out of his original portfolio and lends it at the risk-free rate of 5%. He puts the remaining £50 into portfolio N at 18%, so obtaining a total income of £2.50 plus £9.50 = £12 or 12% on his £100 invested at the original 8%.

Given this reasoning, *all* investors are deemed to hold portfolio N in order to maximise their individual utilities. N is the 'typical', 'average' or 'market portfolio' and so only N need be considered in our analysis from now onwards, not the infinite number of portfolio mixes possible on and within the efficiency frontier.

What are the proportions in which investor A will allocate his funds between portfolio N and the riskless security? Obviously, at point i in Figure 12.17, 100% would be invested in the risk-free bond. At point N, 100% would be invested in the security mix of that portfolio. If he invested 25% of his available funds in N he would expect a mean return of: $\bar{r}_p = 0.75i + 0.25\bar{r}_N$. To obtain this he would accept a risk of $0.25\sigma_N$. Similarly, on a 50:50 split his risk would be $0.5\sigma_N$. If he were to borrow to invest an additional 25% of cash in N his risk would be $1.25\sigma_N$. The straight line through i and N is known as the capital market line (*CML*). It illustrates the extra return which

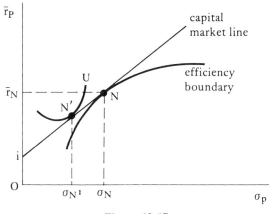

Figure 12.17

is expected for each extra unit of risk, i.e. the measure $(\bar{r}_N - i)\sigma_N$ is also the market price of risk, the slope of the *CML* (which we shall call α).

The *CML* dominates the efficiency boundary. That is, it is everywhere superior (except at *N*) to the efficiency boundary in indicating optimal portfolios of a mix of risky and risk-free securities. Thus, not only has the *CML* concept enabled us to limit the analysis to only one risky portfolio (*N*), it has also provided a way of isolating that portfolio from the individual's indifference curves. This is known as the separation theorem. The security mix indicated by *N* is now chosen irrespective of any individual's risk preferences. Only the amount lent or borrowed at rate *i* is affected. The optimal portfolio of risky securities (in this case *N*) depends only on $\bar{r}_N$ and σ_N. It is *not* the minimum variance portfolio.

The individual can thus be seen as taking a two-step decision: first, deciding on the optimal portfolio of risky assets; and second, determining the proportion of his portfolio which will consist of risk-free securities and the market portfolio. Only the latter depends on his utility function. Risk averters will choose points to the left of *N* (i.e. will lend), risk preferrers to the right (i.e. will borrow).

All investors consequently hold the same mix of risky stocks. This is the market portfolio. This may appear unrealistically presumptive, but since all the risky securities available must be held by someone, and since the market is assumed perfect, then their individual prices will adjust so that the expected return and risk characteristics of each ensure it will be bought by someone. If, given its risk, a security's price is too high. it will be sold until its price is lower, and vice versa if the price is too low. (Thus the assumption of complete divisibility of risky securities is made, and at the limit the proportion which the market portfolio may amount to of a risk-averse investor's total portfolio can be zero.)

From this we can say that when investors contemplate their portfolios:

(i)   They are usually better off if they borrow or lend to change the mix of the given portfolio N to N *plus or minus* a risk-free security. This does not always hold (e.g. if it is tangential at N) but provided their decisions are correct they will not be worse off by borrowing or lending.

(ii) *Two-fund separation exists*: that is, every investor regardless of his risk preferences will hold some combination of two funds (the so-called 'market portfolio' N, and the risk-free security).

(iii) In equilibrium, the marginal rate of substitution (*MRS*) between return and risk is the same for all managers, regardless of their individual risk preferences. (The *MRS* is, of course, simply the slope of the indifference curve U.)

Now if the *MRS* between risk and return is the same for *every* manager or investor in equilibrium, then the slope of the *capital market line* is the equilibrium or the market price of risk:

i.e. $\alpha = MRS$ (12.7)

(bearing in mind that the *MRS* of risk for return is defined as the extra return required per additional unit of risk borne by the investor and that each investor will have the same *MRS* in equilibrium).

We have already shown that in equilibrium all portfolios (as now defined) must lie on the *CML*, and that the slope of the *CML* is the market price of risk. We have also shown that the return required for any mix of the market portfolio, N, and riskless securities in equilibrium is dependent on the weighted average return of N and the risk-free investment. Thus if $(1-x)$ is invested at risk-free interest rates, x is invested in N and α is the slope of the *CML*, then:

$$\alpha = \frac{\bar{r}_N - i}{\sigma_N} \qquad\qquad (12.8)$$

and $\bar{r}_p = (1-x)i + x\bar{r}_N$ at a risk of $x\sigma_N$

and $\sigma_p^2 = x^2\sigma_N^2 + (1-x)^2\sigma_i^2 + 2x(1-x)\rho_{Ni}\sigma_i\sigma_N$
$$= x^2\sigma_N^2 \quad (\text{since } \sigma_i = 0)$$

The extra return per unit of risk required by an individual for investing in N is calculated by dividing the change in overall return by the change in total risk. So, if we assume our investor moves from a totally riskless portfolio to the one described, then the resultant calculation is:

$$\frac{(1-x)i + x\bar{r}_N - i}{x\sigma_N} = \frac{-xi + x\bar{r}_N}{x\sigma_N} = \frac{\bar{r}_N - i}{\sigma_N} = \alpha$$

Each unit of risk accepted by an individual will thus be rewarded by a premium over i of α, or generally:

$$\bar{r}_p = i + \alpha\, \sigma_p \tag{12.9}$$

which is simply the equation of the *CML* (P is any portfolio of N plus or minus an unknown number of risk-free securities). The premium thus reflects the portfolio's unique risk (σ_p) and the market's own risk–return trade-off (α).

12.5   The Capital Asset Pricing Model

The capital asset pricing model is derived directly from portfolio theory and the notions of systematic and unsystematic risk. It provides (if one accepts all the underlying assumptions) a superior measure of the cost of equity because, unlike the equation $K_e = D_0/P_0 + g$, it explicitly embraces the risk attached to a security as well as future returns.

The *CML* equation (12.9) as a whole can now be used to derive a valuation model for each individual security in the market portfolio. The *CML* applies only to efficient *portfolios*. It does not describe the relationship between individual *securities* and their riskiness.

The *CAPM* states that the expected return on any *security* (or portfolio) is related to the riskless rate of return and the expected market return. The general expression summarising this is:

$$\bar{r}_j = i + \beta_j(\bar{r}_N - i) = i + r_j^* \tag{12.10}$$

where r_j is the expected return on security j, and β_j, the beta coefficient, is a measure of the sensitivity of that security's return to movements in the overall market's return. Figure 12.18 plots this equation which is known as the security market line (*SML*). Obviously, if a value for β can be obtained for a security, then its rate of return can be calculated. Under the *CAPM* all portfolios *(efficient or otherwise)*, including the market portfolio as well as all individual securities, lie on the *SML*.[3] Thus in the case of the market portfolio where $(\bar{r}_N - i)$ is known already from overall market data:

$$\bar{r}_N = i + \beta_N(\bar{r}_N - i)$$
$$\therefore \ \beta_N = 1 \tag{12.11}$$

The risk premium of security j is (from 12.10):

$$\bar{r}_j - i = \beta_j(\bar{r}_N - i) \tag{12.12}$$

---

3   Appendix 12 explains how the *SML* is mathematically derived, given the *CML*. Here we rely on intuition rather than algebra.

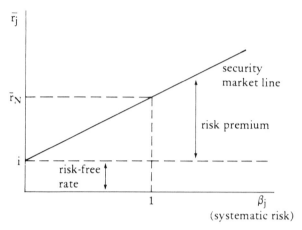

Figure 12.18

or β_j times the risk premium on the market portfolio. Given that all efficient portfolios, including the market portfolio, lie on the *CML* and the *SML*, then for any efficient portfolio, *P*, we obtain:

$$CML \equiv \bar{r}_p = i + \frac{(\bar{r}_N - i)}{\sigma_N} \sigma_p \tag{12.13}$$

and

$$SML \equiv \bar{r}_p = i + \beta_p(\bar{r}_N - i) \tag{12.14}$$

and so, for efficient portfolios like *P* where the *CML* = the *SML*:

$$\beta_p = \frac{\sigma_p}{\sigma_N} \tag{12.15}$$

where either β_p or σ_p can be used as a risk measure. But since individual securities and most portfolios will rarely lie on the *CML*, their spread of returns will not be perfectly correlated with the market's. In terms of Figure 12.18, neither their returns nor their β will lie exactly on the *SML*.

Equation 12.15 is thus an inadequate measure of Beta for individual securities. Any variation of return on such assets not explained by market movements is unsystematic risk. Beta explains only systematic risk since, as we saw in Figure 12.11, most unsystematic risk will be diversified away by careful portfolio construction. As a corollary, only systematic risk should be considered in determining the risk premium of a security.

To calculate β as a measure of a security's systematic risk in practice involves plotting expectations about the future responsiveness of that share's return against changes in the market's return. Since the future is unknown, historical data must be used as a substitute (say monthly returns as measured by dividend yield plus capital appreciation for the share for a period of years). The market portfolio is also unknown, but some widely accepted share index could be used as a proxy. From such data a *characteristics line* can be plotted and its equation estimated by normal *OLS* analysis. Thus in Figure 12.19 the characteristics line for a particular share is shown. Point *X*, for example, is an observation in a given month when the security provided a return of 5% less than risk-free treasury bills and the market a return of 10% more than such a risk-free security surrogate.

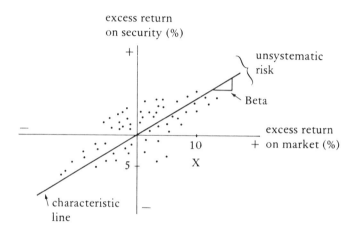

Figure 12.19

Both intuitively and empirically one finds that the characteristics line typically slopes up from left to right. That is, the greater the expected return for the market, so too one would expect a greater expected excess return over the risk-free rate for the stock. Theoretically the line passes through the origin since the excess return on the market portfolio not due to market movements is diversified to zero. Similarly, since the market portfolio's average of zero is simply the weighted average of shifts in the non-market inspired individual share returns, these too will sum to zero. Arbitrage will ensure that no individual share has a negative average excess return over time. Thus each share's average must in turn equal zero.

Where $\beta_j = \sigma_j/\sigma_N = 1$, it means that the stock has the same systematic risk as the market (see equation 12.11). Where $\beta_j > 1$, the stock's excess return varies more than proportionately with the excess return of the market portfolio, and vice versa. Historically calculated Betas have proved useful proxies for calculating future Betas. Thus if a stock's β in a given month was 2.5, and the market excess return was 2%, this would imply an expected excess return for the stock of 5%. This 5% cannot be diversified away.

Beta's significance as far as stock market buying and selling is clear. High-value shares should be bought if the market is expected to rise since they will rise faster than the market. They have a high 'upside potential'. Conversely, if the market is expected to fall, high β value shares are unattractive prospects. They have a high 'downside risk'. The opposite holds in both cases for low β value securities.

The Cost of Equity Again

We noted (equation 12.6) that the expected rate of return for security j was $i + r_j^* = \bar{r}_j$ where r^* was the price of systematic risk. We also now know (equation 12.10) that $K_e = \bar{r}_j = i + \beta_j(\bar{r}_N - i)$. Geometrically β_j can be measured by the slope of the characteristics line. The slope of any line ($y = \hat{m}x + c$) where y is regressed on x is:

$$\hat{m} = \rho_{yx}\frac{\sigma_y}{\sigma_x}$$

which in this specific instance implies that $\hat{\beta} = \rho_{jN}(\sigma_j/\sigma_N)$

$$\therefore \quad \frac{\sigma_N}{\sigma_N}\hat{\beta} = \rho_{jN}\frac{\sigma_j\sigma_N}{\sigma_N^2} = \hat{\beta} \tag{12.16}$$

and so (recall equation 12.5):

$$\beta = \frac{\sigma_{jN}}{\sigma_N^2} \tag{12.17}$$

Algebraically, what equations 12.16 and 12.17 tell us is that both in theory and in the way the estimate of β, $\hat{\beta}$, is derived, β, the measure of responsiveness of j's excess returns to the market's excess returns, is the ratio of the covariance between the possible returns for j and for the market divided by the variance of the market's probable returns (where $\rho_{jN}\sigma_j\sigma_N$ is the covariance of returns for j with the market's returns, and ρ_{jN} is the correlation coefficient between the relevant expected returns). By substitution of this result in equation (12.15) we obtain:

$$K_e = i + \frac{\bar{r}_N - i}{\sigma_N^2}(\rho_{jN}\sigma_j\sigma_N)$$

The significance of this equation as far as *capital* investment appraisal is concerned is that each project should be evaluated in terms of its expected return and its own unique systematic risk in relation to the market portfolio.

The traditional weighted average cost of capital equation provides only one discount rate applicable to all projects. The cost of capital calculated using the *CAPM*, however, will vary from project to project. Thus projects acceptable by one yardstick may prove unacceptable by the other and vice versa.

The difference between the two criteria is highlighted in Figure 12.20.

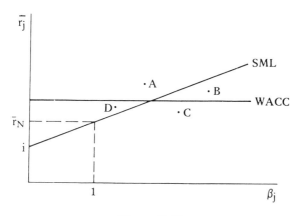

Figure 12.20

Assume that the weighted average cost of capital (*WACC*) is given a constant value for all projects being considered. That is, we are assuming either that the firm is optimally geared, as in the traditional approach, or that gearing is irrelevant, as in the Modigliani−Miller approach. Under *WACC* the cost of capital calculation provides only one discount rate for all projects being considered. Under *CAPM*, the higher the project's systematic risk (β_j), the higher is the required rate of return. The equation for *SML* (from equations 12.14 and 12.6) being:

$$SML = \bar{r}_j = i + \beta_j(\bar{r}_N - i) = K_{ej} = i + r_j^*$$

Clearly, a constant *WACC* and varying *CAPM* criteria will result in conflicting results. Thus in Figure 12.20 the *WACC* yardstick would accept projects *A* and *B*, reject *C* and *D*, while the *CAPM* approach would differ, by accepting *D* but rejecting *B* as being respectively above and below the relevant risk-adjusted cost of capital.

Several objections to the *CAPM* can be raised. First, it rests on the very dubious assumptions of a perfect capital market. Second, as so far developed, it is essentially only a single-period problem. Third, it assumes that firms should diversify their portfolio of investment projects in the same way as investors diversify their portfolios of securities. But if investors can diversify to minimise their risk, there seems little point in firms doing so too. Under portfolio theory, corporate diversification and individual investor diversification are effectual substitutes. Of course, if one relaxes some of the assumptions then clearly diversification by firms can result in higher profits or lower risks for the firm given its own peculiar resource and opportunity situation. Similarly, individuals cannot always hold a portfolio large enough to diversify away all unsystematic risk. Thus, although portfolio theory and the *CAPM* are still in their infancy in assisting managers to assess the cost of capital, their practical and conceptual weaknesses at the level of the individual investor may mean that their strengths should not be ignored by corporate managers in investment appraisal. Finally, and a major weakness for capital budgeting purposes, relative to stock exchange portfolio analysis, the β values for each investment proposal must of necessity be far more subjective in their construction and in their comparisons with the portfolio of ongoing projects than will the Betas calculated from historic stock market data.

12.6   Dividend Distribution

The level of dividends paid to equity holders is the most obvious link between a firm and its owners. Moreover, given that the objective of the firm is to maximise shareholder wealth we know from equation (12.18) just how important dividends are to that objective:

$$P_0 = \frac{D_0}{r - g} \tag{12.18}$$

Consider Figure 12.21. The curve *AB* is the *physical investment line* (*PIL*) open to the firm in a two-period model and connects all possible physical investment: dividend distribution combinations in time t_0. Thus at point *D*, *OC* is distributed, *CA* is retained, and *OE* is the amount available for distribution in t_1 as a consequence of retaining and reinvesting *AC*. Projects available to the firm are assumed to be ranked in descending order of attractiveness.

Thus projects which could be funded with *AC* are more attractive than those which can be funded with *OC*. Hence the curve is simply a variant of a product transformation curve, the two axes representing shareholder consumable income in t_0 and t_1. The appropriate dividend can be obtained by superimposing on the figure shareholder indifference curves which would reflect owners' time preferences. (These would be convex to the origin.)

The highest indifference curve (U_3) would then indicate the optimal level of distribution. However, if we introduce the *financial market line*, *FG*, it is possible because of the presence of capital markets, where shareholders can borrow and lend to increase shareholder utility, and/or take account of different shareholders having different time preferences. This development is a corollary of the separation theorem employed in Figure 12.17.

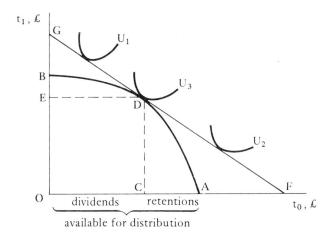

Figure 12.21

It enables us in this instance to ignore all possible distribution:retention combinations except the existing one at point D. It assumes a perfect capital market and the angle GFO is consequently equal to $1+r$ where r is the rate of interest in that market. Thus to the left of C, U^1 is a utility indifference curve of a shareholder still receiving his proportion of OC in dividends, but whose time preference indicates that he will lend to the capital market to reduce his income today in order to increase it tomorrow. U_2 is a utility indifference curve of a shareholder dissatisfied with the current level of dividends (and so his proportion of OC) but who borrows today to increase his current income.

Thus if shareholders can use the capital market in this way, firms should simply invest all available distributable funds in all projects with a positive *NPV*, i.e. they should always move from A to D. This notion underlies the Modigliani and Miller 'dividend irrelevancy' notion.

Again MM depends on the assumptions of a perfect market and again their propositions have provoked controversy. If we introduce market imperfections into the discussion, the argument that dividend policy is irrelevant as a financing decision becomes less tenable. First, there are information effects. Managers are generally reluctant to cut dividends. Thus, any rise in the dividend rate carries with it the presumption that it will be maintained. The increase itself consequently carries information to investors that management has higher expectations for the future, due to his (i.e. the manager's) possession of more intimate knowledge of the firm's prospects. Conversely this information perceived to be carried by the dividend can be faulty or misinterpreted. Static dividends may conceal more than they reveal.

Second, we have tax effects. Depending upon the individual investor's marginal tax rate, he will or will not prefer frequent income distributions to capital accretion. Clearly, this will depend upon the mix of both current and potential shareholders in the firm. Finally, transaction costs exist. It is much cheaper administratively for a firm to retain profits than to raise sums through the new issue market. Conversely, the individual investor may prefer generous dividends since, to him, to realise capital for current consumption purposes involves the brokerage costs of selling shares. The picture is very muddy.

This concludes our discussion of capital budgeting. Of all the topics covered in this book, this is the area where the theoretical advance has been most rapid in the last two decades. Whether practitioners have kept up with these advances, indeed whether it is practical so to do, is regarded by many as an open question.

Additional Reading

Allen, David E. (1983) *Finance: A Theoretical Introduction*, Martin Robertson.
Brealey, R. and Meyers, S. (1985) *Principles of Corporate Finance*, 2nd edn, McGraw-Hill.
Bromwich, M. (1976) *The Economics of Capital Budgeting*, Penguin Books.
Copeland, T.E. and Weston, J.F. (1983) *Financial Theory and Corporate Policy*, 2nd edn, Addison-Wesley.
Gordon, M. (1962) *The Investment Financing and Valuation of the Corporation*, Irwin.
Hawkins, C.J. and Pearce, D.W. (1971) *Capital Investment Appraisal*, Macmillan.
Levy, H. and Sarnat, M. (1978) *Capital Investment and Financial Decisions*, Prentice Hall.
Lumby, S. (1981) *Investment Appraisal*, Nelson.

APPENDIX 12A
The Derivation of the Security Market Line

How do we actually derive the *SML* from a known *CML*? In other words, we know the *CML* provides an expression for the equilibrium return of an efficient portfolio (or security) plus either lending or borrowing at the risk-free rate. We still do not know how the *SML*, showing the expected return on an *inefficient* portfolio (or security), can be arrived at.

Consider the situation where a market equilibrium exists in the sense that all available securities are held in some firm's portfolio (or their prices and returns adjust until they are): then, in equilibrium, supply and demand will be equal and the market portfolio will consist of all securities held in proportion to their value weights. The equilibrium proportion of each security in *N* must then be:

$$W_i = \frac{\text{market value of individual security}}{\text{market value of all securities}}$$

An inefficient portfolio consisting of $x\%$ invested in risky security j and $(1-x)\%$ in N has the following mean and standard deviation:

$$\bar{r}_p = x\bar{r}_j + (1-x)\bar{r}_N$$

$$\sigma_p = \sqrt{[x^2\sigma^2_j + (1-x)^2\ \sigma^2_N + 2x(1-x)\sigma_{jN}]}$$

Now note that *N* already contains (perhaps only hypothetically) security *j* according to its market value weight. The opportunity set provided by various combinations of the risky asset and the market portfolio is *jN* in Figure A12.1. The change in mean and standard deviation respectively with respect to the percent of the portfolio invested in product *j* is determined thus:

$$\frac{\partial \bar{r}_p}{\partial_x} = \bar{r}_j - \bar{r}_N \tag{A12.1}$$

$$\frac{\partial \sigma_p}{\partial x} = \tfrac{1}{2}[x^2\sigma^2_j + (1-x)^2\ \sigma^2_N + 2x(1-x)\sigma_{jN}]^{-\frac{1}{2}} \cdot [2x\sigma^2_j \tag{A12.2}$$

$$-2\sigma^2_N + 2x\sigma^2_N + 2\sigma_{jN} - 4x\sigma_{jN}]$$

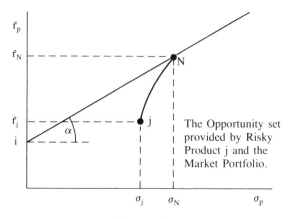

Figure A12.1

The last result is arrived at using the chain rule for differentiation thus:

$$y = f(u) \quad \text{where } u = g(z)$$

$$\Rightarrow \frac{dy}{dz} = \frac{dy}{du} \cdot \frac{du}{dz}$$

Here u is the term under the square root sign. Hence

$$\frac{\partial \sigma_p}{\partial \sigma_x} = \frac{\partial \sigma_p}{\partial \sigma_u} \cdot \frac{\partial \sigma_u}{\partial \sigma_x}$$

But we have assumed that in equilibrium the excess demand or supply for any security j must be zero, hence the above two equations (A12.1 and A12.2) when x, (excess demand) equals zero (or, the same thing when jN is tangential to the *CML* at point N) can be re-expressed as follows: When $x = 0$:

$$\left.\frac{\partial \bar{r}_p}{\partial x}\right|_{x=0} = \bar{r}_j - \bar{r}_N$$

$$\left.\frac{\partial \sigma_p}{\partial x}\right|_{x=0} = \tfrac{1}{2}(\sigma^2_N)^{-\frac{1}{2}} \times (-2\sigma^2_N + 2\sigma_{jN}) = \frac{\sigma_{jN} - \sigma^2_N}{\sigma_N}$$

So the slope of the risk-return trade-off evaluated at N, market equilibrium, as x changes is:

$$\frac{\partial \bar{r}_p / \partial x}{\partial \sigma_p / \partial x} = \frac{\bar{r}_j - \bar{r}_N}{(\sigma_{jN} - \sigma^2_N)/\sigma_N}$$

But, since the left-hand side is also the slope of the *CML*, then (from equation 12.13):

$$\frac{\bar{r}_N - i}{\sigma_N} = \frac{\bar{r}_j - \bar{r}_N}{(\sigma_{jN} - \sigma^2_N)/\sigma_N}$$

Rearranging, we can now find an expression for $\bar{r}_j$:

$$\frac{\bar{r}_N - i}{\sigma^2_N} = \frac{\bar{r}_j - \bar{r}_N}{(\sigma_{jN} - \sigma^2_N)}$$

$$\Rightarrow \sigma_{jN}\bar{r}_N - \sigma_{jN}i - \sigma^2_N\bar{r}_N + \sigma^2_N i = \sigma^2_N\bar{r}_j - \sigma^2_N\bar{r}_N$$

$$\Rightarrow \frac{\sigma_{jN}}{\sigma^2_N}\bar{r}_N - \frac{\sigma_{jN}i}{\sigma^2_N} - \bar{r}_N + i = \bar{r}_j - \bar{r}_N$$

$$\Rightarrow \bar{r}_j = i + \frac{\sigma_{jN}}{\sigma^2_N}(\bar{r}_N - i)$$

which is the equation for the *SML*, and $\sigma_{jN}/\sigma^2_N = \beta$

This equation is the capital asset pricing model.

Appendix 12B: Table of Discount Factors

This table shows the present value of £1 discounted for different numbers of years and at different rates of discount

Rate of discount	5%	6%	7%	8%	9%	10%	12%	14%	16%	18%	20%
Year											
0	1.000	1.000	1.000	1.000	1.000	1.000	1.000	1.000	1.000	1.000	1.000
1	0.952	0.943	0.935	0.926	0.917	0.909	0.893	0.877	0.862	0.847	0.833
2	0.907	0.890	0.873	0.857	0.842	0.826	0.797	0.769	0.743	0.718	0.694
3	0.864	0.840	0.816	0.794	0.772	0.751	0.712	0.675	0.641	0.609	0.579
4	0.823	0.792	0.763	0.735	0.708	0.683	0.636	0.592	0.552	0.516	0.482
5	0.784	0.747	0.713	0.681	0.650	0.621	0.567	0.519	0.476	0.437	0.402
6	0.746	0.705	0.666	0.630	0.596	0.564	0.507	0.456	0.410	0.370	0.335
7	0.711	0.665	0.623	0.583	0.547	0.513	0.452	0.400	0.354	0.314	0.279
8	0.677	0.627	0.582	0.540	0.502	0.467	0.404	0.351	0.305	0.266	0.233
9	0.645	0.592	0.544	0.500	0.460	0.424	0.361	0.308	0.263	0.225	0.194
10	0.614	0.558	0.508	0.463	0.422	0.386	0.322	0.270	0.227	0.191	0.162
15	0.481	0.417	0.362	0.315	0.275	0.239	0.183	0.140	0.108	0.084	0.065
20	0.377	0.312	0.258	0.215	0.178	0.149	0.104	0.073	0.051	0.037	0.026
25	0.295	0.233	0.184	0.146	0.116	0.092	0.059	0.038	0.024	0.016	0.010

13
Product, Market and Corporate Strategies

The extent to which a firm produces different kinds of output is a major strategic decision. Ansoff, using Figure 13.1 subdivides the problem into four. First, market penetration involves increasing sales without departing from an original product market. The firm either sells more to existing customers or obtains new ones with identical requirements. Second, market development is the strategy where the firm adapts its product line (say by modifying characteristics) to satisfy customers with different requirements from those in M_0, the original market. An example of market development is the adaptation by an aeroplane firm of a passenger plane into a freighter for sale to air cargo lines. Product development, a third alternative, improves or adds to product characteristics in order more effectively to satisfy the needs of M_0 the original market. The development of a 'stretched' fuselage to provide greater carrying capacity in an aircraft is an example.

Diversification differs from these strategies. Both the existing product line and market(s) are departed from. Invariably the firm has to acquire a greater or lesser degree of new marketing, technical and administrative expertise. Within the concept of diversification there are three distinct activities. These are horizontal, vertical and lateral integration. Horizontal integration can refer to the action by which a firm introduces new products which, while not contributing to the present product line, cater for market needs which lie within the industry of which the firm is a member. For example if an aircraft firm extended its interests from the civil to the military market entirely different planes would be required. Nonetheless cross elasticity of supply is high. Vertical integration can be either backward or forward in nature. Backward integration is where the firm begins to manufacture products previously purchased from others in order to utilise them in making its original product line. The firm begins to carry out different but successive stages in the production of its original output. Where the firm moves nearer the final market for its product and carries out a function previously undertaken by a customer, the activity is called forward integration. Vertical integration means that the firm has chosen to conduct certain activities within its organisation rather than through the market place. When and why a firm will prefer administered transactions to arm's length trading will depend on the costs

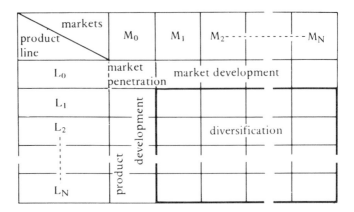

Figure 13.1

and consequences. Lateral integration or 'pure' diversification occurs when the firm moves into areas totally unrelated to its existing activities, either on the side of supply or demand.

13.1 The Decision to Integrate Vertically

Security

Traditionally the main reason for vertical integration is 'a search for security' (E.A.G. Robinson). When demand conditions are high and competing manufacturers are outbidding each other for supplies it may make good sense to integrate backwards and have an assured source of materials of a quality and quantity one can dictate. Conversely, if demand is slack and manufacturers are competing for business it can be sensible to integrate forwards and so be assured of 'customer' loyalty.

Efficiency

Where vertical integration results in cost reduction it is a form of scale economy since, *ceteris paribus*, a vertically integrated firm is larger than a non-integrated one. Four main sources of such increased efficiency are available.

(i) *Engineering Economies* The classic example is the combining of iron production with rolling mill operations into a single integrated steel manufacturing process. The need to reheat the iron is removed if the processes are carried out in quick succession.

(ii) *Marketing Economies*   Clearly delivery charges are reduced if plants are located in close proximity. Savings are also possible without physical nearness. Advertising and sales promotion expenditure can be pruned when the loyalty of 'customers' is guaranteed. Economies also arise when transactions are carried out continually between the same people. Search and negotiation efforts are reduced when transactions become habitual. Repetition fosters the development of routine, reliable, and so low-cost information flows.

(iii) *Financial Economies*   Capital costs are lower in an integrated firm because stocks can generally be held at lower levels. An integrated firm can co-ordinate rates of production and consumption in the various stages of the firm so as to lessen the need to hold contingency and buffer stocks. A firm can also find it easier and cheaper to raise capital if it can gain investors' confidence by indicating that one particular element of risk has been reduced (namely by a guaranteed source of supply or a captive market).

(iv) *Administrative Economies*   To the extent that successive stages of production each with an individual administrative framework can be combined under a single unit of supervision, then there will exist administrative economies.

Predatory Reasons

Predatory causes of vertical integration can be seen as the desire for security writ large. Forward integration can secure a market but it can also foreclose it to competitors. One cannot buy McEwans beers in a pub owned by Watneys. Backward integration can guarantee a reliable source of supply but it can also prevent rivals gaining access to that source; or it can ensure that their costs are raised disadvantageously if the price charged to them is higher than the price charged in an intra-firm transfer. By this analysis, vertical integration is a deliberate investment in entry barriers.

Recordable Costs of Vertical Integration

A firm which is integrated backwards in times of low demand may be disadvantaged. It will have forfeited flexibility in its purchasing policy. Production runs in earlier stages may become too short to achieve minimum unit costs. Relative to outside sources of supply, it may also find itself committed to the use of obsolete production technologies. Conversely, a firm which is integrated forwards in times of high demand may find that it is tied to relatively inefficient and poorly located markets or outlets. The administrative costs of co-ordinating successive stages of production may be greater than the savings. To the normal difficulties of co-ordination will be added the costs of acquiring skills in a relatively strange technology, be it at a preceding or succeeding production stage. Quite apart from learning costs, which can be overcome in time, the administrative skills required for additional stages may prove to be incompatible with those already possessed.

Opportunity Costs

Vertical integration diverts company funds from alternative sources of action. For example they can no longer be used to expand a product line nor for 'pure' diversification. Similarly the opportunities to expand in the same product area, horizontal integration, and the gains from scale economies which may go with it, are forfeited.

Close Alternatives to Vertical Integration

What openings are available to firms which enable them to capture some of the benefits without incurring the costs of formal integration? We will examine three: partial vertical disintegration, exclusive franchising and the exercise of countervailing power.

Partial Vertical Disintegration Here the firm would vertically integrate large portions of its business, but it would stop short of total integration. One example of this is provided by the Walls ice cream division of Unilever. Walls is also in the transport business with a large fleet of refrigerated trucks. In order to avoid having large numbers of expensive lorries lying idle in winter (when demand is low) Walls own a basic fleet, but in times of high demand, rents refrigerated vehicles.

Exclusive Franchising The granting of sole rights of resale to a particular customer in a specific trade or locality provides many of the economies in transportation and promotion which are obtained by ownership of outlets without the associated costs of capital outlay and day-by-day management. Moreover a poor dealer can probably be dispensed with and replaced more readily than a poorly located but wholly owned retail site. Motor car distributorships and dealerships are common examples of this type of franchising operation. Car firms tend only to award franchises to garages who adhere to certain standards of stock holding and who provide specified service facilities.

The Exercise of Countervailing Power A firm may be able to exercise buying strength if it is large relative to suppliers. It can force prices down to a near competitive level. Simultaneously it can ensure that supplies are tailored to its own specification and requirements. This is a relationship not unlike that which Marks & Spencer had for many years with the then highly fragmented garment manufacturing industry. Conversely size and bargaining power may permit charging relatively high prices to diffuse purchasers and so provide much the same profit increase as formal forward integration would. In a bilateral oligopoly the firm should at least be able to share oligopoly profits, and agree on other mutually favourable terms by negotiating from a fairly equal position of strength. To understand the principles of bargaining, consider Figure 13.2. Stage II is a monopsonist of a given commodity and Stage I a monopolist of that commodity.

Stage II has a maximum budget of £60,000 with which to purchase the commodity (hence the dashed line terminating the vertical axis in Figure 13.2(a)). Figure 13.2(a) is an isoquant map for Stage II. The isoquants are curves of equal profitability. Each is a locus of money: commodity purchase combinations which would prove equally profitable to Stage II. The points

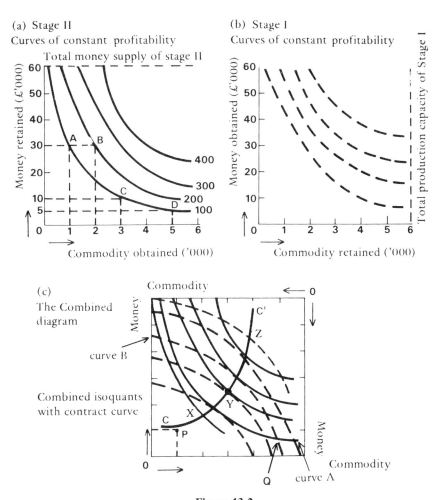

Figure 13.2

on the isoquants indicate combinations of money remaining in hand and goods obtained. Thus at point A, Stage II would make £100 profit and would have in hand £30,000 and 1,000 units of the commodity. At point B profits would equal £200, money in hand would be £30,000 and there would be 200 units of the commodity in stock. To find what Stage II paid for the commodity we must read down the vertical axis. To read up the axis tells us how much money Stage II has retained from the original £60,000 budget. This must be deducted from the original budget to ascertain how much was paid out. Thus at point C, £50,000 would be paid out for 3000 units (£16.66 per unit) and profits of £100 would be made. At point D, £55,000 would be paid out for 5000 units (£11 per unit) and profits would again be equal to £100.

Figure 13.2(b) is a similar figure constructed for Stage I, the monopolistic supplier. Here the y-axis indicates money received from the purchaser, Stage II, and the x-axis shows the production capacity of the commodity left in hand after supplying Stage II. The dashed line intersecting the horizontal axis closes off the figure on one side at the 6000 unit limit of Stage I's productive capacity. The isoquants indicate points of equal profitability to Stage I (profit at any point being equal to the revenue obtained from Stage II less the cost of production of the relevant quantity of output at that point). To obtain the price per unit received by Stage I at any point, we must read backwards along the horizontal axis to obtain the volume of goods sold and divide this figure into the relevant money obtained figure.

Figure 13.2(c) shows the two earlier figures superimposed. Figure 13.2(b), however, has first been swivelled through 180°. The ends of the axes have been joined in such a way that finite limits have been imposed on the figure — namely Stage II's budget constraint and Stage I's production capacity determine the lengths of the money and commodity axes respectively. This figure (known technically as an Edgeworth box) simultaneously indicates where both stages will end up after a trade. For example point P is the point where Stage II buys 1000 units for £50,000 and Stage I conversely sells 1000 units and obtains £50,000 in exchange.

The curve CC' is the contract curve. It is drawn to connect the points of tangency between the two sets of isoquants. The contract curve possesses two main properties. First, for every trade point off it there will exist trade points on it which are advantageous to both stages. For example, consider point Q where the isoquants A and B intersect. The area enclosed by A and B contains a multitude of other trade possibilities, all of which will be on higher profit isoquants than either A or B. Thus any point on CC' between A and B will be preferable to Q to both parties. Second, any move along CC' from an agreed trade point on it can only be at the expense of profits forgone to either Stage I or Stage II. Movement to the left results in lower profits for Stage II. Movement up and to the right is disadvantageous to Stage I.

This does not mean, however, that all trades must lie on the contract curve, even although it could be to the advantage of both parties if they did.

Edgeworth box analysis can narrow down the number of possible trading points and it can isolate that section of the contract curve on which it would be advantageous to trade but no more. The ultimate trade point decided on will be indeterminate in terms of this theory.

The point at the top left corner represents the situation where no trade is made at all. Stage I does not part with any goods, Stage II does not part with any cash. Two isoquants one for each stage, pass through this point. Clearly neither party will engage in a trade which would leave them on an inferior profit isoquant to that which can be attained with no trade at all. The only possible trading agreements must lie within the area bounded by these curves, and the relevant section of the contract curve in this case is the segment XZ. If a trade is made at point Q we can narrow the range of outcomes still further. Both parties could improve their profitability by renegotiation and moving on to the contract curve, say to Y. However, if one stage feels in a very weak bargaining situation he may fear that renegotiation will result in a trade on the contract curve so near to X (or Z) that it will be on an inferior profit isoquant to that on which Q lies.

13.2 Managerial Implications of Vertical Integration

Two main areas of managerial discretion are of interest once the integration decision has been taken. How should the firm price in its final market? Under which conditions should the divisions of the newly integrated firm trade with each other?

Final Market Behaviour

Whether price (and conversely output) should rise, fall or remain unchanged after integration depends on the firm's original decision and the reasoning behind it.

Security Motivation

If an integration exercise is carried out for security reasons alone, then price will remain unchanged. We need consider only three cases under differing initial conditions or market structure to illustrate this.[1]

(i)   *Vertical Integration between Two Perfect Competitors*: Consider the

---

1   Under any other type of market structure combination than those considered here (e.g. the combination of two oligopolists, or a monopolist integrating with an imperfect competitor) there would exist, to a greater or lesser extent, predatory benefits from integration.

perfect competitor operating at the earlier stage of production (Stage I) and the similar firm operating at the later stage (Stage II). After integration the combined firm faces an unchanged final demand situation and since costs are unchanged has an identical aggregate cost function. The price and output of Stage II will consequently remain unaltered. If the price at which the intermediate product is transferred from Stage I to Stage II changes as a result of integration, this will affect the profits earned by the individual stages but not the aggregate profit of the firm.

(ii)   *Vertical Integration between a Monopoly and One Perfect Competitor*: The outcome in this situation would be the same as in case (i) above and for analogous reasons.

(iii) *Vertical Integration between a Monopoly and all Firms in a Perfectly Competitive Industry*: Consider firstly the situation where the monopolist is operating at Stage II and the competitive industry is responsible for the earlier stage. Given his costs of production, including the cost of purchasing the output of Stage I, the monopolist will already be operating at the profit-maximising $MR = MC$ output level. That part of the monopolist's average cost (AC) curve which represents the inputs bought from the competitive industry will be equal to the competitive industry's supply curve (i.e. the prices at which the competitive industry would supply certain outputs). After integration this is still the case, except that these inputs will no longer be bought in but will be manufactured within the one firm. The AC curve and so the MC curve will remain unaltered.

Consider secondly, the situation where the monopolist is operating at Stage I, and integrates forward. It might seem in this situation that output would be reduced as Stage II is monopolised. However, the impact of monopoly at Stage I will already have affected the price:output decisions of the competitive industry at Stage II. Integration will merely result in a change of ownership of Stage II (assuming no cost change as a result of monopolisation).

Figure 13.3 explains this argument. For simplicity we assume that one unit of output of Stage I is required to produce one unit of output of Stage II. This enables us to make direct comparisons between the revenue and cost functions of each stage. Also we assume a horizontal AC_{II} curve. Before integration the monopolist's demand curve (D_I) is derived from the given market determined final demand (D_{II}) by deducting the cost (AC_{II}) of transforming the monopolist's output into the final product. (AC_{II} is defined so as *not* to include the purchase costs of inputs from Stage I, it is the AC of *processing* raw materials bought from Stage I. Since Stage II is perfectly competitive, each firm's price level will be equal to its marginal and its average costs in equilibrium. Thus at any price, say P_0, that price will equal average processing costs (AC_{II}) plus the monopolist's raw material selling

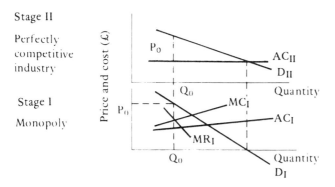

Figure 13.3

price — the average costs of buying raw materials.) Given this derived demand curve the monopolist will produce at output level Q_0 where $MR_I = MC_I$ at price P_0. After integration the monopolist's demand curve becomes D_{II} (i.e. $D_I + AC_{II}$) and his unit cost curve becomes $AC_I + AC_{II}$. For both D_{II} and $(AC_I + AC_{II})$ there will be corresponding marginal functions (MR_{II} and MC_{II}). Where these functions are equated the monopolist will maximise profits. This must be at output level Q_0. At that output level the corresponding marginal values for D_I and AC_I were equated. But if at Q_0 $MR_I = MC_I$ (which it did) then the slope of TR_I = the slope of TC_I at Q_0, but both D_I and AC_I have been increased by the identical value AC_{II} in order to obtain D_{II} and $(AC_I + AC_{II})$. If at any Q both TR_I and TC_I have been raised by the identical amount $Q \times AC_{II}$ to give the corresponding total values TR_{II} and TC_{II} for the integrated firm, then between any two output levels, say a and b, the increase in TR_b minus the increase in TR_a equals the change in the slope of TR between a and b (ΔMR) as a consequence of integration.[2] By analogy between a and b the change in TC, pre-, and post-integration, is merely the change in MC. Therefore since the changes in TR and TC at any output level result in identical changes in MR and MC, the output level where $MR = MC$ is also unchanged.

2 This is proved as follows: consider the attached figure. $\Delta TR_a - \Delta TR_b = WZ - XY = WV + VZ - WV - WU = VZ - WU$. And new slope less old slope equals change in slope or ΔMR. That is $(VZ/a-b - WU/a-b) = \Delta MR = (VZ - WU/a-b)$. At $a - b$ equal to unity $\Delta TR_a - \Delta TR_b = MR_{II-I}$. QED.

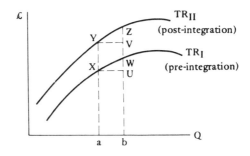

Cost Reduction

What if the motivation behind the vertical integration is that of increasing the efficiency of the combined firm? This will happen, for example, if the *AC* function of the integrated firm is lower than the simple arithmetic sum of the *AC* functions of the individual stages.

If the integration exercise is carried out for cost saving reasons only, and if the cost saved is an overhead or fixed cost, then output will remain unchanged. This can happen, for example, if two firms at succeeding stages integrate and the combined firm does away with a fixed cost such as a now redundant head office for one of the stages. Where the cost saving is invariant with output, the *TC* curve is reduced by an identical amount at each and every output level. The slope of the *TC* curve is consequently unchanged, marginal cost remains the same. Given our original assumption of unchanged demand conditions, the output level where $MR = MC$ will also be unchanged. If the cost saving is one which varies with output (e.g. the elimination of the need to reheat each unit of output between Stages I and II) then *MC* will be altered. Generally when the cost saving rises with output, *MC* will shift to the right, price will be lowered and output will be increased. Alternatively on the rarer occasions when the costs saved fall with output, *MC* will move to the left and output will be reduced.

Predatory Reasons

Two sets of circumstances exist where a vertical integration exercise can result in a changed pattern of industrial behaviour without any accompanying change in demand or cost conditions. One is where an opportunity to practise price discrimination emerges as a result of the integration exercise. The other is where the integration is between the two sides of a bilateral monopoly.

The Emergence of an Opportunity to Practise Price Discrimination   Forward integration may make price discrimination possible for the first time. If a monopolist in Stage I acquires some customers operating in Stage II, he can ensure that there will be no leakage or resale between subsidiaries and extra-group customers operating independently in other segments of the market which is Stage II. Before integration the segments might have been insufficiently sealed off, one from the other, to enable the monopolist to charge discriminatory prices.

In some conditions (for example those of Figure 9.4 in Chapter 9) output will remain unchanged, only the allocation of that output between market segments will differ as a result of the price discrimination. In others, however, the given cost and demand conditions facing Stage I may be such that the practice of price discrimination will result in output being increased. This is illustrated in Figure 13.4.

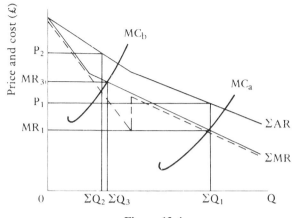

Figure 13.4

Consider first the situation before integration. There are two (or more) market segments with differing demand elasticities, but price discrimination is not possible. For practical purposes the firm is consequently faced not with two differing demand curves, but with one, ΣAR which is obtained by summing the individual demand curves in each segment horizontally. The relevant marginal revenue curve for ΣAR is the discontinuous version of ΣMR (represented by a dashed line). The finite discontinuity in ΣMR is caused by the kink in ΣAR which in turn has resulted from the horizontal summation of the demand curves in the individual segments.

The unintegrated firm with a marginal cost curve of MC_a will produce at output level ΣQ_1 and price P_1. Similarly the unintegrated firm whose marginal cost curve is MC_b will produce at output level ΣQ_2 and price P_2. In both cases these are the relevant price:output combinations indicated by the intersection of the relevant MC curve and the discontinuous version of ΣMR.

After integration and the appearance of the opportunity to price discriminate between segments, ΣAR ceases to have practical relevance. The firm is now interested in and can take advantage of the demand curves in the individual segments. For decision-making purposes the relevant ΣMR curve is now obtained by summing the MR curve in each segment horizontally to obtain the continuous line version of ΣMR.

The integrated firm with MC_a as its MC curve will continue to produce ΣQ_1. The prices charged in the market segments will be found by setting output in each segment at the level where the respective MRs equal ΣMR and the prices then obtained from the segment demand curves accordingly. The integrated firm whose cost conditions are represented by MC_b, however, will increase its output from ΣQ_2 to ΣQ_3 where MC_b intersects the continuous version of ΣMR. Price and output levels in each segment will be found in the usual way by equating each segment's marginal revenue at MR_3.

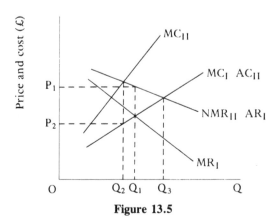

Figure 13.5

Vertical Integration between a Monopolist and a Monopsonist   This is the situation of bilateral monopoly. Consider a monopolist at Stage I before integration, with marginal cost curve MC_I in Figure 13.5. At fixed or agreed prices he would be prepared to supply the quantities indicated by this curve, since then his marginal cost would equal his (constant) marginal revenue. A monopsonist at Stage II must then regard MC_I as the unit (net of processing) purchase cost curve facing him for the product AC_{II}. The curve marginal to this, MC_{II}, is consequently the marginal purchasing cost of the product to the monopsonist. Given that the monopsonist's net marginal revenue curve (net of processing costs) is indicated by NMR_{II}, the unintegrated monopsonist would profit maximise at output level Q_2 where NMR_{II} and MC_{II} intersect. This would require an agreed transfer price of P_2.

On the other hand NMR_{II} indicates the quantities the monopsonist would be willing to purchase at any given fixed or agreed price, since then his net marginal revenue would equal his (constant) marginal purchasing cost for the product. A monopolist at Stage I must then regard NMR_{II} as the demand curve facing him for the product AR_I. The curve marginal to this MR_I is consequently the seller's marginal revenue curve. As a result, the monopolist's profit-maximising output level is Q_1 where MR_I and MC_I intersect. This would require an agreed transfer price of P_1.

The objectives of the two firms are inconsistent. Without integration we can only indicate that the agreed price will lie somewhere between the two extremes of P_1 and P_2. Where the agreement will be will depend on factors such as bargaining skill and negotiating expertise. After integration, however, output will be higher than either Q_1 or Q_2. The two stages will then maximise joint profits by exploiting their suppliers and customers and not as in the earlier discussion also attempting to exploit each other. This case is discussed more fully under the topic of transfer pricing below (pp. 382–384).

Transfer Pricing

When firms integrate vertically they may suffer from managerial diseconomies of scale. One way out of this problem is to retain the divisional structure of the firm and make managers responsible for their own profit and loss account. Each division is a profit centre in its own right. The inefficient manager is then no longer 'concealed' in the overall accounts of the company, and the efficient manager is more highly motivated because his merits are highlighted. However, divisional autonomy creates its own problems, one of which is transfer pricing. What price should be charged by one division for the products it sells to another? Should the sister division be compelled to buy at the price asked? The way these questions are answered will influence overall profits. They will also affect divisional profitability and so management morale and the long-run efficiency of the integrated firm.

Transfer pricing policy should have as its prime objective the maximisation of group profits. A second objective is to permit divisional managers to profit maximise as autonomous units. The transfer price rules which group management lay down must be such that both of these objectives can be pursued simultaneously. The general rule to accomplish these goals is that the transfer price should be equal to marginal cost, except when the transferred product can be bought and sold in a competitive market when it should equal the market price.

Transfer Pricing of a Product with a Competitive Market   Consider two independent firms: T, the earlier firm in the production process and F, the final or transferee firm, which processes the transferred product before selling it in the final market. In Figure 13.6, let D_T be the demand curve in the perfectly competitive market for the transferred product. MC_T is the marginal cost curve of firm T and NMR_F is the net marginal revenue curve of firm F.

It is obtained by deducting from the marginal revenue curve of F the marginal costs of processing and distribution which F incurs (i.e. all F's

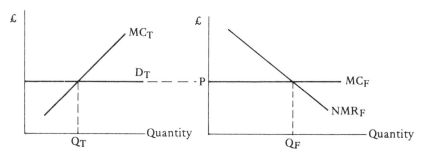

Figure 13.6

marginal costs but exclusive of the costs involved in purchasing the transferred product). MC_F is consequently equal to P, and is the cost of purchasing the good to be processed. The quantity axes are drawn on the same scales and unit for unit production is assumed. Both firms operate at their respective $MR = MC$ points, i.e. at Q_T and Q_F.

Now assume the firms integrate vertically. This is illustrated in Figure 13.7, where the panels of Figure 13.6 are superimposed on each other. The transfer price rule tells us that the divisions should continue to behave as if they were independent firms. The market price P should be selected as a transfer price and Q_T and Q_F produced by the respective divisions. This results in a shortfall of the transferred product of $Q_F - Q_T$. This should be made up by purchasing on the open market. No other position results in the group as a whole profit maximising. If, for example, T was compelled to make up the difference $Q_F - Q_T$, then the additional costs to T can be represented by the polygon $Q_T XZQ_F$. Purchase in the open market, conversely, merely costs F the area $Q_T XYQ_F$. Group profits would be diminished by the triangle XYZ if T was compelled to produce Q_F. Similarly, if F restricted its output to Q_T units, then the group would suffer a loss in net profits equal to the triangle WXY. Q_V might appear to be the optimal output at first glance since there $MC_T = NMR_F$, or, adding the marginal costs of processing to both sides of this equation, it is where the group's $MC = MR$. But this is only the case if the external market is ignored, and to produce at Q_V would lose the firm XVY in profits. If, as in Figure 13.8, the optimal solution results in over-production of the transferred product for F's requirement of $Q_T - Q_F$, then the surplus is merely sold in the open market.

If T restricted its output to Q_F it, and so the group, would forfeit net profits equal to area WXY. If F were compelled to absorb, process and sell Q_T units then the overall loss of profits would equal XYZ. (The additional net

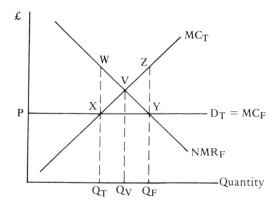

Figure 13.7

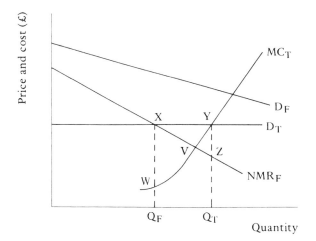

Figure 13.8

marginal revenue F would gain would equal the polygon Q_FXZQ_T. The addition to total costs of buying in the transferred product would, however, equal Q_FXYQ_T.) Similarly, where group MR = group MC, at Q_V, XYV would be forfeited if the external market were ignored.

When there is a perfect external market, transfer pricing is accomplished in practice by following the above rules and using the relevant calculus. Thus stage I equates its own MR and MC. For this its own TC function is required and differentiation applied to obtain MC. Stage II's demand function is transformed in the usual manner into MR by differentiating TR (or with a linear demand curve doubling the slope). Since MR is a sterling value expressed in terms of Q — for example

$$MR_F = 100 - 0.5Q_F$$

then, to obtain NMR by deducting processing costs, the entire MR curve must be lowered on the monetary axis by that amount. Thus if the marginal processing costs are

$$MC_F = 10 + 0.1Q_F$$
$$\Rightarrow NMR_F = MR_F - MC_F = 90 - 0.6Q_F$$

The MR_F curve has been lowered by 10 along its length and the gradient increased by $0.1Q$. If the market price of the transferred product is $P = 10$, then this is set equal to NMR_F of stage II and the optimal output of stage II is found. Thus:

$$10 = 90 - 0.6Q_F$$
$$\Rightarrow Q_F = 133.33$$

If the MC_T of stage I is

$$MC_T = 5 + 0.01Q_T$$

then stage I's output is where

$$P_T = 10 = 5 + 0.01Q_T$$
$$\Rightarrow Q_T = 500$$

(A surplus of approximately 366 units to be sold on the open market.)

Transfer Pricing with no External Market   Here interdivisional transfers should
be priced at the level of the marginal cost of production. The external market
does not exist and so must be ignored. Figure 13.9 illustrates that group profit maximisation is at output Q_v where $MC_T = NMR_F$. This is true because
if we add the marginal costs of processing and distribution to both sides of
this equation we deduce that group marginal costs equal MR_F, which in this
case is also group marginal revenue since the only demand curve the group
faces is D_F. The objectives of the group in this instance include the desire
to prevent the divisions exploiting each other at group expense as the firms
did in the bilateral monopoly of Figure 13.5. To achieve this, two additional
constraints are required. Either F or T must have its pricing freedom removed, and conversely and simultaneously T or F must not be permitted
monopolistically to restrict output or monopsonistically to restrict purchasing by constructing marginal curves to NMR_F and MC_T respectively. (As the
firms did in Figure 13.5.) This is explained below.

Remember that NMR_F equals the marginal revenue received by F after
the marginal cost of distributing has been subtracted. Therefore NMR_F is the
remainder of F's marginal revenue to be set equal to the marginal cost of
buying in the transferred product. Now consider Figure 13.9. Suppose that

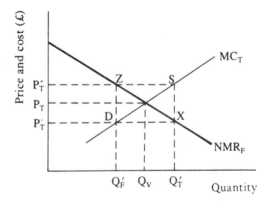

Figure 13.9

both T and F are forced to accept a single transfer price which is fixed no matter how much of the good is transferred. Suppose also that this price is below P_T, say P'_T. Then the horizontal line at P'_T represents the marginal cost to F of buying in from T and also the marginal revenue to T of selling to F. To maximise its profits F will wish to produce Q'_T (point X) and T will wish to produce Q'_F (D). If the transfer price were higher than P_T, say P_T'', then F would wish to produce $Q'_F(Z)$ and T, $Q'_T(S)$. In both cases the two quantities differ from each other and from the quantity which would maximise the profits for the group as a whole. However, if the transfer price were set at P_T, the quantity which T wished to sell, Q_v, would equal the amount which F wished to buy and also the amount which would maximise the group's profits. Therefore P_T is the optimal transfer price which would lead to the transfer of the profit maximising amount of intermediate product.

In practice the transfer price rule can be implemented in either of two ways. Firstly, T can be given the NMR_F schedule and told to use this as its demand curve to determine both the transfer price and the transferred quantity to maximise its own profits. That is, at any transfer price T would be forced to produce a quantity given by NMR_F. In addition, F would be instructed to accept T's chosen price and accordingly would demand a quantity shown by NMR_F. T will wish to set the transfer price at P_T and to sell Q_v to F. To understand this, consider a transfer price below P_T, say P'_T. If T chose P'_T, it would be forced to produce Q'_T but would wish to produce Q'_F (D): it would make an avoidable loss of DSX. If T chose a price above P_T, say P''_T, it would be forced to produce at Z but would wish to produce at S: it would forego profits of DZS. Hence, if the transfer price is greater than MC_T, T could increase its profits by expanding its output and reducing the transfer price. But if T set the price at P_T, the amount it would wish to produce and the amount it was forced to produce would be equal: Q_v, which is also the profit-maximising output for the group. Therefore, to maximise its profits, T would set the transfer price at P_T. Notice that the line P_TV, and not a line marginal to NMR_F, is T's marginal revenue curve.

Alternatively, the same outcome can be arrived at by providing F's managers with the MC_T schedule and telling them to use this as their supply curve to determine both the amount to buy from T and the transfer price. That is, at any price F would be forced to buy an amount given by MC_T. In addition, T would be instructed to accept F's chosen price and accordingly would supply a quantity given by MC_T. F would wish to set the transfer price at P_T and to buy Q_v from T. The explanation is similar to the last case. Again, in Figure 13.9, if F set a transfer price below P_T, say P'_T, F would be forced to buy Q'_F (D) but would wish to buy Q'_T (X) and so would forego profit of DXZ. If F set a price above P_T, say P''_T, it would be forced to buy Q'_T (S) but would wish to buy Q'_F (Z) so making an avoidable loss of ZSX. Hence, if the transfer price is less than NMR_F, F could increase its profits by increasing the amount bought and reducing the transfer price. But

is where $\Sigma MR = NMR_F = MR_T$, that is, at output levels Q_F and Q_T. Price P_E will be charged in the external market, and P_T will be the relevant transfer price. A price of P_T will ensure that division F voluntarily purchases Q_F from T and so the group as a whole maximises profits.

13.3   The Decision to Diversify

Avoidance of Risk

One major reason to diversify is to spread risk. The probability of loss in two markets simultaneously is always less than the probability of loss in either individually. Moreover, we know from equation (12.4) that the less closely markets (or securities in that instance) are correlated in terms of profit variability, the more stable will be the profit performance of a firm operating in each.

More specifically, firms can be affected by seasonal, cyclical and irregular factors, and by the direction of the overall market trend itself. If the trend is falling, a specialised firm will clearly wish to diversify so that total sales will not decline along with those of its primary market. Diversification to minimise the impact of seasonal, cyclical and irregular factors can also be undertaken.

Firms in seasonal goods industries will diversify in order to keep plant fully utilised for the 12 months of the year; or to avoid having to build up stocks in seasons of lean demand; or to avoid the need to shed and re-engage labour, none of which are costless alternatives. The ideal is obviously to produce goods with a seasonal fluctuation inversely related to that of the original product (e.g. Christmas card firms may diversify into summer postcards).

Firms in industries with a cyclical pattern of demand may diversify into areas with a sales pattern the reverse of the original. This may not prove as easy as with seasonal fluctuations but another way to obtain a sales cushion is to diversify into a cyclically stable industry. Irregular factors, of course, are wholly unpredictable. Diversification to avoid such uncertainty rests on the desire of the firm to avoid having all its commercial eggs in the one basket.

Growth and Diversification Economies

Firms also diversify because it appears to be a suitable route for corporate growth. Figure 13.11 illustrates why on occasion straightforward expansion of the existing product line is more profitable, and why at other times diversification is to be preferred. In Figure 13.11(a), the firm's product transformation curve is FF'. Profit (or sales) maximisation occurs at point F, with production of OF units of Y and zero output of X. If the firm now expands its production capacity, its product transformation curve will shift out and up, say to GG'. If there are constant returns to scale then the curve must

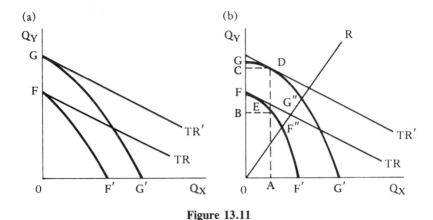

Figure 13.11

move outwards exactly in the same proportion along any straight line through the origin. This must be so to enable output to increase in exact proportion with the extra input resources. The curvature of GG' will be the same as that of FF'. The marginal rate of product transformation ($MRPT$) will consequently be the same at G as it was at F. Given unchanged prices, the point of tangency between GG' and an isorevenue line, such as TR', must then again be at the intersection with the y-axis. In this case it pays to remain a single product firm.

Now consider Figure 13.11(b). Here the curvature of GG' is greater than FF'. Constant returns to scale are not present. If output of Y (or X) alone was increased by movement along the y- (or x-) axis, this could only be done by a smaller proportionate amount than could an increase in output of any combination of the two products by moving along a straight line such as OR (i.e. $FG/OF < F''G''/OF''$).

When diminishing returns are present the $MRPT$ will not be the same at G as at F. Expansion of the scale of operations will result in diversification. The optimal tangency point is now at D and production of both X and Y has become worthwhile.

What industrial realities underlie the figure? Why does GG' have a different curvature from FF'? Two interlinked factors are operating simultaneously. Diminishing returns have arisen in the production of Y, and economies not previously available have become present in the production of X. Even if there are economies of large-scale manufacture, the marketing costs associated with any particular output will probably rise with scale of production. Markets will become increasingly saturated. Advertising and promotion will become progressively less successful and the firm will move well up its S-shaped sales response function. (Alternatively, price will have to be reduced to clear the extra output. This changes the shape of the isorevenue line not the product transformation curve, but the result is the same.) Consequently, as the costs of producing Y increase, it is becoming cheaper, in opportunity cost terms, to produce X. In Figure 13.11(b) OA = one unit of X. Before growth, on curve FF', to move from F in order to produce one unit of X, FB units of Y had to be forgone. After growth, at G, in order to produce one unit of X only GC units of Y have to be forfeited.

In addition there is what Penrose called 'the continuing availability of unused productive services'. Briefly this can be subclassified as follows. First, there is the balance of processes. This is a principle generally explained by reference to the size of manufacturing plant required to utilise fully a range of machine types with differing and indivisible throughput capacities. Throughput must be large enough to equal the least common multiple (LCM) of the various maximum outputs from each machine type.

If we take this principle further and consider the whole range of resources in a firm (managers, accountants, market researchers, sales force workers, engineers, research and development staff, and so on) it becomes apparent that to utilise fully all of these resources, human and/or physical, the LCM will be very large indeed in terms of output. In the presence of market saturation and the like, it is not surprising that diversification may often prove to be the most profitable way to achieve this large LCM.

Second, there is the very similar economy of fully utilising specialised services. For example, if two products have common costs, a specialised firm in one product may diversify into the other so that it can achieve economies at the stage of common cost. This need not mean taking up slack as in the LCM case; it can do, but it can also include the attainment of any scale economies available at that point of common cost. Thus, a tinned soup manufacturer with his own tin can factory may diversify into tinned fruits in order to lower the costs of the essentially service factory which produces the tin containers. Penrose has argued that the ability to achieve economies through diversification is, as a result of these two factors, rarely, if ever, exhausted.

Other Factors

Firms also diversify because external market opportunities change and this, coupled possibly with one or more of the other motivating factors, induces diversification. One obvious illustration of this two-edged motivation for diversification is the possession of a research and development department. This provides the firm with a built-in engine of diversification which is constantly producing new technological ideas which need not be related to the firm's original market.

The possession of marketing expertise can also be seen as an under-utilised specialist resource merely awaiting a market opportunity to arise in order to exploit it by diversification. For example, possession of the financial wherewithal, desire to grow, expertise in the mass marketing of consumer durables, plus a known brand name resulted in Hoover diversifying out of vacuum cleaners into washing machines, refrigerators, dishwashers and other household equipment.

13.4 Managerial Implications of Diversification

Optimising the Product Mix

Eli Clemens argued that firms should expand output on each product to the point where the least profitable unit will be produced at marginal cost. His model, reproduced in Figure 13.12 assumes a low cross-elasticity of demand between a firm's products.[3] Each product is produced until its *MR* is equal to the *MR* of every other product, and prices are selected accordingly. At the limit, *EMR* (equal marginal revenue) = the firm's *MC* curve. (The products whose demand is most elastic have the lowest margin over *MC*. Only on products which have some sort of differential advantage can more monopolistic prices be charged.)

The two-product model of Figure 13.13 is more restrictive, but shows implicitly how linear programming can be applied to the problem, and hence how the multi-product Clemens model can be applied in practice. *FF* is a product transformation curve. It is the locus of output or product mix combinations of products *Y* and *X* which can be obtained from a given amount

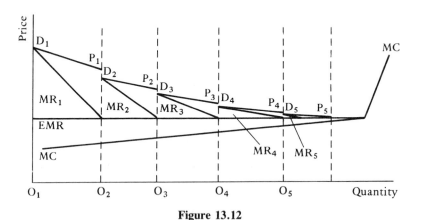

Figure 13.12

3   Note the quantity axis is somewhat unusual in the Clemens model. It is obviously not measuring homogeneous output units. Rather, the demand curves relate price received to the number of units of homogeneous production inputs used in order to provide for the successive markets.

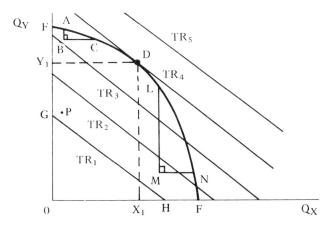

Figure 13.13

of input. The input could be regarded as the firm's total resources at a given point in time. If the firm produces, say, at point P then it is under-utilising its resources. The firm, however, is unable, through lack of resources, to produce any combination of Y and X above and to the right of FF.

FF slopes downwards since any increase in output of X must be accompanied by a decrease in output of Y. FF is also concave to the origin. This is indicated by the rising $MRPT$ of X for Y, which is the direct outcome of the presence of heterogeneity in the fixed input. Thus, for example, as output of X increases, resources which previously were used to produce Y will have to be transferred to the production of X. More and more of Y will have to be forgone to provide the resources which are required to produce (in an increasingly technologically inefficient manner) one unit of X. The reverse will hold as the output of Y is increased at the expense of X. This argument is illustrated geometrically. $BC = MN =$ one unit of X. At A, to increase the output of X by one unit, AB units of Y must be forgone. At L, however, LM units of Y must be forgone to increase the output of X by one.

We can now determine the optimal output mix of the firm by superimposing on Figure 13.13 isorevenue lines. These represent the locus of all possible combinations of the two outputs which result in the same total revenue. They will be higher in value the further they are from the origin. They are straight on the assumptions that the products are unrelated on the demand side of the market and that they are sold in perfectly competitive conditions with prices which are invariant with respect to quantity. The point of tangency, D, between TR_4 and FF determines the optimal output mix of Y_1X_1, which gives the firm the highest total revenue for its given level of expenditure on input resources.

The highest total revenue, given costs, automatically implies that profits are also maximised. Thus both a profit maximiser and a sales maximiser will, given the level of costs, choose an output mix where the marginal rate of product transformation between every pair of outputs is numerically equal to the inverse ratio of their prices.

Algebraically the slope of TR_4 (the same as the slope of TR_1) $= OG/OH = P_X/P_Y$. But the slope of $FF = \partial Q_Y/\partial Q_X$. Thus at D:

$$\frac{\partial Q_Y}{\partial Q_X} = \frac{P_X}{P_Y} \text{ or } P_X \partial Q_X \ (= MR_X) = P_Y \, \partial Q_Y \ (= MR_Y) \qquad (13.1)$$

for both types of firm. Any differences between the output mix or resource allocation of the two types of firm must consequently be due not to reallocation of a given level of costs or revenues, but to the larger outputs (and so larger TC and TR) which can be expected to accompany sales maximisation. This is a trite conclusion as it stands. However, when one bears in mind that a sales maximiser 'forfeits' profits in order to operate up to a profit constraint, the fact that equation (13.1) is valid indicates that profit optimising behaviour will still be pursued. In the case of the sales maximiser, however, absolute profits will not be maximised, but relatively unprofitable input and output mixes continue to be avoided.

If we now compare Figure 13.13 with Figure 8.4 of Chapter 8 it will be apparent that once again there is a close relationship between marginal analysis and linear programming. In the two-product examples of the figures, the boundary of the feasible space is analogous to the product transformation curve. Similarly the iso-contribution lines are analogous to the iso-revenue lines. (Revenue $= P \times Q$, Contribution $= (P - VC \times Q)$. Both concentrate on incremental revenues and costs, and recognise the irrelevance of fixed costs. LP concentrates on contribution maximisation, conventional economic analysis concentrates on $MR = MC$, where MC is the benefit foregone at the margin by cutting back output on one product to increase output of the other. Both thus implicitly or explicitly take opportunity cost into account. With LP, the iterative corner-by-corner comparison of the additional revenue gained by bringing a new product into the solution (or increasing output of an existing one) is contrasted with the sacrifice of earnings from the products that must be given up (or outputs that must be reduced).

The major differences in the two approaches are that the boundary of the LP feasible region is curvilinear only because it is composed of segments each of which is perfectly linear in its own right. Each input type is assumed to be homogeneous. Product transformation curves permit input heterogeneity *within* groups of inputs. Second, linear isorevenue lines require a fixed output selling price and zero demand cross-elasticity between outputs. But linear

isorevenue lines are *not* essential to economic analysis. Linear isocontribution lines *are* necessary to *LP*, and in addition constant variable costs are
assumed which in turn implies constant input prices and constant input marginal
productivity. Third, product transformation curves assume that output mixes
can be smoothly and continuously varied. *LP* restricts itself to a finite number
of alternative mixes which may be more realistic and certainly facilitates
calculation. Finally, scale economies are not possible with *LP*, constant returns
are essential.

Joint Product Pricing

When a multi-product firm sets a price for any one product it must also consider the impact on revenues of any other member of its product range which
is related to the original: either as a substitute or as a complement. In short,
cross-elasticities of demand must be taken into account.

Consider a simple two-product case, where a firm produces x and y. The
firm's total revenue function is:

$$TR = P_X Q_X + P_Y Q_Y$$

The values of MR_X and MR_Y are obtained using the addition and multiplication rules of differentiation, thus:

$$MR_X = \frac{\partial TR}{\partial Q_X} = P_X + Q_X \frac{\partial P_X}{\partial Q_X} + P_Y \frac{\partial Q_Y}{\partial Q_X} + Q_Y \frac{\partial P_Y}{\partial Q_X}$$

$$MR_Y = \frac{\partial TR}{\partial Q_Y} = P_Y + Q_Y \frac{\partial P_Y}{\partial Q_Y} + P_X \frac{\partial Q_X}{\partial Q_Y} + Q_X \frac{\partial P_X}{\partial Q_Y}$$

The first two terms of each equation are the marginal revenues directly arising from each product. The final two terms arise from the presence of demand
cross-elasticities. If the products are substitutes, the sum of these two terms
will be negative; if complements, the net sum will be positive. Thus, for
example, the third and fourth terms of the MR_X equation show the change
in revenue from product y when an additional unit of x is sold. This point
is discussed also on pp. 276–277 where incremental analysis is examined.

In addition to demand cross-elasticities, firms must consider supply cross-
elasticities. Joint products can be produced in fixed proportions, as in the
case of sides of beef and cow hides, or pineapple rings and pineapple juice;
or in variable proportions, where a decision can be taken as to how many
units of product A should be produced and the decision does *not* have a corresponding effect on the output of product B.

Pricing Joint Products Produced in Fixed Proportions

For marketing and pricing purposes, joint products produced in fixed proportions are separable entities. From a production viewpoint, however, it makes sense to regard them as one package. Appropriation of costs to one product or the other is both an impracticable and an unnecessary exercise. Determination of separate and individual prices, on the other hand, is necessary to enable the firm to maximise total profits in the two distinct markets in which the products are sold.

Figure 13.14 shows how the theory of marginal equivalency can be applied to this problem. D_1 and D_2 are the demand curves for products 1 and 2 in their respective markets. MR_1 and MR_2 are the corresponding marginal revenue curves. MR_1 is not continued below the quantity axis, because under no circumstances does it make sense to sell more than Q_2 units of product 1. Beyond Q_2 marginal revenue for product 1 becomes negative, that is, total revenue decreases. ΣMR is obtained by aggregating MR_1 and MR_2 vertically. At Q_2 and beyond, MR_2 and ΣMR are, of course, one and the same.

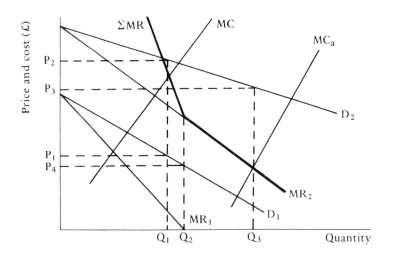

Figure 13.14

The summation of marginal revenue curves is vertical, not horizontal as when the practice of price discrimination was examined in Figure 9.4. Vertical summation gives the added revenues for both products. In the case of joint product pricing, we wish to ascertain the total marginal revenue obtainable at any given output level, and how that ΣMR is distributed. In the case of price discrimination, we wished to ascertain the total quantity at a given MR level, and how that quantity was divided.

Note also that since the two products are assumed to be produced in fixed proportions, the units of measurement on the quantity axis refer to both goods 1 and 2. The profit maximising output level is Q_1 where $MC = \Sigma MR$. Q_1 units of each product are sold and are priced at the levels indicated by the relevant demand curves, P_1 and P_2 on D_1 and D_2 respectively.

It is possible that with a given cost schedule, the marginal cost curve could intersect ΣMR to the right of Q_2, as does MC_a. In this case profit-maximisation procedures require a total production of Q_3 units, with product 2 selling at price P_3. Total revenue from product 1, however, is maximised at output Q_2, not Q_3. Given this, product 1 should be sold at price P_4 which would leave a quantity equal to $Q_3 - Q_2$ as surplus to requirements. This surplus must be withheld from the market in some way (e.g. dumping or destruction) to permit product 1's total revenue to be maximised. Alternatively, it may be more profitable to advertise and increase demand for product 1 so that redundant output is avoided.

The calculus can be used to accomplish optimal joint product pricing. Suppose A and B are produced on a 1:3 basis with the following demand functions:

$$Q_A = 1 - P_A$$
$$\Rightarrow P_A = 1 - Q_A$$
and $$Q_B = 2 - P_B$$
$$\Rightarrow P_B = 2 - Q_B$$

The latter must be re-expressed as:

$$P_B = 2 - 3.0 Q_B^1$$

where the prime sign is an indicator of 3 units of B, the amount produced in relation to A in the joint product. The demand function for B is rearranged as shown since the monetary intercept is unchanged. (Zero units of B will be sold at a price of 2 whether B is sold singly or in the larger package of $Q_B^1 = 0.333 Q_B$.) The new demand function, however, relates to packages which number Q_B^1 where Q_B and Q_A are going to be compared on a diagram with the same horizontal scale. Namely each of Q packages contains one unit of A and three units of B, i.e. $Q = Q_A = Q_B^1 = 0.333 Q_B$. The slope of the demand function with respect to Q_B^1 must, therefore, be three times as steep as that for Q_B, if Q_A and Q_B are to be compared on the same diagram where the quantity axis relates to the fixed proportion joint product.

$$\Rightarrow TR_A = P_A Q_A = Q_A - Q_A^2$$
$$\Rightarrow TR_B = P_B Q_B^1 = 2Q_B^1 - 3Q_B^{12}$$
$$\Rightarrow \Sigma TR = Q_A - Q_A^2 + 2Q_B^1 - 3Q_B^{12}$$

But since $Q_A = Q_B^1$

$$\Sigma TR = 3Q - 4Q^2$$

The firm's TC function is, of course, constructed for Q_A and Q_B^1 jointly and $\pi = TR - TC$. Assume:

$$TC = 100 + 2.75Q + 0.1Q^2$$

then $\pi = 3Q - 4Q^2 - 100 - 2.75Q - 0.1Q^2$
     $= 0.25Q - 4.1Q^2 - 100$

$$\Rightarrow \frac{d\pi}{dQ} = 0 = 0.25 - 8.2Q$$

$$\therefore Q = 0.03$$

The optimal solution, therefore, is to produce

0.03 units of A
and   0.09 units of B (recall $Q_B^1 = 0.333Q_B$)

provided that the values of MR_A and MR_B are positive at these outputs. This can be ascertained by evaluating MR_A and MR_B from the relevant demand curve as follows:

$$MR_A = 1 - 2Q_A = 1 - 0.06 = +0.94$$
$$MR_B^1 = 2 - 6Q_B^1 = 2 - 0.18 = +1.72$$

Both values are positive and hence $Q = 0.03$ is the appropriate solution. The respective selling prices are found by substitution in the demand equations. Thus

$$P_A = 1 - 0.03 = 0.97$$
and $P_B = 2 - (3 \times 0.03) = 1.91$

Had either A or B had a negative MR at 0.03 and 0.09 units of output respectively then an excess production problem would have existed. In which case the relevant MR equation for determining optimal output is that for the other product. That is, MC for the joint product would be set equal to MR for the single product with no excess production problem. This would give optimal output. The output rate for the product with the excess production problem would be determined by setting MR equal to zero.

Pricing Joint Products Produced in Variable Proportions

Consider Figure 13.15. It contains a range of product transformation curves for the firm, each curve representing the production possibilities at a different scale of operations. The range of isorevenue lines is drawn as before on the assumption of given prices. At the points of tangency the marginal costs of

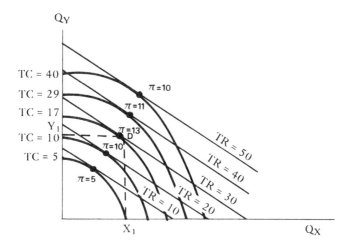

Figure 13.15

producing the products are proportional to their marginal revenues. At each tangency point the condition $MR_Y = MR_X$ holds true. MR_Y is the marginal revenue obtained from selling an increment of Y and this is the marginal cost (i.e. the marginal revenue forgone) incurred by forfeiting the sale of an increment of X in order to release the resources to produce Y. Given knowledge of the total revenues and costs involved in the isoquant map, the total profits (π) at each point of tangency can be calculated. The output scale and product mix selected will consequently be where the value of π is greatest, namely point D, with an output mix of Y_1, X_1.

This analysis, however, assumes that the firm's problem is one of choosing either scale or product mix rather than price. Let us rather consider the situation where scale is given (i.e. the product transformation curve is fixed, at least in the short run) but prices and quantities remain to be determined. We know that optimally $MR_X = MR_Y$ in a two good situation.

In Figure 13.16 a given product transformation curve appears (flipped 180° over on the X-axis), together with demand and MR curves for product X and for product Y, (in the latter case flipped 180° to the left). Quadrant iii contains a 45° line for guidance purposes. The problem is to find the prices P_X and P_Y which will equate MR_X and MR_Y while remaining on the firm's product transformation curve. No other rectangle other than the one traced in on the figure satisfies these conditions. In practice, in a multi-product world, the problem can be solved either by the calculus or by linear programming.

In all three diagrammatic expositions (Figures 13.12, 13.15 and 13.16) we arrived at the same equimarginal result. That is, firms should produce and price two goods, X and Y, where $MR_X = MR_Y$. This is somewhat

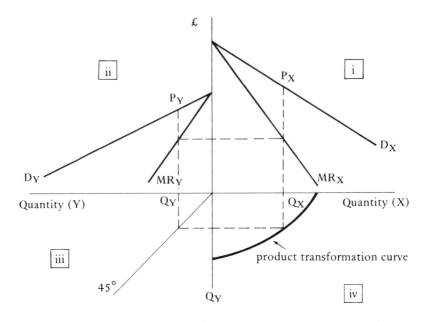

Figure 13.16

simplistic, however. In Figure 13.12 the Clemens model defined the quantity axis in terms of inputs not outputs, hence permitting an identical and diagrammatically uniform MC schedule for each product, whence $MR_X = MR_Y$ was inferred. In Figure 13.15, however, the firm was assumed to be a price taker, albeit at different possible scales and so with different isorevenue lines. The problem was one of selecting scale, not price. There, however, at $MR_Y = MR_X$, MR_X was defined so as to equal MC_Y, the opportunity cost in equation (13.1) of forfeiting revenue from Y to release resources to produce X. As we saw, this can result in a least-cost product mix, but not necessarily in profit maximisation. In Figure 13.16 we moved away from the price-taking situation to downward-sloping demand curves. There again $MR_Y = MR_X$ and from quadrant iv one could analogously deduce that when this is so, $MR_Y = MC_Y$ and $MR_X = MC_X$. Similarly, in quadrants i and ii, if the functions MC_X and MC_Y were to be inserted, they would intersect MR_X and MR_Y above Q_X and Q_Y respectively. But Figure 13.16 is a contrived situation with optimal scale given. Scale may not be optimal.

In brief, the equimarginal revenue per product rule assumes too much. Rather, price quantity decisions should be taken so that, first, the ratios MR_X/MC_X and MR_Y/MC_Y should be equal (verbally the firm should receive the same incremental revenue per pound spent on each product) and second,

MR should equal *MC* for each product, otherwise a profit maximising (as opposed to a least-cost) product mix and scale will not have been achieved. This can be more elegantly phrased using calculus. Assume zero cross-elasticity of demand. Then:

$$\pi = P_Y Q_Y + P_X Q_X - TC\,(Q_Y, Q_X)$$

To maximise profits take the partials and set equal to zero:

$$\frac{\partial \pi}{\partial Q_Y} = P_Y + Q_Y \frac{\partial P_Y}{\partial Q_Y} - \frac{\partial TC}{\partial Q_Y} = 0$$

$$\frac{\partial \pi}{\partial Q_X} = P_X + Q_X \frac{\partial P_X}{\partial Q_X} - \frac{\partial TC}{\partial Q_X} = 0$$

or

$$P_Y + Q_Y \frac{\partial P_Y}{\partial Q_Y} = \frac{\partial TC}{\partial Q_Y}$$

and

$$P_X + Q_X \frac{\partial P_X}{\partial Q_X} = \frac{\partial TC}{\partial Q_X}$$

or

$$MR_Y = MC_Y \text{ and } MR_X = MC_X\,[4]$$

As an example, assume $TC = 500 + 5Q^2_Y + 2Q^2_X - Q_X Q_Y$

$$P_Y = 100 - Q_Y$$
$$P_X = 200 - 2Q_X$$

Hence
$$\pi = 100Q_Y - Q^2_Y + 200Q_X - 2Q^2_X - (500 + 5Q^2_Y + 2Q^2_X - Q_X Q_Y)$$
$$= 100Q_Y - 6Q^2_Y + 200Q_X - 4Q^2_X - 500 + Q_X Q_Y$$

$$\frac{\partial \pi}{\partial Q_X} = 200 - 8Q_X + Q_Y = 0$$

$$\frac{\partial \pi}{\partial Q_Y} = 100 - 12Q_Y + Q_X = 0$$

---

4 The *MC* functions for each of the joint products can thus be identified although the average costs can still not be disentangled.

Solving these equations and substituting to obtain prices[5]:

$$Q_Y = 10.5, \; Q_X = 26.0, \; P_Y = 89.5 \text{ and } P_X = 148.0$$

Innovation and Product Differentiation

Figure 13.17 depicts the firm in Figure 13.12 in a subsequent period when it has successfully introduced a new product significantly better in consumers' eyes than existing products. Demand curve D_6 represents this innovation. While the firm was developing this product, competitors could readily see the profit potential of the product associated with, say, D_1. They had an incentive to enter with products of their own, and such entry would cause the elasticity of D_1 to become greater. The introduction of the new product, D_6, alerts competitors to the profit potential of the innovation also. At the same time as the firm in the figure is introducing its significant new product, it could also be entering product areas of competitive firms (D_7) with demand curves like D_5 in Figure 13.12 or any other product area in which price is greater than marginal cost. This in turn increases the elasticity of the demand curves faced by these competitors. This approach to innovation or brand addition to a product range is a straightforward development of conventional theory. An alternative approach has been developed by Lancaster who claims that the satisfactions which consumers desire are provided by the

5   We can now demonstrate our verbal conclusion that, given scale, the profit-maximising prices are where the marginal revenues are proportionate to the marginal costs of production. Maximise:

$$\pi = P_x Q_x + P_y Q + \lambda(TC_k - TC(Q_x Q_y))$$

where TC_k is fixed total expenditure as given by the product transformation curve.

$$\frac{\partial \pi}{\partial Q_x} = P_x + Q_x \frac{\partial P_x}{\partial Q_x} - \lambda \frac{\partial TC}{\partial Q_x} = 0$$

$$\frac{\partial \pi}{\partial Q_y} = P_y + Q_y \frac{\partial P_y}{\partial Q_y} - \lambda \frac{\partial TC}{\partial Q_y} = 0$$

or

$$MR_x = \lambda MC_x \text{ and } MR_y = \lambda MC_y$$

Hence

$$MR_x/MR_y = MC_x/MC_y \text{ or } MR_x/MC_x = MR_y/MC_y$$

QED

Scale should be altered, and the constraint should be increased or decreased in the long run should either $MR_x \neq MC_x$ or $MR_y \neq MC_y$. When this long-run optimal scale situation is accomplished, then the equimarginal revenue position of $MR_y = MR_x$ of Figure 13.16 must be attained.

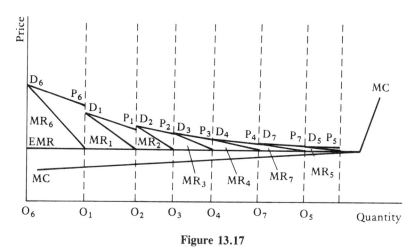

Figure 13.17

attributes or characteristics of goods, and not by the products themselves. A product, in short, is a bundle of satisfactions or characteristics, and not merely a good or service, *qua* good or service.

The demand for tins of Irish stew, for example, depends on characteristics such as the quantity of meat and the quantity of vegetables in each tin as well as on product price. Table 13.1 gives a hypothetical characteristic rating for three brands, and two characteristics.

Table 13.1

	(I) *Quantity of meat*	(II) *Quantity of vegetables*	*Ratio*
Brand A	80	40	2.0
B	40	80	0.5
C	60	60	1.0

In Figure 13.18 the three brands are depicted in characteristics space as rays emanating from the origin. The slope of each ray is determined by the ratio of characteristic I to characteristic II. A consumer of brand *A*, for example, would always 'consume' these characteristics at a ratio of 2:1 no matter how much of brand *A* he bought. The points *A*, *C* and *B* represent respectively the characteristics he could purchase were he to allocate his entire budget to any one brand. Thus points *A*, *C* and *B* depend on his (fixed) budget and the (different) brand prices. The line joining points *A*, *C* and *B* is called the

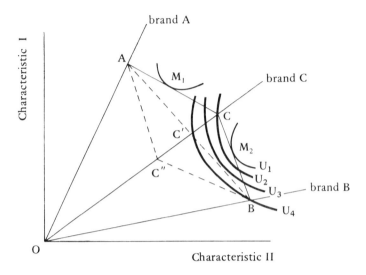

Figure 13.18

efficiency, or *characteristics possibility frontier*. Not only do points *A, C* and *B* themselves represent an exhaustion of the individual's budget, but so too would any intermediate points such as M_1 or M_2. This is so since it is assumed (unrealistically, but as we shall see, usefully) that the characteristics themselves are separable and therefore, hypothetically at least, can be bought in whatever proportions the consumer subjectively desires. Thus if only brands *C* and *B* were available, the line *CB*, if extended to the characteristics axes, is analogous to the price line of normal consumer theory. The consumer's *subjective* tastes for bundles of characteristics can be introduced using conventional indifference curves. To maximise his utility, for example, he might select point M_2.

But M_2, while hypothetically attainable using all of the consumer's budget to buy characteristics I and II, is apparently unobtainable in fact. No brand exists which provides this bundle of characteristics in the proportion he wishes. But, in fact, the model is analogous to linear programming and production theory. Characteristics are viewed as the inputs into a production process of which the output is consumer utility, while the goods are the 'processes' by which this output is obtained. The consumer's individual preference determines which combinations of characteristics he wishes to provide himself with and in what quantities. But there is also an objective 'consumption technology' which relates inputs with processes. This technology is available to each consumer and he will try to attain the characteristics frontier given his subjective tastes. If the consumer is willing to combine brands, however, he can attain a characteristics bundle equivalent to that at M_2. The brand mix

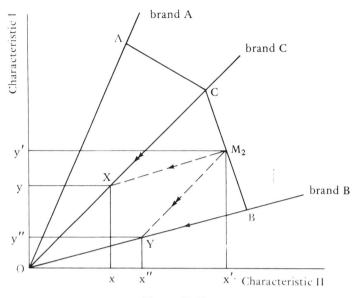

Figure 13.19

can be found, as with our earlier example of linear programming by drawing a line from M_2, parallel to OB until it hits OC (as in Figure 13.19). Similarly, another line, parallel to OC is drawn from M_2 until it meets OB. The budget is thus spent on brand C until the consumer reaches point X, when he will have acquired y units of characteristic I and x units of characteristic II. He will then switch to brand B and spend his remaining budget on it to acquire in total the characteristics ratio indicated at point M_2 (namely $y':x'$). This will be accomplished since the line XM_2 along which he is now moving provides the characteristics in the same proportion as brand B (it has the same slope). This move provides him with an extra $(y' - y = y'')$ units of I and $(x' - x = x'')$ units of II to add to the y and x units he already has at point X. This is so since the move from X to M_2, is, as the opposite side of a parallelogram, equal to OY in characteristics space. By similar reasoning he could consume the brands along the path OYM_2, consuming brand B first. Either pathway exhausts his budget, given the position and slope of CB.

Returning to Figure 13.18 we can see the effect of a price change on consumer behaviour. Depending on his preferences the consumer will be lying on the line ACB. At M_1 he will combine brands A and C, at M_2 C and B. He will reject the possibility of combining brands A and B alone, since this would not enable him to purchase the highest possible characteristic combination. If the price of C increases so that only OC' can be bought with the given budget, the frontier becomes $AC'B$ and combinations of A and B

also become efficient. If the price rises still further so that only OC'' can be bought, then only combinations of A and B are efficient, combinations A and C, and B and C now lying within the AB frontier. As a corollary any budget increase would shift ACB outwards to the right.

Two factors emerge from this discussion of particular relevance to product policy. First, the concept of brand loyalty can now be better understood. This is so since it is definitely not the case that consumers will always and for each product type be willing or able to mix brands to attain a desired characteristics bundle. Thus consider again Figure 13.18 with only brands C and B available. The highest indifference curve, U_1 passing through M_2 is hypothetically attainable but brand mixing is unacceptable to the consumer. Instead he will spend his budget entirely on brand C, achieving U_2. Now C can be progressively raised in price but the consumer will continue to spend his budget on it alone. Given a fixed expenditure he is forced on to progressively lower indifference curves, but not until C's price has risen so that OC' exhausts his budget, will he consider switching brands to B to achieve the same satisfaction on U_4.

Second, if M_2 cannot be achieved in reality by combining brands, then provided there are sufficient customers, it may well pay a firm to launch a new brand, say brand D, which combines characteristics I and II in the proportions shown at M_2. A ray OD would then be drawn on Figure 13.18 passing through M_2, and provided the brand was priced so that the consumer's budget was exhausted at point M_2, or more accurately, anywhere upwards and to the right of U_2 on ray OD, then brand C would be dropped by the consumer in favour of D.

'Loss Leader' Policies

Firms, particularly retailers, often pitch the price of one item in a range of products at a deliberately low price in order to generate sales of other items in the product range. Sometimes, the price set is so low that it is below marginal costs and the term 'loss leader' is applied. Ronald Coase analysed the problems facing the firm in such cases of inter-related costs and demands.

Consider Figure 13.20(a). Assume the figure relates to one product, X, in a two-product company, and it is the product which will be used to promote total corporate sales. Assume also that there is complementarity of demand such that lowering price on X attracts a larger clientele, all of whom buy as many units of Y relative to X as does the original clientele. Given this, a corrected or net marginal cost curve (NMC_x) can be drawn, as in Figure 13.20(a). NMC_x is MC_x less the marginal profits earned on the complementary good, Y, consequential on a change in sales of price-reduced good X. The profit-maximising price and output of X is P_2Q_2 instead of the original P_1Q_1.

Sometimes, given sufficiently high elasticity and cross-elasticity of demand,

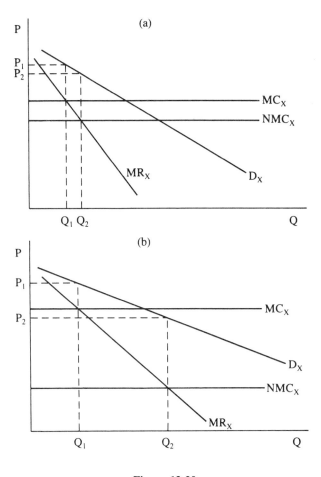

Figure 13.20

the optimal promotional price cut results in a 'loss' being made. Figure 13.20(b) shows this situation. In fact, however, a more accurate term would be 'profit leader', since although the optimal price P_2 is less than MC_x, it is well in excess of NMC_x. Note that NMC_x would have to be reconstructed every time an alternative price was chosen for Y. That is, the higher the price of Y, the higher are Y's marginal profits and so the lower would be the optimal price of X.

13.5   The Growth:Share Matrix

We have already seen how, within the concept of diversification, there are three distinct activities. These are horizontal, vertical and lateral integration.

The motives associated with each differ, and some argue that only lateral integration is truly diversification. The semantics are not of great importance — the managerial rationales are. Again, we use a diagram put forward by Ansoff to highlight these differences in strategies. The *x*-axis of Figure 13.21 represents the alternative integration strategies in decreasing order of affinity with respect to the firm's existing business activity. The hypothetical firm used as an illustration is an aircraft manufacturer. The *y*-axis represents the degree to which such a firm might realise these alternative objectives.

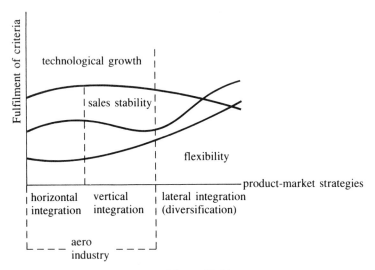

Figure 13.21

Horizontal integration can refer to the action by which a firm introduces new products that, while not contributing to the present line in any way, cater for market needs lying within the industry of which the firm is a member. This would occur, for example, if our aircraft firm extended its interest from the civil to the military market. Entirely different aircraft would be required. The company's sales stability would rise as it would no longer be dependent on only one market segment. Its technological know-how would also remain high, as there would inevitably be a substantial spillover of expertise from the one area to the other. Given that the firm is remaining in the one industry, however, its flexibility, its ability to be swift-footed in the face of unexpected economic contingencies in that industry, would remain low. Given the cyclical nature of the aircraft industry as a whole, sales stability would also begin to decline if over-extensive horizontal integration took place.

Vertical integration, say backwards into electronic components for the aircraft industry, would further reduce the firm's sales stability. However, the ability to sell such components in other markets might raise the firm's flexibility of response to unfavourable exigencies. It would also provide the firm with a broader technological base.

Sales stability as a result of not being overly dependent on one market, and the flexibility that accompanies it, can only really be achieved through 'pure' diversification, namely lateral integration. The company now moves entirely out of the aero industry into, say, chemicals or foodstuffs. In turn, this means that for sheer probabilistic reasons, if no other, the firm would no longer be in the forefront of all the technologies on which it depends.

Figure 13.21, although by no means rigorous, provides a useful introduction to the area of diversification. It is merely a suggestive (and limited) model of the integration alternatives facing one firm in one industry, and is not necessarily universally applicable. However, it again highlights the basic fact of managerial life, namely that objectives often conflict.

If any strategy is pursued, it must generally be done at the expense of objectives which other strategies could achieve more efficiently. Awareness of the non-applicability problems in the above discussion led to the development of the growth:share matrix as an aid to managerial decisions. The growth:share matrix was first developed by a firm of American managerial consultants (the Boston Consulting Group) and is displayed in simple form in Figure 13.22. Products are identified as 'stars', 'cash cows', 'problem children' or 'dogs' and placed in the relevant quadrant.

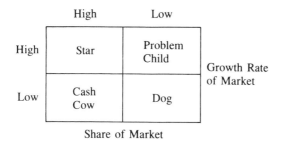

Figure 13.22

Market growth is measured, in real (inflation-adjusted) terms, as the growth rate per year of the overall market for the product. The rate can be calculated either as an *absolute* figure or *relative* to that of real GNP.

Market share of the product in its own industry can also be measured in two ways: either as a straight percentage or as that percentage deflated by that of the leading firm. (Thus a product that has 10% of a market might be reckoned to have a 'high' share relative to one with only 5%. On the other hand, the former product might be competing against a brand leader with a 50% share, 10/50 = 0.5; the latter might have no competitor stronger than a rival with a 2% share, 5/2 = 2.5. This would reverse the quadrant allocation.)

At the end of the day, there are no hard-and-fast rules on how to place products in the growth:share matrix — the law of the situation must hold. That is, the yardstick chosen should be the most helpful to the decision maker and not simply selected because it was successful in a previous, but possibly dissimilar, marketing environment.

Underlying the growth:share matrix philosophy is the product life-cycle concept (see pp. 118−119). In early (rapid growth) stages, purchasing behaviour and brand loyalty are deemed to be fluid and a large market share can be obtained at a relatively low cost in marketing expenditures. In maturity, an increase in market share is more difficult to obtain: consumers are more inert and firm growth involves obvious encroachment on competitors who will therefore be provoked to resist. In this situation (cash cow) funds should be redirected to research and development (R&D) for totally new products, to finding new uses or new markets for the existing product to prevent decline (a move to a dog), or towards other existing products in the right-hand column. Figure 13.23 summarises this discussion.

Figure 13.24 illustrates how this process can appear from the perspective of a given product over time, from product launch to the position where (hopefully) a product rapidly becomes a star, albeit initially a relatively small part of a firm's total sales. As maturity approaches the product becomes a

MARKET SHARE
(Absolute or relative to leading firm)

	HIGH	LOW
HIGH MARKET GROWTH RATE (Absolute or relative to annual GNP growth, in constant money)	STAR Moderate cash generation, high cash requirements to maintain or enhance position	PROBLEM CHILD Use cash to move towards Star category or treat as a Dog via segmentation
LOW	CASH COW High level of cash generated; redirect to R&D or Problem Children	DOG Harvest, i.e. cut back support costs; divest or abandon; or identify segment of market to exploit

Figure 13.23

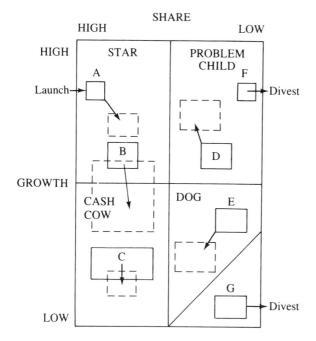

Based on Day, George S. (1977) 'Diagnosing the product portfolio', *Journal of Marketing*, Vol. 41(2), April.

Figure 13.24

cash cow. A moderate or high share has been obtained but growth has ceased or slowed. The company hopes it will remain in or reach that quadrant and not be a problem child on launch, nor degenerate into one. The marketing tools to adopt for problem children or dogs range from identifying new target segments and exploiting them (which is costly although it may ultimately prove worthwhile) to cutting losses by divesting oneself of the product by sale to another firm which itself wishes to diversify.

In Figure 13.24 the solid squares indicate a current position. The dotted squares indicate forecast positions. The areas are approximately and hypothetically suggestive of contributions to corporate sales.

Day (1977) suggests that when a firm is using the growth:share matrix to help assist in corporate strategy it should use cash to support *A* (in order to achieve the higher forecast sales indicated by the dashed lines); adopt policies to maintain *B* and *C* which are about to achieve, or have already achieved, significant sales volumes; and aid *D* by further product acquisition or range widening (hence increasing its growth rate and its sales contribution). Conversely, with *E*, which has a lower initial growth potential than *D* had, Day suggests a narrowing of range in order not to dissipate managerial effects but rather to harvest what can be obtained from those specialised market segments where E is doing well, and hence, as the dotted lines indicate, increase total sales contribution of E. In the cases of F and G, Day's diagram suggests divestment since market share and sales are either so small or growth so low that potential returns would appear to be less than are further development costs. These of course, are only conceptualised guidelines, which may well need to be varied situation by situation. Furthermore, even if the suggested strategies are correct, they are not clear-cut for products in the centre of the matrix. Then there is the human or behavioural problem that managers may not like being associated with dogs, and leave; or conversely, segmentation may be excessively costly but be embarked upon by managers wishing to 'save' their products from divestment or abandonment and so their jobs. Similarly, non-profitable acquisitions may be embarked upon.

The Experience Curve

The emphasis of the growth:share matrix on 'growth' and 'share' led the Boston Consulting Group (BCG) to develop the experience curve. We have already discussed the learning curve on pp. 208—9. The experience curve is a direct derivative. Figure 13.25 contrasts the two. In Figure 13.25(a) we have the conventional learning curve where direct labour costs per unit are plotted against total accumulated units produced. Every time production occurs, unit labour costs fall. The BCG extended this concept to all manufacturing costs. The reasons put forward include learning, but also embrace increased specialisation and improved methods, redesigned products, standardisation, scale and factor substitution. Clearly the experience curve is different from

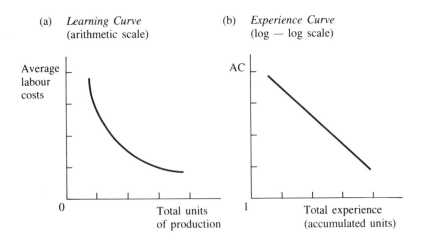

Figure 13.25

the conventional *LRAC* curve where experience accumulation is precluded by definition; technology is constant and the product is homogeneous and constant.

There are two major implications of the experience curve relating to growth and share. First, costs will presumably be lower the higher the market share. Other things being equal, therefore, the higher the market share, the higher the profitability of the firm relative to competitors. Second, costs should fall faster than those of competitors if growth is faster. Faster growing firms will thus be more profitable, other things being equal, than slower growers.

This BCG analysis (the growth:share matrix and experience curve) is not accepted uncritically by economists since it often appears to be based more on observation than on demonstrated theory. Irrespective of this scepticism, we believe that it can provide useful assistance to firms. Further, for economic researchers it provides a set of theories, or at least propositions whose validity may be tested. Indeed, in recent years, strategic planners and managerial economists have had not only these BCG guidelines but also a rich set of statistics to test them against. This has been provided by the *PIMS* data base.

Profit Impact of Market Strategy (PIMS)

The *PIMS* model and data base were developed by the Strategic Planning Institute (SPI) using a number of major firms in the USA and Europe. Participating firms are subdivided into over 2,000 line-of-business or product-type accounting entities. The aim of *PIMS* is the use of the accounting data provided (confidentially) to ascertain how firms behave, in what types of competitive environment, and with what resulting profitability. The intention then is to provide normative advice for managers. The *PIMS* data, using a single-equation model, have identified 28 'profit-influencing' factors. Among the 28 are growth rate, market share, market concentration and labour and capital productivity. Again, the alleged relevance of growth and share is highlighted. Participating firms receive *PIMS* reports at periodic intervals. They can compare themselves with other firms and with the 'profit-influencing' factors, so identifying their own strengths and weaknesses.

13.6 The Decision to Invest Abroad

Firms trading in other markets than their domestic or 'home' country can do so either horizontally or vertically. When vertical integration occurs the reasons are usually similar to the general cases we have already discussed — market or raw material security. Horizontal integration, however, has a less obvious rationale. This is so because of the costs involved in direct investment overseas. The indigenous firm always has a cost advantage over the incomer because it already knows the economic, social and legal conditions of the market. This knowledge is costless (or relatively so) to the indigenous firm. It must be acquired, probably in a costly function, by a foreign firm. For direct investment to be worthwhile, not only must the foreign firm have some more than compensating advantage over the indigenous company, it must also find foreign production preferable to either exporting or licensing.

The advantages a foreign firm generally has if it decides to do business overseas are those of product differentiation. Its product must be protected from precise duplication by trade marks bolstered by skilful marketing (e.g. Scotch whisky, Coca Cola), or high costs of physical imitation (e.g. electronic capital goods), or both (e.g. continuously improving pharmaceuticals).

In its decision the firm must not only weigh this balance of advantage, but also take into account tariff barriers, tax structures, transport costs, and not least, the stage of the foreign market's development. The model depicted in Figure 13.26 draws all of these threads together and is based on arguments put forward by Buckley and Casson.

Consider quadrant III which is a normal cost–quantity diagram whose axes have been twisted (to the right) through 180°. When the firm is exporting, fixed costs are low and limited possibly to the establishment of a distribu-

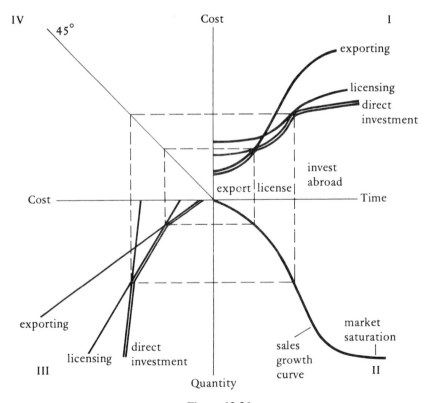

Figure 13.26

tion network. Variable costs will be high and will embrace production costs 'at home', agent's commission (if appropriate), international transport costs and tariffs. Because licensing excludes the last two costs, it will have lower variable costs than exporting, hence the slope of the licensing cost function is less than that of exporting. The fixed costs of licensing are likely to be lower than direct investment because of the start-up and sociological learning costs already mentioned. On the other hand, the variable costs of foreign direct investment are likely to be lower than under a licensing agreement; at the very least the cost of a per unit royalty to the licensee will be avoided. Thus in quadrant III the cost functions take the positions and shapes indicated. (Average variable costs are assumed constant, hence the functions are straight; this simplification is not essential even diagrammatically.)

In quadrant II is plotted the normal S-shaped market or product life cycle curve, flipped over on the time axis by 180°. The combination of quadrants II and III enables the construction of quadrant I to be carried out. This illustrates dynamic cost functions for the overseas trading decisions, and shows how the costs of trading overseas vary with the stage of market development.

At any one output level, as shown in quadrant I, there is one optimal method of trading overseas. (The thick line connecting the lowest segments of each cost function shows which.) However, the quantity sold depends also on the maturity of the market, and the various market strategies being followed through the sales growth curve. These strategies, and time itself, influence the position and shape of the S-shaped curve. Given this, the least-cost method of servicing overseas markets varies not only with quantity sold, but quantity sold varies with time. Thus the decision as to invest directly, license or export depends on when the 'least-cost envelope' of quadrant I's dynamic cost functions indicates that each is optimal.

Figure 13.26 is, of course, stylised. Each method of overseas trading would be engaged in in turn. This need not be the case, and either cost or demand conditions could indicate, for example, an immediate market entry via the licensing route and ignoring the exporting mode altogether. The decision is further complicated by currency market fluctuations, varying international tax treatments, non-identical input costs at international level, the growth or decline of rivalry, and so on. Again we restrict ourselves to the partial equilibrium approach. Full corporate optimisation is, as we remarked earlier, either improbable or is an achievement of indefinite complexity as a modelling objective.

An alternative method of approaching the multinational investment decision is to adapt the growth:share matrix developed by strategic planners. Strategic planning is defined by Harrell and Kiefer as the activity which 'seeks to match markets with products and other corporate resources in order to strengthen a firm's competitive stance'.

At an international level, this implies focusing on *markets* and the firm's *total* strength in such markets rather than on individual products. To attack the international investment problem, Harrel and Kiefer adapt the growth:share matrix as in Figure 13.27. The axes are linear combinations of factors determined from check lists relating to the country's commercial attractiveness and the firm's competitive strength in that country. Country attractiveness can be gauged, for example, by awarding points to market size, market growth rate, and degree of government regulation in areas such as price control, local content rules and dividend repatriation possibilities, and economic and political stability in terms of inflation, balance of trade and political unrest. For competitive strength, firms could examine factors such as market share, market ranking (thus, to be firm number one with a 20% share is qualitatively different from being firm number two in size with a 40% share), product fit (i.e. how well does the domestically designed product fit the needs of the foreign market?), contribution profit per unit, and the degree of market visibility and dealer or after-sales or promotional support. Using a numerical check list for the firm's product portfolio and for countries, national markets can be plotted on the matrix. Those countries falling in the right upward-sloping cell require selective funding strategies, while those in the upper left should receive resources for growth and those in the bottom right are candidates for harvest or divestment.

'Investment and growth' countries require commitment to a strong market position. A high share of a fast-growing market requires considerable financial backing, and commitment to personnel. Local production will often be required for the sake of prompt delivery and good service. Adaptation of products to fit local requirements may be necessary. Marketing support must be strong.

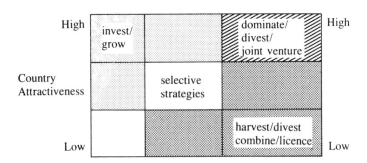

Source: Harrel, G.D. and Kiefer, R.O. (1981) 'Multinational Strategic market portfolios', *MSU Business Topics.*

Figure 13.27   Product Plotting Matrix

'Harvest/divest/licence/combine' nations should not see profits forfeited to maintain market share. Short-run profits should be concentrated in such low-growth, low-potential situations until the operation can be sold or terminated. Cash flows can be increased by cutting support costs and possibly even raising or maintaining prices.

'Dominate/divest/joint venture' nations provide alternative strategic choices. The firm is weak, yet the market is attractive. Moving the firm to a position of strength could be costly, yet if this cost is avoided by divestment the opportunity cost of selling out at a low price and the forfeiting of future profits may be incurred.

'Selectivity strategy' nations also pose difficult choices: should the firm regard the national market as a cash cow or as a potential star with further investment expense required?

13.7 Planned Obsolescence

To conclude this chapter on product market strategy we show why it may often be unwise for firms to build 'planned obsolescence' into their products. Only sometimes is this a profit-maximising action. (The arguments used below are part of the 'oral tradition' of Aaron Director and Armen Alchian.)

Consider Figure 13.28 which shows two demand curves. D_1 is the market demand curve for a product which can be used in only one time period.

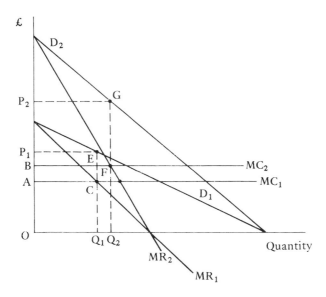

Figure 13.28

The product could be a textbook which physically falls apart after one academic year. The price any buyer is willing to pay, as always, is the present value of that book's educational services to him. D_2 is the market demand for a more durable product, say a textbook which is physically stronger and so can be sold in the second-hand market and used, for simplicity, by one future generation of students. D_1 and D_2 intersect on the Q axis since the maximum number of copies which can be sold to this year's students at a zero price is identical with the student population (assuming no booksellers or others buy for stock and resale in future years). D_2, however, intersects the P axis at a much higher level. Why? Again this year's students will be willing to pay prices which reflect the present value of the book to them. On this occasion, however, that is equal not only to the present value of the educational services but, and in addition, also to the present value of the second-hand price to next year's students. Because of discounting through time, this second component in today's price will be less than the first component. It will also be less since the second-hand price will, irrespective of discounting, be less as well. (The second-hand buyer will value the educational services less since the book will be marked, torn and otherwise less valuable.)

So D_2 will not be twice D_1 even in the simple two-period model we are restricting ourselves to. But notice, when the publisher produces a durable book (or any product) he is able to capture today the market's valuation of all future services that product will render. If he produces a non-durable product the price today is considerably less. To be sure he can receive that same price at the beginning of period 2 when he sells a second non-durable book, but to do so he must incur the costs of production twice. Certainly a durable product will cost more than a non-durable one, but often the differential will be slight. Which course of action a firm should take will depend on the precise cost and demand schedules it faces.

Consider again Figure 13.28. We assume that all durable products have a two-period life, that all are sold on the second-hand market and that MC_2 > MC_1, since it costs more to make the more durable product. The relevant profit-maximising prices for the two alternative strategies are P_1 for the non-durable, and P_2 for the durable. The profits from the two are P_1ECA and P_2GFB respectively. Provided that P_2GFB is greater than P_1ECA plus P_1ECA discounted to present value from period 2, then it is more profitable *not* to engage in production of the non-durable product. Certainly the firm would prefer to sell Q_2 units at P_2 in period 2 as well.

But it cannot do this in the presence of a second-hand market. It can try to kill off the second-hand market by bringing out a new edition of the book at the end of period 1. Students might then buy the new book in case they missed any significant advances in the new edition. But the publisher would only get away with this once. Consumers would realise what was happening and their demand curves would decline to D_1. Thus 'planned obsolescence' can be a short-sighted policy.

Additional Reading

Abell, D.F. and Hammond, J.S. (1979) *Strategic Market Planning*, Prentice-Hall.

Ansoff, I. (1958) 'A model for diversification', *Management Science*, Vol. 4.

Brownlie, D. (1985) 'Strategic marketing concepts and models', *Journal of Marketing Management*, Vol. 1.

Buckley, P.J. and Casson, M. (1981) 'The optimal timing of a foreign direct investment', *Economic Journal*, Vol. 91.

Caves, R. (1971) 'International corporations, the industrial economics of foreign investment', *Economica*, Vol. 38.

Coase, R.H. (1946) 'Monopoly pricing with inter-related costs and demands', *Economica*, Vol. 13.

Hirshleifer, J. (1956) 'On the economics of transfer pricing', *Journal of Business*, Vol. 29.

Lancaster, K. (1966) 'Change and innovation in the technology of consumption', *American Economic Review*, Vol. 56.

Needham, D. (1978) '*The economics of industrial structure, conduct and performance*', Holt Rinehart and Winston.

Penrose, E.T. (1980) *The Theory of the Growth of the Firm*, Basil Blackwell.

Reekie, W.D. (1979) *Industry, Prices and Markets*, Philip Allan.

14
The Location Decision

The aims of this chapter are firstly to evaluate *a priori* theories which have been proposed to predict the location of a firm, secondly, to describe the governmental Regional Policy measures which may affect the location which a manager chooses and finally to assess the effects of past governmental policy on the level of unemployment and therefore on the rate of industrial expansion in aid-receiving regions.

14.1 Factors Influencing Location

The manager faced with a location decision must take four variables into account: input costs; the location of the market; transportation costs; and miscellaneous factors.

Input Costs

Inputs include land, labour, capital, power, materials and enterprise. Only rarely are the attributes of a particular piece of land critical in determining the location of a firm. Bedrock may be essential if heavy equipment is used. A plentiful supply of water may be required in some industries for cooling or waste disposal purposes. But more generally, other features of land costs such as access roads, sewers and power supply lines can be minimised easily by careful choice *within* an area or region, and can be regarded as roughly and ubiquitously uniform, at least in an advanced economy such as Britain.

Capital is a highly mobile resource with an insignificant cost of transfer. It is risk differences rather than location differences which result in varying costs of capital. Power, too, is a relatively mobile resource. Gas and oil pipelines, and the electric grid system have reduced the importance of pithead location for the power-hungry, formerly high coal-consumption, company.

For socio-cultural reasons labour is a relatively less mobile input than capital or power. Skill availability will depend in part on the nature and history of employment of any given area; in part on the schools and technical colleges of that area; in part on current levels of employment and unemployment; and given the joint supply of male and female labour, on the mix of male and female employment opportunities already present in the area. Labour costs will obviously depend on the ruling wage rates in the area but caution must be exercised in wage rate comparisons. Productivity differences may more than offset any apparent gain in lower wage levels. It is not uncommon to find that the regions with the lowest wage *rates* are the regions with the least favourable efficiency wages.

Clearly, all raw materials are not uniformly available everywhere. Yet they vary enormously both in their bulk and in their perishability. The more costly they are to transport, the more firms will be attracted to locate near to them. Nevertheless, over the last few decades, the importance of raw materials as a location factor has been falling. Firstly, cartage costs have been steadily declining with improving transportation technology. Secondly, those industries with a low material content, but high 'brain' content in the finished product (e.g. electronics), have been taking a steadily larger share of total industrial output and are, by their nature, less dependent in cost terms on transportation inwards of bulky raw materials. Thirdly, large numbers of modern industries draw on a multiplicity of raw material sources and then engage in complex assembly or process operations. This diminishes the need to be irrevocably linked to *one* main material source. Finally, finished goods often tend to be bulky and relatively valuable and so require greater care in transportation than do the raw materials. For this reason, a one-ton motor car is costlier to transport than the one-ton of sheet steel and other materials which go into its manufacture. These reasons all combine to minimise the 'pull' of the raw material source *vis à vis* that of the market.

Finally, enterprise. There is little one can say with confidence about this particular input. By definition, the supply of enterprising people should be highly mobile. If we restrict the definition to highly qualified personnel, however, then it is often said that these are relatively immobile. For example, graduate scientists and engineers, and other higher calibre executive staff are allegedly more readily attracted to the South-east of England than to other parts of the country.

The Market

In the last few decades 'being close to the market' has become of increasing importance as a location factor. Materials, power, and high transportation costs are no longer major factors keeping firms *away* from large urban centres. Conversely, the affluence of the town as a market, the relatively high costs of transporting bulky, but valuable and complex finished goods to that market, and the advantages of being close to customers for service purposes, especially in high technology industries, have all combined to pull firms towards their major sales locations.

Transportation Costs and Miscellaneous Factors

Transportation Costs   It has been seen above how transportation costs, although an important variable in location decisions, are not as critical as they have been in the past.

Governmental Regional Aid   This will be discussed in detail in Section 14.3 of this chapter.

Historical Accident   In many instances no rationale can be given for a location decision. For example, what causes other than historical accident, or possibly personal preference, can be cited for the location of Player's tobacco works and Morris' motor factory at Nottingham and Oxford, respectively?

Agglomeration Economies   Agglomeration is one of the most obvious features of economic activity. Firms tend to cluster together in cities and towns. There are three main types of cost saving open to a firm as a result of such clustering or agglomeration. First, *internal economies*, as the firm takes advantage of scale economies open to it due to the size of the immediate market. The firm moves down its long-run average cost curve. Second, *localisation economies*; these are economies which are external to the firm but internal to the industry. Thus, if several closely related firms are located together they benefit, since common facilities which all can draw on would not have been available had the agglomeration not existed. Examples of such economies include common research facilities; technical colleges with specialist courses tailored for the industry in question; the presence of a component supplying industry and other specialised service and consultancy industries made possible by the aggregate demand of the firms. Third, *external economies* to the industry itself; these are gains to all firms in all industries which result from locating together. They include the presence of a highly developed infrastructure of roads, railways, ports and airline facilities; a well-developed banking and capital market; financial, management, and market-research consultancy industries; a pool of management expertise which can be 'poached' from other firms if necessary; and pleasant and developed social and cultural amenities. There are, of course, diseconomies of congestion. But the balance of advantage is probably still heavily in favour of net cost savings.

14.2 Theories of Location

The conventional theory of price, as depicted, for example, in Chapters 5 and 9, is spaceless. We now outline theories which predict the location of a firm.

Weber's Theory

The father of industrial location theory is generally acknowledged to be Alfred Weber. He assumed perfect competition in all respects except that labour, materials and markets had fixed and immobile locations. Implicitly there are no physical constraints on the supply of inputs or demand for outputs at the ruling market prices. In this situation only transport and labour costs, and any agglomerative economies or diseconomies, influence location.

The least-transport-cost (*LTrC*) location can be obtained by resort to the locational triangle. For example, in Figure 14.1(a), take one point of consumption *C*, select the most advantageous deposits of the two necessary raw materials, M_1 and M_2, and the *LTrC* location (*P*) is found by minimising the

(a) A locational triangle

C = point of consumption
M_1 = source of material 1
M_2 = source of material 2
L = a cheap labour location

a, b and c are mileages
x, y and z are tons

the least transport cost location
is where xa + yb + zc is
minimised.

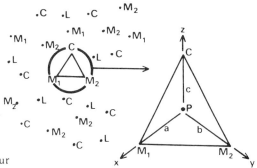

(b) The introduction of labour
cost differences requires the use
of isodapanes (i.e. curves of
equal marginal transport costs)

(c) Economies of agglomeration

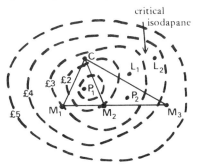

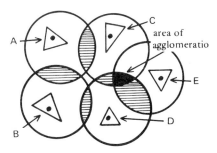

L_1 is a source of cheap labour which
would save £3 on labour costs per unit.

The critical isodapane is that which
has the same value as the savings in
labour costs

A minimum of three firms could attain
economies of £20 per unit through
agglomeration. Only the critical (£20)
isodapanes are shown in the diagram

Figure 14.1

total ton-miles involved in getting materials to the factory and the end product to the market. If the pull of any one corner is greater than the sum of the pulls of the other two, then P will be at that corner.

P, however, will not be optimal if a suitable supply of labour is unavailable. This would be so if any labour cost savings gained by relocating more than offset any incremental transport costs incurred. To analyse this situation Weber introduced isodapanes. These are lines joining points of equal marginal transport costs if the factory was located anywhere other than P_1, the $LTrC$ location, in Figure 14.1(b). Assume that isodapanes are known per unit of production from £1 to £5. Then, since L_1, a location where cheap labour is available, is nearer P_1 than the £3 isodapane, it would be worth relocating at L_1 if labour cost savings there were £3 per unit. If L_1 lay outside this critical isodapane, like L_2, movement would not take place. Movement, of course, introduces further complications. Assume M_3 is a source of material 1. Then M_3 becomes a possible source of material 1 which previously had been too distant. A new locational triangle must be set up, CM_2M_3, and P_2 becomes the $LTrC$ location with a unique set of isodapanes. The process must then recommence until a final and optimal solution is obtained.

Finally, agglomeration economies are treated in a similar manner, namely as reason for movement from the $LTrC$ point. In Figure 14.1(c), A, B, C, D and E are five firms located at the $LTrC$ points of their respective triangles. The firms find they can cut unit costs by £20 if at least three of them have the same location. But in order to gain from this, their average marginal transport costs must not exceed £20. The critical £20 isodapanes show that only C, D and E will find it worth their while to relocate.

Hoover's Theory

Hoover's theory can be explained with the aid of Figure 14.2. In practice transport costs are rarely linear. That is, although they increase with distance they tend to do so less than proportionately. Not only will the cost per ton-mile decrease the greater the distance, but probably also more efficient forms of transport will be used (rail rather than road, sea rather than rail, and so on).

In Figure 14.2 the firm uses one raw material, located at M, and serves the one point of consumption, C. The line $a'a$ is the transfer cost gradient of transporting the finished goods to the market. Thus, if the plant were situated at C, the transfer costs would be limited to Ca', the so-called 'terminal costs' of distribution, off-loading from factory pallets and so on, into the hands of consumers. The distance Ma indicates the total transport costs of moving the finished goods to the market if the factory were located at M. The line $a'a$ has the curvature indicated because of a diminishing transport cost rate per ton-mile. The line $b'b$ is the transfer cost gradient of transporting the raw materials to the factory. Clearly, such assembly costs would be minimised if

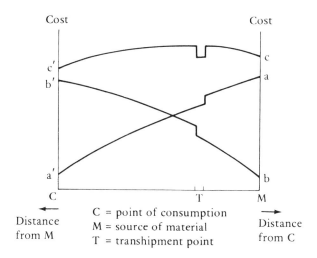

C = point of consumption
M = source of material
T = transhipment point

Distance from M

Distance from C

Figure 14.2

the plant were located at the material source and maximised if the plant was located at the market. The distance Mb is the terminal loading and off-loading charge incurred in transferring the raw material from the source to the plant.

The total transport cost of assembly and distribution of raw materials and finished goods is given by $c'c$, the aggregate of $a'a$ and $b'b$. Given the curvatures of the latter two lines, the least-cost location must be at an end point, such as C or M.

The introduction of a trans-shipment town T, because, say, the goods must be transferred from sea to rail, results in both $a'a$ and $b'b$ 'jumping' by the amounts involved in the appropriate terminal charges of off- and on-loading. A location at T, however, avoids such additional terminal or trans-shipment charges. (A location *away* from T means that Ca' and Mb must be incurred again, namely at T.) Thus the most favourable location can now be either an end point, or a trans-shipment point. Thus, on Hoover's analysis, a location within the Weberian triangle is unlikely except where trans-shipment junctions occur.

Spatial Demand Curves

A normal demand curve is spaceless. It depicts a relationship between price and quantity at a point and imposes no further constraints, making the implicit assumption of perfect resource and factor mobility. In fact, a consumer positioned nearer a seller will purchase more than one further away because the price for the latter includes the cost of movement to the seller. The sloping demand curve has not one, but two determinants — price and location.

August Lösch was the first writer to attempt to develop a theory of spatial demand. In his initial model Lösch assumed an agrarian economy on a uniform plain with uniform transportation costs in all directions, and an even distribution of population and raw materials. Trade is introduced for the first time when some of Lösch's self-sufficient farmers attempt to sell a surplus of their home-made beer to others.

His arguments are illustrated in Figure 14.3. Assume a Löschian plain with a retailer wishing to sell good X at price p. It costs consumers mt to visit the store, where m is the distance in miles and t represents the transport cost rate. So the price paid by each consumer is $p + mt$. Each (identical) consumer has an identical demand curve for X (Figure 14.3(a)). Thus, at price $\bar{p}$, a consumer living next to the store will buy q_1 units, a consumer m miles away will buy q_2, and a consumer r miles away will buy nothing. Since consumers are distributed evenly around the store r is the radius of a perfect circle depicting the market boundary. Thus, as in Figure 14.3(b), it is possible to draw a demand *cone* around the seller, according to which quantity bought drops off with distance. The volume of this cone multiplied by an indicator of population density gives the quantity demanded in the market area at price $\bar{p}$. If the exercise is repeated at different prices, differently sized demand cones which are associated with a specific location of a firm will be obtained. Hence a price:quantity schedule can be calculated which takes into account transport costs and distance. DD in Figure 14.4 represents such a schedule, or *spatial demand curve*.

Profit-Maximising Theory

Since Lösch assumed uniform transport costs in all directions, an even distribution of population and that all consumers have identical demand curves, total revenue is the same in all locations. The revenue maximisation location

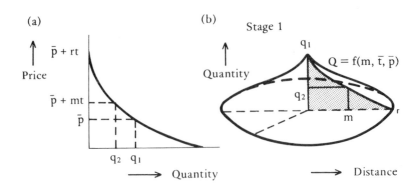

Figure 14.3

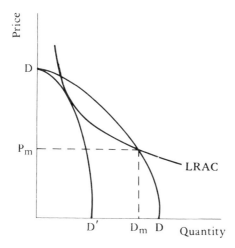

Figure 14.4

is indeterminate. Since it is additionally assumed that factors are perfectly mobile and uniformly distributed, total costs are the same everywhere. The profit-maximising location is also indeterminate.

In contrast, the profit-maximising theory argues that both *TR* and *TC* vary with location. This has been most eloquently explained by Smith and Richardson who we follow here. Figure 14.5 shows curves of these variables.

The *TR* (or Space Revenue) curve shows *TR*, as given by an (adjusted) Löschian demand cone, when the plant, and hence the origin of the cone, is

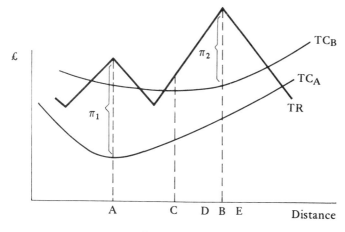

Figure 14.5

located at different places. Some of Lösch's assumptions concerning the demand cone are relaxed. Firstly, we allow population to be more concentrated in some areas than in others. *Ceteris paribus*, the greater the population density within a market area, the greater the total revenue it yields. In addition, the volume of the cone would not be multiplied by a simple population density indicator. Population density is likely to be higher closer to the plant rather than further from it and each of those living close to the plant would be expected to buy a greater quantity than each of those living further from it (due to differences in transport costs). Therefore the population density factor would have to be weighted to reflect the locational distribution of population within the area. Market areas with different distributions of population, even if both had the same total population within their boundaries, may have different population density factors.

Secondly, we relax Lösch's assumption of identical individual demand curves by allowing average income to vary with location. Assuming that the income elasticity of demand is positive, quantity demanded is positively related to mean income. Thirdly, if the transport cost rate decreases with distance from the plant, *ceteris paribus*, the gradient of the cone's upper surface will become flatter as m increases.

Combining these factors and assuming that price is fixed, a slice through a modified demand cone may appear as in Figure 14.6. The flattening of the edges is due to assumed decreasing transport rates. The kinks in the edges are due to differing population densities and average incomes.

If, instead of plotting Löschian demand cones at points along the distance axis, we plot the Richardson style total revenue associated with each cone, as in Figure 14.6, we derive for a given price, the space revenue curve, *TR*, of Figure 14.5. (This figure may be regarded as a slice through a three-dimensional diagram with distance coming out of the page.) The peaks correspond to locations of relatively high density population, high mean incomes, etc.

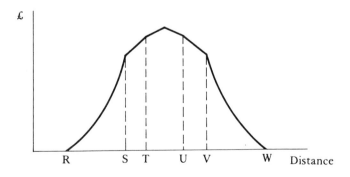

Figure 14.6

Each space cost curve, TC_A and TC_B in Figure 14.5, is constructed under the assumption of a given output. It may be derived from the corresponding average (per unit of output) space cost curve. Average costs in space equal the sum of average basic and average location costs. The former are the average production costs if the firm pays the lowest possible price for each input. Location costs are the premium over these prices which must be paid to gain the factors in a particular spot, rather than where they have the lowest price and the necessary transport costs of these inputs. (Note the output transport costs to market are included in the TR curve.)

If we assume that all inputs are available at all locations at the same price except one which is available only at K in Figure 14.7, and suppose the only additional costs of using this resource at other locations are those of transport, then the line AC of Figure 14.7 represents average space costs. If we now relax the assumption of uniform availability of resources and assume that they may occur in isolated locations, then as one moved, average location costs would at first rise, then fall, then rise, etc.

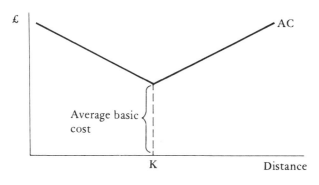

Figure 14.7

Multiple minima may then occur. (This assumes factor ratios are unchanged.) In addition, if at different places the ratio of average costs of two (or more) inputs changes, the isocost line in an isoquant figure (see Chapter 7) will change gradient and the constant output could be produced at different cost levels. Again multiple minima may exist. If we assume that there is only one AC minimum and that transport costs are not linear with distance the average total cost curve can be U-shaped. Since the AC curve is drawn for a given output, if we multiply AC by this output we gain a curve of the same shape but representing TC.

Now return to the TR curve of Figure 14.5. Given price, this shows how output, i.e. the volume of a demand cone multiplied by a population density factor, differs between locations. But the TC curve relates to a single output.

Therefore corresponding to each single point on the *TR* curve, and hence each single output, there is a complete *TC* curve. Hence in Figure 14.5, to simplify the figure we show only two curves. TC_A relates to the *TR* level at location *A*, and TC_B relates to the *TR* level of location *B*. The minimum of different *TC* curves *may* occur at different outputs because of possibly differing optimum factor ratios. The profit-maximising location occurs at location *A* where the difference between the *TR* level and the corresponding *TC* curve is greatest. Notice that one cannot compare the *TR* at *C* with either of the two *TC* curves drawn. Neither *TC* curves relates to the output corresponding to the *TR* level at that place.

If an input is subsidised in certain locations, but not in others, the total costs of producing the same output in that location will decrease. The *TC* curve over those locations will be lower than it would otherwise be. For example in Figure 14.5, if an input was subsidised in locations between *D* and *E*, both *TC* curves would fall in that range *only*. π_2 would then increase and may exceed π_1. (We have ignored any effect on the *TR* curve of a movement of employment into the area *DE* which may increase the population density there.)

Locational Interdependence

A criticism of all of the previous theories is their lack of consideration of rivalry. Using a simplified analysis (see Figure 14.8) we explain Hotelling's discussion of locational rivalry. To facilitate analysis a homogeneous product, perfect market information and linear transportation rates are assumed. A linear market (rather than a point of consumption) and *given* plant locations are also assumed. The two sellers are identified as, and located at, *A* and *B* respectively. The arms beginning at *A'* and *B'* represent the (linear) transportation costs from the two locations. The boundary between the two market areas is at *X* where the delivered product price from *A* and *B* is equal, where the gradients of delivered price intersect. Thus, on the linear scale, *A*'s market is *OX*, *B*'s market extends from *X* to some boundary undefined in this figure.

The assumption of a linear market can be readily relaxed if one visualises Figure 14.8(a) as being merely a cross-section through a three-dimensional diagram. Figure 14.8(b) represents a bird's eye view of such a situation. The lines surrounding *A* and *B* join points of equal delivered price and are known as isotims. The market boundary, where consumers are indifferent as to the source of supply, is formed by the intersection of isotims of equal value.

Let us now relax the assumption of given locations and ascertain how competitive interdependence affects the location decision. Hotelling used a model consisting of two ice-cream vendors, with uniform production costs, selling their products to a uniform linear market (a beach) with inelastic demand where each consumer would buy exactly one ice-cream. He postulated

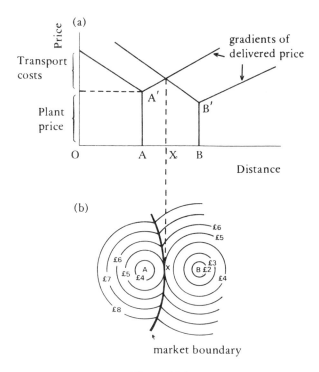

Figure 14.8

that the two vendors would end up in the middle of the beach in a back-to-back situation (Figure 14.9(a)). One firm could capture the entire market by locating anywhere, but two could only share the market equally by locating together. Thus in Figure 14.9(b), firm *B* is located non-optimally.

This model can be criticised on a number of grounds, however, as being too restrictive. Firstly, the market can be shared evenly if the firms locate at the quartiles, as in Figure 14.9(c). If a third firm entered the market, this type of symmetrical dispersion is even more likely, since the back-to-back situation would be inherently unstable with more than two competitors.

If we relax the assumption of infinitely inelastic demand, price reductions will increase quantity sold. A two-plant monopolist or two firms in collusion would then reject the back-to-back situation and locate at the quartiles in order to minimise transfer costs. In Figure 14.9(c), continuing our ice-cream analogy, the average distance walked to purchase a cone is halved compared with Figure 14.9(a)'s back-to-back situation. Superimposing Figures 14.9(a) and 14.9(c) in 14.9(d) illustrates graphically this net saving in transfer costs. The cross-hatched areas (transfer cost savings) exceed twice the dotted area (transfer cost increases as a result of quartile location).

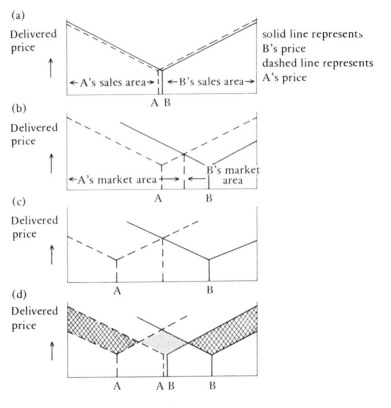

Figure 14.9

We can now relax two further assumptions in our model, those of uniform production costs and identical price policies. In Figure 14.10 firm *A* sets up in the centre, and consumers buy at the prices indicated by the gradients of delivered price. If *B* enters, locates at *B* and has production costs of *BB'* he will be unable to compete with *A* and has chosen an unprofitable location. At *C*, a firm's costs are again higher than *A*'s, but low enough to enable *C* to undercut *A* from *O* to *X*. *C* can now attempt to extend his market by geographic price discrimination. In area *OC*, price can be raised to *OC"*, provided *OC"* is below *A*'s gradient of delivered price. The extra revenue so obtained can be used to lower prices to the right of *C*, giving a gradient extending from, say *C'''*, thus moving the market boundary to *Y*. *A* would inevitably react by price cutting also and the process would continue until an equilibrium situation was reached.

One assumption that we cannot relax is that of homogeneous products. If product differentiation is introduced to our model then, instead of rigid market boundaries, only blurred and uncertain areas are predicted.

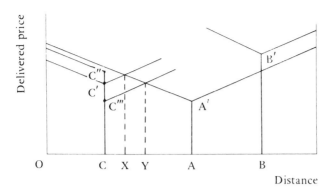

Figure 14.10

Lösch, in later models, also introduced concepts of competitive inter-dependence, profit maximisation and customer reaction. Consider again the spatial demand curve of Figure 14.4. If the retailer's *LRAC* curve is now added, the conclusion is that the optimum size of store is one providing for an aggregated demand of D_m at price p_m (otherwise, there would be either excess supply or demand, and given a situation of free industry entry this would be a situation which could not persist).

Lösch believed that with the entry of competitors, circular market areas would become hexagonal and so all unclaimed space would be occupied and no market overlaps would occur. As a result *DD* must fall to *DD'* (Figure 14.4) tangential to *LRAC* for perfect hexagonal matching. Figures 14.3(b), 14.11(a) and 14.11(b) illustrate the derivation of this pattern.

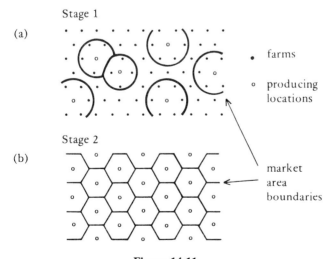

Figure 14.11

The market radius differs for different goods. Partly this is due to the need, on the supply side, for different scales of production. Partly it is due, on the demand side, to consumer preference to search for and to compare different sources of expensive and/or infrequently purchased goods or services. Thus, some centres in Lösch's 'economic landscape' (the metropolii) will have each and every industry's hexagonal pattern centred on them. Others, villages, towns and cities, will each have relatively fewer such coinciding producing locations.

Greater appreciation of the importance of time, distance and market boundaries can be obtained from Figure 14.12. Assume a homogeneous product, two producing areas, perfect information, consumer immobility, and linear transportation costs. Region A's supply and demand curves are shown in the traditional manner. Region B's are reversed and juxtaposed with region A's. The transfer costs between the two regions are shown by the distance MN. Since B is the lower priced region, any product movement would be from B to A, and B's portion of the figure is elevated against A's by MN, the unit cost of transfer.

The 'excess supply' curves ES_a and ES_b can be obtained for the relevant regions by subtracting the quantity demanded at any price from the quantity supplied at that price. These show the amount by which regional supply exceeds demand at any given price. Clearly, there is zero excess supply in each market at their respective equilibrium prices. The intersection of the excess supply curves indicates the unique price at which B will willingly supply

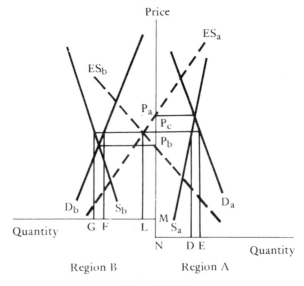

Figure 14.12

a surplus to its own regional requirements ($GF = LM$) and at which A will willingly purchase that surplus to match its supply deficit ($DE = LM$). Thus, provided the difference in market prices in the two regions is greater than the transport costs, trade will occur. Conversely, *prices can differ between two regions* and trade will not occur *provided the differential is less than the transfer cost.*

This is the rationale behind the basing point[1] or uniform delivered price system operated for many years by the Portland Cement Makers Federation in the United Kingdom. The system provides for the same delivered price at the same point of delivery for all brands of cement, irrespective of the works from which the cement may come. The number of cement works in Britain and the number of prices have not always been identical. Factories near each other, for example could have the same base price. Radiating from each basing point is a series of concentric circles at four or five mile intervals. The circles from each point continue until they meet the circles radiating from another point. The delivered price per ton increases within each of the circles by an agreed increment. The map of Britain is covered with a network of isotims after the fashion of Figure 14.8(b). Thus every buyer at a particular point will pay exactly the same price for cement. Every manufacturer is encouraged to minimise transportation costs by selling as close to his works as possible. The further away he delivers, the more likely it is that he will run into isotims controlled by another basing point and the amount he receives will begin to decrease.

For the system to be effective, the isotims and the base prices must be known to everyone in the trade; the product must be homogeneous and so be perfectly substitutable; and spatial differentiation of the product, namely high levels of transfer costs relative to delivered price, is essential.

14.3 Regional Policy

Current Policy

Current regional policy is of relevance to managers because it can alter the profit-maximising location, as shown in the last section. Therefore if a manager wishes to maximise profits he should, when deciding on plant location, include consideration of the available grants, etc, in some areas and the restrictions on locating in others.

Tables 14.1 and 14.2 summarise the main legislation of past and present policy. Assistance is currently available in Development Areas and Intermediate Areas. In addition, assistance is also available in Enterprise Zones — areas

---

1   Basing point pricing has been held to be illegal in the United States. The British attitude depends on the circumstance of the case. The Cement Makers Federation agreement was upheld in 1961 by the Restrictive Practices Court.

Table 14.1 The Main British Regional Measures since 1960

Legislation	Areas Designated	Financial Incentives	Development Controls	Other Features
Local Employment Act, 1960	Replaced DAs with Development Districts — areas with over $4\frac{1}{2}\%$ unemployment.	Loans and grants without 'lender of last resort' restrictions. Building grants.	IDCs to favour DDs.	Industrial estates reorganised.
Local Employment and Finance Acts, 1963	As 1960 Act.	25% building grant, 10% plant and machinery grant. Accelerated depreciation.	None	Advanced factories programme stepped up.
1965			IDC limit lowered in Midlands and South East.	
Industrial Development Act, 1966	Back to DAs: most of Scotland and Wales, Merseyside, Cornwall, north Devon and north of England.	40% investment grants replace all investment tax allowances.	Office Development Permits introduced.	
1966			IDC limit raised to 3,000 sq ft in Midlands and South East.	

1967	Special DAs added: Northumberland, Durham, Cumberland and Scottish and Welsh coalfields.	REP introduced for DAs and SDAs. 35% building grants in SDAs. Investment grants raised to 45% 1967–8 only.		Extra help for hard-hit areas in SDAs, e.g. collieries.
Local Employment Act, 1970	Creation of Intermediate Areas: Leith, north-east Lancashire, Yorkshire coalfield, north Humberside, Notts/Derby coalfield, south-east Wales and Plymouth.	25% building grant, training grants.		Advanced factories.
1970–71	SDAs extended to include: Clydeside, Tyneside, north-west England and south Wales.	Investment grants replaced by 'free depreciation'. Larger building grants. 30% operational grants in SDAs.	IDC limit raised to 5,000 sq ft in Midlands and South East, 10,000 sq ft in other non-assisted areas.	£160m allocated to 'public works' in DAs and SDAs.
The Industry Act, 1972	DAs and SDAs remain the same.	Back to investment grants 20% in DAs, 22% in SDAs; free depreciation to remain.	IDC limit raised to 10,000 sq ft in South East and 15,000 sq ft in other non-assisted areas. IDCs abolished in DAs and SDAs.	Regional executive created with power to give additional grants and loans; budget of £250m.

Legislation	Areas Designated	Financial Incentives	Development Controls	Other Features
1974	SDAs extended to include Merseyside; parts of N.W. Wales, Edinburgh and Cardiff become DAs.	REP doubled to £3.	IDC limit tightened: 5000 sq ft in South East, 10,000 sq ft in other non-assisted areas.	
1975 Industry Act				Planning agreements: if made by firms with government would enable benefits to be received.
1975		European Regional Development Fund created. Grants and rebates on European investment. Bank loans in depressed areas.		
1975 Scottish Development Agency and Welsh Development Agency Acts				Scottish and Welsh Development Agencies established with powers to make loans and grants, make land and plant available, to form companies, to guarantee obligations, etc. *Budgets:* ScDa £200m–£300m WDA £100m–£150m

1976			IDC limits raised: 12,500 sq ft in South East, 15,000 sq ft in other non-assisted areas.	
1977	REP abolished.			
1977 Assisted Areas Order	Minor adjustments and rescheduling of areas into/out of SDAs, DAs, and IAs.			
1979	SDAs and DAs reduced over 3 years.	Rate of Regional Development Grant to be reduced by £230m over 3 years.	IDC limits raised: 50,000 sq ft in non-assisted areas. Office Development Permits abolished.	Regional Economic Planning Councils abolished in England. Concentration of funds in areas with worst problems.
1979 Industry Act				ScDa budget raised to £500m. WDA budget raised to £250m.
1980	Creation of Enterprise Zones: Corby, Dudley, Hartlepool, Ise of Dogs, Newcastle/Gateshead, Salford/Trafford, Speke, Wakefield, Lower Swansea valley, Clydebank, Belfast.	New and existing firms in EZs gain (until 1990): 1. Exemption from development land tax and general rates. 2. 100% capital allowances on buildings for tax purposes.	IDCs abolished in EZs (until 1990).	New and existing firms in EZs gain (until 1990): 1. Exclusion from Industrial Training Board requirements. 2. Speedier government administration.

Legislation	Areas Designated	Financial Incentives	Development Controls	Other Features
1981 Industry Act				ScDA budget raised to £700m. WDA budget raised to £450m.
1981				Office & Service Industry Scheme
1982 Industrial Development Act		Regional Selective Assistance made more selective. Regional Development Grant rate reduced in DAs. Building Grant in IAs abolished.	IDC abolished.	
1982	24 new Enterprise zones created.			
1984	SDAs abolished. DAs & IAs drastically changed to cover 15% & 20% respectively of Britain's working population.	Higher rate of RDG aid removed. IAs no longer qualify for RDG. RDG now subject to max. grant per job but would be waived for small firms. Services become eligible for RDG.		

Sources: Economic Progress Report, HMSO; H. Armstrong and J. Taylor, *Regional Economic Policy and its Analysis*, Philip Allan, 1978; P. Randall, 'The history of British regional policy', in G. Hallet, P. Randall and E.G. West, *Regional Policy for Ever*, Institute of Economic Affairs, 1973.

within certain cities with particularly high levels of unemployment. Table 14.1 subdivides past policies into 'sticks' and 'carrots'. The principal 'stick' has been the Industrial Development Certificate which was required for any industrial building of over 50,000 square feet constructed outside the Assisted Areas. An implicit hope of this negative control was that if an IDC was refused, the building could be constructed in a Development Area. The IDC was abolished in 1982. The principal 'carrots' have consisted, and continue to be, a range of grants and loans.

Effects of Regional Policy

One aim, though by no means the only one, of regional policy is to reduce the level of unemployment in the Development Areas (DAs). We shall now survey studies which have attempted to assess the effects of regional policies on the level of unemployment in DAs and the movement of firms into them. A summary of results is given in Table 14.3.

Levels of Employment   Several methods have been used to estimate the effects of policy on employment but all have the same general idea. The actual level of employment, A, is compared with a hypothetical level, E, which it is estimated would have occurred if no policy had been adopted. Moore and Rhoades (1973) multiplied the size of each industry in the development area in 1963 by the national growth rate of the same industry. For years prior to 1963, industry sizes were similarly reduced at the national compound rate. The hypothetical sizes of all industries in DAs were aggregated for each year. The resulting time series (E) gave the industrial size of each DA if all of its industries had grown at the national rate. The difference between the actual and the hypothetical series ($A-E$) values for the passive policy *before* 1963 were extrapolated *beyond* 1963 into the 'active period'. The differences between this extrapolated series and the non-extrapolated series were taken to indicate the effects of regional policy.

   Armstrong and Taylor (1978) have criticised this approach, arguing that the difference between the observed ($A-E$) series and the extrapolated ($A-E$) series may be due to factors other than regional policy, for example, improved transport links to DAs, lower rate of wage rate increases, discovery of a new raw material source, and so on. A further criticism is that Moore and Rhoades's extrapolated trend did not allow for cyclical behaviour in the passive period's employment series and so for this reason also it may not accurately reflect the correct counterfactual position. This possibility was corrected in a later study (Moore, Rhoades and Tyler 1977).[2] However, jobs created by early

2   Moore, B., Rhoades, J. and Tyler, P. (1977) 'The impact of regional policy in the 1970s', *Centre of Environmental Studies Review*, Vol. 1.

Table 14.2   Main Investment Allowances and Incentives for Industry in the
Assisted Areas

February 1987

REGIONAL DEVELOPMENT GRANTS

Available only in DAs. Value is the higher of:

(a) 15% of expenditure on new capital assets with a maximum for projects employing over 200 full-time equivalents of £10,000 per new job.

(b) £3,000 for each f.t.e. job created with a maximum for manufacturing of 40% of initial project investment.

REGIONAL SELECTIVE ASSISTANCE

Available in DAs and IAs.

(a) Project Grants

Two forms available, the amount being negotiable but related to:
(i) the fixed capital costs
(ii) the number of jobs created and will be 'the minimum necessary for the project to go ahead on the basis proposed'. Projects must 'make a net contribution to the regional and national economy'.

(b) Training Grants

Available for training which is 'essential for project success'. Value is up to 40% of eligible training costs and is matched by a further grant of the same amount from the European Social Fund.

TAX ALLOWANCES

(a) Industrial Buildings

A writing down allowance of 4% throughout UK can be set against profits before tax. Regional Development Grants not treated as income for tax purposes.

(b) Machinery and Plant

A writing down allowance of 25% per year throughout UK. Regional Development Grants etc. again not treated as income for tax purposes.

EUROPEAN INVESTMENT BANK

Loans for up to 50% of fixed capital costs for projects which create or safeguard employment.

EUROPEAN COAL AND STEEL COMMUNITY	Loans for up to 50% of fixed capital costs for projects providing jobs in coal and steel closure areas.
EUROPEAN REGIONAL DEVELOPMENT FUND	Grants available for industrial, service and tourist activities and for infrastructure projects. Projects must qualify for UK grant aid. For administrative reasons in practice this does not increase the amount available to a firm.

Sources: Department of Trade and Industry, undated, *Regional Selective Assistance: Does Your Project Qualify?*; Department of Trade and Industry (1985) *Regional Development Grants: Guide for Applicants*; Commission of the European Communities (1983/5) *Finance from Europe*.

regional policy initiatives may no longer exist in later periods, but Moore, Rhoades and Tyler calculated only the cumulated 'net' number of jobs created, not the actual gross number regardless of how long they lasted. The latter was estimated by Moore, Rhoades and Tyler (1986). Arguably, the most accurate estimates put the gross number of jobs created in the 1960s at around 310,000 and in the 1970s at around 268,000.

Table 14.3

(a) NUMBER OF JOBS CREATED

Authors	Period	Estimated Effect
Moore & Rhoades (1973)	1963–70	Net 150,000 manufacturing
Moore, Rhoades Tyler (1986)	1960–71	Net 309,000 manufacturing Gross 336,000 manufacturing
	1971–81	Net 221,000 manufacturing Gross 268,000 manufacturing

(b) NUMBER OF MOVES INTO DAs

Moore & Rhoades (1976)	1960–71	Due to IDC:	540–552
		Investment Incentives:	288
		REP:	104–160
		SDA:	0–80
Ashcroft & Taylor (1977)	1961–71	787–456	
Twomey & Taylor (1985)	1960–77	977	

Firm Movements   Two methods have been used here: a micro approach using questionnaires and a macro approach relating to firm moves in aggregate. Questionnaire studies show regional policy instruments not to have been very important in the decision to *move* but to be moderately important in the choices of *final destination*. For example, a survey of factors affecting the decision to move by 531 firms during 1964 to 1967, reported to the House of Commons Expenditure Committee,[3] found that 80% of firms gave as a major reason for a move 'to permit an expansion of output' and only 27% gave 'inducements and facilities made available by official bodies' (ranked fourth) and 12% that they expected or had been refused an IDC. Alternatively, in their destination choice, 48% gave as a major reason 'Knowledge or expectation that Industrial Development Certificate will be obtainable' (ranked second) and 39% gave 'Availability of government inducements' (ranked fourth). More recently, Allen, Begg, McDougall and Walker (1986) found 36% and 31% of their sample of around 50 firms (who responded to those questions) regarded Regional Development Grant and Regional Selective Assistance respectively as crucial to their final investment decision.

Several methods have been applied to estimate the effect of regional policy on the aggregate number of moves into DAs (MDA). For example, Moore and Rhoades (1976) regressed MDA on various regional policy variables and an indicator of demand. By substituting the value zero for the regional policy variables into these equations, hypothetical values of MDA are derived for the no-policy situation. Comparison with the actual value indicates the policy effect. Ashcroft and Taylor (1977) have criticised Moore and Rhoades's model for not incorporating the idea that firm movement is simply new investment which is being carried out in DAs. By relating the ratio of MDA to total moves to regional policy variables and relative attractiveness variables and a further equation explaining total moves to, *inter alia*, investment, revised estimates were made. A more sophisticated method still has recently been used by Twomey and Taylor. Estimates as to the number of firm moves differ markedly between the investigators, with arguably the most accurate being that from 1960 to 1977 around 980 moves were due to regional policy.

Additional Reading

Allen, Begg, McDougall and Walker (1986) *Regional Incentives and the Investment Decision of the Firm*, HMSO.
Alonso, W. (1964) 'Location theory' in J. Friedman and W. Alonso (eds) *Regional Development and Planning: A Reader*, MIT Press. Also in L. Needleman (ed.) (1968) *Regional Analysis*, Penguin Books.

3   House of Commons Expenditure Committee (Trade and Industry Sub-Committee) (1973) *Minutes of Evidence*, HMSO.

Armstrong, H. and Taylor, J. (1978) *Regional Economic Policy and its Analysis*, Philip Allan, (Chapter 10).

Ashcroft, B. and Taylor, J. (1977) 'The movement of manufacturing industry and the effect of regional policy', *Oxford Economic Papers*, no. 29.

Berry, B.J.L. (1967) *Geography of Market Centres and Retail Distribution*, Prentice Hall.

Devine, P.J., Lee, N., Jones, R.M. and Tyson, W.J. (1985) *An Introduction to Industrial Economics*, 4th edn, Allen & Unwin.

Diamond, D. and Spence, N. (1983) *Regional Policy Evaluation: A Methodological Review and the Scottish Example*, Gower.

Martin, R.L. (1985) 'Monetarism masquerading as regional policy? The Government's new system of regional aid', *Regional Studies*, 19(4).

McCrone, G. (1969) *Regional Policy in Britain*, Allen & Unwin.

Moore, B. and Rhoades, J. (1973) 'Evaluating the effects of British regional economic policy', *Economic Journal*, (83).

Moore, B. and Rhoades, J. (1976) 'Regional economic policy and the movement of manufacturing firms to development areas', *Economica*, (43).

Moore, B. Rhoades, J. and Tyler, P. (1986) *The Effects of Government Regional Economic Policy*, HMSO.

Richardson, H.W. (1969) *Regional Economics*, Weidenfeld & Nicholson.

Smith, D.M. (1971) *Industrial Location: An Economic Geographical Analysis*, John Wiley.

PART V

Competition Policy and Decision Evaluation

15

Monopoly and Restrictive Practices Legislation

Managerial knowledge of monopoly and restrictive practices legislation is important for several reasons. Firstly, the manager who has such knowledge has an idea as to which actions are illegal or are likely to be prohibited. Secondly, an examination of past investigations by the Monopolies Commission or Restrictive Practices Court helps the manager decide whether, if the activity of his company was referred, it would or would not be likely to be sanctioned. Hence the questions arise: why does monopoly policy exist? What is the current legislation? What criteria have the Monopolies Commission (MC) and Restrictive Practices Court (RPC) used to decide whether or not to allow an activity to proceed?

15.1 Rationale

Government policy is usually aimed at improving economic performance. This presupposes that such performance is poor. Why might this be so, and what defects is policy aimed at? The concept of consumers' surplus can help provide an answer. Consumers' surplus is the value (or utility) consumers obtain from buying goods, which is over and above the total price they pay the supplier. It arises because of the fact that the price paid for each unit is the same, but is, in turn, equal to the utility of only the last unit bought, while earlier units have all provided greater utility. (This is explained by the two economic laws, the law of diminishing marginal utility and the marginal equivalency principle of consumer equilibrium which states that the marginal cost (price paid) must equal the marginal benefits obtained (or utility).) Geometrically, in the special case where utility can be measured by money, consumer surplus is the triangular area. DP_1A under the demand curve and above the revenue rectangle OP_1AQ_1 in Figure 15.1.

Now assume that the perfectly competitive industry of Figure 15.1 is monopolised and that a higher price is charged by virtue of the monopolist's

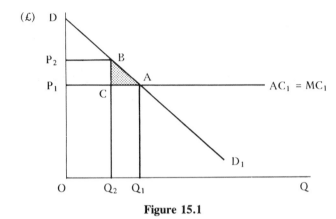

Figure 15.1

increased market power. Output is reduced from Q_1 to Q_2. The original consumer surplus triangle is considerably reduced in size to DP_2B. Part of the original triangle, the rectangle P_2P_1CB, is transferred to the monopolist as additional profits at output level Q_2; the remainder is lost to society as a whole, to both consumer and producer. This area, the shaded triangle ABC, is the deadweight loss from monopoly.

However, the monopolised industry may get the benefits of scale economies, and so lower costs, say AC_2 in Figure 15.2. In this case the net welfare loss (or gain) to the economy is the difference between the two shaded areas, ABC and P_1CDE. The shaded area P_1CDE is a further addition to monopolistic profits. (We have ignored the fact that the profit-maximising output with scale economies would be greater than Q_2 because the original MR curve would cut the lower AC curve at a greater Q.) Because of the scale economies arising from monopolisation, Q_2 can be produced with fewer real

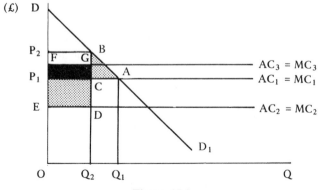

Figure 15.2

resources than otherwise. Resources are released to increase output of other products elsewhere in the economy.

On the other hand, monopolisation may have the reverse effect. Market power often enables high cost producers to remain in business. Competition, by mounting pressure on firms' profits, tends to discipline both management and employees to utilise their inputs and to put in more effort more effectively and more energetically than is the case when this pressure is absent. Thus monopolisation may raise costs, say to AC_3.[1,2] The solid rectangular area P_1FGC is here a deduction from maximum monopoly profits at Q_2. The net welfare loss is now represented by this area plus the deadweight loss triangle. More real resources are being used to produce Q_2 than would have been in perfect competition.

The case for antimonopoly thus rests in the first instance on the presence of deadweight loss resulting from monopolistic price and output practices. When scale economies are present as a result of the monopoly, however, the situation is less clearcut. A welfare trade-off is required between the deadweight loss to the consumer and the cost savings accruing to the producer. Simplistically, a merger should be allowed if the cost savings which will result are greater than the consequent loss of consumer surplus, and *vice versa*. Where scale economies do not exist, the presence of X-inefficiency reinforces the arguments in favour of antimonopoly policy. By extension, when X-inefficiency and scale economies are both present, then any welfare trade-off must be less favourable to the monopolist than it would be in the absence of X-inefficiency.

This is a very abstract explanation of the rationale behind government competition policy. More practically, we can summarise the case for and against increased industrial concentration and monopoly power as follows:

Factors in Favour of Increased Concentration:
(i)   increased monopoly profits provide both the incentive and the wherewithal to conduct research and development and to innovate;
(ii) attainment of scale economies;
(iii) avoidance of capacity duplication.

---

1   This is the concept of X-inefficiency. It is nothing more than the normal 'inefficiency' which businessmen and laymen have always talked about. Economists, however, have reserved the word 'efficiency' for discussions relating to allocative efficiency. They have, moreover, made the assumption that firms always employ all factor inputs in the technically most efficient manner. Our discussions in Chapter 7, for example, rested on this assumption and suggest that in imperfectly competitive circumstances firms may well work within their production possibility frontiers.
2   We again ignore the fact that the profit-maximising output would now be less than Q_2.

Factors in Favour of Diminished Concentration:
(i)   avoidance of X-inefficiency;
(ii)   avoidance of red tape;
(iii)   avoidance of price:output levels leading to resource misallocation.

It should be noted, of course, that these sets of arguments are *not* restricted to the polar extremes of pure monopoly and perfect competition, and consequently are not necessarily mutually exclusive.

15.2   Government Policy

Restrictive Practices

British legislation against restrictive practices dates back to 1948, to the *Monopoly and Restrictive Practices Act*. This Act created the Monopolies and Restrictive Practices Commission, (MRPC). The Board of Trade (BOT) could refer to the MRPC any goods produced, supplied or exported where at least one third of the UK market was supplied either by one person or several colluding companies. The MRPC were asked to examine whether or not the referred practices were against the 'public interest' and if so what action they wished to recommend. In deciding this, the MRPC were to examine 'all matters which appear in the particular circumstances to be relevant' and 'the need ... to achieve ... the production, treatment and distribution by the most efficient and economical means of goods of such types and qualities, in such volume and at such prices as will best meet the requirements of home and overseas markets'.

A second piece of legislation followed in 1956, the *Restrictive Trade Practices Act*. This Act set up the Restrictive Practices Court, composed of High Court Judges and experts to replace the MRPC for the consideration of restrictive practices. The Act required any agreement between two or more persons who manufactured or supplied goods in the UK where the agreement related to the prices charged or paid, the terms or conditions on which goods were to be produced or supplied, the quantities or descriptions of the goods, the manufacturing process or the persons to be supplied, to be registered with the Registrar of Restrictive Trade Agreements. The Registrar would take proceedings against the persons involved, in the RPC.

All agreements which were taken to court were *presumed* to be against the public interest unless the Court was persuaded that two conditions held. Firstly, the agreement had to fulfil at least one of seven 'gateways':

(i)   that the restriction is necessary to protect the public where the use of the goods requires special knowledge or skill;
(ii)   that the removal of the restriction would deprive buyers and users of substantial benefits;

(iii)   that the restriction is a necessary defensive measure against other restraints imposed on the trade by persons outside it;

(iv)   that the restriction is a necessary defensive measure against an outside monopoly;

(v)   that the removal of the restriction is likely to have an adverse effect on the general level of employment in some area;

(vi)   that the removal of the restriction is likely to cause a substantial reduction in the export trade of the United Kingdom;

(vii)   that the restriction is necessary to maintain another restriction which the Court finds to be not contrary to the public interest.

Secondly, the Court must also be satisfied 'that the restriction is not unreasonable, having regard to the balance between those circumstances and any detriment to the public or to persons not party to the agreement ... resulting from or likely to result from, the operation of the restriction'.

Experience since the 1956 Act, especially the possibility of operating unwritten price agreements, resulted in the *Restrictive Trade Practices Act* of 1968, which amended the 1956 legislation in three ways. First, price *exchange information* not registrable under the 1956 Act, can have much the same effect as a *price fixing agreement*, although only the latter was registrable (and usually declared illegal). The 1968 Act empowered the Board of Trade to call up any such information agreements for registration (i.e. this would still not be compulsory). Second, an additional 'gateway' was added. A restriction can now be defended on the grounds that it:

(viii)   does not directly or indirectly restrict or discourage competition.

Third, the government was permitted to make orders providing exemptions for certain agreements from registration provided that either:

(i)(a)   the agreement is aimed at promoting a scheme of substantial importance to the economy;

  (b)   its main object is to promote industrial efficiency or to improve production capacity;

  (c)   an agreement is necessary to achieve this object within a reasonable time;

  (d)   only those restrictions which are reasonably necessary to achieve this aim will be allowed; and

  (e)   on balance the agreement is in the national interest; or

(ii)   the agreement was designed to restrict price increases or to gain price reductions.

The 1973 *Fair Trading Act* repealed the 1948 *Monopolies and Restrictive Practices Act* and amended the 1956 and 1968 Acts. The Registrar of Restrictive Practices was replaced by the Director General of Fair Trading. The Director's duties were 'to keep under review commercial activities with a view to becoming aware of, and ascertaining the circumstances relating to, monopoly situations or uncompetitive practices'. In addition, restrictive agreements and information provisions within service industries were brought under the 1956 Act.

Finally and currently in force is the *Restrictive Practices Act* 1976 which consolidated and only slightly amended earlier legislation. All agreements and information provisions relating to prices charged or recommended, terms and conditions of supply, quantities to be supplied, process of manufacture (form of provision), persons or areas to be supplied or purchased from for both manufacturing and service industries are, with certain exceptions, to be registered with the Director General of Fair Trading. Information provision on costs is also included. The exceptions include those first exempted under the 1968 Act and certain others. The unexempted registrable agreements or provisions are *presumed* to be contrary to the public interest unless the RTP Court is persuaded that at least one of the previously existing 'gateways' applies and that the 'tailpiece' of the 1956 Act is also fulfilled. If the DGFT believes that an agreement is not sufficiently significant to merit court proceedings, he can apply under Section 21(2) of the Act to the Secretary of State to issue directions to this effect.

In 1980 the *Competition Act* broadened the scope of anticompetitive legislation. The Director General, with the Secretary of State's approval, was given power to carry out an investigation into any conduct which appears to be 'anticompetitive', regardless of whether or not a monopoly situation might exist. A person is acting 'anticompetitively' according to the Act if either his conduct alone or when considered with that of others has, or is intended or likely to have, the 'effect of restricting, distorting or preventing competition in connection with the production, supply or acquisition of goods in the UK . . .' If the Director decides that anticompetitive behaviour exists, those concerned may give undertakings of restraint. If these are rejected by the Director he may again, subject to approval, make a 'competition reference' to the MMC. The MMC will investigate whether the person referred had in the preceding 12 months acted as the Director claims, whether such action was 'anticompetitive' and whether the action was 'expected to operate against the public interest'. The MMC may add suggested remedies and, if the referred person does not act upon these suggestions from the Secretary of State, the latter may legally prohibit the activity.

The 1980 Act also empowered the Secretary of State to refer any question of the efficiency, service provided or possible misuse of monopoly situation by a bus service, water authority, agricultural marketing board or any body whose members are government appointed and any organisation with a statutory duty to supply any of these goods or services. By December 1985 the Director General had initiated 18 investigations, in which three companies were found not to have acted anticompetitively. In nine cases the firm concerned gave acceptable undertakings or the practice was too insignificant to merit a full reference.

Resale Prices

The 1956 *Restrictive Trade Practices Act* prohibited *collective* enforcement of resale price maintenance. However, it effectively increased the powers of manufacturers enforcing *individual* RPM (namely the practice whereby the manufacturer stipulates the resale prices of his goods and where he can enforce these prices by withholding supplies from retailers who do not adhere to his terms). The 1964 *Resale Prices Act* prohibited RPM on all but 'exempted' goods.

The Restrictive Practices Court was allowed to exempt goods where it believed that without RPM:

(a) the quality or variety of available goods would be reduced 'to the detriment of the public'; or

(b) the number of outlets for the goods would be 'substantially' reduced 'to the detriment of the public'; or

(c) the price would in the long run rise 'to the detriment of the public'; or

(d) 'the goods would be sold by retail under conditions likely to cause danger to health'; or

(e) necessary after-sales service would be reduced to the detriment of the public.

The *Resale Prices Act* 1976 consolidated earlier legislation. The same conditions for exemption apply.

Monopolies

The 1948 *Monopolies and Restrictive Practices Act* was the first UK legislation against monopolies. Its provisions have been described above.

The 1956 *Restrictive Trade Practices Act*, dissolved the MRPC and for 'monopolistic' situations created the Monopolies Commission to which the BOT could again refer the same situations as it could under the 1948 Act. The onus was still on the Monopolies Commission to show that the situation was against the 'public interest', the definition of which remained unchanged from the 1948 Act. The 1965 *Monopolies and Mergers Act* made service industries subject to the 1948 Act.

The most significant change in monopoly legislation since 1948 was contained in the 1973 *Fair Trading Act* which is currently in force. The Director General of Fair trading may, subject to veto by the Secretary of State, refer monopoly situations which are believed to exist to the Monopolies and Mergers Commission (the MC, renamed under this Act). The Act altered the definition of a monopoly situation to a situation where:

(i) one person supplies or buys at least 25% of a market in the UK; or

(ii) a group of interrelated companies supplies or buys at least 25% of a market; or

(iii) agreements exist which prevent parts of the UK from being supplied with the good at all; or

(iv) at least 25% of the UK market is supplied by several persons who restrict or distort competition.

The same criteria apply to services. Monopoly situations in exports may be referred, where these occur when at least 25% of UK production of the expected good is produced by one person or a group of related firms. The Monopolies and Mergers Commission (MMC) may be asked to investigate whether a monopoly exists and if it does whether it is in manufacturing services or exports, who benefits, whether any uncompetitive activities are maintaining the monopoly and whether the monopoly allows the firm(s) to operate in a particular way. The MMC may additionally be asked whether any of the monopoly's activities 'may be expected to operate against the public interest'.

The Act made the 'definition' of the 'public interest' which was hitherto contained in the 1948 Act, more specific:

> ... the Commission shall take into account all matters which appear to them in the particular circumstances to be relevant and, among other things, shall have regard to the desirability
>
> (a) of maintaining and promoting effective competition ...
> (b) of promoting the interests of consumers, purchasers and other users of goods and services in the United Kingdom in respect of the prices charged for them and in respect of their qualtity and the variety of goods and services supplied;
> (c) of promoting, through competition, the reduction of costs and the development and use of new techniques and new products, and of facilitating the entry of new competitors into existing markets;
> (d) of maintaining and promoting a balanced distribution of industry and employment in the United Kingdom; and
> (e) of maintaining and promoting competitive activity in markets outside the United Kingdom on the part of producers of goods and of suppliers of goods and services, in the United Kingdom.

If the MMC finds that a monopoly's activities are against the 'public interest', the Secretary of State may ask the DGFT to gain voluntary Undertakings from the party(s) concerned or he may issue Orders preventing or modifying the practices concerned.

Notice that it was only after the passing of the 1973 Act that antimonopoly policy explicitly stated that the process of competition should be regarded as a normative goal.

Mergers

Anti-merger legislation began with the 1965 *Monopolies and Mergers Act*. The BOT was empowered to refer mergers to the MC who would be asked to investigate whether 'the fact of the enterprises having ceased ... to be distinct enterprises, operates or may be expected to operate against the public interest', the definition of the 'public interest' being that of the 1948 Act. Notice that the onus is again on the MC to show that the merger is against the public interest.

Currently in force is the 1973 *Fair Trading Act* which, in repealing the 1948 and 1965 Acts, redefined the circumstances in which an acquisition may be referred. Nowadays the Secretary of State may refer a merger involving manufacturing or service industries — again, which is only proposed, or which occurred within the preceding six months, but where either the value of acquired assets exceeds £5m. or the resulting combine supplies or is supplied by 25% of the market. Unlike the case of monopoly, the Director General may only advise the Secretary of State as to which firms to refer. The MMC would be asked to decide whether the situation qualified for investigation and, if so, whether the creation of the combine would be likely to operate against the 'public interest' as redefined in the Act. In 1980 the £5m. size limit was raised to £15m. and in 1984 to £30m. Again, if the MMC finds the merger against the public interest. The Secretary of State may require undertakings from the firms concerned or prohibit the merger or require the firms to separate.

15.3 Evaluation

Restrictive Practices

Various criticisms have been made of existing legislation and procedures. We shall consider firstly the prevalence of restrictive practices, secondly arguments relating to the appropriateness of the gateways, thirdly arguments concerning justifiability, fourthly arguments concerning the rulings of the RTPC and, finally, empirical evidence concerning the effects of the legislation.

Elliot and Gribbin (1977) have argued that in the early 1950s some 50% to 60% of manufacturing output was cartelised. Between 1956 and December 1985, 4,342 goods agreements were registered and 3,335 terminated either by Court Order or by the firms involved. During the period 1976 to December 1985, 1,153 service agreements were registered and 371 ended. (*Annual Report* of the Director General of Fair Trading, 1985, HC 403.)

The eight gateways of the 1976 Act (the first seven from the 1956 Act and the last from that of 1968[3]), through one of which a restrictive practice must pass before the Court will declare it legal, have varying degrees of support in economic logic.

Gateways (i) and (ii) (p. 448) are unexceptional in terms of economic theory. But as the Green Paper on Restrictive Practices reports, Stevens and

---

3   The 1976 Act related these gateways to both restrictive agreements *and* information provisions.

Yamey (1965) have argued that the first gateway is redundant because legislation exists against situations which may put the public at risk and where it does not, the gateway is insufficient anyway.

Gateways (iii) and (iv) both pertain to countervailing power and a restrictive practice allowed through either can be justified on the grounds that the monopoly power so permitted is necessary to offset monopoly power existing elsewhere. Despite the view suggested to the Green Paper group by the National Federation of Retail Newsagents that gateway (iv) should be widened, the group concluded that it would appear that this gateway already deals sufficiently with equality of bargaining power.

Gateway (v) relates to employment. it can be argued that the general level of employment in an area is a responsibility of either macro or regional economic government policy and not that of a group of firms operating a restrictive practice. The reverse argument could also be put that the provision of employment may often benefit many and therefore, in a decision on the desirability of an agreement, such an effect should be allowed to offset any detrimental effects which a restriction might have.

The Green Paper argued that the two tests of gateway (vi) are 'discriminatory'. (*Review of Restrictive Trade Practices Policy* (1979), A Consultative Document, Cmnd. 7512 (HMSO) p. 111.) The first test, that removal of the agreement would reduce export earnings or volume by a substantial amount *relative to aggregate UK exports*, it is argued, favours firms in industries with a relatively large share of UK exports over those in industries with a relatively small share. The second test that removal would reduce export earnings or volume by a substantial amount *relative to the total business of the industry* was argued to 'discriminate against large industries especially where they have a small export trade' (*op. cit.*, p. 111). The Green Paper adds further that the gateway was not presented in a way which would achieve its intended objective of improving the balance of payments. This is because there is no gateway which would enable a restriction to pass due to its causing a reduction in imports, due to greater efficiency, although greater inefficiency *per se* is included in gateway (ii).

In its evidence to the Green Paper group (*op. cit.*, p. 112) The National Consumer Council argued that the final gateway (viii) was unnecessary because it undermined the legal presumption against restrictive practices. The Green Paper replied that the clause should be retained because it allowed insignificant agreements which reached the Court to be continued.

The Green Paper also noted that the current legislation deterred some significant agreements, which were in the public interest, from being made. Such agreements would either have to pass through a gateway which some firms may believe to involve great expense and time or to be sanctioned on the grounds of efficiency in the national interest which applies only to agreements 'of substantial importance to the national economy' (*op. cit.*, pp. 46–7).

The Green Paper noted a further problem with the Act; that many registrable agreements are not registered. A failure to register is not a criminal offence but it does mean the agreement cannot be legally enforced and does render the colluding parties open to civil proceedings by anyone who has consequently suffered a loss.

Stevens and Yamey (1965) have given several reasons why they believe that a judicial court is an inappropriate forum for determining whether a restrictive practice does or does not pass through one of the gateways and the tailpiece. Firstly, some agreements may have socially beneficial or detrimental aspects and the Restrictive Practices Court is required to make a value judgement as to the net effect where this comparison is not based on legal logic. Secondly, since none of the members of the Court is an economist, it has been doubted whether they could correctly appreciate some of the economic arguments made to determine acceptable values for economic variables such as 'the reasonable price'. Thirdly, it has been argued that the Restrictive Practices Court is an inappropriate institution to set down economic policy which it does when making decisions as to the acceptability of certain economic behaviour. It is also inappropriate to lay down political policy which it would do if deciding in favour of one group rather than another on grounds of, for example, the effects of an agreement on unemployment. In its place, Hunter (1965) has suggested an Administrative Tribunal, presumably including economists and politicians. However, since one effect of the Acts has been to lead to the termination of agreements *before* they are presented to the RTP Court, this issue of 'justiciability' has been less important than it might be.

Thirdly, much discussion has questioned[4] some RTP Court decisions. For example, in the case of the supply of magnets, some have questioned whether the price agreement allowed by the Court was necessary to maintain the existing technical co-operation and hence the rate of technical progress. In the case of the Black Bolt and Nut Association, the Association had its price-fixing agreement upheld on the grounds that all sellers offered a buyer the same price. Thus the buyer was saved the cost of shopping around. No consideration was given to the benefits the buyer might get by such shopping around. And no reasons were given in the Court's verdict as to why the Association should be treated any differently from any other industry.

Finally, several empirical studies of the effects of the 1956 RPT Act have been conducted. Swann *et al.* (1974) carried out case studies of 40 industries: 18 in depth, 22 less so. Of the former group, in four the agreement was upheld by the Court, in six the agreement was struck down by the Court and in eight the agreement was abandoned voluntarily before it was tried in Court. Swann *et al.* consider the impact of the Act at different times relative to its implementation. The study found that, of 60 agreements existing before the Act, eight

---

4   See Devine, Lee, Jones and Tyson (1985).

were not registered after it and were suspected of having been abandoned. Various cases of agreement modification were observed around the time of the passing of the Act. For example, in the case of batteries, agreement to engage in exclusive dealing was removed, but price fixing continued. In some industries agreements were substantially unchanged but reworded to appear more acceptable and in some, home agreements were discontinued but those on exports remained. Immediately after the passing of the Act instances of agreements breaking down were observed, probably due to anticipated additional future competition, for example in surgical dressing manufacturing.

Further, events in industries where the agreement was struck down were considered. Of 34 such industries, between 61% and 53% experienced competition, mainly in prices and discounts, as for example wire ropes manufacturing. This was partly due to the entry of new substitute products and to greater import penetration. In 50% of the industries information agreements were introduced, often to prenotify other parties of a price change or of a tender price, e.g. Tile Mileage. In other cases, price leadership followed termination, e.g. electric cables (leader BICC), and in some cases, supply agreements with a large buyer.

In the longer term, after termination in some industries, behaviour paralleled the shorter-term effects. In some, information agreements were ended (frequently before the 1968 call for registration). The greater competition was found to lead to reduced capacity and greater cost consciousness. In many cases, in the long term greater competition was due to innovation. Swann et al. list 13 industries from their sample where this occurred. However, 'on a not inconsiderable scale', collusion rather than competition resulted. Price leadership became more evident in the longer term than in the short term, for instance in steel drum manufacturing. Swann et al. also found that the Act led indirectly to greater merger activity to reduce excess capacity which followed the termination of agreements, and possibly also to reduce competition.

However, two major weaknesses of the Swann et al. study have been proposed by Clarke (1985). Firstly, case studies are not based on comparable quantitative data; comparisons are therefore made based on impressionistic interpretations. Secondly, no rigorous method of indicating that some of the observed behaviour was actually due to the Act was adopted: in many cases, such as mergers, it could have had some other cause.

Finally, O'Brien et al.. (1979) selected a sample of firms in industries which were known to be affected differently by the 1956 RTP Act. These firms fell into four groups: (a) those in an industry where a restrictive practice(s) was upheld; (b) those in an industry where a restrictive practice was struck down by the Court; (c) those in an industry where agreements were voluntarily abandoned and (d) those in an industry where no restrictive practice had operated — the control group. Three subperiods were considered: a pre-Act period, 1951−58, and two post-Act periods: 1959−67 and 1968−72.

By comparing the groups within any one period and the performance of groups between different periods, and by standardising variables for groups (a) to (c) by the values for the control group − to account for changes in the macro-economy rather than the change in the law — the effects of the 1956 Act were estimated. The authors concluded that:

(a) Although the rate of return on assets or on sales decreased between the earliest and later periods for groups (a) to (c), most of this could be attributed to changes in the macroeconomy and only some of it to the change in RP legislation.

(b) The group whose restrictive practice had been struck down had slower asset growth in the earlier period than in the post-Act period, whereas the group whose restrictive practices were upheld by the Court grew more slowly in the later period compared with the earlier period. In terms of sales, firms which retained their restrictive practices grew slowly relative to the control group in both periods, whereas firms in the groups whose restrictive practices changed grew more rapidly.

(c) In case the removal of restrictive practices due to the Act made industries more competitive and hence led to firms merging to increase their profit-ability by economies of scale or monopoly power, comparisons of merger activities were made. For no group were significant differences in merger activity between the earliest and later periods found, and very few differences between the groups were found either. In fact, the control group had the greatest proportion of acquiring and acquired firms in all three periods.

Monopolies

It is possible to classify conduct of which the MMC has approved or disap-proved in several ways. Table 15.1 offers one classification based on ten recent reports, all referred under the 1973 Act. By considering a large number of reports, Devine *et al.* (1985) have suggested the general position of the MMC to be as follows. 'Deliberately anticompetitive' conduct, for example exclusive dealing and entry-preventing behaviour, has been consistently criticised, as have restrictions on the sale of competitors' goods, forms of discount payments to disadvantage potential competitors, tie-in sales and full line forcing. In addition, Devine *et al.* reported that price discrimination has usually been condemned. They also reported that 'very high profits have usually been con-demned'. These generalisations are consistent with the classification of 'prac-tices found against the public interest' by the MMC during the period 1959−78 made by the government's Green Paper (1978).

The Green Paper also notes that MMC investigations impose a considerable burden on the firm(s) concerned in both time and cost. Monopoly references

Table 15.1

CRITERION	REPORT	JUDGMENT OF THE COMMISSION
PROFITABILITY AND PRICING	Ready Mixed Concrete	(a) Acceptance

COMMENTS: Commission had no reason to believe that RMC Ltd was pursuing price policy contrary to the public interest — RMC and others could raise prices at remote depots and practise price discrimination — but do not.

(b) Acceptance

COMMENTS: Mean profitability of RMC was 13% on CCA (1975—80) — 'high by the depressed levels of the United Kingdom' — but was not in itself considered to be evidence of monopoly power and no other evidence of abuse of monopolistic power was found.

	Diazo Copying Materials	(a) Acceptance

COMMENTS: The MMC found that Ozalid acquired trade houses and offered them preferential terms which were not expected to correspond to any additional post-acquisition costs incurred by the trade houses. This led to more effective distribution at the expense of competitors but (i) the trade houses also buy from competitors (ii) Ozalid claimed it did not manage the trade houses and (iii) only one fifth of the Diazo materials business is done through the trade houses, therefore the effects were judged small.

(b) Ambiguous

COMMENTS: Ozalid's profitability 1974—5 on average was 15% (without machines), 7% (with machines) (CCA). Ozalid argued that because the machines sold at little or no profit, the profitability figure used to form a conclusion should be for machines plus copying materials. On whatever basis one uses, the company has made 'profits which we consider to be higher than might have been expected in fully competitive conditions in an industry characterised by excess capacity and declining demand in a period which included some years of general economic recession' said the MMC. But because it was unclear if some of Ozalid's activities were registrable under the Restrictive Practices Act of 1956, the MMC were unable to determine the extent to which these profit levels have been obtained due to limitation of price competition and to what extent they were due to the monopolistic position of Ozalid.

(c) Approval

COMMENTS: Special discounts, i.e. lower prices, individually negotiated, for large customers: these the MMC felt 'contribute substantially to competition'.

CRITERION	REPORT	JUDGMENT OF THE COMMISSION
	Petrol	Ambiguous

COMMENTS: The MMC argued that some wholesalers gave selective price support to outlets in some areas affected by competition from low-priced petrol and that this distorted and restricted competition. But because of the administration cost of enforcing its abandonment, and because the time taken to clear the changes in agreements may itself restrict competition, it was found not to be against the public interest.

	Credit Cards	(a) Mild disapproval

COMMENTS: Profitability of National Westerminster's Access division was 'very high' 1977 and '78, and the profitability of Midland Bank's Access division and of Barclaycard were 'good' by comparison with non-financial companies and were comparable with those of financial companies — all when allowed for risk said the MMC. But none were excessive, since on a DCF calculation, which allows for past losses also, the rates of return were not very great. The MMC argued that the profitability of the credit card business of American Express and Diners Club in the UK has been 'high' in recent years.

The MMC decided that charges to traders were not as closely related to costs as one would find in a hghly competitive market — price discrimination existed, i.e. the smaller traders were at a disadvantage since they had little bargaining power.

		(b) Against the public interest

COMMENTS: Credit card companies prevented traders charging ordinary customers less than card customers. This was against the public interest argued the MMC because it prevented a trader from competing with other traders by offering different prices to credit card users vis-à-vis other customers. This reduced customer choice and may have generally raised prices concluded the MMC.

	Roadside Advertising	Against the public interest

COMMENTS: Range of profitability 1974–9: 19 to 64% on capital employed — 'these returns are very high' MMC (para. 10.24).

	Foreign Package Holidays	Against the public interest

COMMENTS: The MMC estimated that 75% of the total market for foreign

CRITERION	REPORT	*JUDGMENT OF THE COMMISSION*

package holidays which were sold by tour operators through travel agents was subject to prohibitions on the agent discounting the holiday price or offering other inducements to attract custom, e.g. free insurance. The MMC found that, whilst the operator's control of his prices was in the public interest, the prohibition on inducements was not and was restricting price competition between agents.

	Tampons	Acceptance

COMMENTS: Despite (i) Tambrands' rate of return varying between 22% and 39% (CCA) and Southalls' return of 14%−24% (CCA) during 1979−84 (relevant industry averages 12% to 19%) and (ii) the prices of both firms' products rising faster than the RPI after 1980, the MMC concluded that their tampon prices were not operating against the public interest. Reasons: (i) no barriers to entry or anticompetitive practices were found, the MMC arguing 'in these circumstances high profits may be attributable to superior entrepreneurial ability, successful innovation and more efficient techniques of production and organisation' (8.31); (ii) competition from external protection products and own brands was increasing, as was the probability of entry. The high profit rates were seen as 'a magnet to attract new suppliers'.

	White Salt	Against the public interest

COMMENTS: During 1976−86 every price change by one of the duopolists, British Salt and ICI, was followed by the other. Since 1980 all leads were by the higher cost producer, ICI, enabling British salt to earn 'high profits'. Each duopolist notified the other of price changes in advance. The MMC concluded that this mechanism indicated lack of competition which resulted in prices being higher than they would be with competition and against the public interest. British salt's argument that it had not undercut ICI for fear of retaliation was rejected by the MMC as indicating competition.

	Postal Franking Machines	Against the public interest

COMMENTS: The MMC found Pitney Bowers (PB) — with 60% of the market — to be a price leader which neither Roneo Alcatel (RA) or new entrants could challenge and that prices were higher than they would be 'in conditions of more effective competition'. Real prices had increased and the large discounts used to gain orders from big users suggested that PB's prices for the rest of the market provided it with 'comfortable margins'.

Competition was restrained by a failure by both firms to issue price lists.

CRITERION	REPORT	JUDGMENT OF THE COMMISSION
COMMUNICATION	Credit Cards	Likely to reduce competition

COMMENTS: Joint Credit Card Company and Barclaycard had, in the past, discussed policy, e.g. the rates to be paid by cardholders who took extended credit, whether or not to introduce an annual charge etc. The MMC decided that these were likely to lessen the degree of competition since they were likely to make traders liable to pay higher charges for a franchise and to accept franchises on terms which were less beneficial to them and possibly disadvantageous to their customers.

	Roadside Advertising	(a) Against the public interest

COMMENTS: Members of British Posters (who collectively control approximately 80% of all panels) held discussions. The MMC believed that these 'led to a more rapid and orderly upward adjustment in prices generally than would otherwise have taken place and to more consistency in pricing between individual members' (10.23).

This and higher profitability resulting were judged to be against the public interest (10.48).

		(b) Against the public interest

COMMENTS: The MMC argued that less competition between contractors in the Association has enabled them to put pressure on landowners so as to pay lower prices than otherwise, so giving contractors one way of gaining higher profits (10.48).

		(c) Against the public interest

COMMENTS: British Posters members agreed to make panels available for small packages of line by line adverts but to exclude Independent Poster Sales — a non-member of British Posters. The MMC felt that this restricted competition (10.48).

		(d) Against the public interest

COMMENTS: If a dispute arose between a landowner and contractor the
contractor would notify his Association about the difficulty and no other
contractor would try to obtain the site. Therefore the sitting licensee had a great
advantage over the landowner in the negotiations. The MMC found that this
seriously restricted competition, held down rentals and reduced the sites which
landowners would supply (10.41, 10.42). It also enabled some contractors to get
some landowners to accept their model agreements — this, where it occurred
was 'an abuse of monopolistic power' (10.43). The Associations have said that
now, (following entry by non-Association contractors) revised codes of conduct
do not bar enquiries about sites which are currently licensed. The MMC thought
that the revised codes were still likely to lead to the restriction of competition
(10.46).

EFFICIENCY	Wholesaling	(a) Acceptance
	Newspapers	
	and	
	Periodicals	

COMMENTS: The MMC argued: 'it is in the public interest to have a
distribution system . . . which makes available by delivery to homes and offices
or by collection from newsagents, before normal office hours, the maximum
number and variety of newspapers at the cheapest practicable cost for such a
service' (para. 182). The MMC argued that wholesalers refuse to supply some
retailers where they would expect the current circulation to be divided between
more retailers. This is not what the MMC would expect to occur if several
wholesalers competed in one area. But if every retailer was supplied who could
provide a margin covering the increase in wholesalers' costs there would
probably be a decline in retailers providing home deliveries and sales. Also,
increasing the number of retailers but not the circulation would increase
wholesalers' costs in relation to turnover which they would have eventually to
meet by seeking higher margins from publishers or retailers. Therefore the price
to the reader would be likely to increase. The MMC argued that bearing in
mind the special need for economy and the importance of home deliveries, the
public interest, as given above, would be best served by wholesalers limiting the
number of retailers supplied and to select them on the basis of location and
standard of service they are prepared to provide.

(b) Acceptance

COMMENTS: The MMC was concerned that by limiting competition in
retailing, wholesalers may have reduced the incentive for retailers' efficiency but
argued that this was unlikely because wholesalers could threaten to supply new
retailers.

(c) Approval

COMMENTS: The MMC was concerned that recent acquisitions and
rationalisations had reduced the number of wholesalers in certain areas thereby
reducing competition. But the Commission concluded that such rationalisation
reduced the cost of wholesaling and enabled wholesalers to give more reliable
service and that competition had not been antisocial.

CRITERION	REPORT	JUDGMENT OF THE COMMISSION
	White Salt	Disapproval

COMMENTS: The lack of price competition posed by the more efficient British Salt to the less efficient ICI enabled ICI to continue without investing £300,000 in efficiency increasing plant despite an IRR of 70%.

RESEARCH AND DEVELOPMENT	Ready Mixed Concrete	Indifference

COMMENTS: The MMC found no evidence to suggest that RMC's scale of monopoly was the cause of the conservatism of the UK construction industry to use admixtures.

	Diazo Copying Materials	

COMMENTS: The state of technology is 'such that the size of manufacturer does not appear to be of very special advantage in research and development' argued the MMC. Brand loyalty to Ozalid was found to be weak.

	Foreign Package Holidays	Against the public interest

COMMENTS: The MMC found that travel agents' attitudes and the operator-imposed constraints on them to offer client-attracting inducements have deprived customers of choices of prices and services most suited to their needs.

EXPORTS	Diazo Copying Materials	Approval

COMMENTS: Ozalid, like other firms, 'has achieved substantial success in the exporting of Diazo materials'.

VARIETY	Roadside Advertising	Against the public interest

COMMENTS: The MMC found that British Posters' packages of panels lacked flexibility and were more general than would be the case if the market were competitive.

BARRIERS TO ENTRY	Diazo Copying Materials	Acceptance

COMMENTS: Ozalid's market share and size was unlikely to give it sufficient economies of scale to be a substantial barrier.

CRITERION	REPORT	JUDGEMENT OF THE COMMISSION
	Wholesaling Newspapers and Periodicals	Acceptance

COMMENTS: The MMC considered the possibility that wholesalers who owned retail outlets might refuse to supply other retailers to prevent their own retailers facing competition, but concluded this was not occurring.

	Tampons	Approval

COMMENTS: Despite the high profit rates of Tambrands and Southalls (see above) and advertising:sales ratios of 13% and above, no entry barriers were detected. In these conditions (together with no anticompetitive behaviour) high profits may indicate 'the characteristics of competition which the Fair Trading Act seeks to promote'.

	White Salt	Acceptance

COMMENTS: For five reasons entry was unlikely, but these reasons were not due to behaviour by British Salt or ICI. These reasons were: (i) economies of scale necessitating a substantial market share for viability; (ii) a lag of up to 5 years before full efficiency for technical reasons; (iii) planning proposals favouring larger producers; (iv) foreclosure of markets; (v) likely continuation of the current excess demand.

	Postal Franking Machines	Against the public interest

COMMENTS: The Post Office regulation that maintenance must be carried out by the supplier or his agent and that equipment must be inspected 4 times annually was thought to prevent dealer distribution rather than direct selling and prevented the entry of independent maintenance service companies.

OTHER	Petrol	Acceptance

COMMENTS: The MMC argued that if retailers had engaged in competitions or stamp trading under pressure from wholesalers and against their better judgment so that the terms of sale offered to retail customers were different from what they might otherwise be, retail competition would be distorted. The MMC concluded that in this industry no such distortion existed.

OTHER	Petrol	Acceptance

COMMENTS: The MMC argued that if wholesalers owned a very high percentage of retail outlets, there would be little or no opportunity for new wholesalers to enter except by creating new outlets which might not get

CRITERION	REPORT	*JUDGEMENT OF THE COMMISSION*

planning permission. Acquisitions by wholesalers could reduce price competition. At its 1977 level, company ownership of wholesale and retail outlets was not found to operate against the public interest.

	Greyhound Racing	Against the public interest

COMMENTS: (a) The MMC found that the National Greyhound Racing Club's (NGRC) requirement that registered greyhounds may not run at non-NGRC tracks was against the public interest. Reasons: (i) it prevented independent promoters from identifying dogs to an audience by their stud name (so restricting the form information which gamblers receive; (ii) it restricted competition between tracks; (iii) it prevented licensed trainers not attached to a NGRC track from taking their greyhounds to independent tracks.

(b) The NGRC's rule that only greyhounds in the charge of a course's Attached Trainers may run in graded races (90% of total races) at that course was against the public interest, since in comparison 330 nonlicensed trainers had to compete with licensed trainers for only 8% of races (open races) and with 1,000 other trainers for races at Permit Tracks.

	Postal Franking Machines	Against the public interest

COMMENTS: Pitney Bowers (PB) owned PB Leasing which was exclusively recommended by PB salesmen when leasing equipment and which charged higher rates than other leasing companies. The MMC found this against the public interest because it was thought to be intended to maintain PB's monopoly.

specify time limits: usually 18 months or two years. A firm's situation could change significantly during this period and additional salary and legal costs have to be expended over this period to prepare the case.

Some have criticised the vagueness of the definition of 'the public interest', for example, Allen of the 1948 Act. But even in the 1973 Act, the guidelines as to the 'public interest' include as a preamble the need to take account of 'all matters which appear . . . in the particular circumstances to be relevant'. This Act also contains, as one consideration to be included in the Monopolies and Mergers Commission's judgement, 'the balanced distribution of employment'. This guideline would seem to be more relevant to an Act relating to regional rather than to monopolies policy. It might confuse the workings of the Commission, and in certain circumstances may place it in a position where there is a need to take a decision favouring either more or less competition subject to providing less or more regional assistance. It is debatable whether such questions of distribution should be left to politicians or to their non-elected, but specialist, advisers in unrelated areas.

The consistency of the MC Reports has also aroused discussion. Sutherland (1969) compared the consistency of the MC in three Reports under the 1948 Act and decided that 'differences in the facts cannot account for differences in the Monopolies Commission's conclusions about Pilkington on the one hand and Courtaulds and Kodak on the other'.

With reference to more recent reports, Clarke (1985) has argued that the MMC has been 'extremely liberal in its treatment of monopoly profits'. For example, in the Cat and Dogfoods Report (1977) the MMC accepted that Pedigree Petfood's average rate of return on capital (on historic costs) of 47% in 1972–75, compared with an average for all manufacturers of 16%, was reasonable, despite the fact that they had 50% of the market. Pedigree had argued that their high rate of return was due to high efficiency, and the MMC found no anticompetitive practices. Other instances of MMC approval for rates of return much higher than the average for UK manufacturing industry are Rank Xerox (36% on historic cost) and Tambrands (55%–80%).

However, it is often claimed that the pragmatism and flexibility of British policy (particularly in comparison with the dogmatic approach of the American antitrust laws, where market share alone is often regarded as a sufficient ground on which to produce an unfavourable judgement) is its strength: each case may be individually considered with advantages offsetting uncompetitive behaviour.

Little work has been carried out to discover the effectiveness of UK monopoly policy. However, Shaw and Simpson (1985) considered case studies of eight markets for which MMC reports were published between 1959 and 1970. They found that the recommendations of the MMC and ensuing undertakings by the firms concerned had 'only a minor impact on the process of competition': increases in competition and losses of market share would have occurred without the Report. However, they cautioned that their findings did not remove the need for monopoly investigations: in some cases the reports came too late to hasten competition, and in most markets the MMC report did encourage entry barrier reduction and price restraint.

Mergers

In the case of mergers the MMC must usually pass judgment on whether their effects are *likely to be* against the public interest in the future, whereas in the case of monopolies the Commission must decide whether the past or current effects *have been (are)* against the public interest. Therefore accurate merger vetting is often more difficult than the examination of monopolies.

The Director General of Fair Trading asks the Merger Panel to examine any proposed merger which the Director believes might be referred to the MMC. Confidential guidance as to the liklihood of referral is given by the OFT in advance of a bid, on request. Upon the advice of the Panel, the Director advises the Secretary of State and with the latter's permission the Director refers the merger. The Green Paper (*A Review of Monopolies and Mergers Policy* (1979), A Consultative Document, Cmnd. 7198, HMSO) notes that of just over 1500 referable mergers between 1965–77 only approximately 3% per year were actually referred.

The Commission is allowed six months in which to make its prediction of the likely state of the post-merger market and to come to a judgment on the basis of that prediction. The merger can be subject to 'standstill' powers by the government until the report is issued. Enforced delays of this sort while awaiting judgment have resulted in the firms calling off the merger. Either the possibility of a negative verdict or changed market conditions in the interim can explain such breakdowns. Table 15.2 shows the outcomes of the referred mergers.

Table 15.2 Mergers referred to the MMC (other than newspapers) 1965 — December 1985

	No. of Mergers Referred	No. of Mergers Abandoned Without Report	No. of Mergers Against the Public Interest	No. of Mergers Not Against the Public Interest
Total	85	23	27	32

Source: *A Review of Monopolies and Mergers: A Consultative Document.*
Appendix 7, Cmnd 7198. HMSO; and Annual Reports of the DGFT.
Note: Rival bids for the same company are counted as one merger.

In practice the MMC has typically examined the effects of a merger on all aspects of competition as well as examining effects on efficiency, employment, the balance of payments and other factors which may differ between cases. Thus, despite the absence of a reduction in competition in the UK market, the likely reduction in exports, employment and the diffusion of skill through the economy were thought to be uncompensated for in the Enersch Corporation/Davy Corporation Ltd case. Also the failure of the adverse effects of likely reduction in competition amongst finished products, service to customers and in the desire to re-refine used oils, to be outweighed, led the Commission to declare the BP Ltd/Century Oils Group Ltd merger to be against the public interest.

Little direct evidence as to whether the MC (and later versions) have applied the same general criteria to mergers and monopolies alike exists. Sutherland

(1969), in his examination of the five MC reports on monopolies under the 1948 Act and eight merger reports under the 1965 Act, concluded that, whilst for mergers there was a presumption that conduct and performance would not deteriorate despite decreases in competition, in the case of monopolies the MC wished to encourage entry and competition without sectoral change. Again, on the issue of consistency of the MC towards mergers, only Sutherland's study is known; and he concluded that the within-study variations in interpretation prevented between-study comparisons.

A recent study by Fairburn (1985) has attempted to summarise the MMC's attitude to certain issues. Support for defending management, when presented, was found to be on the grounds of reduced efficiency and morale, should the merger occur. Fairburn reports that, if a company is thought to be efficiently run, it would be expected to improve the balance of payments. A concern for career prospects in the regions, especially Scotland, was detected, as were arguments to restrict foreign takeovers such as the Bank of England's control over the money supply, and the view that it was 'advantageous' to have a British transatlantic shipping company.

Fairburn also considered competition issues. When, on the few occasions, cross-subsidisation has been relevant, the MC generally accepted firms' arguments that this was irrational. Vertical mergers, by a firm with great market power, have caused the MC concern. In the case of product or market extension mergers, he notes that the MC has only rarely considered potential entrants — though the recent developments of contestable market theory (see page 471) may lead to greater concern for entry. Furthermore, he argues that in their attitude towards horizontal mergers the MMC has adopted qualitative definitions of markets, 'non-systematic' analyses of entry, and has not considered the trade-offs between lower costs and higher prices to the extent to which the legislation allows. Further, Fairburn argues that when, since 1978, it considers a merger involving the firm with the largest market share, the MC has concentrated on the likely effects of the merger on *competition calculated according to market share* and little on *conduct*.

On a different issue, the Green Paper (Cmnd 7198, 1978) argued that current legislation is biased in favour of mergers taking place because it is based on the assumption that few will be referred to the MMC. Since much empirical evidence suggests that, on average, mergers result in lower profitability (Singh 1971, Utton 1974, Meeks 1977 and recently Kumar 1984),[5] the possibility that mergers should not be allowed unless net benefits could be expected was considered. This possibility was rejected because (a) it would have led to around 90% of mergers being referred to the MMC, (b) the MMC would find most mergers to be in the public interest, and (c) because the whole procedure may

5   The evidence on the effects of acquisitions on the share price of the acquiring firm is mixed — see Firth (1979), Dodds and Quek (1985) and Franks and Harris (1986).

act as a deterrent to socially desirable mergers. Instead, it proposed a neutral approach which would recognise the disbenefit of reduced competition and benefits of larger size. A greater emphasis would be placed on the effects of a merger on competition. Two new clauses relating to the desirability of maintaining competition and international competitiveness of British industry were to be added to the 1973 Act's definition of the public interest.

In the event, this proposal was not adopted — perhaps because of a change in government. However, a further but unpublished review was carried out by the Department of Trade and Industry which resulted in a statement in July 1984 by the Secretary of State, Norman Tebbitt: that 'my policy has been and will continue to be to make references primarily on competition grounds'.

15.4 Further Discussion

In this section we discuss more fully whether anti-restrictive practices, monopoly and merger legislation covering final product markets is necessary to improve any current, or to avoid any potential, misallocation of resources.

Estimates of Welfare Loss

The neoclassical approach to the necessity for competition policy was given in section 15.1. The existence of price distortion has been found by the MMC on a firm-by-firm level of analysis and at aggregated levels for different nations by Cowling and Mueler (1978), Sawyer (1981), Jenny and Weber (1983), Masson and Shaanan (1984), Bergson (1973) and Harberger (1954). To illustrate the technique, consider again Figure 15.1. The area of triangle ABC, the value of the deadweight loss, (DWL), may be written as:

$$DWL = \tfrac{1}{2} \cdot \Delta P \cdot \Delta Q$$

But $\eta_p = \dfrac{\Delta Q}{\Delta P} \cdot \dfrac{P}{Q} \Rightarrow \Delta Q = \dfrac{\Delta P}{P} \cdot Q\eta_p$

$$\therefore DWL = \tfrac{1}{2}\Delta P \left(\dfrac{\Delta P}{P} \cdot Q \cdot \eta_p \right)$$

$$= \tfrac{1}{2}\left(\dfrac{\Delta P}{P} \right)^2 Q \cdot \eta_p \cdot P$$

The values of ΔP, P and Q may be estimated and η_p assumed. Using a more sophisticated version of this technique, Cowling and Mueller have estimated that the welfare loss was between 3.9% and 7.2% of corporate output in 1968–9.

The Austrian Approach

The Austrian School believes that the neoclassical rationale is misconceived. It argues that the necessary condition for the neoclassical optimum allocation of resources — price equal to marginal cost — is deduced from the assumption that firms have full knowledge of their cost and demand curves. But, it is argued, in reality this is never the case. It is the role of the entrepreneur to discover situations where goods/services can be bought for one price and resold at a higher price. Such acts of discovery are a process whereby situations of supply and demand prices being uncoordinated move towards an equilibrium situation where such prices are coordinated. Hence it is the expectation of achieving profits equal to the difference between these two prices which stimulates entrepreneurial alertness to discover the differences and so match consumer demand with supply.

If an entrepeneur buys all the resources used to produce a good, i.e. has a monopoly due to entrepeneurial action, the Austrians argue that this should not be removed from him by, for example, competition policy, because this would remove the incentive for other entrepreneurs to seek differences in prices in the hope of gaining such profits. Similarly, if entrepreneurs use their own (human capital) resources to innovate, and so gain monopoly profits by bringing a new product to the market with a difference between supply and demand prices, this also should not be removed by competition policy, because of the disincentive it would offer. Hence Littlechild has criticised Cowling and Mueller's estimates of the deadweight loss. He argues that if an entrepreneur perceives an opportunity for selling a new product for a higher price than the cost of employing others to produce it and is able to charge a monopoly price, it is inappropriate to consider the deadweight loss as a reduction in social welfare. The alternative source of supply is not by perfect competitors because no perfect competitors have noticed the opportunity of gaining the profits from the production of the good. The *relevant* alternative is for the good *not to be supplied at all*. Since it is produced, the entrepreneur's action is to be interpreted as a social gain equal to the producer's plus consumers' surpluses to which production and consumption gave rise.

Austrians continue that, in the absence of government restrictions, the prospect of making profits will always induce an entrepreneur to enter an activity. Hence, in the long run, monopoly profits will be eroded and competition policy is inappropriate. Mergers, advertising, and other forms of market conduct, are simply methods by which the competitive process occurs to coordinate demand and supply prices: again, policy is not applicable.

George (1985) has replied that, when information costs and transactions cost exist, it will benefit a firm to advertise, and so on, to build up goodwill amongst customers which *will* create entry barriers. Secondly, George notes evidence that positions of dominance can persist for decades and (although conflicting evidence also exists) if this is so there is a need for a pro-active competition policy.

The Contestable Markets Approach

Baumol defined a contestable market as one for which entry and exit are costless: barriers to entry do not exist.[6] Therefore, if the industry's price exceeded average cost, entry would occur and price would be bid down to the minimum of average costs (and hence marginal costs). At a price below marginal costs exit would occur. Hence, in equilibrium, price equals marginal cost and social welfare is maximised. Notice that the theory does not relate necessarily to a specific number of firms in a market. A monopoly or an oligopoly could be contestable. Secondly, since entry and exit are costless, if only a temporary profit could be made an entrant might 'hit and run'. Baumol argues that if entry costs are negligible, an industry with high concentration but no past entry is behaving optimally and therefore, by implication, should not be subject to monopoly legislation. However, as George argues, in practice it may be extremely rare to find an industry where entry and exit are costless.

6 Baumol characterises this situation as one with an absence of 'sunk costs'. If sunk costs exist, an entrant could not exit immediately after entry and before production without loss. An example of such a loss would be a decrease in the market value of a plant because of its installed location.

APPENDIX 15
European Community Competition Policy

Restrictive Practices

Restrictive practices legislation is contained in Article 85 of the Rome Treaty. This states that 'all agreements between undertakings, decisions by associations of undertakings and concerted parties which may affect trade between Member States and which have as their object or effect the prevention, restriction or distortion of competition within the Common Market' are incompatible with the Common Market. Examples of such practices include price fixing and restrictions on output and technological development, etc. Such agreements are void. Restrictions are exempt if they 'contribute to improving the production or distribution of goods, or to promoting technical or economic progress while allowing consumers a fair share of the resulting benefit', provided that they are necessary for the attainment of the objective and do not remove competition for a substantial part of the goods concerned. Suspected violations of Article 85 are examined by the EC Commission. Firms are able to notify agreements (a necessary qualification for exemption) which thereafter have temporary validity until or unless the EC Commission finds the agreement to be void under Article 85.

Notice that in general EC law is more restrictive than UK law. The EC law contains a narrower range of exemptions, and exempt behaviour is only allowed provided it does not remove competition for a substantial part of the goods concerned — a condition which does not exist when deciding on exemption within the UK.

In a survey of past cases Swann has considered a number of actions which the Commission has condemned. These include price agreements, common sales syndicates, the application of output or sales quotas, geographic market sharing, practices which have excluded part of the Common Market to some sellers, and information exchanges.

Monopoly

Article 86 of the Rome Treaty states that:

> Any abuse . . . of a dominant position within the Common Market or in a substantial part of it shall be prohibited as incompatible with the Common Market in so far as it may affect trade between Member States.

Examples of abuse include the imposition of 'unfair' purchase or seller prices or trading conditions, etc. Application of Article 86 is made by the EC Commission. One ambiguity of this Article is that no definition of 'dominant position' or 'substantial' is given in the Act. Case studies suggest that a market share as low as 40% may qualify though the level seems to depend, *inter alia*, on the share of the second and third largest firms in the market and the height of entry barriers. Secondly, as George and Joll (1975) note, the Article does not condemn the *position* of dominance of a firm, but only the *conduct* which may result. Cases suggest the range of abuses which have been criticised. These include rebates conditional on sole supply, refusal to supply, and geographic price discrimination.

Mergers

In 1972 the European Court accepted that Article 86 could be applied to mergers. It was concerned that control of a market by collusion could be banned under Article 85 but, if control were obtained *by merger*, this might otherwise pass Article 86. Thereafter it was accepted that there may be abusive behaviour if a dominant firm gains further dominance such that its control 'substantially obstructs competition'. In fact, only one merger between 1972 and 1983 was banned under Article 86.

However, Article 86 cannot be invoked until a dominant position has been achieved. But this would occur after the acquisition and prevention of such mergers was desired. To correct this and other problems with Article 86 as applied to mergers, new merger legislation was proposed in 1973. Under it, any merger where the acquirer gained power to hinder effective competition between Member States was to be banned. In 1981 the Commission offered an alternative proposal, but by 1983 it had still not been accepted.

Additional Reading

Bergson, A. (1973) 'On monopoly welfare losses', *American Economic Review*, Vol. 63 (5).

Clarke, R. (1985) *Industrial Economics*, Basil Blackwell.

Cowling, K. and Mueller, D.C. (1978) 'The social costs of monopoly power', *Economic Journal*, (88).

Devine, P.J., Lee, N., Jones, R.M. and Tyson, W.J. (1975) *An Introduction to Industrial Economics*, Allen & Unwin.

Dodds, J.C. and Quek, J.P. (1985) 'Effect of mergers on the share price movement of the acquiring firms: a UK study', *Journal of Business Finance and Accounting*, Summer.

Elliott, D.C. and Gribbin, J.D. (1977) 'The abolition of cartels and structural change in the United Kingdom' in A. Jacquemin & H. De Jong (eds) *Welfare Aspects of Industrial Markets*, Vol. 2, Martinus Nijhoff.

Fairburn, J.A. (1985) 'British merger policy', *Fiscal Studies*, 6(1).

Firth, M. (1979) 'The profitability of takeovers and mergers', *Economic Journal*, Vol. 89, No. 354.

Franks, J.R. and Harris, R.S. (1986) *Shareholder Wealth Effects of Corporate Takeovers: the UK Experience, 1955–85*, London Business School, Mimeo.

George, K.D. (1985) 'Monopoly and merger policy', *Fiscal Studies*, 6(1).

George, K. and Joll, C. (eds) (1975) *Competition Policy in the UK and EEC*, Cambridge University Press.

George, K. and Joll, C. (1981) *Industrial Organisation*, Allen & Unwin.

Harberger, A.C. (1954) 'Monopoly and resource allocation', *American Economic Review*, Papers and Proceedings, Vol. 44, May.

Hunter, A. (1966) *Competition and the Law*, Allen and Unwin.

Jenny, F. and Weber, A.P. (1983) 'Aggregate welfare loss due to monopoly power in the French economy: some tentative estimates', *Journal of Industrial Economics*, Vol. 32 (2).

Kumar, M.S. (1984) *Growth, Acquisition and Investment*, Occasional Paper No. 51. Cambridge University Press.

Littlechild, S. (1981) 'Misleading calculations of the social costs of monopoly power', *Economic Journal*, (91).

Masson, R.T. and Shaanon, J. (1984) 'Social costs of oligopoly and the value of competition', *Economic Journal*, Vol. 94, September.

Meeks, G. (1977) *Disappointing Marriage*, Cambridge University Press.

O'Brien, D.P., Howe, W.S. and Wright, D.M. with O'Brien, R.J. (1979) *Competition Policy, Profitability and Growth*, Macmillan.

Pass, C.L. and Sparkes, J.R. (1980) 'Dominant firms and the public interest: a survey of the reports of the British Monopolies and Mergers Commission', *Antitrust Bulletin*, 25(2).

Rowley, C.K. (1971) *Antitrust and Economic Efficiency*, Macmillan.

Sawyer, M. (1980) 'Monopoly welfare loss in the United Kingdom', *Manchester School, of Economics and Social Studies*, December.

Sawyer, M. (1981) *The Economics of Industries and Firms*, Croom Helm.

Shaw, R.W. and Simson, P. (1985) 'The Monopolies Commission and the process of competition', *Fiscal Studies*, 6(1).

Shaw, R.W. and Simson, P. (1986) 'The persistence of monopoly: an investigation of the effectiveness of the United Kingdom Monopolies Commission', *Journal of Industrial Economics*, Vol. 34 (4).

Singh, A. (1971) *Takeovers: Their Relevance to the Stock Market and the Theory of the Firm*, Cambridge University Press.

Stevens, R. and Yamey, B. (1965) *The Restrictive Practices Court*, Weidenfeld & Nicolson.

Sutherland, A. (1969) *The Monopolies Commission in Action*, Cambridge University Press.

Swann, D.P. (1983) *Competition and Industrial Policy in the European Community*, Methuen.

Swann, D.P., O'Brien, D.P., Maunder, W.P.J. and Howe, W.S. (1974) *Competition in British Industry*, Allen & Unwin.

Utton, M.A. (1974) 'On measuring the effects of industrial mergers', *Scottish Journal of Political Economy*, Vol. XXI, No. 1.

Utton, M.A. (1986) *The Economics of Regulation*, Basil Blackwell.

Williamson, O. (1968) 'Economies of scale as an antitrust defence', *American Economic Review*, (58).

Williamson, O. (1969) 'Reply', *American Economic Review*, (59).

A Review of Monopolies and Merger Policy (1978) Cmnd 7198 HMSO.

A Review of Restrictive Trade Practices Policy (1979) Cmnd 7512 HMSO.

16
Profits

Business firms provide an investment home for the savings of individuals (directly or *via* the institutions); they provide employment for managers and workers; but first and foremost they exist to produce goods or services which meet the requirements and needs of their actual or potential customers. Profits are the ultimate yardstick of management's ability to coordinate, plan and act in the interest of the consumer. The word 'profit', however, means different things to economists, to accountants, to businessmen, to politicians and to tax collectors. What is profit?

16.1 The Meaning of Profit

In income distribution theory all income is classified according to source. Wages are income from direct labour; interest is income from allowing others to use one's money; rent is the excess of the value produced by a productive factor over the payment required to induce it to work; and profit is the excess of income over the cost of production. In a perfectly competitive economy in a state of equilibrium, profits do not exist. But in reality competition is dynamic, not static. Given this, three main groups of theories have arisen to explain the presence of profits.

First, there is the view that profits are a reward for bearing risks and uncertainties. Most people prefer to avoid these, yet in general, businessmen are unable to do so. Firms must take actions today with a view to satisfying consumer needs in a risky or uncertain tomorrow. Consequently, a higher reward is required as the risk and/or uncertainty in the situation increases. Without this reward firms would avoid such situations and so market wants tomorrow would remain unsatisfied. A second theory is that profits are the result of market frictions and imperfections. They exist because of disequilibrium and imperfect competition. They tend to persist because the economy can rarely adjust instantaneously to changes in cost and demand conditions. This is the monopoly theory of profit. Third, there is the view that profits are the reward for innovation. Innovations are those new products or processes (Schumpeter went so far as to include all 'different things') which increase national income more than they increase national costs. The difference is profit. All factors of production involved in producing the innovation are paid their opportunity costs and the entrepreneur who crystallised and organised the new idea into a marketable good or service receives this surplus of income over costs as his reward. After a time imitators will appear (what Schumpeter colourfully called the 'Perennial Gale of Creative Destruction'), price levels will tend to be forced down to a perfectly competitive level and the innovative profits will be 'washed away'. More realistically, of course, a further innovation will appear on the scene before equilibrium is attained and the cycle will commence again.

The risk and innovation theories of profit pose a challenge to the public's attitude to business, and to the businessman's attitude to his own activities. By these theories profits are an objective measure of the social value both of new ideas and of the acceptance of uncertainty by others. Not all new ideas are approved of by every individual, but the consensus view is to be found in market performance (subject to the usual qualifications regarding externalities and imperfections). From the manager's own stance, pursuing non-profit-maximising objectives can thus be regarded as anti-social.

Economic Costs and Accounting Costs

Profits are the excess of income over costs. But the cost concepts used by accountants differ from those which would be used by economists. The accountant ignores opportunity costs.

One obvious example of this discrepancy is in the treatment of interest on the shareholder's capital. The accountant does not deduct this as a cost. The economist would impute it as a cost to be deducted from revenues in order to arrive at the profit figure. The rate of interest the economist chooses might be the market rate on 'risk-free' investments such as gilt-edged securities, or it might be a rate which reflects the risk and uncertainty of the operations of the firm in question. In the latter case, any remaining profit would presumably arise only from the rewards of innovation or the presence of market imperfections. Another common example is the case of smaller, owner-managed firms. There the accountant ignores the opportunity cost of the income that owners could earn if working elsewhere. Thus accounting profits, represent an exaggeration of 'true' profits.

In addition to any failure to impute opportunity costs, there are even more serious errors arising out of deficiencies in accounting techniques themselves. These all have a common root. The 'true' profitability of any investment or business cannot be determined until the ownership of that investment or business has been fully terminated. Yet accountants must produce interim profit figures for shareholders (who need information on the progress of their investment), for managers (who need information upon which to judge past or base future decisions), and for the Inland Revenue (who need information on which to calculate the firm's tax liability). As a consequence, accounting figures are produced which are based upon arbitrary allocation of both revenues and costs to a given accounting period. There is a major conceptual conflict here. The economist looks to the future when placing a value on today's assets. To him, and for that matter to the business-man, the past is irrelevant. Profit, in an economic sense, is the *difference between the cash value of the enterprise today and its cash value at the end of its existence.*

Sunk costs are regarded as irrelevant and forecasts of net income into the indefinite future must be made. Accountants define profits as the differ-ence between revenues and costs over a given period, say a year. Both revenues and costs are calculated on an accrued basis, they are allocated to the time period in which they are earned or incurred. Historical, not anticipated, cost and revenue data are used for the calculation. In balance sheet terms, profits calculated in this way represent *the difference between a firm's net worth* (i.e. total assets minus reserves and liabilities) *at the beginning and end of a year.*

These two definitions highlight some of the differences and similarities between accounting and economic profits. The economist is concerned with income expectations: the accountant aims at producing historical records within the constraints of company law and professional practice. We can now proceed to examine in more detail three specific problems met with by economic analysts of company accounts as a result of certain accounting conventions. These are (i) depreciation, (ii) the treatment of capital gains or losses, and (iii) the evaluation of inventory.

(i) The Problem of Depreciation   To the economist, depreciation is capital consumption. (Economically depreciation also includes the opportunity cost of capital equipment, namely, the most profitable alternative forgone by putting it to its present use.) The cost of capital consumption is the replace-ment cost of equipment that will produce comparable earnings. To the accountant, depreciation is an allocation of capital expenditures over time. Allocating the historical capital expenditure on the original plant over time will only equal replacement cost under wholly unrealistic assumptions of stable prices and certain obsolescence. Moreover, the methods of allocating original cost themselves differ and so in turn produce varying levels of profits as reported by accountants.

To illustrate this, consider a firm purchasing a new machine for £1000, with an estimated life of 10 years. The firm has a choice of at least three alter-native methods of allocating this expenditure over time. Under the straight line method the cost of the machine is spread equally over its expected life (i.e. £100 per annum). Under the reducing balance method the firm can choose among an infinite range of depreciation rates (say $x\%$). Instead of deducting the same amount of profits annually, $x\%$ of the price of the machine is allocated against year 1 profits, $x\%$ of the balance is allocated against year 2 profits and so on. Clearly, under this system the £1000 will never be wholly written off. The sum-of-the-year's digits approach is a variant on the reducing balance method. The years of expected asset life are aggregated $(1 + 2 + 3 + \ldots + 10 = 55)$ to give an unvarying denominator. In year 1 the depreciation ratio used is 10/55. As a fraction of £1000 this is £181.80. In year 2 the depreciation ratio becomes 9/55; 9/55 of £1000 is £163.60. This process continues until year 10 when the depreciation has fallen to 1/55. None of these methods bears any relationship to charging depreciation according to the replacement cost of the asset. Moreover calculated profit must vary widely according to which of the three accounting conventions are used.[1]

(ii) The Treatment of Capital Gains or Losses   The way capital gains or losses ('windfalls') are handled also affects a company's reported profits. Examples of windfalls include the bankruptcy of a major creditor not allowed for in bad debt reserves, or the unanticipated rise in share price of a firm in whom the company has a minor stake. By traditional accounting practice a capital gain is not made until the property is sold, irrespective of fluctuations in its value during the period it is held. Thus the entire gain or loss is treated as though it had occurred in the ultimate year of ownership. Clearly, were the actual loss or gain reported annually, whether or not it was realised, this would have an impact on the firm's reported profits over the years in question. The economist is not concerned with which accounting convention is selected for the recording of historical events. The important fact is that management should be aware of the magnitude of such windfalls, long before they become precise enough to be acceptable to accountants. Only then can the manager make valid decisions with regard to the future based on the value of net assets which he will have at his disposal when the decision is activated.

(iii) The Evaluation of Inventory and Stocks   The Inland Revenue requires, and most British accountants practise, even in internal accounts, the evaluation of stocks and inventory by the FIFO (first in first out) method. Stocks consequently appear in a firm's balance sheet at their actual cost price — or market value, if lower. This system correctly represents the physical facts. It assumes that the raw materials which a firm consumes during the course of a

---

1   It should be noted that the Inland Revenue accepts neither the economist's nor the accountant's version of depreciation cost. Standardised capital allowances are permitted as charges against profits for tax purposes. These are now inextricably bound up with regional policy and were referred to in Chapter 14. Accountants consequently compile two sets of accounts — one for shareholders and management and one for the Inland Revenue, where the internal depreciation charge is 'added back' to profits and the legally permitted capital or investment allowance is deducted, producing a net figure on which tax is computed.

year will always be the oldest in stock. Only when earlier purchases have been consumed will later purchases be turned to. However, the FIFO system results in an exaggeration of reported profits over 'true' profits in a time of rising prices.

The system known as LIFO (last in first out), on the other hand, more closely approximates the economist's desire to see replacement costs used in the calculation of profits rather than historic costs. LIFO assumes that the most recently purchased stocks will be the first to enter the manufacturing process. Under LIFO the prices of the most recently purchased stocks become the costs of the raw materials in current production. Given stable inventory levels, the costs of raw materials applied at any point in the calculation of profits is always close to market or replacement value; only when stocks fall do the prices paid for earlier purchases enter into the calculation. Consequently, in times of rising prices the LIFO approach results in a higher level of costs being used in the calculation of profits, and thus deflates profits closer to their 'true' level. Conversely, in times of falling prices, LIFO shows a higher profit than would FIFO.

LIFO has certain disadvantages, however. If stock levels fall, the figure 'cost of materials' becomes increasingly obsolete. If stock levels rise, the figure 'cost of materials' becomes a jumble of different figures, possibly as complex as that produced by the FIFO method. It can also be argued that FIFO produces a more realistic (closer to replacement value) figure for stocks in the balance sheet. At its simplest, if stock levels are static then under LIFO the financial value of stocks in the balance sheet will remain unchanged year by year. This is not a serious objection since LIFO can still be used for the calculation of 'cost of materials' in the profit and loss account, while closing stocks at the year end can be revalued for balance sheet purposes, putting the excess to a capital reserve.

Both LIFO and FIFO, however, are historic cost accounting techniques. To attain full economic realism stocks should be valued in constant pounds.

Accounting for Inflation

Discontent with conventional accounting standards is not new. But it has spread and, with the rising rates of inflation common to most of the western world in the later 1960s and 1970s, it has been accentuated. Profits, as reported by accountants and as inflation has increased, have departed further and further from reality. Table 16.1 highlights and summarises some of the major areas of concern.

Current operating profit is defined as the excess of current sales over the current costs of inputs. This plus realised capital gains (or losses including the accountant's depreciation charge) in the current period is accounting profit. The difference between accounting profit and money income is made up of those accrued capital gains (or losses) which have not yet been realised,

Table 16.1

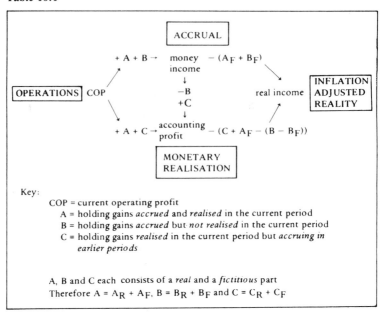

Key:

COP = current operating profit
A = holding gains *accrued* and *realised* in the current period
B = holding gains *accrued* but *not realised* in the current period
C = holding gains *realised* in the current period but *accruing in earlier periods*

A, B and C each consists of a *real* and a *fictitious* part
Therefore $A = A_R + A_F$, $B = B_R + B_F$ and $C = C_R + C_F$

less those capital gains (or losses) which accrued in previous accounting periods but were realised in the current period.

Neither money income nor accounting profit make allowances for the change in the general price level. Real income does. How can we move, in practice, from accounting profit figures to real income figures? For planning and control purposes this is the critical question to which the manager needs an answer. Several alternative routes have been suggested — none is uniquely agreed upon. Ideally replacement cost accounting is the optimal method, the difficulty is to find an operational definition which would be universally accepted. Replacement cost (*RC*) accounting is not one technique. It is a term which covers a range of alternative methods of accounting for inflation.

The advocates of *RC* accounting argue that adjusting figures in the balance sheet by the Retail Price Index, or even some less aggregated but still high level Index Number, has little relationship with the replacement costs of stocks of finished or semi-finished goods or of raw materials.

Replacement costs, they claim, vary widely, and often whimsically, from firm to firm and year to year, depending on the mix of finished goods, work-in-progress, and raw materials in any particular company. In like manner, no one Index can be regarded as an adequate substitute for the replacement costs of capital assets. Indices are merely weighted averages of the prices of selected goods. They are prisoners of the selected items whose prices go to make them up; and whose prices in any event themselves deviate from the Index they make up. A cursory comparison of the RPI and other indices, such as the various wholesale and commodity price indices would indicate frequent and irregular differentials between their respective trends. Thus for some firms index number adjustments in given years might still leave their accounts far from realistic reflections of market values. And in some industries, indexed corrections might move firms away from greater accuracy rather than towards it.

A further problem is the treatment of monetary items, or net indebtedness. The consequences of failure to take account of losses on monetary assets (and profits on current liabilities) as a result of shifts in the general level of prices can be illustrated by the following abstract example. Consider a firm with no transactions between the two dates t_0 and t_1, and let p be the percentage rise in prices between t_0 and t_1. The firm's financial position at t_0 is:

$$N + M - L = C \qquad (16.1)$$

where N is the firm's non-monetary assets, M is monetary assets, L is current liabilities and C is the value of the shareholders' interest or net worth. Now multiply equation 1 throughout by $(1 + p)$ to recognise the effect of the rise in prices between t_0 and t_1:

$$N(1 + p) + M(1 + p) - L(1 + p) = C(1 + p) \qquad (16.2)$$

By assumption, however, the firm's holding of physical assets is the same at both times, and, in particular, the 'counts' of both monetary assets and current liabilities are the same. Transpose Mp and Lp to the right-hand side of equation 2 and the position of the firm in t_1 becomes:

$$M - L + N(1 + p) = C(1 + p) - Mp + Lp \qquad (16.3)$$

So, in a situation of rising prices, so long as current liabilities exceed monetary assets $(L > M)$, the measure of shareholders' interest or net worth (the right-hand side of equation (16.3)) will represent a larger command over goods and services than did C in equation (16.1). If $L < M$ the reverse is true. This complies with the well-known fact that in conditions of inflation it it better to be a borrower than a lender. So, in order to assess the real value of the shareholders' interest in the company in t_1, it is necessary not only to supplement it by Cp, but also to subtract from it $(Mp - Lp)$, the loss on the holding of monetary assets after allowing for the gain on current liabilities. In extreme situations, companies which calculate apparently attractive profits on the basis of historic costs may distribute them all as dividends to shareholders and ultimately discover that when machines have to be replaced, the cash flow is no longer available to permit asset purchase. Alternatively, its entire cash flow might be absorbed by high replacement costs, high profits would be indicated by the accounts, but no cash would be available for dividends. In this situation the shares would be worthless, high profits would be shown in the accounts and the firm could only be valued on a break-up basis. These are absurdities which can arise through the practice of historic cost accounting. The basic objective of inflation accounting then is to provide a measurable yardstick, unaffected by changes in the real value of money, which can enable objective comparisons to be made between the changes in the real net worth of a business firm.

The economist's version of profit requires an estimate of the present value of all future cash flows. This is an impossible attainment in an uncertain world, and if it were attainable, management would cease to be a decision-making task and become merely one of stewardship. *RC* accounting shows fixed assets and stocks, with depreciation and cost of sales at current replacement values. The shareholders' equity interest is also adjusted for the general price level change, as is net monetary indebtedness. Replacement costs can be arrived at by estimating current market values for replacing each individual asset; or (less satisfactorily) by applying one of the many available specific price indices relating to capital goods and published by the government, each of which was believed to be a reasonable indicator of the replacement cost of the asset or group of assets concerned.

An alternative (or variant) of *RC* accounting is the net realisable value (*NRV*) method. Here assets are priced in the balance sheet at the value they would realise if sold on the open market, not at the price a replacement asset would cost. The attractions of *NRV* to the economist are that it embraces the concept of opportunity cost and, secondly, particularly in the case of current assets held for realisation in the short term, it must come close to *PV*, the discounted present value of the cash flow to be expected from their sale price in the near future.

Adjusting the Discounting Formula for Inflation

Failure to correct the *DCF* formulae for inflation can result in biased estimates and hence incorrect project choice. The solution is to be consistent in both numerator and denominator. That is if future cash flows do not take account of inflation, then neither should the discount rate. If they do then so should the discount rate. Which approach is the easier? Since the numerator in the *DCF* formulae contains a multiplicity of different figures (revenues and costs) before it is reduced to a single value in each time period, it is probably more difficult to estimate all outlays and inflows in today's pounds (i.e. in real terms) for every future period. If the numerator is, therefore, expressed in current pounds in each period, then to be consistent, this requires that the value $(1 + r)$ in the *DCF* formula also be expressed in nominal terms. But today's interest rates on which capital costs are based already embody anticipated changes in the price level (i.e. inflation). Irving Fisher argued that:

$$r_n = r_r + I_r$$

where r_n, r_r and I_r are the nominal and real interest and inflation rates respectively. Thus, instead of employing a figure based on r_r in the *DCF* formulae, the denominator should simply be expressed in terms of r_n: the nominal rate which already accounts for inflation.[2]

Now that we have examined the meaning, significance and measurement of profit we turn to two of the ways in which managers use profitability figures for purposes of planning and control: the break-even chart and the rate of return on investment.

16.2 Profit Planning and Control

Break-even Analysis

Break-even analysis studies the relationship between the volume and cost of production on the one hand, and the revenue and profits obtained from the sales of the product on the other.

The break-even point, price being given, occurs where total cost equals total revenue. Figure 16.1 depicts a linear break-even chart. The similarities between this figure and the economist's single-period, profit-maximising cost and revenue diagram (Figure 3.1, Chapter 3) are readily apparent. The

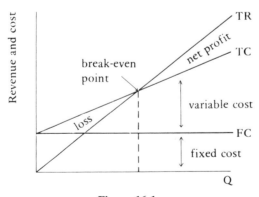

Figure 16.1

2 If inflation is not correctly treated, profitable projects may be rejected, or vice versa. For example, for much of the 1970s, real interest rates were negative. That implies possible project profitability even if the sum of undiscounted cash flows is less than the outlay. For example, consider a negative real rate of 8%, outlay of £100 in t_0, and income of £50 and £40 in t_1 and t_2 (all in constant pounds). Present value = $50/0.92 + 40/0.92^2 = 54.35 + 47.3 = £101.65$.

main differences are the assumptions of a given price and constant variable costs. Over certain ranges of output for brief periods of time these additional assumptions may not be too restrictive.

The break-even production volume can readily be determined from the chart by dropping a perpendicular from the intersection of TR and TC to the Q-axis. Alternatively, it can be calculated algebraically by the following formula:

$$Q = F/(P - V)$$

where Q is the quantity produced and sold, F is total fixed costs, P is the price per unit sold, and V is unit variable cost. (The break-even quantity occurs where $TR = TC$ or $P \cdot Q = F + V \cdot Q$ which becomes $(P - V)Q = F$ which produces the desired result.)

(i) Contribution Analysis   In the short run, where many of the firm's costs are fixed, businessmen are often interested in determining the contribution additional sales make towards fixed costs and profit. Contribution analysis provides this information. Total contribution profit is defined as the difference between total revenues and total variable costs, which equals price less average variable cost on a per unit basis. Figure 16.2 rearranges Figure 16.1 to highlight the meaning of contribution profit. Total contribution profit, it can be seen, is also equal to total net profit plus total fixed costs. Figure 16.2 contains most of the information needed for contribution analysis.

Contribution profit analysis provides a useful format for examining a variety of price and output decisions. For example, consider the situation where the variable costs of a product are £5 per unit and the selling price is £12. The unit contribution profit is consequently £7. Assume the company has a profit target of £12,000. How many units of the product must it sell to meet the target? The answer is found by using the following formula:

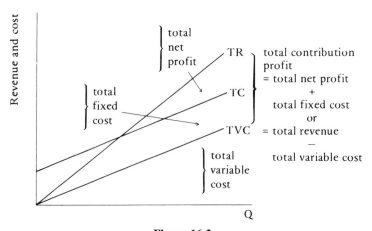

Figure 16.2

$$Q = \frac{(F + \pi^*)}{A\pi_C} = \frac{(F + \pi^*)}{(P - V)}$$

where F is total fixed costs, π^* is the total profit and $A\pi_C$ is the unit contribution profit. With total fixed costs of £9,000:

$$Q = \frac{(£9,000 + £12,000)}{£7} = 3,000 \text{ units}$$

(This can be easily corroborated. 3,000 units produce a total revenue of £36,000. Total cost equals F plus $V \cdot Q$ equals £9,000 + £15,000, i.e. £24,000, leaving a profit $(TR - TC)$ of £12,000.)

(ii) Operating Leverage Break-even analysis can also be useful in appraising the financial merits and demerits of differing production systems. In particular, it highlights how total costs and profits vary with output as the firm operates in a more or less mechanised manner and so substitutes fixed for variable costs.

Operating leverage reflects the extent to which fixed inputs are used relative to variable inputs in production operations. Consider the three alternative production techniques, X, Y and Z, which can be used in producing any given product. X is a highly automated technique, Y is labour intensive, and Z is moderately automated. The break-even charts for the three techniques are given in Figure 16.3. The TR line is the same in each case, given an identical product sold at the same price. The fixed costs, however, differ according to the degree of automation, with X having the highest TVC. The variable costs also differ. The labour intensive technique, Y, has the most rapidly rising level of total variable costs. X, conversely, has a TVC line which rises more slowly than either Y or Z. As a result of these differences the break-even points occur at different volumes of output. Given that the three pairs of axes are drawn on the same scale:

X breaks even at $x_1 > y_1 < z_1$
Y breaks even at $y_1 < z_1 < x_1$
Z breaks even at $z_1 < x_1 > y_1$

Other things equal, capital intensive operating procedures have higher break-even points than labour intensive procedures. Once break-even point is reached, however, the profits of the capital intensive operation, X, rise more rapidly than either of the other two, Y and Z. This is indicated visually by the rise of the angles at x, (36°), y, (13°), and z, (23°).

Operating leverage is measured more precisely as the percentage change in profits that results from a percentage change in units sold. That is:

degree of operating leverage $= \dfrac{\Delta\pi \cdot Q}{\Delta Q \cdot \pi}$

Effectively, operating leverage is an elasticity concept relating to profits.

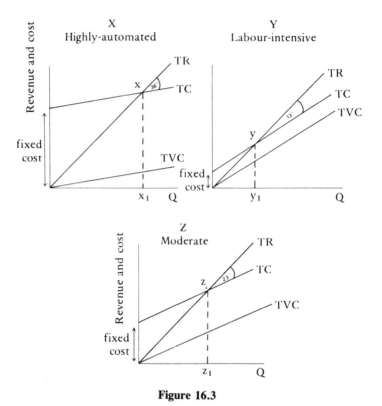

Figure 16.3

Since it is based (here) on linear *TR* and *TC* curves it will vary along the length of any particular pair of curves, and will be largest near the break-even point where π is close to zero.

More generally, operating leverage at any level of output Q, is measured thus:

$$\text{degree of operating leverage at point } Q = \frac{Q{\cdot}A\pi_c}{Q{\cdot}A\pi_c - F}$$

where $A\pi_c$ is unit contribution profit, and F is total fixed costs.[3]

3   This is proved as follows:

the initial profit is $Q{\cdot}A\pi_c - F$

Thus the percentage change in profit is

$$\frac{\Delta Q{\cdot}A\pi_c}{Q{\cdot}A\pi_c - F}$$

but the percentage change in output is $\Delta Q/Q$ so the ratio of the change in profits to the change in output is:

$$\frac{\Delta Q{\cdot}A\pi_c}{Q{\cdot}A\pi_c - F} \cdot \frac{Q}{\Delta Q} = \frac{Q{\cdot}A\pi_c}{Q{\cdot}A\pi_c - F}$$

If we calculated the operating leverage for our three alternative procedures X, Y and Z for any given output level Q, we would discover that X had the highest leverage and Y the lowest. The profits of procedure X are much more sensitive to changes in sales volume than those of either Y or Z.

Break-even data are consequently of considerable value to decision makers, both in their provision of information relating to contribution profit, and in the assistance they give in analysing the implications of different degrees of operating leverage. However, they often require to be modified before they can be of practical use. To embrace different prices, either a series of charts with different TR functions must be constructed, or a curvilinear analysis used. Cost changes, either once for all or varying with output, can be embraced in similar modifications.

Ratio Analysis

Return on capital employed is one of the most common methods of appraising business performance. It is a ratio and, like all ratios used for control purposes, it will generally be compared either with the same ratio at other points in time, or the same ratio for other firms at the same time. Ratio analysis rests on the belief that some normality or abnormality will be found in the process of such a comparison and that managerial action will be taken accordingly.

Ratio analysis makes for readily quantifiable inter- or intra-firm comparisons. The ease with which it can be carried out has encouraged its use. Like all management tools, however, ratio analysis is no stronger than the accuracy of the information on which it rests. Since most ratios spring from the ubiquitous profit expressed as a rate of return on assets, it will be obvious from our earlier discussion that ratios should be used with considerable care. Ratios can only be fully understood in practical use. However, we will list some of the more common. They fall into two groups: line management and financial ratios; both are related to return on capital employed.

(i) Line Management Ratios   Line management ratios are of value to top management and the relevant line managers. Return on capital is the root of all line management ratios. It can be defined as the percentage of:

$$\frac{\text{profits (before deduction of interest and Corporation Tax)}}{\text{total assets less current liabilities}}$$

or

$$\frac{\text{profits}}{\text{shareholders' interest (including reserves) plus fixed interest capital}}$$

Return on capital employed indicates how effectively the firm's resources are being utilised. Both the numerator and the denominator are within the

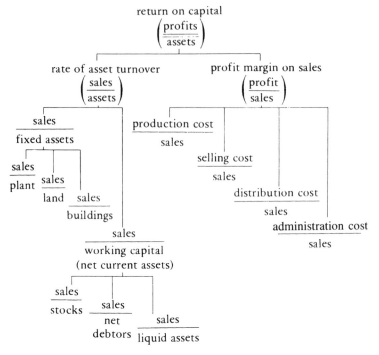

Figure 16.4

control of management. Figure 16.4 indicates how any deterioration in return on capital employed can (in theory) be traced through the firm. Any change in the return on capital ratio depends on a change in one or both of the ratios 'rate of asset turnover' and 'profit margin on sales'.

The profit margin on sales ratio depends in turn on one or more of the various cost/sales ratios. If any one of these have altered for the worse over time, or compare unfavourably with similar ratios in comparable firms, then specific management action to reduce, say, the administrative cost/sales ratio will, other things being equal, raise the profit margin on sales and so the return on capital.

The rate of asset turnover indicates how often the profit margin on sales has been earned on each pound of assets. The higher the figure (i.e. the lower the value of the denominator given a level of sales) the higher is the return on capital. Again, if a deterioration in the return on capital is perceived to arise from a change in the rate of asset turnover, then the specific asset class which has caused this can be pinpointed and managerial action taken to right the situation (say by reducing the value of net debtors by urging more rapid payment from debtors and delaying payments to creditors, or by pruning stock levels).

(ii) Financial Ratios   Financial ratios are of value to top management, financial managers and outside investors. We have already defined return on capital employed. It will be recalled that in Chapter 12 we defined the earnings yield as the percentage of:

$$\frac{\text{profits (after interest and after Corporation Tax) per ordinary share}}{\text{current share price}}$$

The inverse of the earnings yield is the price/earnings or P/E ratio. Financial vernacular talks of the P/E ratio as representing the 'purchase of x years' profits'. The higher the P/E ratio, other things being equal, the greater is the expected future growth of earnings and dividends.

Dividend yield indicates the current income that a shareholder can expect in the absence of any alteration in dividend policy, share price or taxation rates. It is the percentage of:

$$\frac{\text{dividend per share (after Corporation Tax)}}{\text{current share price}}$$

A useful additional ratio which increases the usefulness of dividend yield and earnings yield is dividend cover. This is the ratio:

$$\frac{\text{profits per share}}{\text{dividends per share}}$$

It indicates the extent to which the company retains earnings and does not distribute them to shareholders. It thus also indicates the extent to which the company's profits can fluctuate without it being forced either to prune its dividend payment or to dip into reserves in order to maintain it.

This chapter concludes our discussion of managerial economics. As a conclusion few topics could have been more appropriate than the above discussion concerned with the measurement of income and with the elements of profit management.

Additional Reading

Baxter, W.T. (1962) 'Inflation and accounts', *Investment Analyst*, Vol. 43.

Dean, J. (1951) *Managerial Economics*, Prentice-Hall.

Edwards, E.O. and Bell, P.W. (1972) *The Theory and Measurement of Business Income*, California University Press.

Haynes, W.W. and Henry, W.R. (1974) *Managerial Economics*, Richard D. Irwin.

Hill, S. and Gough, J. (1982) 'Discounting for Inflation', *Managerial and Decision Economics*, Vol. 2.

Merrett, A.J. and Sykes, A. (1974) 'How to avoid a liquidity crisis', *The Economist*, 3 August.

Newbould, G.D. (1969) *Business Finance*, Harrap.

Study Questions

Chapter 1: Introduction to Maximisation and Optimisation

1. Find the first derivatives with respect to x of the following:

   (i) $y = 15$
   (ii) $y = 7x^4$
   (iii) $y = 4x^2 - 3x^3$
   (iv) $y = 6x(x^2 - 2)$
   (v) $y = \dfrac{x^2 - 1}{2x^3 + 3}$
   (vi) $y = \sqrt{(x + 4)}$

2. A firm has the following profits (π) function:

   $$\pi = 10000Q + 150Q^2 - 0.25Q^3$$

   where Q denotes output per period (units)

   (a) Derive the average and marginal profits equations.
   (b) Find the outputs at which profit is at an extremum and identify which is a maximum and which a minimum.
   (c) Show that average profits equal marginal profits when average profits are at a maximum.

3. A firm has estimated its demand function to be:

   $$Q = 1000 - 0.5P + 2A + 0.01Y$$

   where Q = Quantity demanded per period (units)
   P = Price (£)
   A = Advertising expenditure per period (£)
   Y = consumers' *per capita* income per period (£)

   (a) find $\partial Q/\partial P$, $\partial Q/\partial A$, and $\partial Q/\partial Y$;
   (b) defining the price, advertising and income elasticities of demand as

$$\eta_P = \frac{\partial Q}{\partial P}\frac{P}{Q}, \ \eta_A = \frac{\partial Q}{\partial A}\frac{A}{Q} \text{ and } \eta_Y = \frac{\partial Q}{\partial Y}\frac{Y}{Q} \text{ respectively, calculate}$$

η_P, η_A and η_Y when $P = 10$, $A = 400$ and $Y = 4000$

4. A firm's production function is:

$$Q = 3K + 2L - LK - 0.5L^2 - 1.5K^2$$

where Q = output per period
   L = labour inputs per period
   K = capital inputs per period

Find the (unconstrained) maximum output which the firm could produce. (Assume the second order conditions are fulfilled.)

5. Solve the following maximisation problem using a lagrangian multiplier: a firm has £100,000 to spend on labour and materials in the coming year; the cost of labour is £2000 per unit per year; the cost of materials is £1000 per unit. The firm, therefore, has the following budget constraint:

$$2L + M = 100$$

where L is the quantity of labour and M the quantity of materials purchasable.
   The firm's output (Q) is related to inputs thus:

$$Q = 5LM$$

(i.e. this is the production function). What input mix of L and M will maximise Q? What is the value of λ? (You may assume that the second order conditions for a maximum are satisfied.)

Chapter 2: Decision Analysis Under Conditions of Risk and Uncertainty

1. A firm's management wishes to maximise profits. It must choose from three investment strategies I_1, I_2 and I_3 and knows that its profits will depend on which of three future states of the economy S_1, S_2 or S_3 prevail. The company's payoff matrix in £000 profit is:

	S_1	S_2	S_3
I_1	12	8	5
I_2	10	20	0
I_3	1	10	15

Which strategy should the management choose if it used:

    (a) the maximin criterion
    (b) the minimax regret criterion
    (c) the Principle of Insufficient Reason
    (d) the Hurwicz α-criterion (assume $\alpha = 0.4$)?

2. Repeat Question 1 but suppose that, instead of aiming to maximise profits, the management aimed to maximise utility where:

    (a) $U = 2\pi$,
    (b) $U = \log_{10}(1 + \pi)$

    where U = managerial utility (in 'utils')
          π = profits (in £000)

3. Using the same data as in Question 1, which alternative would have the highest EMV if S_1, S_2 and S_3 had probabilities of 0.3, 0.4 and 0.3 respectively?

    Calculate the standard deviation of the returns for each strategy. Plot the standard deviation EMV point for each on a graph and arbitrarily apply indifference curves to show project 3 with the greatest utility.

4. Suppose that the probabilities of S_1, S_2 and S_3 are again 0.3, 0.4 and 0.3 respectively, that the payoffs *in £000 profits* are given in Question 1 and that the cardinal utility function of a manager has been found to be:

    (a) $U = 2\pi$,
    (b) $U = \log_{10}(1 + 2\pi)$

Using the Von Neumann–Morgenstern *expected utility* criterion, which strategy would the manager prefer?

5. When considering two projects a firm has estimated the following payoffs:

	S_1	S_2	S_3	S_4	S_5
P_i	0.50	0.20	0.30	0.20	0.15
I_1	25	50	100	50	25
I_2	10	20	100	70	50

Calculate the standard deviation, coefficient of variation and the semi-standard deviation of the payoffs for each project. Which do you consider to be the riskier project?

Chapter 3: Business Objectives

1. Defining Q as output produced and sold and given the following total cost and demand functions:

$$TC = 150 + 10Q - 0.5Q^2 + 0.02Q^3$$
$$Q = 37.7 - 0.91P$$

(a) find the total profit function in terms of Q,
(b) find the profit-maximising output level,
(c) find profits and price at that level,
(d) if fixed costs rise from 150 to 200, determine the effects of such an increase on the profits of the firm, on its price policy and on its output level.

2. Using the cost and demand functions of Question 1 determine the MR and MC functions. Show that at the output level determined in (b) $MR = MC$.

3. For the company in Question 1, what are its:

(a) unconstrained price and output levels if its objective is sales maximisation and its profit at that output?
(b) its price and output level if a profit constraint of 100 is imposed?

4. An owner–manager initially owns 100% of the equity in CLV Enterprises. The market value (V) of his firm if he takes no perks is £10. He maximises his utility by taking a value of perks whose present value (P) is £0.50, with the market value of his equity consequently being £9.50. Now suppose he sells 10% of his equity to a Pension Fund for a mutually acceptable price and that at that price the manager's indifference curve is given by the equation $V = P^{-1} + 0.5$. What is the monetary value of the 'residual loss' due to the new agency relationship?
(Hint: find the coordinates of the relevant points in Figure 3.16 in the text.)

Chapter 4: Forecasting

1. This month and last month the quantities demanded of a firm's product were 1000 units and 990 units respectively. Estimate next month's demand using the following naive forecasting techniques:

(a) $\hat{X}_{t+1} = X_t + \Delta X_t$
(b) $\Delta X_{t+1} = 1.09(\Delta X_t)$
(c) $\hat{X}_{t+1} = 900 + 100\,(t+1)$ (currently $t = 0$)

2. XYZ Ltd has presented you with the following data. Plot the data on a graph.

UNITS SOLD (X_t)

| | Quarter | | | |
	1	2	3	4
1987	800	900	900	950
1988	1900	2600	3100	2900
1989	3200	3000	2650	2300
1990	2600	2550	2500	2800
1991	3350			

Using the time series model

$$X_t = T_t C_t S_t$$

predict $\hat{X}_{t+1}$

Note: To find $\hat{a}$ and $\hat{b}$ in the equation $T_t = \hat{a} + \hat{b}t$ use the formulae analogous to equations (6.7) and (6.8)

i.e. $\hat{b} = \dfrac{n \sum\limits_{t=1}^{17} X_t t - \sum\limits_{t=1}^{17} t \sum\limits_{t=1}^{17} X_t}{n \sum\limits_{t=1}^{17} t^2 - \left(\sum\limits_{t=1}^{17} t \right)^2}$

$\hat{a} = \dfrac{\sum\limits_{t=1}^{17} X_t}{n} - \hat{b}\, \dfrac{\sum\limits_{t=1}^{17} t}{n}$

and where $n = 17$ (the number of observations)

3. XYZ has presented you with the following data. Plot the data on a graph and establish what, if any, cycle exists.

Sales in month (£'000)	1987	1988	1989
January	10	11	12
February	12	13	15
March	13	14	16
April	15	15	18
May	16	17	20
June	15	17	19
July	14	16	19
August	17	18	22
September	18	19	23
October	20	23	27
November	21	25	29
December	22	26	33

Calculate the 12-month moving averages and forecast the value for January 1990.

4. In mid-1985 Grampian Aluminium Ltd was evaluating the merits of building a new factory, in order to meet the needs of the North Sea oil industry's component supplies. The alternative is to use additional overtime and/or to reduce other production. The company already supplies the aircraft, motor, agricultural equipment and domestic appliance industries and will want to add new capacity only if the total economy appears to be expanding. Forecasting UK economic activity is consequently an essential input to the firm's decision process.

The firm has collected the data and estimated the following relationships for the UK economy:

Last year's total profits (all firms) P_{t-1} = £50 million
This year's government expenditure G = £100 million
Annual consumer expenditure C = £40 million + $0.5Y$
Annual investment expenditure I = £2 million + $0.75P_{t-1}$
Tax receipts T = 0.25 GNP
National income Y = GNP − T
Gross National Product $GNP = C + I + G$

Assume that random disturbances average out to zero, and forecast each of the above variables from the simultaneous relationships experienced in the equation system.

5. The Input–Output transactions matrix for the Island of Trespass for last year has been calculated to be (in £ million):

	Inputs to Agriculture	Inputs to Manufacturing	Inputs to Services	Exports	Govt.	Households	Gross output
	———Producers———			———Final Demand———			
Agriculture	3	8	5	1	3	45	65
Manufacturing	7	50	20	50	40	140	307
Services	1	30	25	15	60	90	221
Government	15	29	21				
Wages	25	150	120				
Profits and Depreciation	14	40	30				
Gross input	65	307	221				

(a) Calculate the direct inputs technology matrix.
(b) Calculate the direct and indirect inputs technology matrix.
(c) Suppose that the value of output which households will take from each industry is 5% greater this year than last year. Predict this year's output for each industry.
(d) How might the manager of each firm on the island use these IO matrices?

6. Suppose that the market for washing powder is supplied by only 3 brands: X, Y and Z. Suppose that the flow of customers between these three brands between the end of the first quarter and the end of the second quarter of this year were:

Brand	Number of Customers at end of 1st quarter	Gains from			Losses to			Number of Customers at end of 2nd quarter
		X	Y	Z	X	Y	Z	
X	30,000	0	5,000	20,000	0	15,000	5,000	35,000
Y	50,000	15,000	0	10,000	5,000	0	5,000	65,000
Z	65,000	5,000	5,000	0	20,000	10,000	0	45,000

(a) Calculate the market shares of each brand at the end of the first and second quarters.
(b) Calculate the number of customers which each brand retained between the two quarters. Hence calculate the probability of retention for each brand.
(c) Calculate the transition probability matrix. What does each element in this matrix represent?
(d) Using a first order Markov process, estimate the market shares at the end of the third quarter. What assumptions are you making when doing this?
(e) Calculate the equilibrium shares for each brand.

Chapter 5: Demand Theory

1. A firm estimates the following demand functions for its two products as:

$$Q_1 = 200 - 2P_1 - 3P_2$$
$$Q_2 = 450 - 6P_1 - 2P_2$$

At $P_1 = £2$ and $P_2 = £4$

(a) what is the demand elasticity for Q_1 with respect to P_1,

(b) and for Q_1 with respect to P_2,

(c) and for Q_2 with respect to P_1,

(d) are the products substitutes, non-related, or complements?

2. An analysis of income data for the Manchester area resulted in the equation $Y_m = 0.02\,X^{0.706}$, where Y_m and X are respectively Manchester's and UK's disposable *per capita* income. This means:

(a) the relationship is log-linear,

(b) a 1% change in the nation's disposable income may be expected to result in about 0.7% change in Manchester's disposable income,

(c) the elasticity is given by the exponent in the equation,

(d) the equation may also be written:

$$\log Y_m = \log 0.02 + 0.706 \log X,$$

(e) all of these.

3. Hazzods, the department store, found that the average daily demand for shirts was given by the equation $Q = 60 - 5P$.

(a) How many shirts per day will the store sell at £3?

(b) If the store has a target of 20 shirt sales per day what price should it charge?

(c) What would demand be if the shirts were given away?

(d) What is the maximum price at which shirts can be sold?

(e) Plot the demand curve.

4. Kuzzy's Ltd, a major TV chain store, does not rent sets to customers but only sells them outright. In addition it provides an optional insurance plan for its customers whereby a one-year or two-year service contract can be entered into. The contract provides for an unlimited number of otherwise free-of-charge service calls to repair broken or faulty sets. The company has decided to review this strategy and the following data have been collected from one of the branch stores:

	Premium for 1-year contract (£)	Premium for 2-year contract (£)	No. of 2-year contracts taken out	Average household income
1970	35	50	1000	5000
1971	35	55	950	5000
1972	40	55	1000	5500
1973	45	55	1050	5500
1974	35	50	1000	5500
1975	40	50	1050	5500
1976	40	50	1000	5000
1977	40	60	1050	5500
1978	35	60	950	5500
1979	35	65	900	5500
1980	40	65	1000	6500
1981	40	65	1050	7000

What inferences can be drawn from this table in general terms? How would you back up these inferences by computing elasticity measures? Which elasticities would you calculate and what are their values? Why would you restrict yourself to these specific elasticities?

Chapter 6: Demand Estimation

1. The marketing department of Goldmine Inc. has collected the following data on the demand for its product:

TIME PERIOD t	QUANTITY DEMANDED (UNITS PER PERIOD) Q_t	PRICE (PENCE) P_t
1	26	2
2	4	16
3	12	13
4	16	16
5	4	23

(a) Assuming the model:

$$Q_t = \alpha + \beta P_t + \epsilon_t$$

relates to the population of possible Q_t values at every given value of P_t, use OLS to estimate values of α and β, $\hat{\alpha}$ and $\hat{\beta}$, on the basis of this sample;

(b) draw the resulting estimated curve and plot the observations;

(c) calculate the price elasticity of demand at the mean values of Q_t and P_t in the sample.

2. The ABC company has estimated its demand function using OLS to be:

$$Q_t = 1992.9 - 4.845P_t \qquad R^2 = 0.949$$
$$ (37.776) \quad (0.264) \qquad n = 20$$

where Q_t = quantity demanded per week in week t
  P_t = price in week t
  n = number of observations
and the number in brackets is the standard error of $\hat{\beta}$.

(a) Calculate the t-statistic for H_0: $\beta = 0$,
(b) using this t-statistic test the null hypothesis:

$$H_0 : \beta = 0$$
against $H_1 : \beta < 0$

(look up the critical t-statistic in a statistics or econometrics text),
(c) interpret the R^2.

3. The market research section of your company has collected the following data on the demand for your product:

TIME PERIOD	QUANTITY DEMANDED (UNITS PER PERIOD) Q_t	PRICE (PENCE) P_t
1	10	45
2	30	45
3	40	30
4	60	30
5	70	15

(a) Assuming the model:

$$Q_t = \alpha + \beta P_t + \epsilon_t$$

relates to the population of possible Q_t values at every given value of P_t, use OLS to estimate values of α and β, $\hat{\alpha}$ and $\hat{\beta}$, on the basis of this sample,
(b) draw the resulting estimated curve and plot the observations,
(c) calculate the t-statistic for the null hypothesis $H_0 : \beta = 0$,
(d) can the null hypothesis

$$H_0 : \beta = 0$$
against $H_1 : \beta \neq 0$

be rejected? (Look up the critical values of t in a statistics or econometrics text),
(e) calculate the R^2 and interpret it.

4. The marketing section of a firm has collected the following statistics:

PERIOD t	(QUANTITY PER PERIOD) Q_t	PRICE CHARGED P_t
1	2800	39
2	3700	32
3	3250	32
4	3100	39
5	2750	44
6	3750	26
7	4500	15
8	4000	20
9	4750	15
10	4250	23
11	2500	47
12	4000	30
13	3400	34

Suppose that the firm *knows* that the supply but *not* the demand curve has shifted over time. Now:

(a) estimate α and β for the hypothesised demand function
$$Q_t^D = \alpha + \beta P_t + \epsilon_t,$$

(b) test the null hypothesis

$$H_0 : \beta = 0$$
against $H_1 : \beta \neq 0$

using a t-test,

(c) repeat (b) using an F-test,

(d) calculate the R^2 and interpret it,

(e) find the price elasticity of demand at the means of Q_t and P_t in the sample,

(f) use the Durbin–Watson test to examine the possibility of auto-correlation (look up the critical values of the t, F and DW statistics in a statistics or econometrics text).

5. The following data on sales and prices have been collected by the market research section for the past five quarters:

Quantity sold (units) Q_t	Price (£) P_t
146	9.00
153	8.50
160	8.00
167	7.50
175	7.25

The supply function is *known* to be $Q_t = 110 + 4P_t + 9t$ where Q_t, P_t and t are quantity demanded in quarter t, price in period t and quarter t respectively.

(a) Plot the family of supply functions at values of t of 0, 1, 2, 3 and 4. Why might t be included in the supply function?

(b) Plot a line *by eye* fitting data in the table.

(c) Under what conditions associated with the completeness of the demand and supply curves (i.e. excluding consideration relating to the 'by eye' estimation technique) is this line an approximation to the demand function for the product?

6. (a) Use the data of question 3 but *instead* of assuming that the model $Q_t = \alpha + \beta P_t + \epsilon_t$ relates to the population of possible Q_t values, assume that the model:

$$Q_t = aP_t^b U_t$$

where a and b are constants to be estimated

u is a multiplicative error term

is applicable and estimate a and b.

To estimate a and b take logarithms of both sides of the equation:

$$\log_{10}Q_t = \log_{10}a + b\log_{10}P_t + \log_{10}U_t$$

then substitute:
$$Q'_t = \log_{10}Q_t$$
$$\alpha = \log_{10}a$$
$$\beta = b$$
$$P'_t = \log_{10}P_t$$
$$\epsilon_t = \log_{10}U_t$$

Hence one has:

$$Q'_t = \alpha + \beta P'_t + \epsilon_t$$

Assume this model fulfils the assumptions of the OLS technique and so estimate α and β in the usual way. Then take the antilog of $\hat{\alpha}$ to derive a.

(b) Plot the value of Q_t which the estimated equation predicts, $\hat{Q}_t$, at values of P_t given in the data table.

(c) Calculate the values of $e_t = Q'_t - \hat{Q}'_t$ at each P'_t value.

(d) Plot these e_t values against time. Can you distinguish a pattern or not?

Chapter 7: Cost Theory and Measurement

1. Find the input values in terms of financial outlay which lie on the firm's expansion path given the production function $Q = Y^2X^4$ and input

prices P_y = £4 and P_x = £12. (The objective is consequently to maximise Q subject to the constraint $4Y + 12X = TC$, using a lagrangian multiplier expression.)

2. Electricity may be produced with either a high grade coal (low sulphur content) or a low grade coal (high sulphur content), with the low grade fuel giving off a much higher air pollution element. If XCX Plc, a large chemical firm, generates its own power, and has the choice of technology defined by the isoquants in Figure 1, find:

   (a) the optimal input mix if the firm is trying to minimise the cost of producing 200 megawatts when prices are P_L = £40 per ton, P_H = £80 per ton,
   (b) what price would the government have to instruct British Coal to sell low grade coal at to induce XCX Plc to switch to the low pollution process?

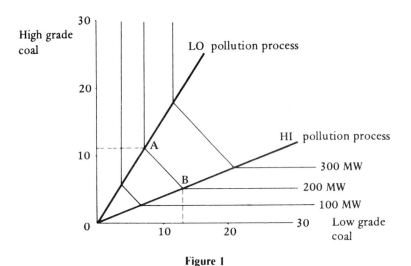

Figure 1

   (c) what financial penalty would XCX Plc incur if a law was passed forbidding the use of the high pollution process at the original prices?

3. Show that the following production functions are homogeneous:

   (a) $Q = aL + bK$
   (b) $Q = \gamma[\delta K^{-\rho} + (1 - \delta)L^{-\rho}]^{-1/\rho}$ (a Constant Elasticity of Substitution production function)

where γ = an efficiency parameter
ρ = a substitution parameter
δ = a distribution parameter

4. Which of increasing, constant or decreasing returns to scale does each of the production functions of Question 3 have?

5. ABC Ltd has estimated its production function to be

$$Q = -71.202 + 63.250K - 0.078K^2 - 37.894L$$
$$(63.103) \quad (28.602) \quad (0.036) \quad (20.463)$$
$$+ 0.034L^2 - 0.00000008LK$$
$$(0.019) \quad (0.00000002)$$

$R^2 = 0.988 \qquad n = 13$

where the number in the brackets denotes standard errors.

(a) Using the formula (6.11) calculate the t-statistics for each coefficient for the null hypothesis that each population coefficient equals zero.
(b) Test these null hypotheses against the alternative hypotheses that each is not equal to zero.
(c) Find expressions for the marginal products of labour and capital.

6. Using the engineering approach Goldrush Inc. believes that its long-run total cost function is:

$$TC = 3.54Q^{0.85}$$

(a) If this is the correct function does Goldrush have economies of scale or not?
(b) If Goldrush is a management consultancy company, what problems would it experience in trying empirically to derive its long-run average cost curve using the engineering approach?

7. Windfall Corporation has estimated its STC curve using accounting data and OLS to be:

$$STC = 380.32 + 2.72Q - 0.003Q^2 + 0.000001Q^3$$
$$(27.82) \quad (0.15) \quad (0.0002) \quad (0.00000007)$$
$$R^2 = 0.993 \qquad n = 25$$

(Numbers in brackets are standard errors.)

(a) Calculate the t-statistics for the null hypothesis that the population coefficient of each variable equals zero. Test these hypotheses for each coefficient separately against the alternative hypotheses that each coefficient is not equal to zero.
(b) The firm has also estimated its demand curve as:

$$Q = 2317.4 - 671.77P$$
$$\quad\ (47.89)\quad (19.65)$$
$$R^2 = 0.981 \qquad n = 25$$

(Numbers in brackets are standard errors.)

Using the estimated coefficients in both regression equations, form the profits function and find the profit-maximising level of output.

(c) Why might the output which you have calculated in (b) not in fact be the level which maximises profits?

8. The following data have been taken from the UK Census of Production. Using the Survivor Technique, deduce the plant sizes at which the technique would suggest the LAC is lowest. Discuss any sources of inaccuracy in this procedure.

Plant Size Distribution for the UK Motor Vehicle Manufacturing Industry

Size Range (No. of employees)	Net Output (£000) 1968	1979
1 – 99	61,034	200,836
100 – 199	36,558	114,143
200 – 299	24,671	72,097
300 – 399	23,776	65,412
400 – 499	25,611	61,387
500 – 749	46,205	105,880
750 – 999	37,757	125,828
1000 – 1499	86,223	267,655
1500 – 1999	55,914	150,514
2000 – 2499	35,044	91,767
2500 – 2999	44,558	121,271
3000 – 7499	186,502	177,852
7500+	281,718	2,711,262
	945,571	4,265,904

Sources: Business Monitor, Census of Production (1979) Vol. PA381.1, Table 4 and Census of Production (1968) Vol. 82, Table 2.

Chapter 8: Linear Programming

1. For the following linear programming problem for π_C, Q_A and Q_B:

Maximise $\pi_C = 3Q_A + 2Q_B$

$3Q_A + Q_B \leqslant 16$
$Q_A + 2Q_B \leqslant 20$

$Q_A \geqslant 0$
$Q_B \geqslant 0$

π_C = contribution profits from the production of A and B
Q_A, Q_B = output of products A and B respectively

(a) Represent the two constraints graphically, indicating the set of feasible solutions.
(b) Solve the problem using the arithmetic method.
(c) Solve the problem using the Simplex algebraic method.
(d) Solve the problem using the Simplex matrix method.

2. Offequip Ltd produces two types of spring clip, the Bulldog and the Poodle are their brand names. Bulldogs sell for £10 per pack. Poodles for £9.50. The VC of Bulldogs is £5 per pack and of Poodles £5.50. Both products go through the stamping department and the assembly and packing department. The former has 9,600 minutes per day available, the latter 12,000. Each Bulldog pack takes 4 minutes to stamp out and 2 to assemble and pack. Each Poodle pack takes 2 minutes to stamp and 10 minutes to assemble and pack. What is the optimum product mix? Find the optimal outputs of both types of clip if their selling prices changed so that the contribution became £7 per Bulldog pack and £3 per Poodle.

3. Potbanks Ltd manufactures two types of vase, Tall and Spherical. The prices of Tall and Spherical are £9 and £7 per vase respectively. The VC of Tall and Spherical are £5 and £4 per vase respectively. The production of each vase requires inputs of labour time, machine time and clay. Each Tall vase requires two minutes of labour time, one minute of machine time and two pounds (weight) of clay. Each Spherical vase requires one minute of labour time, $3\frac{1}{2}$ minutes of machine time and four pounds (weight) of clay. Potbanks has only 1000 minutes of labour time, 4000 minutes of machine time and 2,100 pounds of clay available per day. What is the optimal daily output of each type of vase?

4. (a) Find the dual of the primal shown in Question 2. Interpret the new objective function, the constraints and the new variables. Represent the constraints of the dual as a graph and indicate the set of feasible solutions.
   (b) Formulate the dual of the dual which you found in part (a). Interpret its objective function, constraints and new variables. Compare this formulation with Question 2.

5. (a) Solve the dual problem of the primal given in Question 3. Interpret the dual variables.
   (b) Calculate the values of the slack variables and interpret them.

6. A revenue (R) maximiser manufactures two types of towel: a bath towel and a hand towel. The prices of each are *fixed* at £7 and £4 respectively. Each towel must pass through three production stages: weaving, printing and cutting. Each bath towel requires 4 minutes of weaving, 5 minutes of printing and 3 minutes of cutting, whereas each hand towel requires 3 minutes of weaving, 2 minutes of printing and 3 minutes of cutting. There are only 70,000, 50,000 and 60,000 minutes of capacity per week available for weaving, printing and cutting respectively.

   (a) Find the optimal value of R, R^*.
   (b) Formulate the dual of this primal.
   (c) Find the optimal value of the objective function of this dual and compare it with R^*.

7. Solve the following linear programming problem for C by solving its dual:

   $$\text{Minimise } C = 60P_X + 100P_Y + 55P_Z$$

   $$\text{Subject to } 5P_X + 3P_Y \geqslant 5$$
   $$2P_X + 4P_Y + P_Z \geqslant 4$$

   $$P_X, P_Y, P_Z \geqslant 0$$

Chapter 9: Price Policy

1. A firm selling the same commodity to two or more groups of customers who cannot trade between themselves (because of cost, information imperfection, or characteristics of the commodity) is in a position to practise price discrimination if not restricted. Suppose two markets are geographically separated, with demand schedules $Q_1 = 20 - P_1$ and $Q_2 = 50 - 2P_2$, where the firm's marginal cost schedule is $MC = 2Q$ where $Q = Q_1 + Q_2$. What are the profit-maximising prices in each market? What are the demand elasticities in each market at the selected prices? Are profits with price discrimination more than profits without? If so, by how much? (Assume fixed costs are equal to £2.) Note that this problem has an interesting twist: it will be discovered that one segment is not worthwhile selling into if uniform prices are charged. (This type

of situation often exists, for example, when considering whether to export or not. Exporting is often only profitable if the price overseas is much less than the price charged at home. On the other hand, consciously deciding *not* to export or to do so only if identical — and high — prices are received, both at home and abroad, may prove non-optimal.)

2. Welcome Brewers dominates the liquor industry, although there are 50 small competitors scattered throughout the country and strongly supported by the Campaign for Real Beer (CAMRB). The CAMRB brewers each have an identical total cost function: $0.03+2Q+1.75Q^2$. The market demand for beer has been found by Welcome's market research arm to be $P = 3-0.03Q$. Welcome's total cost function is $1+Q+0.01Q^2$. What price should Welcome set in order to maximise profits? What price level should the CAMRB brewers set? What will be the profits made by Welcome? What quantity will Welcome produce? And the small firms?

3. Two grocery groups control virtually all food sales in a given local newspaper area. Each Thursday evening they provide the local paper with advertising material indicating which product will be on cut price offer that weekend. Experience has indicated that detergent or coffee is the most effective good with which to attract customers for the weekend sales. Suppose that past data show that sterling sales over all goods are gained or lost as shown:

		B cuts price on: detergent	coffee
A cuts price on:	detergent	0	100
	coffee	150	− 50

Given sales gains as an objective, what price strategy will *A* settle on? What do you think *B* would do?

Chapter 10: Public Utility Pricing

1. It is often argued that the role of regulation in the case of British Gas is (should be) to keep the price above what management would set it at, while in the case of British Telecom the regulator's role is to restrain prices. Why does this apparent conflict exist?

Chapter 11: Advertising

1. Suppose there are two large supermarkets in Inverness. The nearest
   similar shops are 90 miles away in Aberdeen. Both begin to consider
   heavy advertising and/or price cutting in order to take business away
   from their rival. Both firms are assumed to be astute market share maximisers. The following market share payoffs are estimated to be the
   outcomes from various combinations of actions:

	Supermarket A			
	Doubles advertising	Cuts prices	Both	Neither
Supermarket B				
Doubles advertising	+ 2	− 10	− 20	+ 10
Cuts prices	+ 10	+ 4	− 10	+ 15
Both	+ 15	+ 5	+ 6	+ 20
Neither	− 5	− 10	− 15	0

What decision will each firm come to?

2. Suppose a press and TV advertiser calculates that by spending an extra
   £1000 on TV he can increase the number of viewers who see his adverts
   by 600. For an extra £500 in either of two papers (or both) he can increase
   the number of readers by 400, each of whom has an average probability
   of noting of 0.5. What should the firm do, assuming no audience overlap,
   homogeneity of viewer and reader characteristics and equal probable
   purchase response? Would your view be altered if the advertiser had
   engaged an extremely creative copywriter?

3. Calculate the marginal advertising response function for a four-night TV
   campaign with adverts appearing at 9.00 p.m. (when on average 50% of
   all viewers recall advertisements). The product is toilet soap. There are
   20 million housewives in the population, of whom 6 million watch ITV
   one night in four, 4 million watch two nights in four, 3 million watch
   three in four and 2 million nightly. Assume constant returns to scale
   from repetition.

4. Express your answer to the last question in the form of a linear programming problem, given a total budget of £10,000, a choice of a TV or press campaign with a maximum of five TV nights and/or six press pages. One night's TV advertising costs £1500, one press page costs £1000. The marginal response function for press is 20%, 20%, 20%, 15%, 2%, 0.3%.

5. A necktie manufacturer estimates his demand function to be:

$$Q = 100,000P^{-3}A^{0.5}$$

Unit costs are £6.66. What are the optimal price and advertising levels? (Hint: in the Demand Theory chapter we find that elasticities are given by exponents in multiplicative expressions.)

6. A firm making electronic games forecasts that its required turnover next year will be a sales figure of £5 million. It estimates that price and advertising elasticities respectively will be 0.9 and 0.08. At what level will it set its advertising budget for the coming year?

Chapter 12: Capital Budgeting

1. A firm makes the following cash flow calculations for two mutually exclusive projects, X and Y; cost of capital is 10%:

Year:	0	1	2	3	NPV	IRR
X	− 1000	475	475	475	181	20%
Y	− 350	0	0	684	164	25%

Which project should it choose?

2. A firm makes the following cash flow calculations:

Year	0	1	2	3	4	IRR
Cash flow	− 200	100	100	173.3	− 110	20%

Its cost of capital is 10%. How should the calculation have been performed? Why?

3. An investor is considering purchasing loan stock which pays interest of £10 a year for ten years and a capital repayment of £100 simultaneously with the last interest payment. The first interest payment is in one year's time.

    If the investor requires a return of 12%, what is the maximum amount he would be willing to pay for the stock?

4. A company is introducing a new product, whose production run will be 10,000 units/year for the next 10 years. The manufacturing process requires welding which may either be carried out on the company's existing equipment or by the purchase of new equipment. Two sorts of new equipment are available, depending on whether a low or high level of automation is selected. The company's cost of capital is 10%. The existing equipment has a book value (original cost less accumulated depreciation) of £50,000, though if sold on the open market it could only fetch £20,000. Equipment that would introduce low-level automation would cost £240,000, though the supplier in this case would be willing to give an allowance of £40,000 if he took the existing equipment in part-exchange. Equipment for a high degree of automation would cost £300,000.

    Costs of production with the different processes would be as follows. All costs are direct. None of the equipment would have any value at the end of 10 years.

	Existing	Low automation	High automation
Material cost/unit (£)	5.00	4.00	4.00
Labour cost/unit (£)	7.00	3.50	2.00

    (a) What are the payback periods of the two investments?
    (b) What *IRR* does each offer?
    (c) What is the *NPV* of each investment?
    (d) What is the company's optimal investment decision? Is any further information needed before this decision can be made?

5. A landowner is considering whether to plant oak or pine on land which he is committing to forestry. Oak can be sold for £8 per cubic metre, and pine for £4. These prices are expected to remain constant. The land will carry equal numbers of oak or pine trees to the acre and the growth expected from the two types of tree is as follows:

Cubic metres of wood	Pine	Oak
after 5 years' growth	1.5	0.5
10	5.0	2.0
15	9.0	4.0
20	12.0	7.5
25	14.0	10.0

Costs of planting and felling the trees may be ignored. The landowner's cost of capital is 10%.

(a) What is the optimum length of time to let oak trees and pine trees grow (consider only the values given in the table)?

(b) What is the present value of the cash flow from each type of tree if it is planted now and allowed to grow for the optimum period?

(c) Which type of tree is more profitable to grow?

6. In the last 5 months excess returns over (or under) the risk-free rate were the following (i) for the market index and (ii) for XYZ Ltd.

	1	2	3	4	5
(i)	0.04	0	0.08	−0.02	0.06
(ii)	0.02	0	0.04	−0.04	0.12

Using this historic data as a proxy for the future and given that the risk-free rate was 5% what is:

(a) the value of XYZ Ltd's Beta coefficient?

(b) XYZ Ltd's cost of equity capital under the assumptions of the capital asset pricing model?

7. In the context of *CAPM* what is the expected return for ABC Ltd if it and the market have the following characteristics?

σ_{ABC}	= 0.2
σ_N (market portfolio)	= 0.1
$\bar{r}_N$ (market portfolio)	= 0.15
i (risk free rate)	= 0.03
ρ between possible returns between security ABC and the market portfolio	= 0.9

What happens if $\rho = 0.9$ changes to $\rho = 0.1$?

If ρ remains at 0.9, but σ_{ABC} rises what happens to the required rate of return, $\bar{r}_{ABC}$?

8. Securities A and B have the following characteristics:

	$\bar{r}$	σ
A	0.2	0.1
B	0.12	0.3

ρ_{AB} is expected to be 0.8

Calculate the risk and return of the following portfolios:

(a) 100% of A
(b) 50% A, 50% B
(c) 25% A, 75% B

Which portfolio is optimal? What results would be obtained if $\rho_{AB} = 0.2$?

Chapter 13: Product, Market and Corporate Strategies

1. Kezzoggs Ltd has a farming division and a cereals division. The corn grown by the farming division can be sold (or bought) on the open market at £20 per 100 kilograms. The farming division's cost function is $TC = 10,000 + 0.0005\ Q_f^2$ where Q_f is in hundreds of kilograms. The cereal division can process corn into flakes which will cost £30 per 100 kilograms, exclusive of the cost of corn. Assume one kilogram of corn produces one kilogram of flakes. The demand schedule for the cereal division is $P = 85.5 - 0.00002\ Q_c$. What should be the transfer price? How much corn should the farming division produce? How much cereal should be produced? Where should it be sold? What price should it be sold at?

2. IBI Ltd is divisionalised into a fine chemicals and a pharmaceutical division. The latter sells a patented drug which requires a unique raw ingredient made by the former. No other firm has been licensed to sell the drug. The demand equation for the drug is $P = 20 - 0.003\ Q_p$. The tableting process costs £0.005 per unit. The cost function for the fine chemical ingredient is $TC = 400 + 0.005\ Q_F^2$. What quantity of the medicine should be produced? At what price? What should the transfer price be? Assume unit for unit production.

3. MacSporran Publishers Ltd has best-selling textbooks in both History and French subject areas. Each has about 65% of the market. A recent market study suggests that the elasticity of demand for each is about the same. Moreover, the MC of production of each text is equivalent and constant over the relevant range. About twice as many copies of the History book are sold as of the French, yet the prices are the same. Is the firm's pricing policy correct? (*Hint*: recall the definition for MR given

in Chapter 6.) Assume (a) that the firm is working at capacity (i.e. that output level at which the firm is working on its constant and flat MC curve has now reached the point where the MC curve becomes a vertical line) and (b) that the firm has slack resources for both printing and distribution.

4. Whisky Distillers Ltd produces malt whisky of two grades, special and rest. Rest is considered to be a relatively low quality variant of special and is sold to the large household brand bottlers for blending with grain whisky. Special is bottled by Whisky Distillers Ltd for direct sale under their own label. The demand functions for the two are:

$$Q_s = 500 - 5P_s$$
$$Q_r = 2500 - 10P_r$$

Total cost is:

$$200 + Q_s = TC$$

What is the optimal output ratio? At what prices should the products be sold?

5. Chicken farmers have two products to sell: feathers and meat. If each bird produces on average 2 kilograms of meat and 1 kilogram of feathers, if storage is not practicable, if each chicken costs £0.50 to rear, and if the demand schedules for meat and feathers are $Q_m = 4000 - 1000P_m$ and $Q_f = 2000 - 1000P_f$ respectively, determine the optimal quantity of birds for the industry to produce and the prices of meat and feathers. (The demand schedules are specified for price per kilo.)

Chapter 14: The Location Decision

1. Integrate into the profit-maximising theory of location:

   (a) a subsidy receivable by firms only in certain areas,
   (b) a lump sum tax to be paid by firms which locate in certain areas.

2. The US coal industry has demand and supply schedules of $P = 11.5 - 0.697Q_D$ and $Q_s = 2.3P - 7$ respectively. The British coal industry's equivalent fractions are $P = 30 - 0.937Q_D$ and $Q_s = 8 + 0.3P$. The shipping cost of coal over the Atlantic is £3 per ton. Will a large British customer such as the CEGB or the BSC be prepared to buy American coal? What f.o.b. price would the market settle at? How much American coal would be imported?

Chapter 15: Monopoly and Restrictive Practices Legislation

1. Is it socially desirable for an economy to have a Monopoly and Merger Policy?

2. 'A complete assessment of firm conduct and market performance is so fraught with difficulties that a purely structural approach to monopoly and merger policy is more desirable than a cost–benefit approach'. Discuss.

3. Do you agree with the MMC's analysis and conclusion in its 1986 Report on the tampon market?

4. Compare the US and UK approaches to merger policy.

Chapter 16: Profits

1. For ABC Ltd the following relations exist: for each unit, selling price is £75; for output up to 25,000 units fixed costs are £240,000, and variable costs are £35 per unit.

    (a) What is the firm's gain or loss at sales of 5,000 units and of 8,000 units?
    (b) What is the break-even point?
    (c) What is ABC's degree of operating leverage at sales of 5,000 units and of 8,000 units?
    (d) What happens to the break-even point if price rises to £85? What significance does this have?
    (e) What happens to the break-even point if variable costs rise to £45 per unit (price £85)?

Subject Index

(Author listings are given on chapter references pages)